1986

LIVING
The process of adjustment

The Dorsey Series in Psychology

Advisory Editors

Wendell E. Jeffrey
University of California, Los Angeles

Salvatore R. Maddi
The University of Chicago

LIVING

LIVING

LIVING

The process of adjustment

Philip R. Newman

Barbara M. Newman
The Ohio State University

1981

THE DORSEY PRESS   Homewood, Illinois   60430
Irwin-Dorsey Limited   Georgetown, Ontario   L7G 4B3

© Philip R. Newman and Barbara M. Newman, 1981

ISBN 0-256-02300-X
Library of Congress Catalog Card No. 80-67664
Printed in the United States of America

1 2 3 4 5 6 7 8 9 0 H 8 7 6 5 4 3 2 1

To Sam, Abe, and Rachel

Preface

Our purpose in writing this book is to raise basic issues about human adjustment for a wide audience of undergraduate students. We have focused on three dimensions for understanding adjustment: the person; the environment; and the interactions between people and their environments.

We have presented the normal challenges to adjustment as they occur during people's lives. The book is organized into four parts. In Part One the orientation of the book and the basic processes for coping with life are described. The second part focuses on the person. The self-concept and the notion of competence are central to the view of coping and adaptation that is presented. Part Three examines the scientific evidence that demonstrates the ways that environments influence adjustment. We have looked at six environments that are central to most people's personal growth. In each of these chapters, the emphasis is on the demands for coping and the patterns of adjustment that develop. Part Four is devoted to crisis and personal growth. Our intention is to understand how life challenges threaten effective functioning and how people manage to respond to them without losing their sense of self-worth and personal control. In a final chapter, some of the more serious problems in adjusting to life are described. Under some circumstances people will give up a realistic view of themselves, the environment, or both in order to protect their inner sense of meaning.

There are several resources in the book that are intended to add to its usefulness as a stimulus for new learning. The living laboratories are designed to increase the student's powers of observation about life in natural settings. They draw from personal experience and new observation to encourage the assimilation of new information. Readings by outstanding scientists provide another set of voices to the text, taking ideas a step further. We have made liberal use of case material to help increase the vividness of issues raised in the text.

We live in a time when increasing information and a promise of a long, healthy life are enormous human resources. At the same time, rapid technical and cultural change create uncertainty, anxiety, and some degree of personal and social disorganization. This book has been an opportunity for us to consider the ways that people make use of their resources to face and even redirect challenge so that it leads to new growth. We are impressed by the enormous capacity for resilience that people exhibit as they live their lives.

In the development of this book, we were benefited by the thoughtful comments of the following people:

Professor Wendell E. Jeffrey, *University of California, Los Angeles*
Professor Salvatore R. Maddi, *University of Chicago*

Kenneth Yee

The photography of H. Armstrong Roberts

Arthur Tress

The photography of H. Armstrong Roberts

Professor Robert C. Bennion, *Brigham Young University*
Professor Robert Petty, *Santa Clara University*
Professor Richard Hirschman, *Kent State University*
Professor Corinne Carson, *Macomb County Community College*
Professor William E. Gibson, *Northern Arizona University*

Ethel Levin, Judy Woodall, and Sarah Twitty helped with manuscript typing. Luan Wagner Stewart, Susan Kugel, Lisa Lines, and Sharon Dougherty helped us in other aspects of manuscript preparation.

Philip R. Newman
Barbara M. Newman

Contents

PART ONE
INTRODUCTION:
ADJUSTING TO LIFE

Kenneth Yee

Chapter 1
Introduction

Two roads diverged in a yellow wood,
And sorry I could not travel both
And be one traveler, long I stood
And looked down one as far as I could
To where it bent in the undergrowth;

Then took the other, as just as fair,
And having perhaps the better claim,
Because it was grassy and wanted wear;
Though as for that the passing there
Had worn them really about the same,

And both that morning equally lay
In leaves no step had trodden black.
Oh, I kept the first for another day!
Yet knowing how way leads on to way,
I doubted if I should ever come back.

I shall be telling this with a sigh
Somewhere ages and ages hence:
Two roads diverged in a wood, and I—
I took the one less traveled by,
And that has made all the difference.

Robert Frost, *The Road Not Taken,* 1916

From *The Poetry of Robert Frost,* edited by Edward Connery Lathem. Copyright 1916, © 1969 by Holt, Rinehart and Winston. Copyright 1944 by Robert Frost. Reprinted by permission of Holt, Rinehart and Winston, Publishers.

United Press International

For reflection

1. What are some major choices you have made in the past? Which ones have had an impact on your life right now?

2. Do you feel that you are in control of the flow of your life? Do you feel that your life is determined by the demands of others?

3. What is your own definition of personal adjustment?

4. Can you think of any very stressful experiences that have helped you become a stronger person?

Turning difficulties into opportunities for growth is no easy matter. One must come to terms with strong emotions. Careful thought and analysis are required. The challenges of life often demand a new view of one's self, one's purposes, and one's values. The goal of adjustment is not merely to be shaped and buffeted by the variety of forces trying to set your course. Adjustment means taking hold of the direction of your life. Resolving uncertainty, developing new skills, and being willing to take uncharted paths or unpopular stances are all part of the process.

As we think about our lives, we are often filled with fears and doubts about decisions that we have to make. Most people learn to realize that making the best life decisions involves overcoming the fear that they will not choose wisely. In this book we hope to teach students about the process of living which involves making significant life choices and decisions.

The person, striving to live an effective, meaningful life, is in continuous interaction with an active, dynamic environment. Both the person and the environment are real. They have boundaries. They have structures. They have resources and limitations. They continue through time, showing both stability and change. Environmental factors may change people. To study this we focus on the mechanisms people use to adapt to the environment. This may involve:

1. Learning to speak the language of the group of which you are a member.
2. Learning to perform the skills that are required for a certain job.
3. Creating a shelter that will protect you from the unique elements of the climate where you live.

In each of these examples the person must respond to environmental demands.

People may also act to change their environments. Behavior is not only determined by external demands. People impose their own visions, goals, and definitions on the world. By choosing a particular kind of work, by deciding to marry or to remain single, or by supporting political candidates or working for legislation, people try to shape their lives.

Case 1·1

LIFE CHOICES

In the following excerpt from her autobiography, Golda Meir shares the conflict she experienced in making a major life decision. We feel that the decision was difficult. She anticipated some of its consequences, but not all. She chose to give up certain life goals in order to achieve others. We sense that as the decision was being made she was guided by the strength of her own belief in herself and her abilities.

At all events, I was delighted (and very flattered) when one rainy day, as I stood talking to someone outside the Histadrut offices in Tel Aviv, David Remez (who had suggested four years earlier that Morris and I work for Solel Boneh in Jerusalem) asked me if I was interested in returning to work and whether I would like to become the secretary of the Moetzet Hapoalot (Women's Labor Council) of the Histadrut. On the way back to Jerusalem I made up my mind. It wasn't an easy decision to take. I knew that if I took the job, it would involve considerable traveling both in Palestine and abroad and that we would have to find a place to live in Tel Aviv—which was difficult. But, hardest and most serious of all, I had to face up to the fact that going back to work would spell the end to my attempts to devote myself entirely to the family. Although I wasn't yet prepared to concede total defeat, even to myself, I had already realized in the course of those four years in Jerusalem that my marriage was a failure. Taking on a full-time job, under the circumstances, meant reconciling myself to this,

and the thought frightened me. On the other hand, I told myself that perhaps if I were happier and more fulfilled, it would be better for everyone—for Morris, for the children and for me. Perhaps I would be able to cope with everything: save what was left of my marriage from going farther downhill, be a good mother to Sarah and Menachem and even have the kind of purposeful, interesting life for which I so yearned.

It didn't work out quite that way, of course. Nothing ever works out exactly as one expects it to. But I can't honestly say that I have ever regretted that decision or that in retrospect I think I was wrong to have made it. What I do regret—and bitterly so—is that although Morris and I remained married to each other and loving each other until the day he died in my house in 1951 (when symbolically enough, I was away), I was not able to make a success of our marriage after all. The decision I took in 1928 actually marked the start of our separation, although it didn't become final for almost ten years.

The tragedy was not that Morris didn't understand me, but, on the contrary, that he understood me only too well and felt that he couldn't make me over or change me. I had to be what I was, and what I was made it impossible for him to have the sort of wife he wanted and needed. So he didn't discourage me from going back to work, although he knew what it really meant.

Source: Golda Meir, *My Life* (New York: Dell Publishing, 1975), pp. 106–7.

Some people even create theories, inventions, organizations, or laws that significantly modify the environment for themselves and for many others.

People direct the course of their lives through the choices they make. These choices may be heavily influenced by the resources and limits of the environment, and by experiences with past choices. For each new choice, the person actively imposes an interpretation on events. Based on this interpretation, the person selects a course that is viewed as pleasurable, protective, and/or most meaningful.

This book takes a very straightforward, practical view of adjustment. We see the main task of living as the ongoing process of adaptation to the basic human environments of life and the creation of better environments for living. In order to appreciate that process, we are going to look in detail at three factors:

1. The psychology of the individual.
2. The demands, resources, and structures of relevant social environments.
3. The unique challenges of living.

We want you to approach this topic with a blend of scientific objectivity and practicality. Basic questions are raised about how people change

"Personally, I liked your old lifestyle better."

Reprinted by permission The Wall Street Journal

and grow through life. You will learn how people satisfy their strong needs for companionship, for effectiveness, and for feelings of self-worth. You will also learn how people struggle and cope with the difficulties, disappointments, or disasters of life. We base our discussion on scientific theory and research. We have selected material that applies most directly to the efforts of people at all life stages to adapt to the realities of their lives. These are the kinds of questions that are most relevant to students. How do people function in families? How do friendships change and grow? What kinds of adjustments do we make to schools? How do we develop a sense of identification with a community? What are the demands and opportunities of intimate relationships? How do we adjust to work settings? These are the essential themes upon which an understanding of adjustment must be built.

THE ORGANIZATION OF *LIVING*

The book is organized into four parts. Part One includes two chapters. An overview of the book and basic concepts of adjustment are presented. Plan to read these chapters again, or at least review them, at the end of Part Two and again at the end of Part Three. If you can do this, the task of applying principles of adjustment to specific life challenges will be much easier.

Part Two includes three chapters in which personal capacities are discussed. Chapter 3 is about the self-concept which is the organizing and integrating force during the life of a person. Motives and emotions are treated in Chapter 4. This discussion of the person includes a presentation of the dynamic inner life which is filled with fantasies, fears, wishes, and feelings. Motives and emotions sometimes provide energy and sometimes impose barriers to action. In Chapter 5, the capacities to cope and adapt are added to the picture of the person. Resources for coping account for much of the ability of people to direct and shape the course of their lives.

United Press International

Part Three focuses on the environments where growth takes place. Adjustment takes place in these contexts for most people. The important challenges of living occur against a backdrop of social relationships. This may be in a two-person relationship between lovers or among many people in a complex governmental agency. We have identified six social contexts that most people must adapt to in American society. These are treated in Chapters 6–11. These contexts include family, friends, school, intimate relations, work, and community. Each of these can take many forms. Their importance can change over one's lifetime. Nonetheless, these social contexts provide basic sources of life satisfaction, stress, and opportunities for growth in the lives of most people.

Ken Firestone

Part Four includes three chapters on crisis and growth. Here the emphasis is specifically on challenges to adjustment and opportunities for growth. Normal life challenges are treated in Chapter 12. These are the crises that take place in the lives of many people and that are more or less predictable during the life course. Chapter 13 is devoted to the

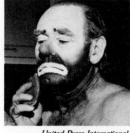

United Press International

United Press International

The photography of H. Armstrong
Roberts

United Press International

The photography of H. Armstrong
Roberts

Jean-Claude Lejeune

United Press International

U.S. Department of Housing and
Urban Development

United Press International

The photography of H. Armstrong
Roberts

Ken Firestone

unique challenge of cultural change. Here we expand the picture of adjustment to include the special demands of moving from one culture to live in a new culture or a new era. The primary emphasis of this book is on adaptation and growth. In Chapter 14, however, we consider some of the maladaptive responses to life challenges and techniques that have been devised to help people begin more effective coping.

SPECIAL FEATURES OF *LIVING*

Living laboratories

In order to encourage the use of scientific inquiry, we have included Living Laboratories in each chapter. These exercises bring concepts from the chapter under the scrutiny of your own experience and evaluation. They provide ways of adding your own analysis to the concepts of the course. Living Laboratories are all designed in the same format. The purpose states quite specifically the goal of the activity. The method explains what you are to do. The results section offers suggestions for organizing your observations. The discussion raises questions about the meaning of your observations. You can work on each Living Laboratory by yourself, as part of a class activity guided by your teacher, or with a small group of other students. All the materials needed for the activities are included in your book. By spending some time in the Living Laboratory you will begin to understand the way in which the logic of the scientific method increases your understanding of life.

Readings

At the end of every chapter there is an original reading from the works of a great scientist. They have been selected not only for their content, but because they shed light on the way these scientists think about the important questions of adjustment. These readings reflect the ideas of some of the major theorists who have written about personality and the process of adjustment. No single course can provide the answers to all the questions you will raise. However, after having participated in this course you will be aware of the wealth of information that exists and where to find it. You will also recognize some of the people who have given serious thought to issues of adjustment. You will also see how their thinking has influenced your own ideas about health and personal effectiveness.

Cases

A major source of evidence for our work comes from the study of individual lives. Case material is used throughout the book. You can use these cases as a basis of comparison for your own experiences. You will find them useful in learning about the variety of responses that people make to life's challenges.

Glossary

As you read, you will find some words defined in the margin of the page. These words appear at the end of the book in the glossary. You can find the page number where the definition was given next to the word on the glossary page.

Suggested readings

At the end of each chapter you will find some suggested readings. These are for students who want to pursue some subjects in greater depth.

Some of the classic articles in the field include:

Allport, G. W. The mature personality. *Pastoral Psychology,* 1952, *2,* 19–24.

Erikson, E. H. Growth and crisis of the healthy personality. *Psychological Issues,* 1959, *1* (1), Monograph 1, 50–100.

Jahoda, M. Toward a social psychology of mental health. In *Symposium on the healthy personality,* Supplement II: Problems of Infancy and Childhood, Transactions of Fourth Conference, March 1950, M. J. E. Senn, Ed. New York: Josiah Macy, Jr., Foundation, 1950.

Two texts which present personality theories are:

Hall, C. S., & Lindzey, G. *Theories of personality* (3d ed.). New York: Wiley, 1978.

Hjelle, L. A., & Ziegler, D. J. *Personality theories: Basic assumptions, research, and applications.* New York: McGraw-Hill, 1976.

For an interesting selection of readings:

Readings in personal growth and adjustment 80/81. Guilford, Cohn.: Dushkin, 1980.

Reading

THE EARLY LIFE OF CHARLES DARWIN: THE PERSON, THE ENVIRONMENT, AND THE PROCESS OF COPING

Charles Darwin, too, got along poorly with his father. The elder Darwin was also a famous and respected man—as a physician he managed to make a considerable fortune. His success and greatness overwhelmed the boy, who felt that his father made too great demands upon him, even in purely superficial matters. He described his father as the biggest and most difficult man he had ever seen; he had "a corpulent appearance" (6′2″ tall); "when he last weighed himself, he was 24 stone [336 pounds], but afterwards increased much in weight." The son was deeply hurt and humbled when his father once reproached him: "You care for nothing but shooting, dogs, and rat-catching, and you will be a disgrace to yourself and all your family." It took the boy a long time to get over this rebuke.

Charles Darwin was born in Shrewsbury and entered school there at the age of eight. His autobiography reveals: "I have been told that I was much slower in learning than my younger sister Catherine." During his first year at school one could already observe a characteristic in Darwin that hinted at the later natural scientist: "By the time I went to this day-school my taste for natural history, and more especially for collecting, was well developed. I tried to make out the names of plants, and collected all sorts of things, shells, seals, franks, coins, and minerals. The passion for collecting which leads a man to be a systematic naturalist, a virtuoso, or a miser, was very strong in me." Yet it took quite some time until Darwin found the road meant exactly for him.

He attended this school for one year, then went to a boarding school, where he remained until he was seventeen. The school was in Shrewsbury, a little less than a mile away from home. Thus he could come home frequently: "I very often ran there in the longer intervals between the callings over and before locking up at night," and he felt that this opportunity of a continuing close tie with his parents and home had been "advantageous" to him. Evidently he almost always stretched the visits to the last minute: "I remember . . . that I often had to run very quickly to be in time, and from being a fleet runner was generally successful; but when in doubt I prayed earnestly to God to help me, and I well remember that I attributed my success to the prayers and not to my quick running, and marvelled how generally I was aided."

The boarding school in Shrewsbury was based on humanistic convictions, and in later years Darwin expressed his extreme dissatisfaction about not being able to attend a school specializing in the natural sciences, especially since he showed no gift for languages, although in his last year he suddenly found great pleasure in Horatian odes. His great preference, however, remained the hunt. "In the latter part of my school life I became passionately fond of shooting; I do not believe that anyone could have shown more zeal for the most holy cause than I did for shooting birds."

When Darwin left school, he was not considered particularly intelligent, and no one expected anything spectacular of him, including his father, who sent him to Edinburgh to study medicine. Darwin later wrote that they thought him "a very ordinary boy, rather below the common standard in intellect."

Nothing came of his medical studies. Darwin not only found the lectures "intolerably dull and dreadful," but what was worse, he could not bear the sight of the corpses in anatomy class or endure observing operations. After a while he thought he would try theology, which meant taking a special course in Greek because he had completely forgotten what he had learned in school. But the attempt to become a theologian finally, as Darwin said, "died a natural death, when I . . . went on board the *Beagle* as a natural scientist." It was more by accident than by design that at the age of twenty-one he was offered a part in the *Beagle* expedition, a trip around the world that would last five years. This trip was the beginning of Darwin's career as a natural scientist and provided the observations upon which he constructed his theory of evolution.

Source: G. Prause, translated by Susan Hecker Ray, *School Days of the Famous* (New York: Springer Publishing Co., Inc., 1978), p. 58–60.

Chapter 2
Basic concepts of adjustment

What I must do is all that concerns me, not what the people think. This rule, equally arduous in actual and in intellectual life, may serve for the whole distinction between greatness and meanness. It is the harder because you will always find those who think they know what is your duty better than you know it. It is easy in the world to live after the world's opinion; it is easy in solitude to live after your own; but the great man is he who in the midst of the crowd keeps with perfect sweetness the independence of solitude.

Ralph Waldo Emerson, *Self-Reliance*, 1841

For reflection

1. What special skills or talents do you have that have made a difference in your life experiences?

2. Why do your friends react differently to criticism than you do?

3. How does your home life differ from your best friend's home life? How has that difference affected your adjustment to college?

4. Can you identify a personal crisis in your life? Are there any ways that this crisis became an opportunity for new growth?

THE PROCESS OF ADJUSTMENT AS ADAPTATION AND GROWTH

The concept of adjustment refers to active, creative efforts to live effectively. Five aspects of adjustment are of special importance:

1. Effective living requires *gaining skills* through interaction with one's world. Riding a bicycle, driving a car, reading a book, and planning a career are some examples.
2. Effective living requires a *degree of control* over one's daily life. Adjustment depends on the ability to make life decisions and choices.
3. Effective living requires redefining difficult situations in order to *successfully meet the challenges* of life.
4. Effective living requires *self-understanding*. Self-understanding allows one to determine which life choices are most likely to result in personal growth. Accurate assessment of personal characteristics enables one to form realistic *aspirations*.
5. Effective living requires the ability to make accurate judgments about the people and places in one's life.

● *aspirations*— ambitions or desires for achievement.

In the chapters that follow, adjustment is viewed in relation to the growth and adaptation that is made to specific life *contexts*. In order to consider this complex process adequately, we need to keep in mind three aspects of the total picture:

● *context*—the interrelated conditions in which something exists or occurs.

1. The person.
2. The environment.
3. The crises and stresses encountered at various phases of life.

● *dynamic*—marked by continuous activity or change. This activity is often energized by the conflict of opposites.

In the remainder of this chapter, basic concepts about the person, the environment, and the concept of crisis will be discussed. Living is *dynamic*. It is filled with contradictions, ironies, and surprises. The concepts we offer here are intended to provide a framework for summarizing or condensing life's peculiar unpredictabilities into some general categories. They are offered in the hopes of clarifying the factors that stimulate personal growth. In no sense are they intended to detract from the vivid, complex scenario of an individual's own personal life story.

THE PERSON

The concept of competence refers to any area of skill that would permit a person to be effective and controlled. A person is described

The emergence of competence

as competent when he or she is able to manage most tasks or challenges in a straightforward, skillful manner. Areas of competence range broadly from mathematical abilities to driving a car. One does not begin life with all the skills necessary for effective adult functioning. This does not mean that competence cannot be seen in infants and young children. Rather, it means that we must try to understand competence as a changing factor that is closely tied to one's stage of life.

The sense of competence is an internal psychological state. It is a result of feelings about: (1) one's ability to perform; and (2) the quality of one's performance.

The individual asks, "In relation to the way I have performed in the past, what do I expect my future performance will be like? How good will this performance be? How good am I?" We feel competent and at the same time we may wonder if we are going to be competent to meet future challenges. Our *sense of competence* is not the same as our *actual competence.* Someone may be very competent at what they do. Yet, they may not feel that they are going to do well or that they will be capable of meeting future challenges.

Ernest Hemingway is considered to be an outstanding author, certainly one of the most widely read of his time. He was often uncertain about his ability to write his next book. He constantly questioned his

Reprinted by permission. The Wall Street Journal

competence as an author. Even though his actual competence was confirmed, his sense of competence would not recognize this reality. In fact, a closer examination of Hemingway's life (Hotchner, 1966) reveals the author's pattern of continually testing himself in order to see if he was competent.

The understanding of behavior that results from understanding competence is complex. The relationship between actual competence and sense of competence needs to be considered. One might construct a table (see Table 2.1) showing some possible relations.

TABLE 2·1
Sense of competence

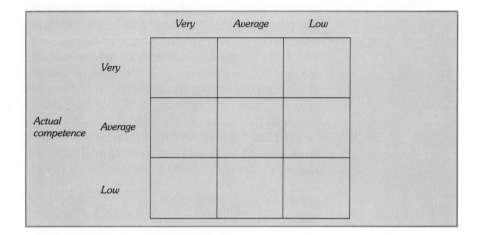

People vary on actual competence and sense of competence. Someone who *is* very competent may feel very competent, of average competence, or not very competent. Most people know individuals who think they are very competent but who do not do a very good job. We are also familiar with people who think they are competent and who are competent. Finally, there are people who think they are very competent, but who, in fact, are of average competence.

One's sense of competence influences not only what one does but how one does it. The relationship between actual competence and sense of competence has an impact on effective adjustment. We recognize that an objective assessment of a person's skills does not tell the whole story. We also need to know how the person evaluates his or her own ability to perform. A feeling of personal confidence can go a long way to compensate for a lack of skill.

Basic mechanisms of adjustment

Sensing and perceiving. Through the five sensory systems, sight, hearing, touch, taste, and smell, we take in information about our environment. Human beings have comparable sensory abilities. In other words, even though some people are farsighted and some are nearsighted, none can see behind their back the way an owl can. Each sensory mode shows the ability to adjust to the environment. Our eyes adjust to different levels of illumination so that we can see pretty well in a very dark room and in the bright sunlight. We can soak in a hot tub and grow comfortable in the warm water. After a while, a strong smell like fried fish or gasoline fumes becomes less noticeable. Each sensory system has adaptive capacities. However, each system also has limits to its adaptability. Intensely bright light can injure the eye. Intense, prolonged sound can injure one's hearing. We cannot adjust to total darkness, as in a cave, or to extreme heat or cold. What humans have done is to recognize the limits of their sensory systems and develop technologies to expand those limits. The microscope, the X ray, sonar, and the electric eye are all examples of techniques that extend our sensory capacities.

Perceiving organizes sensory information into meaningful concepts. We not only see a red color but recognize it as *red*. In fact, there are a whole array of colors that will be categorized as red unless the perceiver is really trying to make a distinction among shades. Perception, the capacity to impose meaning onto experience, is a companion to sensing in the process of adjustment. We understand things about what we see, hear, smell, touch, and taste. In seeing and hearing, we learn to judge size and distance by using sensory cues. We recognize components as part of a larger element. Upon entering the house, a certain smell, the sight of activity in the kitchen, the sounds of holiday music on the radio, all combine to say that the Christmas dinner is in the oven.

Sensing and perceiving aid adjustment in every phase of functioning. From recognizing a familiar face to habits like jogging or driving a car, sensory information is received and interpreted. We make use of what we know about our senses to create pleasurable experiences. Perfumes, paintings, music, clothing, and foods are all created to stimulate the senses. We also make use of what we know to design work settings, machines, roads, shopping areas, and advertisements to alter behavior.

Thinking.   Thinking is private mental activity. It involves the creation of mental imagery. Some thinking is not tied to real experience. It may bring together ideas, sensory experiences, or images that have never occurred together in reality.

Thinking requires the ability to represent sensory and motor experiences in a symbolic form. All normal humans have this capacity. Very young children may not be able to differentiate the symbol from the thing itself. A thought can be very frightening if the child does not know that the thought does not make something happen. Eventually people gain the skill to separate the symbol from the thing itself. In many cultures, symbols continue to be viewed as possessing power as a source of energy in themselves. This is what gives an idol, a totem, an amulet, or a ritual their value.

Thinking brings a degree of unity to past, present, and future experiences. One can transcend time in thought. Thinking also provides an

Jean-Claude Lejeune

outlet for behaviors through fantasy and imagination that might not be acceptable in reality. A person can imagine giving a tongue lashing to a superior, seducing a neighbor, or sailing the South Seas while sitting studiously at the library. Directed thinking is an essential element of problem solving. In thought, one can review, organize, and evaluate information. One can generate alternate solutions and consider their impact. In thought, one can suspend the demands of reality in order to consider what might be an ideal solution.

Thinking is vital for adjustment. It allows us to explore alternate solutions to problems before we take action. In deciding about a major, selecting a marriage partner, or choosing a career, we rely on thought to make effective choices. Through thought we understand ourselves and others. Even when we are under extreme stress, our ability to think things through is a major resource.

Reasoning. Reasoning refers to the ability to identify the logical implications of a statement, event, or relationship. In addition to thinking about experiences humans can also impose reason. They can assess information and evaluate whether or not the information is likely to be correct. They can attempt to predict cause-effect relationships. They invent sciences and philosophies based on the principles of logic. They make controlled observations and infer laws from those observations. Eventually, principles of logic and scientific law become more real, more convincing than our perceptions. For example, we understand that the world is spinning rapidly in space, whirling about the sun. Even though we do not perceive ourselves to be spinning or whirling, our belief in the logic of the scientific method forces us to overcome our experience of reality. We believe what we know to be true rather than what we experience.

Reason is a basic component in the process of adjustment. It permits one to think through a problem to a solution. Through reason we can question assumptions, seek new facts, weigh alternatives, and predict the outcome of our choices. Of course, as adults we also recognize the uncertainty of the future. Our reason itself tells us that no prediction is certain.

Learning. One of the most important processes that helps us adjust during our lives is learning. Behavioral scientists have identified different kinds of learning. These include the following:

Classical conditioning: associations that form primarily without conscious awareness. Example: feeling hungry at around 6 o'clock P.M.

Operant conditioning: habits or chains of behavior that form as a result of repetition and reward. Example: learning how to use a dictionary.

Avoidance conditioning: associations that lead to flight or withdrawal in order to avoid stimuli. Example: not touching a hot stove burner.

Observational learning: behaviors that are learned through imitation of successful behaviors of others. Example: imitating the voice of a famous singing star.

Insight: new behaviors that occur after reviewing possible responses mentally. Example: deciding on a birthday present for a good friend.

Learning how to learn: learning the general pattern of correct responses or rules that would apply across situations. Example: knowing how to take multiple choice tests.

Learning, however, almost always involves changing behavior as a result of one's experience. New knowledge, new skills, or new associations may be learned. These help people to behave flexibly and more effectively. Rather than making the same responses in every situation, humans learn to make different responses where they are appropriate. Hopefully, we make better rather than poorer responses as a result of learning. Learning is a process which allows us to break free from the control of instincts. We are able to make informed choices that allow us to build our own lives. Adjustment to life through learning is possible for all healthy humans.

Feeling.   All human beings have emotions. These emotions have a physical base in the hormone system. They also have a behavioral expression and a cognitive meaning. Feelings provide a bridge between the sensory and perceptual system, and the cognitive system. They alert us to the possible meaning of experiences. Basic feelings of anxiety, anger, and love are intimately tied to survival in human and other animal species.

Feelings are central adaptive mechanisms that serve as cues to oneself and to others. As cues to oneself, they alert us to possible sources of threat and comfort. As cues to others, they alert members of the social group to one's inner state. We send signals about needing help, about danger, or about vulnerability through the expression of feelings. The capacity for empathy links humans to their social group. When we recognize the same feelings in ourselves and in others we begin to understand more about human nature.

Identification.   Identification means becoming like someone else in attitudes, values, and behavior. Identification often takes place without much awareness and planning. It can also be deliberate. In the former case, we may take on the attitudes of our parents, teachers, or religious leaders out of a desire for their approval and love. In the latter case, we may try to be like an idol or hero in order to achieve his or her level of success.

Identification is a process that is central to socialization. Children take on the views of their parents. Citizens identify with their political leaders. Believers identify with their religious heroes or teachers. Workers identify with their superiors. Without having to spell out and teach every aspect of what is desirable, identification produces a more socialized group member. Through identification the person's personality is enriched. In the process of taking on the ideals and style of an admired person, one's own character is modified.

Coping.   When confronted with challenge, we tend to respond with increased effort and concentration. Coping is a general term for the many strategies people use to overcome obstacles. The tendency to cope, like the tendency to identify with others, seems almost automatic. There is something in the tension of a challenging situation that brings out renewed effort. A child struggles to open a closet door. An adolescent draws up the courage to ask a girl for a date. A new parent reads books, talks to friends, or visits the pediatrician to find out about the course of normal development. An older adult insists on keeping his own apartment, preparing his meals, and walking the mile and a half to the market to preserve his independence.

Even though coping skills differ at each life stage, the tendency to cope is always present. As such, it is the force that propels us toward growth. It brings skills that are well developed into contact with new problems. Through coping we may try to alter some aspect of the environment. We may also try to alter some aspect of ourselves. The goal of coping is preserving a sense of personal effectiveness. When one is coping, whether it is planned or a reaction to some sudden demand, the self is experienced as an agent in control of life choices.

Social responsiveness. The final mechanism for adjustment that we will discuss is social responsiveness. Humans are born into an active social system. From birth they are able to respond to social stimuli. Babies like to be held and rocked. They smile at the sound of the human voice. They focus on the human face with interest. The social motive is very strong. Simple things like smiling at a person, nodding one's head in an affirmative gesture, or saying uh huh, can serve as rewards for learning. People tend to cluster together. In a wide space they will build their homes together. People seek companionship at school, at work, in the community, and even in institutions like jails or mental hospitals.

One of the most painful experiences of life is loneliness. People try to avoid being lonely. They may even fear loneliness. From the earliest attachment of the infant to the mother, to the widower who seeks a new wife at age 80, people strive for a sense of relatedness. This does not mean that there are no loners. The need for social interaction is of varying strengths in different people. However, everyone is able to make social contact and wants to be understood by others. Our social needs draw us toward groups, toward friends, and toward lovers. Many of life's choices reflect the person's need to have relationships with others.

Sources of individuality

● *genetics*—the study of heredity.

There is enormous variability in the human species. Four sources of individuality are discussed: genetics, temperament, talent, and intelligence. Each adds resources that help us adjust to life challenges.

Genetics. Individuality is built into the species through the mechanisms of heredity. Each adult couple has the potential for producing vastly different children. There are three ways that genetic information can contribute to individual variability. First, genes control the tempo or rate of development (McClearn, 1970; Dworkin et. al., 1976). Age at the onset of puberty, the age at menopause, and the tempo of aging are examples of ways in which genetic information regulates physical changes. The rate of development has powerful implications for the emergence of competence in relation to one's age mates. Both early and delayed patterns have important psychological consequences.

Second, genetic information is responsible for the presence of individual traits. In addition to physical attributes like eye color, height, or weight, there appear to be genetic determinants of psychological characteristics as well. In studies comparing fraternal and identical twins, such variables as activity level, memory, and intelligence all show greater similarity among identical twins (Willerman, 1973; Wilson, 1974, 1975).

Finally, many abnormalities have a genetic cause (Reed, 1975). Some of these abnormalities result in fetal death early in pregnancy. Still, a large number of genetic disorders are expressed in living children who must strive to adapt to these irregularities. From the mild irregularities, like a shock of white hair or an elongated toe to disorders that lead to deafness or mental retardation, genetic variations create continuous challenges to adaptation.

Temperament. Gordon Allport (1961) defined temperament in the following way:

> Temperament refers to the characteristic phenomena of an individual's nature, including his susceptability to emotional stimulation, his customary strength and speed of response, the quality of his prevailing mood, and all the peculiarities of fluctuation and intensity of mood, these being phenomena regarded as dependent on constitutional makeup, and therefore largely hereditary in origin (p. 34).

There are three ways that a person's temperament can influence the responses of others (Buss & Plomin, 1975).

1. Temperament "sets the tone" for interactions. People who are sociable and who enjoy interacting with others will communicate a different mood as they encounter others than will people who are more reserved.
2. Temperamental differences will determine the kinds of behaviors a person may initiate. Active people are likely to engage in a continuous series of activities that will bring them into contact with a variety of objects and people. Because of this constant initiation others are more likely to be aware of the presence of active people. They are also more likely to interact with them.
3. Each temperamental quality may reward or discourage the responses of others. Others may react either positively or negatively to the person's temperamental qualities. Some parents feel rewarded by their child's high level of emotionality. They are acceptive and supportive when their child expresses joy, anger, or anxiety. These parents are likely to repeat those behaviors that stimulate the expression of emotion. Other parents are embarrassed or disgusted by overt emotional expressions. They are likely to punish those expressions or avoid situations that evoke them.

We see then that temperament has at least three means of influencing the environment. By setting the tone, initiating, and reinforcing or discouraging the responses of others individuals with different temperaments create different environments.

Talent. Individuality is expressed through the development of talent. By talent, we mean any human skill at which the person may excel. In order for an area of skill to be identified as a talent, the person should experience both pleasure and competence in doing the activity. The kinds of talents that have captured the interest of the scientific community tend to be related to intellectual and scientific excellence. The concept of talent, however, can extend to a wide range of capacities that have the potential to serve as a special resource for adaptation.

The variety of talents in a population appears to be almost infinite. Of course, some talents have greater application within a family, school, or community setting than others. The city dweller who is skillful at climbing steep, craggy cliffs, or at recognizing bird whistles may find little opportunity to exercise that talent and little social recognition for those special skills. The talent exists, nonetheless, and is important for the person in two ways. First, any skill feeds into the person's general sense of effectiveness.

Success in an area of talent provides a relatively conflict free sphere of behavior through which the person experiences competence. Second, the recognition of a particular talent contributes to the self-concept. The person who likes to sing and who sings well begins to appreciate singing as one feature of his or her uniqueness. This particular talent may provide an avenue for achieving excellence in adulthood that is not available to those who do not share this aptitude.

Talents may be nurtured or ignored by the society. In addition to providing the person with a sense of competence and self-definition, talents provide a diverse set of valued activities for groups of people. When cultures are complex and specialized as ours is, there is a need for people with particular talents to fill unique roles (Buss & Poley, 1976). The fact that the particular skills are important for the functioning of the group does not mean that every person needs to acquire the same set of skills. It does mean that individuals who have important talents be allowed to develop them.

Intelligence. Individuality is expressed through differences in intelligence. *Intelligence* is a general term for all those skills involved in finding meaning in information from many sources and planning responses.

One element of intelligence is thought. Thought is the mental activity that is necessary to analyze, integrate, organize, or compare information. People differ in how much they attend to inner mental activity. Not all people are equally likely to use symbols to represent sensory and motor experiences (Singer, 1966, 1973). Some people spend more time thinking than others. For some, thought is more vivid than it is for others. Differences in the preoccupation with thoughts and reflections will result in different strategies for coping with impulses and for problem solving.

Another element of intelligence is knowledge. As people encounter different life events, they gather different kinds of information. The degree of freedom a person has to explore, to ask questions, and to experiment will influence the kinds of information that are gathered. People also may have different degrees of access to information. Knowing where information is stored and how to retrieve it broadens one's knowledge base. Even if you do not know something, you may know how to find out about it when you need to. Through formal education, students learn

John Penzari

Access to information contributes to individuality.

to identify sources of new information. They learn the mechanisms for finding out what is known about a particular topic (Hyman, 1975).

A third element of intelligence is reasoning. Individuals differ in their capacity to identify the logical implications of ideas or information. Some people readily evaluate each situation objectively. They search for the logically best interpretation or solution. Others tend to approach problems more intuitively. They depend on their sense of the social meaning or the emotional tone of an event rather than the principles of *logic*. Finally, some people approach problems in a patterned, rather rigid way. They rely on the opinions of authorities, superiors, or parents rather than exercising their own reasoning abilities.

Genetics, temperament, talent, and intelligence all contribute to differences in the emergence of adaptive strategies. As we strive to appreciate the process of adjustment, we must keep these inner resources in mind.

● *logic*—the discipline dealing with the methods and standards of correct reasoning.

Each person's capacity to understand and to react to life experiences will be influenced by these powerful sources of individuality.

Recapitualization

People acquire competence in the use of each of the basic mechanisms of adjustment mentioned earlier. Individuality is achieved by the way in which genetics, temperament, talent, and intelligence affect the basic mechanisms. People with different degrees of competence use basic mechanisms for adjusting to life. The sources of individuality ensure that each person adjusts in their own way. This is summarized in Figure 2.1.

FIGURE 2·1
The person: Competence, basic mechanisms of adjustment, and sources of individuality

Basic mechanisms of adjustment	Sources of individuality			
	Genetics	Temperament	Talent	Intelligence
C O M P E T E N C E — Sensing and perceiving, Thinking, Reasoning, Learning, Feeling, Identification, Coping, Social responsiveness	What role does biology play?	Are you active, difficult, . . . ?	What do you do extremely well?	How good is your mind?

THE ENVIRONMENT

In our discussion of the person we emphasized three concepts:

1. The emergence of new competences at each life stage.
2. Basic mechanisms of adjustment.
3. Sources of individuality that influence the preferences, strengths, and weaknesses of each person.

These concepts take us a long way toward an understanding of the process of adjustment. They are incomplete, however, without a framework for understanding the environmental contexts in which adaptation occurs.

Definitions of environment

● *ground*—the background in a perception.

● *figure*—the focus of attention.

12,436

The concept of environment requires definition. Five ways of thinking about the environment are presented here. In the broadest sense, the notion of the environment is similar to the gestalt concept of *ground*. It is everything else outside the boundaries created by the *figure*. If we are focusing on an infant as the figure, then the parents, siblings, the home setting, and the community are all elements of the environment. If we focus on the whole family group as the figure, then the home setting and the community would be the environment or the ground. A second view of the environment focuses on the physical dimensions of a setting (Ittelson et al., 1974; Proshansky et al., 1976). They include the architectural design of spaces, the amount of space available per person, and physical aspects of a location including landmarks, unique sounds and smells, and paths for moving through the setting. A third view of the environment focuses on the organized contexts for social interaction (Newman & Newman, 1978). The person moves through a sequence of environments from the family to the nursery or day care, to the elementary, junior high, and high school, and so on. At each new life stage, the person will be involved in a greater number of environments. Each of them generates expectations for a higher level of functioning than was the case at earlier stages. Not until later adulthood does the number of settings begin to decrease. Even then, reduced participation depends on the person's health and on earlier preferences for social involvement.

A fourth view of the environment focuses on the perceived environment or the life space (Lewin, 1935). In this view, the important elements of the environment are only those of which the person is aware. What is more, the environment is seen as meaningful only insofar as the person imposes organization and meaning upon it. Many people, settings, and events may exist in an objective account of reality of which the person is not aware. These aspects of the environment would not "count" from this point of view. Only if these elements of the environment make an impact on the person's awareness, would they become components of the perceived environment.

Finally, there is the definition of the environment as behavior settings (Barker, 1963; Gump, 1971). The concept of behavior setting brings together the views of the physical environment and the psychological environment. Behavior settings are meaningful patterns of activity that take place in a bounded, identifiable space. They have shared meaning to all the participants. They are more limited than total social organizations. Rather they are the units of which the larger organization is composed. Behavior settings in a home might include the dining area at mealtime, the bedroom when the family watches television, the bedroom when the people are sleeping, or the bathroom when the children are having their bath. The idea is that the activity and the people who are involved influence the meaning of the setting just as much as the physical aspects of the space.

Behavior settings have meaning because of the activities that are taking place, qualities of the physical space, and the relation between present, past, and future activities in the setting. Environments may function as different settings depending on what behaviors are occurring. The cafeteria of a high school may provide the physical context for a large, all-school lecture, for daily eating, for a spring prom, or for a study hall. Each of these behavior settings is unique despite their common location.

Environments are defined in part by the social systems to which they are linked. They are also defined by the uses people make of them. The backseat of a car can be transformed into a setting for sexual intimacy. The hallways of a school building can be a quiet setting for social interaction. They can also be a congested tunnel of rushing and pushing depending on the organization and rules of the school system. The total environment is defined by the collection of behavior settings in which the person participates. The effects of the environment depend on the demands for performance in each behavior setting and the kinds of settings to which the person has access.

The concept of a psychosocial system

Frequently when we think about adjustment, we tend to emphasize the response the person makes in order to cope with the stable or unalterable challenges of life. Environmental events are viewed as the cause and personal change as the consequence. On closer inspection, however, we see that this is not the whole picture. People frequently cause environmental change. What is more, environments, especially social groups, do not generally impose demands that ignore the needs of the participants. The person and the social environment are part of an interactive network or psychosocial system. The person brings certain resources and needs to the social organization. The social organization offers resources and makes demands on the person. In order for the person to survive and thrive, certain needs must be met. Likewise, in order for the social group to survive, the individual members must make the commitments necessary to maintain group values and skills (Kelly, 1968). This means that the group's resources must be channeled so that members can consume what they need. These resources may be material, like food, money, or clothing, or they may be psychological, like encouragement, a feeling of freedom, or love. As resources are channeled through a psychosocial system, they are not exhausted. Rather, supplies are consumed in one form and transformed into another form to be fed back into the system. For example, money, benefits, and encouragement paid out by the employer are transformed into energy, time and commitment fed into the work setting by the employee.

Both the person and the system must be able to change or adapt. A family may increase in size. A school finds new ethnic or economic groups moving into its district. A business requires new competences of its employees in order to flourish. Each of these social groups must be able to change when necessary in order to remain effective. Adaptation is therefore not only a characteristic of persons but of surviving social systems (Moos, 1976). Sometimes the press for change comes from outside the social group as when a job transfer requires a family to move. Sometimes the press for change comes from within the social group as when a couple decide to start a new business or to move to a larger house. In either case, the openness to change and the ability to make the most adaptive responses to new demands will improve the social group's chances for continuation and growth.

Donald Smetzer

Succession. Chief Tau ili ili (at left with ula around neck) is being installed. Honors must also be paid to the most elderly man in the village. He sits next to the three-tiered birthday cake that has just been presented to him.

A psychosocial system must also be able to provide mechanisms for succession. Succession refers to each group's concern with its own continuation. Societies need adult who want to bear children, to care for them, and to provide the resources necessary for children to eventually take on adult roles. Religious groups need to have members who will be committed to teaching the beliefs and customs of the religion to the next generation. Businesses need mechanisms to pass on the leadership from one executive to the next. Governments have mechanisms for the placement of people who hold public office. In any social group, there will be socialization pressures aimed at building commitment to the group. Part of the process of adaptation is learning the norms for each social

● *norms*—collective expectations, or rules for behavior, held by members of a group or society.

system. Another part is internalizing those *norms*. They become part of one's own goals as well as the goals of the group. In these ways, persons are changed through their participation in social systems. Of course, individuals may also shape the socialization process through their own contributions. By demonstrating certain competences, a certain style of leadership, or certain values, individuals can alter the mechanisms for succession. Based on one person's contributions, the system may encourage new behaviors in future generations.

The flexibility or rigidity of environments

We assume that there is a dynamic interaction between individuals and their social groups. Both the person and the group are involved in a process of adaptation. Changes in individuals may stimulate changes in the psychosocial system and changes in the system may stimulate changes in the person. Just as persons demonstrate individuality, so do psychosocial environments. Not all systems are equally open to change. Not all systems are equally responsive to the contributions of members. Not all systems have adequate mechanisms for making the transition from one generation to the next.

The notion of the flexibility or rigidity of the environment refers to the degree to which individuals can make a meaningful impact. Think of families that operate under different patterns of parental authority. The very authoritarian parents do not encourage their children's participation in family decision making. Children's needs and ideas are only responded to when parents think it necessary. The family in this instance can be viewed as very rigid from the child's point of view. In contrast, very permissive parents do not offer any systematic structure for family life. Children experience acceptance for any behaviors, expressions, or impulses that may arise. The system in the permissive family is open to change, perhaps even to the point of creating confusion.

Systems may also differ in the speed with which change can occur. In the late 1960s Ralph Nader brought the matter of automobile safety to the attention of the government and the public. What followed were discussions about government standards for safety, the development of designs for safety equipment, a process of testing new safety devices, and the gradual addition of such devices into new models. More than a decade later, some safety features are standard equipment in every automobile and some are still being developed. The industry has negotiated a timeline for providing the safety features to meet government standards. In this example, it will probably be close to 20 years before the demands for change actually result in effective safety features. What is clear from this example is that it has not been easy for the automobile industry to respond quickly to demands for change. However, with continued pressure from government and from consumers, the industry can be made to be responsive.

Large organizations need not be slow to change. For example, when the United States entered World War II there was a rapid conversion of industry and manpower from a peace-time economy to an economy designed to support the war effort. New priorities for production, rationing of supplies, and mobilization of a large military force all occurred within a relatively short period of time.

The degree of flexibility of the environment will have an impact on personal adjustment. Members of highly structured, rigid social systems may feel helpless about the possibility of bringing about change. They may encounter more conflict as they run up against resistance to change. Or, they may feel that the only way to meet personal needs is to leave the inflexible group. In contrast, members of highly flexible, poorly defined social systems may feel frustrated that the channels for influence are so unclear.

Resources in the environment

● *socioeconomic status*—one's ranking on a number of social and financial indicators, including years of education, kind of work, and salary.

Another dimension along which environments differ is the availability of resources. If we think of a family group, the parents' education, their salaries, and their talents could all be considered personal resources. Children might contribute their own talents, energy, and information as personal resources. We know that the resources parents bring to the family have significant impact on the development of children. For example, in a sample of 26,000 children who were followed from birth through age four, the *socioeconomic status* of the family and the mother's education were the best predictors of the chidren's intelligence at age four (Broman, Nichols, & Kennedy, 1975). Marital satisfaction, another form of personal adjustment, is positively associated with family income and level of education (Blood & Wolfe, 1960; Renne, 1970). Families with more resources have better access to information. They can function with more flexibility. They are less preoccupied with the chronic stresses of hunger, illness, and poor-quality housing.

Just as families differ in the amount of resources they control, other social systems differ in their access to resources. Communities may not have adequate funds to maintain a full school program. Countries may not produce enough food to feed all the citizens. Businesses may lay off employees as their profits decline. In these and other circumstances, people are faced with the challenge of adapting in a resource poor system. The lack of resources may prompt behaviors that would not be observed in a more plentiful environment. The threat of reduced resources or the actual lack of resources will focus more of life's energy on seeking these resources. Less energy will be available for the satisfaction of conceptual, artistic, or spiritual needs (Maslow, 1954, 1962).

● *objective*—existing independent of the mind.

● *subjective*—from the person's own point of view.

We see the environment, then, as a mixture of physical, social, and organizational structures. The environment has *objective* as well as *subjective* realities. The objective environment includes the dimensions of the physical space, and the existence of social settings about which many people can agree. The physical terrain, the climate, and the population density are all examples of the objective reality of the physical space. The presence of certain stores, certain social groups, and certain resources

Climate is one aspect of the objective environment that influences adjustment.

Living laboratory 2·1

THE ENVIRONMENT

Purpose: To apply the concept of channeling of resources to a specific environment.

Method: Identify a social environment with which you are familiar, either a family group, a high school, or a neighborhood. List all the resources you know about in the specific environment.

Results: Try to draw a flowchart showing how resources are channeled from one member, group, or other source to another.

Discussion: Do all participants of the system contribute resources?

Do resources retain their form or are they changed as they are used by the different groups or members?

Do you identify resource-rich and resource-poor members of the system? What would you say are the consequences of this kind of inequity?

in the community are examples of the objective reality of the social settings. The subjective reality includes all the personal meanings and private experiences associated with the environment. The subjective environment extends to the limits of the person's awareness. If a social group exists but the person is not aware of that group's existence, then that group is not an element in the subjective reality.

Settings, characteristics of terrain, or even specific changes in temperature are experienced differently by different people. The significance of any aspect of the environment depends on how it is interpreted by the person. Of course, when the same environmental events are viewed in the same way by many people, then we can have confidence that the environment is having a clear impact on adjustment. If the temperature drops to 12° F. and many people put on heavy coats, hats, and gloves, we can attribute their behavior to an environmental change. If the temperature is 70° F. and one person begins to add layers and layers of clothing, we can attribute the adjustment to some failure in the person's own temperature regulating mechanism.

In thinking about the process of adaptation, it is necessary to take a dynamic view of persons and environments. Adaptation is a product of people's needs and resources in interaction with the resources and expectations of the psychosocial system. Within this framework, specific aspects of the environment, especially its flexibility and its resources, will have direct impact on personal adaptation.

CRISIS AND GROWTH

The model of adjustment we have presented thus far includes a picture of a developing person with a variety of inner resources. The person is involved with one or more complex psychosocial environments. The challenge of living involves meeting personal needs and experiencing a sense of personal effectiveness while, at the same time, meeting the expectations of the relevant psychosocial environments. Now, we add to this picture the theme of crisis. Crisis involves periods of tension, painful confusion, and intense emotions.

The life history: A unique sequence of circumstances and responses

In order to understand crisis, we must consider the personal life history in which the crisis occurs. As lives progress through time, a personal history is acquired. Each person has many, many experiences. The order, sequence, and intensity of experiences varies greatly from person to person. No two histories are the same. The personal history becomes a factor in determining the pattern of subsequent life events. We carry with us memories of early interactions, of pleasant or unpleasant settings, and of decisions and their outcomes. At each new stage we have memories of a younger, less experienced self. We also remember the way others behaved who were at the particular life stage we now enter. We remember an older brother, an uncle, a parent, or a grandparent.

In the case of Mr. White (Case 2.1), the memories of the depression

---

Case 2·1

THE LIFE HISTORY: MEMORIES OF THE DEPRESSION

How can you know what people went through here, during the Depression? I was a young kid when my father lost his job and all his money. It was horrible, believe me. Millions of people went on relief. We didn't go around hungry, mind you; but it was awful. I remember my mother crying. Once, even my father cried. He ran around looking for a job, any job, and came back home empty-handed. He stretched out on the couch in the living room and cried like a child. "I cannot provide for my family,"

he cried. My mother had a bug for cleanliness; she would never let anyone lie down on the couch with shoes on. My sister wanted to say something to my father, but my mother whispered, "Leave Daddy alone. You can see how he's crying. We may have to sell our furniture—the couch, too."

I will never forget this scene: my father on the couch, my mother and sister crying . . . this scene comes often to my mind. Last night I felt like crying; I don't know why. . . .

Source: B. B. Wolman, *Victims of Success: Emotional Problems of Executives* (New York: Quadrangle/The New York Times Co., 1973), p. 7.

---

haunt him in his adult life. He is plagued by fears about money. The image of his father's pain is a source of insecurity about his own success.

Beginning in adolescence and continuing through adult life, we make deliberate decisions that alter the course of future life events. The decision to marry and the choice of a partner, the decision to have children, or the choice of a specific work role entwine us in a pattern of interactions. Each decision has powerful consequences for our own psychological growth. Our own personal history becomes an increasingly important element in our psychology. For some, the personal history is dominated by experiences of successful coping and effective decision making. They confront life challenges with the confidence that earlier success provides. For others, the personal history is dominated by negative consequences following life choices, repeated failures, and maladaptive coping strategies. These people approach new life stages with a sense of doubt and hopelessness that is a product of earlier failures. It is always possible that a

---

Living Laboratory 2·2

THE PERSON

Purpose:	To enhance understanding of the concept of life history.
Method:	Make a chart of your life history. On the left side of a sheet of paper list each of the years of your life. Across the top, make columns labeled family, school, friends, historical events, and other. Fill in the table identifying circumstances that you perceive to have had a formative impact on your own adjustment. You may want to include the learning of new skills, kinds of school settings, special family events, crises, successes or failures, or unusual opportunities and experiences.
Results:	Do you see increased use of certain columns during specific life stages? Are all columns used every year? Using the chart as a basis, divide your life into stages. How many stages are there? What made you separate one period from another?
Discussion:	Do you see any patterns emerging from your own life history?
	Are there some periods that appear more critical in your own development than others?
	How do family and school forces interact in your own life story? Do they tend to compliment or conflict with each other?
	To what extent did historical events have an impact on the immediate experiences of your life?
	Did any events occur close together in time that may have had a special impact because of this coincidence?

---

single failure at a particular life challenge can motivate a person to future success. A chain of failures, on the other hand, is likely to produce a self-attitude that interferes with future growth. For most of us, the personal history is neither a stairway to the stars nor a dismal tragedy. It is the mix of successes and failures, the blend of meaningful, highlight events that guide our choices. The lessons of experience become more and more useful as our personal goals for adjustment are clarified.

The concept of crisis

Although theorists differ in their definition of normative crisis, in general they refer to predictable stress points that tend to occur when competences do not match environmental demands. Four views of normative crisis are discussed:

1. The psychosocial crisis.
2. The dialectic view of crisis.
3. The field theory approch to crisis.
4. The concept of crisis as natural interventions.

The psychosocial approach emphasizes the discrepancy between cultural expectations and personal resources (Erikson, 1950; Newman & Newman, 1979). At every life stage, new growth occurs. This growth is a result of the tension between the person's level of development and the society's pressure for greater integration or greater effectiveness. Painful as they are, these psychosocial crises may stimulate a higher level of psychosocial functioning.

In the dialectic view, crisis occurs when there are strong, competing claims for limited resources. It can also occur when uncertainty in one role leads to poor performance of other roles (Riegel, 1975). For example, starting a new job and having a new baby at the same time may be viewed as a crisis. Retirement and widowhood, if they occurred together, would be a potential source of crisis. Many of life's events appear to move in harmony with new skills building neatly on earlier achievements. However, a normal life can also be seen as filled with a considerable amount of *contradiction*. One may be hired for a job for which one is not qualified. One may marry a person who does not share one's personal goals. One may live in a community where one is a victim of racial or ethnic prejudice. The examples of potential life conflicts are numerous. The important point is that individuals are not necessarily devastated by these conflicts. In fact, some people seek out conflict. They prefer the tension of conflict to the boredom of predictability. The existence of this kind of conflict in life forces a rethinking of goals and resources. This thoughtful reworking is likely to stimulate important adjustments.

The third view of normative crisis is derived from field theory (Lewin, 1936, 1946, 1951). In this theory the environment and the person are described as divided into regions, each with its own boundaries. Inner regions of the person represent areas of information and competence. Regions in the environment represent people, objects, social groups, or physical settings that populate the life space. Uncertainty exists when experiences are encountered for which no bounded regions exist. Thus normal life crises would be viewed as sudden increases in experiences that do not have well-defined regions. Uncertainty and its partner, anxiety, persist whenever there is a serious gap between the concepts the person holds about the environment or the self and the range of daily experiences.

● *contradiction—* **inconsistency.**

United Press International

Natural disasters can set life on a new course.

Any marked shift in roles, major physical changes, or movement to a new town would generate a period of crisis due to the inadequacy of existing concepts.

A final view of normative crisis includes events that can be called natural *interventions* (Feldman & Feldman, 1974). These events are less predictable than psychosocial crises. Such events as parental divorce, unemployment, or death of a spouse can be seen as relatively common occurrences for the society as a whole. They are unusual stress points in the life of any single individual. Some natural interventions are crises that touch the lives of many people at the same time as in the case of a plane crash or an earthquake. Because the events run contrary to our hopes and to what is viewed as the normal pattern of life events, they

● **intervention—an event that alters the course of one's life.**

catch us off guard. Once they occur, the course of life may be dramatically altered. One usually cannot prepare for the onset of these natural interventions.

Some kinds of stress are a product of a major shift in cultural context. The culture, like the air around us, often goes unnoticed. When we experience extensive cultural *discontinuity* the consequences can be profound. Even when we can prepare for this kind of crisis, it may still bring experiences of uncertainty, value conflict, and feelings of isolation. Culture change can pose a serious challenge to personal resources and coping skills.

● *discontinuity*—a break in the normal flow.

Adaptation and maladaptation

When we think about crisis, one question that arises is how well does the person cope. To what extent can we describe a particular response to life events as adaptive? In order to appreciate the process of adjustment, we must have some criteria for evaluating adaptation. What does it mean to say that a response is adaptive or maladaptive? If someone throws a stone at you, how adaptive is it to close your eyes? Yet, this is a common response to threat.

In biology, adaptation refers to the process whereby a plant or animal becomes fitted to the environment. This may involve a variety of structural changes in the organism. These changes permit the organism to make use of changing resources or to survive changes in ecological conditions such as temperature, vegetation, or *terrain* (Ford, 1971). Adaptation may require movement to a new environment. It may require the modification of the environment so that it is better suited to the biological attributes of the organism.

● *terrain*—the physical features of a tract of land.

From this view, we can still ask about more or less adequate forms of adaptation. All organisms are not ideally suited to their surrounds. What are the clues that adaptation is most effective? Darwin (1859, 1871) suggested that the criteria for "fitness" was reproductive success. He argued that the most well-adapted members of a species would contribute more of their *genes* to the gene pool of the next generation than would the less well-adapted members. Rather than survival itself as the criteria, "reproductive vigor" was taken as the most important evidence of successful adaptation.

● *genes*—the smallest units of heredity information.

When we shift from a biological to a psychological definition of adaptation, the concept becomes more complex. Phillips (1968) offered the following definition of adaptation:

> In our view adaptation implies two divergent yet complementary forms of response to the human environment. The first is to accept and respond effectively to those societal expectations that confront each person according to his age and sex. . . . In another sense, however, adaptation means more than a simple acceptance of societal norms. It implies a flexibil-

Living laboratory 2·3

CRISIS AND GROWTH

Purpose: To clarify the meaning of different kinds of crises.

To identify the differences between adaptive and maladaptive responses to crisis.

Method: Give three or four examples of each of the following kinds of crisis:

1. Psychosocial crisis.

2. Crisis of life contradictions.

3. Natural intervention.

4. Crisis of cultural change.

5. Disaster.

Results: Take one of the examples and write a description of an adaptive and a maladaptive response to the same crisis event.

Discussion: What are the differences between the adaptive and the maladaptive responses?

Are there some responses to crisis that might be adaptive in the short run and maladaptive if they were carried on for a longer time?

---

ity and effectiveness in meeting novel and potentially disruptive conditions, and of imposing one's own direction on the course of events (p. 2).

This definition suggests that the criteria for successful adaptation include fitting into the psychosocial system. Fitting in means developing the expected skills and internalizing the values of the social group. In addition, adaptation includes the ability to exercise one's will, to make independent decisions.

To this view of adaptation we would add a psychological counterpart to the biological notion of reproductive vigor. Another way to evaluate adaptation would be to determine the degree to which the adjustment or change contributes to the quality of life for future generations. The most effective forms of adaptation would have a positive impact on future generations. In other words, personal growth is not the only criteria for adaptation. One must also be concerned about the implications of personal change for one's own children, the children of the larger community, and the subsequent direction of social evolution. If you will, this criteria provides ethical guidelines for the process of adaptation. Without it, the *psychopath,* the tyrant, or the dictator could be seen as outstanding examples of personal adaptation having ultimate control over a wide array of resources and imposing their will to direct the course of life events.

● *psychopath*—a person who displays aggressive antisocial behavior and feels no guilt.

Chapter summary

This chapter provides the groundwork for an understanding of how adjustment happens. It is necessary to understand that the things we've talked about to describe the person are all happening at the same time. How thinking and feeling influence each other will differ from person to person. We described *eight* processes of adjustment that we all use. What we must remember is that the ways these processes are used by people is so different. There are no two people alike. We talk about what results from thinking, sensing, perceiving, reasoning, learning, feeling, identifying, coping, and interacting as adjusting to life. The person experiences the results as a total person. When we try to adjust we have different genes, temperaments, talents, and intellects that make it absolutely certain that our efforts are ours alone. We live in a world which we did not make and cannot control. Living brings us into contact with people, places, and things all the time. From our lives we develop a sense of competence. We have a rating of how good we are at doing things based on what we've done. The sense of competence is important because it sets up an expectation in our minds about what is *going* to happen when we do something. One thing research tells us is that what we think is going to happen influences what we do. If we think we are going to do something well, we approach it differently than if we think we are going to fail. The approach may be as important as anything else in determining success. Thus, the sense of competence produces future experiences of competence by the way it helps us approach a problem or crisis. Crises happen to all of us. They often have a very strong effect on us because of the intensity with which they happen. Knowing you can handle it even when it's something completely new and overwhelming helps produce growth from crisis.

SUGGESTED READINGS

For a more detailed introduction to the study of learning, *the following will be helpful:*

Bolles, R. C. *Learning theory* (2d ed.). New York: Holt, 1979.

Hintzman, D. L. *The psychology of learning and memory.* San Francisco: Freeman, 1978.

For a more detailed introduction to the study of personality, *the following will be helpful:*

Maddi, S. R. *Personality theories: A comparative analysis* (4th ed.). Homewood, Ill.: Dorsey, 1980.

Mischel, W. *Introduction to personality* (2d ed.) New York: Holt, 1976.

For a more detailed introduction to the study of development, *the following will be helpful:*

Newman, B. M., & Newman, P. R. *Development through life: A psychosocial approach* (2d ed.). Homewood, Ill.: Dorsey, 1979.

For a more detailed introduction to environmental psychology, *the following will be helpful:*

Barker, R. G., and Associates. *Habitats, environments and human behavior.* San Francisco: Jossey-Bass, 1978.

Ittelson, W. H., Proshansky, H. M., Rivlin, L. G., & Winkel, G. H. *An introduction to environmental psychology.* New York: Holt, 1974.

For a more detailed introduction to coping and adaptation, *the following will be helpful:*

Coelho, G. V., Hamburg, D. A., & Adams, J. E. (Eds.). *Coping and adaptation.* New York: Basic Books, 1974.

Reading

ON HEALTH AND GROWTH

We have, in the last few decades, learned more about the development and growth of the individual and about his motivations (especially unconscious motivations) than in the whole of human history before us (excepting, of course, the implicit wisdom expressed in the Bible or Shakespeare). Increasing numbers of us come to the conclusion that a child and even a baby—perhaps even the fetus—sensitively reflect the quality of the milieu in which they grow up. Children feel the tensions, insecurities, and rages of their parents even if they do not know their causes or witness their most overt manifestations. Therefore, you cannot fool children. To develop a child with a healthy personality, a parent must be a genuine person in a genuine milieu. This, today, is difficult because rapid changes in the milieu often make it hard to know whether one must be genuine *against* a changing milieu or whether one may hope for a chance to do one's bit in the way of bettering or stabilizing conditions. It is difficult, also, because in a changing world we are trying out—we must try out—new ways. To bring up children in personal and tolerant ways, based on information and education rather than on tradition, is a very new way: it exposes parents to many additional insecurities, which are temporarily increased by psychiatry (and by such products of psychiatric thinking as the present paper). Psychiatric thinking sees the world so full of dangers that it is hard to relax one's caution. I, too, have pointed to more dangers than to constructive avenues of action. Perhaps we can hope that this is only an indication that we are progressing through one stage of learning. When a man learns how to drive, he must become conscious of all the things that *might* happen; and he must learn to hear and see and read all the danger signals on his dashboard and along

the road. Yet he may hope that some day, when he has outgrown this stage of learning, he will be able to glide with the greatest of ease through the landscape, enjoying the view with the confident knowledge that he will react to signs of mechanical trouble or road obstruction with automatic and effective speed.

We are now working toward, and fighting for, a world in which the harvest of democracy may be reaped. But if we want to make the world safe for democracy, we must first make democracy safe for the healthy child. In order to ban autocracy, exploitation, and inequality in the world, we must first realize that the first inequality in life is that of child and adult. Human childhood is long, so that parents and schools may have time to accept the child's personality in trust and to help it to be disciplined and human in the best sense known to us. This long childhood exposes the child to grave anxieties and to a lasting sense of insecurity which, if unduly and senselessly intensified, persists in the adult in the form of vague anxiety—anxiety which, in turn, contributes specifically to the tension of personal, political, and even international life. This long childhood exposes adults to the temptations of thoughtlessly and often cruelly exploiting the child's dependence by making him pay for the psychological debts owed to us by others, by making him the victim of tensions which we will not, or dare not, correct in ourselves or in our surroundings. We have learned not to stunt a child's growing body with child labor; we must now learn not to break his growing spirit by making him the victim of our anxieties.

If we will only learn to let live, the plan for growth is all there.

Source: Erik H. Erikson, "Growth and Crises of the Healthy Personality," *Psychological Issues,* (vol. 1, no. 1 (1959), pp. 50–100. From *Identity and the Life Cycle* by Erik H. Erikson, by permission of W. W. Norton & Company, Inc. Copyright © 1980 by W. W. Norton & Company, Inc. Copyright © 1959 by International Universities Press, Inc.

PART TWO
THE PERSON

The photography of H. Armstrong Roberts

Chapter 3
The self-concept

One's-self I sing, a simple separate person,
Yet utter the work Democratic, the word En-Masse.

Of physiology from top to toe I sing,
Not physiognomy alone nor brain alone is worthy for the
    Muse, I say the Form complete is worthier far,
The Female equally with the Male I sing.

Of Life immense in passion, pulse, and power,
Cheerful, for freest action form'd under the laws divine,
The Modern Man I sing.

Walt Whitman, *One's-Self I Sing*

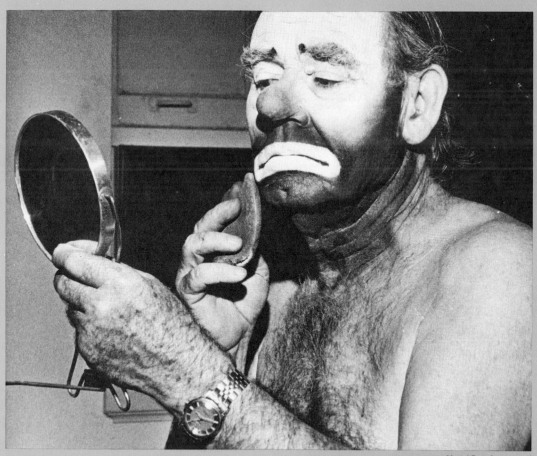

United Press International

43

One morning when two-and-half-year-old Jim was ready to get dressed, his mother brought in a box of clothes that had belonged to a slightly older neighbor, Freddy Stone. The clothes were too small for Freddy, and Jim's mother was glad to add them to Jimmy's wardrobe. As she slipped on each item, Jim would ask: "Is this Freddy's shirt?" Is this Freddy's pants?" "Is this Freddy's socks?" to which his mother smiled and said, "Yes, this was Freddy's." When Jim was all dressed, he looked up at his mother for a moment and said: "This is Freddy Stone's shirt and pants and socks and jacket. Am I Freddy Stone?"

The self-concept is a gradually evolving set of thoughts and feelings about oneself. It provides an organized structure against which to evaluate personal stability and change. As adults, we experience the self as a familiar core of memories, behaviors, thoughts, and preferences. As our example suggests, however, the self-concept does not emerge fully formed. It is built on interactions with the social and physical environment, self-reflection, and cognitive and emotional maturity. In this chapter, three major questions are addressed:

1. What are the dimensions of the self-concept? What are the factors that contribute to the total self-concept?
2. How does the self-concept change over life?
3. How vulnerable or flexible is the self-concept in the face of social pressure?

DIMENSIONS OF THE SELF-CONCEPT

The self-concept is a blend of experiences that Allport (1968) defines as "the self-as-known—that which is experienced as warm and central, as of importance." The self-concept adds integration to the diversity of life activities. It also gives momentum and direction to future growth. There are seven dimensions of the self. Each adds content, depth, and energy to the self-concept.

Bodily self

Focus for a moment on your physical self. The feel of the inside of your mouth; the flow of air through your mouth, nose, throat, and lungs; the tightening and relaxing of muscles; the rumbling of your stomach; each of these and other physical sensations give a continuing physical reality to the self-concept. In addition to these familiar sensations, feelings of pleasure and pain mark the range of physical sensations associated with the self. Parts of your physical self that are viewed as acceptable, including your fingernails, your blood, your mucus, your bowel movements, or your body odor, would be treated as disgusting when they are from another person's body. There is a primitive investment in the bodily self. The body is a basic source of intimate knowledge and commitment to the self.

Self-recognition

Go to the mirror and look at your reflection. Are there any questions in your mind about the identity of the person whose reflection you see? Our response to our reflected image, to our name or to photographs of ourselves are all examples of self-recognition. These familiar experiences add stability to the self-concept. The importance of self-recognition is illustrated by the sense of uncertainty that men experience when they shave away a beard or the disorientation that patients feel after plastic surgery that changes their facial features.

Extensions

The self extends beyond its physical boundaries to objects, spaces, and important people. A child's special blanket, a lifelong home, a prized piece of art work, even a loved parent may be viewed as belonging to the person. Children as young as two or three will guard their prized possessions jealously. They express anger or grief if another child takes away a specially loved toy or sits in a special chair. Identifying the self with specific objects, space, or other people continues into adulthood. People may use objects to prove their importance or their status. They may guard their home or business with weapons. They may even take the lives of others who threaten to destroy valued objects or to dominate personal space.

The reflected self

People make comments about you and treat you in a certain way. These behaviors show their attitudes and notions about who you are. Life is filled with messages from others about who one is thought to be. These include simple things like being recognized by another person or being confused with someone else. Messages from others also include evaluation about one's worth. The reflected self includes the responses from many different people across time. The more roles one plays and the more diverse one's social interactions, the more complex one's reflected image. From the array of reflected images, one abstracts certain *attributes* that are taken to be accurate descriptions of the self. Whether or not these attributes are accurate may be hard to evaluate. As the old saying goes, "If ten people tell you that you are drunk, you had better go home and go to bed." Some people resist the messages that are implied in the reflected self. They may not accept another person's lowly opinion of them. They may struggle to surpass what others describe as insurmountable limitations. Most people, however, are likely to take the opinions of important others quite seriously. These opinions then become part of the person's own definition of selfhood.

● **attributes**—the qualities that are descriptive of oneself and others.

● **feedback**— information that a person receives after doing some action.

It is important to realize that the opinions of others about you may be very arbitrary. They may be a result of another person's jealousy or another person's idolization of you. It may be a grave mistake to believe another person's low opinion of you. Similarly it may be a mistake to trust too heavily the opinions of people who only compliment you. Accurate, honest feedback about one's strengths and weaknesses becomes a very treasured resource that is not easy to find.

Personal competences

The things you do well contribute content to the self-concept. Personal competences continue to emerge at each stage of development. Because of this, the self-concept will be revised now and again to include new areas of mastery. In addition to developmental skills, there are special areas of talent that increase a person's expertise or effectiveness. Competences expand one's sphere of influence. They may provide direct sources of satisfaction through the experiences of mastery. They may also stimulate the positive responses of others. One can think of the exercise of competence as having physical components as in the ability to ride a bicycle or drive a car, as well as cognitive and socioemotional components. In this sense, personal competences contribute to all aspects of the self-concept. What is more, knowledge of one's competences lends a sense of confidence that certain challenges or problems can be managed. A history of the effectiveness should contribute a general tone of optimism to the self-concept.

Similarly, areas of incompetence also feed into the self-concept. Experiences of failure, clumsiness, boredom, or confusion signal areas in which one may not excel. When failure is experienced as very shameful, when it results in public ridicule, the person may be reluctant to strive for excellence in the areas that have produced this shame. Each person's self-concept contains negative elements. These include things the person does not do well or challenges the person does not feel have been adequately met.

Aspirations and goals

One of the components of the self involves the formulation of life goals. This aspect of self is most important during adolescent and adult life (Allport, 1961). The process of deciding on goals lends a forward movement to the self-concept. The person is not content to exist but seeks to grow, to become. The hope of future achievements makes immediate problems endurable. What is more, most people do not limit their self-definition to what they have already achieved. They include a vision about where they are headed. One is not only a college student, but a college student aspiring to be a lawyer or an engineer or a business executive. Take away the goals, the dreams of tomorrow, and the balance of daily activities becomes far less meaningful. For those who are depressed about attaining future goals there is an accompanying depressed feeling about the value of the self.

*Special talents can bring the admiration and
approval of others.*

Self-esteem

For every aspect of the self-concept including the physical self, the reflected self, or the array of personal aspirations and goals, the person makes an evaluation of the worthiness of those characteristics. Feelings of being loved, valued, admired, or successful contribute to a positive sense of worth. Feelings of being ignored, rejected, scorned, or inadequate contribute to a negative sense of worthlessness. Self-esteem can be changed depending on whether one succeeds or fails at an important goal. It can be increased by positive responses from important others and reduced by negative responses. By adulthood a feeling about one's worth is established that sets a positive or negative tone about future life events. Self-esteem contributes to one's willingness to take risks, to

TABLE 3·1
Dimensions of the
self-concept

1. The bodily self	Physical experiences; body boundaries; sensations of pleasure and pain.
2. Self-recognition	Awareness of one's appearance.
3. Extensions of the self	Important objects, spaces, or people.
4. The reflected self	Opinions, comments, or actions of others toward the self.
5. Personal competences	Skills and talents.
6. Aspirations and goals	Meaningful life goals that give a sense of purpose to the self.
7. Self-esteem	Evaluation of the self as worthy or unworthy.

● **expectations—views
held by oneself or by
others about what is
appropriate behavior in
a given situation or at a
given stage of
development.**

expectations about success or failure, and to the belief that one will have an impact on others.

The seven dimensions of the self-concept listed in Table 3·1. Each dimension contributes to the continuity, the creativity, and the persistence of the self-concept. The self is knowable through our physical experiences, our physical appearance, our identification of objects, spaces, and people

Living laboratory 3·1

DIMENSIONS OF THE SELF-CONCEPT

Purpose: To connect the dimensions of the self-concept discussed in the text to the personal experience of selfhood.

To distinguish one's personal experience of self from the self as perceived by others.

Method: Spend five minutes looking at your image in a mirror. Concentrate on what you see, trying to be as objective as possible.

Results: Write ten phrases or sentences in answer to the question: Who am I? When you have finished, take another sheet of paper and imagine that you are your own father. How would your father answer the same question about you? What ten sentences or phrases would be used to describe *you?* Write them down.

Discussion: What kinds of thoughts did you have as you looked at your face? How much is your physical appearance connected to your feelings of selfhood?

What dimensions of the self-concept were reflected in your own answers to the question who am I?

In what ways do you think your father's perception of you differs from your own? To check this, you might want to ask your father to give his own answers to this question.

How is the self as known to others different from the self as known to you? How is it the same?

linked to the self, and in the comments of others about the self. The person's effectiveness is determined by the personal competences and life goals included in the self-concept. Self-esteem influences behavior and expectations about the likely outcome of life choices.

LIFE CHANGES IN THE SELF—CONCEPT

Changes in physical appearance, size, strength, and sexual maturation may all modify the experience of selfhood. Changes in how complicated one's mind is brings new information about the self and new awareness of the components of the self (Epstein, 1973; L'Ecuyer, 1978). Involvement in new roles and more complex social organizations adds new content and new skills to the self-concept. Our inner experience convinces us that we are basically the same person today that we were yesterday. However, we also recognize important areas of growth that have taken place over the years. In fact, as our memories of childhood fade, there are fewer and fewer links between the content of the self-concept during the first decade of life and the content of the self-concept during adulthood. In the discussion that follows, important changes in the self-concept are traced through each of the life stages.

Infancy (birth to 18 months)

An awareness of self comes through the gradual process of adaptation to the environment (Piaget, 1960). As the child explores objects and alters his or her behavior to adjust to those objects, the child is also discovering aspects of selfhood. Trying to put a large block into one's mouth and finding that it will not fit or trying to touch a furry bear and discovering that one's arm cannot reach it are lessons in selfhood as well as lessons about the world of objects. Each encounter with an object that does not readily fit what has already been learned teaches the child about some properties of the self as well as the environment. Every time the child has to change his or her behavior to interact more effectively with an object or a person, the child learns about some new part of the self.

For qualities of behavior emerge during the first 18 months of life that suggest a growing appreciation of self. First, infants are sensitive to events that occur as a direct result of their own actions. As early as one to two months babies are able to use sucking, kicking, or head turning to influence the environment (Bruner, 1968; Rovee & Rovee, 1969).

Second, by three months infants begin to explore their hands, face, and feet. Self-play includes cheerful babbling and chirping, gazing at one's hands, sucking on toes, or gently stroking hair or cloth. All of these behaviors suggest a growing awareness of the pleasures associated with self-stimulation.

A third expression of self-awareness is self-recognition. A child's response to his or her mirror image is an early indication of recognition of self. By five months of age, infants respond to several aspects of the mirror image including eye-to-eye contact, the dependence of the image's movement on the baby's own movement. A smiling expression, faceness, and the similarity of the visual image to past images of the child's own face (Papousek & Papousek, 1974).

Self-recognition is related to a fourth aspect of the self-concept—recognition of other familiar objects. At five or six months infants get very excited when they hear a familiar voice or recognize a familiar place. This growing awareness of familiar experiences is evidence of the infant's understanding of a personal history. "All these things are happening to me. I have experienced them before."

Toddlerhood (18 months to 4 years)

Selfhood is expressed in almost every part of the toddler's life. Language skills allow the toddler to communicate notions of self to the adult world. Language brings not only communication but a growing set of verbal labels and concepts. Toddlers realize that every object, including themselves, has a name. Naming objects serves as a means for creating boundaries in the physical world. Objects can be recognized and sorted by their verbal labels. Initially, toddlers do not separate the name for an object and the object itself. They do not view verbal labels as representations or symbols but as components of the object (Dale, 1976).

Two important verbal labels that toddlers begin to use correctly are the words boy and girl. These are called gender labels. By 36 months of age, children can apply these gender labels to behavior. They are aware of *sex-role stereotypes* that are different for males and females (Thompson, 1975). Another verbal label that has importance to the emerging self-concept is the toddler's own name. The investment that toddlers place in their names is not easily abandoned. One of the quickest ways to offend children is to make a joke about their name. In fact, even in adulthood, we tend to be ruffled if someone forgets or makes a mistake in pronouncing our name. Often, the choice of a first name is associated with characteristics that parents admire. Names of famous people (Moses, Mary, Martin, Luther), beauties of nature (Rose, Dawn), or admired qualities (Faith, Joy, Honor) add specific meaning to the child's self-concept. Jahoda (1954) described the naming practices of the Ashanti of West Africa. The Ashanti thought that children born on different days had different personalities. A child was named for the day on which he or she was born. A boy born on Monday, for example, would be named Kwadwo and would be expected to act in a quiet, calm manner. Jahoda searched police records for evidence of juvenile delinquency among the Ashanti. Boys born on Monday had very low rates. Boys born on Wednesday (a day associated with an aggressive personality) had very high rates of violent offenses.

During toddlerhood, there is an extension of body boundaries to include material possessions and family members. "Mine" and the recognition of personal possessions are clear evidence that the child experiences selfhood (Allport, 1955): Possessiveness is a gauge of the self-concept. (The child who does not have a clear idea of self will not protest or

● *sex-role stereotypes*—an elaborate set of beliefs about what males and females ought to do or be like.

U.S. Department of Housing and Urban Development

Through peer interactions toddlers learn to assert "mine-ness" and to share.

● *subordinate*—to place
in a lower order, class,
or rank.

insist on ownership of material objects.) The child who is in the process of forming a good self-concept may be most insistent on the proper designation of things as "mine" or "not mine." In fact, the child who is working on issues of self-concept may try to attribute "mine-ness" to most every object in sight. Children who have resolved their uncertainty about the boundaries of self may be more willing to entertain notions of generosity, sharing, and taking turns. These concepts require some reduction of "mine-ness" in the service of "our-ness."

All through life there are setbacks in a person's capacity to *subordinate* "mine-ness" for "our-ness." If toddlers do not like to share or take turns, one need not look far to find adult models who do not like to share or take turns either. In the adult community, this can be regarded favorably as "individualism." In childhood, it is often condemned as selfishness or, at best, condoned as childishness. In adulthood, childish selfishness can be transformed into acceptable business practices.

In toddlerhood, the self-concept is stabilized by giving it a name. It is amplified by acquiring possessions. A third element in the self-concept of the toddler is the beginning of a capacity to scan and respond to inner states. The toddler can identify mood states and changes in mood. Toddlers will engage in fantasy play. Occasionally, toddlers will share a memory, giving evidence of their attention to the flow of inner mental activities. Toddlers begin to experience and report nightmares. All these examples of the toddler's awareness of mental activity support the view that toddler's self-concept includes a private, inner world. At the same time as toddlers are imposing their selfhood willfully on others, they are awakening to the many inner states that mark their separateness.

Toddlers are sensitive to the first social components of the self-concept—the self as it is reflected in others (Allport, 1961; Rogers, 1959). Children hear other people talk about them, praise them, or criticize them. If these comments are repeated frequently, they may form the core of the reflected self. Children who are repeatedly told they are cute, smart, devilish, or a bother will begin to include these characteristics in their self-concept. Rogers (1961) has argued that during toddlerhood, children begin to recognize that some of their behaviors are valued and others are not. This means that children learn that they are loved and valued when they behave according to certain expectations. They feel they are not loved when they disappoint these expectations. Parents, relatives, adults in the community, and even older siblings impose these conditions of worth. As a result, children begin to question just how lovable or valuable they really are.

Finally, toddlers often think they can do just about everything. In every aspect of life, toddlers exert their will. "I can do it," "Let me try," "It's my turn." Successful coping is accompanied by a surge of good feeling (Murphy & Moriarty, 1976). Because toddlers have a limited point of view about the difficulty or skill required for most tasks, they approach life with a sense of all-powerfulness. Over time, children experience differences between their competences and the kinds of challenges they attempt. From these differences children form a clearer idea of their actual competences.

The kind of caregiving the child experiences is an important element in the outcome of early coping (White and Watts, 1973; Smith, 1968). Depending on parental responses, children can feel that they are entitled to express their willfulness or that their will must always be suppressed. Children can learn that starting new things will result in danger or that it may frequently result in success. Parents contribute to the child's positive self-image by providing a safe, intriguing world to explore. Parents help children clarify their self-concept through verbal and nonverbal recognition of the child's worth.

Early school age (5 to 7)

During early school age the child's self-concept develops in several ways that are basic to successful psychosocial development. Changes in cognitive maturation, sex-role development, and moral thought each contribute to new personal expectations. Often, these changes in competence and self-definition are accompanied by new expectations from adults for more mature, controlled, and responsible behavior (Erikson, 1950; Whiting & Whiting, 1975).

During early school age, new intellectual competences give children tools for thinking about the self (Piaget, 1970). Classification skills allow children to understand notions of family, kinship, friendship, and association. Their relationship to others and to socially organized units is clarified. An understanding of oneself, one's group(s), other groups, and the orderings among these forces begins during early school age. The ability to order and think about relationships directly influences self-concept development (Rubin & Maioni, 1975).

By the age of four or five, children have learned what is expected from boys and girls in their culture (Masters and Wilkinson, 1976; Flerx, Fidler, & Rogers, 1976). Through observation, imitation, and conversation, children learn the kinds of behavior that are valued for males and females in their culture. During early school age, children begin to form a sex-role preference. They are able to assess the advantages and disadvantages of their own sex role. They begin to consider how well their own inner temperament and talent match the cultural expectations for sex-role behavior (Lynn, 1966).

In early school age, the ideal self becomes part of the self-concept (Freud, 1963; Hartmann, 1964). Children begin to appreciate the moral implications of behavior. They develop categories of desirable and undesirable behavior. The early-school-age child, eager for approval, is sensitive to social messages about what others expect of the ideal child (Kohlberg, 1964).

A final contribution to the development of the self-concept during early school age is a sense of initiative (Erikson, 1950). In social situations some people learn to view themselves as initiators of activity and interaction. Others do not. The view of the self as an effective or ineffective initiator that has been evolving since infancy is crystallized in this phase. The view one takes of oneself as a vital originator of action has a major influence on self-concept for one's entire life.

Early-school-age children may experience rapid changes in feelings of self-worth (Long, Henderson, & Ziller, 1967; Yamamoto, 1972; Gordon, 1972). They are increasingly aware of differences between their own skills and the skills of older children. Children may question their identity. They may feel worthless, restless, bored, or depressed. Children are more willing to have unfavorable thoughts about themselves. Changes in self-esteem may lead to changes in the child's self-concept.

Middle school age (8 to 12)

● **norms—collective expectations, or rules for behavior, held by members of a group or society.**

We begin the discussion of self-concept in infancy with an emphasis on the physical experiences of selfhood. There is no question that the physical changes associated with puberty result in a new self-image that is filled with emotional reactions (Clifford, 1971). As children approach puberty, they must include all they know about sexuality in a new point of view about the self as a sexual object. Cultural *norms* about body type influence the positive or negative value placed on the changes that are taking place (Jourard & Secord, 1955). Children who perceive themselves as too fat, too thin, too bosomy, or too clumsy for the norm, may begin to hold negative attitudes toward the self as a result of body changes. Most children at this age make comparisons between their body

Luis Medina

Admired heroes give content to the young child's ideal self.

and the mature adult body. Often, children do not understand that maturation will continue to alter their appearance for five to eight more years. Children may feel unhappy about their attractiveness on the basis of the first, uneven changes in appearance that occur at age 11 or 12. They may have difficulty revising those evaluations when adult stature has been attained (Dwyer & Mayer, 1968–69).

During the first years of middle school age, children show an eagerness for a great variety of new activities. These activities lead to the development of new skills. Manual dexterity, self-control, peer cooperation, planning, and prolonged concentration are some of the skills the middle school age child develops. Erikson (1950) has described the psychosocial accomplishment of this stage as a sense of industry. Industry refers to the child's joy in work and work-related activities. Children begin to sense the ways they might contribute to their social community through the achievement of valued skills.

The underside of this picture of growing competence is the child's

Donald Smetzer

A young Samoan boy learns to scrape taro,
a basic food in his family's daily diet.

increasingly realistic capacity for self-evaluation. Middle school age children are highly sensitive to social expectations (Shantz, 1975). After the delight of learning new skills, a sense of the criteria for excellence emerges. For every activity, the inexperienced child discovers that there are some people who are excellent at that particular activity. One must decide if one has the talent to become excellent. If so, one must also evaluate whether one has the resources and the motivation to pursue this excellence. A child learns to sail a boat or play a guitar at age eight. By age 10 or 11 that child must begin to evaluate how important that skill is to his or her continued sense of competence. The theme of skill development and skill evaluation provides the final childhood content to the image of oneself as a person who initiates activities.

Early adolescence

Many methods have been used to evaluate developmental changes in the self-concept during adolescence. The interpretation of research on the self-concept is made somewhat difficult because every method uses a different definition of the self-concept. The studies that we will review here suggest some of the dimensions along which the self-concept is being revised during early adolescence, from puberty until about age 18.

To study developmental changes in self-concept, Montemayor and Eisen (1977) asked subjects in grades 4, 6, 8, 10, and 12 to give 20 responses to the question "Who am I?" The answers were coded into 30 categories. The categories reflected roles, personality, activities, membership in groups, and physical characteristics. From childhood to adolescence there was significant increase in the use of five categories:

1. Existential, I am myself.
2. Abstract category, a person, a human.
3. Self-determination, ambitious, a hard worker.
4. Interpersonal style, friendly, nice.
5. Psychic style, happy, calm.

The biggest change came between the fourth and sixth graders. Sixth graders responded more like 12th graders than they did like 4th graders.

Three subjects' responses give a feeling for the common changes

---

Case 3·1

BRUCE C.

My name is Bruce C. I have brown eyes. I have brown hair. I have brown eyebrows. I'm nine years old. I *love!* Sports. I have seven people in my family. I have *great!* eyesight. I have lots! of friends. I live on 1923 P. Dr. I'am going on 10 in September. I'am a boy. I have a uncle that is almost 7 feet tall. My school is P. My teacher is Mrs. V. I play Hockey! I'am almost the smartest boy in the class. I *love!* food. I love fresh air. I *love* School.

Case 3·2

A GIRL

My name is A. I'm a human being. I'm a girl. I'm a truthful person. I'm not pretty. I do so-so in my studies. I'm a very good cellist. I'm a very good pianist. I'm a little bit tall for my age. I like several boys. I like several girls. I'm old-fashioned. I play tennis. I am a *very* good swimmer. I try to be helpful. I'm always ready to be friends with anybody. Mostly I'm good, but I lose my temper. I'm not well-liked by some girls and boys. I love sports and music. I don't know if I'm liked by boys or not.

---

in self-decriptions at ages 9, 11½, and 17 (Montemayor & Eisen, 1977, pp. 314–19).

These first responses are from a nine-year-old boy in the fourth grade. Bruce describes very concrete aspects of his self. Note the references to his sex, age, name, territory, likes, and physical self.

The next statement is from a girl, age 11½, in the sixth grade. It describes her interpersonal style and her personality as well as physical qualities.

The final example is from a 17-year-old girl, in the 12th grade. Note the emphasis on interpersonal style, mood states, and the many references to political and personal beliefs.

These three examples illustrate the changing quality of the concepts that are viewed as central to the self. The youngest subject gave many actual qualities of the self. The self is described in reference to things the subject likes or likes to do. The self is defined by the specific people or settings with which the person is directly associated. The latter two examples make more reference to values, personality, and social relationships. The oldest subject includes political and religious qualities in her self-description. She even includes her own self-conscious feelings of uniqueness in her description.

Other studies of the self-concept during early adolescence confirm these changes. There do appear to be both personal and social dimensions to the self-concept. Adolescents are sensitive to the difference between

---

Case 3·3

A TEENAGER

I am a human being. I am a girl. I am an individual. I don't know who I am. I am a Pisces. I am a moody person. I am an indecisive person. I am an ambitious person. I am a very curious person. I am a confused person. I am not an individual. I am a loner. I am an American (God help me). I am a Democrat. I am a liberal person. I am a radical. I am a conservative. I am a pseudo-liberal. I am an atheist. I am not a classifiable person (i.e.—I don't want to be).

their ideal selves, what they think they ought to be like, and their real selves. Sometimes, this difference creates anxiety. Adolescents may despair about whether they will ever measure up to their idealized concept of adult competence and adult social relationships. One of the most impressive qualities of early adolescence is the intense concern with the self. Self-consciousness, including both critical and admiring thoughts about oneself, increases. Self-consciousness draws adolescents inward. It may even impose barriers between adolescents and their parents and peers.

Later adolescence

In later adolescence, from about 18–22, much of the uncertainty of the earlier period is resolved through formation of a personal identity. Erik Erikson has provided a discussion of the meaning and functions of personal identity. Later adolescents struggle with questions about their nature in much the same way that early-school-age children puzzle about their origins. In their efforts to define themselves, adolescents must blend their bonds to the past with their hopes for the future. Identity serves as an anchor point. It allows the person a basic sense of continuity in social relationships. Erikson (1959) states:

> . . . The young individual must learn to be most himself where he means the most to others—those others, to be sure, who have come to mean most to him. The term identity expresses such a mutual relation in that it connotes both a persistent sameness within oneself (self-sameness) and a persistent sharing of some kind of essential character with others (p. 102).

Erikson believes one's culture influences identity. Personal identity will reflect the values of groups the individual wants to be a member of. It will also reflect the values of one's country. Americans feel that certain values (which are, in fact, American values) are part of their psychological makeup. The resolution of the search for identity is, therefore, the final step in the internalization of cultural values.

As young people move through the stage of later adolescence, they find that the family, neighborhood, teachers, friends, ethnic group, or nation hold certain expectations for the behavior of a person at this age. There are expectations to work, marry, serve the country, attend church, and vote. The persistent demands of important people produce certain decisions that might have been made differently or not made at all if the individual alone was involved in identity formation. There is, in fact, a threat to identity formation which results from these external demands. People may slip easily into roles that are expected of them, without ever feeling a strong personal commitment to those social expectations. Erikson quotes from the autobiography of George Bernard Shaw in making this point:

> I made good in spite of myself, and found, to my dismay, that Business, instead of expelling me as the worthless imposter I was, was fastening

upon me no intention of letting me go. Behold me, therefore, in my 20th year, with a business training in an occupation which I detested as cordially as any sane person lets himself detest anything he cannot escape from. In March 1876, I broke loose (p. 103).

For those who do not "break loose," the situation described by Shaw is called *identity foreclosure* (Marcia, 1966). This is one form of resolution of the identity crisis. It involves premature decisions about one's identity, often in response to the demands of others. Young people may decide early in their adolescence that they will become what parents or grandparents wish them to become. They never question this decision in relation to their developing personality. Individuals may be firm in their commitment to these decisions without fully understanding whether or not the decisions will be enhancing to their continued growth.

Sometimes the cultural expectations and demands provide the young person with a clearly defined self-image that is completely contrary to cultural values. This is called a negative identity (Erikson, 1959). Phrases like *failure, good-for-nothing, juvenile delinquent, hood, greaser,* and *burnout* are labels that are applied to certain adolescents. In the absence of any signs that success would be possible, the young person may accept these negative labels as a self-definition. The person proceeds to establish this identity by acting in ways that will strengthen it. The negative identity can also emerge as a result of a strong identification with someone who has been devalued in the family or the community. Identification with a loving uncle who is an alcoholic can lead to a view of the self as one who shares these undesired qualities.

The foreclosed identity and the negative identity are both examples of resolutions of the identity crisis that fall short of the goal of a positive personal identity. They do provide the person with a concrete identity. Role diffusion is a resolution of the identity crisis that can lead to serious problems. In this state, young people are unable to make a commitment to any single view of themselves. They cannot blend the various roles they play. They may be torn by opposing value systems. They may lack confidence in their ability to make meaningful decisions. The resulting diffusion arouses anxiety, apathy, and hostility toward the existing roles, none of which can be successfully adopted.

Dolores, an unemployed college dropout, describes the feeling of meaningless drifting that is associated with role diffusion.

In the process of forming a personal identity, we all experience moments of confusion and depression. The task of bringing together the many elements of experience into a clear self-definition is difficult and time-consuming. Adolescents experience self-preoccupation, isolation, and discouragement, as the pieces of the puzzle are shifted and reordered into the total picture. For all of us, identity achievement will be the result of some degree of role confusion. The outcome of role diffusion is one in which no commitment is made to a single view of the self. In this

Case 3·4

DOLORES

I have two sisters, and my father always told me I was the smartest of all, that I was smarter than he was, and that I could do anything I wanted to do . . . but somehow, I don't really know why, everything I turned to came to nothing. After six years of analysis I still don't know why. (She looked off into space for a moment and her eyes seemed to lose their train of her thought. Then she shook herself and went on.) I've always drifted . . . just drifted. My parents never forced me to work. I needn't work even now. I had every opportunity to find out what I really wanted to do. But . . . nothing I did satisfied me, and I would just stop . . . Or turn away . . . Or go on a trip. I worked for a big company for a while . . . Then my parents went to Paris and I just went with them . . . I came back . . . got married . . . divorced . . . drifted. (Her voice grew more halting.) I feel my life is such a waste. I'd like to write, I really would; but I don't know. I just can't get going (Gornick, 1971, 77–84, 209–10).

The photography of H. Armstrong Roberts

Some adolescents experience role diffusion. They cannot settle on any single view of themselves.

case, individuals have the persistent fear that they are losing hold on themselves and on their future. The inability to formulate and commit oneself to a positive personal identity is a major obstacle to subsequent adjustment.

Early adulthood   Two studies of the life course during adulthood provide evidence about the kinds of changes in the self-concept that are likely to occur in early and middle adulthood. Levinson (1977; Levinson et al., 1977) studied the lives of 40 men. They were selected from each of the following professions: hourly workers in industry, business executives, academic biologists, and novelists. Each person was interviewed for 10 to 20 hours. The interviews were designed to reconstruct the person's life between the ages of 18 and 45. They focused on the sequence of events, the way they were experienced, and the interconnections across events. R. L. Gould (1972, 1975) administered a questionnaire about major life concerns to 524 male and female subjects between the ages of 16 to 60. Each person was asked to rank the importance of 16 life concerns. Age groupings, or patterns of development, were determined by mapping those age periods during which many statements changed their rank order.

Table 3.2 shows the life phases that emerged from these two studies and the main issues described by Levinson and Gould. While the age ranges studied are not identical, the descriptions suggest some important aspects of adult development.

1. Growth of autonomy.
2. Tension between hopes and achievements in work, marriage, and child rearing.
3. Confrontation with established expectations for success.
4. Assessment, reshaping, and search for the life structure that will provide personal meaning.

In early adulthood there appear to be two major phases (Phases II and III). The first phase involves expansion, autonomy, and acting on the basis of values established during later adolescence. The second phase finds conflicts among life roles. Young adults experience dissatisfaction with the outcome of some initial life choices. They try to set things straight by modifying commitments so that they more accurately reflect personal values.

Several changes in the self-concept can be inferred from these patterns. First, there is an opportunity to perceive oneself as an active agent who can determine the course of one's life. This experience of control is expressed in such varied activities as selecting a marriage partner, selecting employment, choosing a place to live. Young adults distinguish themselves from children and adolescents who have less freedom of choice anf from older adults who have more responsibilities and less energy. Third, because young adults begin so many new roles at the same time, they have an increased sense of their lack of

TABLE 3·2
Phases of adult life

		Levinson	Gould
Phase I		Ages 18–21	Ages 17–22
		Early adult transition: Moving out of pre-adult world Experimenting and choosing adult roles	Growing, independence from family, openness to new ideas
Phase II		Ages 22–28	Ages 22–28
		Entering the adult world: Exploring options Developing a stable life structure	Stabilization of concerns, autonomous, engaged in work, confident
Phase III		Ages 29–36	Ages 28–33
		The age 30 transition: Making efforts to improve or correct the life structure Peaking of marital problems and occupational shifts	Increasing dissatisfactions, more self-reflection, dissatisfaction with marriage, increasing investment in children
Phase IV		Ages 37–43	Ages 33–40
		Settling down: Establishing a niche and "making it" Identifying the steps on the ladder of success; strives to achieve authority and independence Reappraising goals and achievements	Quiet desperation, time is finite, concerns about health increase, concerns arise about one's own parents
Phase V		Ages 45 and over Restabilization	Ages 40–50 Stabilization of personality, increased involvement with spouse, children and friends; an acceptance of the way things are

experience. The constant supervision and evaluation in the role of worker, potential conflict of goals in the marriage, or anxiety and fatigue in the role of parent may prompt serious reevaluation of personal goals. Toward the end of early adulthood, people evaluate their aspirations and goals. The results of this evaluation will set the direction of future life choices. The self-concept is actively adapting to information that emerges as the person's lifestyle is called into question.

Middle adulthood

In middle adulthood, at about the age of 40, there is a focused effort to make things count. The "quiet desperation," as Gould describes it, comes from the anxiety that perhaps important goals will not be reached. Depending on one's point of view, life is either half gone or half more to go. There are two major adjustments in the self-concept during the middle adult years. The first involves redefining one's standards for success. The second involves evaluating the meaningful activities and relationships in one's life. During these years one begins to set aside

● *reciprocal roles—*
**behavior patterns that
permit the players to
alternate the specific
parts they play, as in
batter, fielder, pitcher or
the hiders and seekers.**

some of the constraints of social norms and be more oneself. With support from others in *reciprocal roles,* especially co-workers, children, and marriage partner, it is a time to enjoy one's own lifestyle and personal philosophy. Some adults find that other people are critical or rejecting of their role behavior. If there are constant feelings of inadequacy, then middle adulthood can become a time of unpleasant preoccupation with oneself and one's immediate needs.

A number of researchers have raised questions about sources of satisfaction, stress, or perceptions of well-being in adulthood. These studies begin to fill out the picture of the way people value different aspects of life experience. They find patterns of satisfactions at various phases of adult life. Daniel and Lachman (1975) asked subjects in the age range from the teens to the 70s, "What would you consider to be your prime of life and why?" Older subjects were likely to see the prime years in the past, middle adults were likely to see the prime years in the present, and younger subjects were likely to see the prime years in the future. There was a drop among those selecting the future in the age range 40 to 50. There was also an increase in those selecting the past during those same years. This suggests that the decade from 40 to 50 may be an important *subjective* transition point in perceptions of happiness or satisfaction. Interestingly, at any age no more than 40 percent of subjects was the present as the prime of life. This suggests that many people fall into the trap of looking ahead or looking back to the times of greatest enjoyment and satisfaction.

● *subjective—*from the
person's own point of
view.

Later adulthood

Most older adults tend to feel *more* satisfied with their marriage and parenting roles, their work accomplishments, and their overall lifestyle than younger adults do (Gurin, Veroff, & Feld, 1960; Veroff, Melnick, & Kulka, 1977). In general, older adults feel as positive about themselves as younger adults feel about themselves (Moore, 1975; Riley and Foner, 1968). In four surveys, however, older adults perceived themselves not as "elderly" but as "middle-aged" (Streib, 1968). Resistance to seeing oneself as elderly implies that adults make a distinction between being an older adult who is still active, healthy, and involved (the "middle-aged" older adult) and being one who is irritable, ill, and passive (the "elderly" older adult). Two studies found that older adults who perceived themselves as "old" were more maladjusted than those who saw themselves as young or middle aged (Busse, 1961; Jyrkila, 1960). In other words, one way of adjusting to aging is to resist seeing yourself as old. Identification with the label of old is linked with the convergence of several stressful life events, including poor health, suddenly reduced activity, widowhood, or declining income (Ward, 1977). We would expect, that the self-esteem of older adults, particularly those who have come to later adulthood with a sense of acceptance about their past life, would be high. Studies of the relationship between self-attitudes and age have bearing here. Back (1971) asked adults in the age range 45 to 70 to describe their self-concept. Women tended to use more personal back-

Older adults with high morale do not see themselves as old.

ground characteristics to describe themselves. Men used more personality characteristics or values. As children left the home, women tended to identify their self-image more with their own abilities and feelings than with background variables. There was increased similarity between their real and social selves. For men, differences between the real and the social self increased as they struggled with the issues of retirement.

Women appear to become less self-critical and more confident during their 50s (Gurin et al., 1960; Lowenthal & Chiriboga, 1973). Older women begin to show less "feminine" characteristics, especially of the type that tend to be devalued by both men and women. Some of the freedom from role constraints permits women to enjoy their own personalities. They feel more comfortable with the competences they have already developed (Turner, 1977).

In the case of Therese Carter, we see how a middle-class woman who describes herself as "just a housewife" looks forward to her adult-

Case 3·5

THERESE CARTER

I enjoy cooking. If it was a job, maybe I wouldn't like doing it. As low on the totem pole as I consider being a housewife, I love every minute of it. You will hear me gripe and groan like everybody else, but I do enjoy it.

I'll also enjoy it when the kids are all gone. I always had the feeling that I can *really*—oh, I don't know what I want to do, but whatever that would be, I can do it. I'll be on my own. I'm looking forward to it. Just a lot of things I've never taken the time to do.

I've never been to the Art Institute. Now that might be one thing I might do. (Laughs.) I've grown up in Chicago and I've never been there and I think that's terrible. Because I've never gotten on the train and gone. I can't spend all that time there yet. But pretty soon I'll be able to.

I haven't been to the Museum of Science and Industry for ten years at least. These things are nothing special to anybody else, but to me they would be. And to sit down and read one whole book in one afternoon if I felt like it. That would be something!

When the kids leave I want it to be a happy kind of time. Just to do the things I would like to do. Not traveling. Just to do what you want to do not at a certain time or a certain day. Sewing a whole dress at one time. Or cooking for just two people.

That's what makes me feel guilty. Usually when kids go off and get married the mother sits and cries. But I'm afraid I'm just gonna smile all the way through it.

Source: S. Terkel, *Working* (New York: Pantheon Books, a Division of Random House, Inc., 1972, 1974) p. 302.

hood. She sees it as a period of time when she can indulge herself in the things she likes to do and to rediscover feelings of selfhood.

Summary of the life changes in the self-concept

In infancy, the self-concept is primarily an awareness of one's independent existence. The infant discovers body boundaries, learns to identify recurring needs, and feels the comfort of loving contact with caregivers. These experiences are gradually included in a sense of the self. In toddlerhood, the self-concept grows through an active process of self-differentiation. Children explore the limits of their skills and the nature of their impact on others. The toddler's self-concept depends upon being competent and being loved. There is little concern about the perceptions of others, cultural norms, or future plans.

During early and middle school age, the child becomes more aware of differences in perspective. Knowledge about logical relationships feeds into a clearer concept of cultural norms. The child is also aware of moral principles that define good and evil. All these cognitive gains make the child more sensitive to social pressure, more likely to experience feelings of guilt or failure, and more preoccupied with issues of self-criticism and self-evaluation. At the same time, children between the ages of 5 and 12 remain dependent upon adults for material and emotional resources. Thus, the self-concept is likely to be quite vulnerable during these years. Children continue to need reassurances about their skills and about being loved. They can think about the future concretely enough to begin to worry about the kinds of responsibilities that will be expected of them as adults. The fact that they will have increased skills and resources to meet those future expectations may not be entirely obvious to children.

The self-concept is strengthened during later adolescence. As young people achieve autonomy from their parents, they begin to review their childhood skills, values, and goals. Adolescents are able to organize their self-concept around a set of values, goals, and talents that are more relevant to their personal temperament and to the culture in which they live. The anxiety and tension surrounding the crisis of identity result from two simultaneous factors: (1) conceptual and emotional separation from many of the attractions of childhood; and (2) a commitment to a view of oneself persisting in a future which is largely unknown. If personal identity can be achieved at this stage, then the self becomes an important structure that guides the person toward future goals.

Once identity is achieved the individual becomes self-governing. Adults can undergo extreme stress and still preserve a sense of their personal motives and goals. They can perform in roles that are unpleasant, meaningless, or humiliating and still protect a part of themselves from these negative experiences. The self is protected by the formation of a value system that has meaning, regardless of daily events. As adults perform new roles in which they invest energy, the content of the self expands. It incorporates new skills, new sources of life satisfaction, and changes in values and beliefs.

● *integration*—the process of putting diverse elements together.

In later adulthood the process of introspection brings renewed attention to the components of the self-concept. During this stage, the content of the self-concept remains rather stable. Self-esteem is most likely to fluctuate. As adults approach the tasks of developing a point of view about death and accepting their own past life, they are likely to have strong feelings of depression and lack of worth. They cannot change the direction that their adult life has taken, but they may feel regret about it. As they become more resigned to their past, their esteem will rise. With extreme age the process of self-differentiation that began in birth shifts to a gradual process of self-*integration*. In that process, older people attend less to the differences between themselves and others and more to the similarities between themselves and others. Because of their perspective on time, very old people are able to identify with people of other ethnic groups, other historic periods, and other cultures. In the aging process, the self serves less to preserve one's uniqueness and more as evidence to link each person with the rest of humanity.

We have offered a view of the self-concept as acquiring new attributes at each developmental stage. Each new skill, each new role relationship, each encounter with novel historical events has the potential for bringing about revisions in the self-concept. At any single moment, however, the self-concept serves as an anchor point for the assessment of external events and for guiding future activities.

Living laboratory 3·2

LIFE CHANGES IN THE SELF-CONCEPT

Purpose: To identify some of the changes in the self-concept across three life stages.

Method: Select two people at each of three consecutive life stages to interview. For example you might interview people in middle-school years (8–12), early adolescence (13–17) and later adolescence (18–22).

Ask all your subjects the following three questions:

1. What kind of person are you?
2. What do you think is special about you?
3. How do you think you will change in the future?

Results: Using the five categories described by Montemayor and Eisen (1977, p. 21) compare the answers of your six subjects. Is there any evidence of developmental change in their responses?

Discussion: Are there consistencies across ages in the importance of some dimensions?

How well do these people's perceptions of themselves correspond to your perception of them?

What dimensions are most likely to be perceived as changing?

VULNERABILITY AND RESILIENCE OF THE SELF-CONCEPT

We have described the self-concept as a multidimensional concept about one's attributes, skills, hopes, and behaviors. This concept is continuously revised. Yet at any single moment it retains a convincing stability. In this section we will consider three approaches to the question of just how easy it is to change or alter the self-concept. Does the self-concept really remain a focusing point for interpreting and directing life events? Is the self-concept readily changed by success and failure, by the treatment and opinions of others, or by pressures to conform?

The impact of information about success or failure on the self-concept

We tend to assume that the feelings of self-worth we experience are the product of a history of successes and failures. In order to evaluate the impact of success and failure on the self-concept, three sources of evidence will be considered.

First, there are studies where false information about success or failure is given. Subjects might receive false scores on a test. They might be asked to solve impossible tasks. They might be told that tasks which, in reality, are extremely difficult are well within normal range for a person of the subject's age (Archibald & Cohen, 1971; Rule, Rule, & Rehill, 1970; Zellner, 1970). The consequences of these conditions depends on at least two important factors. First, failure has a greater negative effect on self-evaluation if the skill was one that the subject viewed as important and central to the self-concept. Failure at a task which is not very important to the peson does not lower one's self-esteem. Failure in an important area of talent may lower one's self-esteem (Newman &

Newman, 1979). Second, failure does depress the self-esteem of individu-als who already have a low or middle level of self-esteem. People with high self-esteem are not influenced as negatively by failures. In this sense, feelings of self-worth provide a protective shield for the self. The person with high self-esteem will explain failures by looking for causes outside themselves. They point to the task, the amount of time to work, the other people involved, or the criteria that were used for evaluating success and failure. In contrast, people with low self-esteem see their failure as another bit of evidence about their lack of worth (Wells & Marwell, 1976).

Another approach to the study of the effect of success or failure is described by Rosenfeld (1978). Instead of giving false information about successes and failures, Rosenfeld trained sixth-grade students to

"It's not me, Dad. It's the system that failed."

Reprinted by permission of The Wall Street Journal

recall and report their daily schooltime successes and failures. One group was asked to report successes for 20 school days. Another group reported failures. A third group reported their teacher's successes. Each strategy had a different impact on the high and low self-esteem students. The only group that benefited from recalling successes was the group that began with high self-esteem. Low self-esteem students showed movement toward a positive evaluation when they reported their own failures or the teacher's successes. Reporting failures led to decreased esteem for the high self-esteem students.

This study highlights two aspects of the self-concept. First, it is possible to influence one's self-evaluation by drawing attention to one set of behaviors and ignoring others. Second, the positive effect of emphasizing successes depends on the pattern of successes or failures among other members of the group. If one child has many fewer successes than the other children in the class, emphasizing successes points out a *deficit* for this child.

● *deficit*—a deficiency.

A third source of evidence about the impact of success and failure on the self-concept comes from information about the effect of repeated school-related successes or failures. Kifer (1978) asked school age children to compare their school ability to other children in their grade. At every grade from second through eighth, two groups of students were compared, those who had received grades of A and B and those who had received grades of D and E. Figure 3·1 shows the self-rating of ability

FIGURE 3·1
Observed means for successful and unsuccessful students by grade level

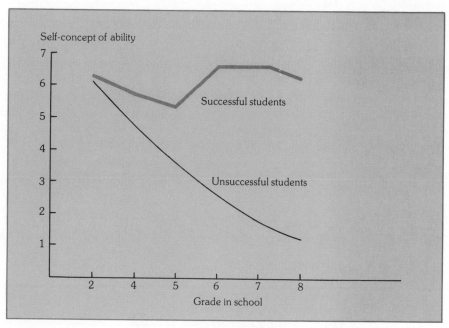

Source: E. Kifer, "The Impact of Schooling on Perceptions of Self" (Paper presented at Self-Concept Symposium, Boston, September 1978), p. 3.

by successful and unsuccessful students. In the early years, success and failure as measured by grades are not linked to different self-ratings of school ability. After eight years, the accumulation of evidence about success and failure has a strong relationship with at least one component of the self-concept. By the time students reach eighth grade, their assessment about their ability to perform on school-related tasks is almost irreversible.

The question of how the child's assessment of school-related skills influences other components of the self-concept is not fully understood. For students who succeed in school, school-related ability is likely to provide a strong source of positive evaluation. For some of these children, school success may be a central competence, highly valued by the child and others. For others, desires for popularity or athletic skill may overshadow the importance of school success. Often, *peer* norms operate to ridicule the students who work for good grades or who are involved in academic efforts. In these conditions, school success may not add to a feeling of worth. Even if school success is not highly valued, school failure may bring a general sense of worthlessness. If the child values academic achievement, failure will have a strong impact. For many students, however, parents and peers provide support for the importance of other competences. School failure has less impact if the student and the peer group make nonacademic skills important for peer acceptance.

● *peer*—a person belonging to the same group, often on the basis of age or grade.

Living Laboratory 3·3

VULNERABILITY AND RESILIENCE OF THE SELF-CONCEPT

Purpose: To identify success and failure experiences in your own personal history.

Method:
A. Think back to your earliest memory of failure. Describe it in as much detail as possible. Try to think about how this experience contributed to your feelings of worth.

B. Think back to your earliest memory of pride in accomplishment. Try to think about how this experience contributed to your feelings of worth. Describe it in as much detail as possible.

Results:
A. When does this memory take place? Who was involved? Does this experience relate to any current concerns about failure and evaluation?

B. When does this memory take place? Who was involved? Does this experience relate to any current goals, aspirations, or sources of satisfaction?

Discussion: How do past successes or failures affect adjustment to life?

What are the benefits of experiencing successes? What are the costs?

What are the benefits of experiencing failures? What are the costs?

Chapter summary

Throughout our lives, we construct a complex understanding of ourselves and our personal reality. The self-concept is a blend of seven parts: the bodily self, self-recognition, extensions of the self, the reflected self, personal competences, aspirations and goals, and self-esteem. At every life stage, changing skills, new social roles, a history of past successes and failures, and new mental abilities change the exact nature of the self-concept.

The importance of the self-concept to the process of adjustment cannot be underestimated. The self-concept defines meaning and goals, even in conditions that might appear meaningless or hopeless. In concentration camps, as slaves, as prisoners of war, or as victims of earthquakes and floods, people remain committed to create their own reality. The self-concept acts as a guide, selecting which experiences are important and which are not. We are the focus of our own attention. We take care of ourselves and of others. Our societies set laws to regulate us and tell us about compromises that have been made. Our society depends on people taking care of themselves. The basic American belief is that people should be trusted. This encourages the development of individual selves. The self-concept helps us to identify what is special about us and what will work for us.

SUGGESTED READINGS

A collection of papers on theory and research about the self-concept is:

Gordon, C., & Gergen, K. J. *The self in social interaction.* New York: Wiley, 1968. Vol. 1. *Classic and contemporary perspectives;* Vol. 2. *A Socio-cognitive approach.*

Two works that review and evaluate research on self-concept are:

Wells, L. E., & Marwell, G. *Self-esteem: Its conceptualization and measurement.* Beverly Hills, Calif.: Sage, 1976.

Wylie, R. C. *The self-concept.* Vol. 2, *Theory and research on selected topics.* Lincoln, Neb.: University of Nebraska Press, 1979.

Reading

IS THE CONCEPT OF SELF NECESSARY?

Does psychological science need the concept of *self?* Philosophy may need it; theology may need it, but it is entirely conceivable that a concept useful to philosophy or theology may turn out to be merely an impediment in the path of psychological progress.

Since the time of Wundt, the central objection of psychology to *self,* and also to *soul,* has been that the concept seems question-begging. It is temptingly easy to assign functions that are not fully understood to a mysterious central agency, and then to declare that "it" performs in such a way as to unify the personality and maintain its integrity. Wundt, aware of this peril, declared boldly for "a psychology without a soul." It was not that he necessarily denied philosophical or theological postulates, but that he felt psychology as science would be handicapped by begging so important a question. For half a century few psychologists other than Thomists have resisted Wundt's reasoning or his example.[1] Indeed we may say that for two generations psychologists have tried every conceivable way of accounting

Reading (continued)

for the integration, organization, and striving of the human person without having recourse to the postulate of a self.

In very recent years the tide has turned. Perhaps without being fully aware of the historical situation, many psychologists have commenced to embrace what two decades ago would have been considered a heresy. They have reintroduced self and ego unashamedly, and, as if to make up for lost time, have employed ancillary concepts such as *self-image, self-actualization, self-affirmation, phenomenal ego, ego-involvement, ego-striving,* and many other hyphenated elaborations which to experimental positivism still have a slight flavor of scientific obscenity.

We should note in passing that Freud played a leading (if unintentional) role in preserving the concept of ego from total obliteration throughout two generations of strenuous positivism. His own use of the term, to be sure, shifted. At first he spoke of assertive and aggressive ego-instincts (in a Nietzschean sense); later for Freud the ego became a rational (though passive) agency, whose duty it was to reconcile as best it could through planning or defense the conflicting pressures of the instincts, of conscience, and of the outer environment. With the core concept thus preserved, even with stringently limited meanings, it was easier for dynamically inclined psychologists, including the neo-Freudians, to enlarge the properties of the ego, making it a far more active and important agent than it was in the hands of Freud.

There still remains, however, the danger that Wundt wished to avoid, namely that the ego may be regarded as a *deus ex machina,* invoked to reassemble the dismembered parts of the throbbing psychic machine after positivism has failed to do so. The situation today seems to be that many psychologists who first fit personality to an external set of co-ordinates are dissatisfied with the result. They therefore reinvent the ego because they find no coherence among the measures yielded by positivistic analysis. But unfortunately positivism and ego-

theory do not go well together. Bergson has criticized the use of "ego" in this face-saving way by likening the process to the dilemma of an artist. An artist, he says, may wish to represent Paris—just as a psychologist may wish to represent personality. But all he can do with the limitations of his medium is to draw this and then that angle of the whole. To each sketch he applied the label "Paris," hoping somehow that the sections he has ablated will magically reconstitute the whole.[2] Similarly in psychology we have a state of affairs where empiricists, finding that they have gone as far as possible with analytic tools and being dissatisfied with the product, resort as did their predecessors to some concept of self in order to represent, however inadequately, the coherence, unity, and purposiveness they know they have lost in their fragmentary representations.

I greatly fear that the lazy tendency to employ self or ego as a factotum to repair the ravages of positivism may do more harm than good. It is, of course, significant that so many contemporary psychologists feel forced to take this step, even though for the most part their work represents no theoretical gain over nineteenth-century usage. Positivism will continue to resent the intrusion, and will, with some justification, accuse today's resurgent self-psychologists of obscurantism.

The problem then becomes how to approach the phenomena that have led to a revival of the self-concept in a manner that will advance rather than retard scientific progress.

A possible clue to the solution, so far as psychology is concerned, lies in a statement made by Alfred Adler. "What is frequently labeled 'the ego,'" he writes, "is nothing more than the style of the individual."[3] Life-style to Adler had a deep and important meaning. He is saying that if psychology could give us a full and complete account of life-style it would automatically include all phenomena now referred somewhat vaguely to a self or an ego. In other words, a wholly adequate psychology of growth would discover all of the activities and all of the interrelations in life, which are now either neglected or consigned to an ego that looks suspiciously like a homunculus.

The first thing an adequate psychology of growth should do is to draw a distinction between what are matters of *importance* to the individual and what are, as Whitehead would say, merely matters of *fact* to him; that is, between what he feels to be vital and central in becoming and what belongs to the periphery of his being.

Many facets of our life-style are not ordinarily felt to have strong personal relevance. Each of us, for example, has innumerable tribal habits that mark our life-style but are nothing more than opportunistic modes of adjusting. The same holds true for many of our physiological habits. We keep to the right in traffic, obey the rules of etiquette, and make countless unconscious or semiconscious adjustments, all of which characterize our life-style but are not *propriate,* i.e., not really central to our sense of existence. Consider, for example, the English language habits that envelop our thinking and communication. Nothing could be of more pervasive influence in our lives than the store of concepts available to us in our ancestral tongue and the frames of discourse under which our social contacts proceed. And yet the use of English is ordinarily felt to be quite peripheral to the core of our existence. It would not be so if some foreign invader should forbid us to use our native language. At such a time our vocabulary and accent and our freedom to employ them would become very precious and involved with our sense of self. So it is with the myriad of social and physiological habits we have developed that are never, unless interfered with, regarded as essential to our existence as a separate being.

Personality includes these habits and skills, frames of reference, matters of fact and cultural values, that seldom or never seem warm and important. But personality includes what is warm and important also—all the regions of our life that we regard as intimately and essentially ours, and which for the time being I suggest we call the *proprium.* The proprium includes all aspects of personality that make for a sense of inward unity, even though these aspects are at times in conflict. Unity does not necessarily mean harmony.

Psychologists who allow for the proprium use both the term "self" and "ego"—often interchangeably; and both terms are defined with varying degrees of narrowness or of comprehensiveness. Whatever name we use for it, this sense of what is "peculiarly ours" merits close scrutiny. The principal functions and properties of the proprium need to be distinguished.

To this end William James over seventy years ago proposed a simple taxonomic scheme.[4] There are, he maintained, two possible orders of self: an empirical self (the *Me*) and a knowing self (the *I*). Three subsidiary types comprise the empirical Me: the material self, the social self, and the spiritual self. Within this simple framework he fits his famous and subtle description of the various states of mind that are "peculiarly ours." His scheme, however, viewed in the perspective of modern psychoanalytic and experimental research, seems scarcely adequate. In particular it lacks the full psychodynamic flavor of modern thinking. With some trepidation, therefore, I offer what I hope is an improved outline for analyzing the propriate aspects of personality. Later we shall return to the question, Is the concept of *self* necessary?

[1] Until about 1890 certain American writers, including Dewey, Royce, James, continued to regard self as a necessary concept. They felt that the analytical concepts of the New Psychology lost the manifest unity of mental functioning. But for the ensuing fifty years very few American psychologists made use of it, Mary Whiton Calkins being a distinguished exception; and none employed "soul." *See* G. W. Allport, "The Ego in Contemporary Psychology," *Psychological Review, 50* (1943), pp. 451–478; reprinted in *The Nature of Personality: Selected Papers* (Cambridge: Addison-Wesley, 1950).
[2] H. Bergson, *Introduction to Metaphysics* (New York: G. Putnam's Sons, 1912), p. 30.
[3] A. Adler, "The Fundamental Views of Individual Psychology," *International Journal of Individual Psychology,* vol. 1 (1935), pp. 5–8.
[4] William James, *Principles of Psychology* (New York: Henry Holt, 1890), vol. 1, ch. 10.
Note: Footnotes were renumbered.
Source: Gordon W. Allport, *Becoming: Basic Considerations for Psychology of Personality* (New Haven, Conn.: Yale University Press, 1960).

Chapter 4
Motives and emotions

Men, in their primitive conditions, however savage, were undoubtedly gregarious; and they continue to be social, not only in every stage of civilization, but in every possible situation in which they can be placed. As nature intended them for society, she has furnished them with passions, appetites, and propensities, as well as a variety of faculties, calculated both for their individual enjoyment, and to render them useful to each other in their social connections. There is none among them more essential or remarkable, than the passion for distinction. *A desire to be observed, considered, esteemed, praised, beloved, and admired by his fellows, is one of the earliest, as well as keenest dispositions discovered in the heart of man.*

John Adams, *The Passion for Distinction,
The American Enlightenment* 1965

United Press International

For reflection

1. Why do two swimmers on a swimming team compete against each other?

2. Why do some of your friends need to have so much approval from others?

3. How can you tell when a person is faking an emotion or trying to disguise an emotion?

4. What level of anxiety do you find best for good decision making?

5. Why do mothers of the bride cry at weddings?

● *arousal*—a physical state of alertness.

Motives and emotions surface throughout our waking hours and even during our dreams. Motives direct behavior toward specific goals. They may bring a general increase in *arousal*. They may prompt a series of specific behaviors designed to satisfy the motive. Motives may energize a set of plans designed to achieve satisfaction. Motives can be gratified or frustrated. They can move one toward or away from action. They can be in agreement or not in agreement with the social goals of one's family, social group, or culture. The questions Why does she want to do that? What will she get out of it? What is in it for her? all reflect the underlying assumption that behavior is motivated. They imply that behavior has at its origin the goal of meeting some need. The first half of this chapter focuses on motivation. The concept is defined in more detail. Four theoretical views of motives are described. Two examples are given to illustrate the process of socialization involved in the strengthening of motives.

Emotions are experienced as changes in feeling states along three dimensions: positive-negative; strong-weak; and active-passive. Emotions result in part from changes in hormone level. They also result from training. Emotions may cause a person to act. The direction of behavior is not as clear as in the case of motivation. In the process of adaptation, one must learn how to recognize emotions that signal danger or safety, pleasure or pain. One learns how to express and to control the expression of emotions. One learns ways to create emotional states that are pleasurable and to limit emotional states that are unpleasant.

The second half of the chapter is about emotions and their place in the process of adjustment. We consider the gradual increase in the number of emotions one can identify and express. Anger, loneliness, and love are used as examples of learning of emotions. Finally, the relation between adaptation and emotion is analyzed in a discussion of two emotions, self-esteem, and anxiety.

MOTIVES

A definition of motivation

Motivation is the inclination to engage in some form of mental activity or observable behavior (Atkinson & Raynor, 1974). The inclination or motive is not itself observable. Instead, motives are inferred from behaviors, the goal of those behaviors, and the events that alter the pattern of behavior (Murray, 1938; Birch, Atkinson, & Bongort, 1974). For example, let us say that a child grows restless, starts making sucking movements, stuffs his fist in his mouth, and eventually begins to cry. His mother may infer that the child is hungry. If she offers a breast and the infant sucks eagerly, she will assume she was correct. Now suppose that after 15 minutes of nursing, the infant begins to gaze around, coo and babble, and shows little energy for nursing. The mother may assume that the infant is no longer hungry. We have theories about the motives that are directing the behavior of others.

Some theorists describe certain motives as unlearned and others as learned. Unlearned motives or instincts are thought of as more central to survival (Hull, 1943; Dollard & Miller, 1950). Once a motive is actually expressed in behavior, the distinction between learned and unlearned motives becomes less relevant. Learning occurs in regard to all motives. People learn many ways to satisfy a particular inclination. They learn about the ease or difficulty in achieving a goal. They learn what happens when they try to satisfy a need.

Concepts related to the nature of particular motives include the acceptability of the motive, the strength of the motive, or the ease with which a motive may be expressed in behavior. Each of these are closely related to qualities of the environment. In particular, motives are labeled by the culture. They are linked to the availability of resources needed to satisfy the motive. They are encouraged or discouraged by the cultural approval for particular motives. Let us think about the motive to achieve. We might assume that all people have a motive to experience effectiveness, to manipulate and control events successfully (White, 1960). However, the extent to which individuals begin to think about their own skills in terms of successes and failures, winning and losing, best and worst depends on the way in which their skills are interpreted and evaluated by others (McClelland, 1961).

Motives and incentives

The two concepts *motives* and *incentives* are frequently confused. Motives for action originate within the person even when they have previously been learned. They are experienced as inner needs that press for satisfaction. Incentives originate outside the person. They are the rewards and resources that can be obtained after specific behavior has taken place. In order for an incentive to work, it must be related to a motive. Let us say that a company offers an additional bonus to employees who stop smoking. In order to be an effective incentive, the bonus must be attractive enough to want to give up a satisfying habit for it. The bonus must be large enough to meet some perceived needs that are as strong if not stronger than the need to smoke.

Sometimes repeated exposure to an incentive can create a motive. For example, children do not usually come to school with a strong need for gold stars to be glued to their work. After weeks of exposure to the use of gold stars as a reward, children begin to desire them. They may even alter their behavior in order to obtain them. The gold stars take on incentive value because the teacher establishes them as tokens of recognition. Students who value this recognition will support the teacher's use of stars by valuing them and by exerting pressure on other students to value them.

In this example, we can begin to see that the ways motives are satisfied can become very specific. While most people have a need for love and approval, each person seeks to satisfy that motive in a special way. Most people want love from the people they care about. Being loved by a stranger or by someone we do not admire may not satisfy this need. Incentives can work with some people and not with others. As every advertising specialist knows, the coupons, rebates, or special offers that are intended to generate greater sales do not prompt additional purchases from every person who learns about them. We each have preferred ways of satisfying our needs. From the array of incentives dangling in front of each of us, only a limited number will set the wheels of need gratification into motion.

Motivation and behavior

● *homeostasis*—a relatively stable state of equilibrium.

Motives direct behavior toward doing things that will satisfy the need that has been aroused. The hunger motive directs us toward eating. The need to be with others directs us toward social interaction. The competence motive directs us toward activities that provide a sense of mastery and effectiveness. Two models of motivation have been described that take different approaches to the way that motives activate behavior. The first approach, often referred to as the *homeostatic model,* describes motives as if they functioned like a thermostat. In this model, a certain state of satisfaction is viewed as ideal. As the need becomes stronger, the energy devoted to satisfying the need increases. Hunger appears to conform to this model. After a number of hours of not eating, the need to eat increases to the point where eating takes priority over a number of other possible activities. Eating continues until the tension created by hunger is reduced. At that point, the hunger drive returns to a comfortable level and another motive emerges to direct behavior.

The other model of motivation is referred to as the growth or fulfillment orientation (Maddi, 1976). Not all motives have tension reduction as their goal. Some motives such as the need for stimulation or the need for competence may direct the person to seek increased levels of arousal and tension. These motives help us increase our information, skills, and social relations.

These are four ideas about motivation that are essential for understanding the process of adjustment. First, one cannot always infer the same motive from the same behavior. Infant crying may be a signal of hunger, pain, overstimulation, or boredom. A boy may ask a girl on a date to satisfy needs for social interaction, sexuality, peer group status, or to avoid loneliness. When a boss shouts at a secretary, the boss may be motivated by a need to exercise his or her authority or by a need to express hostility at another target (perhaps his or her own supervisor).

Second, the same motive may not always be expressed in the same behavior. For example, let us say that children desire adult approval. They may act very independently on some occasions to demonstrate their self-sufficiency and thereby gain approval. The same children may try to get attention from adults by acting helpless, rebellious, or angry depending on the responsiveness of adults to each of these strategies (Murphy & Moriarty, 1976).

Third, the importance of particular motives changes as the person develops new skills and as the expressed expectations of others change. The infant's insistence on food gives way to a desire for *autonomy* in the feeding situation. Babies will insist on feeding themselves at around seven or eight months of age, even though this method results in less food making its way from the tray to the stomach (White, 1960). In childhood, the desire to play a game gives way to a desire to play by the rules (Piaget, 1965). By adolescence, the emerging need for peer friendship may dominate the need for adult approval (Damon, 1976).

● **autonomy—the ability to behave independently; to do things on one's own.**

Fourth, adults and children may approach the same event with quite different motives. These differences are based on their understanding of the situation and their expectations about future events. Let us consider the example of moving to a new house. We may find that the parents are very positive and optimistic about the move, but the children are anxious and reluctant. Adult motives for a better income or improved social status that might be gained by moving are not immediately relevant to children. For children, strong needs for their friends or the comforts of their home are threatened by the prospect of moving.

An understanding of the motive base of any person requires careful and prolonged observation. Because motives are not directly observable, we must use behavior as an indication of what may be operating inside the person. Different theories make different assumptions about what motivates behavior.

THEORIES ABOUT PRIMARY MOTIVES

In the following section, the basic concepts of four views of motivation are explained. From among the many theories of personality, the thinking of Sigmund Freud, Abraham Maslow, Henry Murray, and Gordon Allport were selected for two reasons. First, motivation plays a central part in each of these theories of human personality. Second, each theory adds a special emphasis so that the concept motivation is quite distinct in each.

Freud's psychosexual theory

Freud assumed that all behavior is motivated. Freud acknowledged the possibility that some behavior occurred as a result of fatigue. He was convinced, however, that much of what people claimed to be a result of accident or chance was really expression of a motive of which they were unaware. One of Freud's most powerful concepts was the unconscious. The unconscious includes all the wishes, motives, and fears that are not readily accessible to conscious thought. Freud believed that

The photography of H. Armstrong Roberts

Many motives play a part in human relationships.

there were conflicts between unconscious wishes and learned norms for when these wishes could be acceptably expressed. The motivating force of mental life was the tension caused by these conflicts.

The two motives that Freud identified as having primary impact on psychological functioning were sexuality and aggression. Freud also referred to these motives as the life instinct and the death instinct. In his view, these motives and wishes were not only in conflict with societal wishes, but they were in conflict with one another. The total quantity of motivational energy fluctuates between a thrust toward life and growth, and thrust toward death and destruction.

In Freud's model, energy shifts from the mouth in infancy, to the anus in toddlerhood, to the genitals in early school age. At each stage of development, sexual and aggressive satisfaction are expressed in new patterns of interpersonal relations and new forms of mental activity. During the oral stage, the mouth is the major source of satisfaction. Oral behaviors including sucking, biting, licking, gumming, and chewing all provide pleasure and outlets for aggression. Social relations are marked by reliance on others, passivity and lack of boundaries between the self and others. During the anal stage satisfaction is experienced by holding on and letting go of feces. Controlled use of the sphincter muscles becomes a way to experience pleasure and also to express aggression by messing deliberately. During the phallic stage, children focus on the penis or the clitoris as sources of physical pleasure. Masturbation is a means of experiencing pleasure. For boys, the penis is also a focus of fear that the penis could be mutilated or removed. Personal relationships during the phallic stage are characterized by curiosity and outgoingness on the one hand, and secrecy and guilt on the other. The final stage of personality development occurs during adolescence. The outcome is the total expression of sexual impulses in a heterosexual, loving relationship.

One of Freud's most significant contributions, and one that continues to generate controversy, is the importance he placed on the first six or seven years of life for the formation of personality. Freud (1953) argued that from infancy children had strong sexual and aggressive impulses. At any one of the childhood stages, the child's efforts to gratify basic instincts can be severely frustrated. If this frustration is quite prolonged, the person would continue to seek gratification of those wishes at later life stages. We recognize that no person could possibly satisfy all of his or her wishes and impulses at every life stage. Freud argued that because we each experience frustration in childhood there are important childhood origins to contemporary conflicts, anxieties, and personal habits.

Even though the source of motives remains the same, the mode of expression can change. For every action impulse there are at least four avenues of expression—thought, *symbolic* thought, direct action, and symbolic action. For example, let us say that a young girl has a strong wish to be intimate with her father. She might think about lying in bed with her father. She might imagine that she is a famous movie star and that lots of men are in love with her. These are thoughts that could satisfy the wish. She might go into the living room and cuddle up on her father's lap while he is watching television. She might bring a special gift to her male teacher at school. There are actions that could satisfy the wish.

A person's most profound wishes remain in the unconscious. They are inaccessible to conscious thought. These wishes can never be fully satisfied without suffering the anxiety and guilt associated with a violation of conscience. In this view there is lifelong involvement with the gratification of sexual and aggressive wishes. This implication is probably the

● *symbolic*—**stands for something else.**

one most often attacked in analyses of Freudian theory. These ideas link the motivational base to a set of needs and satisfactions that are characteristic of very early childhood. Even during the childhood years, these motives are only a small part of all the sources of satisfaction and pleasure children experience. This theory does not deal with basic needs for social interaction, needs for meaning, and pleasures in exploration and novelty as they are expressed in childhood or adult life.

Maslow's need hierarchy

● *self-actualization*—in Maslow's theory, the highest of human motives, the motives for making the most of one's competences and for realizing one's potential.

Maslow's approach to the study of personality focused on the creative, growth potential of the person. Maslow argued that in order to understand human potential one must study the experiences of healthy, even exceptional people. To this end, Maslow became involved in the study of the lives of 49 famous, prominent people whom he considered to be examples of three groups: fairly sure cases of *self-actualization;* partial cases; and potential cases. In justifying his selection of these individuals for intensive study, Maslow (1969) makes the following comments:

If we want to answer the question how tall can the human species grow, then obviously it is well to pick out the ones who are already tallest and study them. If we want to know how fast a human being can run, then it is no use to average the speed of a "good sample" of the population; it is better to collect Olympic gold medal winners and see how well they can do. If we want to know the possibilities for spiritual growth, value growth, or moral development in human beings, then I maintain that we can learn most of studying our most moral, ethical or saintly people (p. 726).

In trying to explain the forces toward self-actualization, Maslow proposed a new model of motivation. At its core here is an appreciation of the "fully functioning" person. Maslow believed that human beings are in a constant state of striving. There are few if any moments of total satisfaction. Once one kind of need is satisfied, another emerges to direct behavior.

Two motivational systems are described that exist in every person. The first group of needs, that Maslow referred to as deficit needs, include physiological needs, safety needs, needs for being with others and love, and esteem needs. Each of these needs are critical for survival and for psychological health. Physiological needs including needs for food, oxygen, drink, and sleep must be satisfied before focus will shift to safety needs, and so on. (See Figure 4.1.) Disruption in the satisfaction of more basic needs will detract from efforts to achieve satisfaction of needs that are higher in the hierarchy. At the top of the hierarchy are needs for self-actualization. These needs refer to efforts to realize one's potential, to become everything one is capable of becoming.

Emerging from the deficit system, there exists a growth system that Maslow described as meta-needs or being-needs. These needs for justice, goodness, beauty, order, or unity lead to expansion of the person's potential. They contribute to an inner tendency toward growth.

FIGURE 4·1
A schematic representation
of Maslow's need-hierarchy
theory

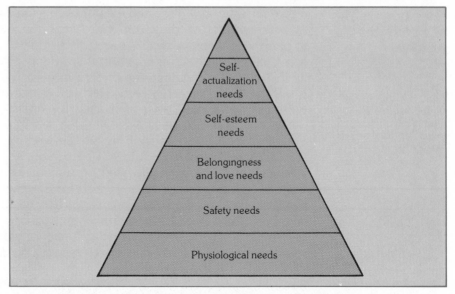

Source: L. A. Hjelle and D. J. Ziegler, *Personality* (New York: McGraw-Hill Book Company, 1976), p. 256.

The need hierarchy has clear developmental implications. The needs must be satisfied sequentially. One can assume that earlier life stages are more concerned with the physical, survival needs. It is not until adolescence or even adulthood that one can really begin to focus on the search for self-actualization. We might also infer that, in agreement with Freud's view of motivation, childhood is an unstable time for the gratification of basic needs. If there is constant anxiety about meeting needs for food, safety, or love then the chances of moving past these needs toward a state of self-actualization is less likely. On the other hand, if one can hold a level of satisfaction with regard to basic needs, then there is the promise of further growth. The search for meaning, for the expression of values, and for the achievement of creative forms of action draw people toward a life of continued personal enhancement.

● *adversity*—a
condition of suffering or
hardship.

How literally can we take the concept of a hierarchy of needs? First, we know that there are people who emerge successfully from a childhood of *adversity* (Goertzel & Goertzel, 1962). The lives of James Baldwin, Viktor Frankl, or Sarah Bernhardt instruct us that relative deprivation in physiological, safety, or belongingness needs may not prevent the emergence of talent or the pursuit of self-actualization (Maddi, 1976). Second, there are people who relinquish basic needs in order to achieve what they believe to be higher levels of awareness or fulfillment. Thoreau's retreat to the woods, or Ghandi's fasts show a willingness to sacrifice more basic needs for higher ones. Maslow's model expresses an optimism about growth that is lacking in the Freudian system. It still falls short of a satisfying analysis of the ways that motives achieve priority in orienting human behavior.

Murray's profile of needs and presses

● *affiliation*—the connection or association of oneself with others.

Murray (1938) discussed the human personality in terms of a variety of psychological needs which were organized differently from person to person. Some of the needs Murray discussed include affiliation, achievement, dominance, autonomy, nurturance, and aggression. Even though all the needs he described are present in human beings, not every need is equally strong in each person. The need operates to motivate behavior. For example, if one has a high need for *affiliation,* one will seek out others and to try to have a relationship with them. If one has a high need for dominance, one will try to gain control of one's environment and of the people who are in it. The person who has a high need for affiliation and relatively little need for dominance will behave differently from the person who has a high need for dominance and relatively little need for affiliation. These two people will behave differently from a person who has a high need for both affiliation and dominance.

Murray classified needs along a number of dimensions. For example, some needs are described as viscerogenic. This means that they stem

United Press International

Some people give up safety needs for social approval or self-esteem.

from biological requirements for survival. Other needs are psychogenic. They refer to motives for certain kinds of relationships, for preserving personal integrity, or for exercising control over the environment. Murray listed 28 psychogenic needs as central to human motivation.

Needs were also described as covert and overt. This distinction refers to the degree to which the specific need could be openly expressed within a culture. A third distinction was the proactive-reactive dimension. Sometimes needs arise because of the changing state of the person (proactive). Other times needs are stimulated by events, changes, or new stimuli on the environment (reactive). It can be seen that with a large number of needs, there are a wide variety of individual differences in motivation that are possible, according to Murray's theory. Murray's concept of personality suggests that one would need a motivational profile for each individual in order to be able to understand that person's behavior.

Murray's analysis of motivation would run into difficulty if it did not also consider the environments in which the person behaves. Murray theorized that the arousal of needs was sometimes the result of intra-psychic conditions (the person's temperament, talent, needs, or conflicts). Sometimes, however, needs are the result of the situation. Each motivational profile would have to include the demands of the situation that the person faces, as well as the person's dominant needs. The concept Murray used for the contribution of the environment was press.

> The press of an object is what it can do to the subject or for the subject—
> the power it has to affect the well-being of the subject in one way or
> another (1938, p. 121).

Environmental press can facilitate or frustrate a particular need. The pattern of behaviors a person exhibits is a product of the interaction of the dominant needs and the most powerful environmental press.

For example, the person who had a strong personal need to achieve success would be highly motivated in a school setting where standards for success and failure were clearly defined and where a demand was made for excellence. In this situation the person's behavior would be vigorous, persistent, and directed toward reaching the goal. The same person in a different situation, for example at a party, might appear to be aimless, uninvolved, and uncomfortable. The latter situation does not, in fact, arouse a very significant part of the individual's motivational base. His behavior may reflect this lack of motive. According to Murray, in order to understand a person's behavior one must assess the fit or lack of fit between the person's central motives and the situational demands the person faces.

It may be possible to evaluate the press of an environment objectively. Murray's system, however, marks a difference between the perceptions of the environment from the person's point of view (beta press) and the objective environment (alpha press). A person with a high need for power may see more demands to assume authority than a person who has a low need for power. The theory does not clarify how environmental presses modify the person's motivational profile? Do those presses just alter the strategies the person uses to satisfy an unchanging array of needs? Or do alpha presses eventually create corresponding needs? In other words, the theory does not clarify the process of motivational change based on continuous interaction between the person and the environment.

Allport's theory of the self

At the center of Allport's theory of personality is the self, which he refers to as the proprium. Allport defines the proprium as "the self-as-known—that which is experienced as warm and central, as of importance" (Allport, 1968, p. 4).

As we discussed in Chapter 3, the self provides continuity and energy for personal growth. It directs behavior toward specific goals, it influences life choices, and it offers a context for the interpretation of life events. In a word, the self permits each person to influence the outcome of his or her own development. These processes are viewed as conscious, rational, and purposeful. Allport has identified what he believes to be four requirements of a theory of motivation.

1. The theory must account for motives as they exist in the ongoing, present experiences of the person. A motive must guide the contemporary array of behaviors in order to have meaning for the person.
2. A theory of motivation must recognize a variety of motives.
3. The person's own ways of thinking of things have motivational properties. For example, our aspirations can direct our behavior.
4. A theory of motivation must allow for similar motives to function in unique ways in different people.

For example, the need for success may be expressed in private achievements, in a search for public acclaim, or in a commitment to the growth and accomplishments of one's children. All of these criteria combine to express Allport's view of the person as one who is forward moving and unique. Allport's emphasis on individuality is very important to the theory of motivation.

> Now it is certainly sure that we often wish to use universal and group norms. We want to know whether Bill, relative to others, is high or low in intelligence, in dominance, in affiliativeness. But although Bill can be compared profitably on many dimensions with the average human being or with his cultural group. Still he himself weaves all these attributes into a unique idiomatic system. His personality does not contain three systems, but only one. Whatever, individuality is, it is not the residual ragbag left over after general dimensions have been exhausted. The *organization* of Bill's life is first, last, and all the time, the primary fact of his human nature (Allport, 1968, p. 87–88).

The concept that Allport offered to express his view of motivation is called the functional *autonomy of motives.* "A given activity may become an end or goal in itself in spite of the fact that it was originally engaged in for some other reason" (Allport, 1961, p. 227). Even if goals begin in the service of biological or survival needs, those drives do not necessarily continue to be the energizing forces behind such behavior. The motives for self-fulfillment are unique to each person. They are constantly changing as the person's life goals change. At first, a person may perform a behavior because of some deficit need. For example, a person may take a job in order to earn enough money to support a family. Over time the behavior itself becomes pleasurable and valued. The person begins to enjoy the work and to value it for its own sake. The valued behavior, in this case-

In Allport's view, motives change as people's life goals change.

work, becomes a "functionally autonomous motive." The person will engage in work because of the satisfactions it brings. In an extreme example, the person may refuse a higher paying job because of the pride and commitment that is already associated with the ongoing work activities. The situation might also be reversed. The person works because of a need to earn money in order to support a family. The person becomes good at making money and finds the process pleasurable. The pursuit of wealth becomes important in its own right. It takes priority over commitments to any particular job and, perhaps, even to the family.

This way of thinking about motives means that a person's motives are flexible and open to change. The same behavior may be directed by different motives in two people. Similar motives may be expressed in quite different behaviors. In Allport's view, it is the capacity to plan and to value that dictate the nature of one's motives.

Contrasting the four views of motivation, these observations can be made. First, the four views differ in the degree of stability they attribute to motives through the life span. Freud has identified a narrow range of motives, the life instincts and the death instincts, that motivate behavior throughout life. Maslow takes an intermediate position, describing an ordered set of needs that emerge during childhood, adolescence, and adulthood. The behavior of adults is the result of different motives than the behavior of infants and young children. Murray's theory views personality as the result of the relationship between personal needs and conditions in the environment. Allport suggests that a person's motivational base is changing all the time. Changing motives are the result of personal values and contacts with the environment. His theory argues that adults are different from children in their primary needs. In addition, each person has a unique set of experiences that lead to new motives.

Second, Freud's theory has frequently been contrasted to Maslow and Allport's theories. In Freud's view, motives press for satisfaction through fantasy or direct action. Once expressed, the intensity of the drive subsides until a new buildup of tension occurs. These drives, tied to biological survival, are never fully satisfied. They go through cycles of tension buildup, expression, and tension reduction. Maslow and Allport both recognize that some motives operate according to this drive reduction model. However, they both suggest that some motives produce a level of activity or social involvement that is best for the person. The focus on growth is not entirely absent from Freud's model. In fact, the concept of a life instinct is just such a motive—an urge toward growth. We can conclude that all the theories acknowledge the existence of an inner commitment to growth. It continues to motivate the person throughout adulthood. It is not only present during periods of physical maturation. It is assumed to help the person adapt to life.

A third area of comparison is the relative emphasis on the biological, emotional, and cognitive components of motivation. While no theory disregards these three sources of motivation, each view emphasizes a different domain. Allport has the most intellectual orientation. His theory includes an appreciation of the motivating properties of personal plans, values, and goals. As the person discovers a new reality, the related motives vary. Maslow is most concerned with an emotional source of motives. Feelings of belongingness, self-esteem, and self-actualization can all be considered emotional states that guide behavior. The higher level needs seek understanding or meaning in life. The search for self-actualization, however, is a state of being which is desirable. Freud's view is most clearly biological. Sexuality and aggression are the main motives. They are expressed from infancy. Even before the person is capable of investing feelings in others or of thinking realistically about the physical or social environment, motivational energy exists to direct behavior. Murray's system probably comes closest to giving equal weight to all three components. His list of needs includes biological, emotional, and intellectual motives. What is more, his emphasis on press recognizes the perceived reality and the objective reality as the main factors in the expression of motives in behavior.

Living laboratory 4·1

THEORIES ABOUT PRIMARY MOTIVES

Purpose:
1. To identify the unique contributions of the theories of motivation discussed in the text.
2. To clarify the explanatory value of motivation in the study of adjustment.

Method: Read the following case study (Case 4·1).

Results: After you have read the case, explain how each of the four theories would interpret Sharon's behavior.

Discussion: What is the relationship between motives and body movement?

What are the motivational origins of competition according to each theory?

THE SOCIALIZATION OF MOTIVES

When we say that learning occurs with regard to all motives, we are really saying that motives can be shaped through experience. Parents, teachers, friends, and bosses can modify how important different motives are. They can offer rewards that make some behaviors worth more than others. In Freud's model, some motives or wishes are thought to be so unacceptable that they are pushed from conscious awareness. In Allport's system, motives are shaped through experience. Adults can be expected to develop new motives through their experiences in adult roles. One important element in the process of adjustment is finding ways for needs that are strongly felt to be gratified through socially acceptable strategies. In order to identify what is important in learning new motives, we are going to discuss two kinds of motivation that have been studied by psychologists.

Case 4·1

SHARON: THE PRESCHOOL YEARS

In contrast to Sharon's stressful infancy, the pace of her physical and cognitive development during her preschool years was not markedly unusual, although motor development continued to lag in some respects. In retrospect, it seems likely that part of her stiffness may have been a residue of her prematurity, yet her inadequacy in this area may have been increased by her "reluctance" (her mother's word) to interact with new people in the preschool period.

At four and a half, Sharon was seen by a male psychologist, who administered projective tests. En route to the examining center, Sharon sat wordlessly beside her mother and younger sister. Upon arrival, both children remained silent but moved freely, gracefully, and with apparent pleasure. When Sharon was separated from her sister for an individual examination, her movements became stiffer. Her posture was uncomfortably erect throughout the session. Communication was at first restricted to nodding. Later, Sharon spoke very softly and used as few words as possible. Most of her CAT responses were exclusively enumerative, with rare flashes of appropriate feeling tone, which resulted in a meager test protocol showing only that she was a sad, lonely, and apparently angry little girl with limited outlets for expressing her feelings.

A week later, with a female psychologist, Sharon behaved like a mannequin from a fashionable children's store. Her expensive, well-fitting clothes accentuated her feminine delicacy, but aside from her beauty, she was not charming or appealing. While one could empathize with the apprehension and confusion she felt in a new situation, as reflected by her sobbing, tremulousness, and inability to communicate verbally, she radiated such an undercurrent of coldness, resistance, and hostility that even her misery seemed calculated to control or to defy adults and to express impatience as much as shyness. On two occasions, she managed to keep

the familiar adult who accompanied her (once her mother and once her paternal grandmother) within her view, rather than to allow her frightened younger sister their comforting presence. In each instance, she expressed slyly sadistic pleasure that it was the sister who must be "all alone with two strange people." Having won out over her sister, she was able to handle structured tests with considerably efficiency and occasionally a modicum of pleasure.

She used only one-word sentences and sometimes refused test items with a shrug of her shoulders or inexpressive silence; when she spoke, however, her words were clear, of normal intensity, and without articulatory errors. She visually explored everything within range, curiously peeking under and behind test materials and quietly ignoring instructions not to her liking.

She worked rapidly and vigorously at nonverbal tasks involving puzzles, blocks, or toys. At times, there was a breathless hurry, with the accompanying tension most clearly visible in her rigid and unrelaxed postures or the tightness of her fingers. She frequently delayed responding for several minutes or reacted with a facial expression implying that she would do what she wanted when she wanted.

When the mother was present, Sharon made no demands on her. With the grandmother, who offered numerous critical suggestions, Sharon moved physically closer to the examiner. She whispered or turned away to talk directly to the examiner or cast a conspiratorial smile in the examiner's direction as she continued an activity the grandmother had protested. Sharon was quick to understand verbal instructions and had a fairly good vocabulary despite her frequent failure to communicate. It seemed clear that she had at least average capacity to recall and to reason, but her capacity to solve number problems was very limited. Finger coordination was average, although speed and impatience with minor difficulties sometimes led to errors. Her over-all intelligence, as tested, was of high average quality (IQ, 113).

Five months later, when examined by a female pediatrician with the mother and younger sister present, Sharon played intermittently with toys while the mother and doctor talked. She allowed herself to be undressed and submitted to the examination with moderate interest and cooperation. She spoke clearly, but often with a whining quality. She directed most of her comments to her mother, whom she teased occasionally, or to her sister, whom she addressed sharply, as though temporarily assuming the role of a critical mother.

Although short and of delicate bone structure, Sharon was considered relatively healthy at five. There were, however, indications of physical vulnerability in several bodily systems. For example, she continued to be more susceptible to colds than most children. A systolic cardiac murmur, of low intensity and probably functional in origin, was found, as were flattening of the arches and toeing in. It was also reported that Sharon had been hospitalized for four days at the age three with complaints of inability to urinate and a bloody discharge from the genital area. Her white blood count had indicated infection, but the source of bleeding was not determined. According to Mrs. J., Sharon reported scratching herself, but no evidence of this was found. A urinalysis at that time was negative, although during the preceding year two series of terramycin had been given for urinary tract infection. The mother felt that Sharon had not been sick enough to warrant the intensive medical work-up. Comparing Sharon to her siblings, Mrs. J. felt that the child was "alert in her mind, but physically weaker than the others."

A month later, with a male psychiatrist and in the presence of her sister, Sharon seemed more upset. In the psychiatrist's words:

> All Sharon's positions are stiff, uncomfortable, angular, always correct, but never free or adapted. Similarly, her movements are rigid, jerky, and lack grace.

Her constant tension interferes with her coordination so that she only barely is up to her age level, be it in finger or in gross coordination. One soon understands the source of this rigidity. Her frequent caresses of her sister much more resemble the caresses of a chimpanzee than of a human being. They frequently looked like aggressive approaches which were stopped in the last minute and converted into their apparent opposite. It was noticeable that Sharon carried out tasks which did not have aggressive implications far better than tasks which were, or could be, aggressive. While coloring, for example, she managed to stay inside the line surprisingly well, while her handling of the peg board was just as remarkably awkward. She held the hammer by the head and never produced one honest stroke.

The gross difference in her motor coordination observed by the female psychologist and a male psychiatrist suggest several speculations. It is possible that Sharon could express her motor skills more freely in the presence of a woman. Or, she may have found the structured tests less threatening, or at least less emotionally toned, than the psychiatric play sessions. Or, the presence of her sister, which she demanded to enable her to come to the session, may have raised competitive issues, especially since Carol was much more skilled motorically for her age than was Sharon (Sharon had exhibited considerable jealously toward more motorically skillful children in nursery school).

Summarizing the findings of these sessions with respect to Sharon's physical health and cognitive resources at the preschool period, we note improved general health over the years, although there were constitutional weaknesses in the respiratory and urogenital systems and some deformities of the feet. There were also indications of moderate lag in motor development, associated with vulnerability and deterioration under stress, as observed in the psychiatric session. Cognitive resources, both as reflected by test scores and performance in the psychiatric play session, were essentially average, but cognitive functioning was rarely comfortable or fully effective. Her general knowledge and her memory, although age-adequate, were in no way spectacular. Her functioning was so often dimmed by overwhelming feelings that the content of her thinking was unclear. Her massive verbal inhibitions and her motoric variability were particularly outstanding.

Riley W. Gardner and Alice E. Moriarty, *Personality Development at Preadolescence. Explorations of Structure Formation.* (Seattle: University of Washington Press, 1968), pp. 285–88.

Achievement motivation

● *projection*—the attribution of one's own ideas, feelings, wishes, or attitudes to other people and situations.

Let us define achievement motivation. The need for achievement is the inner state of arousal that leads to active, persistent, goal-directed behavior when a person is asked to perform a task. Task performance must be evaluated in relation to some standards of excellence (which may be defined by the person or by others), where there are possibilities for success or failure (Atkinson & Birch, 1978; Atkinson & Raynor, 1974). Achievement motivation is not aroused in every situation. It is a meaningful motive only in specific situations.

There are individual differences in the strength of the achievement motive. The origins of these differences have been linked to parental child-rearing practices. Winterbottom (1958) conducted a study with 29 eight- to ten-year-old boys. She obtained need-achievement scores for each boy by asking them to tell stories about situations that she presented. The boys *projected* their own motives into the stories they told. Their stories were then coded for the presence of themes that would suggest the arousal of the achievement motive. Winterbottom also interviewed the boys' mothers. She asked them to recall specific aspects of their child-rearing practices. Mothers of boys who scored high and who scored low on the need-for-achievement measures were equally likely to expect their sons to be independent. However, the mothers of the high group tended to make earlier demands (before the age of eight) for many behaviors. The mothers of the low group made their demands later (after the age of eight). Mothers of the high group tended to use more intense rewards when their sons met their expectations. They used more physical signs of affection. Mothers of the high group also tended to evaluate their son's behavior more positively than did mothers of the low group.

Rosen and D'Andrade (1959) visited 40 families in their homes. Twenty of the families had a son who had been identified as high in the motive to achieve success, and 20 others had a son who had been identified as low in the motive to achieve success. All the boys were between 9 and 11 years old. The boys and their parents were presented with five tasks that involved interaction between the child and the adults. During the problem solving, parent-child interactions were coded.

Parents of boys who had a high need for achievement actually gave their children achievement training. They set clear standards of excel-

The achievement motive is aroused when the person is striving toward a standard of excellence.

lence. They expected greater competence, and showed more signs of approval after success than did parents of boys who had a low need for achievement. Mothers of boys in the high group tended to emphasize achievement by encouraging and punishing in response to the quality of the boy's performance. The fathers of boys in the high group tended to allow the boys more independence. They valued self-reliance and mastery. Boys who show a strong need for achievement are likely to learn the permissiveness that allows for the development of competence from their fathers. They learn the goals or standards of excellence that direct their behavior from their mothers.

The child-rearing environment of children who show strong achievement motivation includes three elements:

1. Early and continued encouragement for achievement.
2. Permissiveness toward exploration.
3. Reward or praise for achievement efforts (Smith, 1969; Stein & Bailey, 1973).

In addition to child-rearing practices, the presence of role models influences achievement motivation. Adults or older siblings who show children how things are done or who express satisfaction in experiencing excellence help children to build a personal motive for achieving success. The presence of men and women models who have high achievement aspirations will foster strong achievement motives and the expression of achievement-related behaviors.

The need for social approval

    The need for social approval has two components: a desire to obtain the approval of others; and a desire to avoid disapproval (Millham & Jacobson, 1978). The person with a high need for social approval does not want to risk criticism from others. People who have a strong need for social approval may be readily influenced by the opinions of others. They are responsive to the positive or negative comments of others, and reluctant to risk failure (Mehrabian, 1970; Milburn, et al. 1970; Thaw & Efran, 1967). In fact much of the experimental research on this motive has demonstrated how people try to avoid disapproval or rejection. Little evidence exists about how the need for social approval prompts more positive, personally satisfying social interactions.

    In order to understand the functioning of this powerful motive, we must look back to the family context. As Carl Rogers (1959) has pointed out, all children begin life with a feeling of worthiness. Self-involvement and self-love are qualities of the initial human condition. It would be ideal if life would continue along a path of mutual acceptance. However, the conflict between parental expectations and the child's impulses and skills results in setting conditions of worth. This means that each child discovers that love and approval are conditional. One's behavior, one's language, and even one's wishes are subject to social evaluation. Not all thoughts or actions are equally valued by others. Some may even be punished. By the period of toddlerhood, the child experiences feelings of shame at having failed to meet adult expectations. Shame, the emotion linked with having been caught in a misdeed, is the negative emotion that energizes the desire for social approval. In order to avoid feelings of shame, we do what is expected of us. The more intensely one experiences shame and the broader the range of behaviors that have been the target of shaming, the greater will be the motive for social approval.

    The next step in the socialization of the need for approval is the internalization of social values and expectations. Through identification, parental values are firmly intwined into one's personal belief system. These values provide a core for determining the worth, the morality, and the benefit of specific actions. Strong identification with one's parents provides the child with confidence that he or she knows what is right and what is wrong. Sometimes identification is filled with ambivalence. Whether it is because the parent is rejecting or indifferent or weak, the child has less commitment to a particular set of values. Therefore, the child depends more heavily on the approval of others to judge his or her own behavior. We expect adults to have a personally defined moral philosophy that provides the inner voice of approval and guidance. In childhood, however, the ability to resist pressures toward conformity or to direct actions according to internal standards depends on the strength of parental identification and the clarity of parental values.

Finally, the intensity of the need for social approval is shaped by the pattern of school evaluations. Within the school environment there are repeated experiences of evaluation. One begins the school career strong on energy and weak on skill. Teachers, peers, and parents are constant judges of one's progress. Successes and failures become matters of peer comparison and public approval or rejection as well as for achievement motivation. It is not enough for children to struggle privately with their limitations. Criticism, reprimand, and even ridicule are common aspects of classroom interaction. Public shame and accompanying doubts about one's own skills heightens the school child's dependence on the approval of others. In extreme cases, children rely on the teacher's judgment of what is a correct response and disregard their own opinions. They would rather be liked than be right.

In these examples we see the convergence of family and culture in shaping the person's motivational profile. Motives may be encouraged or inhibited through child-rearing practices. Imposed on the pattern of family socialization are the other cultural influences, especially the school, mass media, and the visible community leaders. These cultural forces encourage or discourage the expression of specific motives.

EMOTIONS

The main difference between motives and emotions is that motives are goal oriented while emotions are not. Motives direct behavior toward some action, whether it involves sleep, sex, stimulation, or success. Emotions do not generally direct us toward a specific goal. One can sit in a chair, watching a television program and experience sadness, delight, vengeance, pride, and disgust. None of these feelings necessarily lead to new behavior. This is not to say that emotions play no role in behavior. In fact, one could argue that the basic motive underlying all behavior is to increase feelings of happiness or pleasure and to avoid feelings of unhappiness or pain. However, emotions tend to play a reactive role. They tell us whether an event, a thought, or an action is positive and pleasurable or negative and unpleasurable. Emotional reactions are bits of information that guide subsequent behavior. If the roller coaster ride evokes intense fear, I will not buy another ticket. If the ride evokes excitement and delight, I will. Emotions provide signals that we learn to interpret. They also provide social signals for others. The behavioral components of emotion, including facial expressions, posture, and hand gestures give information to others about the person's inner state.

The emotions of childhood

Early in life our emotions are not very distinct. In infancy, we might describe three initial states: calm; aroused alertness; and crying. During the first month or two, only the crying state shows levels of intensity. Babies may cry softly or whimper and fuss or cry loudly, shaking their entire body. During the second month, babies begin to smile. We would call this the emergence of happiness as a positive emotion that balances the expressions of distress. Smiling usually occurs during the aroused, alert period. It is sometimes observed after feeding during what might be called the calm state. Smiling is a single expressive behavior that has several interpretations during infancy. It can signal satisfaction, recognition of a familiar object or person, or sensory delight at being touched, tickled, or spoken to.

During toddlerhood, the variety of emotional responses increases. The loud, hard cry is transformed into anger. Anger itself is differentiated into more subtle expressions from willful resistance (I'm not going!) to full-bodied rage (the temper tantrum). The whimper and fuss become pouting, worrying, and feelings of helplessness. The soft cry may become a cry of pain and a cry of fear.

Fear itself begins in the startle reflex and the Moro reflex, both inborn responses to potential threat. The startle reflex is described as a reflexive jerk in response to a loud noise. Usually it is followed by crying. The Moro reflex is a response to sudden loss of support. Babies spread their arms out and then clutch them close to their bodies. This response too is usually followed by crying. During infancy and toddlerhood, fear is expressed by clinging, crying, or hiding the face. By the age of three, fear of objects, people, and places is joined by fear of imaginary creatures. Somewhat later, children begin to play with fear. They engage in activities that are mildly frightening. Frightening stories or games become entertaining. The emotion of fear is influenced by the factor of control. Threats that can be changed or easily avoided may be exciting. Threats that are sudden and unavoidable create a more intense, painful reaction.

The positive emotions of happiness, excitement, surprise, and pride are also more clearly separated during toddlerhood. These emotions can be evoked as a response to the child's own accomplishments. They may arise in response to the praise, kindness, or loving actions of another.

As the range of emotions expands, children also get better at interpreting the emotions of others. Empathy is the *vicarious* experience of an emotional state that is being expressed by another person. Just by observing the facial expressions, body posture, and vocalizations of another, children can identify and experience that person's emotions.

The capacity for empathy is first demonstrated in the newborn nursery. When one infant starts to wail, it sends a rippling effect through the other babies who also begin to cry (Sagi & Hoffman, 1976; Simmer,

● *vicarious*—an experience achieved through the imagined participation in events that happen to another person.

United Press International

Terror, grief, and desperation can all be seen in this woman's face and body.

1971). Three- and four-year olds can recognize the emotional reactions that children might have to specific problem situations. In a comparison of American and Chinese children, both groups were able to recognize happy and unhappy reactions by age three. The ability to distinguish between *afraid, sad,* and *angry* emerged slightly later. Specific cues for these feelings were different in the two cultural groups. Nevertheless, it was clear that the youngest children in both cultures were able to recognize an emotional state in another person (Borke, 1973).

The ability to identify pleasurable and unpleasurable emotions in others and to empathize with those feelings makes the young child vulnerable to moral teachings. Empathy can make a child willing to help another person. Empathy can also produce remorse for having caused an emotional state in another person. In either case, because children are able to experience how others feel, they are more willing to modify their behavior (M. L., Hoffman, 1975).

For every emotion, there are physical, behavioral, and cognitive components. The physical component may include a change in heart rate, tightening or relaxing of certain muscles, release of adrenaline, constricting of blood vessels, or excretion of stomach acids. These changes occur as the body readies itself for action. Although we may recognize these bodily changes as the physical components of a certain emotional state, the physical components are not markedly different for each emotion. For example, the physical changes that occur during intense anger are quite similar to those that occur during intense fear. Even though we experience the two emotions as distinct, they are not easily separated at the physical level.

The behavioral component refers to the outward signs of the emotion. We will discuss those in more detail in the next section. Let us point out here that there are both universal and culturally specific body modes for expressing emotions. One aspect of our social development is learning to express and to disguise certain emotions. We learn to put on the "pokerface" in order to block communication or to "put up a good front" in order to mislead others about our inner state.

The cognitive component involves labeling and interpreting emotions. This dimension is probably responsible for the greatest amount of differentiation in our emotional life. Levels of emotional intensity can be captured by different words. Take the terms we use for a low-energy sadness. We can be *down, blue, depressed, sad, grief-stricken, or despondent.* Each emotion requires a match between a verbal label and a set of feelings and events. The pattern of all the components has a personal meaning as well as a social meaning. Even though the specific pattern might be different for each person, each label has some degree of shared meaning. When you tell someone you feel depressed, they can honestly say "I know how you feel."

Emotions and nonverbal behavior

As we mentioned earlier, the behavioral part of emotional expression helps communicate our inner state. A smile is part of feeling happy. A pout or a frown are parts of feeling sad or troubled. The overt expression also alerts others in the social group that some change of state has occurred. For parents, the infant's smile lets them know that the baby is happy. It tells parents that whatever they are doing or have just done succeeded in making the baby comfortable. Expressions of anger, including the clenched jaw, the scowl, or the tightened fist, alert others that an aggressive act may be forthcoming. Sobbing and crying are signals that help is needed. When we see another person cry, it arouses an empathic response that stimulates our own desire to provide help.

● **universality—** applying to all human groups.

The study of emotions shows that there is some universality in emotional expression. This *universality* can be explained by the primitive animal origins of some emotional expressions. There are two questions about the expression of emotion. The first is whether we recognize the emotion being expressed in certain faces made by other people. Would everyone understand, without previous learning, that a smile means pleasant feelings? The second question is whether we produce certain faces in certain situations. Do all people make similar faces when they accidentally step on a sharp object with a bare foot?

In one experiment (Ekman, 1972), these questions were studied in American and Japanese college students. First, students from both countries were photographed while they watched movies. Half of the students saw a movie showing surgery; and the other half saw a travelogue. The researcher assumed that watching an operation would be an unpleasant and stressful experience, whereas watching a travelogue would be a neutral and unstressful experience. Would the students from different cultures make similar faces in response to the two kinds of movies? To answer this question two other groups of American and Japanese students looked at the photographs taken of the students who watched the movies. Their task was to guess which movie the students were watching. Would there be differences? Would they be able to guess the emotions of people from their own countries?

The results showed that students from the two countries had similar facial expressions to each of the two movies. Their faces reflected unpleasantness while watching the surgery movie and had a neutral expression while watching the travelogue. Their fellow students had no trouble correctly judging which movie was being watched while the photographs were taken. Furthermore, they were as accurate in judging the expressions of students from the other country as they were in judging those from their own. This study supports the idea that there *are* natural tendencies to produce a certain facial expression in response to certain emotional states.

People may also be able to interpret the facial expressions of people from other cultures without being trained to so do. The study just described leaves some uncertainty about this point. First, the two emotional categories used were quite broad: unpleasant, and pleasant or neutral. Can a greater variety of expressions be produced and recognized? Second, there is a large amount of communication between Americans and Japanese. There is an exchange of visitors, magazines, movies, and television programs. There are many opportunities to learn about the use of facial expressions in each other's culture. These problems were overcome in the following study.

Facial expression was studied in New Guinea in order to reduce the possibility of cross-cultural learning. The people who were observed had little contact with other cultures. They had no movies, television, or any other way of learning about the facial expressions in other cultures. The researchers told stories that had different emotions as themes. For example, the happy story was about friends who came together after a long separation. The people were asked to select a photograph of a face that showed how the person in the story felt. Their choices of photographs were the same as the choices made by people of other cultures.

To study the production of expressions, the researchers told another group the same stories and asked them to make faces that reflected the emotions of the characters in the stories. They produced the same faces as subjects in other cultures. From this research we have learned that faces representing six basic emotions appear to have the same meanings across cultures. The emotions are happiness, sadness, fear, anger, disgust, and surprise.

If there are natural tendencies for the production and recognition of certain facial expressions, how can we explain that fact? One approach is to consider these expressions as movements of muscles that serve biological needs. The angry face can be interpreted as a protective movement. The lowered brow and tightened eyelids protect the eyes from injury in a fight. The lips press together in order to force air back into the lungs to prepare for strenuous activity. The mouth may be open and the teeth exposed for biting.

Charles Darwin, who spent much of his life studying evolution, offered an evolutionary interpretation of facial expressions. Darwin compared the facial gestures and expressions of primates with those of humans. He concluded that they began with primitive activities like drawing back their lips for biting. He believed that those primitive activities evolved into threatening displays to other animals. The form of facial expressions may have changed through evolutionary changes in facial muscles. The meanings of the expressions may also have changed. The function of facial expressions became communication. They were passed along through each stage of evolution, giving the human face remarkable communication skills.

The frown provides a rather simple example of the evolution of expressions. This expression derived from intent staring at an object close to the face. In the frown, the eyebrows are typically lowered in the dog, the capuchin monkey, and many other mammals including man. The function of the lowered brows is unclear. Perhaps it serves a protective function. Perhaps it helps focus the eyes on the object. In most mammals this direct stare is a good indication of concentrated interest and little or no fear. Often those interested stares immediately precede attacks. So the intent stare with lowered brows has become an expression of confident and unafraid threat in monkeys, apes, and humans.

The grin appears to have a far more complicated history. It has at least two primitive origins. One of these origins seems to be a protective response to something that startles the animal. The lips are drawn back to bite or to spit out something unpleasant that has been swallowed. Many mammals show this response when they are startled. Under those circumstances it is a grimace. You will recognize this expression by noting each others' expressions to the sound of a nail scraping on a blackboard.

The primitive grin can also be connected to high-pitched screams in animals. Some suggest that the tensing of the neck muscles that accompanies a grin may serve to strengthen the neck against the vibration that accompanies vocalization. One can see this action in the expressions

Living laboratory 4·2

EMOTIONS AND NONVERBAL BEHAVIOR

Purpose:　　　　To assess the capacity to interpret nonverbal signals.

Method:　　　　A. Find two pictures, one of a male and one of a female, that illustrate each of the six emotions listed below:

　　　　　　　　1. Anger.　　　4. Fear.
　　　　　　　　2. Disgust.　　5. Happiness.
　　　　　　　　3. Surprise.　　6. Sadness.

　　　　　　　　B. Get three adult judges to tell you what emotion is portrayed by each photograph.

　　　　　　　　C. Show the photographs to children aged 4, 8, 12, and 16.

Results:　　　　What emotions do the adults and children see? How do the interpretations of the children coincide with those of the adult judges?

Discussion:　　How easy is it to read a person's face?

　　　　　　　　Can you tell when someone is faking an emotion or trying to disguise an emotion?

　　　　　　　　What are the cues that the face is insincere?

of wailing children during a quarrel. The grin, when it accompanies screaming, generally signifies a threat in social animals, including humans. Often the advanced primates do not vocalize at all, but grin in such circumstances.

The evolution of the primitive grin into the human smile has only been traced partially. Physically, the smile is clearly related to the grin. The connection of vocal laughter with the grin is quite clear. However, it is difficult to understand how the grin or the smile became associated with pleasure. The grin is seen in baboons and humans as a defensive gesture. By grinning the animal tries to assure the other of friendly intentions. Picture a man holding a fixed smile in response to the verbal attacks by a superior. Think of the bland smile one prepares when meeting a stranger. These are illustrations of defensive reactions. In these examples, the grin is part of a cautious or submissive stance. We usually do not consider the human smile as a submissive behavior. Yet, one researcher found that in interactions between high-status and low-status children, the low-status children smiled more often (Krebs, cited by Jones, 1972). Perhaps you can think of situations in which adults smile frequently when they are trying to please someone.

We see then that emotional expressions have a long history of contributing to the process of adaptation. In many cases, emotions serve as an outlet for energy even when the person is trying to maintain control. The fact that there are common facial expressions used in many different cultures lends support to an evolutionary view of emotional responses.

The socialization
of emotions

● *innate*—born with.

Every emotion, even those that have their origin in an innate reflex, are subject to socialization. Let us use fear as an example. We have identified the origins of fear in the startle response or the Moro reflex. During the second six months of life, infants show fear of strangers by clinging to their caregiver, crying, or rejecting interaction with strangers. From these universal beginnings, the experience of fear travels a different course in each society.

Each society teaches its children that different objects or events are sources of danger. In the United States, the automobile is a dangerous object for little children. Children are warned to watch carefully for moving cars, and never to dash out into the street. In one small group called the Semang who lived on the Malay Peninsula similar caution was exerted to prevent children from committing a variety of sins. Among these sins were killing a sacred black wasp, mocking a tame animal, playing with birds' eggs, or combing one's hair during a thunderstorm. Each of these sins was viewed as very dangerous. It could bring on the anger of the most powerful god Karei who could slay them with his thunderbolts (Murdock, 1934). Children were warned of these fearful acts and urged not to do them.

In each culture objects, people, or activities are treated differently as stimuli for emotions. Different norms exist for the expression of emotions. One culture may encourage bravery. Adults model an indifferent response to fear or pain. Another culture may encourage crying, writhing, or moaning as the appropriate response to fear or pain. In our own culture, that distinction is made in response to male and female children. Crying and whinning, while viewed as undesirable signs of dependency or helplessness, are generally more acceptable for females at every age than for males. At this point in our evolution, human emotions are closely linked to thought. Since culture influences thought, the labeling and the expression of emotions take on unique qualities in each society.

In the following sections, we will describe the socialization of three emotions: anger, loneliness, and love. Each emotion provides a slightly different view of how the control or expression of emotions is learned.

Anger. Anger is a feeling of strong displeasure usually accompanied by hostility toward some object. Anger, like other emotions, can vary in intensity from being annoyed or "peeved" to being enraged. Angry feelings can be expressed in a variety of forms from silent withdrawal to physical aggression. In every society, angry feelings are a threat to group support. Therefore, they are an important target for socialization. The expression of anger frequently creates tension between parents and children. There are many causes for the child's anger. Inability to perform a task, limits imposed by parents, and unwillingness of a sibling to share a belonging may all stimulate angry feelings. The expression of anger is often unpleasant even when it is understandable. Parents who have encouraged their children to be independent, to try new things, and to express their thoughts may still find it difficult to accept their children's

"If you're looking for violence and excitement, how about bathing the dog?"

Reprinted by permission The Wall Street Journal

angry feelings. In order to manage their aggression, children need acceptable outlets for the expression of anger as well as strategies for the control of anger.

Two "Commonsense" strategies for controlling anger are catharsis and punishment. Catharsis refers to draining aggressive energy through activities that are emotionally arousing but not harmful. Activities including competitive sports, television, movies, imaginative play, or listening to stories about aggression all provide opportunities for catharsis. Unfortunately, the research evidence does not support the notion that this strategy reduces aggression (Berkowitz, 1973). For example, Feshbach (1956) found that boys became more aggressive after freeplay experiences rather than less. Aggressive play toys increased the child's use of aggression after the play session more than neutral toys. Laboratory studies of the effects of viewing filmed violence also report that viewing violence stimulates children's preference for violence. Rather than being drained of angry motives, exposure to violence tends to increase the likelihood of the child imitating the violent actions (Bandura, Ross, & Ross, 1961, 1963; Lovaas, 1961). Viewing filmed violence may also increase children's tolerance for real-life aggression (Drabman & Thomas, 1974).

Punishment of aggression also does not consistently improve the child's ability to control aggression. Studies of parent discipline suggest that if parents use physical punishment their children are likely to be physically aggressive (Becker, 1964). Parents who use physical punishment serve as models for aggression that is rewarded by the child's own compliance. While the punishment may inhibit the immediate action, the child observes that aggression is an effective and rewarded strategy. One study focused on the timing of punishment. Half the children were punished as soon as they reached for an attractive toy. The other children were punished after they touched the toy. When the children were left alone, more boys from the first group resisted the toy than did boys from the second group (Walters, Parke, & Cane, 1965). Punishments that come early in the action and that are administered consistently appear to be effective in controlling aggression (Berkowitz, 1973).

The problems with punishment are many.

1. Punishments illustrate to the child the usefulness of aggression.
2. Punishments produce many emotions in the child that are related to what happened just before the punishment. While some of those emotions may be remorse or guilt, others may be anger and revenge.
3. A rapid punishment does not allow the child to explain his or her point of view.

Frequently, the child is punished for a behavior that the child meant to be helpful or kind. For example, one morning parents found their two-year-old son spreading toothpaste on the windows. It turned out that he wanted to give them a good cleaning. He had seen a television advertisement in which toothpaste made things sparkle. An abrupt punishment in that case would have tied a negative feeling to something the child meant to be helpful.

There are a few strategies that do appear to reduce the expression of aggression (Berkowitz, 1973). First, ignoring aggression reduces the expression of aggression (Williams, 1959; Brown & Elliott, 1965). Sometimes ignoring aggression is combined with a brief period of isolation where the child is taken to a "time-out" room. Ignoring aggression is only effective when the child understands that the adult's failure to respond is not a sign of approval. Second, other emotions that are incompatible with anger can be evoked. These include feelings of sympathy for the victim, defining the aggressive actions as bad, or arousing the child's needs for affiliation (Gordon & Cohen, 1963). Third, watching aggression that is punished may reduce aggressive behavior. Finally, aggression can be reduced by limiting the child's exposure to aggression. This includes aggressive toys, exposure to hostile interactions among adults, and viewing televised or filmed aggression. Clearly, it is not possible to avoid all exposure to aggression. Children need to encounter some aggression in order to learn how to manage feelings of anger and rage. However, adults can be sensitized to the provocative features of certain stimuli. They can help their children to understand the meaning of these stimuli. Parents and other adults can also help to interrupt the expression of aggression by increasing the child's empathy with the victim.

Loneliness.   The origins of loneliness are bound up with the desire for social interaction. Babies not only have the competencies to participate in social interactions, but interactions are an important source of pleasure. The human voice is one of the earliest stimuli to evoke an infant's smile. Tickling, rocking, and holding a baby closely are ways of soothing and delighting an infant. The human face becomes a target of interest and pleasure within the first six months of life. All this is merely to emphasize the early origins of pleasure in human contact that exist for babies in all cultures.

Loneliness is an emotional response to a difference between the desired level and the actual level of social interaction (Peplau & Perlman, in press). One of the earliest experiences of loneliness is called *separation anxiety.* At about nine months, infants show attachment to their caregivers by expressing rage and despair when the caregivers leave. Separation can lead to two different kinds of behavior. Under some conditions, separation from the caregiver will lead to efforts to find the adult and to restore physical contact. Separation can also be the cause for protest, despair, or detachment depending on the length of the separation (Ainsworth et al., 1971; Bowlby, 1960). When babies are separated from their mothers and placed in an environment where there is little sensory and interpersonal stimulation, they become withdrawn and listless (Spitz, 1945, 1946). Babies who were transferred from a foster mother to an adoptive mother after eight months of age responded to this change with strong negative reactions (Yarrow, 1963, 1964, 1967). These observations provide evidence of the very young child's capacity to grieve over separation from loved ones. In its adult form, loneliness reflects a modified form of grief over separation.

Peplau and Perlman (in press) distinguish between events that may bring out feelings of loneliness and personal qualities that make individuals likely to feel lonely. Some events that can prompt feelings of loneliness include: ending a close relationship; physical separation from loved ones; retirement; children leaving the home; or a promotion that involves separation from friends. Personal qualities can also produce feelings of loneliness. If a person is socially unacceptable to others (whatever the reason), they are likely to feel lonely. Some people have inadequate interpersonal skills. They may be shy, lack verbal skills, or be very self-conscious. Any of these qualities may lead them to be unwilling to take the risks necessary to seek out others.

Lonely feelings may be the result of what one expects from a situation. We do not expect to have many interactions during a movie or on a bicycle ride. At a party or at a holiday resort, however, we may expect to meet new people and have opportunities to interact. When what we expect does not come true, feelings of loneliness are likely to result. We learn what to expect in social situations. Over time, we become aware of norms for social relations in certain settings and for certain roles. Adolescents, for example, are expected to start dating, to go to parties, and to "hang around" with friends. Young adults are expected to form serious heterosexual relationships. When early adolescents are isolated from their peers, or when young adults are unable to make a loving commitment to someone, feelings of loneliness may arise. These feelings are not only the result of the lack of interaction. They are also the result of feelings of failure to meet expectations for people your age.

One's self-concept influences feelings of loneliness. People who are quite anxious about letting people "come too close" will have trouble reaching out to others. Some people have a negative self-concept. They may define themselves as undesirable, awkward, unattractive, or even harmful to others. People with low self-esteem are unlikely to initiate interaction. They lack hope about being positively responded to by others. We are reminded of the shy, self-conscious adolescent who approaches his first try at asking a girl for a date by saying: "You don't want to go to the movies on Saturday, do you?"

Generally, our culture treats loneliness as a negative experience that is to be avoided (Peplau et al., in press; Weiss, 1973). Isolation is often used as a punishment. It can range from temporary time away from the social group (being sent to your room) to extended separation from all forms of social contact (solitary confinement). Feeling misunderstood, having failed to make meaningful contact with others, or being shunned by others may make someone lonely. The prospect of loneliness itself generates fear. The fear of being lonely leads to anxiety that adds to the distress of the loneliness. The socialization of loneliness combines the original feelings of grief over separation with feelings of shame and fear about not having enough social contacts.

Loving. Love is a deep emotional commitment to some person, object, or activity. Usually, it is thought of as the love that is felt between two adults as they establish *intimacy*. Love has its origins in childhood. We first learn about love with our family. The first objects of our love are usually parents. Through repeated interactions, infants form an attachment to the people who take care of them.

● *intimacy—the ability to experience an open, supportive, tender relationship with another without fear of losing one's own identity in the process of growing close.*

There are three things that show that a social attachment has been formed. The infant: *(a)* tries to keep close to the people who care for them (Ainsworth, 1973); *(b)* shows distress when the people who care for them are absent (Schaffer & Emerson, 1964); and *(c)* can identify people who take care of them and tell the difference from other people. Babies who are attached are more relaxed and comfortable with the person to whom they are attached and more fretful with people to whom they are not attached (Bronson, 1973).

This kind of love can be established between the infant and several adults or older siblings. Lamb (1976), for example, has described the qualities of attachment that infants show to their mothers and fathers. Babies tended to have more playful interactions with their fathers. They have more comforting interactions with their mothers. When only one parent was present, babies showed attachment to that parent. When both parents were present, babies had different patterns of interacting with each.

The social attachment that occurs during infancy is very important for the development of interpersonal relationships. Without the establishment of this bond, experiences of trust and closeness are difficult to establish. Attachment serves as evidence to the child of his or her capacity to love and of the capacity of others to return that love. It is on the basis of this lesson that later friendships are formed.

The capacity to give and to receive love is expanded during childhood as children establish close friendships. Loving peer relationships bring early experiences of giving affection to someone outside the family network. The "best friend" relationship can become quite intimate. Children share private jokes, develop secret codes, tell family secrets, set out on dangerous adventures, and help each other in times of trouble. They also fight, threaten each other, break up, and reunite in the course of the friendship. Sullivan (1949) has pointed out how important intimate childhood friendships are for adult heterosexual relationships. They provide one basis for our ideas of intimacy without the sexual component. When children experience love for a friend, they have the chance to work on some of the conflicts of intimacy with someone of equal power, status, skill, and access to resources.

One of the most difficult times for learning about love is early adolescence. In the midst of physical, cognitive, and social changes, the young adolescent is expected to have heterosexual relationships. There is the challenge of learning to express new sexual impulses in an acceptable way. There is the struggle to overcome self-consciousness. Being engrossed in one's own issues makes it hard to make contact with another person. There are peer pressures to establish a social reputation and relatively strict criteria for popularity. Records, novels, television, and movies tell young adolescents how wonderful sex and love are. Parents encourage their adolescents to be social, to be involved with friends. High schools provide social activities and informal settings for adolescents to be together. In the corridors, at the lockers, and in the parking lots, high school students see their peers experimenting with love. For many adolescents who are not college bound, high school is the last opportunity to meet potential marriage partners. The pressure is on at least to experiment with loving if not to make a final commitment.

In our society, the expectation that is permanent loving commitment will be made to someone one's own age is reserved for young adulthood. It is during this period (from approximately 22–30) that the vast majority of men and women marry. More important than marriage itself is the expectation that the young adult will experience a sense of intimacy (Erikson, 1950, 1974).

> In youth you find out what you care to do and who you care to be—even in changing roles. In young adulthood you learn whom you care to be with—at work and in private life, not only exchanging intimacies, but sharing intimacy. In adulthood, however, you learn to know what and whom you can take care of (Erikson, 1974, p. 124).

The establishment of intimacy is an active process. While we refer to the onset of a loving relationship as "falling in love," it seems more appropriate to speak of the active process of establishing intimacy as "making love." Intimacy includes the ability to experience an open, sup-

The photography of H. Armstrong Roberts

Childhood friendships bring closeness without the "confusion" of sexuality.

portive, tender relationship without fear of losing one's own identity. Intimacy in a relationship supports independent judgments by each person (Stone, 1973). Establishing intimacy depends on the confidence that people have in themselves.

Intimacy implies the ability for mutual empathy and mutual regulation of needs. One must be able to give pleasure and to receive pleasure within the intimate context. Although intimacy may be established within the context of marriage, marriage itself does not, by definition, produce intimacy. In fact, during the early years of marriage, several forces are disruptive to the establishment of intimacy. These include:

1. The early period of mutual adjustment.
2. The birth of the first child.
3. The social expectations of members of the extended family.

Differences in patterns of socialization for men and women lead to different meanings of intimacy for each. Men and women have different problems in the establishment of intimacy (Bernard, 1971). Boys are taught during childhood to restain their expressions of dependence and to limit their emotionality. During middle school age and early adolescence, the emotional life of boys may be guided into expressions of competitiveness and self-reliance. Adolescent boys often resist expressions of tenderness toward their family members. There are tender moments shared by adolescent couples. However, boys are likely to resist any pressure toward long-term commitment until they have confidence in their own independence. The demand for intimacy during young adulthood may be very difficult for young men to meet. They have been socialized to resist intimate relationships. Achieving an intimate relationship provides a man with a chance to express emotion in a safe, supportive environment. The home may be the only place where a man can express his feelings in an open and direct way.

Women are better prepared for the emotional demands of intimacy. They are likely to have been rewarded for being expressive, nurturant, and supportive. Women are more willing to express dissatisfaction with their personalities than men are. They are likely to feel quite delighted about having a relationship with someone who will hear their problems and support them. If anything, women may enter an intimate relationship with too many needs for support. They rely on their husbands for reassurance. Women may, in fact, be disappointed to discover that their husbands are not as strong or as resourceful as they had expected.

● *reciprocal*—each participant influences the responses of the other.

The sense of intimacy, a sustained, *reciprocal* love between two people, is difficult to achieve. The high divorce rate, an estimated one third of all first marriages (Norton & Glick, 1976b), is testimony to the transience of loving feelings. Frequently love is replaced with hostility or boredom. On the other hand, adults continue to seek involvement in loving relationships. Most adults who have been divorced remarry (Glick, 1977). For the most part, failures or disappointments in love do not inhibit the desire to experience loving. As the saying goes: " 'Tis better to have loved and lost than never to have loved at all."

THE INFLUENCE OF EMOTIONS ON ADJUSTMENT

Emotions signal one to move ahead or to flee, to be open or guarded, to relax or to be alert. The intensity of emotions can influence the amount of reasoning or information gathering one can do. For example, a boy who is attracted to a girl may try to find out more about her, involve her in conversation, or call her for a date. A boy who is overwhelmed with sexual and loving impulses may be unable to even approach the girl. He may pursue her without taking time to find out anything more about her. In general, both intense and minimal emotional arousal are linked with less effective decision making than is a moderate level of emotionality. The extent to which emotions disrupt effective coping depends on: (1) the kind of activity or behavior that is required; and (2) the person's skills for controlling or changing emotions (Janis & Mann, 1976; Lazarus, 1974). Self-esteem and anxiety are two emotions that provide evidence of the relationship between emotional state and behavior. Research about these emotions show the adaptive and maladaptive roles that emotions play in the process of adjustment.

Self-esteem and risk taking

Self-esteem has both cognitive and emotional content. The emotional content is associated with positive feelings of pride and worthiness and negative feelings of shame and worthlessness. Feedback about failure or inadequacy produce feelings of shame and worthlessness. When the feedback is directed to skills that the person believes relevant to the task at hand, it is more likely to influence their hopes for success. Negative information about intelligence will lower expectations about one's performance on a course examination while negative information about sociability will lower expectations about having a good time at a mixer (Wylie, 1961; 1974; Wells & Marwell, 1976). One impact of lowered self-esteem is lowered confidence about one's skills. As one approaches an uncertain situation, lowered self-esteem is likely to lead to caution and efforts to preserve the status quo. If there is little to gain and much to lose, this kind of conservation may be quite adaptive. If there is as much to gain by change as there is to lose, the conservative strategy may not be a good one. Thinking of certain high-risk life decisions, like the decision to marry, or the decision to leave a secure job for one that has greater potential, one's self-esteem may provide the inner voice of confidence or doubt about which option is best.

Anxiety as a productive and disruptive emotion

Anxiety can be viewed as an emotion that signals threat. The threat may be a real danger to the person. The threat may be a perceived danger. In either case, anxiety should set into motion some form of protective behavior. Two different kinds of studies show the influence

United Press International

Anxiety is a signal of threat. One common response to threat is flight.

of anxiety on adaptation. First, anxiety has been studied for its influence on learning. Tasks that were judged as low, moderate, and highly complex were given to two groups of students. One group was high in anxiety and the other low. Students who were high in anxiety did well on the simple tasks. Students low in anxiety did well on the most complex tasks (Montague, 1953). Doing simple tasks that are already well within the person's competence is not disrupted by anxiety. The arousal caused by anxiety keeps attention focused on the details of the task. Complex tasks require much more thinking. Anxiety makes it difficult to concentrate on the task.

The second approach was to study the way anxiety affects attitude change. In a series of studies, Janis and Feshbach (1953) evaluated the impact of fear-arousing messages on attitude change. High school students heard a high, moderate, or low fear-arousing lecture on tooth decay and dental care. Students' attitudes were measured one week before the lectures, immediately after, and one week after the lectures. The group that heard the high-fear lecture were most impressed by it. They said that the lecture should be given to all students, and that the lecture made them worried about their own dental health. Students who heard the low-fear lecture were not very impressed by the talk. Few students, however, found the lecture unpleasant or became worried about their dental care. Two additional steps revealed the effect of these messages on adaptation. The high-fear lecture group was less likely to improve their toothbrushing one week after the lecture while 50 percent of the low-fear lecture group said they were brushing better. In fact, 20 percent of the high-fear lecture group was doing worse than they had done before the lecture. After the lecture students were exposed to different information which was opposed to the information presented in the dental care lecture. The high-fear lecture group was much more likely than the low-fear lecture group to change their attitudes in the direction of the new message. These studies show that fear-arousing messages may interfere with effective coping if they are too intense. In order to avoid the anxiety aroused by these messages, some students avoided behaviors like toothbrushing. They eagerly switched to a less-threatening message when it was available. Intense threat and anxiety can make it hard to gather new information.

Living laboratory 4·3

THE INFLUENCE OF EMOTIONS ON ADJUSTMENT

Purpose: To trace the influence of anxiety on adjustment.

Method: A. Describe your own physical and behavioral signs of anxiety. How do you feel when you are anxious? Write it all down.

B. For the next three days, keep a log of your experiences of anxiety. Keep a record of the decisions you make or the behaviors you engage in while you are feeling anxious.

Results: Write down when you feel anxious; how intense the anxiety is on a scale from one (not too anxious) to five (extremely anxious); and how long you feel anxious. After the three days are past, go back and evaluate these anxious moments.

Discussion: What conditions are likely to prompt anxiety for you?

What level of anxiety do you find best for good decision-making?

How are your choices or decisions influenced by anxiety?

Do you have any ways of reducing anxiety when it is interfering with what you are doing?

Chapter summary

Motives direct people toward specific actions or thoughts. Even though many motives originate from physical needs, psychological motives play a powerful role in directing behavior.

Four theories of motivation highlight different aspects of the function of motives in personal adjustment. Freud identified sexuality and aggression as the primary psychological motives.

Maslow described a need hierarchy to explain the "fully functioning person."

Murray's model emphasizes the relationship between personal needs and environmental pressure.

Allport's theory recognized the fact that a continuous revision of motives takes place during life.

Learning about motives is illustrated in the literature on achievement motivation and the need for social approval. Personal needs to express competence and to feel connected to the social group are shaped and modified by family, school, and culture.

In contrast to motives, emotions have a reactive quality. They do not necessarily guide us toward a specific action that will reduce the emotion. Often emotions are a signal about some dangerous, undesirable, or pleasant kind of experience.

Every emotion has a physical, a behavioral, and a cognitive component. While the physical component may be quite similar across emotions, the behavioral and cognitive components are usually easier to distinguish.

The nonverbal components of emotions provide an outlet for the expression of emotional energy. They also serve as a social signal about one's inner state. There is some degree of universality in the expression of emotions. Especially the emotions of happiness, sadness, fear, anger, disgust, and surprise have readily recognizable facial components.

Just like motives, emotions are modified by socialization. The discussion of anger, loneliness, and loving illustrate ways that emotions are learned. Child-rearing practices, age norms, and learned expectations about the behavior appropriate for specific settings all shape our emotional life.

SUGGESTED READINGS

Some good books on motivation include the following:

Korman, A. K. *The psychology of motivation.* Englewood Cliffs, N.J.: Prentice-Hall, 1974.

Weiner, B. *Theories of motivation.* Chicago: Markham, 1972.

Some good books on emotions include the following:

Izard, C. E. *Human emotions.* New York: Plenum, 1977.

Strongman, K. T. *The psychology of emotions.* 2d ed. New York: Wiley, 1978.

Reading

ON VIOLENCE

What we need is an intelligent recognition of "the nature of the beast." We shall not be able to deal capably with violence until we are ready to see it as part of human nature. When we have gotten well acquainted with this idea, and have learned to live with the need to domesticate our violent tendencies, then through a slow and tenuous process we may tame them successfully, first in ourselves, and on such basis also in society. But we shall never succeed in taming our violent tendencies as long as we proceed on the assumption that because violence *should* not exist, we might as well act as if it did not.

Violent action is, of course, a short-cut toward gaining an objective. It is so primitive in nature that it is generically unsuitable to gain for us those more subtle satisfactions we seek. That is why violence stands at the very beginning of man's development into a socialized human being. The heroic sagas marking man's entry into a more civilized and humane world are dominated by themes of violence; and it is also characteristic of our own entrance to life. Often violent temper tantrums, so typical of the child about to become a complex human being, show both: how violent and destructive outbursts preceded our developing ability to master inner drives and deal constructively with the problems presented by the fact that the external world is often frustrating; and the need to achieve such mastery if we are to cope well.

Although we do not wish to acknowledge how universal this really is, a birthday party of happy, normal children could instruct us. The birthday child, in his natural eagerness to get at the enticing present, will tear the wrappings off the package to get at the toy. If the box he is ripping should be part of the game, so much the worse for the box. Thus desire begets violence, and violence may destroy the object desired. In this sense, as in many others, violence is both natural and ineffective. It rarely reaches its goal or else, in getting at it, destroys it. True, discharge itself is a goal—but then once we have discharged our anger, we no longer question what caused it, nor do we seek better ways to deal with the causes. Then nothing prevents what enraged us from happening again, leading once more to an outburst of violence.

To recount the evils of violence here is unnecessary. What is to be considered is whether our attitudes toward violence are reasonable given our goal to contain it, and what ways might better serve our ends.

The obvious is often neglected when we think about violence: whether or not it will be used or avoided depends entirely on what alternative solutions are known to a person facing a problem. Aeschylus understood this, and thus I evoked his *Oresteia.* In it Athena offers a substitution for ancient revenge for murder which is better than another murder. Violence is the behavior of someone who cannot visualize any other solution to a problem that besets him; this shows up most clearly in gang warfare.

Today we are constantly bombarded by images of the "good life" of ownership and consumption, but for a great number of people the means of consumership are slim. This is particularly true of many young people before they find a secure place both in our economic and our social systems, and even more so if they are from marginal or sub-marginal backgrounds. They often feel helpless to provide themselves with what they feel is even a minimal satisfaction of the demands we create in them. So they see no alternative for reaching their goals except through violence, and the pressures of frustration—and the very real chance that they might get away with using violence—only tempt them more to use it. Nothing in their education has equipped them to contain their violence, because during their whole educational life, its existence has been denied.

Source: Bruno Bettelheim, from *Surviving and Other Essays*. Copyright 1952, 1960, 1962, 1976, 1979, by Bruno Bettelheim and Teude Bettelheim as trustees. Reprinted by permission of Alfred A. Knopf, Inc.

Chapter 5
Coping and adaptation

A crow, so thirsty that he could not even caw, came upon a pitcher which once had been full of water. But when he put his beak into the pitcher's mouth he found that only a little water was left in it. Strain and strive as he might he was not able to reach far enough down to get at it. He tried to break the pitcher, then to overturn it, but his strength was not equal to the task.

Just as he was about to give up in despair a thought came to him. He picked up a pebble and dropped it into the pitcher. Then he took another pebble and dropped that into the pitcher. One by one he kept dropping pebbles into the pitcher until the water mounted to the brim. Then perching himself upon the handle he drank and drank until his thirst was quenched.

Application: necessity is the mother of invention.

"The Crow and the Pitcher," Aesop's Fables

THE MEANING OF COPING

Coping refers to a person's active efforts to resolve stress and to create new ways of handling new situations at each life stage (Erikson, 1959). This idea emphasizes the importance of the personal resources and competencies that are used to deal with new challenges. Coping emphasizes mastery of the situation while defense emphasizes protection of the self. This is not to imply that coping occurs with no regard for the self. The coping process requires an effective person who actively engages each life challenge.

White (1974) identified three components of coping. First, coping requires that the person be able to gain and process new information. New information is needed to understand a difficult situation more fully or to establish a new position in the face of threat. Second, coping requires that the person be able to maintain control over his or her emotional state. This does not mean doing away with emotional responses. Rather, it suggests the importance of correctly interpreting emotions, expressing them when necessary, and limiting their expression when necessary. Third, coping requires that the person be able to move freely in his or her environment.

The goals of coping include the desire to maintain a sense of personal integrity, and to achieve greater personal control over the environment. In each situation, the person uses physical, cognitive, social, and emotional resources to understand what is needed. Then they modify some aspect of the situation or the self in order to achieve a more adequate person-environment fit. Coping, then, is behavior that occurs after the person has had a chance to analyze the situation, take a reading of his or her own emotions, and move to a closer or more distant position from the challenge.

The meaning of defense

In order to understand defense, we must begin by knowing why defenses are used. By and large, defenses are used to protect the person from anxiety. Anxiety leads to concern and worry. Normally, anxiety serves as a signal of threat. When a person is anxious, he is preparing both physically and mentally for possible conflict, attack, punishment, or harm. Anxiety usually results in greater activity, muscle tension, increased heart rate, and increased production of adrenal hormones. All of these physical changes prepare the person to respond to danger. When the danger is real, that is when there is an objective threat, the anxiety is followed by some self-protective response. The person may run away, freeze, strike out against the attacker, figure out some way to reduce the threat, change the threat into something more controllable, or overcome the source of threat.

Anxiety is not always a response to a real threat. Frequently, anxiety is a response to fear or to frustration. Sigmund Freud (1959a) thought that anxiety would also be experienced when a person was in conflict about expressing a desire. If the desire is thought to be very bad, as in the case of a desire to harm a parent or to be sexually intimate with a sibling, the person may experience anxiety without being able to recognize where it comes from. In this case, efforts to protect the self are directed at reducing the anxiety rather than at the source of threat itself.

Defenses work to protect the person from anxiety by distorting, substituting, or completely blocking out the source of conflict. Table 5·1

TABLE 5·1
Defenses

Process	Defense mechanisms	Problem solving
Discrimination: Ability to separate idea from feeling, idea from idea, feeling from feeling.	**Isolation:** Keeping apart ideas and/or feelings that belong together.	**Objectivity:** Separation of ideas from feelings to achieve objective evaluation or judgment.
Means-end symbolization: Ability to analyze the causal texture of experience, to anticipate outcomes, to entertain alternative choices.	**Rationalization:** Offering plausible causal content for unconscious true reason.	**Logical analysis:** Ability to analyze thoughtfully, carefully, and cogently the causal aspects of situations and proceed systematically in exposition.
Selective awareness: Ability to focus attention.	**Denial:** Refusal to recognize painful percepts, thoughts, or feelings.	**Concentration:** Ability to set aside recognizably disturbing feelings or thoughts in order to stick to the task at hand.
Sensitivity: Apprehension of others' feelings or ideas.	**Projection:** Attributing objectionable internal ideas or feelings to others.	**Empathy:** Ability to imagine how others feel.
Time reversal: Ability to recapture past experiences, feelings, ideas.	**Regression:** Avoidance of anxiety by reverting to age-inappropriate behavior.	**Playfulness:** Utilization of ideas and feelings not directly required by present situation.
Impulse restraint: Ability to control impulse.	**Repression:** Total inhibition of affect or idea.	**Suppression:** Impulse held in abeyance and controlled until appropriate time, place, and object appear.
Fantasy: Ability to imagine nonexistent events, ideas, experiences.	**Wish fulfillment:** Imagining the satisfaction of frustrated motives.	**Divergent thinking:** Imagining possibilities for the tasks at hand.

Source: W. J. McKeachie, C. L. Doyle, and M. M. Moffett, *Psychology*, 3d ed. (Reading, Mass.: Addison-Wesley Publishing Co., Inc., 1976), Table 13–1, p. 412. © 1976, Addison-Wesley. Reprinted with permission.
Note: The first six items are modified from Kroeber (1963).

lists some of the more common defenses. As the table illustrates, some of the same processes can be used in a defensive manner to protect the self or in a problem-solving manner to cope with conflict.

When behavior is described as defensive, psychologists are usually implying that the consequence of the behavior is a short-term reduction of anxiety. No progress is made on understanding the conflict. While this may be protective when used occasionally, it cannot really lead to new learning. A person who fails an exam may blame the failure on the unfairness of the teacher (projection). If repeated failures are handled in a similar manner, the fact that the student may need to study harder or that the course material may be too difficult for the person will not be noticed. The person will continue to fail. Teachers will be blamed. Nothing effective will be done to handle the situation.

People develop personal strategies for handling anxiety. Some people will use one or two defenses over and over again. One person may use projection. Another person may use denial. A third person may use isolation and rationalization. If we met people like these, we would observe that the first person was often blaming others. The second would insist that there was no problem. The third person would appear to be rather cold and detached. A defensive style represents an individual's way of dealing with anxiety.

A comparison of coping and defense

● *distortion*—a deviation from the real meaning.

Coping and defense are different. Defense protects the person in the face of threat. Fears of vulnerability are so strong that the person has to use *distortion* in order to be protected from harm. The extent of the distortion can vary. For example, in rationalization there is only a little distortion. The unacceptable wishes or threatening events are recognized, but they are explained away through a series of arguments. These arguments may be convincing to the person. To the outside observer they appear illogical and highly subjective. In contrast, repression involves a great deal of distortion. The stressful event or thought is simply removed from conscious awareness. The person has no conscious awareness of the event at all. Whether the distortion is great or small, defenses change the person's perceptions of the self or of the environment. Threat is reduced by refusing to allow some aspects of the situation to come into awareness.

Coping involves continued experiences with the environment. Rather than changing one's perception of reality through distortion, one may try to change some aspect of reality itself. Coping includes efforts to change reality so that it poses less of a threat or offers more of the resources the person needs. Coping also includes efforts to change the self so that a threat can be faced with more resources.

In the short run, defenses may help the person. They shield the person from intense grief, fear, or rage. They permit the person to go on by isolating the impact of one serious threat. Defenses may help

"Ms. Ryan, send me in a scapegoat."

postpone the impact of an unpleasant reality until the person has the resources for integrating that information. After a terrible accident or the death of a loved one, a person may refuse to believe that the crisis has occurred. They continue to expect to see their loved one healthy and normal. Denial protects them when the pain of the reality might be overwhelming. However, defenses are always imperfect. They do not really change the source of the threat. As long as the real source of the threat remains, energy will be needed to maintain the defense. No real progress in gaining control or reducing personal vulnerability is made.

Coping involves change. One uses information, emotions, and movement to alter some element of the situation so that it becomes less of a threat. In this sense, coping can actually bring the tension of a life stress to an end. Rather than coping with the same stresses again and again, one is able to master threatening situations and move on to new challenges.

Coping as a response to psychosocial conflict

At each stage of life the society within which one lives makes certain psychic demands upon the individual. These demands differ from stage to stage. Toddlers are expected to become more independent. Adolescents are expected to make a commitment to a peer group. Middle adults are expected to make commitments about the future generations of the society. The demands are experienced by the individual as mild but persistent guidelines and expectations for behavior. Toward the end of each stage, people are forced to make some type of resolution. They try to adjust to the demands of society even as they translate social demands into personal terms. This produces tension that must be reduced in order for the person to proceed to the next life stage. It is this tension state that causes the psychosocial crisis. The psychosocial crisis forces the person to use skills that have only recently been mastered. Table 5·2 lists the crisis of each of the stages of life, from infancy through later adulthood.

TABLE 5·2
Psychosocial crises of nine life stages

Life stage	Psychosocial crisis
Infancy (birth to 2 years)	Trust versus mistrust
Toddlerhood (2–4)	Autonomy versus shame and doubt
Early school age (5–7)	Initiative versus guilt
Middle school age (8–12)	Industry versus inferiority
Early adolescence (13–17)	Group identity versus alienation
Later adolescence (18–22)	Individual identity versus role diffusion
Young adulthood (23–30)	Intimacy versus isolation
Middle adulthood (31–50)	Generativity versus stagnation
Later adulthood (51–)	Integrity versus despair

This format suggests the nature of a successful or unsuccessful resolution of the crisis at each stage. The likelihood of a completely negative outcome is quite small. On the other hand, some negative elements are experienced by each person.

In fact, the negative outcomes offer opportunities for understanding oneself and one's social environment. One would not recommend a steady diet of mistrust. However, it is important to be able to evaluate situations and people for their trustworthiness. One must be able to recognize the cues that are being sent about the safety or goodwill of an encounter. It is an advantage to be able to anticipate that some people are not concerned about your needs or your welfare.

In the transitions from stage to stage, there will be periods of increased uncertainty about meeting new demands. People may resist leaving the stability of an earlier stage. The combination of uncertainty and resistance produces developmental anxiety. This anxiety reflects doubt about one's capacity to succeed at the tasks of each new life stage. The capacity to cope with developmental anxiety transforms these cultural challenges into opportunities for expansion and fulfillment.

Living Laboratory 5·1

THE MEANING OF COPING

Purpose: To translate the concept of coping into real-world terms.

Method: Read the situation below and generate a list of strategies that would be considered examples of coping with the challenge that is described.

Mary is an adult who is returning to college to complete her undergraduate degree. She is scheduled to make a class presentation on sex education. She is extremely anxious about the presentation because she is so much older than the other students in the class. She did not have sex education when she was a student. She and her husband have not openly discussed sex with their children. Mary very much wants a good grade in the course. How might Mary *cope* with this conflict?

Results: Generate a list of coping strategies. Try to think of as many different ways to handle this conflict as possible.

Discussion: Do your suggestions include an attempt to gain new information?

How is the situation redefined through coping?

Can you see new growth emerging from these coping efforts?

COPING COMPETENCIES THROUGH THE LIFE SPAN

The capacity to cope changes as the person achieves new physical, cognitive, social, and emotional skills. At the same time, the challenges that call forth coping efforts change at each phase of life. Infants do not have the conceptual ability or the physical strength to handle the stresses of household management. However, no one expects infants to assume those responsibilities. The growth of coping skills involves making effective use of existing skills to resolve stress. The ideal relationship between stress and coping occurs when the stress requires some new actions. When the stress is so intense that it cannot be mastered no matter how much energy is expended, coping efforts will most likely result in a sense of failure. The following discussion highlights some of the resources that can contribute to coping at four phases of development: infancy, school age, adolescence, and adulthood. We will see that many kinds of personal strengths can contribute to effective living.

The coping capacities of infants

● *reflex*—an unlearned connection between a specific stimulus and a specific response.

Lois Murphy describes coping behavior in infancy as: "A process, involving effort, on the way toward solution of a problem, as contrasted on the one hand with ready-made adaptational devices such as *reflexes,* or on the other hand, with complete and automatized mastery and resulting competence" (1974, p. 76). Control of stimulation and soothability, are two means available to infants through which they can shape their environment and reduce stress.

Control of stimulation.   Infants have a number of ways to control or change *stimulation.* These strategies may be aimed at increasing or at limiting stimulation. Infant searching and scanning behavior, even in the dark, is an attempt to supply additional information and complexity (Haith, 1968). Infants often cry or fuss when they are laid down on their back or if their head is covered by a cloth. Their protest reflects a desire for more control over what's happening to them (Freedman & Freedman, 1969; Korner & Grobstein, 1966). In the first few weeks of life, Brazelton and his co-workers (1974) observed at least four strategies for coping with unpleasant situations. These include:

- ● *stimulation—* **excitement of new activity.**

1. Active withdrawal.
2. Rejection by pushing the object away.
3. Decreasing sensitivity by moving toward sleep.
4. Fussing and crying.

Each strategy was used by all infants in the study to some degree.

Several experiments were designed to allow infants to deliberately alter their stimulus environment. In one study, the more rapidly infants sucked, the brighter a visual stimulus became. Infants quickly learned to increase their sucking rate in order to maintain brightness (Siqueland & DeLucia, 1969). In another study, a cord was tied between an infant's ankle and a mobile hanging over the crib. The *frequency* and intensity of leg movements could make the mobile move. Another group of infants saw the mobile move, but movement was produced by the experimenter, not by the infants' leg movements. There was almost three times as much leg movement when infants had direct control over the mobile's motion (Rovee & Rovee, 1969).

- ● *frequency—***a number of occurrences per unit of time.**

In most cases, infant behaviors do not produce changes in the environment. When they do, as is the case when sucking produces milk or when crying brings a caregiver, infants respond very favorably to this *contingent relationship.* The infant's power to begin or end events cannot be underestimated. Researchers who do studies using infant subjects know about an infant's capacity to bring an experimental session to a close by crying, struggling, or falling asleep (Gregg, Clifton & Haith, 1976; Bell, 1974). Spitting out unwanted food and refusing to suck are other ways that babies have to control the situation.

- ● *contingent relationship—***the effect of a behavior consistently producing a specific outcome.**

Soothability.   The time required to achieve a calm, alert state from a crying, fussy state has been called the infant's soothability. Many techniques have been tested for their soothing value (Birns, Blank, & Bridges, 1966). A low-frequency, moderately loud tone, a sweetened pacifier, gentle rocking, and placing the infant's foot in warm water are all effective in soothing babies. Infants may show a preference for one soothing experience over the others, but there is no single way of soothing that was best for all babies. Newborns who are readily soothed by one method are readily soothed by all. Babies who are difficult to soothe with one method are generally hard to comfort. Irritability and soothability are components of the infant's behavior that have important consequences for the kinds of responses babies get from their caregivers (Bell, 1974). The caregiver's response to a fussy child will be shaped by the kinds of soothing strategies that work best.

Infants contribute to the quality of care they receive. By crying, by rejecting, by startling, and by becoming upset, they influence a parent's responses. They also contribute to the quality of their care by rewarding their caregivers. When the baby calms down after a diaper change or smiles in response to a familiar voice, caregivers feel that they are effective. Caregivers feel good when they see the pleasure and comfort that these familiar experiences give the infant.

● *vocalizations*— sounds or utterances one makes.

Specific infant qualities are linked with specific caregiving behaviors (Murphy & Moriarty, 1976). Babies with high-energy and frequent *vocalizations* receive more frequent facial and verbal expressions from their mothers. Robust, healthy babies have mothers who are more successful at breast feeding than do small, frail babies. Babies who are very sensitive to stimulation have mothers who are less successful at breast feeding. Babies who are active and expressive have more responsive caregivers. These examples illustrate the baby's impact on the quality of care they receive.

Coping behavior in childhood

● *gratification*—a source of satisfaction or pleasure.

Resources for coping increase dramatically during the childhood years. Reading and arithmetic skills, intellectual development, physical growth, and language are some resources which increase coping effectiveness. In this section, one kind of intellectual ability, fantasy, will be discussed in detail. Fantasy is a resource for coping that provides avenues for *gratification*, creativity, and bouncing back from adversity.

Fantasy is a form of symbolic thought. It can be expressed verbally, in mental images, or in action. The content of fantasy thought is not limited by reality, but it may be directed toward reality. Fantasy is one type of conscious processing of inner mental activity. Once a fantasy unfolds, it can become the stimulus for continuous fantasy or for reality-oriented reasoning.

Freud identified some qualities of what he called "primary process thought" that describe the nature of fantasy. In primary process fantasy, one image or symbol may represent more than one object. The same object may be repeated in a variety of forms. Fantasy may blend time. Past, present, and future may occur all at once or with the future coming before the past. Conditional relationships that are present in reality-oriented thought may be ignored in fantasy (Freud, 1958). Fantasy could reasonably be prefaced with a silent "as if" (Singer, 1973). When a child imagines bending a steel bar, the child is really acting "as if" they were strong enough to bend steel.

Fantasy thought, like memory, reasoning, or information processing, is a skill that is within the potential of all children. It is more highly developed in some than in others. Fantasy serves three functions for the child. First, it provides a way of bringing reality into the intellectual system. Complex adult expectations, technology, and information bombard the child daily. All of this information can be taken in piece by piece through fantasy without concern for reality demands. The following story is told by a boy four years and ten months old. It suggests some of the ways that specific details of the world are brought into the child's idea of reality through fantasy activity.

Case 5·1

DENNIS H.

Well, this covered wagon just started out one day and it had six or even seven horses to pull them, but that was because it had such a long, long journey to go. They were going west to find gold and silver and pirate treasure. As they went along they came to a tremendous rock slide, and they can't go any further for one month. So they let the horses eat for one month so they would be very strong, but then they forgot to hook up them to the wagon, and so a tremendous rain storm came and washed the wagon and all the people down a tremendous cliff, and it was a covered wagon crash, and the horses went on and left it. But after while then the horses went back and found a covered wagon, and it was the same one because it had the same people in it so they pull and heaved and that was the state of Oregon.

Source: E. G. Pitcher and E. Prelinger, *Children Tell Their Stories* (New York: International Universities Press, Inc., 1963).

In his story, the disasters can be recovered from even if they might not be recovered from in real life. Cause and effect do not have the same logic in fantasy that they have in reality. The story can take directions that even Dennis might recognize as impossible in real life.

The second function of fantasy is drive reduction (Freud, 1958). When a motive is blocked from direct expression one way of continuing to gratify the motive is through fantasy. Even though Freud saw fantasy as an expression of only two motives, sex and aggression, it makes sense to assume that children who use fantasy do so to satisfy a range of frustrated motives. For example, a three-year old is watching his older brother learn to read. Reading is a skill that gives his brother a personal sense of accomplishment and a good deal of parental praise. The younger child pretends to read, overcoming his own intellectual limits through fantasy. Much of the imitative play of toddlers is a willful expression of autonomy. Children transform into make-believe activities that they are not yet competent to perform in reality. "I may not be able to drive the car, but I can act as if I know how."

The idea that frustration of motives activates fantasy has its limits. Children who have many motives repeatedly frustrated may be so aroused that it would not be possible for them to engage in fantasy. For some children, survival depends on carefully observing and responding to environmental events. They will not be free to sample the flow of inner experience on which fantasies are built. Usually, children can use fantasy to express moderate frustrations. They can compensate for some of the ways in which reality limits the satisfaction of motives through fantasy. Frustrations can be redefined and potential solutions can be thought about. The fantasy process may delay the immediate reaction to frustration. It provides a format for exploring the consequences of many possible reactions (Biblow, 1973).

The third function of fantasy is to provide avenues for private work on personal effectiveness. Fantasy is a way for working out the blend of temperament, motivation, intelligence, and talent that makes the person unique. The child's make-believe activities can be viewed as potential solutions to the "who am I" question. Taking an heroic figure, a parent, a beloved friend, a relative, or a pet as a focal point, children work out meaningful dramas. These dramas are built on their sensitivity to stimulation and activity, important motives, the roles they are enacting, and the talents that they recognize in the hero or in themselves. These fantasies provide the child countless opportunities to evaluate their personal qualities. Through these fantasies they discover the exact blend of qualities that feels most comfortable.

Living laboratory 5·2

COPING THROUGH THE LIFE SPAN

Purpose: To recognize the contribution of fantasy to coping in childhood.

Method: Read the fantasy described below. Then identify the ways that the fantasy may satisfy the three functions described in the chapter: assimilation, drive reduction; and personal integration.

In a fantasy of Wonder Woman, a two-year-old boy concentrates on whirling around in circles, waving the invisible rope, and slipping in and out of his mother's half-slip. In each adventure, Wonder Woman appears to stop disaster. "She" rushes to some adult to inquire "What's happening on earth? which means what disaster is happening. Depending on what the parent replies, Wonder Woman runs off whirling in circles and throwing the invisible lasso around the culprit.

Results: Divide a paper into three columns. Label the columns assimilation, drive reduction, and personal integration. Under each heading, show how elements of the fantasy might serve that function.

Discussion: How are the elements of the fantasy related to developing competences in a two-year-old child?

Why might a young boy select a woman as a hero for imitation?

What conflicts might be resolved through this fantasy? What part does fantasy play in the life of an adult?

Fantasy is a potential form of thought for all children. Not all children make use of this resource. The use of fantasy depends on a child's willingness to spend time sampling internal experience and the support of the environment for such activity. Fantasy activity has the potential for contributing a number of strengths to the formulation of coping strategies.

1. Fantasy provides an avenue for finding novel solutions to complex problems.
2. Through the world of fantasy, children gradually integrate novelty into their mental constructs without losing a sense of control and competence.
3. Fantasy offers a vehicle for personality integration so that the forces of temperament, motivation, intelligence, and talent compliment each other.

Coping strategies in adolescence

Moriarty and Toussieng (1976) documented the adolescent coping styles of the sample initially studied in infancy, in toddlerhood, and in preadolescence (Escalona & Leitch, 1952; Murphy, 1962; Murphy & Moriarty, 1976).

Four coping styles were identified. They reflect the ways adolescents use sensory information and the intensity or energy of their coping style. Two groups were described as *censors,* the obedient traditionalists and the ideological conservatives. These two groups limit sensory experiences. They reject information that does not confirm their traditional values. Two other groups were described as *sensers,* the cautious modifiers and the passionate renewers. The sensers, comprising 72 percent of the sample, were more likely to be influenced by experience. They would seek out new experiences that would alter their values.

In this sample, puberty was followed by a brief period of "rebelliousness" that ended by about age 14 or 15. From that point, censors tended to clarify their parents' values. They tried to discover what was viewed as acceptable in adult society. This effort generally meant controlling and limiting social experiences. Censors rejected the companionship of peers. They discounted much of their school experiences. The sensers were also seeking a value position. Their strategy was to engage people, to try out new activities, and to question inconsistencies. This group resisted any final or firm definition of personal identity. They held the view that coping with reality requires a changing value structure.

Another approach to the coping process in early adolescence is illustrated in an analysis of adaptation to two midwestern high school environments. Over 30 researchers utilized tests, survey questionnaires, interviews, demographic data collection, field observation, and field experimentation to observe adolescents and their school environments (Kelly et al., 1971; Kelly, 1979).

James Kelly (1969) began with a concern for coping preferences among adolescents in different social environments. Social exploration,

*Most adolescents seek out new experiences
to help clarify their values.*

the desire to actively find out about the people in one's environment, was identified as a personality variable that guides the process of adaptation within a specific setting. During their eighth-grade year in junior high school, a sample of high, moderate, and low explorers who would enter the same high school were selected in each of two communities.

The two schools were selected because they were different in several ways. School 1 was seen as a relatively changing environment, with a population exchange rate of 18.7 percent per year. School 2 was seen as a relatively stable environment with a population exchange rate of 8.0 percent per year (Goldberg et al., 1967; P. Newman, 1970, 1979; Rice & Marsh, 1979). Population exchange was calculated by dividing the number of students who entered or left the school during the school year by the total student population. There was more student involvement and identification with the school in school 1 than in school 2. New students experienced greater confusion as they tried to adjust to school life in school 2 than in school 1. In relation to a new authority figure, boys at school 1 were more willing to interact. They were more enthusiastic about having an opportunity to meet with a small group of other students than were boys at school 2. These observations illustrate the differences in the social atmosphere of the two schools. Similar data provided a sense of the boys' competences and their feelings of self-worth. The boys show individual variation in the levels of social and problem-solving skills they brought to the task of adaptation. They also differed in the ways they used their skills in the school setting. One particularly interesting pattern, for example, shows that high explorers at school 1 found many opportunities to express their interest and initiative within the school. High explorers at school 2 were more reserved, less openly expressive, and more involved in deviant behavior than other groups or high explorers at school 1. They found more chances to follow their interests outside of school. This study shows that the schools provide different ways for people with similar personality characteristics to express themselves. High explorers develop different ways of being effective when they go to school 1 than when they go to school 2.

Adulthood and the integration of coping competences

The quality of coping changes from adolescence to adulthood. Adults face more complex roles and responsibilities. This requires a new perspective on life activities and new beliefs and actions. Maturation continues into adulthood. It brings an expansion of awareness, an increased capacity for commitment, and an identification of meaningful life goals (Vaillant, 1977).

In an analysis of adulthood, we (Newman & Newman, 1979a) consider three phases of adult development: early adulthood, middle adulthood, and later adulthood. Table 5·3 lists the developmental accomplishments of each stage, the psychosocial crisis of the stage, and the central process through which the crisis is resolved.

Let's look at three topics which lead to new coping skills: (1) lifestyle; (2) social skills; and (3) multiple roles. The creation of a lifestyle in early adulthood requires developing a balance between work requirements, temperament, and the needs of others. The lifestyle is an expression of values. It reflects one's values about work and leisure, the importance of peer interactions, the importance of family, and the kind of community that would most likely lead to personal growth. In adulthood, the demands of work, home, and child rearing require the ability to manage resources. There are demands to anticipate the needs of others, to assign responsibility, and to make plans for the future. The philosophy of life that is formulated in middle adulthood is an expression for the person of what makes life meaningful. Finally, in later adulthood there is a need to take

TABLE 5·3
The tasks and crises of
adult life stages

	Developmental tasks	Psychosocial crisis	Central process
Early adulthood (23–30)	Marriage. Childbearing. Work. Lifestyle.	Intimacy versus isolation.	Mutuality among peers.
Middle adulthood (31–50)	Management of household. Child rearing. Management of a career.	Generativity versus stagnation.	Person-environmental fit and creativity.
Later adulthood (41–)	Redirection of energy to new roles. Acceptance of one's life. Developing a point of view about death.	Integrity versus despair.	Introspection.

a broad view of life successes and failures. The person must arrive at an analysis of life events that is in agreement with personal ideals and with reality.

Adulthood also leads to the growth of social skills. Social relationships take place at many levels. Adults are capable of maintaining relationships at different levels of intimacy. Children can make different responses to people, depending on their age, role, or closeness. In adulthood, levels of intimacy are even more clearly defined. We recognize good friends, colleagues, associates, and opponents. For each level of closeness, adults develop a social style.

In the work setting there are a number of ways in which social skills are essential for success. The ability to lead, to participate in team efforts, and to cope effectively with the demands of many authorities are all components of adult social relationships. As careers advance, new social demands are made for administrative, executive, and teaching skills. Adults seek not only to improve themselves through social contacts but to help others as well.

In adult life we have a number of social roles that have rather specific prescriptions for behavior. Family roles provide a set of relationships and behaviors that exist throughout life. One moves from child to parent to grandparent within this system. At every point, we learn our own role and the roles of the other members of the family. Age roles are also important for lifelong development. Each culture has a unique set of expectations for young males, older males, young females, and older females. These role expectations provide ideals to strive for and restrictions that prevent behaviors thought to be destructive to the culture. A number of roles are defined by participation in social institutions. Student, voter, religious believer, and worker are all examples of social roles that serve to define the individual for the culture.

*Shock, grief, and disbelief are three re-
sponses to sudden crisis.*

As the dominant roles that occupy an individual's energy change or end, the person is left with behaviors, habits, and motives that may no longer be of personal use. At each age, people must shed the roles that are no longer relevant. They turn their energy to maintaining current roles and to learning new roles.

Some examples include the end of the student role in later adolescence, the end of the dependent-child role in later adolescence, the end of the active parenting role in middle adulthood, and the end of the work role in later adulthood. Changes in social roles bring tension and anxiety as old habits are discarded and new behaviors are acquired. The pattern of learning roles and changing roles is important throughout the lifespan.

COPING STRATEGIES

● *denial*—refusal to admit the truth or reality.

There are different strategies for coping with stress. There is no single, widely accepted model for categorizing differences in coping styles. There are studies which observe responses to specific kinds of stress. These studies point out the contribution of personality to the coping process. One of the repeated themes in these studies of coping is the role of *denial* in response to stress. People differ in how seriously they treat stress. People differ in how fully they are willing to accept the severity of the situation. They also differ in how much they allow themselves to be hurt by conflict.

● *mortality*—the quality of life that involves one's eventual death.

Janis (1962) found that people responded in two different ways to a close brush with danger. Some felt very anxious about their own *mortality*. They had never realized how capable of being hurt they were. Others saw the same situation as evidence of their adaptability. Having come so close to death, they felt that their survival was evidence that they were meant to continue living. Similar feelings were held by combat pilots, civilians who survived an air raid, and survivors of a tornado. The narrow escape made some people increasingly nervous about the threat of potential disasters. Others became more convinced that they could not be hurt (Janis, 1974).

Wolff et al. (1964) observed the bereavement process of parents whose children were dying of leukemia. Some parents used denial to minimize the stress. They felt sure that their child would not die and that some cure would be found. Other parents did not deny the seriousness of their child's illness. They showed far greater emotional and physical signs of stress. They were not able to use denial to lose the pain of the crisis.

● *detach*—to withdraw or remove oneself from involvement.

Buffering oneself against intense feelings can protect some people from the stress related to illness, anxiety, and fatigue. In an experimental test of this concept, subjects were shown pictures of woodshop accidents where serious injuries occurred. Half the subjects were instructed to *detach* themselves in a later situation. The other subjects were given the opposite instructions, *involvement* preceding *detachment*. All subjects were given the same instructions in situations 1 and 2. Despite the pain and serious consequences of the accidents, subjects in both conditions were able to control their feelings. Measures of heart rate and the subjects' own reports of emotional experiences showed that cognitive strategies were effective in minimizing the impact of stress (Koriat et al. 1972). Those who were told to detach themselves actually felt less upset by the visual images. In real situations, without the benefit of coaching or instructions, people seem to differ in their natural capacity to resist stress. Whether it is the stress of work, separation, or death, the ability to minimize the impact of these crises is associated with better physical health and greater self-acceptance.

So you will not think that coping always involves minimizing the impact of environmental events, let us consider quite the opposite coping strategy. Janis has described a coping strategy he calls "the work of worrying" or "emotional innoculation" (Janis et. al., 1969). This concept was based primarily on observations of patients who were undergoing major surgery. In one study, three groups of patients were identified. The first group showed intense preoperative fear and continued anxiety after surgery. Their feelings about being hurt produced a constant state of emotionality and fear. The second group had little anxiety before surgery. They were cheerful and calm. After surgery, however, they were angry and bitter about their treatment. The third group was described as showing moderate fear before surgery. They were concerned about specific aspects of the operation and tried to find out as much as they could about it. They were somewhat anxious before surgery. They tried to remain calm by distracting themselves with other activities. After surgery this group showed the least emotional upset. They were described as cooperative and generally confident about their recovery. Each group showed a different approach to working through the feelings of threat and pain before they actually occurred. Some amount of worrying beforehand allowed the moderate group to feel reassured after surgery. They felt that things were going along pretty much as they should. Their recovery process was confirmation of their own competence to test reality. It provided evidence that they were not really helpless.

A further test of this concept involved giving extra information about the pain which would follow surgery to one group of patients. This information was not given for the *control group* (Egbert, et al. 1964). A description of the pain, reassurance that the pain was normal, techniques for relaxation that could relieve some of the pain, and information that medication for pain would be available as the patient needed it were given to the first group. After surgery this group required significantly less pain medication. They were released from the hospital an average of 2.7 days earlier than the control group. During their hospital stay, they were rated in better emotional and physical condition than members of the control group. Janis concludes the following about the work of worrying: "A person will be better able to tolerate suffering and deprivation if he worries about it beforehand rather than remaining free from anticipa-

● *control group*—in research design, a group of subjects who do not experience the experimental manipulation.

tory fear by maintaining expectations of personal invulnerability" (Janis et al., 1969, p. 105).

Resilience, the ability to recover from stress, can contribute to effective coping (Kagan, 1976; Murphy & Moriarty, 1976). The concept of resilience is similar to the notion of "vitality" as it is used in describing older adults. It implies a beneficial energy that makes up for physical, cognitive, or socioemotional limitations.

Infants and young children have the resources of energy, self-love, and flexibility that allow them to rebound readily from stress. Most young children are not burdened by memories of past pressures. They do not worry about the outcome of current pressure. They approach each stress without the strong fears generated from past crises. These fears often sap the energy of older children and adults. The resilient child is more likely to approach each crisis with a fresh outlook. Murphy (1974) describes a child of ten named Ann who got polio. After a long operation, Ann had to wear a cast from her chin to her hips. She managed to return to school wearing the cast. Ann made a caricature of her awkward posture. She pretended to be a queen. The other children would carry her books and bend over to reach things to her. This kind of resilience helped Ann and her friends handle her illness.

Resilience can be fostered by the caring responses of others. For example, Murphy describes a nurse who helped Ann during three months

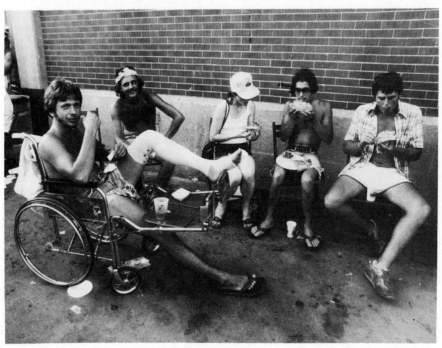

Ken Firestone

Coping requires creativity and flexibility.

● *respirator*—a device for maintaining artificial respiration.

she spent in a *respirator* by making up stories about a little pink rabbit. Adults may demonstrate resilience. They understand the need for behaviors that allow a child to recover from stress. They may replace a lost love with their love. All of these efforts contribute to the child's ability to rebound after crisis. There are important differences between help giving that enhances resilience and help giving that smothers it. Resilience depends on a sense of autonomy. Children have to be able to handle situations by themselves and to ask for help when it is required. Adults who view children as helpless or resourceless can undermine the child's own confidence. The child's doubt will interfere with their ability to reach a good solution to a problem. Resilience shows an inner optimism about the possibility for an improved future.

Coping must be ever present and, at the same time, vastly flexible and creative. It involves a general biological arousal that signals a need for activity. The content of the activity is in part influenced by personal

Living laboratory 5·3

COPING STRATEGIES

Purpose: To learn more about the costs and benefits of particular coping strategies.

Method: Consider the two strategies described by Wolff et al. (1964) for coping with the death of a child. Some families denied that their child would die. They kept looking for new cures. They maintained a cheerful, optimistic orientation while their child was hospitalized. Other families were clearly engaged in grief and mourning before their child died. They experienced the deep feelings of loss, and were not able to generate any optimism.

In the matrix below, try to consider the consequences of these two coping strategies *before* the child died and *after* the child died.

	Before	*After*
Denial		
Grief		

Results: In each box, list the possible consequences for the parents, for the child, and for the parent-child relationship.

Discussion: In this situation, are there social pressures to use one coping strategy in favor of others? How does our culture expect us to cope with grief?

Might different family members have different coping strategies? Could this lead to conflict? Explain.

characteristics, in part by environmental patterns, and in part by chance events which may be either internal or external. The outcome of the activity represents the best responses a person can make in a certain period of time. Each person makes the best judgments possible in order to cope.

Chapter summary

Coping is the capacity to resolve stress and to create new solutions to challenges. Three components of coping include gaining information, maintaining control over emotions, and keeping freedom of movement. Coping is contrasted with defense, which usually involves distortions in the perception of the self or the environment.

One of the central challenges to development are the psychosocial crises. These crises arise at every life stage. They result from a discrepancy between personal skills and resources, and the expectations of the culture. Coping means overriding these discrepancies, and therefore fosters continued growth.

Because challenges and crises occur at every life stage, it is necessary to take a developmental view of coping. Individuals have a changing group of skills and strengths that they can use at each life stage. In infancy, control of stimulation, soothability, and activity level influence the impact of the environment. During childhood, fantasy was emphasized as a major coping resource. In adolescence, the definition of personal values is a major resource. The search for values is approached differently by people who hold to traditional values and people who seek a variety of experiences in order to create values. Social exploration is another coping strategy. In adulthood, new coping skills are developed. These include the formation of a lifestyle, increased social competence, the emergence of administrative skills, the expression of a philosophy of life, and the ability to evaluate one's life achievements.

There is evidence that there are individual differences in preferences for coping strategies. Some of these coping strategies include feeling incapable of being hurt; denial of stress; worrying when you know stress is coming; and resilience in recovering from stress. Individual ways for coping strategies reminds us to keep an open mind in our attempt to understand the process of adjustment. A strategy that would increase stress for one person may reduce stress for another. As each person copes with a stressful situation, his or her temperament, talents, motives, and intelligence will combine to develop unique, personally meaningful strategies. We need to respect and to encourage coping strategies that will be most adaptive for each person.

SUGGESTED READINGS

For those who want to read more about coping and adaptation, the following should be good:

Coelho, G. V., Hamburg, D. A., & Adams, J. E. (Eds.). *Coping and adaptation.* New York: Basic Books, 1974.

Murphy, L. B., & Moriarty, A. E. *Vulnerability, coping, and growth.* New Haven, Conn.: Yale University Press, 1976.

Monat, A., & Lazarus, R. S. (Eds.). *Stress and coping: An anthology.* New York: Columbia University Press, 1977.

Moriarty, A. E., & Toussieng, P. W. *Adolescent coping.* New York: Grune & Stratton, 1976.

Reading

ADAPTATION AND THE TREND TOWARD AUTONOMY

The point of departure for a systematic description of strategies of adaptation should be the broadest possible statement. Let us put it this way: adaptation is something that is done by living systems in interaction with their environments. It is important to emphasize both the noun *systems* and the adjective *living*. Our whole enterprise can founder at the very start if the basic image is allowed to be mechanical rather than organismic. It is characteristic of a system that there is interaction among its various parts, so that changes in one part are likely to have considerable consequences in at least several other parts. A system, furthermore, tends to maintain itself as intact as possible and thus displays more or less extensive rebalancing processes when injured or deformed. This much is true of inanimate systems as well as animate ones, which makes it necessary to qualify the systems under discussion here as *living*. For it is characteristic of living systems that they do something more than maintain themselves. Cannon's historic studies of homeostasis have familiarized us with the remarkable mechanisms whereby animal and human living systems maintain internal steady states, such as body temperature and fluid content, and restore such states when circumstances have forced a temporary departure. But Cannon was well aware that maintaining homeostasis was not the whole story; he saw it as a necessary basis from which living systems could get on with their more important business. This further business consists of growth and reproduction. Living systems do not stay the same size. They grow dramatically larger: the puppy that you once held in your hands becomes the big dog that you can no longer hold in your lap. This increase eventually reaches its limit in any one system, but not until arrangements have been made to start a whole fresh lot of tiny living systems on their way toward maximum growth.

The fundamental property of growth in living systems was well described in 1941 by Andras Angyal. Looking for "the general pattern which the organismic total process follows," Angyal pictured the living system as partially open to the environment and as constantly taking material from the environment to become a functioning part of itself:

> It draws incessantly new material from the outside world, transforming alien objects into functional parts of its own. Thus the organism *expands* at the expense of its surroundings. The expansion may be a material one, as in the case of bodily growth, or a psychological one as in the case of the assimilation of experiences which result in mental growth, or a functional one as when one acquires skill, with a resulting increase of efficiency in dealing with the environment (1941, pp. 27–28).[1]

Thus the life process necessarily entails expansion, but Angyal carried the matter further. Living systems, he pointed out, exhibit *autonomy*. They are in part governed from inside, and are thus to a degree resistant to forces that would govern them from the outside. If this were not true, the whole concept of adaptation would be impossible. Angyal then describes the direction of the organismic process as one toward an *increase of autonomy:*

> Aggressiveness, combativeness, the urge for mastery, domination, or some equivalent urge or drive or trait is assumed probably by all students of personality. All these various concepts imply that the human being has a characteristic tendency toward self-determination, that is, a tendency to resist external influences and to subordinate the heteronomous forces of the physical and social environment to its own sphere of influence (1941, p. 49).[2]

It was an evil day, we may imagine, for the inanimate world when living systems first broke loose upon it. Conservative boulders doubtless shook their heads and predicted gloomily that if this subversive trend gained strength the day might come when living systems would overrun the earth. And this is indeed exactly what has happened. Most of the land surface is completely buried by living systems, and even the oceans are full of them. When we consider this outrageous imperialism it is small wonder that the expansion of peoples and of nations has been a besetting problem throughout human history. And even when we concentrate on strategies of adaptation, we must keep it in mind that human beings are rarely content with maintaining a personal homeostasis. Unless they are very old they are almost certain to be moving in the direction of increased autonomy. It can be a threat of disastrous proportions to discover in the midst of life that all avenues are blocked to further personal development.

Living creatures, in short, will constantly strive for an adaptive compromise that not only preserves them as they are, but also permits them to grow, to increase both their size and their autonomy. Consider an animal as it steps forth in the morning from where it has been sleeping and moves into its daytime environment. If all goes well, it will ingest a portion of that environment, maintain its visceral integrity by homeostatic processes and by eliminating waste material, add a tiny increment to its size, explore a little and thus process some fresh information about its environment, gain a bit in muscular strength and coordination, bask in the warm sunshine, and return at night to its den a little bigger, a little wiser, a little stronger, and a little more contented than it was in the morning. If the season is right, it may also have found an opportunity to set those processes in motion whereby a number of offspring will come into existence. A day like this can be described as one of maximum animal self-actualization. If all does not go well, the animal may return to the den hungry, cold, perhaps battered and bruised, yet still essentially intact as a living system, capable of recuperating during the night and setting forth again in the morning. Of course, it may have failed to keep itself intact or even alive, but we can be sure disaster occurred only because the animal's adaptive repertoire, employed with the utmost vigor, has not been equal to the circumstances. Animals try to go up; if they go down, they go down fighting.

[1] Angyal, A. *Foundations for a Science of Personality.* New York: The Commonwealth Fund, 1941.
[2] Ibid.

Source: Robert W. White, *Coping and Adaptation* (New York: Basic Books, Inc., 1974), pp. 52–54. © 1974 by Basic Books, Inc., Publishers. Reprinted by permission.

PART THREE
THE ENVIRONMENT

Arthur Tress

Chapter 6
The Family

And a woman who held a babe against her bosom said, Speak to us of Children.

And he said:

Your children are not your children.

They are the sons and daughters of Life's longing for itself.

They come through you but not from you,

And though they are with you yet they belong not to you.

You may give them your love but not your thoughts,

For they have their own thoughts.

You may house their bodies but not their souls,

For their souls dwell in the house of to-morrow, which you cannot visit, not even in your dreams.

You may strive to be like them, but seek not to make them like you.

For life goes not backward nor tarries with yesterday.

You are the bows from which your children as living arrows are sent forth.

The archer sees the mark upon the path of the infinite, and He bends you with His might that His arrows may go swift and far.

Let your bending in the archer's hand be for gladness;

For even as He loves the arrow that flies, so He loves also the bow that is stable.

Kahlil Gibran, *"On Children,"* 1963

Reprinted from *The Prophet*, by Kahlil Gibran, by permission of Alfred A. Knopf, Inc. Copyright 1923 by Kahlil Gibran renewed 1951 by Administrators C.T.A. of Kahlil Gibran Estate and Mary G. Gibran.

The photography of H. Armstrong Roberts

For reflection

1. In our culture, why do married people have only one spouse, but in other cultures married people may have more than one spouse?

2. How might children who have only one parent differ from children who have two parents?

3. How do people learn how to be parents?

4. If you are the oldest child, what would it be like to be a younger child? If you are a younger child, what would it be like to be the oldest?

5. Why might you and your grandfather have different, conflicting opinions about premarital sexual practices?

The family is the first and perhaps the most enduring context for growth. Adjustment within the family means identifying with models, accepting values, playing out family roles, developing affection, and eventually distinguishing one's own values and goals from those held by other family members. One central part of life after childhood is discovering all those motives, values, and beliefs that were not accepted within the boundaries of your own family.

KINDS OF FAMILY GROUPS

The term *family* refers to a variety of groupings including (1) a father, mother, and their children, (2) children of a father and mother, (3) a group of people living in the same house, (4) all of a person's relatives, (5) a group of related people, (6) a tribe, (7) one's ancestors (Adams, 1975; Blood, 1972; Winch, 1971). When we speak of "family" we are usually speaking of the group of adults and children who live together for a long time. The main ideas that guide our thinking about the family are these:

1. The family is the main setting for the experiences of the child, particularly the young child.
2. The family is a dynamic set of relationships among all the people who live in the "family."
3. Children's behavior, ideas, thoughts, and fantasies affect the lives of those with whom they live.
4. The behavior, ideas, thoughts, and fantasies of fathers and mothers affect the lives of their children.
5. This group has resources that are used to adjust to life.

The family group is part of a culture. In order to understand the family's impact on a person, one must consider the expectations that adults have about the ideal marriage relationship, the ideal parenting style, and the ideal parent-child relationship. Adults also function as sons and daughters, workers, members of a political community, and participants in religious organizations. All of these roles may contribute to their role as parent or spouse. Finally, adults have access to particular resources because of the work they do, the education they have had, their social status in the community, and their bonds with other family members. The resources that adults bring to their family group will influence adjustment for adults and children in the family.

The nuclear family

● *normative—*
conforming to an average pattern.

In the United States, the most common family type is the monogamous nuclear family. In this kind of family one male and one female marry and live in the same household with their children. Polygamy is marriage that involves more than two people. While polygamy is unusual in our society, it does represent a kind of marriage pattern that is *normative* in 419 of a sample of 554 societies sampled by Murdock (1957). There are three varieties of polygamous marriages:

1. Polygyny, in which one man has more than one wife.
2. Polyandry, in which one woman has more than one husband.
3. Group marriage, in which two or more men marry two or more women.

● *sibling—***brother or sister.**

In each marriage pattern, children experience a different array of adult caregivers, patterns of *sibling* relationships differ, and there are different patterns of adult interaction.

In addition to the many possible marriage arrangements, there are a variety of household groupings. The most common household groups are:

1. The monogamous nuclear family.
2. The joint family, in which sisters, their spouses, and their offspring, or brothers, their spouses, and their offspring live together.
3. The extended family, in which three or more *generations* and their families live together in the same household.

● *generation—***a group of individuals born and living at the same time.**

● *family of origin—***the family to which one is born.**
● *family of procreation—***the family one begins as an adult.**

In each of these family arrangements, the nuclear unit can be viewed as the two parents and their offspring. In an extended family living arrangement, the middle generation would be living with both the nuclear *family of origin* and the nuclear *family of procreation*. The youngest generation would be living in only one nuclear unit and with extended family members (Adams, 1975).

In the United States, the majority of children under 18 years old live in a household with their mother and father (see Table 6·1). The pattern of family groupings is toward small, nuclear families. Young American wives, in the age range 18 to 24, expect to have an average of 2.2 children in their lifetime (U.S. Department of Commerce, 1976). This compares to a 1965 estimate of 3.70 persons. The 1976 estimate of the average family size was 3.39 persons (U.S. Department of Commerce, 1976a). Children are less likely to be in families where adult brothers and sisters or older grandparents are living with them. Both of these age groups, the elderly and the young adults, show a growing preference to live in their own, separate homes (Glick, 1976; Norton & Glick, 1976a).

TABLE 6·1
Persons under 18 years old, by presence of parents and whether living with mother only, by marital status of mother, for the United States: 1975 and 1970 (000s)

Presence of parents and marital status of mother	1975 Total*	1970 Total*
All persons under 18	66,087	69,458
Percent	100.0%	100.0%
Living with both parents	80.3	84.9
Living with mother only	15.5	10.7
Separated	4.9	3.4
Other married, husband absent	0.9	1.3
Widowed	2.4	2.0
Divorced	5.5	3.3
Single	1.8	0.8
Living with father only	1.5	1.1
Living with neither parent	2.7	3.3

* Excludes persons under 18 years old who were heads and wives of heads of families and subfamilies.
Source: U.S. Department of Commerce, Bureau of the Census, "Marital Status and Living Arrangements: March 1975," *Current Population Reports*, p. 20, no. 287 (Washington, D.C.: U.S. Government Printing Office, 1975), p. 6.

● *lineage*—family ancestry.

There are two specific functions of the nuclear family, with respect to the child. First, adults who marry and then have children provide a legitimate direction of lineage through the mother's and/or the father's ancestry. This *lineage* ties the child to past generations of family members. In some societies, it entitles the child to a particular family inheritance. The family lineage links the current generation with a historical past.

Second, the nuclear family guides the child through the process of socialization (Nye, 1976). In some cultures, the biological parents do not actually participate in the process themselves. For example, in Murdock's sample, 125 societies are described as mother-child households in which the father lives in a separate house. In some of those societies, the fathers live far away from the mother and child. He may wander away for long periods of time. In two African societies, the Hebe and the Thonga, the grandmother keeps the child from the time it is weaned for a number of years and then returns the child to his or her parents (Stephens, 1963). In both of these examples, however, at least one of the biological parents is recognized as providing care in infancy. That parent is required to guide the child in making the change from infancy to childhood or childhood to adolescence.

The extended family

The nuclear family is typically embedded within a kinship structure. This structure includes:

1. The parents and grandparents of the child's father and mother.
2. Sisters and brothers of the child's parents and the offspring of those sisters and brothers.
3. Family members related through marriage to either parent or "in-laws."

The traditional picture of the family in the United States is that it is independent of extended kinship relationships (T. Parsons, 1943). A more current look at the family pattern in the United States is that kinship relationships are a matter of choice (Adams, 1967; Winch, 1974). In some subcultures and in some families, the kinship network is an important component of family life. The culture as a whole and the economic system do not require intense kinship group commitments. Frequently, however, these commitments evolve as effective means of coping with life challenges.

The extended family continues to serve at least three important functions for families in the United States. First, they provide historical

Donald Smetzer

The extended family can provide important resources to the nuclear family group.

continuity. We are beginning to appreciate the need to preserve our ethnic backgrounds. Extended family members provide the opportunity to learn about one's cultural heritage. They bring special life to the ethnic rituals or holidays. The extended family, as a group, shares an ethnic identity.

Second, extended family members provide important child care resources. Parents frequently speak to their own parents about problems in child rearing. More directly, grandparents, aunts, and uncles may fulfill a variety of child care functions from daily supervision of the child, to occasional baby sitting. Children learn to feel close to these adults. Children share private thoughts with these relatives that they might not share with their parents. In many cases, grandparents are more receptive to the desires and plans of the grandchild than are the parents (Mead, 1975).

Finally, the extended family is a source of resources that are greater than those held by the nuclear family alone. A child can look to extended family members for areas of expertise, access to settings, and information that parents or siblings do not have. Under extreme stress, extended family members can help the parents and children in many ways.

Single-parent families

In 1975, 80.3 percent of children under 18 were living with both parents; 15.5 percent were living with their mothers, and 1.5 percent were living with their fathers (U.S. Department of Commerce, 1975, p. 20). Approximately one child in seven (14.5 percent) under the age of three was living in a single-parent family (U.S. Department of Commerce, 1976a, p. 20). There are almost twice as many children in single-parent homes now as there were in 1950. Even though the vast majority of American families have two parents present, the rate of single-parent families is increasing. If one parent is absent, it is most likely to be the father. Many psychologists believe that absence of the same-sex parent leads to maladjustment. Several problems in adjustment including delinquency, academic underachievement, and emotional immaturity have been linked with parent absence. Failure to identify with a parent of the same sex has been viewed as a cause for these problems (Biller, 1974; Hetherington, 1966). This theory is appealing. It tends to guide our thinking about such emotional issues as divorce, child care, and family planning. However, the data on one-parent families does not show that parent absence results in poor emotional adjustment for the child.

First, the absence of either the father or the mother changes many aspects of the family. The family's income is reduced, particularly if the absent parent was bringing an income to the family. The remaining parent is forced to take on more child care functions and more work functions. The family becomes open to influence from outside forces including relatives, or social welfare agencies. These forces may undercut the competence of the remaining parent, suggesting that he or she is incompetent to raise a child alone. The single parent may actively seek a new partner. This will have additional consequences for the child. Finally, children

United Press International

The impact of single-parent families on children depends on the meaning of the parent's absence.

may be quickly cast in new roles. Particularly the eldest children may be asked to assume some of the roles of the absent parent. For all these reasons, parent absence cannot be viewed as a single variable. The impact of the parent's absence from the family has the potential for rippling through each family member's experience. The parent's absence increases the competence of some and increases the sense of helplessness for others.

Second, parent absence may be temporary or permanent, socially valued or devalued. Temporary absences may be socially valued. Examples would be the absence of soldiers during wartime or film stars shooting a series of scenes on a distant location. Temporary absence may be socially devalued. An example would be absence due to being in prison.

Permanent absence can also have different meanings to both children and the remaining parent. Widowed fathers more often report that children feel saddened by their mother's loss than do divorced fathers (George & Wilding, 1972). One father who feels his children are better off without their mother says: "They are better off in the emotional atmosphere. There is no parental friction and there is only a single outlook to get used to. Therefore, life is calmer and less confusing." (George & Wilding, 1972, p. 65).

For children whose fathers were absent due to military service, the absence tended to increase the children's idealization of their fathers (Bach, 1946; Baker et al.). Through fantasy play these children had imaginary conversations with their fathers. On their father's return, two consequences of father absence were observed. First, children whose fathers were absent during their first year of life were more aggressive and less friendly than their own siblings. They were also more aggressive than children who did not have absent fathers. Second, the absent fathers were less warm and more critical of the child born during their absence than of other children (Stolz, 1954). Thus, the timing of absence may influence the building of the parent-child bond. If the child already has a relationship established with his or her father, the father's return is far more likely to be associated with favorable changes. These changes include better behavior and better school grades (Baker et al., 1968). The effects of parent absence depends, then, on the permanence of the separation, the social meaning of the separation, and the timing of the separation.

A third factor in understanding the impact of parent absence is the community where the family lives. As one father says: "When he is with other kids and they talk about their mothers, he says, 'I haven't got one,' and it is upsetting for him" (George & Wilding, 1972, p. 64). When a child is the only one of his or her friends who is in a one-parent family, there are many occasions for uncomfortable contrasts and comparisons. In communities where divorce, separation, or abandonment are common, children do not have to apologize or hide their family situation.

Finally, the consequences of motherless or fatherless homes must be viewed in contrast to other alternatives. For example, in a study of factors associated with delinquency in addition to father absence, four qualities of fathers were found to separate delinquent from nondelinquent boys. These included harsh and unsuitable discipline by father, father's indifference or hostility to the child, father's delinquency, and poor work habits of the father (Glueck & Glueck, 1962). Thus, while father absence may be undesirable, so may father presence in some cases.

Furthermore, children in a single-parent family have the chance to observe a caregiver who is committed to their welfare. Children in one-parent families can be certain of a continuing relationship with at least one parent. The integrity of their family group is preserved. The absent-parent situation may not be preferred to the family where two parents are present, involved and effective. Parent absence may be more desirable than other alternatives that involve high levels of conflict or uncertainty.

PARENT RELATIONSHIPS

Every person who occupies the parent role may define that role in light of personal goals, past experiences, and the children's needs. People perform the parent role in many different ways. However, the role of parent is not defined solely by the person who holds that position. Other family members have expectations for the mother's and the father's behavior. Beyond the family group, expectations for the parent role are defined by the community, the school, the mass media, and the legal system. Parents must blend their own view of the role with these other social expectations. Eventually, children themselves make comparisons between their own mother and father and the image of "mother" and "father" that exists in the culture. How adults perform as parents is subject to evaluation and redefinition from their own children, their parents, and their adult peers.

Psychologists and sociologists have offered many ideas about the specific content of the parent role. Adults learn about views of parenthood at home, in school, in the neighborhood, and through the mass media. It is up to each adult to blend those views with the realities of child care and parenting that confront them on a daily basis. In the following section, some of the views of the parental role that have been studied by social scientists are discussed. These include parents as the socialization agents in the family group, parents as protectors and caregivers, and parents as models for imitation and identification. The ways that parents interpret their roles as mother and father have lifelong implications for the adjustment of both adults and children. The adults try to integrate their parent role with the other elements of their self-concept. Children must not only adjust to the ongoing demands of parents. They carry those roles with them into adult life.

Parents as socialization agents

Talcott Parsons (1955) has suggested that mothers and fathers have different functions in the family group. The mother fills expressive functions. This means that she tries to maintain the family's morale and to insure open paths for communication among family members. The father's functions are instrumental. Fathers bring resources to the family from outside through work. Within the family, fathers show their competence by meeting task-related demands of the family members. This difference between the mother's and father's roles is viewed as adaptive. It makes sex-role identification easy for the children and satisfies both the emotional and task needs of the group.

Studies of child-rearing functions find that mothers perform both task and expressive functions within the home (Clausen, 1966). In 1978, about 50 percent of mothers in two-parent families with children under the age of 18 were in the labor force. Women with infants and preschool age children are less likely than others to go to work. Nonetheless, 1978 data indicate that 41 percent of mothers in two-parent families with children under six were working (U.S. Bureau of Labor Statistics, 1979). The tasks performed by women do not all show up in the labor statistics. Interactions with storekeepers and businessmen, the management of the household budget, driving the car, fixing a leaky faucet, and the range of household chores are all examples of activities that are task-related.

Fathers do not perform task functions exclusively. Fathers are involved in the discipline of their children, in play activities, and in the communication of approval or disapproval. Fathers are important sources of support for both sons and daughters. Children report more involvement with mothers than fathers in child-care activities (Bronfenbrenner, 1961).

"No. You are not entitled to one phone call to your grandmother!"

Reprinted by permission The Wall Street Journal

However, it is clear that many fathers are deeply involved in parenting and in their relationship with their children.

Child-rearing practices are the ways that parents transform their definitions of the parental role into behavior. Schaefer (1959) offered a two-dimensional model of child-rearing behaviors. He argued that most parental behavior can be viewed as a blend of two bipolar dimensions, love-hostility and autonomy-control. Love-hostility refers to expressions of affection, support, anger, and criticism. Autonomy control refers to setting and enforcing family rules. Some parents set limits and strictly enforce them. Other parents invite children's opinions about limits and encourage children to reach their own decisions. Baumrind (1966) described three models of parental discipline which illustrate differences in the expression of love and control: permissive, authoritative, and authoritarian discipline. These models are described briefly below:

> The permissive parent attempts to behave in a nonpunitive, acceptant, and affirmative manner toward the child's impulses, desires, and actions (p. 889).

> The authoritative parent attempts to direct the child's activities in a rational, issue-oriented manner. She encourages verbal give and take, shares with the child the reasoning behind her policy, and solicits his objections when he refuses to conform (p. 891).

> The authoritarian parent attempts to shape, control, and evaluate the behavior of the child in accordance with a set standard of conduct, usually an absolute standard, theologically motivated and formulated by a higher authority. She values obedience as a virtue and favors punitive, forceful measures to curb self-will at points where the child's actions or beliefs conflict with what she thinks is appropriate conduct (p. 890).

The two systems of parent practices have been integrated by Buss & Plomin (1975). Figure 6.1 presents the integrated model in which parent discipline techniques can be seen as an expression of hostility or love, and autonomy or control. In a study of 137 families of young twins, the style of child-rearing patterns was found to relate to the parent's temperament (Plomin, 1974). Parents who were very sociable tended

FIGURE 6·1
Integration of two models of parent practices

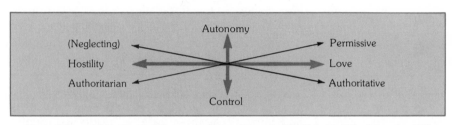

Source: A. Buss and R. A. Plomin, *A Temperament Theory of Personality* (New York: John Wiley & Sons, Inc., 1975), p. 214. Reprinted by permission.

to be high on the love dimension. Parents who were very active also tended to be high on control. Fearful and impulsive parents were low on the love dimension.

It is difficult for parents to help their children know right from wrong. In a sample of 210 families from the state of Washington, 25 percent of wives and 16 percent of husbands said that they often worried about this part of their parenting. There was rather frequent disagreement between husbands and wives on how children should be taught, and what methods were most suitable (Gecas, 1976). Parents often found that their own values were brought into conflict as they tried to make decisions about the care of their children. To the uncertainty about how to respond to a child is added the stress of disagreeing with one's spouse.

Parents as protectors and providers of care

Mothers generally provide most of the infant care during the first six months of life or more. Even in cultures where the mother is highly valued as a member of the labor force, as in the Israeli kibbutz or the Chinese communes, mothers keep their children in their households in order to nurse and care for them for the first few months. In the United States, women feel strong social pressures to have children and to stay with them during the preschool years. Working women with children experience both guilt and anxiety about whether they are providing adequate care in their absence. Many women drop out of the labor force after their first child is born and do not return until their last child enters school (Kimmel, 1974).

One might ask whether families in which the father and the mother are both employed share the responsibilities of child care. Most fathers take little responsibility for the care of their infants. There tends to be a division of responsibilities. Mothers do feeding, bathing, and dressing. Fathers do heavy lifting, repairing toys, and protecting children from danger. In families where both parents work, fathers tend to assume more of the household responsibilities than they do when women are not employed (Gecas, 1976). When both the mother and father are employed, fathers do not tend to assume more child-care responsibilities. Most often these needs are met by a relative or a child-care service (Hoffman & Nye, 1974).

In some cultures like China or the Israeli kibbutz, young infants are cared for by state-supported nurseries or child-care centers after they are weaned. In these societies, neither the mother nor the father is viewed as the expert in child care or socialization. Each adult has an area of competence that is expressed in his or her work. One kind of work is child care, but not every biological parent is designated to pursue that career.

Parents as models for imitation and identification

Freud (1953) suggested that one of the primary functions of mothers and fathers was to serve as a model for identification for their like-sex children. Boys look to their fathers as a first image of what it will mean to be adult. Girls look to their mothers. Children internalize their parents' values, attitudes, and goals. They may also imitate their parents' mannerisms. The two most important factors in determining whether children will identify with their parents are: (1) the parents' status in the family; and (2) the parents' expressions of acceptance, warmth, or approval (Martin, 1975).

Status

The two examples described below give us a sense of the differences in power, competence, and control of resources that children may observe in their family group. In a number of societies, husbands are clearly dominant over their wives. This dominance may be expressed in wife beating, overt signs of respect like bowing or walking behind the male, or customs relating to ownership and decision making. The following excerpt illustrates a male-dominant orientation:

> The wife is expected to take a subordinate position; she should obey her husband and he is entitled to beat her if she does not do so. The household is organized for his convenience; meals should be ready at the times when he likes to eat, and the wife should not cook for herself in his absence. She should ask his permission to go visiting, and if she goes away from home to sleep he fixes the number of days that she may be away (Mair, 1940, p. 13).

In other societies, men and women each have responsibilities, possessions, and rights that give them similar power. The following excerpt suggests a culture in which women have a role that is respected and admired.

> The status of the wife in Hottentot society is far from being that of an inferior. Although as a rule she plays a subordinate role in matters pertaining to tribal life, and in public always walks several paces behind her husband, yet her position in the household is supreme, and the education of the children is wholly in her hands. Upon marriage she is regarded as the mistress of the hut and of all its contents. She even has the right in certain circumstances to forbid her husband to enter it. She has her own property in cattle, some given to her by her parents while she was still a child, others when she was married, and her husband will not venture to sell or slaughter an animal belonging to her without her consent or in her absence. Even if he intends to barter his own stock he usually first consults her, and during his absence she also controls the pasturing of the herds. She supervises or herself does the milking which provides the household with most of its food, and controls all the provisions, allotting to each his food according to status and age, and brooking no contradiction. Her husband may not even take a mouthful of milk without first obtaining her permission, and should he do so, says Hahn, his nearest female relatives will put a fine on him. (Schapera, 1930, p. 251).

Children are sensitive observers of the power relationships that exist in their homes. They sense who controls resources, who makes decisions about their care, who determines their punishments, and who initiates activities. As children observe the pattern of dominance and submission between their parents they form a concept of what typical father-mother and parent-child relationships are like. We carry these concepts from the family where we were children to the family where we raise children.

The analysis of power in a family is not a simple one. In some societies, the parent who controls the most resources, including money, property, education, or material goods may have the most power. However, in other societies, the more highly educated men who also have access to an abundance of resources tend to share their power more fully with their wives. Thus, control of resources is not the only predictor of family power. One must also know what the culture views as the desirable distribution of power in the family.

Warmth

Warmth is expressed by recognizing and responding to children's needs, communicating acceptance, and by being available for interaction. Generally, warmth is communicated in expressions of praise or approval, in nonverbal interactions including patting, touching, stroking, and kissing, and in playful activities. Parents who show these qualities foster stronger identification than do parents who are inaccessible and insensitive. Like status, warmth can be a characteristic of one or both parents' roles.

To the three elements of the parental role already discussed, parent as socialization agent, parent as caregiver, and parent as model, we would add an emphasis on the developing nature of parenting. The roles of father and mother are the products of the specific marriage relationship. Adults enter marriage with their own ideas about these roles and, perhaps, with an idea of societal expectations for "father" and "mother" role performance. In the process of living together, bearing, and rearing children, the couple evolves the actual role content of mother and father. The roles are alterable as the needs of family members change. Flexibility is necessary for successful adaptation. The content of the role may be modified by the role holder, the spouse, the children, and other individuals who are important to the family. The role may also change as children are added or leave the family, as the needs of children change, as the resource base of the family expands or contracts, and as the problems that confront the family change.

● *optimize*—to make as effective as possible.

The general goals of the parental roles include *optimizing* the physical and, increasingly, the psychological well-being of the offspring. The particular behaviors that are necessary to accomplish these goals are not specified. People learn to behave in order to achieve their goals. They bring their own temperament and talent to play as well as their assessment of the changing needs of other family members. Parenting, once it has begun, brings a lifelong relationship. As such the role must be viewed as a changing career rather than as a fixed, stable role (Feldman & Feldman, 1975).

Living laboratory 6·1

PARENTAL ROLES: THE CONTENT OF THE MOTHER AND FATHER ROLE

Purpose: To clarify the components of the parental role.

To evaluate the advantages and disadvantages of sex-role differentiation in parenting.

Method: Spend some time in a public setting where mothers and fathers are likely to be present with their children. This might be a shopping mall, a grocery, a zoo, or a restaurant. Watch for patterns of interaction between mothers and children, and fathers and children. Try to evaluate whether each interaction has as its primary function *(a)* to socialize the child (discipline, share values, explain how to behave); *(b)* to protect or care for the child (wipe, help, feed, or warn the child of danger); or *(c)* to entertain or play with the child (joke, tickle, chase).

Results: Make a table showing how many interactions with mothers and fathers had each function. The table might look like this:

	Mother	*Father*	*Total*
Socialization			
Protection and care			
Play and entertainment			
Total			

Discussion: Are there differences in the ways mothers and fathers interact with children? Describe those differences.

Are there advantages to these differences? Any disadvantages?

Do children come to expect different responses from mothers and fathers?

SIBLING RELATIONSHIPS   The number, spacing, and sex of the siblings in each family influences the pattern of interactions and relationships among family members. In addition, each child in the family has a different perspective on these interactions depending on their position in the sibling order. Family size and sibling order are the two dimensions that have been most closely studied. The size of the family and the position of birth cannot be separated in experience. It is useful, to look at the effects of these variables in order to get some idea of how influential siblings might be in any person's adjustment.

The effects of family size

Both parents and children are affected by the number of children in the family. It is difficult to know whether the number of siblings creates certain parental responses or whether parents of a particular type choose to have a certain number of children. Parents of large families (four or more) tend to function differently than parents of small families. Parents in larger families are more authoritarian, more likely to use physical punishment, and less likely to explain their rules than are the parents of smaller families (Elder & Bowerman, 1963; Clausen, 1965).

Marital adjustment and happiness tend to increase with family size when parents have wanted and planned all their children (Clausen, 1966). However, in a survey of almost 5,000 married adults, marital satisfaction was found to be higher among couples who either never had children or whose children had left home. This finding supports other studies of the impact of children on marital satisfaction (Rollins & Feldman, 1970). Generally, adults who have children have less time for interactions with one another. They have far fewer opportunities to pursue their leisure interests than adults without children. Marital satisfaction is not the result of the number of children present (Renne, 1970).

The effects of family size on children appear to cluster around issues of intelligence, achievement motivation, school performance, and occupational success. This might well reflect the notion that the decision to have a small family is an expression of parental values for upward mobility and achievement. In one study, couples in a Mexican village who were using contraceptives were compared to couples who were not using contraceptives. The former group scored higher on measures of ability and need for achievement than the latter (Keller, 1973). Children from smaller families express more achievement motivation and better school performance than children in large families (Elder, 1962; Rosen, 1961). This finding is particularly true among Protestant families and less accurate for Catholic families (Elder, 1962).

Children from smaller families score higher on tests of intelligence than children from larger families. A study of 4,000 children who were born during the same week in England and Wales found that when these children were tested at ages 8 and 11 years, intelligence was negatively related with family size (Douglas, 1964). The larger the family, the lower the child's score on an intelligence test. Preschool children from small and large low-income families were compared on measures of learning readiness. The children from small families scored higher on all the skills that were measured (Scott & Seifert, 1975). In an analysis of 400,000 Dutch males, intelligence scores decreased as family size increased from two to seven siblings. Only children scored slightly lower than children in two-child families (Belmont & Marolla, 1973).

One might assume that children from large families would excel in some areas of adjustment which the child from the small family lacks. However, evidence of this sort is not available. In one study of children from rural midwest towns, children from families with five or more siblings did more daydreaming, felt lower self-worth, and had more problems in social adjustment than did children from smaller families (Hawkes, Burchinal, & Gardner, 1958). A study of 3,000 French children seen in child guidance clinics found a large group of patients from families with five or more children (Chombart de Lauwe, 1959). Particularly when resources are scarce, the large family is under chronic stress in its efforts to meet survival needs. The strengths that might be found in children from a large sibling group may not develop when the family does not have many resources.

The effects of sibling order

Being the youngest male who is born after three female children is clearly a different experience than being the youngest male who is born after two males and a female. Being second born and 18 months younger than one's older sibling is a very different experience than being second born and five or six years younger than one's older sibling. In the first example, both boys would be described as fourth born. In the second example, both children would be described as second born. However, these categories do not capture the differences in sibling relationships or parent-child interactions that would be experienced in these distinct family groupings.

As one might expect, the clearest sibling effects we know about are for the firstborn. The physical effects of birth order are the most striking. The firstborn experiences longer labor, greater pressure on the skull bones, greater incidence of forceps delivery, and a higher rate of mortality as newborns than do later-born children. Firstborns are smaller at birth and larger at age one or two than later born. By adulthood, these physical birth-order differences disappear (Clausen, 1966). Later-born children have twice as many infectious diseases by age four and one half as do firstborns, but firstborns are more likely to be absent from school due to illness than later borns. The later born have earlier exposure to childhood illnesses and usually are immune by the time they are of school age (Douglas & Bloomfield, 1958; Douglas, 1964).

The literature on intelligence and achievement suggests that firstborns and later borns do not differ in intelligence. However, firstborns are more likely to achieve success and to show academic excellence. When firstborn and later-born elementary schoolchildren were compared, the firstborns scored higher on measures of intelligence, academic achievement, and school motivation. It appeared from these results that the firstborn children were more intelligent. However, when motivation was taken into account, the differences in intelligence and achievement were no longer observed (Adams & Phillips, 1972). Birth order is not a strong or consistent predictor of intelligence (Cicirelli, 1975).

The firstborn speaks earlier and more distinctly than does the latter born (Koch, 1956). The firstborn performs more effectively in school, goes farther in school, and is more frequently identified as an eminent scholar than are later-born children. This excellence does not appear to carry over to sports or business. The academic success of the firstborn may be due to the child's greater opportunities for interaction with adults who verbalize, explain, and reason with the child. It may also be due to the child's access to a greater pool of resources. Many families who have limited funds may help the oldest child to go as far with his or her education as they can. They help the oldest with the understanding that this child will then be in a better position to help the younger siblings (Sutton-Smith & Rosenberg, 1970).

Sibling interaction and the family group

Each new child changes the nature of the family group. In the following section we discuss some of the ways families may function differently depending on the number of children who are present. Our discussion focuses on patterns of interaction, availability of resources, and mobility. Each of these dimensions contributes to the quality of the immediate environment and to the process of adjustment.

Adults are the main people firstborn children interact with. The first child is likely to be watched carefully. Every change is of interest. New parents also watch carefully since they are likely to feel doubts about adequacy as parents. New parents are more likely to view the difficulties of child rearing as abnormal problems that are the result of their own inadequacies or the infant's deviance. They are less likely to have a feel for the pattern of normal difficulties that occur throughout development.

With each new child, the quality of life in the family changes.

We know that parents feel more anxious about their first child than they do about later children (Clausen, 1966). They also may be quite emotionally involved in a positive way with the first child. Each life experience that the first child encounters takes the parents in a new direction. They are probably less prepared and less confident as they accompany their first child through life than they will be with later children. This uncertainty might account for the observations of firstborn children that their parents are stricter and more likely to use physical punishment than are parents of later-born children (Elder & Bowerman, 1963).

Several important changes occur in the family when a second child is born. Parents have to attend to the needs of both children. This reduces some of the intensity of their involvement with the first born. As parents observe familiar patterns of development in the second child, they begin to appreciate some of the regularities of development. They learn to anticipate future changes. Parents also begin to be sensitive to the temperamental differences between their children. The first child may have been more active or more sensitive to touch. The second child may be more calm or more afraid of new things. With two or more children, parents may be able to identify these temperamental characteristics as belonging to the child's "nature." They may begin to be more accepting of both children as they are, rather than persisting in trying to change according to some abstract idea of a "child."

The experience for both children is also quite different. They each have more people to talk to. For the older child, there are opportunities to assume a dominant, teacher role. This teacher role is rarely possible for the child in a two-adult, one-child family (Cicirelli, 1975). The older child may also see the younger as someone to play with. If mother and father are preoccupied or tired, there is another person who might like to play. Generally, one expects that the older child will spend less time alone after the birth of a sibling than before. The addition of a second sibling gives a great deal of life to the children's interactions. Fighting, fantasy, and teasing are all more frequent in sibling interactions than in a child's interactions with parents. The quality of sibling interaction that has attracted attention in child care manuals and developmental textbooks

● *rivalry—competition.*

is *rivalry* or jealousy. Rivalry among siblings is thought to result from two sources. First, older siblings are jealous of love, attention, and time that new babies draw from parents. In this sense, older siblings are said to feel dethroned by new brothers and sisters. Second, younger brothers and sisters are jealous of the advantages in skill and authority that older siblings have (Adler, 1927; A. Freud, 1965).

The intensity of sibling rivalry will be determined in part by the temperaments of the children. Two active, impulsive children are more likely to experience conflict over space, objects, noise level, and privacy than two children who are less active or more reflective. Sibling rivalry is also effected by parental behaviors. Some parents clearly spend less time with an older child once a new baby is born. Some parents repeatedly praise one child and criticize another. Children are likely to identify these behaviors as evidence of parental preference. They will resent their sibling if he or she is openly favored. Some parents are able to intervene in sibling conflicts in a way that is consistent and fair. They point out what principles are involved and how a solution might be reached. Under these conditions children will recognize that the same guidelines for behavior apply equally to both of them (Ihinger, 1975). When parents accept all their children, encourage interactions among children, and apply rules fairly to all, rivalry will be minimized.

The themes that we have raised here can be extended to consider each family pattern. With each additional child, all other family members are older. By the birth of the third child, the oldest may be in school all day. The father or mother may be experiencing a career promotion that involves additional responsibilities. One or more of the child's grandparents may have died. The family is moving through time so that the third child is likely to be born during a different economic and/or political phase that may influence the lifestyle of the family.

Adult-child interaction is less frequent and must be sought more deliberately as family size increases. If one parent is involved in activities that cannot include children, the other parent must supervise three or more children. It is unlikely that each child would be able to have quite as much freedom to do as he or she wished when only one adult is available. On the other hand, in families with three or more children, an older child can serve as the supervisor or teacher instead of a parent. In large families of five or more, by the time the youngest children are born, the oldest children can perform many of the household tasks that had previously required an adult. Whether they are willing to perform those tasks is quite another matter.

One must keep in mind that most families move through phases when the sibling pattern changes. Part of each person's life history includes the adaptation to different patterns of family membership. Of course, the oldest siblings experience more of these changes than do the youngest. Furthermore, as the family changes, the relationships among family members change. If the father was not very involved with his infant son, he may be more likely to interact with this son by the time a second or third child is born. If the first two siblings were very close during their first years together, they may have become more distant by the time a third child is born. The readiness of each family member to respond to a new family member will change as the family grows. Some of the effects of sibling order and family size may be the result of having had different opportunities to observe the family in the process of change.

ACHIEVING AUTONOMY FROM THE FAMILY GROUP

Modern psychologists working in industrialized societies have observed that gaining autonomy from parents is important for adjustment. Many adolescents and adults who should be functioning autonomously are, in fact, operating from beliefs and feelings that are more like those of young children than adults. Childlike ways of thinking and feeling often cause a great deal of psychic pain. The failure to achieve autonomy from parents limits the ability to function effectively as adults. Blos (1962) has suggested that reassessing childhood identifications is one of the fundamental tasks of adolescence. It is essential, from his point of view, for a person to dissolve the uncritical psychological bonds of childhood in order to become a free, autonomous adult. Freedom and autonomy are important for further personality development and for effective behavioral and psychological functioning.

Evolutionary theorists (Darwin, 1859; Huxley, 1941, 1942; deBeer, 1974) point out that humans spend a much longer period of time in physical and biological dependence than do members of other species. Some animals become independent within a few days or hours after birth. Humans remain dependent upon caregivers for many years. In many human societies the transition from childhood to adulthood occurs in a relatively swift manner between the ages of 10 and 13. In these societies *puberty rites* mark the transition from dependence upon others to personal independence. In our own modern, technological society, a long period of development, commonly referred to as adolescence, is devoted to achieving personal autonomy.

● *puberty rites—* **ceremonies that mark the onset of adolescence when the reproductive system matures.**

During the period of later adolescence many young people live outside of their parents' home. Whether it is because they go to college, join the military, or take a job in another community, this independent living is common. The process of leaving one another has strong psychological implications for both parents and child.

Psychosocial development prior to this stage prepares people for taking care of themselves. Skills such as dressing oneself, handling money, cooking, driving a car, reading, and writing have all been mastered. Although we take them for granted, these skills are essential for someone who is living independently. The physical maturation that has taken place also contributes to the possibility of autonomy. Life requires a certain amount of physical strength, coordination, and endurance. These are finally acquired in the physical maturity of adolescence. The person learns what is appropriate behavior through internalization and the learning of parental values. The person's ability to leave the intimacy of the family can also be traced to a growing involvement with the peer group. Peer relations begin to satisfy many of the needs for closeness and support that were initially satisfied only within the boundaries of the family. Finally, the young person's mental development provides a fund of information, problem-solving ability, and capacity to plan for the future. These intellectual abilities are necessary for the person to create a lifestyle that works.

In the process of developing a psychological sense of autonomy, individuals have to realize that they are approaching the end of childhood. They must want to let go of the last threads of dependency in their relationship with their parents. Many young people are ambivalent about this. For example, many college students eagerly leave home for their new adventures but react with dismay when they discover that their bedroom has been turned into a den. Many new jobholders eagerly respond to new responsibilities but still long for their families to prepare their meals and share their evenings. Autonomy is delayed by the unwillingness to give up the support of childhood.

Behavioral autonomy— independence

● *puberty*—the period of physical development at the onset of adolescence when the reproductive system matures.

An analysis of independence and dependence in adolescent-parent relationships requires a view of the family as children emerge into adolescence. Before their children enter *puberty,* parents grow accustomed to a gradually changing, increasingly competent child. Children before puberty are capable of performing tasks that require increased strength, coordination, and planning. They can follow instructions. They see difficult tasks—cleaning the attic or building a boxcar—through to the end. Then, at puberty, the previous picture of stability and skill changes. Young adolescents are experiencing rapid physical changes, expanding intellectual skills, and new challenges in peer relationships. They are physically larger and not easily threatened by their parents' physical power. They are curious, excited, and perhaps somewhat embarrassed by the sexual impulses that accompany puberty. These new impulses lead to new conflicts in heterosexual interactions. They may also bring some competition or jealousy among same-sex peers. Discussions of "sex" with parents are often experienced as a source of tension and caution. Parents do not want to disclose their ignorance, and neither do adolescents. What is more, such discussions often contain some suggestion that the parent suspects the child of "fooling around." Parents may assume the role of the "grand inquisitor." Questions about who will be at a party, how the child will get home, whether alcohol or other drugs will be used, or whether adults will be present are all legitimate parental concerns. At the same time these questions make adolescents feel unprepared. The answer "I don't know" seems weak. Yet more often than not, it is the truth. In order not to appear incompetent or "immature," adolescents make up a story that will appease parents even though it is inaccurate.

In early adolescence young people are likely to have a temporary setback in independence and self-assurance (Newman & Newman, 1979). All of the physical, cognitive, and social changes of this phase open up new areas of uncertainty. Just as parents were beginning to anticipate a stable, predictable relationship, they are confronted with their child's mood swings, withdrawal, secrecy, anger, and helplessness. Adolescents may be so preoccupied with their thoughts that they do not listen to instructions. They may not give the kind of help that they gave in the past. They may daydream, talk on the phone, spend long periods in the bathroom, go for long walks, or become very religious. They may be easily frustrated, disappointed, or hurt. They may feel resentful that parents do not understand them better. Adolescents may feel that their problems are terribly serious. They should be of great concern to parents, siblings, and peers. It comes as quite a blow that mother and father have not even thought about what you are going to tell Joe when he calls or whether you should lend Betty the money she asked for.

In 1955 and 1956 a national sample of boys aged 14 through 16 and girls aged 11 through 17 were interviewed. Douvan and Adelson (1966) have summarized many of the central life themes that emerged from those interviews. Both the boys and the girls showed a pattern of increased independence during early adolescence. For the girls, independence was expressed by increased responsibility for jobs and for work around the house and by more time away from home with friends. Emotionally, independence was gradual. Girls continued to express a tendency to be tied to their parents. As they grew older, however, they tended to be less likely to think of their mothers as someone to confide in and they selected their mother less often as the person whom they most wanted to be like in adulthood.

Conflict between girls and their parents occurs around three themes. Early daughter-parent conflicts were about dress, makeup, and appearance. These conflicts were most frequent before the girls were 14. From 14–16 the disagreements were about dating, friends, or driving the car. Conflicts about ideas, especially religion or politics, occurred at later

Jean-Claude Lejeune

Adolescents become so preoccupied by their thoughts that they seem to withdraw from interaction.

ages. Most often conflicts took place in an atmosphere that the girls perceived as fair rather than extremely restrictive or arbitrary.

Interviewers asked the following: "Jane sometimes wishes her parents were different. What does she have in mind?" The most frequent response made reference to fewer restrictions or limitations. However, another answer suggested that some girls wished for a closer relationship with their parents. This kind of answer was given by 17 percent of the girls under 14 and by 32 percent of the girls who were 17–18. It appeared that the gains in independence that were being made were balanced by feelings of nostalgia or regret about the absence of feelings of intimacy.

The picture of emerging independence is somewhat different for the boys than for the girls. The boys started to date and to earn money later than the girls. However, the boys spent less time at home with parents. They shared fewer leisure activities with parents. They were less likely to see their fathers as their ideal for adulthood. Only 31 percent of the 14-year-olds and 18 percent of the 16-year-olds said that they wanted to be like their fathers when they were adults. The boys were more likely than the girls to resist a parental restriction or to tell a parent that they had disobeyed. In response to the question "Have you ever broken a rule?" 26 percent of the girls and only 10 percent of the boys answered no.

Douvan and Adelson drew the following conclusion about the importance of independence for males and females: "We know that independence is a more prominent issue for boys—they more often speak of it in discussing their conscious concerns, ideals, hopes, and aspirations. They are more actively 'on the move' toward independence during the adolescent period" (1966, p. 168).

Douvan and Adelson approached the issue of the family context for independence by looking at three different matters. First, autonomy could be inferred from the answers to the question "What are the most important things your parents expect of you?" Answers that reflected an expectation for independence in the girls' sample increased from 8 percent at age 14 to 25 percent at ages 17–18. No similar data were available for boys. Parents who expected their daughters to function independently were viewed as more lenient. They were more likely to involve girls in making rules, and more likely to use psychological discipline than physical punishment or deprivation. Nonetheless, it is striking to learn that only 25 percent of the oldest girls saw autonomy as a clear parental expectation.

Another index of autonomy in the family is the question "Do you have any part in making the rules at home?" Data on this question were only available for females. Participation in rule making increased from 45 percent of the girls under age 14 to 62 percent of the girls aged 17–18. Still, at ages 17–18, 34 percent of the girls had no part in rule making. The girls who participated in rule making saw their parents as encouraging autonomy. They experienced little physical punishment.

They appeared to be able to resist adult authorities or to break rules when necessary. Participation in rule making increased their internalization of moral standards. It enabled them to regulate their impulses effectively.

The relationship between independence and parental power has been studied in other samples. Adolescents in grades 7–12 were sampled from a population of 19,200 white subjects from unbroken homes in North Carolina and Ohio (Elder, 1963). The level of parental power and the frequency of parental explanations were studied. Three kinds of families were described: autocratic, democratic, and permissive. In autocratic families, parents tell their children what to do. In democratic families, children are encouraged to make their own decisions, but parents "have the last word." Permissive families, range from asking children to include parents' opinions when reaching a decision to expressing indifference about children's decisions. Democratic and permissive parents are quite a bit more likely than autocratic parents to use frequent explanations for their rules. Four aspects of adolescent independence were related to parental power and the frequency of parental interactions:

1. The greater the amount of parental interaction, the more likely adolescents are to want to be like their parents.
2. Parents who use frequent explanations have children who are more likely to comply with parental wishes in response to a conflict about a friend.
3. The group of subjects who are most likely to feel self-confident and independent in decision making have permissive or democratic parents who provide frequent explanations.
4. Dependence and lack of confidence are greatest in children from autocratic families with low amounts of interaction.

Across all levels of parental power, girls were more compliant than boys in going along with parental objections to a friend.

The adolescent's perception of parental power is associated with the desire to be like the parents. Most adolescents see their parents as having equal power in family decisions (Bowerman & Bahr, 1973). This pattern seems to be most highly associated with strong identification with both parents. Families in which the father or the mother is viewed as most powerful are associated with weaker identification with both parents. Identification with fathers is significantly lowered when adolescents perceive their mothers to have primary power in the family. Uneven power in families generates tension and conflict that make both parents less desirable models for identification.

The pattern of family relationships and its contribution to independence is further illustrated by Kandel and Lesser's (1972; Lesser & Kandel,

1969) analysis of families in the United States and Denmark. Several differences between Danish and American families have been found. First, there are more democratic families in Denmark and more authoritarian families in the United States. American parents have more rules for their adolescent children than do Danish parents. Danish parents talk more with their children and give more frequent explanations than do American parents. Danish adolescents are less likely than American adolescents to turn to their mothers for advice. They feel less close to their mothers, and are less likely to see their mothers as models for adult life. They are more likely than American children to feel close to their fathers and to want to be like their fathers.

Danish adolescents are more likely to believe parental values even without specific rules for behavior. For example, Danish adolescents are more likely than American adolescents to spend two hours or more doing homework when there are no rules about how many hours they should spend. Danish adolescents are also more likely to feel independent. They feel more comfortable than American youth in exercising their own judgment in cases of conflict with parents. In both countries, a greater feeling of independence is associated with fewer rules. Americans' dissatisfaction about freedom is linked to more parental restrictions.

The achievement of independence is clearly linked to the parents' ability to involve adolescents in decision making, to provide explanations

Living laboratory 6·2

ACHIEVING AUTONOMY FROM THE FAMILY GROUP

Purpose: To link the term *autonomy* to shared values in the child-parent relationship.

Method: Review your beliefs in the following areas: religion, politics, sexuality, career goals, and commitments to family. For each area write down five statements that explain your values, what you think is important for your own life, and how committed you are to your beliefs. Ask your parents to each do the same thing. In each area, ask them to write down five statements about their beliefs, values, goals, and commitments. Do not discuss your views with your parents until they have completed their statements.

Results: Now compare your statements with those of your parents. For each area, how many statements had similar content? How many emphasized something different?

Discussion:
1. How would you describe the level of autonomy you have achieved from your parents at this point in your life?

2. To what extent are your values different from your parents? Are your values opposed, complimentary, or similar to theirs?

3. Is similarity or difference of values a good measure of autonomy? Can you think of cases where there is high autonomy and strong similarity of values, or cases where there is conflict of values, but little autonomy?

for rules, and to emphasize independence of judgment rather than conformity with rules. On the one hand, feelings of confidence, freedom, and autonomy are associated with democratic, egalitarian families. On the other hand, adolescents in such families are most apt to be fond of their parents, to want to be like them, and to consider their rules and judgments fair and reasonable. The same conditions that foster a sense of independence also build a bond of closeness and affection between parents and children. The image of adolescence as a period of angry, dramatic conflict is missing from these studies. Rather, identification, in which parents' values are internalized, preserves the adolescent-parent bond. This same identification permits effective, reasoned, autonomous decision making.

ADULTS AND THEIR PARENTS

We tend to think of the task of achieving autonomy from parents as a challenge of later adolescence. During this period, young people try to confirm a sense of independence through their actions and their values. However, the problem of autonomy from and responsibility for parents continues to be a life long theme.

As one ages from 30 to 50, one's parents may age from 60 to 80. From 1970 to 1976 the population in the age range 65 and over increased by 14.8 percent (U.S., 1977). It is increasingly likely that today's young adults will eventually confront the challenge of how to best meet the needs of their own aging parents (Simos, 1973; Trall, 1971).

The challenges are many. Physical problems begin to limit the aging parent's activity and independence. Death of a spouse may leave the remaining parent feeling isolated and depressed. Most older adults will resist the idea of living with their adult children. Nonetheless, they may need to find some new living arrangement if their spouse dies or their health fails. With increased age there is an obvious shift in the parent-child relationship. The parent begins to need more help, care, or financial resources and the adult child has to learn how to give it.

Just because help is needed does not mean it will be received comfortably or willingly. Adult children struggle with the nature of their responsibilities to their parents and how to meet those responsibilities effectively. They must weigh the obligations toward their parents with commitments to their parental, marital, and work roles. They must also resist the urge to treat their parents like children. Finally, they must handle the feelings of sadness and loss at watching a loved one lose his or her vitality in the last years of life. As part of achieving a sense of generativity, or commitment to the quality of life for others, adults must establish a mature relationship with their own parents. The seek means for showing nurturance and responsibility to those who have cared for them.

Caring for one's aging parents is a source of stress throughout the mid-life years (Lieberman, 1978). It is a matter of concern for younger adult children who are likely to share the responsibility for their parents with other older adults. As the years pass, the parents' peers, spouse,

Jean-Claude Lejeune

The care of the aging parent often falls to the adult female child. Adjustment is required by both parent and child to build a mature, caring relationship during these years.

and relatives die. The older adult child may become the only person responsible for an aged parent. At this point, certain very difficult choices may have to be made. Daughters, more frequently than sons, are perceived by parents as the people who ought to assume care for the aged parent (Sussman, 1965; Blenkner, 1965). This care might include having to decide about the housing arrangements, medical care, or financial arrangements of older adults. It may involve refusing or agreeing to parental requests to spend more time together, to live in the same home, or to assume caregiving responsibilities. What is more, the responsibilities for caregiving require additional information about the parents' needs, problems, and resources. These kinds of frank discussions may not have occurred between parents and their children. Adult children may be faced with the task of establishing a new, authoritative stance without adequate information about the parent's situation.

The nature of the relationship between adults and their parents is ambiguous. It is only recently that we have so many healthy older adults in our society. We are just beginning to spell out the expectations of this bond. Older adults may never have anticipated this type of relationship with their adult children. They may not want to give up the parent role they formed during the child-rearing years. At the same time, they recognize new areas of need and fewer areas of authority. Adult children may feel confused about how to meet their commitments to their parents, to their own spouse, and to their children. Often this ambiguity is a result of poor communication. Resolutions are difficult to achieve and risk satisfying no one. When the adult-aging parent relationship has been based on responsiveness and mutual respect in the past, the possibilities for providing meaningful help to aging parents are many (Coward & Kerckhoff, 1978).

Chapter summary

The family provides a major context for adjustment. The kinship system links children of each generation to a particular family history that becomes part of each person's identity. The family group also serves as the primary agent of socialization. Each nuclear family is nested in an extended kinship structure that can enhance or compete with the nuclear family for resources. Of growing concern are the special needs of the single-parent family. The meaning of the absence of one parent, the change in resources, and the community norms will all influence the ease or difficulty with which adjustment to this particular family form takes place.

Within the family group, parents blend their understanding of the culturally defined role expectations with their own past experiences in families, their personal qualities, and their current views of the needs of spouse and children into a personal definition of the parent role.

Parents play three roles that make special contributions to the child's adjustment. These include socialization agent, provider of care, and model for imitation and identification. The parents' status and warmth are major factors in fostering the child's identification.

Adaptation in the family is influenced by the quality of sibling relations. Family size, sibling order, and sibling spacing all influence the quality of sibling interaction. Siblings have lifelong relationships that preserve certain memories and expectations of one's childhood family.

With maturity, one is expected to achieve autonomy from parents. Adolescence is a time to begin value clarification and a review of childhood identifications. In the struggle for adults and aging parents to achieve a satisfying relationship we see that the achievement of autonomy is a continuous process.

SUGGESTED READINGS

Some good books on the family include the following:

Broderick, C. B. *Marriage and the family.* Englewood Cliffs, N.J.: Prentice-Hall, 1979.

Rossi, A. S., Kagan, J., & Hareven, T. K. (Eds.). *The family.* New York: Norton, 1978.

Smart, M. S. & Smart, L. S. *Families: Developing relationships.* New York: Macmillan Publishing Co., Inc., 1976.

For those people interested in the developments in national policy, we would recommend the following:

Advisory Committee on Child Development, National Research Council. *Toward a national policy for children and families.* Washington, D.C.: National Academy of Sciences, 1976.

Reading

THE FUTURE OF THE AMERICAN FAMILY

Over the last century parents have had dwindling control over the resources they need, the people with whom they share the job of raising children. In colonial days, the American family worked together on the farm. The parents had a very large say in the kind of work their children did. Most schooling was done inside the home and not in schools outside the home. Health care was a family matter except in extreme or unusual cases.

Although parents weren't really self-sufficient, at least they didn't have to go to professionals, experts or outside institutions for the normal job of raising children. Today, that's changed very drastically—now it's impossible for any two people to raise children without extensive help.

On the good side, that means that children get a quality of health care that was unimaginable one or two centuries ago. Many people feel, in fact, that education is better, particularly in dealing with kids who have some difficulty in learning. And there is education for everyone today; there wasn't a century or two ago.

On the other hand, it means that parents have to deal with a whole array of professionals and often faceless institutions over which they have very little control. They don't have any say over the way the local schools run, very little say over the kind of advertising on television, of what is on television at all. They confront the pediatrician or the health care person from a position of, often, confusion. They don't really know how to talk to this person.

It's not that families are collapsing, but in the last quarter of a century, there's no question that there have been very large changes going on in families, the way they organize themselves and do their business. You can measure, for example, the increase of women in the paid labor force and that is very dramatic. It's not just an American phenomenon, it happens all over the world. A majority of mothers with school-aged children are out working. A very high percentage, over a third of mothers with preschool children, are working outside the home. So that overall, the typical American woman today is a mother who works—part-time, full-time or a combination of both.

Another crucial factor is the rising divorce rate. It's not that those children live forever in single-parent families, because many people who divorce remarry. But there are two phenomena: the children who spend significant portions of their childhood in the single-parent home, which people estimate is up to 42 percent for children born now. Obviously, some people never remarry, some people do, but there's a period of separation that's going to affect between one third and one half of all American children being born today. About one out of six children in America lives in a single-parent family at the moment, and up to half will spend some time in a single-parent family. And then there is the new phenomenon of a reconstituted family in which one of the parents, usually the father, is a stepfather, so that approximately the same percentage of children are now living in families where they have one biological parent and one by marriage.

But other factors make much more difference to a child's life than marital status of the parents—a lot of those things are immeasurable. Other things being equal, though, it looks like the best arrangement for a child is to be raised by two grownups, a man and a woman who want a child and will care for him. That's a good arrangement, even if one is not a biological parent.

There are strains with stepparents, but they are felt more by the parents than the kids. The stepparent often questions his or her goodness as a parent, but the kids seem to do fine. The worst thing for children is a mother and a father who don't get along well at all, particularly if their not-getting-along involves the child in their conflict.

Many other things are so much more important than a divorce. It is still true in this country that if you want to predict which children are going to have measurably successful adulthoods—do well, say they're relatively happy, have reasonable incomes, not end up in mental hospitals, and so on—the best way of predicting this is the economic and social status of the family in which they're born. The best prediction is that kids who were born well-off and under good circumstances will end up better off than kids who are born in the bottom 30 percent of the population. The richer you are at birth, the better your chances of being rich as an adult: The poorer you are, the smaller the chances.

The other things that matter are very hard to measure. They're not all luck, though luck does play a role. They have to do with the things we've always talked about—the consistency and fidelity of parents toward their children, responsiveness, and the child's ability and resourcefulness, which are inborn. A lot of the research on child development suggests that the most determining things as far as the children's liveliness and interaction with the world has to do with the capacity of the parents to respond to those children as unique individuals. To play with them. To affect and be affected by the children's behavior in some unique way. There are all sorts of technical words—contingency, interaction and so on. It comes down to spending time with and respecting the child. Those things really matter as far as developing a child's sense of the world.

One of the reasons why poverty and being on the bottom of the heap affect people so much is that it takes away energy and attention. The struggle to survive—whether there's going to be enough to pay the fuel bill, how you get food for the kids, how you deal with the welfare agency, find a job—takes so much of a person's spirit and morale that the kind of playful attentiveness that we know is a good thing for parents to develop just isn't there.

Mothers who work have a particularly difficult problem finding enough time to do everything they want to do. The notion that women are working because they're fed up with their families or they're doing it just for spending money or they want luxuries—it's just an enormous fallacy. She works because she needs the money, because the income is important for her family, not against her family. Women are working for reasons similar to men's and that involves income.

There are very few working mother who don't worry about neglecting their children. "What's happening to the children? I should be with them." And there's no question that breaking the role sort of stereotype—the tradition of the stay-at-home mother who has all the cookies ready when the kids come home from school and is always available, always on tap, is very difficult.

The evidence about working mothers and their effect on children doesn't support that. If the mother is forced to stay home against her wishes, against her better judgment and what would be good for the family, herself, and is bored and restless and feels she's giving up too much, then the kids are going to suffer. And they visibly do. They don't do quite as well at school and they're more upset and they have more problems.

There are other mothers, particularly mothers who either don't have husbands or do have husbands but feel compelled to work in order to keep the family finances going at all, who, in their best judgment would be better off at home. They really want to be at home with their kids. That's what is meaningful to them, and if they have to go to work for economic reasons or whatever reasons, their children also seem to suffer. The people who stay home because they want to be at home or are working because they want to be working—their kids seem to do the best.

If you ask, "What makes the working mother feel okay about working?" then you get into some of the more traditional things. Can she find good, adequate care for her children when she's not working? Does her job allow her enough flexibility so that she can still spend time with her husband, so that she can still get to the school conference, take the kids to the dentist, whatever? It's almost always been true, until recently, that when the job and the family conflict, the family has to go.

The job has to be flexible and somehow the mother and father have to juggle the kids. That's one of the things that makes many people unhappy about working—and rightly so. A mother has to be able to respond to what the kids need, when they need it. If they get sick or need her at a school conference, she has to be able to go. This applies to the father, too, if he is raising the children.

Families face many other pressures too, including the pressures of high technology. I think there's a feeling among parents at all levels that living in this very ambiguous man-made universe, where there are all these good things we want, presents great problems. We need appliances, automobiles; electricity comes from atomic reactors somewhere; we put things into foods to prevent spoilage. And at the same time, they're saying all this may be destroying us, poisoning us, wasting our minds.

We don't know how to deal with it. It's too complicated for the average person and above all, we don't have any say. In tangible forms, the thing that every parent faces is what to do about television. What do you allow kids to see? The programs are violent. They deal with adult sex—a whole lot of things you may not want your child to see. Or they're just idiotic and mindless. But how does a parent exercise any influence over this? It contributes to a general feeling of hopelessness. Everybody talks about it, but how can you do anything about it, short of just turning off the television set?

I'm not being optimistic or pessimistic, but I think it's possible for parents to get together and to have some influence of their local television shows, for example. It is possible for parents to say, "Look, we think that standards of radiation activity or chemical safety really ought to be set with the most vulnerable person, say a pregnant woman, in mind." It wouldn't happen automatically, but in the long run it would have an effect.

The parents' roles have been redefined so that the parent is not the coordinator, like an orchestra conductor, who really did have a responsibility for coordinating all these outside forces; for monitoring television, for reviewing teachers, for health care, day care, for periodic checks of this or that, for dealing with special consultants on the other. This was sort of the new parental role. It's caricatured in the picture of the suburban housewife in the sixties who ran around with a station wagon going from one place to another, and spending all of her time—it's always a her—arranging things for the kids, taking them from one lesson to another. The parent as chauffeur. The level of living in a high technology society that has costs and benefits is not going to go away. There's no magic solution for it.

What's terrifically important is the whole so-called changing of sex roles and family goals. It's clear there are more and more women outside the home. Also, there are fewer men working. In fact, the women's labor force is basically going up; men's is dropping slightly. The two lines are coming closer and closer together.

The reality is that not only are women doing things that have been traditionally defined as male, like working outside the home. But men have to take more care of the house. They have to do the shopping. There's more child care shared. There's split-shift marriages, for better or worse. There's a whole kind of personal level at which these big economic changes are affecting people very drastically and painfully.

A lot of people are deciding, "Gee, now that I don't have to be economically dependent, that also raises the question of whether I have to be psychologically dependent. And maybe I don't like this marriage at all." The man who says, "Gee, now that my wife is earning so much, I won't have to support her."

I don't think there will ever be a time when everybody is doing the same thing. There is a biological difference between the sexes, and I think it will be a long time before men spend as much time with small children as women do.

On the other hand, more and more families are deciding who is going to do what. They are achieving some sort of parity, in terms of sharing the household tasks, of sharing the homework, the jobs that women have done in the past. This is coming increasingly without a sense of political consciousness in a lot of cases. There are a lot of people who don't like all this women's liberation stuff necessarily, but they end up changing their roles really because the facts of their lives have changed.

I'm often struck that among professional and highly educated families there is a lot of talk about sharing. And there are some cases where it really happens. But so often a man has a very high level job when his wife goes back to work that somehow when push comes to shove, it's the wife and the wife's job that gives way. They revert to the old roles again.

If there's a question in the family of who stays home—well, obviously, the man says, he's got a very important job, he has to go to a conference, a crucial meeting—then it's the wife again who is in charge of the family.

There is going to be a lot more parity as the wife's work becomes more important financially. It will be no less important than the man's in terms of prestige. As this happens the role will come more in balance with each other, and both the wife and husband will have to decide together how the demands of both of their jobs will affect their homelife.

If you really were deciding what you want a child to have, you'd start with caring parents who want a child. You'd want people who were responsive and loving, who would set limits, yet were flexible. You'd want some sort of great parent-person. You'd certainly want to start with human qualities in the parent-child relationship and in other people surrounding the child.

But those are things which there's no way for a government to guarantee or prescribe. In fact, all the younger parent can do is try to make those things more likely to be there. Conditions that make it more likely to grow or prosper.

And so that means that the government has a rather limited role as far as families are concerned. The role should be to try to provide diffuse support for families. The right way to go about it is to try to provide a kind of general support, particularly for those who need it the most.

Specifically what that means, in terms of the things we can measure that are bad for children, is that the greatest harm to kids occurs in those kids who fall in the bottom quarter of the income levels. Our estimate was that about 25 percent of all American children grow up today in conditions of economic hardship that are really damaging to them and their families, where it is terribly hard to survive. We included a realistic line, which for a family of four is $8,500 now. That's an awfully low income for four people to live on, and anybody who does it knows that they can just barely make it, if that. Also, there are those families where the family is barely above some minimal level because the mother works. The family can't hack it, economically, unless she does work.

There are a lot of things this country should do about that. None of them is going to happen next year. All of them are going to be expensive.

But the first priority would be a full employment policy which is not easy to implement, but if there were jobs for everybody who wanted one, then that would really take care of millions of children who live below the poverty line.

There are lots of ways of redesigning the tax system to give people with below-middle, particularly low-middle income, a break. Just because you're below the poverty level doesn't mean you're not pushing.

The fact is that people of below-average incomes often pay as much or more in taxes than high-income people do. So one way of easing the financial burden a little on families who are earning $12,000 or $13,000 is through tax reforms of various kinds, just to make the taxes a little more progressive.

Another thing that affects families is the problem of corporate mobility. The traditional reaction to this was acquiescence. You didn't think of raising questions. You were just moved every three years and the company explicitly said, "We do this because we don't want you to get too attached to any one place." The wife may have had a nervous breakdown but nobody paid any attention.

I'm struck that many people—some women's groups, men's groups, everybody—are beginning to say, "Hey, look at what you're doing to our families." The corporate or public leaders are much more responsive to that now. People are getting up their courage to say, "Really, I've got my kids to the point where I don't want to move them."

We also can do a lot about becoming far more flexible in the demands that jobs place on people. Businesses and other offices can adjust their hours or work out part-time and shared-time opportunities for people. Husbands and wives can share jobs in some cases.

Employers can be flexible in their demands so that a mother can leave the office, for example, when her child is sick or needs her—if she is then permitted to make up for the work she missed at some other time.

There are some costs. If you get into, say, upgraded part-time work, then the company has to provide prorated benefits and that can be more expensive. Once you start providing job security you're getting into something that a lot of firms don't want to do, particularly in time of economic shakiness. These things are not going to happen overnight, but they will come bit by bit—and they'll make it increasingly possible for mothers to work without feeling they're neglecting their children.

The traditional view of a woman, the stereotype at least, was that she was a helper to her husband and she stayed home and followed him wherever he went and tried to make an attractive home for him. He came home and she had whatever was appropriate on the table. And the children were all clean and ready. And the children and the family were sort of attached to the breadwinner and what went along with it. I think as that concept changes, then the entire society—all of us—will be much better off.

Source: Kenneth Keniston, "The Future of the American Family," *Parents,* August 1978, pp. 46–47, 73–74. Copyright © 1978 Parents Magazine Enterprises. Reprinted from *Parents* by permission.

Chapter 7
Friends

In suburbia friendship has become almost predictable: "Despite the fact that a person can pick and choose from a vast number of people to make friends with, such things as the placement of a stoop or the direction of a street often have more to do with determining who is friends with whom.

William H. Whyte, Jr., *The Organization Man,* 1956.

179

For reflection

1. Why did you and your best friend become friends?

2. When did you begin to feel like the advice of your friends was more important than the advice of your parents?

3. Over the next ten years, which friends from college will you keep in touch with and why?

4. How are your friends and the friends of your parents alike and different?

Little Sally Saucer
Sitting in the water.
Cry, Sally, cry
Wipe off your eyes.
Turn to the East
And turn to the West.
Point to the one who
You love best.

Nursery rhyme

One's circle of friends provides a context for personal growth throughout life. Through peer friendships we learn to care for people outside our families. They help us to see their point of view within a context of mutual support and understanding. The chapter focuses on lifelong changes in friendships. Topics include peer interactions during infancy and toddlerhood, peer evaluation and pressures toward conformity, friendships in adolescence and adulthood. Throughout life friends contribute to self-understanding and help in coping with life challenges.

INFANT AND CHILDHOOD FRIENDSHIPS

Part of the fun of playing is the opportunity to be with peers. Peer interactions have a special quality. Peers are more comparable in their skills, their status, and their life experiences than are parents, other adults, or older or younger siblings. Generally, peer group friendships do not involve long-term responsibilities and commitments. One can play for hours with a friend without having to make promises for the future. There are at least four ways that peer play makes an impact on the developing child. Peer play provides opportunities for: (1) new learning; (2) exploration; (3) experience with changing role relationships; and (4) understanding feelings.

Children learn from other children. They learn motor skills, games, information, language, and even misinformation. As early as 18 months of age, children were able to learn to work a complicated toy by watching another child work it (Poppei, 1976). Children bring different skills, experiences, and beliefs to their play. Interactions with many different playmates can teach a young child about ideas, family styles, and information that might not be learned at home. Sometimes the things children learn from peers are not wholly accepted or desired by parents. In the following example, a four-year-old boy is very convinced about some information he secured from an older playmate.

Coming home from work a father engages in the following conversation with his four-year-old son (Lewis et al., 1975, p. 27).

Son: Did you know God is a woman with many arms?

Father: There is no such thing as God. Who told you such a story?

Son: There is too a God. Linda told me. [*Linda has been the child's best* *friend for the last two and a half years. They live next door to each other and are constantly together.*]

Father: Linda is wrong.

Son: Linda is older than me and she knows better. [*She is six years old.*]

Father: But I'm older than Linda, right? [*long pause*]

Son: It doesn't matter—she told me.

Children learn about the world from each other. Friends spend time at one another's homes. They explore their neighborhood together. In the company of a peer, children are likely to be away from home longer and to wander farther than they might alone. Even at home, a visiting friend brings new life to a familiar environment. They see new uses for familiar toys, new hiding places, and new adventures.

When Jane (age eight) came over to Carol's (age eight) house, she asked if Carol's mother had any aprons. Carol had never bothered to look at her mother's aprons which were tucked away in a kitchen drawer. Soon, the two girls had aprons wrapped around their necks backwards and aprons tied around their heads. They were both Egyptian queens commanding their servants.

Both symbolic play and games with rules involve *multiple roles.* As children play with peers, they have the experience of exchanging roles. One is the hider and then the seeker, the catcher and then the thrower, the statue maker and then the statue. Through peer play, children have an opportunity to experience the give and take of relationships. Many of a child's roles are fixed. In such roles as child, sibling, or student, there is no chance to take another part. In play with peers, children experience multiple perspectives of the same event (Sutton-Smith, 1971; Lee, 1975).

As a result of many encounters in the positive context of play, children form strong emotional ties to one another. The intensity of these ties is illustrated in Freud and Dann's (1951) case example of a group of war orphans. These six children had been together in concentration camps without any parent figure from their second year. The children became intensely attached to one another. They protected each other from danger. They refused to be separated from one another. They shared their gifts and possessions with each other. One child was even willing to give up his security blanket when another child was afraid to go to sleep. They desperately resisted any efforts to separate them or to treat them differentially.

Even under more usual circumstances, children still come to feel deeply for one another. They form intense friendships, grieve at the disruption of those friendships, and delight in forming new bonds. Close friends teach children that it is possible to have an intimate relationship with someone outside the family (Sullivan, 1949).

In adulthood, we strive to blend friendship and sexuality in the formation of intimate relationships. Much of what we seek in a companion has its roots in childhood friendship. In those relationships, we discover the joy of intense closeness, mutual satisfaction, and adventure. All through life, the close companionship of an age-mate can be a great source of happiness.

Infant play

The child's first playmates are his or her family members. Very early in life, play activities between adults and babies acquaint the baby with the form of social play. Laboratory observations of peer play among strangers show that children approach each other with a degree of distance and caution. This may well be related to the unfamiliarity of the play companion or the play setting rather than the age of the child. When 12-month-old babies were observed with a familiar friend and with a stranger, they showed a different play pattern with each. Familiarity was linked with more closeness, more touching, more imitation, and more offering or sharing. Unfamiliarity was linked with more distress, more taking, and more resistance (Lewis et al., 1975).

Peer play becomes more deliberate and responsive in the preschool years. Before that time, many parents do not provide opportunities for peer interaction. The day-care environment illustrates that children who are reared in groups can learn to play with each other and help each other well before age three. However, most American children do not have the chance to exercise these play skills at an early age. Peer play, like fantasy play, is a skill that requires practice in order to be most satisfying.

Fantasy and symbolic play in childhood

Symbolic play is seen from one generation to another and in cultures. Plumb (1971) describes the regret that King Louis XIII of France felt when, at age six, he was asked to abandon play with his toy soldiers and assume more adult activities. In 1896, G. Stanley Hall and his associate A. C. Ellis reported on the importance of doll play in the lives of growing children. Ellis and Hall (1896) report that many objects were used as dolls. These included pillows, bottles, daisies, clothespins, cucumbers, petunias, and pieces of cloth. Sutton-Smith and Rosenberg (1961) compared preferences for different forms of play that were expressed in four different studies from 1896, 1898, 1921, and 1959. The samples in these studies were from Massachusetts, South Carolina, California, and Ohio. Cowboy and Indian games and cops and robbers were most desired by boys in the four periods. For girls, doll play ranked first in the period 1896 to 1898, but by 1959 it had slipped to eighth position. Other fantasy games that girls preferred including house and school remained within the top 30 games. These too became less popular in the most recent study.

The reason certain games are enjoyed and widely shared must be due to the richness of the symbols involved. Symbols are objects or images that represent other things. They may have many meanings. An inanimate object like a doll can become a symbol in the child's imagina-

Through make-believe play children experiment with images of the self and are drawn closer to one another.

tion. The doll may stand for mother, love, and happiness in the child's mind. Piaget (1951) has suggested that there are at least three groups of symbols that are likely to be bound to deep personal feelings. These include:

1. Symbols for the child's body.
2. Symbols for family roles and family feelings.
3. Symbols for the birth of babies.

Intense play reflects the importance of these themes to the child. Through symbolic fantasies children try to understand where they come from, who they are, and how they are related to others.

The enhancing effects of fantasy and symbolic play. Research suggests that imaginative play contributes to adjustment. Singer (1973, p. 59) used a four-question interview to find out how children use fantasy. The four questions include:

1. What is your favorite game? What do you like to play the most?
2. What game do you like to play best when you are all alone? What do you like to do best when you are all alone?
3. Do you ever have pictures in your head? Do you ever see make-believe things with pictures in your mind or think about them? What sort of things?
4. Do you have a make-believe friend? Do you have an animal or toy or make-believe person you talk to or take along with you? Did you ever have one, even though you don't any more?

The children were between the ages of six and nine. Singer rated how much each child was likely to use fantasy. Then the children were told that the experimenter was trying to decide which children might make good space travelers. One criterion for space flight is the capacity to sit quietly in one place for a long time. The children, therefore, were asked to sit quietly in one place as long as they could. The children who used fantasy a lot were able to remain seated and quiet for almost six minutes longer than the children who didn't use fantasy much. After the "space wait" was over, the children were interviewed. The high-fantasy group reported that they had created some kind of adventure related to space travel to occupy their thoughts. They focused less on the time and more on the nature of their imaginary space adventure.

One study points out what can happen when children are taught to play. Rosen (1974) gave 40 hours of play training to children in low-income kindergartens. These training sessions included role playing, creating fantasies, and asking questions about the fantasies. The goal of the training was to help children create more elaborate fantasies. A control group met weekly with the experimenter for ten weeks during which time she led group activities.

Results showed that the children benefited from the training in four ways:

1. The children who had training initiated more symbolic play in free-play observations than those who did not have training.
2. After training the children performed better on a group task involving building blocks. They helped each other and used more building blocks in an interrelated way. They seemed more relaxed and involved in the task after training.
3. After training they worked more cooperatively in a group situation.
4. After training the children showed increased role-taking skills.

The study shows that children can learn how to use play skills.

These studies of symbolic play give us some idea of the usefulness of this kind of activity. In ambiguous, boring, or unpleasant situations, fantasy permits children to create interesting ways of passing time. Some children tend to use fantasy more than others. Children who don't use fantasy will find it harder to handle these situations. For some children, fantasy may help to redefine the meaning of the experience. For other children, fantasy may allow emotions to be expressed. Individuals use fantasy for different purposes. Finally, children can learn to be more active, to consider each other's point of view, and to work together through symbolic play.

Peer interaction and games with rules

Piaget (1951) argues that of the forms of play, games with rules are the ones that persist into adulthood. The rules themselves give these games a social dimension. They provide agreed-on limits, consequences, and rewards for action. The rules structure the play and add to the challenge.

Sutton-Smith (1971) defines a formal game as follows: "an exercise of voluntary control systems, in which there is a contest between powers, confined by rules in order to produce a disequilibrial outcome" (p. 298).

This definition emphasizes five aspects of formal games. Each is relevant to the psychological involvement of children who play.

1. The game is voluntary.
2. There is a contest between powers. This implies that all players have some skill and that the outcome is not totally predictable.
3. The game is confined by rules. Younger children will play a game without concern for the rules. Once rules are understood they become a central element of the game.
4. The contest and the rules combine to create a situation in which one player or group of players wins and the other is defeated.
5. There is an implication that a player engages in game playing in order to create this experience. Some part of the energy for playing a game comes from the possibility of ending the game as a winner.

The definition appears to have two significant limitations. First, as Sutton-Smith (1971) himself observes, there are a number of early games that do not fit this model. These games like "Ring around the Rosie," "Duck, Duck, Goose," or "Farmer in the Dell" are almost like a ritualized form of symbolic play. They have rules that define the part to be played by each participant and the sequence of actions. They do not really include a contest of powers. Without the contest, there is also a less clearly defined sense of a winning and losing. The games of toddlerhood are the most short-lived form of play activity. These games point out the second quality of gaming that is not included in Sutton-Smith's definition. We refer to the social nature of game playing. The game provides a

United Press International

In games with rules, children learn to set agreed-upon limits on their behavior.

comfortable way for having social interactions. Children and adults use games as a way of being together with others. Card games, chess, tennis, or golf are all examples of games that adults use in order to maintain social contact with others. The social encounter is not a part of the rules or contest of the game. It is part of the experience of playing. As such, the game may be secondary to the companionship that game playing provides.

Living laboratory 7·1

PEER INTERACTION AND EARLY PLAY

Purpose: To identify the importance of early play activities for adjustment.

Method: Think back to when you were between seven and ten years old. That would be when you were in the second through the fifth grades. List five play activities you remember enjoying during those years. For each play activity, tell whether it involved other children, whether it involved fantasy, whether it involved rules, whether it involved physical activity, and whether it involved competition or cooperation. You might like to use the checklist below to compare the five play activities as you remember them.

Activities	Friends	Fantasy	Rules	Physical activity	Competition	Cooperation
1.						
2.						
3.						
4.						
5.						

Results: Summarize the characteristics of your early play activities. Try to evaluate their contribution to your adjustment during childhood.

Discussion:
1. Did the play activities you mentioned help you to build new skills? If so, what kinds of skills?

2. Did the play activities help you to cope with stress? If so, in what ways?

3. Were friends and the ability to make friends an important outcome of these early play activities?

ADOLESCENT FRIENDSHIPS

During early adolescence, the peer group is more structured and organized than it was during the elementary school years. Friends are important to the preadolescent. It is less important to the preadolescent to be a member of a peer group. Friends are often found in the neighborhood, local clubs, community centers, or classrooms. Friends tend to be alike in many ways.

During early adolescence, this process begins to change. The adolescent enters high school. There is a reordering of the "leading crowds" from neighborhood schools into a single "leading crowd." Some students find that their social positions are the same or better. Others find that their social positions are worse. A revision in friendships takes place because of these changes.

Popularity and acceptance into a peer group at the high school level may be based on one or more of the following characteristics: good looks, athletic ability, social class, academic performance, future goals, religious affiliation, ethnic group membership, and special talents. Usually the criteria for group membership are not openly stated. Nonetheless, the groups tend to include or exclude members according to consistent standards.

Characteristics of the peer group

Adolescent peer group structure has been described in detail by Dexter Dunphy (1963). He based his analysis on peer interactions in Sydney, Australia, in the period 1958–60. His observations were made "on street corners, in milk bars, and homes, at parties and on Sydney beaches." In addition, he used questionnaires, diaries, and interviews. Together these sources of information led to an understanding of peer group structure. Two aspects of structure were important: group boundaries and group roles. The group boundaries showed two types of groups: *cliques* and crowds. The cliques were small, with an average of six members in each. The crowds were associations of two-four cliques. Feelings of intimacy and closeness extends to the clique. The crowd is needed for social events such as parties and dances. Dunphy observed that clique membership was necessary for crowd membership. Not every clique was included in a crowd, but no one claimed to be a member of a crowd and not a member of a clique.

● *clique*—a small exclusive group of people.

The formation of the crowd changed as the members got older. Adolescents began their group experience in same-sex cliques. The next stage was the interaction of a girl's clique and a boy's clique in some kind of group activity, such as a trip or a volleyball game. In the third stage meetings between leaders of the two cliques and the beginning of dating occurred. After these early boy-girl interactions, the cliques themselves began to be *heterosexual*. They joined with other cliques to form a heterosexual crowd. At this stage most peer contacts, including friendships, dates, and larger group activities, were confined to other members of the crowd. In the last stage, the crowd began to grow apart. Couples who were going steady focused their attention on one another. Separate couples had less need for a large peer group.

● *heterosexual*—sexual desire for one or more members of the opposite sex.

Among American adolescents there are many types of crowds. Petroni (1971) states that students in a desegregated Topeka, Kansas, high school reported the following 12 types of students: "middle-class whites, hippies, peaceniks, white trash, 'sedits' (upper class blacks), elites, conservatives, racists, niggers, militants, athletes and hoods."

Poveda (1975) asked the seniors in a working-class community near San Francisco to rate the student types for girls in their school. The students described two social types, the "high society" girls and the "party" girls. The high society group were much more involved in school activities.

The party girls viewed school as limiting. They were more involved with social life, adventure, and freedom. In between these two groups, there were the "average" girls, who were less visible and less active in school activities. These girls said that they could be friends with anyone. They were not likely to be included in the social activities of the other types. Finally, there were the social outcasts of the female peer structure including about 12 percent of the senior girls. They either looked and dressed differently, did not like to party, or tended to be very critical of others. Another type of outcast was the "tramp," who had a bad reputation. Tramps did not seem to care what others thought of them. In today's student culture, "burnouts" are a new type of outcast. These are students who have used drugs for a long time.

These peer groups have boundaries. Some students try to push their way into a high-status group. Others may fall out of a crowd. Dating someone of a higher status or getting involved in a high-status school activity (athletics or cheerleading) may be ways of moving into a new peer group. When the school population is relatively stable it is very difficult to change one's group identity (Jones, 1976).

The impact of friends on behavior and values

Two important questions are raised about the impact of the peer group on adjustment. First, what determines peer group acceptance? Second, do adolescent friendships draw individuals into conflict with parents?

James L. Coleman (1961) has looked at the first question. His study describes a system of cliques within the American high school. In most schools, status in the peer group structure was based on athletic skills, student activities, and social leadership, but not academic excellence. In this way peer group values determine the acceptance of students in a particular school. The boundaries around clique groupings, and the kinds of behaviors that are likely to be approved, rejected, or ignored are imposed by clique members on themselves and on newcomers.

Kandel (1978) found that high school friends tend to be in the same grade in school and of the same sex and race. Friends were most alike in drug use, educational expectations, and involvement with peer activities. Even friends who had liked each other for more than three years, did not hold the same attitudes about such things as politics, materialism, career aspirations, closeness with parents, or evaluation of teachers. This picture of peer friendships suggests that peer groups tend to be structured around several rather obvious characteristics—age, race, and sex. These friendships are probably fostered by frequent interactions within the school. Similarities in behavior may eventually produce similarity in attitudes. Attitudes do not tend to be the force that binds most adolescent peers together.

The second question about the impact of peer groups on values focuses on the extent to which parents and peers are in conflict. Where

● **hypothetical
situation—**
**circumstances that have
been devised for the
purpose of discussion
and analysis.**

there is conflict, do peers have more influence over adolescents than their parents? One approach to this question has been to survey the attitudes of adolescents and their parents on a range of topics, including sex, drugs, religion, war, law and law enforcement, racism, and politics. In surveys of this kind, attitudes of the parents and their children tend to be similar in most areas (Lerner & Weinstock, 1972; Weinstock & Lerner, 1972).

Another approach has been to pose *hypothetical situations* in which parents and peers offer opposing views of how to behave. The adolescent subjects are then asked whether they would follow the advice of parents or peers. Early studies of this type suggested that adolescents turned to peers when the situation involved a current question about popularity or membership in a club. They turned to parents in deciding about future plans or moral decisions with consequences for the future (Brittain, 1963, 1967–68, 1969).

Later studies came out with a rather different picture. In these studies (Larson, 1972a, 1972b), the subject was asked to tell what he or she would do in a given situation. The situation was described in two different ways. In some cases the parents urged against some behavior that friends supported. In other cases friends urged against the behavior and the parents supported it. The majority of subjects (73.6 percent) were neither parent oriented nor peer oriented. They made their own decisions about the situation and did not change them, regardless of who approved or disapproved. The next largest group (15.7 percent) went along with their parents' decisions in at least four of the six situations. In general, the group of adolescents tested in this situation were strongly parent oriented. They felt that their parents understood them, supported them, and generally had good advice. Nonetheless, when the decision about how to behave in a particular situation had to be made, the adolescents often made judgments different from their parents' wishes.

A third approach to the question of the impact of parents and peers on adolescents' values is to ask adolescents directly how they regard parental advice. Curtis (1975) asked over 18,000 adolescents in grades 7–12 questions about the degree to which they valued father's, mother's, and friends' opinions. At every age, parents were more valued sources of advice and opinions than friends. However, the number of students who gave a high rating to parents declined rather steadily from seventh through tenth grade. At grade 11, the middle-class and working-class boys show an increased rating for their fathers. The value of friends' opinions and advice remained much more stable across ages. About 28 percent of the boys and 50 percent of the girls gave a high rating to their friends' opinions at *every* age. Although friends do not become more important, parents become somewhat less important with age. Rather than becoming more influenced by peers, adolescents adjust to parent-peer conflict by becoming more confident of their own opinions.

United Press International

During early adolescence, friends are a source of companionship, support, and understanding.

An interesting comparison is provided in a survey of friendship among Soviet students aged 14 to 17 (Kon & Losenkov, 1978). The students felt that their friends understood them better than either their mother or father. They also felt more comfortable sharing confidential problems with their friends than with their parents. On the other hand, in response to the question "With whom would you consult in a complicated life situation?" boys and girls both chose their mothers.

We see a picture of adolescent friendship as providing companionship in activities, emotional support, and understanding. In addition, personal judgment emerges as a basis for decisions. Adolescents become better at evaluating situations and making their own choices without guidance from parents or peers.

**Being
understood:
Changes in
friendship
relations during
later adolescence**

There can be no question that friendships made during the college years can provide deep and lasting relationships. Adolescents gradually lose their concerns about the intense pressures of the high school peer group. Friendships begin to reflect a growing sense of personal identity. The hope for intimacy and understanding brings later adolescents together.

As adolescents work on their own identity, it is important for them to find friends who share their values and understand their questions. During later adolescence, young people become more independent in their judgments (Lehmann, 1963; Costanzo & Shaw, 1966; Boyd, 1975). They are less likely to seek peer friendships in order to be accepted by a clique or crowd. Honesty and commitment become the goals of friendship. Soviet adolescents have two main parts to their definition of friendship: "(1) the requirement of mutual aid and loyalty; and (2) the expectation of empathetic understanding" (Kon & Losenkov, 1978, p. 196). The former became less important with age, and the latter became more important. At every age, loyalty was more important to males and understanding was more important to females.

During the college years there is an increased emphasis on friendships that help the person work on understanding who they are. Newcomb (1962) described the process of friendship formation in a student rooming house. At first, friendships were based on the closeness of living arrangements. Men who lived on the same floor or who shared a room became friends. After four months, common values drew friends together. The men felt closest to others who were struggling with the same problems and who had similar beliefs.

Tangri (1972) asked women whom she had typed as Role Innovators to discuss their friendships. The Role Innovators were college women who had selected male-dominated careers. These women had more men among their ten closest friends than did traditional women (women who had chosen occupations with 50 percent or more women). The men who were friends of Role Innovators were likely to support the idea of having a wife pursue a career. Role Innovators also found women friends who supported their career goals. They used their friendships to support them for the directions they had chosen.

A student at a small New England liberal arts college describes the quality of her closest college friendship. In this description we begin to understand that opening oneself up to someone else can lead to self-awareness and personal growth.

"Junior year I formed the closest relationship to anyone I've ever had, not only at Berkshire but anywhere. Lisa and I became extremely close. She cared about what I thought, and many times, even though she had reservations about what I was feeling, she never attacked but asked questions, her questions making me question in turn and generally causing me to at least reevaluate those feelings. We talked hours on end about Berkshire and what was happening to us and everyone else here" (Goethals & Klos, 1976, p. 234).

Friendships between males and females

People differ in the kinds of friendships they desire. Some adolescents have male and female friends. Some only have friends of the same sex and some only have friends of the opposite sex. Some adolescents have only one intimate friendship that combines sexuality and understanding. In the sample of Soviet adolescents discussed above, 75 percent agreed that it would be possible to have a friendship with someone of the opposite sex without being in love. However, among the oldest males (age 20), more than half doubted that this would be possible. In general, among all age groups in the Soviet sample more males preferred same-sex friendships and more females preferred opposite-sex friendships. If this pattern was reflected in real friendship choices, one could expect that more females would feel disappointed in not being able to have the close friendships they desired. This was in fact the case. At every age, the Soviet girls were less optimistic about the possibility of finding a "genuine friendship."

Opposite-sex friendships are desired but they cause problems. In a study of black college students, friendships across sex were more intimate than friendships between members of the same sex (Peretti, 1976). Opposite-sex friendships involved more sharing of personal information, more shared activities, and greater feelings of reciprocity than same-sex friendships. We know from Tangri's (1972) study of Role Innovators that male friends can be very important in supporting women's nontraditional goals. Adolescent males also benefit from close friendships with females. In these friendships it is possible for males to share some of their doubts and weaknesses. They can disclose more of their personal thoughts without being viewed as overly dependent or incompetent.

Both males and females bring stereotypes about the opposite sex that may interfere with the formation of a friendship. Females expect that males will have fewer "feminine" characteristics than they actually have (Nicol & Bryson, 1977). Females expect males to be less supportive, empathic, dependent, or nurturant than males feel they are. For this reason, females may not accept qualities that are part of a male friend's personality. In contrast, males have trouble accepting a bright female friend. Many males have difficulty with heterosexual relationships in which they do not feel more competent (Komarovsky, 1973). Such men may avoid heterosexual relationships that threaten their feelings of competence. They may try to turn their female companions into "good listeners." Some women pretend to be less competent than the male. Some disguise their abilities. This kind of charade is becoming less acceptable among college women. However, it continues to operate in colleges and work settings. Obviously, a good friendship would not be easy to achieve when one partner had to disguise her intellectual abilities.

Living laboratory 7·2

ADOLESCENT FRIENDSHIPS

Purpose: To identify the function of different kinds of friendship bonds.

To characterize the friendship network.

Method: Using the diagram below, fill in the names of people who belong in each concentric circle of friends. The people with whom you are most intimate would occupy the first ring around self, those in the farthest ring would be a group with whom you have friendly but remote relationships.

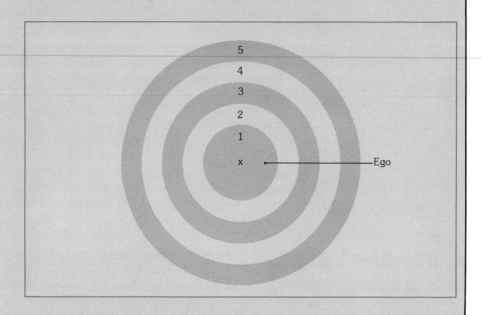

Results: How many people did you name in each category? How many people did you name altogether?

What are the essential differences in the relationships you have with people in rings 1, 2, 3, 4, and 5?

With which level of friends do you spend most of your time?

Discussion: What functions do friendships at each level serve? In other words, what would be missing in your life if there were no one left in a particular category?

What are the interconnections among categories? Do people in each ring know one another? Can they move from one ring to another?

Think about your friends as a self-selected personal environment. Which of your qualities does your friendship environment enhance? Which of your qualities does it try to modify? Which of your qualities does it discourage? Can you imagine a deliberate change in friendship relations that might contribute positively to your own personal adjustment?

As adolescents work toward their own solutions to the challenges of personal identity, it is important to have friends who support them to their full potential. If understanding, support, and empathy are the goals of friendship, then self-doubt, competition, and shame are its pitfalls. It is important that a friendship begin on a foundation of respect and acceptance. Otherwise, the price of companionship may be the abandonment of personal growth.

ADULT FRIENDSHIPS

Adult friendships are varied in nature. Some friendships survive across the years, despite few meetings and many life changes. It is as if the bond of understanding and mutual support lives in the minds of the two friends. Like a cactus that needs minimal watering, the friendship thrives on minimal interaction. Other friendships emerge out of the day-to-day life of the work setting or the neighborhood. These relationships develop because the people are near each other and see each other often. They may talk to each other daily, participate in the same social activities, and share contemporary problems. Yet, if one or the other is transferred to a new location or buys a home in a new neighborhood the friendship may quickly dissolve. Adult relationships may continue

The photography of H. Armstrong Roberts

Adult friendships that are formed in the work setting may never extend beyond that role.

for many years within a work setting and never extend to family or home life. Two physicians, for example, may serve on committees together, see each other frequently at conferences, keep abreast of one another's research activities. These two consider one another good friends, and yet, they may know nothing about one another's parents, brothers, and sisters, or college years.

Some friendships have a more practical function in adulthood. This is similar to the view of a friend as "someone I can count on" that is expressed in early adolescence. Adult friends support one another's business activities. They look after each other's children, or check one another's homes when one is on vacation. The friendship has meaning as a support system that helps the adults meet their many life obligations.

Blending friendship and marriage

In our society it is common to view one's spouse as one's closest friend. It is part of the folk wisdom that it is important to find a lover who can be your best friend. This blending of sexual intimacy and emotional support is difficult to achieve. In some views, it may not even be very desirable. In Case 7·1 Brain (1977) describes the importance of friendship to the Bangwa of West Africa.

Brain suggests that the distinction between marriage and friendship

---

Case 7·1

FRIENDSHIP AMONG THE BANGWA OF WESTERN AFRICA

When I went to live among the Bangwa of western Africa, high in the mountains of Cameroon, I soon found that these non-Western people placed great emphasis on the value of friendship between two persons not related by kinship or sexual attachment. To have a best friend was as important as having a wife or a brother—possibly more important. At first I was taken aback by their fervent, demonstrative attitudes toward friends, being used to Anglo-Saxon coolness. But I had little choice and eventually learned how to be a best friend, by, for example, verbalizing affection, giving gifts, and accompanying my friends on journeys.

Among the Bangwa, best friends are known as "twins." It was explained that the merging of twinship and friendship expresses the unity of the relationship. All Bangwa children have friends. If a boy or girl is not given a best

friend by his or her parents, the children will choose one from among other children their age.

Youth who become friends exchange confidences, discuss their secret plans, hunt together, and plan their endless amorous adventures. The Bangwa speak of ideal friendship as one of reciprocity backed by moral, rather than supernatural and legal, sanctions. He is my friend "because he is beautiful," because he is good. Although there is in fact a good deal of ceremonial courtesy and gift exchange, it is seen as a relationship of disinterested affection. Friends spend long hours in each other's company, holding hands, walking together in the market. For old men, friendships are particularly valued: the most bitter complaint of one old Bangwa man was that he had grown too old to have a friend left to gossip with."

Source: R. Brain, "Somebody Else Should Be Your Own Best Friend," *Psychology Today Magazine*, 1977. Copyright © 1977 Ziff-Davis Publishing Company.

is a healthy one. It allows people to have more than one intense personal bond. This takes some of the pressure off the marriage to serve so many different needs. It may also heighten the sexual quality of the marriage. Having a close friend permits physical intimacy to take a greater role in marriage without the threat that sexuality will interfere with friendship.

In our culture, marriage partners are often threatened by close, loving friendships with others. The range of people one can be close to may be limited to family members. As each family member matures, the adults monitor emerging friendship patterns. Parents impose their own restraints on the intensity and diversity of friendships that should be formed. Salamon (1977) compared the pattern of friendships in Japanese and West German families. In the Japanese families, each family member is permitted considerable freedom to establish friendships outside the family group. This pattern tends to reduce isolation, but it also reduces feelings of closeness between family members. In the West German families, friendships are carefully scrutinized. Contacts outside the family are given low priority in contrast to the time spent with the family. The norm of family unity and closeness puts a strain on all members for value *solidarity*. It may create a strong sense of isolation when one family member is rejected or leaves home.

● *solidarity*—unity.

Making and losing friends during adulthood: The challenge of mobility

One explanation for the pattern of casual friendships in American society is the increased mobility of American families. Involvements in intimate friendships are emotionally costly when these relationships are destined to be disrupted. Company transfers from one city to another, leaving home to attend college or to find employment, or the decision to settle in a new community after retirement are all common events in American life. Movement has become a way of life in the United States. The image of the wagon train taking pioneers west has been replaced by the explosion of campers, trailers, and omnibuses taking family groups from one coast to another. There have been migrations from east to west, from south to north, and, most recently, from north to south. At each phase of history, people respond to the promise of new opportunities and new resources. One price of this mobility is the loss of lifelong friendships.

One of the factors that contributes heavily to family mobility is the practice of company transfers. The following headline in *The Wall Street Journal* February 28, 1979, p. 1, summarizes the problem:

> Family on the Move
> A Manager's Transfers
> Impose Heavy Burden
> on His Wife, Children
> After 9 Moves, Mrs. Klaskin
> Is Tired; Daughter Feels
> She Doesn't Have a Home
> Husband: Is Job Worth It?

Company transfers affect hundreds of thousands of employees annually (Ramirez, 1979). Most of these employees are married and about ⅓ have school age children. Four or five company transfers in a career are not uncommon. They usually occur during the early adult years as companies train their young executives for higher level management positions. The moves are usually viewed as a promotion for the employee. They often disrupt the friendship network of the wife and children. The nonemployed spouse and children achieve their status in the community through informal paths. Having been a leader in a peer group or a valued member of a volunteer organization in one community are not achievements that are readily shifted from one place to the next. One does not arrive on the scene and announce to one's neighbors that everyone liked you at your last community so let's just carry on from there. With each move, there is a new period of testing, which requires finding sympathetic companions.

Adaptation to this kind of mobility takes many forms. In a case study of the Klaskin's that served as a basis for the headline above, the following behavior patterns were attributed to the stress of nine moves in 20 years of marriage.

When friendships are broken up many things can happen. Emotional responses may include depression, lethargy, hostility, and anxiety. Physical

Case 7·2

THE KLASKINS

Barbara, age 13, has moved seven times. She says: "I don't feel I have a home anywhere, because I've grown up in so many different places." She has become sullen, withdrawn, and especially resentful toward her father. She is developing a chronic stomach problem.

Howard, age 16, has moved eight times. He claims to be adjusting relatively easily. "The teen-age mind is programmed to do the same thing everywhere, I feel." However other family members describe his response to this move rather differently. They say he became withdrawn, hostile, and critical of the new community. He had a hard time making friends.

Leona, in her early 40s, has a teaching certificate but has never pursued her career. The brunt of each move falls on her shoulders, especially the task of setting up a new household. She misses the cultural activities and the friendships in her previous community. She says that she would follow her husband if he chose to move again, but she says "playfully" that she is only giving him one move. One of the ways Leona has of expressing her frustration is by grinding her teeth. She wears a retainer to protect her teeth, but she has already had to have 13 teeth capped because of this habit.

Roy, age 42, has a lot of doubts about the impact of his career moves on his family. He is sensitive to the change in his daughter's moods. He is nostalgic about the recent death of his own father and the few chances his children had to get to know his father. As the target for his family's hostility about the move, Roy feels guilty and also confused about what values ought to have priority.

symptoms may occur because of this form of stress. In the case above, the daughter's stomach pains and the mother's teeth grinding are examples. The Klaskins have had practice at moving. Nevertheless, the events of the move and the condition of the house they purchased suggest that they had not anticipated their needs adequately. They moved into a stable neighborhood where friendships were already established. This made it difficult for them to make new friends. The Klaskin family is caught in a lifestyle dominated by corporate transfers. They do not really enjoy moving or adapt effectively. We will have more to say about the Klaskins in Chapter 12 when we look at their case in greater detail.

Friendship in later life: A major source of self-esteem

Maintaining an intimate relationship into later adulthood contributes a great deal to feelings of well-being and self-worth. Some of the satisfaction of such an intimate relationship comes from the values, experiences, and knowledge shared between the two people. Particularly when an adult loses a spouse, friends become a major source of life satisfaction (Flanagan, 1978).

Jean-Claude Lejeune

Having friends and spending time with them is a major source of life satisfaction in later adulthood.

Case 7·3

AN ADULT FRIEND

"Currently, at age 81, J. gives much of her time to her house and grounds. She is an impressive woman, only 5 feet 4 inches tall, but large in build and overweight; with strong features and becoming white hair. She talks endlessly in a loud, raucous voice (she is somewhat deaf) punctuated with occasional ear-splitting guffaws. It is difficult to get a word in edgewise, or to bring the conversation to an end and escape. She is overpowering but consistently good natured and likeable. She rides around on her power mower cutting the grass on her extensive grounds, or rolling the lawn. She drives her elderly friends places in her aged Cadillac (several are younger than she). She has many visitors; and knows hundreds of friends, former students, and business men. She plays bridge regularly."

Source: R. M. Hamlin, "Restrictions on the Competent Aged" (Paper presented at the 85th annual meeting of the American Psychological Association, San Francisco, August 26–30, 1977), p. 22.

Living laboratory 7·3

ADULT FRIENDSHIPS

Purpose: To characterize the pattern of friendships in adulthood. To trace similarities and differences in the friendship relationship from adolescence through adulthood.

Method: Using the diagram in Exercise 7·2, fill in the names of people who are your parents' friends. If you do not know your parents' friends, you might ask them to help you or interview another adult about his or her friendships. Try to answer the same questions for this adult that you answered on page 194.

Results: 1. How many people are in each circle? How many people are there altogether?

2. What are the essential differences in the relationships with people at each level?

3. What functions do the friendships at each level serve?

4. What are the interconnections among categories?

5. With which level does the adult spend most time?

Now compare the patterns for your own friendships in later adolescence and the pattern in adulthood.

Discussion: 1. Does the nature of each level remain the same or appear to change from adolescence to adulthood?

2. Are there more or fewer friends in adulthood than in adolescence?

3. Is more time spent with one circle of friends in adolescence and adulthood?

4. Do friends provide different kinds of resources in adulthood and adolescence or is the function of each level pretty much the same from one period of life to the next?

The experience of being alone in the later years does not appear to be equally difficult for males and females. As part of a larger study of consumer decision making, Bikson and Goodchilds (1978) reported on the social and situational variables associated with living alone at three ages: young (25–35), young-old (65–74), and old–old (75 and older).

Women living alone and both men and women who are still married are in better health and have more regular health care than do men living alone. Fewer single men than the other three groups eat their meals at home. This is especially true for the old–old males. In their leisure time, two thirds of the older men are involved in activities by themselves, whereas two thirds of the women participate in social activities. On a three-point scale where 1 equals most of the time and 3 equals hardly ever, men living alone are the most often lonely ($M = 2.27$). However, no groups describe themselves as lonely most of the time. Another interesting observation was that older *married* women are more likely to feel alone than older married men. Often the responsibilities for health care, meal preparation, and decision making fall on the shoulders of the older married woman. These responsibilities create a more stressful living condition, than does living alone. For this group, the companionship of marriage is outweighed by the demands of caring for an aging partner. For men, living alone is more lonely and more demanding than being married. Many adult men are not prepared for assuming household tasks in later life. Given that only 33 percent of old–old males live with a spouse (Glick, 1977), a great majority of older males are struggling with the many challenges of living alone. These challenges include looking for companionship and help in meeting everyday needs.

Chapter summary

Infants begin their play activities with family members. They soon delight in playing with peers. Early play involves the manipulation of objects and the repeated stimulation of the senses. In toddlerhood, fantasy becomes a new element in play. The capacity to symbolize is developed through imaginative play. "Make believe" becomes an important way of coping with boredom or frustration. The third form of play in childhood is games with rules. These games often involve competition and give an appreciation for the ways that rules structure and limit behavior. Everyone remembers the intensity of play. During the elementary school years, children become increasingly sensitive to close friends for standards and approval. During the high school years, the peer group becomes larger and more structured. Membership in these groups is determined by dress, looks, athletic ability, academic performance, and future goals among other things. One of the critical experiences in these years is the experience of identifying with a close group of friends.

The more work adolescents do on their personal identity the more they can choose friends freely. Later adolescent friendships offer understanding, opportunities for the development of personal standards, emotional support, and physical health experiences. Opposite-sex friendships may be especially difficult to maintain.

Adult friendships are made on many levels. Friendships are not limited by physical closeness. They can be kept over time and across distances. Frequently people feel that their spouse is their best friend. This intensifies the importance of the marital relationship. It also puts heavy demands on marriages. In later life, friendship is an extremely important source of enjoyment.

SUGGESTED READINGS

For further reading on friendship:

Burgess, R. L., & Huston, T. L. *Social exchange in developing relationships.* New York: Academic Press, 1979.

Goethals, G. W., & Klos, D. S. *Experiencing youth: First person accounts.* 2d ed. Boston: Little Brown, 1976.

Lewis, M., & Rosenblum, L. A. *Friendship and peer relations.* New York: Wiley, 1975.

Rubin, Z. *Liking and loving.* New York: Harper & Row, 1973.

Reading

FRIENDSHIP AND LONELINESS

Love, by definition, is so personal. A skilled clinician learns to use his or her own responses to recognize many emotions in others—sadness, anger, fear, pleasure. But the capacity to act lovingly is different. It always takes two to demonstrate. What if the subject finds the clinician unlovable? My private judgment of who was lovable and who was not was perhaps more projection than science.

So I devised a far less satisfactory way to measure love—one in which I, the clinician, could stand aside. It is less real but more believable—a common failing of modern science. Over the years, the men had described their marriages and their use of leisure time every two years. In the interviews, they were asked specifically to describe their oldest friends, the friends they could call on for help, and their patterns of entertaining. On the basis of such information, six objective tasks for loving were set, and a blind judge reviewed the data to see how many tasks each man had carried out. The tasks were (1) getting married without later getting divorced, (2) achieving at least ten years of marriage that neither partner perceived as outright painful, (3) fathering or adopting children, (4) believing that he had one or more close friends, (5) appearing to others as if he had one or more close friends, and (6) enjoying regular recreation with non-family members. (The ratings, made by raters blind to much other data, were admittedly subjective, but in 88 percent of instances, the raters agreed.)

Friends

Twenty-seven men—I will call them Friendly—had carried out all six tasks. Thirteen men, whom I will call Lonely, failed to carry out more than two of the tasks. Some had carried out none. As I compare the blind ratings to my own, I would definitely make a few substitutions; but no one would believe me. However, in all but 4 of the 40 cases, I agreed with the judgment of the less-biased independent rater. Thus, her judgment shall stand.

Of all the ways that I subdivided the 95 healthy men of the Grant Study, the dichotomy between the 27 Friendly and the 13 Lonely proved the most dramatic. At first, this observation seems obvious; but if it were, the study of lifetimes would not be necessary. You see, at points in time each of us is lonely; at other points in time we are loved and loving. We pass from one state to the other, and who is to say if we have more friends than our neighbor, or if we are more caring than our brother? On a cross-sectional basis, judgments about capacity to love are meaningless. But as will become evident, if examined longitudinally, the lifetimes of the Lonely and Friendly were really very different.

The classification of a man as Friendly or Lonely was based principally on whether during his adult life he had achieved a relatively stable marriage and made a few sustaining friendships. These facts alone were usually enough to predict the state of his other relationships at other points in his life (see Table 1).

TABLE 1
Comparison of the adjustment of lonely and friendly men

	27 Friendly men (percent)	13 Lonely men (percent)
Adolescent social adjustment poor	4	62
Distant from family of origin	15	39
Distant from own children	13	50
Childhood environment poor	7	46
Mother dominant in adult life	0	54
Childhood relations with mother poor	30	31
Chronically physically ill by age 52	4	46
Ever labeled psychiatrically ill	11	54
Immature defensive style	11	85
Stints vacation	22	85
10 or more oral vignettes	4	62
Immoderate use of drugs or alcohol	11	39

* Of the eight men who had children; five more lacked children from whom to be distant.

I believe that the capacity to love is a skill that exists along a continuum. In order to make this point clearer, let me develop an analogy. We may like some foods and dislike others, but we all have approximately the same capacity to enjoy nourishment. Love is not like that. Rather, the ability to love is more like musical talent or intelligence. Even in a population chosen for health, the capacity to love—or what social scientists call "capacity for object relations"—was distributed very unequally; but for the individual the capacity possessed considerable longitudinal stability. Granted that we all have a basic need to love and be loved, but if loving were like eating, we might suppose that men not close to wives or friends could substitute their siblings or their children. Instead, as befits the hypothesis that the capacity to love lies on a continuum, this was not so.

In middle life, 20 of the 95 men in the Study had failed to maintain gratifying relationships with their parents or siblings. Such men were three times as likely to be called Lonely as Friendly. Nor could the Lonely substitute their children. All but three of the twenty-seven men one judge called Friendly were rated by another judge as close to their children. In stark contrast, only 8 of the 13 Lonely men had even had children, and 4 of these were distant fathers.

Over half of those men called Friendly at age 50 had ratings of high school social adjustment that fell in the top third of all the men; not even one of the Lonely had fared so well. Over half of the 13 Lonely had high school social adjustments (rated by judges blind to their post-high school lives) that fell in the bottom third; and only one of the 27 Friendly fared so poorly. This association existed despite the fact that the two sets of independent ratings were made on evidence separated by 30 years and that the two sets of ratings were based on very different evidence.

. . . each man's childhood profoundly affected his future ability to love. None of the 13 Lonely but half of the 27 Friendly had childhood environments that fell among the very best in the Study. Only two Friendly but half of the Lonely had childhoods that fell in the bottom quarter. None of the Friendly but half of the Lonely had a mother who continued both to dominate their adult lives and to serve them as a model for identification. Such continued maternal dominance was probably not the cause of their loneliness; rather it reflected the basic difficulty that these men encountered in replacing their mothers with more appropriate and more enduring intimacies. As children their relations with their mothers had seemed as warm as those of the Friendly.

The capacity to love was also associated with subsequent physical and mental health. Half of the Lonely but only one of the Friendly had developed a chronic physical illness by age 52. At some point in their adult lives, half of the Lonely but only two of the Friendly could have been called mentally ill. Not surprisingly, the Lonely were four times as likely to seek psychiatric help, and also far more likely to seek general medical attention. Physicians are loathe to admit it, but they often serve their patients in the capacity of rent-a-friend. Rather than avoid this role, maybe they would do better to learn how to do it well.

Perhaps the biggest difference between the Friendly and the Lonely was that the Lonely were more frightened. In the stage directions for Tennessee Williams's *Glass Menagerie,* the effect of Laura, as she moves away from her dream world and toward people, is indicated by a stage sign that reads "TERROR," and in psychiatric clinics, the schizoid patients are always the most scared. Why? Man has always known that he feared noxious dangers, be they real tigers and dentists' pliers or the more metaphysical states of penury, grief, and sin. However, it is only recently that we have recognized that pleasure, the warmth of sex, and the exultation of victory could also be feared. Child psychiatrists—Erikson with his concept of basic trust, John Bowlby with his examination of maternal attachment, and several who have investigated the fear of strangers anxiety in infants—have all taught us that human fear is not only directed toward the lifeless unknown but also toward the imagined dangers of human intimacy.

Source: George E. Vaillant, *Adaptation to Life* (Boston: Little, Brown, & Co., 1977), pp. 305–308. Copyright © 1977 by George E. Vaillant.

Chapter 8
School

We are convinced that education is history, and therefore has no final end. Education, in its widest sense, including the bringing up, is, in our opinion, that activity of man, which has for its base the need of equality, and the invariable law of educational progress.

Leo Tolstoy, *Tolstoy on Education*, 1862

The photography of H. Armstrong Roberts

For reflection

1. What were the most exciting and stimulating ideas you learned or thought about in school?

2. What difficulties did you experience during the transition from elementary school to high school?

3. What would your life be like now if you had attended a totally different school? For example, if you graduated from a middle-class suburban high school, what would your life be like now if you had attended a rural, one-room school?

4. What were the goals and objectives for educating children in your community's school system?

5. Think about your best friend in high school. How did your adjustment to college or work compare to your friend's adjustment?

Three levels of schooling are considered in this chapter: elementary school, high school, and college. An emphasis is placed on the cognitive and socioemotional growth that is achieved in these settings. One must keep in mind two related concepts when trying to appreciate adjustment within the school. First, students differ in their mental and socioemotional skills, their styles of learning, and their goals for schooling. Second, schools differ in their program, their physical design, and such dimensions as student-teacher ratio, population stability, or the tenure of the faculty. We can describe some of the patterns of adjustment that occur in schools. The experiences of any individual student will depend upon the interaction between the learner and the learning environment.

ADJUSTMENT IN ELEMENTARY SCHOOL

This discussion of adjustment in elementary school focuses on how the classroom group affects young children. Adjustment in elementary school also depends heavily on the skills and resources of teachers. For this reason we are concerned about dimensions of teachers' leadership style and evaluation messages.

The classroom group

The assignment of children to teachers and classrooms creates social groups. In some of these groups the children come to care for each other. Often the teacher makes use of the group to aid learning. A classroom may gain a reputation in the school or even in the community. The children in Mr. T's third grade or Miss V's eighth grade are influenced by this social group. Here we consider group size, the homogeneity or heterogeneity of the group members, the pattern of interaction, and the role of teachers as group leaders as they influence the group.

Group size. Large class size tends to decrease the amount that each child contributes (Hare, 1962; Barker & Gump, 1964). When there are fewer children, there is a greater need to use each child's skills to the fullest. In large classes, students tend to feel anonymous. They do not expect to talk with the teacher. They do not expect the teacher to come to know them as people. Particularly in the primary grades, children who are in smaller class groups score higher on achievement tests than children in large class groups (Jamison, Suppes, & Wells, 1974).

Group composition.   The composition of the classroom group can vary according to age, ability, and the socioeconomic background of the children. Most classroom groups are age graded. There is an assumption that children of the same age will have comparable cognitive and social skills. There is also an assumption that children of the same age will be ready for the same new skills. However, achievement tests and "readiness" tests tell us that there are big differences between children of the same age. Children mature at different rates. Furthermore, some skills are more highly developed than others. This pattern is not identical for all children. When children are grouped by age, there will continue to be a range in the students. This means that some children will be evaluated as below average for their age while others will be evaluated as above average. If no child can count to 100 at age two and almost all children can count to 100 at age seven, does it make sense to make a five-year-old feel inferior because he or she does not yet count to 100? Homogeneous age grading tends to benefit the early maturing children and discourage the slow-maturing children.

The practice of grouping children in classrooms based on their abilities creates another kind of group experience (Shafer & Olexa, 1971). Arguments for ability grouping include the view that teachers can meet students' needs more effectively. A curriculum can be designed that is most adequate for student learning when the children are of similar ability. The arguments against ability grouping include:

1. The negative label of being in a low-ability group.
2. The lack of opportunity to be with competent peers.
3. The lowered expectations for achievement that teachers have for the low-ability groups (Martell, 1971).

Differences in the backgrounds of the children in class affect the norms and standards that operate in the group. For example, Lippitt & Gold (1959) reported that middle-class students liked peers who were friendly, supportive, and helpful. They did not like peers who were aggressive and rebellious. In contrast, Pope (1953) reported that, in a lower socioeconomic class school, students who were aggressive and rebellious were admired by their peers. In classes where children are from lower and middle-class backgrounds, the middle-class values are the standards for the group (Schmuck & Schmuck, 1975). This is probably due to the greater similarity between teacher values and the middle-class children's orientation to the school setting.

The teacher's leadership style.   The ways that teachers use their power will have consequences for the productivity and the morale of their class. In an early study of leadership, Lewin, Lippitt, and White

(1939) described the differences between three kinds of group leadership: authoritarian, democractic, and laissez-faire. Clubs of five 10- to 11-year-old boys were created that operated under each leadership style. The authoritarian leader used discipline and rewards to direct the behavior of the boys in the group. The democratic leader used skill and warmth to produce identification. In the democratic leadership condition boys were asked to take responsibility for some decisions and tasks. In the laissez-faire group, the leader gave up the decision-making power. He permitted the boys to make all the decisions. Different patterns of group behavior occurred. In the laissez-faire group, the boys were frustrated and produced very little. They seemed unable to influence each other. They didn't get to the goal. In the authoritarian group, productivity was high, but so were hostility, competitiveness, and dependency. In the democratic group, productivity was midway between the laissez-faire and authoritarian groups. In this group the boys successfully shared responsibility for completing the task. They expressed stronger group commitment than in the other two groups. The teacher's leadership style can be expected to produce similar outcomes.

● *reinforcement*—the positive consequence that follows a given behavior.

The potential power of the teacher to create and to change qualities of the class is great. Through careful *reinforcement* and positive responses, teachers can increase the social status of low-status group members. They can increase the frequency with which students ask questions. They can increase the curiosity and exploratory behavior of students. They can increase the academic achievement of students who had been underachievers. They can demonstrate ways of being that will be imitated by their students. Teachers may also cause rebellion, defiance, helplessness, and apathy. Their impact on student adaptation depends on their leadership style and the expectations they hold for student performance.

Evaluation

One of the most confusing questions facing a teacher is how to provide students with information about their work that helps them to learn. Think of a child who takes a spelling test, hands in the paper, and two days later receives the paper back. At the top of the paper is a score of 80 or a grade of B or a word Good. Do any of these messages tell the child how to improve or why the mistakes were made? Do these messages help the child to recognize any cues about those words that were spelled correctly and the words that were spelled incorrectly? Do any of these messages make children feel good about what they have learned? Do they make children feel disappointed about what they have not learned? Are the children motivated to improve?

Teachers may evaluate students in many ways (Stainback & Stainback, 1972). They may use praise or nonverbal signs of affection and approval. They may give grades on daily assignments as well as on report cards. They may meet with children for conferences about the work the child is doing. They may meet with parents to discuss the child's work and progress. In general, when teachers respond to their students' efforts, achievement is higher than when teachers are unresponsive (Hughes, 1973; Goldberg & Mayerberg, 1975).

The meaning of evaluation for any single child depends on its context (Crandall, 1963). Some children are used to being praised and rewarded for their work. A single, sharp criticism may be a serious, negative experience. In contrast, a child who is often criticized and reprimanded may become toughened to this treatment. For a child who usually does excellent work, a score of 80 may be a sign of failure. For a child who usually does failing work, a score of 80 may be a victory.

In one comparison of children from graded and nongraded classes, the impact of grading depended on how bright the children were. The bright children who were in nongraded classes didn't like school as well as the bright children in graded classes. The less intelligent children responded just the other way. They liked school better when they were in the nongraded classes (Hicks, Edwards, & Sgan, 1973). Put very simply, children like to hear that they are doing well and they do not like to

The photography of H. Armstrong Roberts

The kinds of evaluation children receive from teachers influence their confidence in themselves as learners.

hear that they are not doing well. If they are doing well, but don't hear about it, they are not very happy.

The question of whether the absence of grading affects performance or achievement has not been fully answered. On intelligence items, students who were told that they had done well in the past tended to perform better. Students who were told that they had not done well in the past scored lower (Bridgman, 1974). The effect of evaluation depends on the nature of the task to some extent. When tasks are very difficult, evaluation may interfere with a child's concentration and persistence (Maehr & Stallings, 1972). The effect of evaluation also depends on the child's anxiety about failure. A great deal of anxiety about failure may interfere with doing well when there is an emphasis on evaluation. Under more relaxed conditions, children who are worried about failure can perform more effectively (Hill & Sarason, 1966).

Often evaluations are influenced by the teacher's past experiences, expectations, and values (Willis & Brophy, 1974). Many of the things children do in class, including writing stories or poems, painting pictures, or asking questions are graded without objective *criteria* for excellence. Teachers rely on their own experience and intuition to make their judgments. First-grade teachers were asked to estimate their students' IQs (Doyle, Hancock, & Kifer, 1971). When a teacher had overestimated a child's IQ, that child also received higher reading scores than the actual IQ would have predicted. When a teacher underestimated a child's IQ, that child received lower reading scores than would have been predicted. Some teachers repeatedly underestimated all students' IQs. Children in these classes all tended to achieve lower reading scores than would have been expected.

● *criteria*—standards on which judgments or decisions are based.

Some of the dimensions that influence grades are the children's race, social status, and sex. One study compared children by sex, race, and social status for intelligence, standardized achievement scores, and teacher's grades. The children's achievement scores were poor predictors of teachers' grades. Grades were consistently lower for boys than for girls. For only one group, low-income black girls, were teachers' grades in keeping with achievement and intelligence. For all other groups, one may infer that the teachers' beliefs and social expectations influenced the grades (McCandless, Roberts, & Starnes, 1972). Children are forced to adjust to evaluations that are not objective reflections of their ability.

School evaluations contribute to a sense of oneself as a competent, skillful problem solver or as an incompetent, inferior problem solver. Several investigators, for example, have found that girls are less confident about their chance of success than boys (Parsons et al., 1976; Dweck & Gilhard, 1975: Maccoby & Jacklin, 1974). When girls receive negative feedback from an adult authority, they tend to blame their failure on a lack of ability. When boys receive negative feedback they assume that they did not try hard enough. The result is that girls do not respond to information that they are not doing well from adults with increased effort.

Boys do. Girls tend to feel that there is nothing they can do and they try to avoid failure experiences (Dweck & Bush, 1976).

Patterns of achievement and failure

Armstrong (1964) analyzed the pattern of school achievement for students in New York state public schools. Forty-five percent of the children had average or above average grades in elementary school but received poor grades in junior high school. Most of these students did not return to their earlier level of performance in high school.

Fitzsimmons and his colleagues (Fitzsimmons, Cheever, Leonard, & Macunovich, 1969) studied the achievement patterns of a group of students who either performed poorly or who dropped out of high school. The students were from a New England community. They attended elementary school for grades kindergarten through 6, junior high school for grades 7 through 9, and high school for grades 10 through 12. For both the dropouts and the poorly performing graduates, failure began early in the elementary years. Failure increased through the later school years. Seventy-five percent of the sample had failed once by the fourth grade, most often in English. There were several important differences between the dropouts and those who graduated from high school. The number of failures for the dropouts began to exceed the number of failures for the group that graduated at the fourth grade. The excess of failures increased through tenth grade. By seventh grade, about 50 percent of the eventual dropouts had failed two or more subjects.

The failure patterns suggest that there is enough evidence by the junior high school years to identify students who will have difficulty completing school. The demands for performance in junior high school appear to be increasingly difficult. Students who are doing poorly began to think that they will not graduate.

It may be that motivational factors rather than intelligence determine whether students will continue to achieve or begin to fail in the junior high school (Finger & Silverman, 1966). Academic motivation, including persistence and a desire for a college education, and low involvement with the peer culture are qualities of people who do well in school. The more autonomous and self-controlled the child is, the more likely the child is to remain in school and succeed academically.

Adaptation to school change

The middle school years give us an opportunity to consider the process of person-environment interaction. We know that two important personal changes begin to occur during this phase of development: formal operational thought and sexual maturation.

In the age range 10 years, 5 months to 12 years, 10 months (comparable to fifth to seventh grades), children begin to use formal operational thought in the solution of problems (Kuhn, 1976). Formal operational thought is a stage of mental development observed by Jean Piaget. It makes use of logical reasoning and thinking about a variety of actions and consequences. The person can test out mentally what might happen

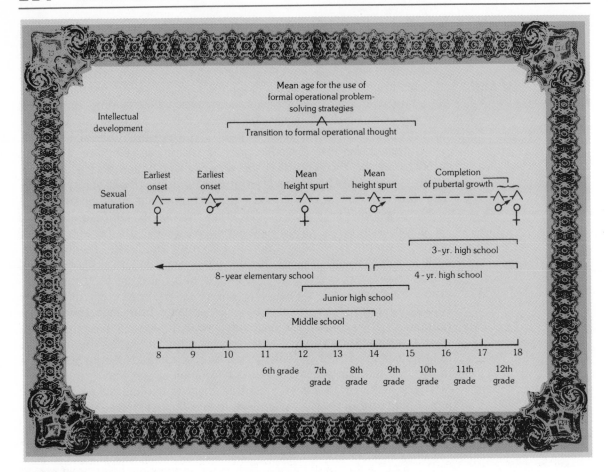

FIGURE 8·1
Intellectual development,
sexual maturation, and
patterns of school change

before they decide to do something. It has been demonstrated that the movement to formal operational thought from the previous level of thinking occurs in a stepwise pattern (Neimark, 1975). Formal operational thought is seen among children who have a mental age of ten years. Most children can use at least some formal strategies by the time they reach a mental age of 15. Beyond the mental age of 12 years, all children can approach some problems with a systematic problem-solving strategy. Children have the potential for making marked improvements or declines in IQ performance around the age of 10 when this intellectual growth begins (McCall, Appelbaum & Hogarty, 1973).

Figure 8·1 shows the mean age and the age-range for the transition to formal operational thought. The mean age and the range for sexual maturation is also presented. Along the bottom of the time line, we have indicated three times when school change may occur: (1) after fifth grade (to middle school); (2) after sixth grade (to junior high school); and (3) after eighth grade (to high school). School changes are stressful. They involve new demands for academic performance, adaptation to a new building, new expectations for responsibility and independence from parents and teachers, and new peers. School changes may also provide new opportunities and resources for the person.

Figure 8·1, then, illustrates some times of stress and some new abilities. Going to middle school, for example, requires a school change at the end of fifth and eighth grades. Formal operational thought will be developed in the middle school. There will be some time for learning to use these skills before the stress of a new school move occurs. For girls who begin puberty early, the move to middle school comes just at the peak of the changes caused by sexual maturation. This adds to the stress of that experience. For most boys, the move from middle school to high school comes just at the peak of these physical changes.

The move to junior high school creates a different situation. The change of setting comes at the same time as the use of formal operational thought and physical maturation for girls. For boys, however, the entry into junior high occurs after the process of sexual maturation is well under way. We would expect the change to the middle school to be better for cognitive growth and for social development for girls. It postpones the stress of school change until girls have had time to adjust to these major developmental challenges. By the end of middle school, girls are better able to use their new cognitive abilities to solve the social problems and the academic challenges of the high school setting. The move to junior high school may be better for social and emotional development for boys. In junior high, boys can experience the changes of physical maturation without direct competition from a more mature male group. The eight-year elementary school pattern seems to put stress on the average and late maturing boys. For other students it presents a familiar setting for the consolidation of developmental gains. One limitation of the eight-year elementary school setting is the limited resources and opportunities that can be provided for the older students. We can see, then, that each school change is a source of stress for the young adolescent. The process of adaptation depends on the person's pattern of growth and the demands of the new setting. One question is whether we consistently make it harder for some children through the predominance of one system.

There is some evidence that this might be the case. In a study of the self-image during adolescence, 1,917 students in grades 3 to 12 were interviewed (Simmons, Rosenberg, & Rosenberg, 1973). Children in the age range 12 to 14 showed significantly more self-consciousness. There was greater instability in their self-image, lower estimates of self-esteem, a more negative view of how others perceive them, and more depressed feelings than children in the age range 8 to 11. Twelve-year-olds who were in elementary school were compared with 12-year-olds in the first year of junior high school. The junior high students showed lower self-

Luis Medina

*In junior high, children adjust to a new,
more demanding school setting. At the
same time, major physical and cognitive
changes are taking place.*

esteem scores, more self-consciousness, and greater instability in their self-image.

The transition from elementary to junior high appears to be more difficult for females than for males. Children in two school systems were compared, one that had a kindergarten to eighth grade and one that had a junior high for grades seven, eight, and nine. More seventh-grade girls in the junior high school showed low self-esteem than seventh-grade girls in the kindergarten to eight setting. The seventh-grade shift to a junior high school appears to be particularly difficult for girls who are maturing sexually during that year (Simmons, Blyth, & Bush, 1977).

Exclusion from school

In a report called *Children Out of School in America* (1974), the Children's Defense Fund (CDF) provided information about the many

Living laboratory 8·1

ADJUSTMENT IN ELEMENTARY SCHOOL

Purpose: To clarify the social characteristics of the classroom group that have an impact on adjustment.

Method: Think back to your *best* and your *worst* years in elementary school. Try to recall as much of the detail about the teacher and the class as you can. Then go back over the variables discussed in the section on the classroom group and try to fill in information on each variable for both the best and the worst class. Your data record might look like this:

	Best class 2d grade	Worst class 5th grade
Class size	About 40.	About 40.
Homogeneity or heterogeneity of group members	Can't remember.	I was the youngest in the class; everyone else had already turned ten.
Pattern of interaction	Lots of chances to talk with others.	No talking or you would lose points.
Teacher's leadership style	Ms. F. let us do lots of group projects; she always smiled a lot.	Ms. T. was very strict. She gave every student a rating on behavior every day.

Results: What are the differences on these variables between the best and the worst class?

Discussion: To what extent are these environmental variables responsible for your perceptions of best and worst class?

Would you say that your own level of development and your own needs were more responsible for your adjustment than the environmental characteristics?

What would you advise a child to do if he or she were in your "worst" class?

Are there any coping strategies that might have helped you in that situation?

children who were not enrolled in school. The data are taken from the 1970 Census and from a CDF survey of 6,500 households in 30 areas of nine states. The census data showed that (U.S. Bureau of the Census, 1970) 1,984,432 children between the ages of 7 and 17 were not enrolled in school. This figure included 85,194 children who were institutionalized. In urban areas 3.8 percent of the children are not enrolled. In rural areas, the percentage is 5.3 percent. Of all white children, 3.9 percent are not enrolled. Of nonwhite children 6.0 percent are not enrolled.

The CDF survey reported a variety of reasons that children were not in school. All states except Mississippi have compulsory school attendance laws. Nonetheless, various states permit exemptions from school attendance for reasons including the following:

1. The child presents a danger to others (a reason for exemption in six states).
2. Completion of a specified grade (a reason for exemption in nine states).
3. Married, pregnant, or a parent (a reason for exemption in two states).
4. Physical, mental, or emotional disability (a reason for exemption in 48 states).
5. Distance from school (a reason for exemption in 13 states).
6. Suspension or expulsion (a reason for exemption in six states).

When children were asked why they were not in school, they gave a number of answers from being afraid to go to school (2.4 percent) to not being able to afford the book rental fees or other school fees involved (4.5 percent). The cases of Dale McCutcheon, age 13, and Theresa Engler, age 12, illustrate some of the personal frustrations that push children away from school (see Case 8·1). For these two children and others, the decision to leave school protects them from continued attacks on their sense of worth. Schools sometimes push away children who are pregnant, who have been expelled, or who enroll too late. Finally, some children who are physically or emotionally handicapped, who live too far from school, or who do not speak English need more assistance in order to attend school than the school is prepared to give.

ADJUSTMENT IN HIGH SCHOOL

The high school is the main setting where adolescents spend time away from home. High schools are large, complex institutions with a variety of educational and socialization goals, yet, these are not the elements of high school that seems to make the deepest impressions on young adolescents. Rather, it is the tempo, the climate, the relationships, and the activities that provide a rich set of images about the meaning of high school. We think of the high school setting as a lively convergence

---

Case 8·1

TWO CHILDREN WHO ARE OUT OF SCHOOL

Dale, 13

Dale McCutcheon, 13, is in the eighth grade of his local public school. He is an eneuretic, a bedwetter.

Dale's school had a policy requiring every eighth grade boy to spend a long weekend in the country to learn to live outdoors. Most boys adore this trip, Dale dreaded it as early as fifth grade after he heard it was compulsory. When the time came, he begged his mother to keep him home, but she refused.

The first night of the excursion, Dale woke several times and cautiously felt around his waist, but everything was dry. The next day his spirits were high and he enjoyed learning how to make food from wild plants and to classify mushrooms. The secret problem he had carried for so long seemingly had vanished.

It was different the second night. He did not awake until morning when the sounds of boys talking and laughing startled him. The two boys sharing his tent had discovered the wetness. They hounded Dale mercilessly and he wept. The boys told the counselors, who lectured him. Later, someone cracked a joke about Dale's accident and all the boys exploded with laughter. Humiliated, he wanted to run away and dreaded the thought of returning to school. The third night he remained dry but the damage had been done.

Dale never told his parents about the incident. He refused to go to school for two days and pretended he was sick. But by the end of the week, his sister had become the butt of other children's insults about Dale, and she reported the incident to her parents who were painfully embarrassed and angry with Dale.

Two weeks after the excursion, the principal of Dale's school asked his parents to come in for a meeting. The principal wasted no time outlining the seriousness of Dale's situation, for the boy as well as for the school. The problem was not, he explained, the other children. "They'll probably forget the whole thing in another week or so. It's Dale's teachers—how do we know he won't just, you know, pop off at any time in one of his classes?" Mrs. McCutcheon explained that it was only a nighttime problem but the principal replied, "We can't take any chances. I can't stop him from going to school. But I can stop him from going to this school and that's exactly what I'm doing. The boy's out for a month, or until a time you can prove to us that he is able to control himself, night and day."

And so Dale was out of school.

"What do we do?" Mrs. McCutcheon asked over and over again. "They don't want him and there's no way of knowing how long he'll be like this. I've read books on it. Everybody says it disappears. But when's that going to be? How do we know he might not be too old for school by the time he's cured? What's going to be worse for him, being a bedwetter or a boy without a proper education? You think people like Dale's principal ever think of that?"

Theresa, 12

Theresa Engler, a 12-year-old black girl from one of Boston's poorest neighborhoods, had been absent from school. No one took much notice of Theresa's absence of several days in October. In November, her teacher reported that she had returned to school but had been absent quite often for weeks thereafter. She had never spoken with her about the absences, or whether the girl was in danger of failing because of them. "There's no time," her teacher said, "I've got 26 Theresas."

Of the 20 or so school days in October, Theresa had missed 15. In the first week and a half of November she attended school once. She was, in effect, out of school. But she was in good health, and no particular incident had happened that would have kept her from attending.

Theresa's grandmother knew what was wrong. "She won't go because she's ashamed that we ain't got anything, in the way of material things I mean. She's afraid that folks will find out just how poor she is, and she don't want them knowing anything about this. Girl has only got a couple of dresses and after she wore them day after day she thought she shouldn't go to school anymore. People would be laughing at her," she said, "cause she always looked the same. Same goes for her shoes. She says they look like boy's shoes, and the other kids are going to laugh at them. The children go to the cafeteria at lunchtime and she never has any money to buy things. She's always hungry and she doesn't have the nerve to ask them for money, otherwise like I told you, they'll see how bad off she is. Then another thing. She used to like to talk in class. But then the teacher started to ask the children about their homes and their families, and what it was like outside of school. She knew they'd get around to her and she'd have to tell them about this house, and the street, and us too. She must have got scared, or ashamed, like I said before. She couldn't do it. I think that's when she stopped going."

Source: Children's Defense Fund, *Children out of School in America* (Washington, D.C.: Children's Defense Fund, 1974). Reprinted with permission of the Children's Defense Fund, 1520 New Hampshire Avenue, N.W., Washington, D.C.

of adolescents and adults, functioning in some moderate degree of order or rhythm. Periodically this rhythm is interrupted by explosive outpourings of feelings, spontaneous laughter, ridiculous antics, and loudspeaker messages from the principal's office.

High school requires a complicated mental map. This map must include settings, people, activities, and time. From the point of view of the students, the important high school settings may include the bus ride to school, the coffee shop across the street, the bathrooms, certain sections of hallway, or a particular set of back hall stairs. These settings may be far more important than the more obvious settings like the classrooms, the athletic fields, and the cafeteria. "Being in high school" becomes a quality of the person. Even when the student is away from school or on vacation, the phrase "I'm a high school student" identifies their life framework. High school is perceived as a time of one's life.

United Press International

The importance of high school social life stems from adolescents' needs to be with others.

Adults often look back with nostalgia at this period. The meaning of this period, the positive and the negative, continues to be important in adulthood. It is a time of physical, cognitive, social, and emotional awakening. It is the arena in which the energy and confusion of adolescent growth influence one's life. Given what we know about psychological development during early adolescence, what are the challenges created by the high school environment for personal adjustment? Our discussion of adjustment in high school will explore daily life, adaptation to the high school, and academic tracking. Because the high school is such a central institution for career choice, we are especially concerned with academic tracking and its effect on decision making.

A typical high school day

Let us look at the daily experiences of a few students as they attend high school. From the following cases we begin to see the interaction between student needs, talents, and school environments.

Case 8·2

BRAD

Brad attends a large, urban high school. He has a vocational curriculum and is in a work-study program. He comes to school on a city bus which is usually crowded early in the morning. After a half-hour ride during which he stands most of the way, Brad goes to his locker and talks with a few friends. He is in his homeroom for attendance by 8:00 A.M. At 8:10 he reports to the machine shop. There is a car that needs a tune-up and a carburetor that needs repair. These projects are the focus of Brad's work for the morning. He works in the shop for an hour and a half. He leaves for two periods for math and English classes. During the math class, one of the kids falls asleep and starts snoring loudly at the back of the room. The class breaks up, and there isn't much more work done that period. In English, a student teacher is in charge of the lesson. She asks Brad to read a poem out loud. When he is done, she asks him to say what it meant. Brad is embarrassed. He just shrugs his shoulders. He tells her that he is working on a big project in the shop. He asks to be excused early to get back to it. He returns to the shop, where he completes his work on the tune-up by noon. He asks his teacher whether he can leave the carburetor for the next day, since he has to be to work by 1:00. The teacher agrees, but points out that Brad works too slowly and that he just has to learn to speed things up.

Question 1. What is the stress on students who are trying to keep a job and at the same time going to high school?

Question 2. What problems might students encounter when trying to function in two very different classroom settings such as machine shop and English class?

Case 8·3

MARY

Mary is a senior at a small, private school in a large, urban area. She also rides the city bus to school, and she meets a lot of her friends along the way. As they ride, they are talking about college applications, where they want to go, and who has already heard from some schools. At school, Mary goes to her locker, grabs the books and notebooks for her first two classes, and goes to homeroom. There are announcements, and a brief discussion about the senior party.

In English class, they are reading the Book of Job. There is a lively argument about why Job suffered. Mary thinks that Job's suffering gave his life meaning. The class ends in an argument between a very religious student and an atheist about why humans believe in God.

In French class, the students rehearse a play. In art class, they begin designing the sets for the senior class play. There is some discussion about the design, Mary offers to draw up some quick sketches so that they can get an idea of how the different plans would look. While she is working, Clark, a boy in her class, sits down next to her. He starts talking about how badly he is going to feel to leave the school. After art class, they go to the students' lounge together and talk for a while more. Mary suddenly feels very sad herself. She is glad to be able to share her feelings with Clark. Then the conversation becomes more personal. Clark tells Mary that he has been fond of her for a very long time. He has always been too shy to say anything. Mary is surprised and confused. She is already

dating another boy. She has never really thought about Clark as anything other than a friend. Soon some other students come into the lounge and Mary goes off to her anthropology class. There are class reports, but Mary's mind wanders. She thinks about the conversation with Clark and the troubled feelings she has about it. Her mind is miles away when the teacher asks if the class has any questions. Embarrassed at having tuned out so completely, Mary looks at the clock and is glad to be moving on. She makes sure to have lunch with lots of other kids that day, trying to avoid Clark's gaze. After lunch there is a long rehearsal for the senior play. While Mary is back stage, Clark comes to talk to her again. He is upset. He tells her how deeply he cares for her. Mary tries to comfort him she explains her feelings, but nothing seems to help. Mary leaves school feeling sad, angry, and a little bit flattered.

Question 1. What are some of the adjustments that students must make in small, private schools that might not be necessary in a large, public school?

Question 2. What are some of the things in a school that foster close relationships with peers?

Case 8·4

PAUL

Paul is the fourth child in a family of six children. His mother and father both work. Mother is on the morning shift and father is on the afternoon and evening shift. Paul usually leaves home without breakfast to ride the school bus to the suburban school he attends. On the way, he is quiet, not interested in joining in the gossip, the teasing, or the conversations about sports that fill the bus. He goes to his homeroom for attendance. Then he goes to his first class, which is biology. Paul has about a sixth-grade reading level. He usually does not read the homework

assignments. If he does read some of them, he usually does not understand much of what he reads. The biology teacher is describing the parts of a plant, and Paul's stomach is rumbling. When it rumbles very loudly, a student in the next seat starts to giggle. Pretty soon the back of the class is giggling. Paul cuts his next class and goes over to the fast-food restaurant across from school. He has a sandwich, plays pinball, and talks with some of the boys who are there. Paul buys a few "joints" from one of them. He goes into the bathroom to get high. When he is feeling good, he walks around the school neighborhood. He wanders around some of the stores, and then drifts back to the school grounds in time to catch the bus back home.

Question 1. What aspects of the high school environment might be contributing to Paul's isolation?

Question 2. In what ways can Paul's behavior be viewed as adaptive?

Case 8·5

TERRY

Terry always goes to bed late after finishing his homework. His parents must work hard to wake him up. Breakfast is ready by the time he struggles into the kitchen. He eats with the family. He gets his homework and books. He thinks about whom he will try to see during the day and what meetings he must go to after school. He is a junior in a large high school in a city of about 100,000 people. His father drives Terry to school. Along the way they pick up two friends. During the drive they talk about courses, the prom, and which parties they will go to after the basketball game on Friday night.

When they arrive at school, Terry proceeds to the main entrance to have a cigarette with some guys who are active in clubs and sports. They talk about activities, team records, and girls. At 8:25 Terry goes to his locker to leave his lunch and pick up his books for his first three classes. He walks to the counselors' office to see his friend the debate coach and Student Council adviser, Mr. Collins. They quickly talk over several matters, and then Terry heads to another locker room to meet his girlfriend. She has been waiting for five minutes. She asks why he can't be there on time. They walk through the halls together. They talk about many things and casually saying hello to other students who pass by. They stop at the school office. Terry picks up a batch of announcements for a Student Council dance on Saturday night. He will post them around the school during the day.

At 9:00 A.M. a bell rings and the students all head for different classes. Terry drops his girlfriend at her English class and arrives at his biology class before the second bell rings. The teacher asks questions. Terry answers periodically to keep things moving and is somewhat bored as the teacher tries to get the slower students to talk. In the ten minutes between classes Terry walks with a few friends to a college preparatory English class. The group talk about basketball, Student Council, romances, and the English teacher.

The English teacher picks a panel of several of Terry's friends. Terry escapes the spotlight. He listens while his friends discuss the play. He feels uneasy when the teacher systematically embarrasses one student after another. Only Mel Garber is able to provide reasonably good answers to her probing questions. Terry is glad to be able to relax during this class.

After English, Terry rushes to meet his girl friend and walk her to history. He is glad to see her. He gets all the information about the first two classes. After he drops her off, he attends his American history class. The teacher talks about the U.S. Constitution. Terry prepares his Debate Club agenda while listening. From history, Terry and several boys go to gym. They play a game that the coaches made up, called "mass murder." Terry plays strongly enough not to be labeled a "sissy" but not so intensely as to risk injury. Terry is very hungry after gym, but he must get through French class before lunch. Luckily, the French teacher is a bit of a comedian. Terry is one of the best students in French, so the teacher rarely calls on him. He tries to keep up to date, but is glad to see the other students called on. When no one else can conjugate an irregular verb, the teacher calls on Terry, and luckily he remembers. The teacher smiles when his hero comes through, and Terry is glad he stayed up late the night before memorizing his French.

After French, Terry goes to his locker to get his lunch. He stands in the "milk" line to get a drink. He then goes to the table where he and some friends always sit. They talk about classes, sports, and girls until everyone is finished eating. Terry then heads toward the school entrance to have a cigarette. After lunch he attends typing class and study hall. During study hall he talks with the teacher about the Drama Club. When the final school bell rings, he meets his girlfriend.

They go to the Debate Club meeting. He is the president of the Debate Club and leads the meeting. He talks with his friend the counselor (who is the club adviser) after the meeting and then goes home. He has dinner with his family. They watch television together. Terry does his homework, talks to his girlfriend on the phone, and goes to bed.

Question 1. What are the responses of teachers and peers to students who are highly involved in school activities?

Question 2. What are the motives that direct Terry's involvement in school?

Adjustment to the high school environment

When one looks closely, one notices important differences among institutions that are called high schools. Differences exist in physical design, school size, curricular emphasis, control or surveillance, and the quality and quantity of interactions among students and faculty. All of these dimensions contribute to the quality of the environment to which a high school student must adjust.

The question of adjustment asks about the ways in which students with diverse abilities and motives respond to the expectations, demands, and opportunities of their school. Through a process of interaction, students change in response to environmental realities. Schools also change in response to the needs of students. Neither the person nor the organization is static. Each has a history and a future.

What are some of the ways students adjust to their schools? The examples that follow suggest only a few. The physical design of the school lends itself to some activities. In the older school buildings, there were locker rooms in which students would congregate. In more modern school buildings, lockers line the hallways, limiting opportunities for student privacy. Students in new schools create their own territories or regions where friendship groups or classmates congregate. In one school, each class met at a certain window ledge or area of the corridor. Sophomores did not sit on the junior ledge (Newman, 1971). Most schools have a deviant group. The students who want to smoke marijuana or drink alcohol may be found in one area of the athletic field, in a bathroom, or in a part of the basement.

Adjustment also takes place in response to the size of the school. In the smaller schools, there is the greater need for students to run activities and to populate school events. This need leads to greater student involvement and stronger commitment. Even students who are not heavily involved in school activities feel a strong sense of obligation to the smaller school. This kind of psychological investment in smaller schools seems to contradict the trend toward eliminating small high schools in favor of larger, centralized schools. The larger schools can offer a greater variety of resources and greater academic expertise. However, the superiority of resources is not matched by greater student commitment. The fact that strong commitments occur in the smaller schools has contributed to the "school-within-a-school" model. These schools are divided into smaller subunits to preserve the atmosphere of the small school.

Schools also differ in the quantity of student-teacher interaction. Where the quantity of interaction is relatively high, students have more personal, informal interactions with teachers. Teachers are more likely to become objects of identification. Students and teachers show more agreement about standards and beliefs. Where the quantity of interaction between students and teachers is low, students are more involved with peers. In such schools, the peer culture determines standards for behavior (P. Newman, 1979; Iacovetta, 1975).

Even within the same school, groups adjust differently to the same resources. Gottlieb (1975) described two such groups as the "elites" and the "deviants." The elites are a high-status group. They are visible participants in school activities and athletics. They are academically competitive. They are concerned about their plans after graduation, particularly their admission to college. The deviants are a low-status group. They are not highly involved in either academic or extracurricular activities. They are identified primarily by their excessive use of drugs.

The elites make use of school personnel for help in problem solving. Because of the involvement of elites in athletics, the coach is an important school adult for them. In contrast, peers are rarely mentioned as sources of help. Elites see peers as troubled by the same problems as they are. They don't have the experience or skills to help.

Deviants look for help from people who are open, sincere, and accepting. This guides them to people who will accept them for who they are, without forcing them to put on a front. Deviants are much more likely to find helpers among friends, siblings, or parents than school personnel. They may identify only one or two school adults as approachable. Any person who can help a deviant gain insight into his or her own problems is a valued helper. Experience, status, or authority do not make school adults resources if these adults view this group critically.

A final example of adjustment is dropping out. One can think of degrees of involvement with school from "highly involved" to "very alienated." Dropping out might be viewed as an extreme expression of alienation. Studies of dropouts suggest that the social status of the student's family is a very strong predictor of who will drop out. Family background is also a strong predictor of school success (Elliott, Voss, & Wendling, 1966; Bachman, Green, & Wirtanen, 1971; Alexander & Eckland, 1975). Students from lower social status levels are less likely to plan to go to college. They are less likely to have good test scores. They are more likely to experience early school failure. Although lower status students may have high aspirations for their future occupation, they are confronted by the daily reality of low status and academic failure. Due to their inability to conform to their teachers' desires and to their feelings that school does not teach useful information, these students become increasingly unhappy at school.

The following responses from students who had dropped out of school suggest some of the ways that the school is seen as the primary *alienating* factor (Bachman et al., 1971, pp. 155,157).

● *alienating*—causing the withdrawal of people's affections from an object of former attachment.

"I was mostly discouraged because I wasn't passing."

"I was failing, so I quit school. I was working and didn't have time to study. I wasn't interested in it either."

"School in general. It didn't teach me true things. It didn't teach me how to cope with society once I got out of the school doors."

"They wanted me to do too much of what they wanted and none of what I wanted."

"They said I could drop out or they'd drop me out. They said I was a rebel. I wore my hair long."

These examples suggest that students can reach a point at which the effort to stay in school no longer seems worthwhile. What is more, the immediate rewards of having a full-time job may seem quite appealing.

How enduring are the above adjustments to school? There is not much evidence which helps answer this question. What there is suggests that it depends on the degree of similarity between the high school and the environments the person gets involved in later. Students at small high schools, for example, are more likely to remain high participants if they attend small colleges than if they attend large colleges (Baird, 1969). Students who receive good grades in high school are likely to achieve greater occupational success than students with low high school grades (Hess, 1963). People are likely to participate in activities if they go on to college or join the military service. These are places where structured activities are made available. They are less likely to endure if people go to work, get married, and have children (Jones, 1958; Hess, 1963).

Adjustments, such as dropping out of school, are not necessarily repeated in the future. Dropouts without a diploma have more trouble finding work than do high school graduates. Those who do find employment do not earn lower salaries. They were as satisfied with their jobs as those with diplomas. The dropouts did not feel the same discouragement and alienation at work that they felt in school. In fact, close to 75 percent of dropouts expected to return to school to get their diploma (Bachman et al., 1971). This suggests what happens after high school can reverse a previous adjustment. A new environment can offer new opportunities for a person to develop their skills.

Academic tracking

Because of the compulsory attendance laws, students who are very different in ability go to high school. Some communities support specialized high schools to meet the needs of students. Vocational schools and schools for the gifted, such as the Bronx High School of Science, are examples of schools that are designed for students with special needs and abilities. Most comprehensive schools use many strategies to adapt to the range of student abilities. Thomas and Thomas (1965) list ten of the most frequent administrative techniques that are designed to respond to the many levels of competence among students.

1. Ability groupings.
2. Special classes for slow learners.
3. Special classes for the gifted.
4. Other special classes.
5. Ungraded classes.
6. Retention and acceleration.
7. Frequent promotion plans.
8. Contract and unit plans.
9. Team teaching.
10. Parallel track plan.

In the parallel track plan, students are assigned to programs that are supposed to match their ability and interests. The tracks are not always the same in different high schools. One plan has four tracks:

1. Basic or Special Academic, for slow learners.
2. General, a vocational program for students who do not plan to attend college.
3. Regular, for college-bound students.
4. Honors, for intellectually gifted students (C. F. Hansen, 1964; Hobson, 1967).

Other track plans offer even more programs. They may provide fine arts, business education, vocational education, practical arts, general, or college-bound tracks (Tanner, 1965). In most track systems, some general education courses are required for everyone. This means that all students will take courses in freshman English, U.S. History, or Biology. Usually these courses are taught at different levels of difficulty in the college-bound general, and vocational tracks.

Assignment to a track is based on six factors: aptitude, achievement, teachers' opinions, elementary and junior high school performance, social maturity, and the student's interests (Tanner, 1965). This assignment usually occurs during junior high school or upon entrance to high school. Two criticisms of the procedures for track assignment have been raised. First, the assignment to tracks often discriminates against low-income and minority-group children. These children tend not to be assigned to the college-bound track.

Second, the assignment to tracks is based on past performance.

The photography of H. Armstrong Roberts

Academic tracking is intended to provide specialized training for post-high-school careers.

There is some evidence to suggest that early maturers perform better on verbal tasks than do late maturers. In contrast, late maturers perform better on spatial tasks than do early maturers (Weber, 1976). Decisions about high school tracking are usually made during the seventh- and eighth-grade years. Young adolescents may be directed toward one educational pattern before their mental abilities are fully developed.

In an assessment of the tracking system, Schafer and Olexa (1971) compared the effects of tracking in two comprehensive high schools. Five findings of this study reflect the impact of the tracking experience at the two schools. First, even when IQ and previous school records were taken into account, students whose fathers held blue-collar jobs were more likely to be in the noncollege-bound tracks than were students whose fathers held white-collar jobs. Second, black students were more likely than white students to be in the noncollege-bound tracks. These track assignments were relatively permanent. Third, about 7 percent of the college-bound students moved into the noncollege programs. About 7 percent of the noncollege students moved into the college-bound programs. These patterns might not be very important if students in all the tracks were having intellectually stimulating, positive academic experiences. However, Schafer and Olexa did not find this to be the case. A fourth finding showed that 73 percent of the noncollege group showed grades in the low or low-average categories. Only 39 percent of the college group had grades in this range. Looking at grade change between the 10th, 11th, and 12th grades, the researchers found that students whose grades were in the 2.5–1.5 range were more likely to show drops in grades if they were in the noncollege track. Students in this same grade range were more likely to show improvements in grades if they were in the college track. These findings suggest that being in a noncollege track lowered the students' records. In contrast, the college track seemed to better the students' records.

Finally, the track system seems to make adjustment harder for some students. As illustrated in Table 8•1, students in the noncollege tracks showed less involvement in extracurricular activities, higher delinquency rates, and a greater dropout rate. It would appear that the school values the college-bound students and prides itself on their future accomplishments. The noncollege-bound students experience less reward and less encouragement for hard work. Involvement in the school and getting good grades have less payoff for a student who is planning to leave

TABLE 8•1
Differences between tracks in extracurricular participation, dropout rates, and delinquency rates, standardized for father's occupation, IQ, and previous achievement

	Activities				
	3 or more	1–2	None	Total	N
College prep	41%	35%	24%	100%	512
Noncollege prep	15	35	50	100	199
	Dropout rate				
	Graduated	Transferred	Dropped out	Total	N
College prep	88%	8%	4%	100%	681
Noncollege prep	74	7	19	100	326
	Delinquency rate				
	Nondelinquent	Delinquent*	Total	N	
College prep	95%	5%	100	708	
Noncollege prep	88	12	100	354	

* Determined by juvenile court records.
Source: Adapted from W. E. Schafer and C. Olexa. *Tracking and opportunity: The locking-out process and beyond.* (Scranton, Pa.: Chandler, 1971), pp. 42, 46, 48.

school for work. Many teachers have lower expectations for the noncollege-bound students.

The tracking system places social stress on some students which makes it difficult for them to succeed. Some students are faced with a dual message that says they should stay in school but that they are not really valued in that setting. Many students cope with this by finding satisfying experiences outside the school setting. They come to hold a negative view of school because the school does not value them or the activities in which they participate. Other students become angry at the school. Others become depressed about their abilities.

ADJUSTMENT IN COLLEGE

The transition from high school to college involves many changes for adolescents. Our discussion of adjustment to college will center on the decision to attend college, the impact of college on cognitive growth, and the college as a setting for the socialization of values. Because the college provides so many experiences for students, we are concerned with the impact of college on personal standards.

The decision to attend college

In 1977, over 11 million Americans were enrolled in some type of college program (*Yearbook of Higher Education,* 1979). American college freshmen can be described as follows: Over 90 percent are either 18 or 19. Over 90 percent have graduated from high school. Almost half of the women and one third of the men have a high school average of B+ or better. They tend to come from families that are relatively well-to-do. Less than one fourth of them say that their parents' annual income is less than $10,000 (Grant & Lind, 1976). In 1978–79, the estimated charges for room, board, and tuition were $1,794 a year at public undergraduate schools and $3,855 at private undergraduate schools (Simon & Frankel, 1976). Because of steadily rising costs, a major concern of college freshmen and their families tends to be financing education.

Going to college is a process of negotiation and decision making for the student and for the college. Some public universities and community colleges have an open admissions policy. These schools will admit graduates of regular daytime high school programs who have a minimum grade point average of C and are residents of the state. Among the private, "prestige" universities and colleges, however, there is an active selection procedure. Selection standards have been developed to get a balanced class of freshmen. There are five groups that try to select schools that have more applicants than they can accommodate (Moll, 1978). The intellects are students who have high Scholastic Aptitude Test (SAT) scores and have earned excellent grades in difficult high school courses. These students are desired by the faculty. They provide the creativity and intellectual stimulation that make college teaching exciting. The special talent group are students who have a skill that is particularly valued by the college. While this skill may be in music, drama, or art, it is usually in sports. Colleges try to select the outstanding athletic talent for the sports they emphasize. The third group is made up of children of alumni. These students bring alumni support. The fourth group is made up of the "all-American kids." These are students who will help run the school organizations, the student government, clubs, and activities. They will carry the reputation of the college to the community. Most applicants fall into this group. They are, therefore, competing against the largest number of other applicants. The last group is called the "social conscience" group. These students are admitted as part of the college's commitment to enroll minority students in proportion to their numbers in the population. In most admissions procedures students do not compete for space against all other applicants. Rather, they compete with the other students who have been placed in a similar admissions category. In this way, each college tries to pick the best mix of groups that it can get.

High school students who are deciding about college make their decisions on the basis of their high school achievements, their career aspirations, the reputation of the school, the geographic location of the school, and financial considerations. Because of rising costs, public education is becoming more attractive. Students have high expectations for a career "payoff" from their college degree. College attendance continues to be a way of improving social status. In 1977, the median income for males 25 years or older who had finished four years or more of college was $20,625. The income for males who had only finished high school was $15,434. The median income for female high school graduates in 1977 was $8,894. The median income of females who had completed four years or more of college was $12,656 (*Yearbook of Higher Education,* 1979). Students continue to believe that a college education helps one to get a good job. College is also seen as the training ground for specialized careers. High school students also expect the college to provide a good social and intellectual atmosphere.

What do high school students expect from a college? Goodman and Feldman (1975) asked high school seniors who had been accepted at colleges to rate their ideal college and the actual college that they would be attending. The qualities of an ideal college were (Goodman & Feldman, 1975, p. 152):

● *ambience*—**the mood or tone of a place.**

Permissive *ambience:* "Permissive attitudes toward drugs," "permissive attitudes toward sexual activities," "opportunity to do just about what you want."

Primary-group emphasis: "Mostly small classes," "close contact with faculty," "friendly student body," "many cultural activities."

Liberal arts emphasis: "Emphasis on liberal arts," "emphasis on arts," "can meet academic pressure without strain."

Specialized and useful training reputation: "Has the special curriculum I want," "good reputation for helping to get into graduate school," "good reputation for getting a job," "a lot of hard work but worth it," "meet different kinds of people."

An inexpensive and convenient college: "Close to home," "relatively mild winter," "low cost."

A high-quality institution: "High scholastic standards," "faculty of high academic quality," "intellectual stimulation," "small city."

Opportunities for student involvement: "An opportunity to become politically active," "student voice in administration," "good athletic program."

In the semester before attending college, seniors felt their ideal college was better than the school that they planned to attend. Two years later, while the students were college sophomores, they were asked to rate their own college and their ideal college again. In four areas, the initial evaluation of the actual college was better than the evaluation of that college after the student had been there for two years. The students reported that there was less primary-group emphasis, less of a specialized and useful training reputation, less emphasis on high-quality instruction, and less opportunity for student involvement than they had expected. The students demonstrated that they had had higher expectations of the college they chose before they entered the college than they had after they had been enrolled in it for some time. Over time the students felt that the quality of the school was less important in their definition of an ideal college. Perhaps they became more sensitive to reality and more suspicious of reputation after having been in college for a while.

Most adolescents are not very well informed when they make a decision about college. Decisions tend to be guided by such things as the reputation of a school, convenience, cost, and the availability of particular professional programs. Adolescents know very little about the quality of instruction, the teacher-student relationship, the availability of laboratory or library resources, or the quality of dormitory life. These and other critical aspects of college life are left to be discovered as part of the "college experience."

One might argue that part of this lack of information is the fault of students and parents who do not actively search it out. Among competent high school seniors, however, it has been observed that a great deal of effort is used in trying to obtain information about college (Silber, 1961). These students wrote to colleges, talked with college-age friends, visited campuses, and talked with teachers or counselors. They actively tried to get a sense of what college might be like.

Many colleges do not tend to provide the most useful information to future students. For example, Speegle (1969) analyzed the kinds of information that appeared in college catalogs. He found no description of the informal social atmosphere of the schools. He also found that most catalog descriptions were not very similar to students' views of

John Penzari

Students have higher expectations about college before they enter than they have after they have been enrolled awhile.

colleges. Baird (1974) tried to make information about colleges more accurate for incoming students. He offered colleges free tests and scoring services for a questionnaire on student and college characteristics. This questionnaire would provide applicants with information about the rules, the amount of faculty-student interaction, student activism, intellectual difficulty, the nonacademic activities, and the flexibility of the curriculum. Only 25 percent of the 200 colleges involved in Baird's project made use of the questionnaire results. Students are left to learn by experience whether their choice of a college will make the contributions to personal growth that they had thought they would at the beginning.

The impact of college on cognitive growth

In order to understand intellectual growth during the college years, it is necessary to look in two different directions. First, as Cottle emphasizes, there is the personal experience of being a student. We must try to get a glimpse of the ways students function in the classroom. We consider their emotional involvements with teachers, exams, and grades. We need to know the extent to which they experience intellectual stimulation. Second, we can look at the more objective measures of academic performance, including grades, honors, graduate study, and evidence of new

---

Case 8·6

REMEMBRANCES OF COLLEGE

If my college days ended two decades ago (in the late 1950s), my dreams of it have not. Several times a year I awake from a fitful sleep, perspiring, anxious. It is always the same dream: an examination is coming up and I am wholly unprepared for it. As I attempt to discipline myself and get down to serious study, I remember my other courses and their examinations and suddenly, with terror, I realize that I cannot pass, that I cannot graduate, that the degree I genuinely thought I had earned was illusory. I remain years away from the successful completion of my studies, while everyone else is progressing normally and successfully. In my dream I tell myself, this is only a dream; you know you have finished your work, you have earned your diploma. No, I tell myself, in the past it was a dream, but this is real; this time it is actually happening. I am still in college, well on my way to abysmal failure, humiliation, and quite possibly dismissal. And it is the most portentious moment in my life."

Source: T. J. Cottle, *College: Reward and Betrayal.* (Chicago: University of Chicago Press, 1977), p. 3. © 1977 by The University of Chicago Press.

---

intellectual skills. The objective measures may be what scholarships, graduate admissions, and hiring practices are based on. They do not tell the whole story of intellectual adjustment to college.

We can begin to understand the process of intellectual adjustment to college by examining some of the student styles that have been observed by researchers. In a study of introductory psychology courses, Mann et al. (1970) describe eight groups of students. These student groups showed different patterns of involvement with the work of the course. They reacted differently to the teacher. They expressed different emotions during the course. For some of the groups, the work of the course did not seem to be very important. Table 8.2 lists the eight groups, the number of males and females in each group, and a description of each group. The largest group, called the anxious-dependent students, had constant anxiety about grades and exams. In class they tried to "please the teacher." At the same time, they suspected that they would not be graded fairly. Becker, Geer, and Hughes (1968) found a similar group in their study of the students at the University of Kansas. These students depend on their

TABLE 8·2
Student styles

Cluster	Males	Females	Description
The compliant students	5	7	Consistently task oriented.
The anxious-dependent students	12	15	Angry on the inside but frightened on the outside; anxious about being evaluated.
The discouraged workers	3	1	Involved in class but discouraged about themselves.
The independents	8	2	Older students self-confident and somewhat detached from classroom issues.
The heroes	10		Involvement in the class includes both productivity and hostile resentment.
The snipers	7	3	Low investment and frequent attacks on the teacher.
The attention seekers	5	6	Social orientation; trying to please by showing off, bragging, or joking.
The silent students	8	12	Fewer than 20 scorable acts for the whole semester

Source: Adapted from R. D. Mann et al. *The College Classroom: Conflict, Change, and Learning* (New York: John Wiley & Sons, Inc., 1970).

grade point average for staying in school, for scholarships, and membership in fraternities or sororities.

The next largest group of students are the silent students. Many students do not take advantage of the opportunities for interaction that college provides. The students in this group are either afraid of the teacher's authority or of their own possible failure. They became passive in order to avoid conflict and failure. Meanwhile, they have private reactions to the class. These private thoughts may include feelings of distance, feelings of being overlooked, and feelings that they will be admired for their silence and passivity.

Finally, there are two groups who are openly hostile toward the teacher. They are called the heroes and the snipers. The hidden anger of the anxious-dependent students and the silent students openly expressed by these groups. The heroes and snipers have strong feelings about the teacher's authority. They attack the teacher's competence. They assert their individuality by not agreeing with the teachers. From the teacher's point of view, the difference between the heroes and the snipers is important. The latter will never become involved in the work of the class. The former can be "won over." They may provide an element of creativity that can make class exciting.

Students seem to resent the way many teachers behave. Mass testing, large classes, and teachers who read their lectures or appear bored with class are a disappointment to most students. As one college junior puts it:

> Yes, I have been turned off by a few professors. They didn't have a positive attitude about what they were doing. To them it was just another class to teach. This was most common in introductory classes, which are primarily designed as distribution fillers. The attitude was that most of the students wouldn't be continuing in that particular area, so why bother spending a lot of time with them? (Michigan Alumnus, 1978, p. 7).

College attendance makes a lasting contribution to knowledge and competence. Hyman, Wright, and Reed (1975) looked at survey data that were collected in the early 1950s, the late 1950s, the early 1960s, and the late 1960s. For each period, they evaluated the answers of people in the age ranges 25–36, 37–48, 49–60, and 61–72. In each period, the less well-educated subjects had less knowledge than the more highly educated people. This was true for topics in civics, domestic policy, foreign affairs, science, geography, history, and the humanities. At each higher level of education from elementary to high school to college, the researchers found a broader range of knowledge and greater efforts to get new information.

Another way of looking at the impact of college on intellectual growth is to evaluate changes in educational accomplishments or goals. Only about 50 percent of entering freshmen actually earn their B.A. or B.S. in four years. Another 12 percent complete a degree in five years. Some students return to school years later to finish their undergraduate degree (Astin, 1977; El-Khawas & Bisconti, 1974). A number of things influence whether or not someone stays in college. These include: living in a dormitory; attending a four-year rather than a two-year college; and involvement in academic or social activities at college (Astin, 1977). Some studies found that students who attend large universities are more likely to drop out of college than are students who attend smaller colleges. The strength of this finding remains in question (Astin, 1975; Kamens, 1971).

Goals for graduate or professional training are also influenced by college. About half of the freshmen students have plans to take a postgraduate degree. This percentage increases to 65 percent four years later (Astin, 1977). The pattern of changes depends on the student's initial plans. About 40 percent of the freshmen expect to stop at the bachelor's degree. By the senior year, 53 percent of these students have plans to go on for a graduate degree. In contrast, about 30 percent of the freshmen plan to go on for a master's degree. Seventy-seven percent of those freshmen have the same plan by their senior year. Students who enter

"What do you mean you still want to be a cowboy?"

Reprinted by permission, The Wall Street Journal

college with plans to be a lawyer, doctor, dentist, or veterinarian are the most likely to keep their initial goals.

The college environment provides different reinforcements for males and females with regard to further education. "Although women earn higher grades than men, they are less likely to persist in college and to enroll in graduate or professional school. Moreover, women's aspirations for higher degrees decline, while men's aspirations increase during the undergraduate years" (Astin, 1977, p. 129).

The impact of the college environment on academic accomplishment must be viewed in light of the student's high school performance. High school grades give a good idea of how someone will do in college. Students who begin college with greater ability are likely to continue to do well. They make greater gains in academic skills and are more likely to graduate with honors (Astin, 1977). This pattern of success keeps on during the early work experiences of young adults. Good college grades often lead to completing postgraduate education and to higher starting salaries in most careers (Astin, 1977). College clearly makes a contribution to intellectual growth. However, the ability and skills that students bring to college also contribute.

College as a setting for the socialization of values

Many studies of the impact of college have looked at changes in opinions, beliefs, and standards. In their analysis of research done over a 40-year period, Feldman and Newcomb (1969) found that attending college had a liberalizing effect on these areas. Decreases in giving opinions as facts, submitting to people in authority, sticking to established religious customs, and rigidity took place in people who attended college. Increasing openness to artistic experiences took place in these people. Questions have been raised about these changes. Is the liberalizing trends the same for students with all kinds of occupational goals and at all kinds of colleges? Does it only hold true for special groups of students at some colleges? Is there a liberalizing trend among noncollege students who are the same age? In other words, is maturation at work, or is the change really due to the college environment? Astin's (1977) 1966–70 analysis provides answers to these questions. The areas of value change that are discussed here are *liberalism* versus *conservatism; altruism;* artistic, athletic, business, and musical interests; status needs; and religious beliefs.

● *liberal*—less constrained by traditional values and more open to accepting new moral standards.
● *conservative*—more constrained by traditional values and less open to accepting new moral standards.
● *altruism*—unselfish regard for or devotion to the welfare of others.

Liberalism versus conservatism.   Both student and college factors were linked with changes on a self-rating of liberal or conservative beliefs. Students who were likely to show increasing liberalism during college: had Jewish parents; were black; had high academic ability; and scored high on tests of artistic interest, altruism, pleasure-seeking, and drinking. The students who were more likely to show an increasing conservatism were female, older than the average freshman, highly religious, and interested in business. Greater increases in liberalism appeared among social science majors than among majors in engineering, mathematics, or the physical sciences. There is some evidence that social science majors begin their college years with more liberal views. These views are developed further by contact with liberal faculty and by campus conflicts over social issues (Rich, 1977).

Increases in liberalism are greatest at prestigious, selective four-year colleges. They are smaller at nonselective public universities, men's colleges, Protestant colleges, and southern colleges. Students who live in a dormitory and participate in student government show greater increases in liberalism. Students who are very involved in academics or athletics become more conservative over the college years.

While in college, some people become more and more open to accepting new moral standards. They become more liberal. Background, interests, personal qualities, major, and qualities of their college work together to produce this change. For many of these people, openness is the direction they were headed in before college. Other people become less open to accepting new moral standards. They become more conservative. Sex, age, religiousness, interests, major and qualities of their college produce this change. Once again, the change is in the direction people were headed in before college. Whether a person is open or closed to new moral standards has important implications for how one adjusts to moral questions in college and throughout the rest of life.

Religious beliefs. During the four years of college, there was decreasing commitment to religious denominations and increasing choice of no religion. Only 9 percent of freshman students had no religion. This group increased by 14.9 percent by the end of college. In contrast, there were 11 percent fewer Protestants, 5.7 percent fewer Roman Catholics, and 1 percent fewer Jewish students. Students who shared their parents' religious beliefs were less likely to drop these beliefs. Students who lived at home were more likely to retain their original religious beliefs. Two groups were likely not to have a religious choice at the end of four years of college. One was students whose parents have no religion. The other was students who attend selective, prestigious, nonsectarian colleges.

Adjustment to college involves value changes in moral standards. The change depends on personal and college qualities. Increased liberalism occurs at the higher status and selective schools. The increase is greater among students who live at school than among commuters. The increase is greater among social science majors, and among participants in student government. The increase in liberalism is less strong among athletes and among "scholars." These two groups may be relatively isolated from some of the more social experiences that produce liberal attitudes. The process of adopting more liberal values may be a result of: (1) greater satisfaction and confidence in one's own worth; and (2) greater awareness of the differences in standards and talents of others. In order for colleges to have a liberalizing influence the college role models must hold liberal views. The students must be in a situation that transmits those values.

With the exception of artistic interests, there is a declining interest in many values and on religion. College students become more selective about which values are really important and which are unimportant to their happiness. The college experience has the general effect of raising students' awareness of artistic experiences. It also increases their interest in business and academic status. It is hard to know what these changes mean. One view would suggest that the college experience produces less interest in traditional values. Another view would suggest that freshmen come to college with an unrealistic and uncritical perspective. Adjustment to college brings more carefully worked out personal standards. College may be a time when practical, worldly values are not as important as they were and as they will be. Students are urged to question things as they are. They are taught to deal with new ideas. Gaining a personal identity requires letting go of values learned from the past. This may occur only for a short period of time and the old values are found to be effective standards for guiding the person's behavior.

Living laboratory 8·2

COLLEGE

Purpose: To identify differences in student style.

Method: Take the student style categories in Table 8.2 to one of your classes. Over a period of a week, try to identify and classify all the students into the eight student styles. Determine the number of males and females in each group. Your chart of student styles could have the following format:

Student styles	Males	Females	Examples of involvement
The compliant			
The anxious-dependent			
The discouraged workers			
The independents			
The heroes.			
The snipers			
The attention seekers			
The silent students			

Results: Compare your results to the results of the Mann et al. study in Table 8.2. What examples of involvement can you cite?

Discussion: What can we learn about the process of intellectual adjustment to college by understanding student styles?

What factors could have influenced the style exhibited by the students?

Why do you think the largest group in the Mann et al. study fell into the anxious-dependent group?

To what extent will students maintain these styles in other classes or over time (that is, for the duration of their college years)?

What factors would be responsible for maintaining or changing a student's style?

Chapter summary

Elementary school experiences are a blend of the curriculum, the physical setting, the method of instruction, and the skills and motives that children bring to the learning situation. Attributes of the classroom like group size and similarity of classroom members and method of instruction will influence the process of adjustment. The teacher's leadership style, student cohesiveness, and the evaluative process also are powerful factors that effect children's sense of themselves as learners.

Over 90 percent of American adolescents attend high school. The effect of high school attendance on intellectual growth can be summarized as increasing information about school-related topics. This gain is highly influenced by initial abilities and continues well into adulthood. Both peers and teachers can influence cognitive growth. Their influence depends on the extent to which they encourage achievement and educational goals. High school attendance influences social development as students participate in a complex social institution. They become involved with school adults, the social status system, and political decisionmaking.

About one-third of all American 18–24-year-olds go on to postsecondary, degree-granting institutions. Another million enroll in noncredit professional programs. The questions raised in this chapter focus on the impact of these college environments on development during adolescence. Students choose their colleges on the basis of comparative ignorance. Students expect some career payoff from their college degree. Their choice of college may also be based on expectations about the social life or the intellectual stimulation that the school will provide. Evidence suggests that students are usually disappointed in regard to these early expectations.

College attendance results in more knowledge and more openness to new information. This is especially true for students who begin with minimal expectations for advanced degrees. College attendance increases educational goals. The impact of college on intellectual growth depends on the student's initial level of ability.

SUGGESTED READINGS

For general readings on education and its impact on adjustment:

Cohen, D. H.   *The learning child.* New York: Random House, 1972.

Lortie, D. C.   *School teacher: A sociological study.* Chicago: University of Chicago Press, 1975.

Pranse, G.   *School days of the famous.* New York: Springer Publishing, 1978.

Tolstoy on Education, translated by Leo Wiener. Chicago: University of Chicago Press, 1967.

Special works on the college environment include:

Astin, A. W.   *Four critical years.* San Francisco: Jossey-Bass, 1977.

Cottle, T. J.   *College: Reward and betrayal.* Chicago: University of Chicago Press, 1977.

Mann, R. D., et al.   *The college classroom: Conflict, change and learning.* New York: Wiley, 1970.

A text in educational psychology is:

DuBois, N. F., Alverson, G. F., & Staley, R. K.   *Educational psychology and instructional decisions.* Homewood, Ill.: Dorsey, 1979.

Reading

THE IMPACT OF COLLEGE

Student change during college

The longitudinal data, derived from studies that collectively involved some 200,000 students (at different periods) show clearly that students change in many ways after they enter college. They develop a more positive self-image as reflected in greater interpersonal and intellectual competence, and they develop more liberal political views and attitudes toward social issues. At the same time, they show less religiousness and altruism and show reduced interest in athletics, business, music, and status. Some of these attitudinal and personality changes are accompanied by parallel changes in behavior. Most dramatic is the decline in religious behavior and the accompanying increase in hedonistic behavior. Freshmen appear to be less studious and to interact less with instructors than they did in high school, but studiousness and interaction with faculty increase with time in college.

Are these changes directly attributable to the effects of college, or does maturation play a part? A change is considered to be dependent on the impact of college if residents show larger changes than commuters, if students with high interpersonal involvement on campus show larger changes than uninvolved students, and if persons who stay for four years show larger changes than persons who drop out after a short time. Maturational effects are assumed to be operating when these differences do not occur and when older students show smaller changes than younger students. Using these criteria as a guideline, a number of changes appear to be attributable to the college experience. Increased interpersonal self-esteem seems most dependent on college attendance. Increased intellectual self-esteem and liberalism and decreased business interest also appear to be primarily attributable to the effects of college. Decreased religiousness and increased hedonism seem to result from a mixture of college and maturational effects, whereas decreased need for status and reduced

interest in music and athletics appear to be entirely maturational. Indeed, college attendance appears, if anything, to impede the decline in status needs occurring among young people during this period of life.

Another factor influencing changes in students during the college years is *changes in the larger society*. Some of the "liberalizing" effects of colleges observed in earlier longitudinal studies appear to be in part a result of societal changes occuring during the same period. Longitudinal analyses covering the late 1960s and the early 1970s show, for example, large increases in student support for women's equality and student autonomy. Independent evidence from successive classes entering college during this period suggests that these changes in support for student autonomy are almost totally attributable to societal changes and that increased support for women's equality represents a mixture of societal and college influences.

Although college attendance is associated with an increase in both academic knowledge and competency across a variety of fields, students' college grades and rate of extracurricular achievement decline from those in high school. Reduced grades in college are attributable in part to the increased competition and higher academic standards of colleges compared with high schools. Reduced chances of achieving in extracurricular fields (music, leadership, theater, writing, athletics, and so forth) occur in part because of increased competition and in part because of the larger size of colleges compared with high schools. The greater the number of students, the less chance any given student has to participate in such activities as athletics or the school paper.

Although many students change career plans after they enter college, the amount of change varies across fields, and the "traffic" between fields is not random. The biggest dropout rates occur among students who initially plan careers in engineering, nursing, medicine, science, and school teaching. Careers that gain substantially in popularity are business, college teaching, law, and homemaking. Although the dropout rate from school teaching is large, that career captures a number of dropouts from other fields.

Students who have well-formulated career plans at college entry are only moderately successful in completing these plans. The greatest degree of success (about two thirds) occurs among students pursuing nursing and school teaching; the lowest success rates (about one third) occur among students planning to become doctors, lawyers, or social workers.

Students seem reasonably satisfied with various aspects of their undergraduate experience, although a significant minority (between 10 percent and 30 percent) reports moderate or extreme dissatisfaction with particular features of the college. The greatest degree of satisfaction is with student friendships, social life, and the college's academic reputation. Students tend to be least satisfied with the variety of courses offered, outlets for creative activities, and advice and guidance from faculty and staff.

Source: Alexander W. Astin, *Four Critical Years* (San Francisco: Jassey-Bass, Inc., Pubs., 1975), pp. 212–214.

Chapter 9
Intimacy

*somewhere i have never travelled, gladly beyond
any experience, your eyes have their silence:
in your most frail gesture are things which enclose me,
or which i cannot touch because they are too near*

*your slightest look easily will unclose me
though i have closed myself as fingers,
you open always petal by petal myself as Spring opens
(touching skilfully, mysteriously) her first rose*

*or if your wish be to close me, i and
my life will shut very beautifully, suddenly,
as when the heart of this flower imagines
the snow carefully everywhere descending;*

*nothing which we are to perceive in this world equals
the power of your intense fragility: whose texture*

*compels me with the colour of its countries,
rendering death and forever with each breathing*

*(i do not know what it is about you that closes
and opens; only something in me understands
the voice of your eyes is deeper than all roses)
nobody, not even the rain, has such small hands*

e. e. cummings, *ViVa*, 1931

Jean-Claude Lejeune

For reflection

1. Why is trust important for an intimate relationship with another person?
2. What personality and physical characteristics do you want your spouse to possess?
3. What would your life be like if you never married?
4. What adjustments must women or men make when their spouse dies?
5. What do you know about the sexual behavior of older adults?

Intimacy is a major goal for people. Feelings of trust, of being understood, of knowing mutual pleasure and support are sources of deep and long lasting satisfaction. Without feelings of intimacy, people feel isolated and depressed. This chapter discusses experiences of intimacy from infant-caregiver relationships to sexual intimacy in later adulthood. The sections follow a developmental sequence:

1. Childhood origins for a capacity for intimacy.
2. Intimacy during adolescence.
3. Marriage as a context for achieving intimacy.
4. Intimacy as it is achieved among "singles."
5. The importance of intimacy during later adulthood.

INTIMACY DURING INFANCY AND CHILDHOOD

The story of the development of intimacy begins with feelings of trust. We start with Erikson's definition:

> The general state of trust, . . . implies not only that one has learned to rely on the sameness and continuity of the outer providers, but also that one may trust oneself and the capacity of one's own organs to cope with urges (Erikson, 1950, p. 220).

Trust is established through interactions between the infant and the people who take care of them. In order for trust to emerge, infants must have their basic physical needs met.

Trust implies some ability to see oneself as different from others. Infants discover that sources of pleasure are outside of themselves. Sigmund Freud (1961) argued that this takes place when there are brief delays in the gratification of needs. In other words, some amount of frustration is necessary in order for the infant to find out that someone else is required to satisfy their basic needs. The next step is to learn that others are reliable and will provide satisfaction. The realization that other people are trustworthy is followed by deep caring feelings for these people. By around six months of age, babies begin to show that they care for the people who take care of them.

Trust is a property of the relationship between the caregiver and the infant. The caregivers show that they can satisfy the baby's needs and that they wish to satisfy the baby's needs in many ways. The baby, in turn, becomes more responsive to the caregiver, more expressive in his or her delight at the caregiver's attention, and more willing to control his or her rage.

Trust has implications for social relationships that last beyond infancy. The toddler's willingness to stay with babysitters, the five-year-old child's acceptance of a teacher, the eight-year-old's capacity to have a close friend, the adolescent's success in dating all build on the early experiences of openness, optimism, and trustworthiness of the infant-caregiver relationship. One's skills as a marriage partner and as a parent depend in part on the degree to which one feels a sense of trust in others and in oneself. This does not mean that each of these relationships is the same. Each one calls for different combination of emotional and social skills. Trust, however, is a necessary condition for any enduring social bond. Without it, the person becomes suspicious and *cynical* of others. Without confidence in oneself and in others there can be no positive social outlook.

● **cynical—deeply distrustful.**

Attachment and the emergence of trust

Attachment refers to an emotional relationship between an infant and at least one caregiver. Bowlby (1958) points out its usefulness for the infant's survival. He believes that attachment generally serves three functions: (1) to maintain closeness with the caregiver, (2) to establish an emotional bond with the caregiver, and (3) to bring out caregiving behaviors. The result is a pleasant emotional bond.

Ainsworth (1973) describes four stages in the development of social attachment (see Table 9•1). In the first stage, which occurs during the first three months of life, infants signal, activate, and bring others to them. They do this by using reflexes such as rooting, sucking, and grasping. They also use behaviors they can control like crying, gazing, smiling, and cuddling. During this phase, infant's have an impact on other people. However, they do not clearly distinguish between or prefer familiar people to unfamiliar people.

In the second stage, which occurs from about three to six months of age, infants show their attachment by being more responsive to a few familiar people than they are to others. This includes more smiling, more delight at seeing the familiar person, and more distress at watching

TABLE 9•1
Four sequential stages in the development of social attachment

Stage	Age	Characteristics
1	Birth to three months	Infant uses sucking, rooting, grasping, smiling, gazing, cuddling, and visual tracking to maintain closeness with caregiver.
2	Three to six months	Infant is more responsive to familiar figures than to strangers.
3	Seven months to toddlerhood	Infant seeks physical proximity and contact with object of attachment.
4	Toddlerhood and beyond	Infant uses a variety of behaviors to influence the behavior of the object of his or her attachment in order to satisfy his or her needs for closeness.

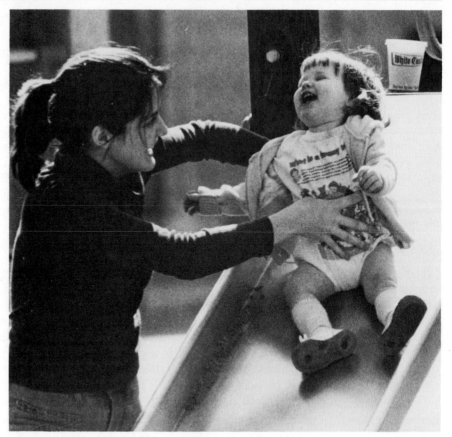

The earliest experience of intimacy is the
love shared between mother and child.

the familiar person go away. During this phase, infants have begun to recognize some of the unique qualities of their caregivers. Thus, infants are saying: (1) I recognize who you are, and (2) I like you.

In stage 3, which occurs from seven months to toddlerhood (about age two), babies stay close to the people who take care of them. They crawl or toddle after them, call to them from another room, cling to their legs or skirts, and snuggle cozily in their laps.

The fourth stage begins in toddlerhood and may extend into middle childhood. Children begin to alter the caregiver's ways of doing things in order to get their own needs met. Children ask their parents to read them stories, give them baths, rub their tummies, and build sand castles with them. Children also become more sensitive to the things their caregivers like to do. They may do things with adults that are pleasant for all. This leads to mutually satisfying relationships.

Sibling rivalry and sibling love

● *ridicule*—to mock or to make fun of.

Sibling rivalry has implications for the development of intimacy. It suggests that there is competition within the family. This competition leads to resentment when one is a loser. A child who has been defeated or *ridiculed* because of the presence of a brother or sister may find it hard to be able to love a peer in adulthood. Resentment may be directed toward the marriage partner.

Brothers and sisters can also have feelings of closeness and love for each other throughout life. The older child may be a teacher for the younger child. This is a role rarely possible in a two-adult, one-child family (Cicirelli, 1975). The older child may also find the younger to be a welcome play companion. If mother and father are busy or tired, there is another person who might like to play. Generally, the older child will spend less time alone after the birth of a brother or sister. The presence of brothers or sisters gives a great deal of life to children's interactions. They are likely to fight with each other, to have fantasies with each other, and to tease each other. These kinds of behaviors are not as likely to be used with parents.

A survey of 8,000 adolescents focused on the quality of emotional attachment among siblings (Bowerman & Dobash, 1974). The results of this survey showed that females like their other brothers and sisters more than do males. Adolescents tend to prefer siblings of the same sex. They like older brothers and sisters better than younger ones. We do not know if these patterns of affection are found among preschool or school age children. They do support the importance of sibling love in learning about intimacy.

Parental identification

● *identification*—a psychological mechanism in which people enhance their own self-concept by including some of the valued aspects of important others, such as parents, into their own behavior.

● *imitation*—repetition of another person's words, gestures, or behaviors.

The concept of *identification* is very important. A common question that is asked is why children become like one of their parents. There are three different theories about motives for identification. Psychoanalytic theory suggests that two different processes are involved: (1) fear of loss of love and (2) identification with the aggressor. The fear of loss of love is a very basic motive. It is based on children's realization of their dependence on their parents. Children behave like their parents in order to keep their parents' love. After a while parts of the parent's personality become part of their own self-concept. Identification permits children to gain some independence from the parent (Jacobson, 1964). If children can be like their parent, they do not need the parent's presence in order to reassure themselves about the parent's love.

Social learning theory defines status and power as the main motives for identification (Bandura, 1977). Studies show that a child is more likely to *imitate* the behavior of a person (model) who controls resources than a person who is rewarded. A feeling of power is experienced by children when they behave in the same way as the powerful person. This feeling is what causes the child to imitate. A model is a person whose behavior serves as an example for someone else.

Kagan (1958) suggested that children behave like their parents in

Parental warmth and responsiveness foster identification.

order to see themselves as more like the adults. Children think their parents have qualities including physical size, good looks, special abilities, power, success, or respect, which they like. Children can more easily share these qualities when they see themselves and their parents as more like each other. These are:

1. Perceiving actual physical and psychological similarities.
2. Adopting parental behaviors.
3. Being told about similarities by others.

The more alike children think they are to their parents, the stronger are their identifications (Mussen, Conger, & Kagan, 1979).

Whatever the cause, identification with parents, we adopt many of our parent's standards, beliefs, and ways of doing things as our own. We see them as the first examples of men and women, husbands and wives, fathers and mothers. As children we want to be like our parents.

Their goals become our goals. In adulthood, we bring these notions of the ideal man and woman with us as we search for our life partners. These ideals are likely to be retained without the benefit of comparison, analysis, or evaluation. They continue to serve as examples of intimacy. They may get in the way of achieving intimacy with someone who does not understand or like your parent's style. This basic process of adjustment causes us to be like someone else. This helps us to gain love and to be effective.

Learning about intimacy with friends

There appears to be three lessons a child learns from daily life with peers. First, children discover that their peers have different points of view.

As children interact with peers who see the world differently than they do, they begin to understand the limits of their own point of view. Piaget (1948) suggests that friends have a big influence in decreasing each other's self-centered outlook. Friends are equals. Children are not forced to accept each other's ideas in the same way as they may feel forced to accept the ideas of adults. They argue, bargain, and compromise in order to maintain friendships. The chance to be in peer groups for work and for play draws children away from the *egocentrism* of early childhood. It encourages flexibility of thought.

● *egocentrism*—**the perception of oneself at the center of the world.**

Second, children become more sensitive to the norms of the peer group. The peer group also evolves norms for acceptance and rejection. Social norms are the rules or guidelines for behavior (Brown, 1965; Schmuck & Schmuck, 1975). Raising your hand to be called on, wearing a jacket and tie at a "fancy" restaurant, or riding your bike to school instead of having your mother drive you are all examples of norms. Each one might work in one setting but not have much meaning outside of that setting. As children become aware of these norms they also experience pressures to do what the norms say. The early school-age child sees the teacher as a source of approval and acceptance. By middle school-age, children are sensitive to their friends as an important audience. Children often "play" to the class rather than to the teacher. The roles of joker, snob, and hero or heroine come out during the middle school years as ways of gaining approval from the peer group. The need for peer approval becomes a powerful force producing acceptance of peer norms (Pepitone et al., 1977). The child learns to dress, talk, and joke in ways that their friends like. Hostility between girls and boys, which is very common during this stage, is kept alive largely by this pressure. If all the fifth-grade boys hate girls, then Johnny is not very likely to admit that he likes to play with Mary.

Third, peer relations usually lead to the formation of friendships that can become quite intimate. Being together, children can begin to make strong commitments. The intensity of childhood friendship was illustrated in the example of the war orphans described in Chapter 7. The children fiercely resisted any effort by adults to separate them or to treat one differently from the rest. Their sense of empathy and support for each other probably was a key to their survival.

With loving parents and a stable home environment, children still form strong friendships. Children share private jokes, develop secret codes, tell secrets, go on adventures, and help each other in times of trouble. They also fight, threaten, break up, and reunite in the course of these friendships. Sullivan (1949) points out the importance of these early friendships as building blocks for later opposite-sex relationships. It is important that children feel love and closeness for a peer rather than for an adult. These relationships allow for mutuality of power and status. The conflicts can be worked out by the children. One child cannot take away another child's allowance or send the child out of the room when a conflict happens. The children must deal with each other on different terms than they deal with adults.

Childhood sexuality

One of Freud's basic observations was that children had sexual concerns. Freud described infants and young children as willing to use many objects for sexual pleasure. Sexuality was part of children's self-stimulation and their playful exploration of the bodies of friends. The concept of childhood sexuality tells us that sexual interests and sexual fantasies do not begin in adolescence. Long before the person is physically mature, wishes and fears about sexual intimacy are part of mental life (Freud, 1953, 1959a, 1959b, 1961, 1964). What is more, the genital area is sensitive to stimulation long before puberty. Kinsey (Kinsey et al., 1953) reported that 28 percent of males and 14 percent of females remembered having some sexual play by the age of nine. A survey of adult sexual behavior conducted by the Playboy Foundation (Hunt, 1974) reported that 93 percent of males and 63 percent of females had *masturbated* to orgasm. About 60 percent of males and 35 percent of females had experienced orgasm through masturbation by age 13. For both sexes, masturbation is a primary way for achieving sexual stimulation. Sexual maturation begins earlier for females than for males. These data suggest that sexual activity of a nonsocial nature plays a more important role for males than for females.

● *masturbation*—erotic stimulation of the genitals commonly resulting in orgasm and achieved by manual or other bodily contact exclusive of sexual intercourse.

Young children also show their curiosity about sexuality through play. It is not uncommon to find five- and six-year-old children involved in a game of "doctor" in which both "doctor" and "patient" have their pants off. Boys of this age are occasionally seen in a game that is won by the individual who can achieve the longer urine trajectory. Girls say that they attempt to urinate from a standing position "in the same way that a boy does." These behaviors show growing curiosity, and pleasure in their body.

Some adults are embarrassed or offended by the sexual implications of the child's exposure of body parts. Their response to the child creates feelings of shame and guilt. From the child's point of view, a good path for play has been stopped by the adult's emotional reaction. From the adult's point of view, something harmful has been stopped. This is an

● *suppress*—to hold back.

area of conflict between the norms of parents and the child's natural leanings. The child learns to *suppress* some ways of exploring in order to avoid embarrassment or parental anger. The parent's skill in this situation involves adjusting to the child's behavior without placing a heavy burden of guilt on the child. The child may understand that there are norms for proper sexual behavior without feelings that sexuality is bad and immoral.

Childhood experimentation with sexuality is important for achieving a sense of intimacy in adulthood for two reasons. First, it tells children something about the potential pleasure of sexual intimacy. Second, it ties sexuality to morality. One's parents' attitudes about sex and sexual behavior are early sources of feelings of shame and guilt. Sexuality is also part of ideals about masculinity or femininity that result from parental identification.

Living laboratory 9·1

CHILDHOOD ORIGINS OF A CAPACITY FOR INTIMACY

Purpose: To increase awareness of one's capacity for intimacy.

Method: Write down everything you can remember about your childhood that helped you develop a sense of intimacy. This might include times when you felt very close to one parent, your feelings about the birth of a new brother or sister, reasons why you prefer one brother or sister, conflicts with your brother or sister over toys, clothing, or privileges, occasions when you really needed to talk to one parent, long separations from parents, the age at which you first left parents for a long time, times when your brother or sister was treated differently than you by your parents, ways you want to be like your mother or father, and ways you want to be different than your parents.

Results: Using the format suggested below, take each period of your life, such as middle childhood, preadolescence, and adolescence, and record events that stand out in your mind. See how your culture, your family members, and your personal history have affected your sense of intimacy. Note your feelings about your parents and siblings. How do they relate to your current sense of intimacy and the intimate relationships you have now?

Life period	Events	Environmental influences	Feelings and thoughts	Current sense of intimacy

Discussion: Who is responsible for developing your sense of intimacy?

How has your past affected your ability to form close, mutually satisfying relationships?

What can you do to increase your sense of intimacy?

What are the advantages of having intimate relationships with parents, siblings, and peers? What are the disadvantages?

How can you help your friends and others develop a sense of intimacy?

**INTIMACY IN
ADOLESCENCE**

By the age of 25, most Americans have experienced their first marriage. For women born in the 1950s, the median age at marriage was 21.2 years (Glick, 1977). Young people in the working class marry somewhat earlier than people in the middle class. There can be no doubt, however, that adolescence is a time for learning about intimacy. A loving relationship usually involves three phases: (1) meeting someone of the opposite sex; (2) making an emotional commitment; and (3) gaining sexual intimacy. These phases do not always occur in order (Gagnon & Greenblat, 1978). The heterosexual relationships of this period have goals of meeting new people, falling in love, and giving and receiving physical pleasure. Many adolescents do not see these relationships as a part of courtship or as getting them ready for marriage. Nevertheless,

The photography of H. Armstrong Roberts

Dating requires new social learning.

these romances help young people to know who they find attractive. It also help them know their own ability to share in a close, emotional relationship.

Dating

Dating is a delightful, troublesome, intense, mysterious experience that serves many functions for the adolescent. Winch (1971) offers six functions of dating that help us understand its importance.

1. Dating is a form of recreation.
2. Dating is a means of gaining status.
3. Dating provides chances to learn about the opposite sex.
4. Dating helps us learn about our own personality and needs.
5. Dating allows us to compare which relationships are satisfying and which are not. This leads to a better understanding of who would be a good mate.
6. In dating, standards about marriage, child rearing, sexuality, and life-style are thought about before a marriage partner is chosen.

We would add that dating helps the person learn about sex. For most adolescents, dating means degrees of physical intimacy from holding hands to having sexual intercourse. In these relationships, young people learn how to handle their feelings of being hurt and their fears about physical contact. They must cope with difficulties that come from sexual demands. They learn how to give and receive physical pleasure without alarming each other (Estep, Burt, & Milligan, 1977).

What do we know about the dating behavior of adolescents? Three topics are discussed in the following section:

1. Learning to date.
2. Who is a desirable date.
3. Emotional and sexual intimacy in dating.

Learning to date

Jackson (1975) asked 11- and 12-year-olds who were not yet dating two questions: (1) What does the word dating mean to you? (2) When you go out on a date, where do you usually go? Table 9·2 shows the answers given by males and females to question (1). As the table shows, most of the children knew what dating was. Eighteen percent of the boys and 5 percent of the girls thought that the whole idea was stupid. When the children were asked what one does on a date, it became clear that they didn't know very much. Forty-three percent of the females and 73 percent of the males did not know what a date involved.

What one does on a date must be learned. Adolescents figure out where to go, what to do, and how to act by going around in large groups at first and then moving into pairs. Some of the problems can be solved in a group before dealing with them in a one-to-one situation.

One of the special problems of dating involves getting permission to go out. In one study of high school sophomore girls, most parents

Females	Frequency	Percent	Males	Frequency	Percent
To go out with opposite sex	101	58	To go out with opposite sex	50	35
To go out with a special person (friend)	32	18	It's "dumb," don't know	27	18
To go to a special place (party)	12	7	It's "fun" (recreation)	26	18
To go out for a special time span	11	6	To go out without parents	14	10
To get to know someone better	11	6	To go to a special place	13	9
It's "dumb," "gross," etc., don't know	9	5	To get to know someone better	13	9

Source: D. W. Jackson, "The Meaning of Dating from the Role Perspective of Non-dating Pre-adolescents," *Adolescence* 10 (1975), p. 124.

TABLE 9·2
What does dating
mean to you?

set 16 as the age when they thought their daughters ought to begin dating. All the girls in the sample tried to get permission to go on a date long before that. Some of the strategies they used to try to convince their parents are given below. They show some ways adolescents adjust to restrictions they are ready to do away with (Place, 1975):

"My parents said I couldn't date until I was 16. Last year I started going steady with Ed. I wanted to go out and we (parents and she) had a fight. I just begged every weekend until she gave up."

"Dad, can I go to the show? (Dad: 'I don't know, ask your mother.') Mom, Dad said it's OK to go to the show if you say yes. Then my Mom says yes, and then I say to my Dad, 'Mom said yes.' "

"As long as I name off a whole group of girls that are going, my Mom let me go, I told her (mother) all the kids were going and if I couldn't go to the city, I couldn't go to the dance. She said, 'OK, but that's once and for all.' But the next time I asked to go to the city, she said, 'OK, go ahead.' "

"I use older brothers and sisters to plead for me. I plead for my older sister when she wants to go somewhere. That way, when my times comes, I can go" (pp. 158–61).

Who is a desirable date?   What do adolescents look for in a date? Waller (1937) described a status system of dating in which both males and females placed higher value on money, dress, or owning a car than on intelligence, consideration, or a good sense of humor. In a recent study, Hansen (1977) asked black and white high school students to choose the 12 most important qualities of a date from a list of 33 items. The students were asked to choose items that were important to their peers, that were important to them for a date, and that were important to them for a mate. Table 9·3 shows the top 12 items for each

Characteristics important to respondents' peers	Characteristics important in a date	Characteristics important in a mate
1. Is pleasant and cheerful.	1. Is pleasant and cheerful.	1. Is pleasant and cheerful.
2. Is neat in appearance.	2. Is dependable.	2. Is dependable.
3. Has a sense of humor.	3. Is considerate.	3. Is considerate.
4. Is dependable.	4. Has a sense of humor.	4. Is honest, straight-forward.
5. Is popular with the opposite sex.	5. Is neat in appearance.	5. Is affectionate.
6. Is natural.	6. Is honest, straight-forward.	6. Is natural.
7. Is affectionate.	7. Is natural.	7. Is neat in appearance.
8. Is considerate.	8. Is affectionate.	8. Has a sense of humor.
9. Has a car or access to one.	9. Has good sense, is intelligent.	9. Has good sense, is intelligent.
10. Knows how to dance.	10. Thinks of things to do.	10. Is a good listener.
11. Is willing to neck on occasion.	11. Is appropriately dressed.	11. Is a good sport.
12. Thinks of things to do.	12. Is a good sport.	12. Thinks of things to do.
		13. Is appropriately dressed.

Source: S. L. Hansen, "Dating Choices of High School Students," *The Family Coordinator* 26 (1977), p. 135. Copyright (1977) by the National Council on Family Relations. Reprinted by permission.

TABLE 9·3
Rank order choices on the dating-rating checklist

set of choices. The students thought that others regarded prestige factors as important but that they were more concerned with personal qualities. The students did see neatness and dress as qualities that make a person a desirable date. In general, there is quite a bit of overlap among the lists. Only four qualities in the first list do not appear on the other lists:

1. Is popular with the opposite sex.
2. Has a car or access to one.
3. Knows how to dance.
4. Is willing to neck on occasion.

It may be reassuring to some and bothersome to others that physical appearance is still an important basis for dating. Good looks, a good build (shapely for girls, muscular for boys), and an attractive face are qualities that both boys and girls rate as important to a person's desirability (Berg, 1975; Place, 1975; Cavior & Dokecki, 1973. There are indications, however, that personal qualities, like understanding, gentleness, and dependability or loyalty, are more important than appearance in girls' judgments of a boy. For boys, physical attractiveness is the most important factor in choosing a date (Hansen, 1977; Konopka, 1976; Berg, 1975).

Dating in college. In college, one of the biggest changes in opportunities for meeting members of the opposite sex is the coed dormitory. An estimated 70 percent of colleges offer this option for students (Pierson & D'Antonio, 1974). These dorms allow students to have casual, *spontaneous* relationships with members of the opposite sex. They also provide more chances for males and females to be in private.

● **spontaneous—** natural or unplanned.

Opportunities for male-female relationships are different for those who do not go on to college and those who do. For the former, high school is the last place where there are many chances for males and females to meet and mix. After high school, contacts between these males and females are much more limited. Work and one's neighborhood are two of the main places for meeting people. The "singles" bar is becoming a new setting for meeting people. Many adolescents who do not go on to college move more quickly toward sexual intimacy and emotional commitment during high school. Soon after graduation many noncollege adolescents are ready to make a decision about who to marry. The period for finding a marriage partner among working-class adolescents who do not attend college is fairly short. If a good partner is not found among high school, work, or neighborhood contacts, the young person may feel the need to move to another town or to take an apartment in a building in which other "singles" are likely to live (Starr & Carns, 1972).

College students have to begin mixing, getting involved, and having physically intimate relations all over again. College-bound students aren't pushed into marriage during high school. College-bound females are also less likely to have sexual intercourse during high school than are females who are not going to college (Simon, Berger, & Gagnon, 1972).

College-bound adolescents do go steady and fall in love. They also set limits on high school relationships because of the promise for meeting new people and for future growth that college offers.

In college, students who resisted serious involvement during high school may be more willing to have long-term relationships. They may even experiment with living together. Loving relationships formed during college are likely to include sexual intimacy. Openness to marriage depends on future career goals and the decision to pursue an advanced degree. The more involved students are with academic goals and the more selective the school is about admitting students, the less likely students are to marry during college (Bayer, 1972).

During college, young people seek close, loving relationships, often with the understanding that these relationships are not permanent. We view adolescent loving relationships as indicating a need for understanding and for sexual expression. In these relationships, important work

● *value clarification—*
process of defining the
standards by which one
lives.

on identity and *value clarification* continues. Away from the supervision of parents and neighbors, college students have the chance to develop intimate bonds with a person who may come from a very different home background, have different political and/or religious views, or have a very different outlook. When they share ideas, the students learn a lot of private things about each other. These ideas are likely to include new information about identity.

Sexual experimentation

We begin this discussion of adolescent sexual intimacy with the observations of G. Stanley Hall (1904) who wrote about adolescence at the turn of the century:

The development of the sex function is normally, perhaps, the greatest of all stimuli to mental growth. The new curiosity and interests bring the alert soul into rapport with very many facts and laws of life hitherto unseen. Each of its phenomena supplies the key to a new mystery. Sex is the most potent and magic open sesame to the deepest mysteries of life, death, religion, and love. It is, therefore, one of the cardinal sins against youth to repress healthy thoughts of sex at the proper age, because thus the mind itself is darkened and its wing clipped for many of the higher intuitions, which the supreme muse of common sense at this its psychologic moment ought to give (vol. 2, pp. 108–9).

Intense romantic involvements are common to adolescent boy-girl relationships. In a national sample of high school seniors, only 35 percent of the white students and 23 percent of the black students had never gone steady during the previous three years (Larson, Spreitzer, & Snyder, 1976). White males were the largest group with no experience in a "steady" relationship (40 percent had never gone steady).

Sorenson (1973) described the basic goals young adolescents have in close relationships. Love is seen as mutual involvement in a satisfying relationship. For adolescents, love does have to last a long time. The partners share feelings of understanding and closeness. This is expressed in part through sexual intimacy. In Sorenson's national sample, 44 percent of the boys and 30 percent of the girls had experienced sexual intercourse before age 16. By age 19, 72 percent of the boys and 57 percent of the girls had experienced sexual intercourse. This reflects a significant increase in sexual experience among girls, especially younger girls, when compared to Kinsey's data from the late 40s and early 50s (see Table 9·4).

The meaning of sexuality in a relationship seems to differ for two groups in Sorenson's sample: the "serial monogamists" and the "sexual adventurers." The serial monogamists do not have sexual relations with others while they are involved in one relationship. However, they are likely to move from one close relationship to the next. The sexual adventurers do not restrict themselves to one partner for sexual relations. They view sex as a pleasurable experience that does not require love or emo-

TABLE 9·4
Adolescent sexual activity as reported by Sorenson (1973) and Kinsey (1948, 1953)

	Percent having sexual intercourse	
	Before age 16	By age 19
Males		
1948	39	72
1973	44	72
Females		
1953	3	20
1973	30	57

Source: R. C. Sorenson, *Adolescent Sexuality in Contemporary America: Personal Values and Sexual Behavior, Ages 13–19* (New York: World Publishing, 1973); A. C. Kinsey, W. B. Pomeroy, and C. E. Martin, *Sexual Behavior in the Human Male* (Philadelphia: W. B. Saunders Co., 1948); and A. C. Kinsey, W. B. Pomeroy, C. E. Martin, and P. H. Gebhard, *Sexual Behavior in the Human Female* (Philadelphia: W. B. Saunders Co., 1953).

United Press International

Most adolescents expect sexuality to be an important part of an intimate relationship.

● *exploit*—to take advantage of.

tional intimacy to be enjoyed. In Sorenson's sample, more people who had intercourse described themselves as serial monogamists than as sexual adventurers. Although the latter had more sex partners, the former had intercourse more frequently.

Whether or not sexual intercourse is part of the relationship, there can be no doubt that sexual intimacy is important, enjoyable, and common in adolescent dating. Even adolescents who do not approve of intercourse before marriage will experiment with sexual activities that may result in orgasm. In general, adolescents see sex as a pleasant, natural part of a tender, caring relationship. Even the sexual adventurers do not intend to use sex to *exploit* or harm others. They see sexuality as a part of personal freedom. It is part of a relationship that is open and natural rather than a relationship that is bound by traditional morality and formality (Conger, 1975). In early adolescence, especially, girls and boys can feel pressured into having greater sexual intimacy than they find really comfortable. Adolescents face peer expectations for sexual openness. These expectations may not match their own needs. Learning to experience sexuality in a satisfying way that meets one's ideals about mutual respect, tenderness, and physical pleasure requires more psychological maturity than many junior high and high school age adolescents can bring to a relationship.

The pattern of increasing sexual permissiveness goes on into the college years. When beliefs and behaviors are studied over the four years of college, males and females become more and more "single standard." That is, they do not identify differences between what is appropriate sexually for males and what is appropriate for females. What is more, this single standard becomes more lenient over the college years. Students move from a standard of restraint or *abstinence* to a standard based on having sex for both sexes (Ferrell, Tolone, & Walsh, 1977).

King, Balswick, and Robinson (1977) compared university students in 1965, 1970, and 1975 in their answers to questions about sexual behavior and attitudes. Table 9·5 compares the percentage of students who had had intercourse and the percentage who had experienced heavy petting at the three time periods. These data suggest that there has been increasing participation in intense sexual activity by both males and females. The increase shows more involvement by females. As sexual experience has increased, there has also been an increase in permissive attitudes toward sex. Over the ten-year period, fewer students viewed premarital sex as immoral. Fewer students felt that having sexual intercourse with a number of different people was sinful or immoral.

The double standard, though fading, continues to contribute to the formation of intimate relationships. Although the gap between males and females has been closing, fewer females than males report being sexually active. Also, both males and females are slightly more critical of women who have many sexual relationships than they are of men who have many sexual relationships (King et al., 1977).

In seeking sexual intimacy, males and females have somewhat different views. They expect each other to act differently. Among dating couples interviewed by Peplau et al. (1977), the males and females believed in the same standards for sexual conduct in a loving relationship. However, more males mentioned sex as the best thing in the relationship or as an important goal in dating. When a couple had not yet had intercourse (which was the case for 42 of the 231 couples), it was usually the female

● *abstinence—* **deliberately not doing something.**

TABLE 9·5
Percentage of students experiencing sexual intercourse and heavy petting at three time periods: 1965, 1970, and 1975

	Sexual intercourse		Heavy petting*	
	Male	Female	Male	Female
1965	65.1%	28.7%	71.3%	34.3%
1970	65.0	37.3	79.3	59.7
1975	73.9	57.1	80.2	72.7

* Manual and oral manipulation of genitals.
Source: Karl King, Jack O. Balawick, and Ira E. Robinson, "The Continuing Premarital Sexual Revolution among College Females," *Journal of Marriage and the Family* 39 (1977), pp. 455–459. Copyrighted 1977 by the National Council on Family Relations. Reprinted by permission.

who restrained the couple. Among couples who had had intercourse, the less sexually experienced the female, the longer the couple dated before they had intercourse.

McCormick (1977) gave students examples of strategies that might be used to have or to avoid having sexual intercourse. The students were asked to guess whether a male or a female would be more likely to use each strategy. Both the males and the females thought the strategies were masculine when they led to intercourse and as feminine when they led to the avoidance of intercourse. When the students described the strategies that they would actually use, both sexes used indirect strategies such as body language, or seduction as a means of moving toward sexual intercourse. Both sexes used direct strategies such as *coercion,* moralizing, or rational argument to avoid having intercourse. Although males and females described their behavior in quite similar ways, they saw the two sexes as using different strategies—males active and females passive.

● *coercion*—**bringing about by force or threat.**

A final view of the double standard can be seen in the ways that males and females act when they have already had intercourse. Carns (1973) interviewed students at 12 colleges and universities in the United States. He assumed that sexual behavior had a different meaning for males and females. He found this difference in the extent to which males and females talked about their sexual experiences with others. Males were quite a bit more likely to talk with many friends. Over half of the males (53.4 percent) had told five or more friends about their first sexual experience. Of the females, 26 percent had told no one and another 29.3 percent had told only one or two friends. Over half of the females (57.1 percent) had never told a parent about their sexual experience. Two thirds of the males had shared this information with parents. Finally, 61.6 percent of the males had talked about the first time they had sexual intercourse immediately or within one month. Only 39.1 percent of the females had told anyone about having sex immediately or within one month.

For males, having sexual intercourse is expected and approved of by peers and parents. Often, they are proud to have had sex. For females, however, sex is something that continues to be clouded by mixed feelings. Females may expect less approval. They also feel that the intimacy of sex is too personal to disclose. Clearly, the sexual script for males and females is still different. Males begin their sexual activity with peer support. They often view sex a conquest and a validation of their masculinity. Females begin their sex life as an expression of intimacy and loving. They still have more mixed feelings about the reactions that such behavior will generate.

Living together

Achieving a personally satisfying sense of oneself as a male or a female is one of the challenges of personal identity. In an effort to have a satisfying relationship with someone of the opposite sex, some young people decide to live together. Most of the data about living together (cohabitation) has been gathered in colleges. In a study at Cornell, about 30 percent of the students had lived with someone for three or more months and shared the same bed or bedroom (Macklin, 1974). When students who had lived together were compared to those who had not, the similarities between groups were striking. Students who lived together were from similar family backgrounds, showed similar levels of academic performance, and had similar views about marriage compared to students who were not living together. Students who lived together thought that they were trying out this living arrangement in order to further the closeness they felt for one another. Only a small percentage thought the relationship would lead to marriage.

We learn more about cohabitation from a national survey of young men born between 1944 and 1954 (Clayton & Voss, 1977). Eighteen percent had lived with a woman for six months or more but only 5 percent were living with a woman at the time of the interview. In comparison with the studies at colleges it was found that living together was more frequent among men who were not in college or who had not attended college. It should be noted that the youngest of these men was 20, so many of them were already past the college years and had attended college.

An interesting finding in this sample was the connection between living together and other forms of experimentation. In comparison to those who had never lived with a woman, men who had lived with someone were also more likely to have lived in a commune, meditated, explored an Eastern religion, tried an organic or vegetarian diet, participated in a political demonstration, studied astrology or ESP, and "bummed around" for a while. In other words, living together can be seen as one example of experimentation with traditional roles. People who experiment in their adjustments during college are likely to do so in many ways.

Living laboratory 9·2

INTIMACY IN ADOLESCENCE

Purpose: To identify factors that increase intimacy in adolescence.

Method: Give the following dating-rating checklist to ten male and ten female college students. The college students will use the checklist to rank the important characteristics of a date and a mate. Each student should rank the characteristics of the date or mate in the order of importance. The most important characteristic should receive a rank of 1 and the least important a rank of 13. Each characteristic should be ranked only once and should not receive the same rank as any other characteristics. The rating checklist, which appears in Table 9·3, was used by S. L Hansen (1977) in a study of the dating choices of high school students. The portion of the checklist to be used in your study follows:

	Characteristics important in a date	*Characteristics important in a mate*
	Is pleasant and cheerful.	Is pleasant and cheerful.
	Is dependable.	Is dependable.
	Is considerate.	Is considerate.
	Is honest, straightforward.	Is honest, straightforward.
	Is affectionate.	Is affectionate.
	Is natural.	Is natural.
	Is neat in appearance.	Is neat in appearance.
	Has a sense of humor.	Has a sense of humor.
	Has good sense, is intelligent.	Has good sense, is intelligent.
	Is a good listener.	Is a good listener.
	Is a good sport.	Is a good sport.
	Thinks of things to do.	Thinks of things to do.
	Is appropriately dressed.	Is appropriately dressed.

Results: For all 20 students, calculate the characteristics important for a date which received a rank of 1, 2, 3, etc. for all 13 characteristics. For example, 14 out of 20 students may have given a 1 rank to the characteristic "is pleasant and cheerful." Do the same for the characteristics important for a mate. Change this number to percentages (e.g., 5 out of 20 = 25 percent). Compare the preferences of your sample of 20 students to the preferences of the sample in S. L. Hansen's study in Table 9•3. Finally, compare the responses of the males and females to each other and to the rank order choices of Hansen's study listed in Table 9•3.

Discussion: What qualities make a person a desirable date or a desirable mate?

Why are some characteristics more important for a date and some for a mate?

How might peer pressures or cultural influences affect a person's perceptions of characteristics that are important for a date or mate?

How would certain characteristics affect long-term relationships?

INTIMACY AND MARRIAGE

Marriage is the relationship within which work on intimacy takes place. Glick (1977) provided a comparison of marriage and childbearing experiences of women in their 40s over the past 80 years. Of women born in the two youngest periods (1940 and 1950), well over 90 percent were married. In fact, while the trend to remain single seems to have increased since the period of the 40s and 50s, fewer adult women remain single in the 70s than was the case during the period from 1900 through the 1920s.

The main change in marriage is that more young adults seem to be postponing it until the end of their 20s. There was an increase from 28 percent (1960) to 40 percent (1975) of women between the ages of 20 to 24 who were single. The increase for single men was 53 percent (1960) to 60 percent (1975) (U.S. Department of Commerce, 1976). There is the possibility that a larger number will remain single than has in the past. In this section, we discuss the decision to marry, stages in

Jean-Claude Lejeune

Marriage is the most usual context for achieving intimacy in adulthood.

the marriage relationship, marital instability, extramarital relationships, and marriage as a source of life satisfaction.

The decision to marry

Through dating one meets many possible partners, some of whom may seem quite attractive on "important" dimensions. What determines whether or not a dating relationship ends in marriage? One very important thing is the readiness of the two people for a long-term commitment. Work on identity must be far enough along so that the possibility of deep emotional involvement with someone else is exciting rather than frightening.

For some young adults, readiness for marriage is a response to the "social clock." Within social groups, there are expectations about the best age for marriage. For working-class groups, the ideal age for marriage is between 18 and 22. Those who are dating seriously during high school are likely to marry soon after graduation. Once these young adults move past the age of 23 or 24, they find far fewer eligible partners. Anxiety about finding a mate increases (Gagnon & Greenblat, 1978). Young people who attend college tend to have a later timetable for marriage. Men are expected to marry somewhat later than women. If a young woman is still single at 25, her family may look at her with questioning eyes. A male can remain single a bit longer, but by 30 the glances turn to him.

Finally, readiness may depend on other goals, such as finishing school, completing military service, or earning a certain income. In each case, the person with these commitments is less open to loving than someone who is looking forward to marriage in the near future. In our culture, people have a great amount of freedom to choose the time of marriage and the marriage partner. Even though the expectations that one will marry are very strong, young adults can at least follow their own timetables.

Once the person is ready to choose a marriage partner, the choice is guided by similarity in personal qualities (Barry, 1970) and similarity of social and cultural background (Brim, 1968; Z. Rubin, 1973). People tend to seek others to share their private worlds who hold similar beliefs, values, and life goals.

Ideally, before the decision to marry is made, the people are each able to bring a capacity for intimacy to the relationship. It is not hard to understand that a person would be on intimate terms with parents, brothers, and sisters. The family is clearly an appropriate place for sharing confidences, expressing love, and revealing weaknesses or *dependence*. The task of young adulthood is to establish an intimate relationship with someone who is not a family member. In fact, the two people who eventually become intimate may begin as total strangers.

● *dependence*—the reliance on another for support.

The formation of intimacy is an active process. Even though we refer to the beginning of a loving relationship as "falling in love," it seems more appropriate to speak of the active process of intimacy as "making love." Intimacy includes the ability to experience an open, supportive, tender relationship with another person. In intimacy, closeness is possible without fear of losing one's own identity in the process. Intimacy in a relationship supports independent judgments by each member (Stone, 1973). The possibility for establishing intimacy depends on the confidence that people have in themselves as worthy, competent, and meaningful people.

Different patterns of socialization for men and women lead to differences in the meaning of intimacy for each and to different problems in the establishment of intimacy for each (Bernard, 1971). Boys are taught not to be dependent and to limit their emotionality. During middle school age and early adolescence, the emotional life of boys is generally guided into competitiveness and self-reliance. Often adolescent males don't express tenderness toward their family members. Relationships with girls are often used to demonstrate virility to friends. Even though adolescent couples share tender moments, the males are likely to resist pressure toward long-term coimmtments until they feel sure of their own independence. Demands for intimacy during young adulthood may be very difficult for young men. They have learned to resist intimate relationships. On the other hand, the successful formation of an intimate relationship provides a man with a chance to express his feelings in a way that is acceptable. The home may be the only place where a man can express his feelings in a direct way.

- **expressive—showing one's feelings.**

Women are better prepared for the emotional demands of intimacy. They have often been rewarded for being *expressive,* nurturant, and supportive. Women are more willing to tell about dissatisfaction with their personalities than men are. They are likely to feel pleased to have a relationship with someone who will hear their problems and support them. If anything, women may tend to enter an intimate relationship with a surplus of dependent needs. They rely on their husbands for reassurance, they may be disappointed to discover that their husbands are not as strong or as resourceful as they had expected.

Some of the stresses of marriage for the female, particularly the nonworking female, come from her isolation in the home, and her view of housework and child care as low-status activities. Women who are not employed may feel a sense of not having a purpose in life. Separated from their husbands for most of the day, women may feel that the demands of the "housewife" are not stimulating enough to keep away feelings of loneliness, aimlessness, or failure.

For some young people, closeness with another person threatens their sense of self. They think intimacy strains the boundaries of their own identity. They cannot let themselves have such relationships. The result is a sense of isolation. People who experience isolation build barriers between themselves and others in order to keep their sense of self. This sense of self results from many experiences in childhood that create rigid, brittle, or diffused sense of identity. Individuals who have a weak sense of identity must constantly remind themselves about who they are. They cannot allow their identity to stand on its own in order to lose themselves, even for a moment, in another. They are so busy maintaining their identity or struggling to make sense out of *diffusion* that they cannot attain a sense of intimacy.

- **diffusion—in psychosocial theory, a failure to integrate roles and past identification.**

Isolation may also be a result of the situation. A young man who goes off to war and returns to find that the "eligible" women in his town are married, or the young woman who rejects marriage in order to attend medical school, may find that desires for intimacy cannot be met. We may say that the lonely person should try harder to meet new people or should develop new social skills. However, it is possible that the sense of being isolated itself interferes with more active coping strategies (Peplau, Russell, & Helm, 1979).

Establishing intimacy in marriage

During the early years of marriage, several things may interfere with the formation of intimacy. These include:

1. The early period of adjustment.
2. The birth of the first child.
3. The social expectations of members of their extended family.

The successful development of an intimate relationship may not occur until a couple has been married for several years.

Once the choice of a partner has been made and the thrill of courtship has passed, the first few years of marriage involve a process of mutual adjustment. These years may prove to be very difficult. Often the young married couple does not anticipate the strains that are to come. They may be quite upset to find their "love nest" filled with the tensions that are part of carving out a life together. In fact, some data suggest that the probability of divorce rises during the first years of marriage and is at its highest somewhere between two to four years (Kimmel, 1974).

Sources of early tension in a marriage are many. The single factor that is most directly related to divorce is income. Lack of financial resources prevents the couple from meeting the expectations for support or protection that are usually associated with the husband's role. Worries about meeting basic needs interferes with the formation of a sense of mutuality and emotional security (Cutright, 1971; Levinger, 1976). If the couple does not share religious, educational, or social class backgrounds, they may have to make many compromises. If the couple does share a small value orientation, certain *lifestyle* decisions will still cause tension. The couple must develop a mutually satisfying sexual relationship. They must work agreements about spending and saving money. They must adjust to each other's sleep patterns, food needs, and toilet habits. Most likely, no single difference will cause a lot of tension. It is the need to adjust to so many things at once that brings conflict into the relationship.

● *lifestyle*—a relatively permanent structure of activity and experience, including the tempo of activity, the balance between work and leisure, and patterns of family and social relationships.

Psychological commitment also must be achieved. The marriage ceremony is intended to make this commitment public and binding. Often the individuals concerned do not fully accept their marriage vows until they have tested their relationship. There is a period of testing during which each partner is likely to put strain on the relationship just to see how strong it is. The question can be posed in this way: "Will you still love me even if I do . . .?" Or "Am I still free to do what I did before we were married?" It is this seesaw between independence and loving that causes a lot of impulsive behavior during the early years. The marriage must be able to handle these pressures from both partners in order to survive. Both people must feel that they still have some freedom. At the same time, they must feel that the limits on their freedom are worth the love they gain in return. As each test is passed, the partners become closer. They trust each other more. They become more sensitive to each others' feelings. Tests diminish as the question of trust is resolved.

The comparison between this testing process and the first psychosocial crisis of trust versus mistrust should be noticed. As an infant, the person learns to count on parents to meet basic needs. As young adults, the marriage partners learn to trust each other. Without trust, the possibility of future growth is seriously frustrated. Despite the challenges and tensions of marriage, young married couples tend to be in a period of satisfaction and positive feelings about their life. In a national survey of adults, Campbell (1976) found that married people were more satisfied with life than unmarrieds. Young married women who had not yet had children were happiest of all. Studies of the early years of marriage find that the husband is important in the success of the marriage because of his strength in the relationship. The woman is generally the partner who has to adjust most to the new situation. She is the one most likely to alter her lifestyle to fit the career and living habits of her mate.

We note a changing pattern of conflict management between marriage partners. Swain (1969) analyzed the handling of conflict at three early stages of marriage: newlywed, pregnancy, and childbearing. In the first stage, men were more likely to be rejecting, forceful in keeping distance, and warmer in closing distance than were women. During pregnancy, husbands were more supportive. Women used more forcefulness to maintain distance and compromise to close distance. Their behavior

Jean-Claude Lejeune

*After a period of testing, couples achieve
a sense of trust in one another.*

was like their husbands as newlyweds. Later, both the man and woman used more logical arguments to handle conflicts.

The successful husband is able to use emotional expression in family problem solving. Women are more uncertain of their identity than are men. Therefore, women are more likely to be threatened by distance during the early years of marriage. As wives feel more confident in their personal identity, they can use more direct strategies in handling conflicts. We would also assume that wives become more comfortable expressing support and agreement.

Divorce

The high divorce rate is evidence of just how hard it is to resolve the conflict of intimacy versus isolation. Almost one third of all first marriages end in divorce (Norton & Glick, 1976b). Three factors that are linked to separation or divorce are income level, differences in between the man and woman, and the husband's ability to express himself.

The divorce rate is higher among low-income men and among couples who marry young. Women with a high personal income are more likely to divorce and to delay remarriage than men (Levinger, 1976). Many studies show that there is a strong relation between social status and both the length of marriage and the partners' happiness (Bernard, 1966; Gurin, Veroff, & Feld, 1960; Scanzoni, 1970). This relation shows how important feelings of security about basic needs are to a sense of intimacy. Doubts about job security, paying bills, or status can undermine the married couple's efforts to meet each other's emotional needs.

Women experience more stress in adjusting to marriage than men do (Bernard, 1964; Gurin et al., 1960). This is based on differences in competences and sense of self between men and women. Many women enter marriage having done less work on their identity than men. Women often have little or no preparation for childbearing and child rearing, which may be their main task. Women are often dependent on their husbands for financial security and social status (Rausch et al., 1974; Rossi, 1968). Because of the differences in power early in marriage, women often experience more emotional strain in the marriage than men.

Finally, mutual satisfaction in marriage depends primarily on the husband's qualities. Stability of the husband's masculine identity, the happiness of his own parents' marriage, his educational level, and his social status all affect marital happiness. "Husbands with strong identities can supply the security their wives need and can support them emotionally in the difficult years of married and parental life" (Barry, 1970, p. 50).

● *inequities*—instances of injustice or unfairness.

Not all evidence supports the view that women experience *inequities* in power and self-confidence in marriage. In surveys of working wives, women in high-status occupations feel confident of their status and independent of their husband's occupational prestige. Working women who have a positive sense of their achievement are less dependent on their husbands for their sense of worth (Hiller & Philliber, 1978).

Marital problems are not always linked to poor adjustment. Four groups of low-income women were compared. The groups were: (1) nonemployed, husband—absent; (2) nonemployed, husband—present; (3) employed, husband—absent; and (4) employed, husband—present. Women whose husbands were absent were less likely than women whose husbands were present to see themselves as a "second" or "submissive" sex (Bendo & Feldman, 1974). They were more efficient, more ambitious, and better at finances. Women whose husbands were present had greater life satisfaction. Their level of satisfaction with work or children was not greater. All women expressed more dissatisfaction with men than with other areas of life. Women whose husbands were absent and more dissatisfied with men than women with husbands. Working women with husbands who were absent had the strongest sense of their own productiveness. They were the most optimistic about possibilities for change, even when their current satisfaction was not very high.

Finally, the likelihood of divorce is greater for men when income and occupational achievement are low. Divorce is more likely for women when income and occupational achievement are high (Levinger, 1976; Norton & Glick, 1976b). Very simply, stresses that women have put up with in the past in adjusting to marriage may be less tolerable as women's autonomy and financial independence increase. The current situation looks distressing. Many marriages fail. Many more young adults fail in their search for intimacy today than they did a generation ago. The long-range picture, however, may lead to more work on identity for both partners, greater mutual understanding, and more mutual respect for competence between marriage partners (Hawkins, Weisberg, & Ray, 1977; Nichols, 1978).

Extramarital relations

● *consensual*—mutual agreement.

Extramarital relations are sexual relations with people besides the marriage partner. Extramarital relations can be agreed upon or not agreed upon. Some authors call the former comarital relations (Libby, 1977) or consensual adultery (Clanton, 1977). This type of sexual activity has been viewed by some as a healthy kind of adult relationship. *Consensual* adultery allows for needs for privacy, self-expression, and sexual experimentation for both husband and wife.

Data on the extent to which couples engage in extramarital relations, whether or not they approve of these kinds of experiences, and the impact of extramarital relations on the marriage are contradictory. Among respondents to a *Psychology Today* survey (Athanasion et al., 1970), 80 percent thought extramarital sex was acceptable. However, those who had actually had extramarital sex was 40 percent for men and 36 percent for women. A *Redbood Magazine* (1975) sample found that 33 percent of women aged 20–29 had participated in extramarital relations. For working women, the percentage was 47 percent.

The impact of extramarital sex on the marriage depends very much on whom one asks and how the behavior is handled in the marriage.

● *furtive—secret.*

Cuber (1969) cited four factors that will determine whether the marriage is helped or hurt by extramarital sex. These are:

A. Whether the adultery is carried on *furtively* or is known by the spouse.
B. Whether the married partners agree to the propriety or expediency of such behavior.
C. Whether one or both participate.
D. Whether the condonement is genuine and based on principle or is simply the result of an ultimatum by one of the two parties (p. 193).

When couples are honest about their behavior and when they accept one another's needs, extramarital relations can be successfully handled in the relationship. On the other hand, for many adults having extramarital relations is a sign of boredom or distance in the marriage (M. Stein, 1974). Stein (1974) interviewed over 1,200 men who were customers of 64 call girls. These men sought sexual excitement. Many felt that their marriages did not provide the emotional closeness or the sexual excitement they needed.

Marriage as a source of life satisfaction

A number of surveys on life satisfaction or psychological adjustment have studied the importance of marriage, parenting, and work in a person's overall feeling of well-being. These studies have asked adults at each of three stages of adult development to describe the areas of conflict, the kinds of needs, and the sources of satisfaction that come from these three basic life activities. The Institute for Social Research at the University of Michigan has done a national survey on personal adjustment in 1957 and again in 1976 (Gurin et al. 1960; Veroff et al. 1977). At each time, people in the age ranges 21 to 34, 35 to 54, and 55 and over were sampled. For these adults, marriage is one of the three most important sources of happiness. Seventeen percent of the sample said their marriage

TABLE 9·6
Comparison of men and women's admission to problems in marriage: 1957 and 1976 (by age)

Age	1957			1976		
	N	M	F	N	M	F
Young: 21–34	268	52%		225	66%	
	368		55%	301		74%
Middle age: 35–54	397	45%		254	63%	
	433		49%	274		60%
Old: 55+	230	33%		216	47%	
	156		43%	156		52%
Total group	897	44%		695	59%	
	961		51%	732		64%

N = number of subjects; M = males; F = females.
Source: J. Veroff, H. Melnick, and R. Kulka, Attributions of Causes of Critical Life Problems. Paper presented at the 85th annual meeting of the American Psychological Association, San Francisco, 1977. Reproduced by permission of the authors.

was a main source of happiness. Only 5 percent said it was a source of unhappiness (Gurin et al., 1960, p. 24).

Men and women were alike in their adjustment to the marriage role. Women, however, experienced more problems and stress in their marriages than men. From 1957 to 1976 there was an increase in the number of men and women who reported problems in their marriage. Table 9·6 compares the percentage of the sample admitting to problems in marriage in the two time periods. In the table, there is a decrease in the percentage of males and females admitting to problems in marriage in the older age group. Perhaps older couples have achieved successful adjustments to the conflicts that disrupt younger marriages.

"Oh, Helen — I saw the counselor today, and he told me to start paying more attention to you."

Between 1957 and 1976 there were more problems in marriage at all age levels for both sexes. There have been changes in the reasons given for marital problems. Most men and women saw the problems as caused by the relationship, not the self or the other alone. However, college-educated men in 1976 were more likely to blame debts, work, or children, as a reason for marital problems. More of the noncollege men shifted to personal blame like "I drink too much" or "I'm too stubborn." In 1976, women were less likely to blame their husbands for marital problems than they were in 1957. At both times women were more likely to blame their husbands than husbands were to blame their wives.

In general, those who were very happy with their marriages thought the relationship itself was a major source of satisfaction. Those who were unhappy thought there was some problem in their life situation, such as lack of money. This was seen as the source of dissatisfaction. There seem to be fewer problems in the very happy marriages. It is not true however, that they are problem-free. A certain amount of stress may even result in greater creativity and involvement in the relationship.

Others have raised similar questions about sources of satisfaction, stress, or well-being in adulthood. These studies begin to show the value people place on different kinds of life experience. They also show the pattern of satisfactions at various phases of adult life.

Flanagan (1978) developed a list of experiences that add to life satisfaction. The list was based on the responses of over 3,000 people. These experiences include:

1. Material well-being and financial security.
2. Health and personal safety.
3. Relations with spouse (girl friend or boy friend).
4. Having and raising children.
5. Relations with parents, siblings, or other relatives.
6. Relations with friends.
7. Activities related to helping or encouraging other people.
8. Activities related to local and national governments.
9. Intellectual development.
10. Personal understanding and planning.
11. Occupational role.
12. Creativity and personal expression.
13. Socializing.
14. Passive and observational recreational activities.
15. Active and participatory recreational activities.

Groups of adults aged 30, 50, and 70 from across the nation were asked to rate each of the above. They told how important it was for the quality of their life and how well their needs in each area were being met. Three factors that were important to 80 percent of men and women at every age were:

1. Health and personal safety.
2. Having and raising children.
3. Personal understanding.

A spouse or opposite sex partner was very important for all but the oldest women, 57 percent of whom were widowed.

Campbell and others (1975, 1976; Campbell, Converse & Rodgers, 1976) have begun to try to understand what factors account for a feeling of well-being or life satisfaction. It is not as easy as one might think to identify the major sources of life satisfaction. Ten factors were included as dimensions that might determine a person's feelings of well-being. They were sex, religion, education, occupation of head of household, family income, working, race, age, urban or rural community, and phase in the life cycle (married, parenting, widowed, and so forth). Campbell felt that this group of factors did not help much to predict who saw life as satisfying and who did not. The one factor that was most related to life satisfaction was the phase in the life cycle. Among the groups with high satisfaction were young, married females with no children, married males over 30 with no children, and married males and females with children over age 17. Those who had the most stress were divorced or separated females and married couples with children under six. Sex differences interacted with life phase to produce feelings of satisfaction and stress. Being young and unmarried was more stressful for females than males. Being over 30 and single was linked with more negative feelings for males than for females. Those who were married experienced greater life satisfaction than those who were single. Being widowed was far less stressful than having children from infancy to 17 years.

Marriage, with its conflicts, is a central source of life satisfaction. This is especially true in the early years before children are born and in the later adult years when children have left the home. Childbearing and child rearing pose *creative* challenges to the intimate husband-wife relationship.

INTIMACY AMONG SINGLES

Just as marriage does not guarantee intimacy, being single does not produce isolation. Being single can be a temporary or a permanent lifestyle. One can be single and isolated or single and fully involved in a complex social network. The case of singles is an example of another pattern of adjustment in the face of what we assume are human needs to experience social interaction and intimacy.

Who remains single?

In 1975, the median age at first marriage was 20.4 for females and 22.9 for males. Almost 92 percent of males and 78 percent of females in the age range 18–19 were single. Of people in their 40s or early 50s in 1975, however, only 5 percent of males and 4 percent of females were single. The majority of single people are late adolescents or young adults who have not yet married for the first time. Since 1970, the rate

TABLE 9·7
Marital status of
males and females
75 years and older:
1976

	Single	Married	Widowed	Divorced
Males	4.9	69.6	23.5	2.0
Females	6.0	22.5	69.7	1.7

Source: Adapted from "Marital Status of the Population by Sex and Age; 1976 U.S. Department of Commerce, Bureau of the Census, *Current Population Reports*, Series P–20, no. 306 (Washington, D.C.: U.S. Government Printing Office, 1977).

of first marriages has been declining. Both males and females are waiting longer to marry than they did eight or ten years ago. This is due to several reasons. More women are seeking advanced degrees and are entering the labor force. Males are concerned about being able to earn enough money. There are about 5 to 10 percent more females in the age range 18 to 24 than males in the age range 20 to 26. This makes marriage less of an alternative for young women (Glick & Norton, 1977). In addition, current attitudes are more accepting of cohabitation. Couples are more likely to agree to the idea of testing a relationship before making a permanent commitment. There are also fewer limits on sexual involvement outside of marriage. Young adults do not feel the pressure to marry in order to have sexual relations.

Another group of singles are those who have been married and are currently divorced. The majority of people who are divorced remarry. There is, however, an increasing tendency to delay remarriage or to remain single after divorce. It is common for adults to wait three years between their first divorce and remarriage. Thus, some singles are in a *transitional* phase moving from one relationship to a new, and hopefully more fulfilling one.

● *transitional*—passing from one stage to another.

The third major group of singles, and one we will discuss further in the next section are widows and widowers. In contrast to those whose marriage ended in divorce, only half of adults who were in their 50s during 1975 were remarried after having been widowed. The marital status of males and females 75 years old and over is shown in Table 9·7. In this age group, the people most likely to be living without a spouse are widowed women.

The last group of singles are the people who never marry. This group is small. It includes brothers and sisters who live together, children who continue to live with their parents, men or women who remain single and live independently, and members of religious orders. These groups probably have the most unusual lifestyle. They have never married. They are unlikely to have experienced the parenting role. They are a distinct minority.

Avenues for intimacy among singles

At one end of the continuum are the interactions among singles that lead to casual sex or "swinging." Roebuck and Spray (1967) studied 30 men and 30 women who were regular customers at a cocktail lounge. While all the women were single, most of the men were married. The

The photography of H. Armstrong Roberts

*Singles meet and find casual encounters
at discos and singles bars.*

women did not seek marriage nor did they want to disrupt the man's marriage. They really came to the lounge for social interaction and to meet someone for sexual pleasure. If they did get married, these women would stop coming to the lounge. The chance to have sexual contact without long lasting social bonds was satisfying for the males and the females. Singles bars, lounges, resorts, and "singles" housing units permit interactions with "ground rules" that limit entanglements.

By and large, sexual encounters are available to the young "never-been-married" singles and to the "transition-between-marriage" singles if they want it. Changing norms about premarital and extramarital sex suggest that more and more people have sex outside of the marriage relationship. Only the oldest group of singles, especially the older widows, are forced into sexual isolation. For this group, there are few eligible partners in their age range and there are norms against relationships between older women and younger men.

FIGURE 9·1
Degrees and dimensions of
sexual lifestyles

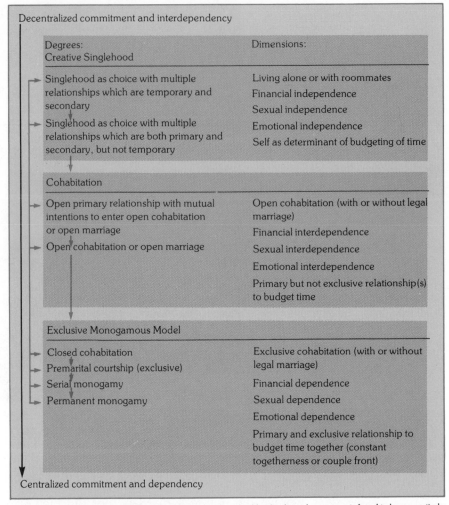

Decentralized commitment and interdependency

Degrees:
Creative Singlehood

	Dimensions:
Singlehood as choice with multiple relationships which are temporary and secondary	Living alone or with roommates
	Financial independence
	Sexual independence
Singlehood as choice with multiple relationships which are both primary and secondary, but not temporary	Emotional independence
	Self as determinant of budgeting of time

Cohabitation

Open primary relationship with mutual intentions to enter open cohabitation or open marriage	Open cohabitation (with or without legal marriage)
	Financial interdependence
Open cohabitation or open marriage	Sexual interdependence
	Emotional interdependence
	Primary but not exclusive relationship(s) to budget time

Exclusive Monogamous Model

Closed cohabitation	Exclusive cohabitation (with or without legal marriage)
Premarital courtship (exclusive)	
Serial monogamy	Financial dependence
Permanent monogamy	Sexual dependence
	Emotional dependence
	Primary and exclusive relationship to budget time together (constant togetherness or couple front)

Centralized commitment and dependency

Note: The dotted lines with arrows indicate feedback loops to other lifestyles if one chooses to or is forced to leave a particular lifestyle. The continuum from creative singlehood to the exclusive monogamous model does not assume a regular progression. People do not necessarily go from top to bottom of the figure; one may stop at any point, or skip lifestyles (they may begin with traditional premarital courtship and end with serial monogamy or permanent monogamy, skipping cohabitation). The arrows indicate the entry points into the various lifestyles.

Source: Roger W. Libby, "Creative Singlehood as a Sexual Lifestyle: Beyond Marriage as a Rite of Passage," in R. W. Libby and R. N. Whitehurst, eds., *Marriage and Alternatives: Exploring Intimate Relationships* (Glenview, Ill.: Scott, Foresman and Co., 1977), p. 51. Reprinted by permission.

At the other end of the continuum is what Libby (1977) describes as "closed cohabitation." Some singles are intensely involved in a monogamous, exclusive relationship in which finances are shared, time is planned together, emotional needs, and sexual needs are all met by the two partners. Figure 9·1 shows Libby's concept of the options open within the single lifestyle. They include the life with temporary and secondary commitments and the life of permanent commitment. Perhaps the most important point about being single is that, like marriage, it is a variable lifestyle.

Adjustment to being single depends on the needs of the person and on the point during the life span at which one experiences it.

Adjustment of singles

Returning to Campbell's study of life satisfaction, we recall several points about the single lifestyle. First, people who were single were less satisfied with their lives than people who were married. Second, young single women felt that they were under more stress than did young single men. Third, single men over 30 were experiencing greater dissatisfaction than were single females over 30. Fourth, one of the two groups experiencing greatest life stress were divorced or separated women. This group of singles is adjusting to three sources of stress at the same time. They include:

1. The loss of an intimate relationship.
2. The *possible* feeling that they might be a failure in the spouse role.
3. Sudden increased demands for self-sufficiency, independence, and competence.

Fifth, being widowed was less stressful than being divorced. It was even less stressful than being the parent of a child between the ages of infancy and 17. In this last group of singles, the loss of intimacy does not imply that the widow was a failure. To compensate for their loss, older women can gain satisfaction from the contributions they make to the lives of others.

INTIMACY IN LATER ADULTHOOD

The impact of widowhood

● *depression*—a state of feeling sad, often accompanied by feelings of low personal worth and withdrawal from relations with others.

In the course of a lifetime, the most difficult adjustment occurs when an adult loses a spouse through death. For many older people, this loss brings severe disruption, grief, and *depression*. The average woman is widowed at age 56 and has a life expectancy of 75. She has almost 20 years when she will be living in a new status (Lopata, 1973: O'Leary, 1977). Because of differences in life expectancy, women are far more likely to experience widowhood than men. There are an estimated 10 million widows in the United States and only 2 million widowers (Lopata, 1978). What is more, almost 70 percent of men 75 years old or older are married whereas only 22 percent of women 75 years old or older are married (U.S. Bureau of the Census, 1977). We see that women are more likely to have to adjust to being a widow. Many women remain single from the time of their husband's death until their own.

Widowhood brings special challenges for those women who have placed strong emphasis on the wife and mother roles. They will be likely to have a decrease in financial resources. They may have no marketable skill and therefore feel uncertain about entering the labor market. They may be uninformed or uncomfortable about using social welfare services in the community. On the positive side, many widows continue to be active in their community and in their family. They may become more involved in the lives of their children and grandchildren. Others establish their own households. For most women, the loss of the husband is felt most keenly as the loss of a vital emotional support. "He is most apt to be mentioned as the person the widow most enjoyed being with, who made her feel important and secure" (Lopata, 1978).

It is important to recognize that widowhood, as painful and confusing as it is, is one life challenge which most women cope with effectively. Recalling the studies of life satisfaction, we see the importance of close friends increasing for older women as the importance of the spouse declines (Flanagan, 1978). According to Campbell, widowhood is less stressful and is linked with less dissatisfaction than the child-rearing years when children are between infancy and adolescence.

Sexuality in later adulthood

What do we know about the sexual behavior of aging adults? Cameron and Biber (1973) surveyed people at different life stages from childhood to later adulthood about their thoughts of sex. They found a decline in thoughts about sex after adolescence that reached a lifelong low among the oldest group, who were 65 and over. If thoughts about sex decrease with age, what about sexual activity? The early Kinsey studies (Kinsey et al., 1948) reported that 2 percent of males were impotent at 35, 10 percent were impotent at 55, and 50 percent were impotent at 75. Of men 75 or older, 60 percent have involuntary morning erections. In a sample where the average age was 71, 75 percent still felt sexual desire. In this group, frequency of sexual activity was as high as three times per week for some people. Sexuality for older males appears to be closely related to the level they had as younger adults (McCary, 1978).

Women experience continued sexual desire at the same level to the age of 60 or older. Continued sexual interest depends on whether or not a woman has the opportunity to remain sexually active. There is no evidence however that physiological changes of *menopause* or even those brought about by hysterectomy reduce a woman's sexual drive.

● **menopause—the ending of regular menstrual periods.**

The key factor for continued sexual satisfaction for both males and females is the presence of a cooperative sex partner. In a comparison of adults in four age groups, 60–64, 65–69, 70–74, and over 75, 60 percent of the married subjects in the first three groups were sexually active. Among subjects who did not have a partner, only 7 percent remained active (Newman & Nichols, 1960). Since women are likely to live longer than men and therefore to have a long period without a partner, they are more likely than men not to have sexual activity in later adulthood. Women may be physiologically more capable of experiencing sexual satisfaction in the later years. Because of the norms for men to marry younger women and for women not to make sexual overtures to men, women are most likely not to have an outlet for their sex drive.

Marriage in later adulthood

When marriage ends in divorce, adults tend to remarry. Today's elderly adults (70 and older) are less likely to have divorced during the early years of marriage than are today's young adults (25–35 years).

Among those 50–75-years-old in 1975 about *85* percent of men and *75* percent of women whose marriages ended in divorce remarried. Fewer adults who are widowed remarry than do those who are divorced (U.S. Bureau of the Census, 1976b).

Remarriage after divorce or widowhood creates several problems. The adult's children may interfere with the couple's efforts to achieve intimacy. In some cases, parents are tempted to devote more attention to their children than to their new spouse. This pattern occurs especially if parents feel their children have been deeply hurt by the divorce or death. Some children really do compete with the new spouse for the parent's affection. The new spouse may resent or dislike the children, adding new levels of hostility and competition to the family.

Finances, especially after divorce, can disrupt a second marriage. If the husband is paying *alimony,* money for the new marriage may be strained. If the wife is supposed to be receiving alimony and does not, her new husband may resent having to assume the expenses involved in the care of her children (Messinger, 1976). Even in marriages among two older adults, perhaps two who have been widowed, the reactions of children and the concerns about finances can create conflict. Although friends may understand and support the marriage, children may look on with concern as a new person enters their lives. The most obvious benefits of these relationships are the opportunities they provide for companionship, sex, and emotional support.

● **alimony—an allowance made to a woman for her support by a man pending or after her legal separation or divorce from him.**

Chapter summary

Intimacy has its origins in the relationship between children and their caregivers. Early experiences of responsiveness and warmth create a bond of affection and a sense of trust.

Interactions with siblings, identification with loving parents, and close peer friendships teach children about the potential for loving relationships. Very young children are clearly able to initiate and respond to loving actions.

In early adolescence and continuing in later adolescence, sexuality is actively woven into the search for intimacy. Even though adolescents do not see a permanent commitment as a condition for sexual intimacy, they view sexual intercourse as an expression of involvement rather than as purely "recreational."

Marriage is the central context for adult intimacy. Differences in patterns of socialization for males and females pose different challenges for adjustment to marriage. Intimacy permits greater openness in engaging in conflict as well as in expressing support.

Divorce is becoming a more common outcome of marriage. It forces us to understand how hard it is to achieve intimate relations during adulthood. For many adults, extramarital relations compensate for qualities that are missing in the marriage. The impact of extramarital relations on a marriage depends on whether or not it is mutually agreed upon and voluntary. Being single permits varied emotional involvements depending on the person's needs and on the person's life stage.

Needs for intimacy go on throughout later adulthood. Widows are especially likely to live without a partner and therefore without opportunities for sexual encounters. Even though adults continue to desire and enjoy sexual activities, the avenues for sexual expression become limited in later life. Remarriage in adulthood is one way to preserve an intimate context. Needs for companionship and sexuality can be met within these relationships, so long as financial obstacles and children's objections can be overcome.

SUGGESTED READINGS

A text with an emphasis on intimacy and sexuality is:

Gagnon, J. H., & Greenblat, C. S. *Life designs: Individuals, marriages, and families.* Glenview, Ill. Scott Foresman, 1978.

A source with a more social, developmental framework is:

Broderick, C. B. *Marriage and the family.* Englewood Cliffs, N.J.: Prentice-Hall, 1979.

For more detailed readings on the process of achieving intimacy:

Murstein, B. I. *Exploring intimate lifestyles.* New York: Springer, 1978.

Raush, H. L., Barry, W. A., Hertel, R. K., & Swain, M. A. *Communication, conflict, and marriage.* San Francisco: Jossey-Bass, 1974.

Reading

LOVE AND EVOLUTION

In love, so richly endowed with bodily and mental satisfactions, social feeling is seen to be the immediate and unquestionable moulder of our destiny. As in friendship and in the relationships with brothers and sisters or with parents, so in love we are concerned with a task for two persons, this time of different sex, with a view to having offspring and continuing the human species. Perhaps no other human problem is so vitally bound up with the welfare and prosperity of the individual in his social environment as that of love. A task in which two persons must be engaged has its own special form and cannot be successfully performed if it is treated as a task for one person alone. It is as though, for the right solution of the problem of love, each of these two persons has to forget his or her own self entirely and give complete devotion to the other; it is as though one life had to be formed from two human beings. To a certain degree we also come across the same necessity in friendship and in activities like dancing and sport, or in work where two persons make use of the same instrument for the same purpose. It is undoubtedly involved in this relationship that questions of inequality,

mutual suspicion, hostile thoughts or feeling must be excluded from it. Moreover, it is of the very essence of love that physical attraction should not be lacking. Undoubtedly, too, it is due to the nature of evolution and its effect on the individual that physical attraction influences the choice of partners in a manner corresponding to the stage of advance that has been achieved by humanity.

Thus evolution puts our aesthetic sense at the disposal of the development of humanity by foreshadowing for us consciously or unconsciously a higher ideal in our life-partner. In addition to the obvious fact of equality in love—still so frequently misunderstood in our day both by husband and wife—the feeling of mutual devotion must also be taken into account. This feeling of devotion is extremely often misunderstood by men, still oftener by girls, as a slavish subordination, and, especially when it is combined with the adoption of the principle of egotistic superiority in the style of life, it deters them from love or makes them incapable of fulfilling its functions. Deficiency in all these three directions—in preparation for a task requiring two persons for its performance, in the consciousness of equal worth, and in the capacity for devotion to another—characterizes all who lack social feeling. The difficulty they experience in this task misleads them into making perpetual attempts to find relief in dealing with the problems of love and marriage—the latter in the form of monogamy, which is undoubtedly the best active evolutionary adaptation. The structure of love just described, being the task and not the end of a development, demands in addition a decision final for eternity, since it is bound to have unending results in the children and in the welfare of humanity. It is a dismal prospect to realize that our mistakes and blunders, our lack of social feeling in love, can lead to our exclusion from everlasting existence on this earth in our children and in our cultural achievements. Such trifling with love as is seen in promiscuity, in prostitution, in perversions, or in the hidden retreat of the cults of nudism, would deprive love of all its grandeur and glory and all its aesthetic charm. The refusal to enter into a lasting union sows doubt and mistrust between the two partners in a common task and makes them incapable of devoting themselves entirely to one another. Similar difficulties, though varying for each individual, can be shown to be a sign of impaired social feeling in all cases of unhappy love and marriage, or of a refusal to perform functions that are justly expected. In such cases only the correction of the style of life can bring any improvement.

Source: Alfred Adler, *Social Interest: A Challenge to Mankind* (New York: G. P. Putnam's, 1964), pp. 59–61.

Chapter 10
Work

No other technique for the conduct of life attaches the individual so firmly to reality as laying emphasis on work; for his work at least gives him a secure place in a portion of reality, in the human community. The possibility it offers of displacing a large amount of libidinal components, whether narcissistic, aggressive or even erotic, on to professional work and on to the human relations connected with it lends it a value by no means second to what it enjoys as something indispensible to the preservation and justification of existence in society. Professional activity is a source of special satisfaction if it is a freely chosen one—if, that is to say, by means of sublimation, it makes possible the use of existing inclinations, of persisting or constitutionally reinforced instinctual impulses. And yet, as a path to happiness, work is not highly prized by men. They do not strive after it as they do after other possibilities of satisfaction. The great majority of people only work under the stress of necessity, and this natural human aversion to work raises most difficult social problems.

Sigmund Freud, *Civilization and Its Discontents*, 1930

Reprinted by permission of W. W. Norton & Company, Inc.

United Press International

For reflection

1. Why do some people choose the same careers as their parents?

2. How people choose careers?

3. If someone said to you, "You can create the job of your dreams," what would it be? Why?

4. If you were unhappy with your job, how would your other life roles be affected?

Our culture defines one's worth by the kind of work one does and by one's income. Work settings may be sources of frustration, disappointment, and conflict. Adjustment to work includes the choice of a satisfying career, involvement in work activities, dealing with problems, and the development of technical, interpersonal, and intellectual skills. Successful adjustment to the world of work may mean pursuing a career in order to contribute to the quality of life. On the other hand, adjustment to work may mean reducing one's focus on the work setting and emphasizing other parts of life. The quality of adjustment depends not only on one's skills, one's education, and one's family background, but on the opportunities open during the years when career choices are made.

The chapter includes five sections:

1. There is a discussion of the sense of oneself as a worker. The development of an inner commitment to work is an ongoing life activity.
2. Early work experiences are described. They add specific content, both successes and failures, to the abstract idea of being a worker.
3. Career choice is treated as a process that may identify goals, point out necessary training, and set early standards for success.
4. There is a discussion of the concrete realities to which one must adjust in specific jobs.
5. We consider the possibility of career change. The work role is not a *static* experience. It is a part of life that changes all the time just as adjustment to the educational setting or to marriage changes.

● *static—fixed*.

THE DEVELOPMENT OF A SENSE OF ONESELF AS A WORKER

We view work as a basic focus of life activity. Work influences social relationships, the development of special skills, the accumulation of financial resources, and the formation of a sense of worth. The components of the work role include personal goals and motives for work, personal abilities and talents, training opportunities and experiences, and the economics of the job market.

Changing concepts of work and working

Two developmental models have been offered that focus on the gradual change of the work role. In the first one, Ginzberg (1972; Ginzberg et al., 1951) describes three ways of thinking about work. In the *fantasy period*, until about age 11, children do not see a difference between what they would like to be and what they can be. The range of career aspirations at this stage reflects the child's awareness of many work roles. It is influenced by the status or "glamour" associated with specific work roles. During the second phase, the *tentative period,* at about 12 to 17, adolescents begin to understand more about the aptitudes and training that a career requires. They also become aware of their own talents, values, and goals that make some occupations more attractive than others. The third phase of career development is the *realistic period.* During this phase, the person tries to match personal talents and goals with the selection of a real career. This may involve experimentation with different jobs and the rejection of certain work activities. These processes can continue well into adulthood. The realistic period may also involve consideration of the current and future demand for certain work roles.

A second approach focuses on changing concepts of the self as a worker. In his description of developmental tasks, Havighurst (1964) has described three stages in the growth of the concept of self as a worker. In the first stage, children identify with workers, especially parents, relatives, and older siblings. During this phase, children may idealize some work roles. Working becomes a major component of the *ego ideal.* In the second stage, children get a sense of industry. The ways of being an effective worker are being learned. These include: planning a task; organizing one's time; enjoying feelings of accomplishment; and beginning to evaluate one's progress. During the third stage, one acquires an identity as a worker in an occupational role. This may come from technical training, on-the-job experience, and experimentation with a variety of work roles.

In Table 10·1, the two views of career development represented by Ginzburg and Havighurst are combined. The top of the table shows the kinds of thinking discussed by Ginzburg. The bottom of the table shows the developmental tasks that promote the concept of the self as a worker. As you can see in the table, both mental processes and developmental tasks contribute to one's ideas about the work role.

Evidence of changes in thinking about the work role are provided by a study of career plans among college women (Harmon, 1971). Stu-

● *tentative*—not certain.

● *ego ideal*—a set of positive standards, ideals, and ambitions that represent the way a person would like to be.

TABLE 10·1
The emergence of the work role during childhood and adolescence

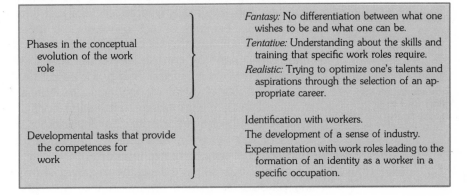

Phases in the conceptual evolution of the work role	*Fantasy:* No differentiation between what one wishes to be and what one can be.
	Tentative: Understanding about the skills and training that specific work roles require.
	Realistic: Trying to optimize one's talents and aspirations through the selection of an appropriate career.
Developmental tasks that provide the competences for work	Identification with workers.
	The development of a sense of industry.
	Experimentation with work roles leading to the formation of an identity as a worker in a specific occupation.

dents were asked whether they had ever considered each of 135 occupations as a career. They were asked the age at which they first thought of it and the age at which they rejected it. The answers showed that the earliest and most popular career choices were housewife and actress. These were first considered in the age range six to nine. Many of the subjects continued to look forward to becoming housewives. Later choices tended to be more specific and indicated greater understanding of actual jobs. For example, careers such as nurse and veterinarian were chosen during the 10 to 12-year range. Biologist, nurse's aid, and physical therapist were chosen at around 15.

These female students expressed interest in a narrow range of career choices. Less than 3 percent of the sample had ever thought of such careers as accountant, governor, dentist, weather forecaster, museum director, children's clothes designer, or hotel manager, to name just a few. The pattern of career choices selected by the students illustrates the narrow range of occupations that most women consider during childhood and early adolescence.

The development of a sense of industry

Psychosocial theory suggests that the person's basic attitude toward work is formed during the middle school age period (8 to 12-years-old). As children learn skills and standards for evaluation, they decide whether or not they will be able to make a contribution to the social community. The concept of industry includes an eagerness for building skills and performing meaningful work. During middle school age, there are many aspects of work that make it attractive and satisfying. The skills are new. They bring the child closer to the skills of adults. Each new skill allows the child some degree of independence. They may bring new responsibilities that add to the child's sense of worth.

There are many sources of reinforcement for skill development. Parents and teachers encourage children to "get better" at what they do through grades, rewards, privileges, or praise. Peers are sources of encouragement for gaining some skills and sources of discouragement for gaining others.

Despite internal and external forces pushing toward mastery and a sense of industry, many middle school age children struggle with feelings of inferiority. Feelings of lack of worth and inadequacy come from two sources: the self and the social environment. Alfred Adler (1935) argued that organ inferiority can play a central role in shaping personality. He suggested that much of the energy for adjustment came from efforts to *compensate* for physical inadequacies. In Adlers view the child, who is small and weak in comparison to the adult, constantly strives to overcome a sense of physical inferiority. By developing skills, drawing attention to his or her behavior, and making demands for love and affection, a child compensates for basic inferiority.

It makes sense to extend the meaning of organ inferiority to include any physical or mental limitation that prevents learning certain skills.

● *compensate*—to make up for; to counterbalance.

A child's sense of industry includes an eagerness to do meaningful work.

When rewards are so closely tied to evidence of mastery, those children who cannot develop specific skills experience increased feelings of inferiority. Individual differences in aptitude and in talent will result in feelings of inadequacy in some areas for everyone. No one can do everything well. Children discover that they will not be able to master every skill they try. Even the child who feels good about work and who finds new challenges to be exciting will experience some amount of inferiority whenever a specific skill cannot be mastered. As Adler suggests, personal limitations can be a challenge that energizes the person toward excellence.

If success in one area could make up for failure in another, then not doing well in one particular area might not matter very much. However, the social environment enters here to provide special reinforcement for success in some areas. In our culture, for example, success in reading is more rewarded than success in tinkering with broken automobile engines. Success in team sports is more highly valued than success in operating a ham radio. A child who does not do well in skills everyone values cannot really compensate through mastery of other abilities.

Social comparisons also add to feelings of inferiority. In the school and at home, children may hear things that compare them to someone else. Children are grouped, graded, and criticized on how their efforts compare to someone else's. The inner motives for doing a task for the challenge conflict with messages that make the child feel self-conscious or competitive. "I like playing ball, but I'm not as good as Ted so I don't think I'll play." During middle school age, some children simply will not try a new activity because they fear that they will not be as good as their peers.

This kind of thinking affects adjustment. At every phase of life there are new challenges and there is the need to develop new skills to meet those challenges. When people approach new skill areas with feelings of inferiority, they may not be able to learn the skills that are necessary for adjustment. This process can go on throughout life. It can reduce the person's flexibility for coping with new life demands. Colleges often have students who decide they are not good at mathematics. Rather than risk failure, these students avoid courses and career programs that depend on mathematical skills. This seriously restricts the students' career options. If one is not willing to take a risk by taking mathematics, then careers in science, engineering, architecture, medicine, nutrition, computer science, or psychology are eliminated. Students who approach mathematics with a more positive attitude soon see its importance for their life goals. Potential risk of failure is outweighed by the new options that math skills open up.

Finally, the social situation produces feelings of inferiority through the negative value placed on any kind of failure. Two kinds of failure messages have been described that add to feelings of inferiority. Some criticize the child's motivation. In these interactions, the person is told that if they had really tried, they could have avoided failure. Other messages criticize the person's ability. They imply that the child does not have the competences necessary to succeed. This criticism is tied to a group of attitudes about the self that has been called "learned helplessness." In response to even a few remarks about lack of ability, children develop a *pessimistic* view about future success (Dweck, 1975; Dweck & Bush, 1976; Parsons et al., 1976).

● *pessimistic—gloomy.*

Middle school age children are often shamed for failure, just as toddlers are shamed when they wet their pants. Feelings of personal doubt and guilt are also caused by feelings of inferiority. Information about failure suggests that there is a standard of perfection which the person did not meet. A few failure experiences can build such strong negative feelings that children will avoid new tasks in order to avoid failure.

In extreme cases, we see the terrible feelings and the withdrawal of children who feel very inferior. These children cannot think of themselves as succeeding. This is very serious. It makes it hard for this person to become a member of a social group. The irony of the conflict between industry and inferiority is that the social environment, which depends on our motives toward mastery for its survival, is a powerful force in working against those motives by sending messages of inferiority.

The importance of work in the culture

In America, adolescence is viewed as the time when most people become workers. For most, adolescence marks the beginning of temporary paid work experiences. Education or training for more permanent careers also begins. In a number of ways, work activities bring adolescents closer to a sense of themselves as adults.

1. Being paid for one's work involves a person in the reality of our economy. Labor → money → resources for purchasing goods → desire for more money.
2. Work is important to Americans. Adolescent workers get a feeling of social worth.
3. Work experiences help adolescents find out what they do well.
4. Work provides adolescents a view of the outcomes of work for future lifestyles.
5. Experimentation in the work role may contribute to a sense of personal identity.

● *postindustrial societies*—societies where technology is highly developed and the emphasis is on human service administration.

● *authoritarian*—a style of decision making in which the leader assumes responsibility for making decisions and assigning responsibility.

Industrial and *postindustrial societies* differ from traditional cultures because of the range of the work needed. There is also a difference in the extent to which children are trained to do those work roles. In American society, there is a lot of freedom to choose one's work. Of course, family finances, community expectations, and personal skills may limit the work roles which an adolescent aspires to. However, the opportunities for training are tremendous. People are encouraged to seek the work goals for which they feel best suited. In more *authoritarian* societies, individuals have less choice about their work. In China, for example, one's work depends on the country's need to have a certain number of people employed in some form of work. The individual's general competencies are matched and channeled through systematic work assignments. In both societies, however, the kinds of work roles that exist are varied, the amount of training necessary for each work activity is varied, and the kinds of lifestyles that accompany different occupations are varied. A person who is trained to repair automobiles may complete training by the age of 18 and feel fully involved in the work of auto repair. A person who is trained as a physician may not complete training until the age of 28 and may not be working in health care until the age of

Jadwiga Lopez

Mexican children help their family by sorting through junk for resale.

30 or 35. In our own society and in other industrial and postindustrial cultures, changes from adolescence to adulthood that are work related are very different.

Compared to other cultures, and other periods of history, modern American society is protective in involving children in work. Gillis (1974) described child labor in peasant families of 16th-century England. At the age of six or seven, children performed major household chores. By the age of nine or ten, they often left home to work for wealthier families. This helped the peasant families to ease the strain of feeding and clothing their other children. It may have helped these families increase their funds through their children's income.

Mead and Newton (1967) described a variety of ways that young children contributed to the economic survival of families in traditional societies. Children are frequently expected to gather food, catch small game, run errands, or help prepare food. Children as young as five or six are asked to look after younger brothers and sisters, carry infants on their backs, and feed younger children. In Samoa, for example, children are expected to perform many tasks for their parents or older relatives. The chores for children under the ages of nine or ten include "fetching water, gathering leaves, cleaning house, building fires, lighting lamps, serving drinks, running errands, and tending babies" (Murdock, 1934, p. 64).

The examples of work done by young children suggest that the adolescent years do not mark the beginning of the ability to contribute to the economic survival of the family group in all societies. We cannot even argue that young children do meaningful work in *traditional societies* but not in technological societies. In China, for example, part of the kindergarten curriculum includes planned experiences in "productive labor." Children at the Yu Yao Road kindergarten spend one period a week wrapping crayons and putting them in boxes or folding crayon boxes into their proper shape. The crayon factory pays for this work, and the kindergarten uses the money to purchase more equipment (Sidel, 1972). The degree to which children and adolescents participate in meaningful work activities depends upon cultural values about the meaning of work and about the part work plays in the development of children.

In American society, the importance of work is stressed from early childhood. Here the emphasis is in the importance of work in adult life. Questions like "What does your Daddy (or perhaps now, your Mommy) do for a living?" or "What do you want to be when you grow up?" are some adults' ways of making contact with young children about the importance of work. Children's activities tend to be viewed as less serious or less meaningful. Play is less worthwhile than work. Work at home for no salary is less worthwhile than work away from home. Work roles that draw mostly women, including nurse, teacher, or secretary are less valued than ← work roles that are filled by males, especially lawyer, physician, engineer, or politician.

From the child's point of view, some of the ideas the culture conveys about work are:

1. One's work determines one's worth.
2. Not all work is equally valued.
3. Not all work roles are open to all people.

What is more, the culture makes it very difficult for children to understand the reality of work. Children are not part of most work settings. Children grow up knowing more about grocery stores, gas stations, and restaurants than they know about architects' offices, newspaper offices, factories, or hospitals. Parents go off to work while children go off to school, to the baby-sitter, or to day care. At the end of the day, the family tries to involve contact with each other. They either ignore most of the experiences that have filled each of their days or they try to understand what each of the family members have experienced. The children are often made to feel that their school experiences are like the parent's work. School is the child's workplace. In making this comparison, however, the essence of the process of education and its place in childhood as well as in adult life is lost.

● *traditional societies*—societies where technology and industry play little or no part.

Living laboratory 10·1

THE DEVELOPMENT OF A SENSE OF ONESELF AS A WORKER

Purpose: To develop an appreciation of the influences of social and cultural values on the importance of work.

Method: Interview one working mother and one mother who works at home who have a child or children the same age. Ask the mothers what household tasks and chores, such as making beds, washing dishes, taking out the garbage, and caring for young children, they expect from their children. Also ask the age at which the child began doing tasks, what tasks the mothers expect their children to undertake in the future, and at what ages the children will assume the additional responsibilities.

Results: What household tasks are the children currently doing?

What tasks are similar? What tasks are different?

Does the working mother expect her child to do more tasks or tasks that require more responsibility than the mother who works at home? If so, why does she expect more?

Compare past and future expectations. How are they similar or different?

Discussion: Do the two mothers equally value the work efforts of their children?

Do you think the child who is expected to do more work around the house will be more likely to appreciate the value of work experiences than the child who is expected to do less?

What differences would there be in the development of a sense of self as a worker between a child who is expected to assume work responsibilities at an early age and one who assumes responsibilities later in life?

What implications do these differences have for the ease of adjustment to the world of work?

EARLY WORK EXPERIENCES

It is clear from the ideas outlined in Table 10·1 that many factors contribute to a commitment to work. What is more, neither system expects that a final decision will be made during early adolescence. This is the time for becoming aware of the requirements and rewards of occupations. It is the time for learning an effective work strategy, and for enjoying the positive aspects of a wide range of productive activities.

Adolescent work experiences

During the age range 14–16 almost all adolescents are still in school. About 25 percent are working in unskilled jobs, including delivering papers, baby-sitting, doing farm chores, or waiting on tables (U.S. Bureau of Labor Statistics, 1967, 1971). Young adolescents are beginning to get work experiences. They are developing a sense of the meaning of work and what they hope for in a job. A poll of high school adolescents shows that active work versus inactive work, work with others rather than work alone, and self-guided work versus work guided by others is desirable (Erlick & Starry, 1972).

Youth face a serious dilemma as they try to identify with work and work activities (Havighurst & Dreyer, 1975). Most young people look forward to work that will be meaningful, that will provide satisfying social relations, and that will not take advantage of them. Their hopes for finding satisfying careers are high. Adolescents from all walks of life aspire to jobs that require a high level of education, involve skill and prestige, and provide good incomes (Kurlesky & Thomas, 1971). However, several barriers stand in the way of these expectations. Many young people who want to work are turned away. The kinds of jobs that adolescents can get often do not provide them with the responsibility, the range of contact with others, or the sense of contributing to meaningful goals that would produce a sense of the self as a worker. The challenge is to create work activities that match adolescent expectations. This challenge requires the adolescent's knowledge of the careers that are possible and of the paths that lead to those careers. It also involves changing work settings so that jobs provide the personal satisfactions that adolescents seek. There is a great need to create meaningful work roles that demand only temporary commitments, as adolescents gain a fuller sense of their own competence as workers.

Vocational education

● *vocational*—relating to a skill or trade to be pursued as a career.

The objective of *vocational* training, "the use of acquired skills immediately on graduation," raises difficult questions. How should work experience by woven into the secondary school program? Should all students be prepared to use some acquired skills immediately on graduation? How can the school make its resources available to students who work?

The goal of vocational preparation has always been a major objective of the American public high school (Deal & Roper, 1979). It has also been the object of constant criticism. Students in vocational programs often do not have other academic experiences. The training for many occupations is outmoded, so that students who graduate from high school do not have the skills they need on the job. The range of careers in the vocational curriculum has been limited, so that adolescents are not free to explore the full variety of careers that may exist in their area.

Recent recommendations on high school reform emphasize the need to work with community industries, business leaders, and professionals in designing the vocational curriculum. Industry might support the purchase of modern equipment so that high school students could receive more up-to-date training. Students might have the chance for some vocational experimentation before choosing one area for training (Porter, 1975; Brown, 1973).

Because of the high cost of a college education and the declining vocational advantage of having a college degree, more and more communities are increasing the vocational emphasis of their high school. One might argue that all students should leave school with a vocational skill, whether or not they plan to attend college. Having a "marketable skill" increases the adolescent's sense of competence, reduces his or her dependence on parents for financial support, and makes college attendance an option rather than a necessity.

Some say that the high school should offer vocational training and a service experience for all students. Students need to feel responsible and to have a commitment to their community. High school students represent a virtually untapped resource of human energy, ideas, and competences that could benefit the community (Havighurst, 1966). Rather than isolate high school students from their communities, this goal would move more adolescents into contact with other age-groups, other socio-economic, religious, and cultural groups. It would give high school students some experience in providing help, entertainment, service, or companionship to others in the community who might benefit from their efforts.

Adolescent unemployment

Since 1960, there has been an increase in the number and proportion of unemployed youth in the United States, especially among nonwhite males and females (Havighurst, 1975). Some changes in the economic and social conditions of the last 15 years have reduced the opportunities for early experimentation in employment. Between 1968 and 1972, the proportion of high school students going on to college dropped from 55 percent to 49 percent (Young, 1973). In 1977, the proportion of high school students going on to college was 26.3 percent (*Statistical Abstracts,* 1978). The drop has been especially large among white males. Several factors may be causing the decrease in college enrollments. The fact that college enrollment no longer is a means of delaying military service, the rising costs of college tuition, and increasing difficulties in finding work after college are a few (Perrella, 1973).

At the same time that the pool of high school graduates who do not go on to college has increased, the availability of jobs for high school graduates has decreased. Businesses that are required to pay a high minimum wage are less willing to hire young employees who come with limited skills and who are likely to leave for another job (Coleman, 1972). Work settings are asking for more educational credentials and they are providing fewer opportunities for part-time work experiences. The impact of these changes are reflected in work patterns of the high school class of 1972. Of the graduates in the labor force who were not enrolled in college, 14.7 percent were unemployed. In addition, of the class of 1972 high school dropouts who were in the labor force, 26.5 percent were unemployed.

Unemployment is especially difficult for adolescents in low-income communities. When those teens look ahead to the young men and women who are only five or ten years older, they often see a life of constant financial problems. They see men who cannot provide for their families. They see women who are forced to take *menial* jobs. They see couples who can barely manage to pay the rent, buy food, or feed their children

● *menial*—lowly or subservient.

The photography of H. Armstrong Roberts

Unemployment is especially high among adolescents.

even when both are working (Liebow, 1966, 1967). Shifts in the job market, the kinds of work available, and the vulnerability of the unskilled laborer to layoffs all make the *work role* a source of frustrations. In Liebow's example of a young street corner man, the future as a worker is seen through the lives of others in the neighborhood.

As for the future, the young street corner man has a fairly good picture of it. In Richard or Sea Cat or Arthur he can see himself in his middle twenties; he can look at Tally to see himself at thirty, at Wee Tom to see himself in his middle thirties, and at Budder and Stanton to see himself in his forties. It is a future in which everything is uncertain except the ultimate destruction of his hopes and the eventual realization of his fears. The most he can reasonably look forward to is that these things do not come too soon. Thus, when Richard squanders a week's pay in two days it is not because, like an animal or a child, he is "present-time oriented," unaware of or unconcerned with his future. He does so precisely because he is aware of the future and the hopelessness of it all. (Liebow, 1966, 1967, p. 66).

CAREER CHOICE

A career can be thought of as any set of work experiences that permits a person to make productive use of talents and skills. The career of an artist, for example, could involve work in many media, including oil painting, sculpture, ceramics, sketching, collages, watercolor, and pen and ink. It is not the medium, the project, or the theme of the work that defines the career. It is the artist's personal definition of all these activities as the expression of a unique set of talents and goals. In the same way, one might think of an entrepreneur's career as a series of involvements in a number of small businesses. A salesperson's career may be selling many different products. The concept of career change needs to be reevaluated.

If a person continues to work, we understand that he or she has a career in the broadest sense of the word. Changes in work activities cause changes in the life structure. They may also result from changes in the life structure. Activities that were once satisfying no longer are. The lifelong occupational career is a changing set of activities. These changes lead to changing competences, new goals, and a changed appreciation of the meaning of types of work and types of reward. From this point of view, it does not make sense to expect that a career decision that is made during adolescence will remain unchanged throughout life. Even if the decision is made in a rational, planned way, a good decision may not be a permanent one. As adults grow and change, their awareness of options and their understanding of their own skills change. The phases of decision making and the factors that may contribute to career choice during later adolescence must account for the likelihood of change. In fact, we expect that a person's career will be the subject of constant attention and adjustment throughout adulthood (Newman & Newman, 1979a).

The decision-making process

In discussing career choice, we are thinking about the purposeful choices and decisions that individuals make in guiding their careers. Career-related tasks may include a decision to attend college, a decision about a major, or a decision about an occupation. Career decisions are made by a process of logical thought about the consequences of particular career choices. They require the ability to consider the suitability of particular career choices and work activities. Planning that leads to career choice is also necessary.

Tiedeman has proposed a model of career decision making that assumes the person is responsible. The goal of *career definition* involves a number of separate tasks during adolescence and early adulthood. With effective problem solving, the person gains increased control over life events. They are better prepared to meet the challenges of the next decisions. Tiedeman's theory offers seven stages in the career decision-making process that are summarized in Box 10·1. Four stages emphasize

Box 10·1

SEVEN PHASES OF CAREER DECISION MAKING

1. Exploration

This stage is marked by unrestricted exploratory considerations. It is characterized by generalized, vague concerns with little or no progress toward choice. Knowledge of self and the occupational world is a felt need, but the individual has developed no strategy or plan of action for satisfying this need. There is an absence or a near absence of negative choices (exclusions of alternatives from the range of possibilities). This stage is accompanied by vague anxieties about the future.

2. Crystallization

This stage represents progress toward choice but not its attainment. The individual recognizes alternative choices and at least some of their consequences. Conflicts are recognized; advantages and disadvantages are weighed; and the bases for a decision are being developed, at least implicitly. The range of possibilities is being narrowed down through negative choices. False steps and inappropriate earlier decisions are recognized and are used as bases for further decisions.

3. Choice

This stage represents a definite commitment to a particular goal. That commitment is accompanied by expressions of satisfaction and relief for having made it. The individual may focus on aspects of self which are evidence that the decision was appropriate. This stage further represents a swing from the pessimism characteristic of the exploratory stage to a kind of naive optimism about the future. The individual usually expresses a singleness of purpose and an unswerving attitude of goal direction, as well as eagerness and impatience to reach the goal. A focus upon the consequences of the decision and further planning are not yet in evidence.

4. Clarification

This stage represents a process of closure in which the individual is involved in clarification and elaboration of the consequences of commitment, as well as in planning the details and next steps to be taken to follow through on the commitment. The individual is usually engaged in a process of elaboration and perfection of the self-image and the image of the future. Although planning and overt action to carry out the commitment are characteristic of this stage, the overt action may be delayed until the environmental conditions are appropriate for action.

5. Induction

This stage marks the beginning of the implementation of a decision, the point at which the individual comes into actual contact with a new environment. One begins the process of accommodating to a new group of people and a new situation in the living out of one's career decision. The primary mode of interaction is passive. The individual is hesitant and is looking for cues from others in the group to determine what the group's values and goals are and what the group's expectations of one are. Although there is a general defense of self and a giving up of aspects of self to group purpose, the individual needs to feel some level of acceptance of one's uniqueness by the group. Gradually, one identifies with the group through the assimilation of one's individual values and goals into the group's values, goals, and purposes. This stage ends when a person becomes aware of being accepted by the group.

6. Reformation

In this stage, the individuals primary mode of interaction is assertive. One is highly involved in the group, enjoins the group to do better, and acts upon the group in order to bring its values, goals, and purposes into greater conformity with one's own values and goals (which have become somewhat modified during induction). One also acts upon the out-group to bring its view of one's identification with the in-group into greater consistency with one's own view. There is a strong sense of self, which is somewhat lacking in objectivity. At the same time, self is abandoned to solutions and group purposes. The result of this stage is a modification of the group's values, goals, and purposes.

| 7. Integration | In this stage, older group members react against the new member's force for change, which causes the individual to compromise or modify intentions. This results in a greater objectivity toward self and toward the group's purposes. A synthesis is achieved which both the individual and the group strive to maintain through collaborative activity. The individual is satisfied, at least temporarily, has an image of self as successful, and is considered successful by the group. |

Source : V. A. Harren and R. A. Kass, "The Measurement and Correlates of Career Decision Making," (Paper presented at the American Psychological Association Meeting, San Francisco, 1977). Reprinted by permission.

planning or clarification of the choices. Three stages involve carry the decisions into action. For each of the career-related decisions, including the decisions about college, major, occupation, job change, and career redirection, effective decision making would involve all seven phases (Tiedeman, 1961; Tiedeman & O'Hara, 1963; Miller & Tiedeman, 1972; Tiedeman & Miller-Tiedeman, 1975). You might think about the decision-making process that has led up to your own choice of major and try to identify how many of Tiedeman's phases were involved.

Styles of decision making. The phases of decision making are probably encountered by every person in the process of choosing a career. However, people use different decision-making styles that determine how they make use of information and how much responsibility they take for the decisions they reach (Dinklage, 1969; Harren, 1976; Lunneborg, 1977).

Harren (1976) has described three categories of decision-making styles. The *Planning style* is the most rational. Planners assume personal responsibility for a decision. They seek out information to assess both personal competences and the qualities of the situation. The *Intuitive* style makes primary use of fantasy and emotion. A decision is reached without much information seeking. It is based on what feels right or best at the time. The *Dependent style* is influenced by the expectations and evaluations of others. Dependent decision makers take little responsibility for their decisions. They see circumstances as forcing their decision or limiting the options.

Harren and Kass (1977) studied the progress of 578 college undergraduates in choosing a career. Their decision-making progress was determined by three tasks: the decision to come to college; the decision about

● **intuitive—knowing or perceiving by quick and ready insight.**

a major; and the decision about a future occupation. Both academic class standing and having made a satisfying decision about one's major or future occupation were closely related to the career decision-making score.

Students identified the Intuitive style as most like their decision-making process. Students responded favorably to items that reflected an instinctive sense of what would be a good career decision. They preferred this strategy to the more tedious activities of the Planning style. Nevertheless, the Intuitive style was not related to decisiveness, to the formation of a vocational self-concept, or to work values. Fantasy, awareness of feelings, and a sense of one's inner states may be highly valued as a path toward personal adjustment, but they are not the most effective coping strategies for career decision making.

Sex role and career choice

In recent years, more and more women have entered the labor force. Many women hold the roles of wife, mother, and worker. There is no sign that this trend toward increased employment of women is

Jean-Claude Lejeune

The title "cameraman" suggests the sex-role bias of that career.

going to decline in the near future. In fact, the census data show that women are delaying marriage and childbearing longer and that more women are voluntarily childless (Glick, 1977). These data suggest a growing involvement in work and a decision to limit the demands of competing roles.

Despite the fact that more women are in the labor force, men and women do not participate equally in areas of employment (Bernard, 1971; J. E. Parsons, 1977). Even though women do as well as men in college, fewer women plan for graduate training (Astin, 1977; Baird, 1976). Women continue to enter a few traditional careers, and many women are "underemployed," considering their level of ability and education (Tangri, 1972; Severance & Gottsegen, 1977).

Several explanations have been offered to account for these differences in participation. Four explanations are presented along with supporting or qualifying evidence.

1. Men and women use different cognitive styles to make career choices. Women use the Intuitive style, and men use the Planning style. As we discussed above, the Intuitive style is a less effective coping strategy. It would, therefore, lead to less carefully planned or less mature career decisions. However, studies do not support this explanation. Comparisons of male and female college students do not find differences in decision-making styles (Barrett & Tinsley, 1977; Lunneborg, 1977; Harren & Kass, 1977).

2. Men and women understand specific careers in different ways. Baird (1977) asked a national sample of college seniors to evaluate five careers: medicine, law, college teaching and research, elementary and senior school teaching, and business. Except for business, men and women see different advantages and disadvantages in these careers. For example, more women than men thought that law provided challenge and interest, that it required a high level of intelligence, and that it offered avenues to contribute to the advancement of knowledge. More women than men saw success in law as affected by one's political views. Women saw law as a high-pressure profession requiring hard work, long hours, and a lot of time away from one's family. In this sense, women may see law as a less desirable career, particularly if they have already made a strong commitment to marriage and family.

3. The absence of women models in certain industries or in highly visible leadership positions contributes to differences in the career aspirations of men and women (Shafer, 1975; Severance & Gottsegen, 1977). Following this hypothesis, Tidball (1973) found a correlation of +.95 between the number of women faculty at an undergraduate college and the number of women graduates who followed successful careers. In the Soviet Union, where there is an attempt to make full use of women in the labor force, 36 percent of engineers and 45 percent of scientific workers are women (Chabaud, 1970). Russian girls are more likely than

American girls to have mothers who are in professional roles and to hear about professional women who are in positions of responsibility.

4. Career aspirations are determined by attitudes, personality, and child rearing experiences. Women who are most committed to the roles of wife and mother will have less *innovative* career aspirations. Tangri (1972) reported that female students who choose occupations which few women choose are likely to have educated, working mothers. These women are autonomous and internally motivated. They have well-developed self-concepts. They have a strong career commitment. They are likely to have support for their career goals from faculty, female friends, and a boyfriend. In a more recent study of female college students, a number of attitudes were important to high career aspirations (Parsons, Frieze, & Ruble, 1975). These attitudes included:

- ● *innovative*—unusual, something new.

1. A belief that women's demands for equality are justified.
2. A sense that men think women's demands for equality are justified.
3. A belief that career and family roles are not in direct conflict.

A woman with high aspirations was likely to have a mother who had a career or a mother who was dissatisfied with her work. In this analysis, the strength of the woman's commitment to her own career was greater when she understood the ways that discrimination had influenced the problems of women in careers.

In summary, men and women bring the same intellectual skills to career decision making. Women do not use a less effective cognitive style than men. Women do tend to have different views than men about the desirability of certain careers. This is most likely due to past differences in the participation of men and women in various professions. The absence of female models reduces the likelihood that women will aspire to some careers. The more women understand how these patterns have come about and the more support they have from parents, faculty, and peers, the more likely they are to seek more innovative careers.

Career counseling

Career decision making can be improved by seeking help from a vocational counselor. This type of counseling is most often used by adolescents and young adults as they enter the job market. Vocational counselors can also be of help to adults who are thinking about a career change or to women who have not had a career and want to begin one during middle adulthood.

There are several ways the vocational counselor works with the client. First, the counselor tries to figure out the client's talents and interests. One test used by vocational counselors is the *Strong/Campbell Interest Inventory* (1974). This test asks about what the person likes to do in a wide range of activities. The person's responses are matched to those of people who are already established in specific careers. One learns how similar or different one is from others who are already in careers in science, humanities, social services, social sciences, journalism, medicine, business, or clerical work (to name a few).

Second, the counselor may test specific skills or aptitudes. Test scores provide information about whether one has the potential to develop skills that might be required in a job.

Third, the counselor may do personality testing in interviews. This information helps the counselor and the client to predict the kinds of work that would be a good fit with the person's motives, temperament, and social style.

Once a career has been identified, the counselor can help the client to learn skills that might help in getting a job. These skills include *resumé* writing, how to react in an interview, how to complete personnel data forms, or how to tell a potential employer about one's skills.

● *resumé—a short account of one's career and qualifications prepared typically by an applicant for a position.*

More generally, the vocational counselor has a broad view of the kinds of jobs that might best match a person's competences. The adult who wishes to change career directions can benefit from this point of view by recognizing other uses for well-developed skills. The person who is just entering a career can be encouraged to consider new work roles that may not have existed during the person's own childhood or careers that were not thought about during the person's educational training.

Adaptation to work settings

Work itself is a complex concept in our society. Each job places the person in a different situation and, therefore, each job can be seen as involving different psychological demands on the individual. The three characteristics of the work setting to be discussed include:

1. Interpersonal demands.
2. Authority relations.
3. Occupational hazards.

Interpersonal demands. Even though the potential for friendship in the work setting is not promoted as a central feature of job incentive, the opportunity for companionship can be important in the decision to take a job. The need for friends and the need to share the uncertainties of the new job with peers are strong motives to seek comradeship in the job. Co-workers who get along with each other, who can relax together, and who can share feelings of accomplishment together can improve the quality of any work setting. In fact, the spirit of friendship on the job may make it possible to tolerate many stressful demands. Of course, some work settings stress competition between co-workers. Incentives increase competition rather than cooperation. In these settings, new workers must handle the stress by themselves. They must learn the game of "one-upsmanship," always taking credit for successes and directing the blame for failures onto others. Depending on the person's motives, the competitive setting may interest some people, whereas a setting that emphasizes collaboration would attract others. New workers must determine the quality of interpersonal relationships and whether or not these relationships meet their social needs.

Authority relations.   Each job involves status positions and hierarchical decision-making relationships. Adjustment to a new job means learning who rates one's work, what criteria they use for evaluation, and what the limits of one's freedom may be in the job. New workers must respond both to the authority structure and to people who occupy positions of authority. With respect to the structure, they must understand the paths for decision making and the ways they can influence decisions. New workers must be able to deal with many personalities in higher and lower positions.

There are many patterns of authority relations in the world of work. The person must identify the authority structure that operates in the work setting and then begin to establish a position in that structure. Advancement in a career involves some increases in responsibility and decision-making power. One cannot advance without having some increased authority. Thus, career development eventually involves the ability to take on the authority role as well as to respond to higher authorities.

Jobs differ in their patterns of advancement. Some careers begin with a long period of working for someone else. This slowly gives way

"Does anyone here have enough sense of security to oppose my suggestion?"

Reprinted by permission The Wall Street Journal

to increased authority. Some careers place new workers in positions of authority quite early and continue to move them up the ladder at a steady pace. Still other careers find the new worker in a position of authority that never changes much. The task for the adult is to recognize the authority pattern and to figure out which skills will be needed for advancement.

Some people do not choose to advance beyond a given point in the authority structure. They find a position in which the responsibility and position in the authority structure are both comfortable. Others find that if they do not choose to advance, their careers suffer. Still others discover that further advancement is not possible. They attain a peak in status which they cannot improve.

The ability to understand the nature of the authority relationships and the expectations of the authority figures in a work setting will in large help to determine success at work. Success, in this sense, means advancement or movement toward material goals and freedom from the demands or the needs for advancement of others.

● *hazards—sources of danger.*

Occupational hazards. During the trial work phase, people learn about the stresses and *hazards* in the jobs that they are trying out. Different occupations create different hazards. The list of ways that a worker might be hurt in a job includes:

1. Sudden demands for new kinds of job performance.
2. Job performance and job security highly dependent on the decisions of others.
3. Rapid obsolescence of knowledge and/or skills.
4. Decreased demand for occupational specialty.
5. Likelihood of transfer by the employer.
6. Early peaking of upwardly mobile opportunities.
7. Lack of preparation for and abruptness of retirement.
8. Limited or fixed salary and benefits.
9. Hazardous working conditions.
10. Continuous exposure to stress.

Jobs differ in the kinds of pressures or hazards they expose workers to. Individuals differ in the danger these hazards present. Some people are more willing to risk danger than others (Gardell, 1977). Each person must decide whether the hazards of a job are tolerable.

The impact of work on other life roles

Management of a career does not occur independently of commitments to one's spouse and one's children. Decisions about more authority, working longer hours, accepting an offer with another company, quitting one's job, or accepting a transfer to a new location are all decisions that will affect the lives of other family members. One of the most draining things about career management is trying to meet the conflicting demands of marital, parental, and work roles (Pines & Kafry, 1977). Family and work life are connected whether one or both adults are employed. In the following example, the same *work-family conflict* is viewed from two points of view.

Work. The atmosphere in the office is serious as three department heads meet to discuss the complaints they have been receiving from one important work team. The focus of the complaints is the employees' travel schedules. Heavy travel during the summer season is a project necessity, but the complaints this year have been particularly bad and the number of sick days and postponed travel schedules have been increasing.

Family. In one of the families in which heavy travel was the issue, the wife makes a demand upon her husband. "The teacher told me today it's very important for you to spend more time with our son. She thinks a lot of his disturbed behavior can be traced to wanting more attention from his father, since he told her you're never home." The husband's response is, "But you know I have to finish up this assignment. Things will be better in the fall" (Renshaw, 1976, p. 250).

Careers differ in the kinds of strains they place on other family members besides the worker. Some women care deeply about their husband's achievement. They experience personal satisfaction from his success. Other women are forced to accept the long hours, frequent moves, or social obligations that come with a job (Papanek, 1973). Even though the long hours, the travel, or the transfers are thought of as stressful, they do not necessarily create marital dissatisfaction (Clark, Nye, & Gecas, 1978; Renshaw, 1976). The degree to which the couple copes with these work-family conflicts depends on three factors:

1. How successful the husband actually is in his work.
2. His income level.
3. The wife's views about what kinds of commitment the husband should have to household or child-rearing activities.

For example, many men who work long hours also earn high salaries. Their salary can be used to buy things for the whole family and to improve the quality of their leisure time together. In these cases, the husband's absence is resented less than it might be if he were earning less.

The work-family conflict is increased when both the husband and the wife are working. Most couples see child care and certain household tasks primarily as the job of the wife (Hoffman, 1974; Stafford, Backman, & Dibona, 1977). When both the husband and the wife are working, the woman may experience a lot of stress as she tries to meet work demands and still have the time to spend with her children. In a study of 200 professional couples, women were more likely to have greater responsibility for the home and family and to put their husband's career ahead of their own (Heckman, Bryson, & Bryson, 1977). The conflict between career aspirations and family commitment is handled for some women by limiting their competitive, achievement strivings.

For other women, work limits achievement through assumptions about a woman's commitment to her family role. Women do not tend to be promoted to high-level administrative or managerial positions where work demands would begin to interfere with family needs (Blaxall & Reagan, 1976). Companies do not like to put women in positions where they may have to be transferred. They assume that the husband will not make the move (Gallese, 1978).

In spite of the stresses of conflict for working women, career development appears to be well worth the effort in the long run. Low-income women who do not have a husband are more confident and more independent if they are employed than if they are not. In a study of women in middle adulthood, the self-esteem of career women was higher than the self-esteem of noncareer women (Birnbaum, 1975). Women who are working are more independent, assertive, and self-assured than those who are not. They do not have to struggle with the self-doubt and uncertainty that confront family-oriented women.

Living laborabory 10·2

CAREER CHOICES

Purpose: To understand the psychology of work.

Method: Visit a factory or other work setting that requires the use of unskilled or skilled laborers. Observe the interpersonal demands of the work setting, authority relations, and occupational hazards.

Results: Keep a log of your observations.

> *Interpersonal demands:* Is there a spirit of friendship in the setting or is competition stressed?

> *Authority relations:* Draw a diagram of the patterns of authority in the factory. What is the likelihood that a factory worker will assume an authority role?

> *Occupational hazards:* What hazards exist in the setting? (See section on "Occupational Hazards.")

Discussion: How does the spirit of friendship or lack of it relate to stressful situational demands?

What type of individual (e.g., psychological characteristics) would fit into an affiliative work setting? What type would fit in a competitive work setting?

What processes occur as individuals adjust to new work settings? If adjustment is difficult, how might other areas, such as family life, of the worker's life be affected?

What psychological factors may be operating to encourage a worker to assume higher levels of authority? To discourage seeking of authority? How would assumption of an authority role affect the worker's relations with co-workers and other interpersonal demands of the setting?

How might long-term stress affect the work performance and nonwork roles of an individual?

CAREER CHANGES

Adults do not always do the same kind of work throughout life. In modern times, career change is often necessary. In the section on career counseling we suggested some of the ways that people find help in changing their career direction. At any point in one's career, adults may do this assessment. They are likely to decide to redirect their skills and talents toward new goals.

Some kinds of career change occur because of development. The period of work search and accompanying experimentation with work roles is part of the early period of work life. The mid-life career change or the decision by women to enter the world of work after a career as parent and homemaker are more likely in the middle adult period. These changes occur as people have time to examine the fit between early personal goals and actual achievements. Changing careers is a kind of risk that may only be possible when accompanied by a *sense of urgency* that comes at mid-life. Similarly, retirement, and redirection of work-related competences to new activities is common in the later adult life phase.

Early adulthood and the work search

Because of the fact that many occupational choices are possible, young people are not usually prepared for a specific occupational role during childhood and adolescence. Most jobs require a period of training for the new employee. The training period may last from a few weeks, in the case of an assembly line worker, to ten years, in the case of a physician. For some people, the stage of young adulthood is passed before training is completed. During the training period, workers are taught the norms and goals of the work setting. This involves learning the technical skills, interpersonal behaviors, and authority relations that are worth something in this job. These are necessary to successful work in this job.

Brim (1968) discusses the "occupational search phase" of this period:

Thus the typical adult during his first years in the labor force experiments with various jobs and passes through his trial work period. People become differentially attracted to occupations on the basis of income, accessibility, and the fit of the job to their skills and their personalities (Inkeles, 1964), so that an individual's discovery of a compatible occupation is a result of his shifting from one line of work to another until he finds work that he likes. Often the individual leaves jobs which he does not like until he stumbles upon something better. It is during this period that he acquires the knowledge and skills suitable for his more mature occupational choice (Form & Miller, 1960) and enters that phase of his occupational history in which he is likely to continue in the same general line of work for the next 30 years (p. 197).

Many things limit which occupations are open to a person during the work search phase. The most obvious include: educational level, talent, and location. Other social and psychological factors may limit a person's work goals or their chance to do certain kinds of work. Let us offer some examples. First, some occupations are *sex-labeled*. Females are more likely to think of nursing, teaching, or library work as suitable careers. Men are more likely to see administration, engineering, or management as fitting them (Oppenheimer, 1968).

Second, women's career goals depend on whether or not they expect to marry and to have children. In a study of a national sample of women, results show that the higher their occupational achievement, the more likely they were to remain single (Havens, 1973; Mueller & Campbell, 1977). In contrast, the more a woman is committed to the family roles of wife and mother, the more likely she is to interrupt her career, to choose a lower status occupation, or to reject graduate training (Astin, 1977; Cartwright, 1977).

Third, racial discrimination continues to affect the participation of white and black men in the labor force. There continue to be limits on school achievement, work status, and income level of blacks that indicate racial discrimination (Hauser & Featherman, 1974).

In summary, we see the period of early adulthood as the time for looking around and for training. By working in several settings, young adults learn about the requirements of specific occupations and environments. They also begin to imagine themselves moving into the future through a particular work role. In this context they begin to weigh the costs and gains of their chosen occupation. The work search is limited by the limits individuals place on the kinds of work they are willing to consider and by the responses of the work world to the diversity of potential employees.

Mid-life career change

The development of a career does not necessarily mean doing the same job or even the same kind of work. There are many reasons to change one's work goals during mid-life. Here, we will consider four different patterns.

First, some careers reach an end during middle adulthood. One obvious example is a professional athlete. Other work roles that require physical strength, speed of reaction, or endurance may force a mid-life career change when these abilities are gone.

Second, some adults cannot handle conflicts between job demands and personal goals. Here we think of the young Chicago executive who decides to buy a farm in Arkansas (Terkel, 1972, 1974) or the public relations aid to a senator who leaves Washington to return to Maine to sell real estate (Sheehy, 1974, 1976). The case of Simeon Wooten, Jr., illustrates this kind of career change. It is guided by careful study and decisions about what is important (see Case 10·1). Wooten was one of the graduates of the Harvard Business School class of 1949. Affectionately called the "49ers," this class met with unusual business success. Sixteen percent of those who responded to a *Fortune* Magazine survey in 1974 were millionaires. Thirty years after graduation, Wooten shows a common pattern of personal understanding and change (Wellemeyer, 1979).

United Press International

Professional athletes expect a mid-life career change.

Third, some workers recognize that they have succeeded as much as they can in their work. Their career change reflects a realization that they are not going to achieve their aspirations in their career. It may take a person several years to reach this understanding. Many adults decide to stick it out in a secure position, even when it falls short of their goals. Others decide to retrain, return to school, or begin in a new field.

Fourth, there are women who have been in and out of the work force who decide to make a greater commitment to career once their children are in high school or college. These women often begin by returning to college to complete a degree or to pursue a new degree. Nearly 40 percent of women who leave work while their children are young and 60 percent of those who have never worked but want to, state a need for more education or training before entering the job market. At every age range from 18–24 to 65 and over, women look for an employment pattern that allowed them to stay home while their children were young. They want to combine career and homemaking before children are born and after they are older (Market Opinion Research, 1977).

Case 10·1

SIMEON WOOTEN

Simeon Wooten Jr., at 52, gave up his comfortable life as president of the Southeast Everglades Bank of Fort Lauderdale to embark on a new career in teaching. Wooten, who calls himself a "new conservative," is worried that the drift toward egalitarianism in the United States is eroding the foundations of capitalism, and he blames this partly on the U.S. educational system. As he puts it: "If I have a voice that has any impact at all, it will be in that system. I'm a very concerned citizen, and I no longer want to be among the silent majority."

Wooten's first stint at teaching came when he was recalled during the Korean War and taught leadership to noncoms. The satisfaction of that experience stayed with him. Once financial commitments to the education of his own three children were taken care of, he began to think about changing careers. After a year as a college instructor, to make sure he still enjoyed teaching,

Wooten enrolled in the fall of 1976 in the doctoral program at the University of Virginia's Darden Graduate School of Business.

Shifting gears hasn't been easy. "If you really want a course in humility, come back to school after 30 years," Wooten remarks. He's found one of his biggest problems to be acquiring the quantitative skills necessary to use computers. And he has had to redevelop the habit of concentrating for hours on a problem. "It's not retirement," he notes. "I thought I would have a nervous breakdown the first year."

Wooten has traded the sailing club for the library, and his wife, Marion, has traded the Junior League for real-estate brokerage. "Obviously our living standard is lower in a material way," says Wooten, who doesn't seem to mind because, "in an intellectual way, life is much more stimulating."

Source: M. Wellemeyer, "Reassessment Time for the Forty-Niners," *Fortune*, May 21, 1979, p. 120.

Many women actually desire a lifestyle that would have a built-in mid-life career change.

In contrast to the mid-life career change, some adults are "locked-in" to their career choice. In a national survey of people 16 years or over who were employed for 20 hours a week or more, almost 42 percent felt it would not be at all easy to find another job with a similar salary and fringe benefits. What is more 62 percent of the sample said they would not be willing to move 100 miles away in order to get a much better job. In fact 26 percent were not willing to move that far for another job even if they were out of work. The risks of trading certainty, even an unpleasant or unfulfilling certainty, for uncertainty are not very appealing to many adult workers (Quinn & Staines, 1979).

Retirement

At the time of retirement there is a new demand to occupy time. Many options for new activities are open at this point. Some people have anticipated the increased freedom. They have activities in mind that they look forward to as the demands of work decrease. For others, retirement comes without being anticipated or prepared for. These adults may experience anxiety or depression at the end of their work. For these older adults, redirection of energy to new roles is a much more complex

● *introspection—*
deliberate self-
evaluation and
examination of private
thoughts and feelings.

● *mandatory—*required.

process of adjustment. It involves personal *introspection* about their areas of skill, their outlook toward the future, and the quality of their social relationships. In order to select activities that will satisfy their interests, they must evaluate their life goals. New directions are sought that will bring greater harmony with personal ways of viewing the world.

Still other workers reject or resist forced retirement. At retirement age, they are still strong, energetic, and involved. Work gives their lives structure and meaning. Their salary permits them to live independently and to maintain their sense of personal competence (Powers & Goudy, 1971; Shapiro, 1977). In 1978, growing resistance to *mandatory* retirement at age 65 resulted in raising the retirement age to 70 among federal government employees.

Let us just note here that some people never retire, they never face this part of career development. Individuals who are self-employed or who are in some creative profession where age is not important may continue at the same work until death. They may discover new skills, they may redefine their work goals, or their standards of success. They never abandon their occupational role (Dennis, 1966; Simonton, 1977).

As adults get close to retirement, many turn to leisure activities to fill their time. Some people decide that tennis, golf, fishing, cards, boating, or administrative work related to these activities will occupy the remainder of their lives. Investment in leisure activities is not exactly a new role; the retired businessman does not think of himself as a golfer. However, the energy spent in these sports can be quite intense. Adults may chose a retirement community that helps them satisfy their leisure interest. They may plan vacations to allow new experiences related to their favorite sport. Involvement with a leisure activity can actually become like a full-time job.

A new interest among many older adults is continuing education. Community colleges as well as four-year schools have begun to respond to the educational interests of the adult population. Older adults are returning to complete bachelor and advanced degrees to develop new skills, or simply to share interesting times with other students (Stetar, 1975).

An interesting new role that has begun to emerge for people who have ended their life work activity is that of retiree. Current publications such as *Modern Maturity* define an older age-group with common, interests in much the same way as *Seventeen* defines early adolescence as an age role. There are groups of people in later adulthood who form active voting blocks and maintain lobbies which attempt to promote the passage of legislation in the interest of older people. Within many companies there are groups of retirees who, as former employees of that company, attempt to administer pension plans and to influence company policy. The presence of these groups is evidence of the continued vigor of older adults. It is also evidence of their ability to identify and promote issues related to their own welfare (Ragan & Dowd, 1974).

National policy also attempts to aid older people by helping them to direct their energies to a wide variety of new roles. The Social Security Act was designed to provide a minimum income to people 65 or older. Benefits now may be obtained by women and by men at their own request before age 65. Social security benefits may then be received continuously until death. To some, the benefits of social security seem to be inadequate. To others, these benefits represent an important source of income. Because this minimum income is secure, older adults who receive them have the freedom to do what they want with their time and energy. They may wish to stop work. They may choose to continue some form of part-time work. Some become absorbed in being a grandparent. Others begin completely new lives. With these benefits, older adults do not need to work a full forty hour week to survive.

Retirement stimulates a person's capacity for introspection. When the day-to-day preoccupations of work are removed, people are freer to let their thoughts wander. They can begin to pay more attention to personal interests. Retirement may also spark a personal evaluation of the work role, job satisfaction, early training, and occupational contributions. As a person seeks solutions to the problem of how to redirect energy to new concerns and activities after retirement, private thinking

U.S. Department of Housing and Urban Development

After retirement, many adults develop new areas of skill.

helps the person to select new interests and to evaluate the available resources for pursuing these interests. Retirement usually means an increase in time that is unscheduled. Most adults feel positively about being relieved of the daily work.

For some, the time made available by retirement is an unwelcome burden. These people may not be ready to retire. They may feel discouraged by the feelings of uselessness that accompany not working. For these people, introspection is more likely to spend time on injustices of the retirement regulations, anxiety about how to maintain a certain financial level, and regrets about a lack of personal control over one's life. Those who do not feel content about this new phase of their lives are unlikely to find sources of satisfaction in their own introspective thinking. Retirement may facilitate the development of a sense of despair (Atchley, 1976).

Living laboratory 10·3

CAREER CHANGES

Purpose: To explore causes of career change.

Method: Read biographical or autobiographical information about an athletic superstar.

Results: Trace the career changes that occur in the athlete's life.

When did the athlete enter into professional sports?

What life events or experiences preceded entry into professional sports?

What work demands were placed on the athlete?

When did the athlete change careers?

What life events precipitated the change?

What similarities and differences exist between the two careers?

Discussion: Some athletes elect to leave their sport and some leave because contracts are not renewed. Do you think there will be differences in adjustment and coping to a new career in these two instances? What adjustments in lifestyle must be made?

What cultural or societal factors would facilitate or hinder a career change?

Chapter summary

The process of adjusting to work begins with the development of a concept of oneself as a worker. In addition, the development of an accurate understanding of the variety of work activities is achieved. A sense of the work role involves three stages. In stage one, the person has fantasies about work and about identification with other workers. In stage two, the person thinks tentatively about specific work roles. The development of a sense of industry also occurs during this stage. In stage three, the person makes a realistic selection of a career. Experimentation with work roles which occurs during this period leads to commitment to an occupational identity.

According to psychosocial theory, the middle school age stage of life is the time when a sense of industry is achieved by most people. The sense of industry creates a self-perception of one who has valued skills and who enjoys exercising competence. This self-perception is essential to the development of the worker role. In contrast, feelings of inferiority create a self-perception that makes the person doubt their capacity to work effectively.

A sense of oneself as a worker is also influenced by the culture one lives in. The importance placed on work, opportunities to work, and the status given to particular occupations are all cultural conditions that shape our image of ourselves as workers.

For most Americans, adolescent work experiences do not teach about the kinds of work or work settings they will experience as an adult. They do provide opportunities to learn about money, about taking responsibility, about the employer-employee relationships. Some adolescents develop specific skills they will use in their adult work. The adequacy of their training depends on the particular community they live in and the collaboration between school and industry in the community. Many adolescents face unemployment.

Seven phases of decision in the process of career choice are identified: exploration, crystallization, choice, clarification, induction, reformation, and integration. Many college age students approach career decision making from an "intuitive" style. They emphasize fantasy and feelings more than information. Career choice is also influenced by sex-role stereotyping of careers and by models who encourage or discourage nontraditional career choices. Career counseling may help identify the range of options and the person's potential strengths and interests. Counselors also teach the problem-solving skills necessary to make an informed decision.

Once a career is chosen, the process of adjustment to the work setting begins. Interpersonal demands, authority relations, and hazards of the work setting all require some compensatory adjustment. What is more, work demands often require a reorganization of personal life. Family, spouse, and peer relations may all be altered because of expectations of the work setting.

Adjustment to work involves creating a fit between the person's skills and needs, and job demands and opportunities. It is not surprising that one's career often includes shifts of emphasis, changes in employer, or even total reorientation. Major change points include the early search phase, mid-life career change, and retirement. Whether these changes are imposed by employers or chosen by the worker may influence later adjustment. Some people avoid change. They willingly survive unpleasant work settings in order to retain job security. Others eagerly move from one career to another. They see career change as a way to remain fresh and vital.

SUGGESTED READINGS

A journal that treats issues related to work and adjustment to the work setting is Monthly Labor Review.

Of interest in the area of women and work are:

Mednick, M. T. S., Tangri, S. S., & Hoffman, L. W. *Women and achievement: Social and motivational analyses.* New York: Halsted, 1975.

Blaxall, M., & Peagan, B. *Women and the workplace.* Chicago: University of Chicago Press, 1976.

Hoffman, L. W., & Nye, F. I. *Working mothers.* San Francisco: Jossey-Bass, 1974.

Other books on specific aspects of work include:

Wolman, B. B.   *Victims of success: Emotional problems of executives.* New York: New York Times Book Co., 1973.

Bryson, J. B., & Bryson, R.   *Dual-career couples.* New York: Human Sciences Press, 1978.

Hall, D. T.   *Careers in organizations.* Santa Monica, Calif.: Goodyear, 1976.

Reading

STRESS AND THE WORLD OF WORK

Individuals or organisms under stress react with complicated and often paradoxical responses. To understand how to personally manage stress, some background discussion of these effects will be useful. What are the physiological signs of stress? What are the behavioral signs of stress? What sustains stress?

Physiological signs of stress are shown in change of appetite or in level of physical activity. Under stress, the appetite moves up or down; you will either eat more food or less food. You will be more physically active or less physically active. You will either want more sleep or less sleep. The reason for this is uncertain. I can't resolve the paradox of why these things tend to go in one direction or another. What are the indicators of physiological stress in you? Which way do your appetites move? Are you more interested or less interested in sex? Are you more interested or less interested in drinking?

One of the generalized reactions to stress is depression, in which case the appetite tends to go down. Inferred from this, very often, is the conclusion that the organism is not aroused. The organism is, in fact, physiologically highly aroused. This arousal is expressed as low appetite, low sex interest, or disturbance of sleep. If a person feels confidence in the ability to control stress, the appetite moves up; a lack of that confidence to control means movement of appetite in the opposite direction.

The first phase of stress is aggression—adrenalin is secreted; you are in an attack phase. However, if at a point you think you have lost control, there is a shift to the other side—the depressed side.

What are the behavioral signs of stress? Irritability is one; you are like a firecracker with a very short fuse, ready to explode at someone. Restlessness is another; things do not seem to move fast enough for you. You do not respond to your environment; sometimes you do not listen to answers to questions you ask. This can be like listening to a telephone message through background noise, or being in an airport control tower with too many planes waiting to land at the same moment; you receive too much information to filter out the main signal.

What sustains stress? Guilt is one factor, and leads to a feeling of ambivalence when unresolved things are carried over from day to day. Hostility is another. You are very angry but cannot or do not express it, either to a senior person in the establishment with whom you are worried about the consequences or to a subordinate (both examples of hostility or denial).

There are people who are very hostile in their talk, but who never take action. Theirs is a passive hostility; they are the "chronic complainers." These people are under high stress.

Resolving conflicting attractions is stressful; this can be a situation where a choice must be made between two equally good job offers, and it can be just as difficult as having a choice between two negative situations. In conflicting attraction and conflicting avoidance there are stresses, though the former is more pleasant. In conflicting attraction your pace will be speeded up, you assume control, and will be more aggressive; you think you are going to win. Nevertheless, you are under stress; there is an adrenalin response to this kind of situation.

Creative procrastination or "When do you win with procrastination?" Is a concept studied at the University of Chicago with successful middle-aged men and women in professional careers. Some were principals of large high schools. They recognized that, while procrastination can be over-used, it is a useful strategy for control of stressful situations. In certain disciplinary problems, for example, letting a problem "ripen" a little might be preferable to immediate intervention.

Goal clarity is another factor to consider: if you have diffused goals you are more likely to be stressed than if they were clearly set; being specific helps. And there is the ability to express feelings related to frustration, especially since there is a notion that feelings are to be controlled and not expressed. Particularly as one moves toward middle age it is less appropriate to express emotions than when younger. As a result of this norm, more time is spent under stress. In the executive position, you are not supposed to have these feelings.

What strategies can be used to handle these chronic stress situations? Talking things out seems a good technique; somehow a drainage of tension occurs which seems to help. There is also the notion that we are stronger emotionally some days than others, and therefore can take more stress on certain days. Another thing that seems to work is the encounter group.

Under stress one's pattern of thought changes, moving heavily toward convergent thinking. Convergent thinking is that which says there is one and only one solution to a problem. Divergent thinking, on the other hand, takes place when one is relaxed and able to choose from alternate hypotheses. A strategy for recognizing stress may be to ask yourself whether you are looking for single solutions or generating alternatives.

On getting stress feedback from physiological or behavioral signs, the first question to ask is, "What is causing the stress?" Try to get some clarification of your goals, and then perhaps take action. On the other hand, perhaps you will see that the things that are causing the stress do not relate to you. Going through the process (maybe admitting you are under stress and talking about it to someone else) cools you down enough to reduce that high state of physiological arousal—to keep the brain relaxed rather than response-prone.

I want to end these comments on a note of hope and faith. Faith has been credited with stress-resistant qualities. Experiments with rats deprived of hope resulted in death, with hypothalmic changes measured through autopsy. Lack of hope made the rats give you the will to live, yet if they had some experience with survival, they would have no longer been vulnerable. Belief has an effect against stress. If you believe things are going to improve, you will be better off than if you did not believe that.

Source: James E. Birren, *Personal Management of Stress.* In R. H. Davis (ed.) *Stress and the Organization.* Los Angeles: The University of Southern California Press, Ethel Percy Andrus Gerontology Center, 1979, pp. 51–53.

Chapter 11
The community

The policeman buys shoes slow and careful; the teamster buys gloves slow and careful; they take care of their feet and hands; they live on their feet and hands.

The milkman never argues; he works alone and no one speaks to him; the city is asleep when he is on the job; he puts a bottle on six hundred porches and calls it a day's work; he climbs two hundred wooden stairways; two horses are company for him; he never argues.

The rolling-mill men and the sheet-steel men are brothers of cinders; they empty cinders out of their shoes after the day's work; they ask their wives to fix burnt holes in the knees of their trousers; their necks and ears are covered with a smut; they scour their necks and ears; they are brothers of cinders.

Carl Sandburg, *"Psalms of Those Who Go Forth before Daylight,"* 1918

From CORNHUSKERS by Cark Sandburg, copyright 1918 by Holt, Rinehart and Winston, Inc.; copyright 1946 by Carl Sandburg. Reprinted by permission of Harcourt Brace Jovanovich, Inc.

U.S. Department of Housing and Urban Development

For reflection

1. In what places do you feel most welcomed in your hometown community? Why?

2. How do we learn what are appropriate and inappropriate ways to act in different settings?

3. Why do some college students always choose to sit in the same seat during every class?

4. What are some of the neighborhood noises you associate with your hometown?

Communities differ in many ways. In order to appreciate the process of adjustment within communities, we must know how well each community serves its people. What are the ways in which communities help people to be more effective and efficient? The chapter approaches this concern with a discussion of four topics:

● *ecological*—dealing with the relationship between living organisms and their environments.

1. There is a description of some of the basic *ecological* qualities of communities. These qualities provide some dimensions across which communities can be compared.
2. The concept of setting access is discussed in some detail. This concept refers to the openness or availability of settings to community members.
3. Some examples of special settings for people with special needs are described as a way of showing strategies communities use to help adjustment.
4. The concept of community mental health and its goals are discussed. The community mental health movement shows the types of programs that communities are expected to have to serve the needs of the population. The main purpose of community mental health programs is to help people use community resources in ways that will allow them to become effective. In this chapter, our emphasis is on mutual influence of the healthy, growing community and the healthy, growing person.

CHARACTERISTICS OF COMMUNITIES THAT AFFECT ADJUSTMENT

People spend their daily lives in many different settings. Think of four children who wake up in the morning, eat breakfast, get dressed, and decide to go out to play. One child leaves the apartment, walks down the hall to the elevator, rides the elevator down 20 floors to the basement, unlocks his or her bike from the bicycle rack, walks the bike out the rear entrance of the building, and rides to the park. The route to the park involves crossing several busy streets and riding through an underground passage beneath a highway.

The second child lives in a house with many other houses nearby. In order to go out to play, the child walks out the back door, gets his or her bike from the garage, and rides across a number of streets to the park.

The third child lives on a 500-acre farm. In order to play with a friend, the child asks his or her mother to drive to the friend's home, ten miles away. The two children play at the friend's house and around dinner time, an adult drives the child back home.

The fourth child lives in a small village in the mountains. When he or she goes out of the home, there are groups of children at play in the open spaces between the huts. Children wander together in the woods, down by the stream, or gather around a mother who is feeding a small baby.

There are hundreds of images that can be called upon to show different neighborhoods. What is more, the same neighborhood may be viewed quite differently by people at different ages, with different resources, or with different backgrounds. A person who is moving from a small, rural village to a city of 50,000 may be impressed by the increase in resources. A person who is moving from a city of 1 million or more might find life in a city of 50,000 slow paced, and perhaps somewhat restrictive.

The study of neighborhood environments as contexts for adjustment is just beginning. There are some dimensions that have been described in some detail. These include the density of the population and the income level of the population. Other aspects of neighborhoods are just beginning to be systematically assessed (Sarason, 1974; Warren & Warren, 1976). The seven concepts discussed below merely serve to introduce some of the relevant dimensions of communities that have implications for adjustment.

Population density

Density refers to the number of people who are living in a specified amount of physical space (persons per acre or persons per room). Freedman (1975) has contrasted density and crowding. Density is an objective quality of a neighborhood that can be measured. Crowding is a subjective experience. It refers to the person's past experiences in settings of varied densities as well as to the expectations for a particular setting. A person can feel crowded in the back seat of a car with 2 other passengers and feel very comfortable on a bus with 40 others. A child can feel comfortable in bed surrounded by stuffed toys, trucks, books, and blocks but feel crowded zipped into a sleeping bag on a camping trip.

We can appreciate just how subjective the experience of crowding is by comparing the relation between population density and signs of stress in different cultures. Schmitt (1963) studied the effects of population density in Hong Kong. In comparison to cities like New York and Boston where high-density areas include 450 people per acre, Hong Kong has 13 census tracts that have more than 2,000 people per acre. Yet in Hong King the rate of hospitalizations for mental illness was 10 percent of the American rate. There were six times fewer cases of murder and manslaughter, and less than half as many crimes. In Tokyo, where there are over 20,000 people per square mile, density is generally not a disruptive factor (Canter & Canter, 1971). Yet when the subway cars in Tokyo became overloaded, passengers burst into violence. There are limits to every person's willingness to adapt to crowding (Ittelson, Proshansky, Rivlin, & Winkel, 1974).

When other aspects of the neighborhood are controlled, including income level, educational background, and people coming and going, high density is not related to unfavorable factors like crime rate, disease, death rate, or mental illness. In fact, Freedman (1975) argued that in low-income neighborhoods, high density is related to lower rates of juvenile delinquency. When there are more people around on the streets, the streets are safer. The presence of many people in a small space provides diversity, opportunities for interaction, and the focus of public resources to specific high-density locations. If many people are drawn

"Don't think 'overcrowded'—think 'the richness of urban life.'"

to a particular location, they most likely see some advantage to living there. High-density areas may have high status. They may also produce strong feelings of unity among the residents.

In contrast, we might ask about the effects of very low-density neighborhoods. What is the effect of having very few people in a given physical space? In some low-density areas, families receive far fewer support services and resources than they would if they lived in more dense areas. Low population density may be related to few opportunities for interaction, more dependence on family members for companions, and more time alone.

Income level

There are some qualities of low-income neighborhoods that influence the opportunities that people who live there have for interaction. Low-income families tend to live in smaller living space. This is true in inner city neighborhoods, in small towns, or in mountain communities. The number of people in the house influences each person's privacy. The more people who live together, the greater the frequency of encounters among family members, and the more they use the same space for several purposes. In an analysis of persons per room, Winsborough (1965) reported that when seven or more people lived in a room, disease and mental illness were high.

Low-income neighborhoods have higher crime rates. This means that people have to be more watchful. They must use more precautions to protect their property and themselves. When juvenile delinquency rates are high, the attitude toward young adolescents becomes one of suspicion. As adolescents move through the neighborhood, they are likely to face mistrusting looks and harsh reprimands. Adolescents often face accusations by store owners, security guards, and customers.

Freedman (1975) made a comparison between high-density, high-income, and high-density, low-income neighborhoods. In the former, like West End Avenue in New York City, the streets are clean, and the buildings are attractively decorated. There are few stores and few pedestrians. In the latter, like Broadway between 72nd Street and 140th Street, the street is filled with garbage. There are all kinds of stores including pizza parlors, bookstores, supermarkets, and cigarette shops. Drunks, dope addicts, and prostitutes hang around the street. Yet, after 10 P.M., it is much safer to walk down Broadway than to walk down West End Avenue. The norm in low-income neighborhoods to use the street, to get out and mingle around, actually protects people. Even though Broadway may be less attractive it is more alive, and therefore safer.

Population stability

Kelly (1966) has argued that how often people come and go in an environment influences adjustment. This influences the roles that emerge, the openness of the people to newcomers, and the attitudes toward novelty in general. When we think about population exchange in a neighborhood, we think about trucks loading and unloading furniture,

The photography of H. Armstrong Roberts

When neighbors are always changing, everyone feels a bit more anonymous.

discovering new playmates, and feeling like a newcomer or feeling like one of the old gang. The degree of transience in a neighborhood influences both those who remain and those who move. When people do not plan to remain in a neighborhood, they tend not to become involved in community activities or projects. Other residents may make fewer efforts to extend friendship if they expect that newcomers will soon leave. Young mothers in transient neighborhoods may feel more isolated than young mothers in stable neighborhoods. Without the bonds to childhood friends or to extended family members, young parents have fewer adults with whom to share the concerns of parenting.

● reputation—overall quality or character as seen or judged by people in general.

In stable neighborhoods, children and families develop neighborhood *reputations*. These reputations may extend to the people on the street, shopkeepers, schoolteachers, or the police. One's reputation can be an advantage or a disadvantage. People may expect more than the person can accomplish. People may also expect less than the person can actually achieve. In highly transient neighborhoods, children and their families may simply be more anonymous. Adjustment to the stable or the transient community depends in part on whether one is a stable or a transient member in each of these contexts. For example, the transient adult may have more feelings of alienation in a stable community. Gaining acceptance is slow and the criteria for acceptance are rigid. The stable resident in a transient community may experience stress and find adjustment difficult as friends and neighbors come and go.

Population diversity

Neighborhoods differ in the extent to which they include people from different income levels, different racial and ethnic backgrounds, different ages, and different educational backgrounds. In most unplanned communities, income level tends to determine who will live in a particular neighborhood. In large cities, it is not uncommon to find neighborhoods that are inhabited largely by Italians, Puerto Ricans, blacks, Jews, Greeks, or Irish.

● homogeneous— sharing the same qualities.

There are two current trends in planned communities. One is the development of *homogeneous* communities designed to meet the needs of a specific population. This includes public housing for low-income families and adult communities for retirees. The other approach is to create neighborhoods that will include residents from a variety of income levels, ages, and backgrounds. Planned communities like Reston, Virginia; Columbia, Maryland; and Roosevelt Island are new urban settings that have diversity of population, function, and design.

Typically, suburban neighborhoods are far from the resources of the city. They are composed of families that are quite similar to one another. Children who grow up in homogeneous communities have few opportunities to interact with children or adults who do not share their experiences or values. Homogeneous communities are low in value conflict and high in ethnocentrism. Children grow up thinking that everyone is like they are. If they are different, they are not as good. The lack of diversity in the population tends to put heavy pressures on individual members to conform. Deviance of behavior or thought is quite obvious in a homogeneous neighborhood. It is important to point out that city neighborhoods can be just as homogeneous as suburban or rural neighborhoods. Although we tend to associate cities with diversity, this is only true when taken as a whole. It is very likely that during the elementary school years, children in the city will interact primarily with immediate neighbors. Those neighbors on the streets, in the stores, and in their school very probably share their cultural, financial, and religious experiences. As adults in the city, people may know of the diversity of the population without ever having more than the most impersonal contacts with members of different ethnic, religious, or economic backgrounds.

Weather

The climate of the neighborhood will determine how people use outdoor space or indoor space. Cold weather climates tend to push people inside for more of the day. During the cold seasons, children use indoor public settings for play if they are available. These include hallways, lobbies, and malls. As the weather gets colder, people spend more time in their homes and less time wandering through the neighborhood. In warm climates, people are outside more. They need more outdoor settings and tend to create settings to meet those needs.

Weather affects mood and energy level. People react to weather conditions like heat, cloudiness, or high humidity with a range of symptoms including irritability, lack of concentration, headaches, and restlessness. Even infants have been noted to react to weather changes with increased whining and irritability (Faust, Weidman, & Welmer, 1974).

Safety

People seek safety in their neighborhood. Feelings of being unsafe are a major source of adult dissatisfaction with respect to their community (Kasl & Harburg, 1972). Ironically, though we usually think of the need to protect children from danger, many adults express a need to protect themselves and their property from children. In several public housing projects, residents felt threatened by children (especially adolescents) who damaged the elevators, made noise, wrote *graffiti* in the hallways, and hid in dark corridors where they would rob and attack residents (Rainwater, 1970).

● *graffiti*—writing or drawing on rocks and walls.

Safety influences the pattern of exploration and the ease with which people can encounter one another. At different ages, parents will set limits on their children's entry into the neighborhood depending on just how safe parents think it is. In some apartment buildings, the corridors and lobbies are safe play areas. In other buildings they are not. In some neighborhoods, the sidewalk in front of one's house is a safe area. In others it is not. In some communities, young children can walk safely to one another's houses without worrying about traffic. In other communities they cannot. Public parks are safe areas in some communities, but not in others. The dangers in a neighborhood depend upon the terrain, the automobile traffic, the diversity and poverty of the population, and the extent to which the neighborhood is open to observation (Gump, 1975).

Noise

Noise is one of the major sources of urban stress. People are bombarded with more sensations and information than they can process (Miller, 1961). The most disruptive kind of noise is high-intensity noise which comes and goes at unpredictable intervals (Glass & Singer, 1972).

It is quite clear that children and adults adjust to noise. Some residents became so used to the noise of the Third Avenue elevated train in New York that they moved near another el station when the Third Avenue el was taken down (Ittelson et al., 1974). Residents of Boron, California live near Edwards Air Force Base where supersonic military planes are tested. The citizens of Boron take pride in the 20 to 30 sonic booms that take place in their town every day (Murray, 1972).

There is some evidence that adjusting to noise takes its toll on children. The hearing abilities and reading ability of schoolchildren who lived in four 32-story apartment buildings built on bridges over an expressway were evaluated (Cohen, Glass, & Singer, 1973). The lower the floor, the higher the noise level. If they had lived in the apartment buildings four years or more, the children on lower floors with more traffic noise made more errors in telling similar sounds apart. Difficulties in hearing were related to poorer reading scores. There was a clear pattern of more difficulty with hearing and reading with increased time living in the building. It is important to point out that none of the children in this study had a hearing loss as tested by an *audiometrist*. The children had adjusted to the noise level of their home environment by tuning out fine sound discriminations. This adjustment had the long-term effect of interfering with reading skills.

● *audiometrist*—a person who measures characteristics of sound, including hearing.

Not all neighborhood noise is "noise pollution." Some of the noises of the neighborhood are part of the vivid image-making stimuli that give character. A study by Southworth (1969) provides an illustration. Students explored the city of Boston in three different groups. Some could see but not hear, some could hear but not see, and some could see and hear. Some sounds added a sense of delight and distinctiveness to certain parts of the city. Boat whistles, bells, birds singing, or water splashing were all meaningful sounds that highlighted the city settings. Memories of our own neighborhoods include the call of the knife sharpener man, the Good Humor ice cream bells, the wind blowing piles of dry leaves, and the fog horns sounding in the night. Over time we get to know the meanings of neighborhood sounds. We recognize some as signals of calm and others as signals of trouble.

PEOPLE AND SETTINGS

In order to study the process of adjustment within communities, we need to identify the units or components of the community. One might use a physical measure such as acres or square feet for this purpose. However, this kind of measure lacks psychological meaning. In a community, just as in a home or a school, there are meaningful settings that engage participants. If we want to understand the resources and barriers of a community, we need to know about the meaningful patterns of interaction that might be available to community members.

Behavior settings

Roger Barker (1963, 1978) has developed the concept of "behavior settings" as a unit for studying environments. A behavior setting is defined by the physical boundaries, the physical entities, and the space-time bound-

U.S. Department of Housing and Urban Development

A behavior setting has shared meaning for all participants.

● *random*—**arranged by chance.**

aries of a particular behavior episode. Barker gives the example of a lecture in a conference room of a Philadelphia hotel. The time and space, the physical boundaries, and components including people, furniture, water pitchers, and microphone, can all be described. The collection of objects and persons is not *random*. The setting has a meaningful unity that can be observed, even without participating in the setting. Other examples of behavior settings might be the family at dinner in the dining room, the bus ride to school, a bank lobby, or a game of baseball in the park.

In order to study an environment, one begins by identifying the behavior settings. Once the settings are described one can trace the patterns of behavior that occur in the settings. Barker and Wright (1955) used four categories to code social behavior in each behavior setting. These included:

1. Occupancy time: the number of hours people spent in the behavior setting during a year.
2. Penetration: the extent of involvement and responsibility of individuals in the setting.
3. Action patterns: typical behavior patterns associated with a particular behavior setting.
4. Behavior mechanisms: frequency of occurrence; tempo or speed, and intensity of thinking, talking, manipulating, looking, listening, motor activity, and emotional behavior.

In order to appreciate the quality of life in a community, one begins by identifying the behavior settings that exist. These will provide an idea of the opportunities as well as the pressures of the community. For example, in an analysis of behavior in an American and a British community of similar size (population 830 in Midwest, 1,300 in Yoredale) there were 146 public behavior settings in the American town and 178 in the British town. In Yoredale, 20 percent of the behavior of the town's residents took place in trafficways, 1 percent in Hays garage, and 2 percent in the National Health Service Office. In Midwest, 7.8 percent of behaviors occurred in trafficways, 3.7 percent in Weylin's grocery store, and 0.3 percent in the county engineering office (Barker, 1978). These data illustrate a method for mapping setting use. They provide a map of the human activity within a community. They also suggest that not all settings are the same in the lives of all community members. From the available settings, residents create their own pattern of relationships. They shape their own lifestyles.

Not all settings are equally open to all community members. For example, in American communities young children are not likely to be active in bars, factories, or hospitals; the elderly are not usually found in day-care centers or elementary schools; and adults do not frequent certain drive-in restaurants or pinball parlors. To some degree, setting use increases with age. Adolescents can go into a greater range of settings than infants or toddlers. Adults can use a greater range of settings than adolescents. In later adulthood, the use of settings declines somewhat. Intensity of involvement in the settings that are used may stay quite strong, however (Barker & Wright, 1955).

The ability to enter a setting also depends on the number of people available to fill the required functions of a setting. Barker and Gump (1964) demonstrated this in a comparison of setting use in high schools that ranged in enrollment from 35 students to 2,300 students. The largest school contained 65 times as many students as the smallest, but only 8 times as many settings. What is more, the largest school contained only 1.5 times as many kinds of settings as the smallest. Students at smaller schools participated in more district events and extracurricular activities than did students in larger schools. A much larger percentage of students in small schools held positions of responsibility in a variety of activities.

Small-school students reported feeling greater pressure to participate in the school than did large-school students.

Differences in satisfaction with extracurricular activities were also mentioned. Students at smaller schools reported satisfaction about their self-competence, including more successes, and being part of an action group. Students at larger groups reported satisfactions of a more passive nature. They were proud to be a part of the school. Students in small schools act on their environment rather than being passive members of their school community.

Barker and Gump found that there is a difference in adolescents' experiences, depending upon the size of the high school they attend. Small schools have relatively "undermanned settings." These involved schools need students to work well. This results in social norms for students to participate in school activities. Participation leads to a greater sense of responsibility among small school students. Students in small schools tend to develop general, well-rounded competences. Students in large schools tend to become specialists in particular activities.

The availability of settings and the chance to participate in settings makes an important contribution to the process of adjustment. The nature of the settings themselves influences adjustment. We develop skills, mannerisms, and preferences in response to the pattern of behavior settings in which we participate. Barker (1978) makes this point quite clearly as he describes possible changes in the behaviors of an inhabitant of Yoredale who might visit Midwest and an inhabitant of Midwest who might visit Yoredale.

> Inhabitants of Yoredale who visit Midwest are quickly identified as foreigners, for many aspects of their behavior differ noticeably from those of Midwest residents. Likewise, visitors from Midwest are seen to be alien within Yoredale. However, if the visits are prolonged behavior differences diminish under the influence of the towns' settings. Natives of Midwest in Yoredale begin to walk more (and more vigorously) in its streets and sidewalks, to express their partisanship at its cricket games by discreet clapping rather than by wild cheering, to drive forthrightly on the left side of its streets, to accept without expressions of surprise meals served at 5 P.M. (tea) and 9 P.M. (supper), and, in general, to adopt the more leisurely pace of Yoredale's behavior settings. And Yoredale natives sojourning in Midwest begin to walk less (and less vigorously) in its trafficways, to raise their voices at basketball games, to drive bravely on the right side of the streets, to eat one evening meal, and to fit into the faster pace of Midwest's behavior settings. The new environments bend some features of the visitors' behavior to the different, prevailing patterns (p. 198).

Territoriality   When people create boundaries and claim the right to control who moves across those boundaries or what can be done inside those boundaries, we describe their behavior as territorial. We cannot call territorial behavior an instinctive response in humans. It is a kind of behavior that is common to many cultural groups (Roos, 1968). As children explore their neighborhood, they begin to learn the ways in which their culture defines territories. They may learn that they can invite children into their home, but that they do not have the right to enter another person's home uninvited. They may learn that a park is open to all children but that another park is only open to people who have a key for the gate. They may learn that the sidewalk is public, but the lawn next to the sidewalk is private.

Territories are claimed by individuals and families. In some neighborhoods, territories may be claimed and defended by gangs, by ethnic groups, or by age-groups. These groups may not own all of the territory. They simply make it very uncomfortable or even dangerous for outsiders to come inside the territorial boundaries (Suttles, 1968; P. Thomas, 1967). Children who grow up in highly territorialized communities learn quickly which settings are controlled by members of a competing or hostile group. As part of the adjustment process within a community, we identify the territories of others. We also create our own sense of ownership of objects, space, or property. One learns how to behave in settings that are controlled by another person or group, and how to defend or protect one's own domain.

● *terrain*—the physical features of a tract of land.

Among animals, territoriality is thought to have adaptive features. It ensures preservation of a *terrain* that is large enough to provide food, shelter, opportunities for mating, childbearing, and child rearing without threat of constant conflict with competing groups. Even among animal groups, however, territories are given up and migration to new feeding grounds occurs. Humans are not bound by instinct to create or to defend a physical territory. Yet we know that humans may become so invested in their own possessions, their own home and property, or even their own space in an office or factory, that they will fight to defend it. In the case of the Holocaust, we saw Jewish families who perished in Germany because they could not bear to give up their land and their homes in order to flee from Nazi persecution. Territorial responses may be a healthy expression of selfhood. They may also limit one's capacity to respond flexibly to danger. Territorial responses may impose unnecessary boundaries between members or groups in a community.

We begin to see that there are many ways that the characteristics of the community where we live have an influence on adjustment. Community settings influence our anxiety level, the quality of our interactions with others, our feelings of relaxation or tension, and our feelings of belongingness or alienation. All through time, people have searched for the perfect community, for a Shangri-La. But the perfect community would be different for different people. For example, high population density might be exciting and stimulating for some, but others would find it oppressive. Some people would want to live in a climate that had extremely cold, snowy winters, but others would want to live in a sunny, warm climate. Stable neighborhoods might encourage feelings of belongingness and welcomeness for some, but others might find them boring.

We would like to point out that person-environment interaction is part of daily adjustment. On the one hand, it is important to adjust to the community. On the other hand, the community can be changed to meet the needs of the people who live there.

When people actively participate in a variety of settings in the community, they begin to make a strong identification with the community. This strong identification becomes a component of the self-concept. A good example is that of a community with a championship basketball team. Members of the community may attend the games, read newspaper accounts of the team's efforts, or contribute to funds for athletic scholarships. As the team's successes continue, fans identify with the team and other members of the community. They make comments like "How do you think we will do tonight?" and "I hope we can get that star high school player to come here." The achievements and resources of the community, in this case a championship athletic team, lead people to identify with other members of the community and to view themselves differently.

Living laboratory 11·1

AN ANALYSIS OF THE USE OF A SETTING

Purpose: To apply the concept of behavior setting to a specific environment.

Method: Identify one behavior setting in your nieghborhood. Choose a grocery store, a local park, or a ride on a bus. Before observing in the setting, write down the behaviors you would expect to occur in the setting. For example, in a church, people sit quietly, but spend a lot of time looking around at others. Go to the setting and trace the patterns of behavior that occur in the setting for one hour.

Results: Record the number of people who use the setting in that hour, episodes of territoriality (see section on "Territoriality"), the age range and sex of the participants, the penetration, action patterns, and behavior mechanisms (see section on "Behavior Settings") of the participants.

Discussion: Do you observe the behaviors you expected to observe?

What similarities and differences in expected behaviors and observed behaviors occurred?

What was it about the setting that influenced the people to act the way they did?

How do people know, or learn, what behaviors are appropriate for particular settings?

**COMMUNITIES
RESPOND TO
PEOPLE**

Two examples illustrate some of the ways that communities create or change resources in order to respond to individual needs. These community responses suggest some ways for increasing the personal growth of community members. By and large, these resources indicate the community's commitment to future generations. They tell us about the commitment of competent adults to create an environment that leads to growth at all developmental levels.

**Play space for the
young**

Neighborhoods provide both planned and unplanned play space for children (Ittelson et al., 1974). The planned play space may include playgrounds, parks, courtyards, or backyards. The first question that must

United Press International

*Children tend to play near their homes.
They create play settings out of the space
available.*

be asked about children's use of planned play areas is: How available are they? For children under age ten, availability means being close. Children tend to play near their home, even if the area near their home is not particularly well suited for play (Littlewood & Sale, 1972). For children under five, planned play spaces must be within the range of mothers to supervise their children. A balcony, courtyard, landing, or deck that opens onto a number of adjoining apartments is more likely to be used for play than a space that is set aside in an isolated area of a building (O. Newman, 1972).

The way a playground is designed will determine the kind of play that occurs there and the children who use it. Some of the qualities of playgrounds that are important for children include: shelter from the wind and the heat; enclosed spaces that permit small groupings of children to feel some privacy; access to water play; sports areas; traditional swinging, climbing, and sliding equipment; some flat space for tricycles, buggies, and wagons; and some opportunity for risky play (Bengtsson, 1970; Ellis, 1972).

Neighborhood parks and playgrounds are not used by as many children as they are intended to serve (Gold, 1972). Children will only use parks if they are nearby their homes and if they are not the territory of another group of children. Children who do come to the park stay an average of only 15 minutes (Wade, 1968). Children find their own, unplanned play settings or play in real-world settings (Ittelson et al., 1974). Alleys, empty lots, shopping malls, and undeveloped woods are places where children can have privacy, meet one another, and feel some sense of territorial control. In these settings play can emerge and yet the children need not feel removed or cut off from the real world.

Probably the most used unplanned play area is the sidewalk. On it children can play hopscotch, jump rope, roller skate, and ride bicycles. They can wait around hoping to meet a friend. On sidewalks, children

---

Case 11·1

PETER

Nine-year-old Peter describes his use of the alley near his apartment.

In the alley it's mostly dark, even if the sun is out. But if you look around, you can find things. I know how to get into every building, except that it's like night once you're inside them, because they don't have lights. So, I stay here. You're better off. It's no good on the street. You can get hurt all the time, one way or the other. And in buildings, like I told you, it's bad in them, too. But here it's o.k. You can find your own corner, and if someone tries to move in you fight him off. We meet here all the time, and figure out what we'll do next. It might be a game, or over for some pool, or a coke or something. You need to have a place to start out from, and that's like it is in the alley; you can always know your buddy will be there, provided it's the right time. So you go there, and you're on your way, man. (Coles, 1968, p. 1315).

can be right in the thick of the real world and yet be separated by the boundaries of their play. Sidewalks are important to the child's sense of the neighborhood (Jacobs, 1961). On them children can be watched and protected by the people in the houses and shops or by people walking by. From the sidewalks, children can learn about the flow of traffic, the different types of people, and the delight of an unexpected meeting with a friendly person. The narrowness of some sidewalks, the amount of traffic, the traffic noise on the adjacent streets, and the density of people walking on some sidewalks makes them unsuitable for play (Appleyard & Lintell, 1972).

One strategy that meets children's needs to play and to be part of the real world is to create safe play settings near the business community. The Fresno Mall is an example of one setting of this type. Children can play right near the stores and offices where their parents are doing business. Another strategy is what Bengtsson (1970) calls "vest pocket" and "portable" parks. Portable parks may be moved from one vacant lot to another, between buildings or on land that has been cleared but is not yet ready for building. Vest pocket parks are small spaces. They are designed around a nature study. A park may have a planetarium, an aquarium, or an aviary as its focus. These play areas draw children. They increase a child's experience in a way that a playground alone might not.

Housing for the elderly

Communities are just beginning to make adequate responses to the housing needs of the elderly. It is no easy task to provide aging adults with good housing arrangements. Table 11·1 summarizes some housing arrangements of adults over 60-years-old in the United States during 1970. As the table suggests, the majority live in single-unit housing with a husband or wife. At any time, only 4–5 percent of people over 65 live in institutions, including old-age homes, mental institutions, nursing homes, or residential retirement hotels and apartments. A far greater

TABLE 11·1
Housing characteristics of persons 60 years old and over: United States, 1970

	Urban	Rural nonfarm	Rural farm
Living alone	23.5%	21.5%	10.3%
In husband-wife families with head 60 or over	53.5	59.6	70.3
In households with head under 60	10.0	7.3	8.3
In single-unit housing	67.0	89.2	97.9
In mobile homes	2.2	5.7	1.1
In group quarters	4.6	4.2	0.1
In owner-occupied unit	64.9	80.7	90.3
In units with incomplete plumbing	4.3	19.5	21.2
Population, in millions (N)	(22.9)	(4.8)	(1.1)

Source: R. C. Atchley, *The Social Forces in Later Life* (Belmont, Calif.: Wadsworth Publishing Co., Inc., 1977), p. 273.

percentage spend at least some time in such an institution, especially if they live past the age of 75.

Many elderly people don't want to move. Less than 20 percent of the population over 65 will move during any five-year period (U.S. Census, 1975). This is not because the elderly have ideal housing conditions. Many of the elderly live in older dwellings, 8 percent lack complete indoor plumbing, and couples spend an estimated 35 percent of their income to maintain their homes. Many couples have lived in their homes for a long time, 20 years or more. Even though the neighborhood has changed, the house may remain attractive because it is close to shopping or to medical care. Especially in the city, getting to public transportation is important in housing satisfaction for the elderly. The comfort, familiarity, and convenience of the old home usually outweigh the drawbacks of living in a deteriorating setting.

What can communities do to help the elderly remain in their own neighborhoods, living as independently as possible in spite of physical and financial limitations? Several responses to this problem appear promising. Some communities have day centers that offer a range of services including health care, meals, financial counseling, transportation, and assistance for housekeeping, shopping, and home maintenance. Adults can go to the center for some services or contact the center for services that must be provided in the home. These centers permit aging adults to retain their independence by using community resources to help them in areas that have become difficult for them. Instead of moving to an institution that provides too much care and not enough freedom, day centers support the adults ability to retain his or her independent housing. Staying in one's own home symbolizes security and well-being (Morris, 1974; Bell, 1973).

Another strategy is to create community settings that provide everything from independent housing to full nursing care. One would purchase or rent an apartment that is designed for an aging adult by including ramps, wide doorways, hand supports in the bathrooms, and cupboard shelves that are easy to reach. If illness prevents independence, one moves first to a setting in the same complex that provides needed assistance. Finally, for those adults who cannot move about or who need intensive daily care there is a third setting that can provide round-the-clock nursing and medical assistance. The advantage of this program is that the setting is a familiar one. The adults maintain their autonomy as long as possible. The closeness of housing units of various kinds permits relationships among the adults who live there to keep going. This kind of arrangement would be especially important to a married couple if one partner becomes more frail. It allows the two to remain together. The ill one can receive the care needed and the healthy spouse is not totally responsible for that care.

Hendricks and Hendricks (1977) have estimated that there are 3,000 organizations qualified under medicare to provide home health care. One

U.S. Department of Housing and Urban Development

Most aging adults try to live in their own homes and retain their autonomy as long as possible.

can add to these the many services to the elderly including warm meals, visitors, telephone contact, employment information, homemaker skills, and financial counseling. Most communities could provide the services that would permit older adults to remain in their homes as long as possible. What is needed is a community-based mental health service that could bring these resources to the attention of those who need them. The next section describes the concept of the community mental health center and its contribution to the process of adjustment.

There are many ways that communities can create or modify resources to respond to the needs of the individual community members such as children or the elderly. For young children, communities provide planned and unplanned play spaces including neighborhood parks, alleys, undeveloped woods, sidewalks, shopping malls, and portable parks. For the elderly, communities provide transportation services, day centers, meals, home maintenance, and special housing arrangements. Once the community locates the members with special needs, new settings can be created. A network of resources can be developed which depends on the community itself.

COMMUNITY MENTAL HEALTH

In 1963 a new piece of legislation brought to life the community mental health movement in the United States. Bloom (1977) has described ten characteristics of that movement that provide an introduction to its flavor and direction.

● *prevention—* **intervening so that something expected does not occur.**

1. Community mental health emphasizes practice at the community rather than the institutional level.
2. The focus is on the total population, not just individual clients.
3. Emphasis is on *prevention* rather than therapy.
4. The goal is toward continuous and comprehensive mental health services.
5. Indirect service, including consultation and education, are preferred to direct service.
6. Another goal is prompt service to large numbers.
7. Community mental health centers operate on the basis of data on the needs, risks, and priorities of specific communities.
8. A variety of professionals and paraprofessionals are used as resources to provide a variety of services.
9. Centers operate on behalf of communities relying heavily on community input for their programs and goals.
10. Sources of stress within the community are identified as potential stimuli for mental disorder.

Goals

The Community Mental Health Centers Act of 1963 required that each center provide five services: inpatient services; outpatient services; partial hospitalization services such as day care, night care, weekend care, emergency services 24 hours per day; consultation, and education. In addition, the 1963 act called for mental health centers to provide diagnostic services, rehabilitative services, pre-care and after-care, training, research, and evaluation. In 1975 a new list of services were added to the responsibilities of mental health centers. These included specialized services for the mental health of children and the elderly. Consultation and education were to be made available to a wider audience including courts, law enforcement agencies, and public welfare agencies. Centers were supposed to see all people being considered for admission to public mental institutions to evaluate whether or not admission was needed. Centers were to develop follow-up services for discharged mental patients. Centers were to develop programs on the prevention, treatment, and rehabilitation of alcohol and other substance abusers. Given the different services provided by community mental health centers, it should be obvious that the centers cannot provide all those services directly. Their main activities include three functions:

1. They assess community needs and community resources.
2. They coordinate and consult with community programs so that they form a more effective network.
3. They supplement existing services by setting up crisis intervention pro- grams, educational programs, or special follow-up services.

One of the central concepts in the community mental health act is the region or community that the center is supposed to serve. Each state was instructed to divide into population areas. These areas were to include a population from 75,000 to 200,000 with a geographically bound area. Each area was to be served by a single mental health center. The idea was to create centers that would be used, that would fit into communities, and that would not be overloaded by large case demands. Limiting the population served to 200,000 was intended to lead to a sense of community ownership and responsibility. From its very concep- tion, the idea of using the geographical units, the cultural atmosphere, and the resources of the community as a way of delivering mental health services was central to the community mental health movement.

The methods

The main goal of community mental health is to build healthy com- munities through prevention of problems. The meaning of prevention is clarified through Gerald Caplan's (1964) application of public health principles to mental health. There are three levels of prevention: primary, secondary, and tertiary. The latter is closest to what is considered by most people to be the common form of mental health activity. Tertiary prevention refers to reducing the rate of mental illness. This is achieved through programs aimed at shortening people's stay in hospitals, building skills among patients, and providing help returning from the mental hospi- tal to the community.

Secondary prevention involves locating people who might run the risk of having mental problems before those problems become mental disorders. Early detection might be done, for example, by evaluating large numbers of employees in a high-risk occupation. Those who show signs of serious conflict could be referred to professionals before the conflict interferes with the person's ability to be effective. Early detection has been carried out in schools where children who might have problems are identified. Programs are created to build their strengths.

Primary prevention is the most far-reaching concept of all. It suggests that the rate of mental disorder can be lowered by eliminating conditions that cause mental illness. People using this method try to develop commu- nity resources and make sure they are shared by everyone in the area. Today the method attempts to promote "wellness" by teaching people how to be competent and effective in their lives. The emphasis is on helping people be stronger so that when difficulties occur they can be handled more easily.

The process of prevention involves three steps: assessment, interven-

● *diagnosis*—the conclusion concerning the nature or cause of the problem.

tion, and evaluation. The first two steps are similar to what we do to keep physically healthy. Assessment is *diagnosis*. An attempt is made to find out what the problem is. The problem must be carefully described. Symptoms are noted. Community diagnosis means that we are concerned with groups of people who may develop problems. Survivors of a disaster may be likely to have difficulties coping with their experience. Finding out about what happens to them can help us design programs to allow these people to obtain proper guidance for their difficulties in dealing with their emotions, including the guilt of having survived. Diagnosis in primary prevention programs may involve studying the personality characteristics of normal people. Understanding what things help them to function well allows the community mental health specialist to use this information for the benefit of all. We know that adolescents may have strong mood swings because of the development of the endocrine system. Adolescents, themselves, don't usually know this. The unexpected mood swings can produce great fear about being normal or being sane. Creating education programs for adolescents, parents and teachers allow us to make them aware of what's going on. This awareness can help many adolescents understand what is happening to them. This knowledge reduces the worry and fear that may have led to emotional problems.

The second step, intervention, is similar to the idea of treatment. Based on a diagnosis of the difficulty, the populations involved, and the settings where the problems exist an intervention can be designed. The design of the intervention depends on the level of prevention desired as well as the nature of difficulties or needs. Primary prevention calls for an intervention designed to change conditions that lead to a particular difficulty. Tertiary prevention, in contrast, would try to limit the bad consequences of the difficulty and bring a rapid return to normal. An intervention might be direct, like lengthening the time a green traffic light is on so that elderly pedestrians have more time to cross a busy intersection. An intervention might be quite complicated and involve a variety of groups including lawmakers, mental health specialists, educators, and families. An example would be the recent demands for "mainstreaming" developmentally delayed and physically impaired children in regular classrooms. Interventions are usually designed with a target population and a target need in mind. They may have benefits beyond the target audience. They may also have negative impact beyond the target audience. Whether they achieve their goals and how adequately they achieve them is studied in the third step, evaluation of the intervention.

● *accountability*—being held responsible for one's actions and interventions.

Evaluation is, at once the most difficult and the most unique part of the community mental health approach. It reflects the scientific orientation of community mental health leaders. Community mental health professionals are committed to *accountability*. Evaluation involves gathering data about the effect of an intervention and whether it accomplished its goals. This can be done by tracing the rate of occurrence of a problem before and after the intervention. It can compare a population that was influenced and one that was not influenced by an intervention. Evaluation might look at both short- and long-term effects of an intervention. It might weigh the costs of intervention against the costs of treating the problem. Evaluation might also measure the points of view and behaviors of community members as they have been changed by the intervention. The goal of evaluation is to determine whether the intervention was effective in changing the community in a desired and helpful way.

Consultation. Two of the most frequently used methods for achieving community mental health goals are consultation and intervention. Both of these methods are intended to reach a large population rather than to provide service on a one-to-one basis from professional to client. Both are also intended to change the competences of the people involved so that the professional does not need to continue providing these same services to these same clients forever. Consultation can be aimed at at least four different levels (Caplan, 1970):

1. *Client-centered case consultation* in which the consultant helps the client to analyze and cope with a specific problem. A consultant might work with a parole officer about problems with a specific parolee.
2. *Consultee-centered case consultation* in which the consultee develops new skills that can be used to cope with a variety of problems that interfere with effective functioning. An example might be teaching time management skills to a group of young executives.
3. *Program-centered administrative consultation* in which the consultant helps design program methods and goals.
4. *Consultee-centered administrative consultation* in which the consultant helps to develop the consultee's administrative skills.

Consultation has some unique properties that make it different from other mental health roles (Bloom, 1977):

1. The consultant may not be an expert in the consultee's profession.
2. The consultant usually has no power over the consultee.
3. The consultee is free to accept or reject the consultant's suggestions.
4. The consultant has no special long-term commitment to the consultee's institution, the program, or the goals toward which the consultee is striving.

The consultant uses the consultee's desire to seek advice as a primary motive for change. If, however, the program for change conflicts too greatly with the consultee's values or competences, the consultee is likely to resist change.

Intervention. Intervention is a method for bringing about change. Interventions can be quite minimal such as changing the pattern of chairs in a room or adding a 15-minute break for informal discussion in a lecture. Bloom (1977) describes a program he developed to help college freshmen cope more effectively with the stresses of the first year of college life. One of the main objectives of the program was to give students

The photography of H. Armstrong Roberts

*Consultation is a major method of
community mental health.*

information about their incoming class. The assumption was that knowing
how their classmates were thinking and feeling would help students adjust
to college.

The program included six ways of helping to improve adjustment
(Bloom, 1977):

1. Establishing a sense of membership in a group and thus reducing
   feelings of isolation.
2. Giving group members some facts with which to compare themselves
   to others.
3. Giving students the chance to express their feelings and reactions to
   the university.
4. Giving students some intellectual tools to better understand the stresses
   acting on them and their reactions to these stresses.
5. Giving students a chance to think through their own beliefs.

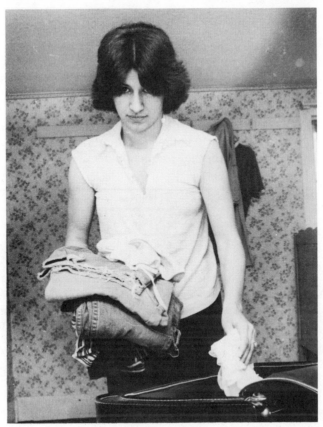

Bloom's intervention was intended to prevent feelings of isolation so that students would stay enrolled in college.

6. Providing a resource person for the students to talk with in the event of a crisis (p. 97–98).

Questionnaires were given out during orientation week and four more times during the freshman year—after one month, after Christmas vacation, after the beginning of the second semester, and before second semester finals. Students received letters showing the responses of males and females to the questions. Students also received copies of the comments made by one another after Christmas vacation. Finally students received copies of six articles about mental health, sexuality, and political activity among college students.

There is some evidence that the intervention was successful in improving adjustment. Some new students were included in the program and others were not. More students in the program remained in school longer than those who were not in the program. Of those who left the college, more students who had been in the program continued their studies in another school rather than dropping out. Of those who left school, more students from the program continued to live independently in their own apartments rather than return to their family's home. This intervention provided information and skills to students that would help them handle the crises of the first year with more competence. It also helped to create communication that would counteract feelings of alienation that frequently occur in the freshman year.

Living laboratory 11·2

COMMUNITY MENTAL HEALTH

Purpose: To become aware of the mental health services in your community.

Method: Look in the yellow pages of your local telephone directory. Try to determine the number and variety of community mental health services in your community. Be resourceful. Look under a variety of headings.

Results: Record the number and variety of services available. Select one agency to find out more about. Try to pick a community mental health center if one is present in your community. Call the center for a visit and try to find out the following: Are the services geared to certain age groups or people with special needs? What types of services are provided by the agency (diagnostic, intervention, rehabilitative, pre-care, and so on)? Is the service available for free, sliding scale (fee based on income), or a flat charge? Does the agency provide transportation to the service or must consumers find their own? Does the agency go to the consumer?

Discussion: Are community mental health centers needed? What are the benefits to a community? What are the costs?

Should the people in the community provide financial support for the services or should the individuals who use the services be completely responsible?

Would you use a community mental health center? Why or why not?

Do you think there is a stigma or negative stereotype associated with use of community mental health services in your community? If so, what can be done to change such a stereotype?

Chapter summary

In order to understand the importance of this chapter, please allow yourself an exercise in fantasy. Think of a community as living. Is it possible? What does it do? How do you know it lives? Suspend the logic which says a community does not live. Create a fantasy of a community that is alive. Try to make your fantasy as realistic as possible.

The task for the scientist is to use the fantasy technique to make the image realistic. If he can imagine it correctly, then he will understand something even if no one else does. We have made the assumption throughout this book that the environment exists and can be understood. In this chapter we have identified several ways a person can understand the influence of communities on adjustment.

Do any of the characteristics of community we have discussed indicate that communities do things? The noise level is something we make, even if we do not mean to. The sounds of the place where we live are the music or the pollution of our background. The places where we can go are important to us. You can see that cultural differences can be scientifically charted by looking at the ways people use settings. What we find in our democracy is that the community reflects the will of the people. Essential services and protection are the products of communities.

We have discussed community mental health as an example of a new service planned by governments. It represents the doorway to adjustment for people in crisis and the diagnosis of maladjustment for those who need it. As the years go by, the community mental health efforts will focus more and more on the concept of "wellness." How people grow as individuals will be better understood through the evaluation efforts.

Have we found a fantasy that enables us to see a society as living? What is the energy source? The Americans have argued that the energy comes from the people. The American democracy attempts to get everyone active. Arguing, discussing, doing things were thought to be important to creating a community that worked. Channeling this energy into a structure was believed to be the key to creating a society that worked.

SUGGESTED READINGS

For a further analysis of environments and their impact on adjustment:

Altman, I. *The environment and social behavior.* Monterey, Calif.: Brooks/Cole, 1975.

Barker, R. *Habitats, environments, and human behavior.* San Francisco: Jossey-Bass, 1978.

Bengtsson, A. *Environmental planning for children's play.* New York: Praeger, 1970.

Freedman, J. L. *Crowding and behavior.* San Francisco: W. H. Freeman, 1975.

Ittelson, W. H., Proshansky, H. M., Rivlin, L. G., & Winkel, G. H. *An introduction to environmental psychology.* New York: Holt, 1974.

Muñoz, R. F., Snowden, L. R., Kelly, J. G., & associates. *Social and psychological research in community settings.* San Francisco: Jossey-Bass, 1979.

Wicker, A. W. *An introduction to ecological psychology.* Monterey, Calif.: Brooks/Cole, 1979.

Reading

WHAT IS A SOCIETY?

At this point it is useful to explain more fully Parsons' conception of a society. Recall that he regards a social system as one of four analytically distinct aspects of human behavior—specifically the one concerned with the coordination of mutually responding actors with one another. Most social systems—local communities, schools, firms, families—are not societies but *subsystems* of a society. He defines a society as a special type of social system, one characterized by the highest level of *self-sufficiency in relation to its environments,* including environing social systems. Self-sufficiency in relationship to environments means that, although the society is dependent on its environments, it is *less* at the mercy of its environments than are most social systems. That is to say, a society can control interchanges with its environments fairly successfully so as to promote societal functioning—and thereby societal survival. Consider this relative autonomy in relation to each of the various environments of a society in turn.

1. *The physical-organic environment,* being the source of the resources which the society can utilize to satisfy the needs of its members, must be controlled or adapted to. Self-sufficiency with respect to the physical-organic environment implies sufficient control over the economic-technological complex so that, for example, food and shelter can be obtained. A family is less self-sufficient with respect to the food and shelter supply than is American society as a whole.

2. The *personalities* of members of the society are also part of its environment in the sense that the society must be able to count on its members to contribute to societal functioning. Just as the society must maintain some control over the physical-organic environment through technology, so it must maintain some control over the personalities of its members so that most personalities can assume roles in the society without undue strain. The society could not be considered self-sufficient with respect to environing personalities if the majority of its personalities were radically alienated. All societies guarantee a favorable personality environment by shaping personalities (largely in the family) through the socialization process. As a result of socialization, personalities learn adequate motivation for participating in socially valued patterns of action, and these internalized norms help to solve the problem of social order. Parsons assumes that American society is more self-sufficient with respect to its constituent personalities than are smaller social systems like schools or business firms.

3. The *symbolic environment of a society* (cultural systems) includes empirical knowledge, expressive symbol systems, religious ideas and practices that define the society's collective identity, and conceptions of the desirable (values). Self-sufficiency with regard to the symbolic environment means that the institutions of the society are legitimated by the cultural system. Enough members of the society have made commitments to the values and other symbols of the culture so that a sociological observer could infer a sufficient level of consensus on the legitimacy of institutions. Of course, no social system is self-legitimating; all social systems must appeal for legitimation of their norms to the larger culture. But a *society* is in a stronger position to obtain legitimation than more limited social systems because the cultural elements embodied in its institutions are routinely internalized in personalities in the course of socialization.

4. The *social environment* of society includes all the environing social systems with which it must deal. Other societies are obviously part of the social environment, but the social environment of a society is far more inclusive. Some social systems cut across societies (such as the organization known as the Roman Catholic Church), and other social systems, though fully included within a society, must be adapted to, for example, the millions of individual families, schools, governmental organizations, and voluntary associations of American society. Self-sufficiency with regard to the social environment means (1) that clear boundaries exist defining who is a member of the society and who is not, and (2) that greater solidarity exists among members than between members and nonmembers. These criteria, while not so difficult for a small social system to fulfill, are extremely difficult to fulfill on a large scale. That is why problems in the "societal community"—Parsons' term for the fulfillment of these two conditions—are often the most serious problems faced by a society.

Source: Talcott Parsons, *The Evolution of Societies,* Jackson Toby, ed., © 1977, pp. 6–8. Reprinted by permission of Prentice-Hall, Inc., Englewood Cliffs, New Jersey.

The photography of H. Armstrong Roberts

Chapter 12
Coping with normal life challenges

. . . let me make a general observation—the test of a first-rate intelligence is the ability to hold two opposed ideas in the mind at the same time, and still retain the ability to function. One should, for example, be able to see that things are hopeless and yet be determined to make them otherwise. This philosophy fitted on to my early adult life, when I saw the improbable, the implausible, often the "impossible," come true. Life was something you dominated if you were any good. Life yielded easily to intelligence and effort, or to what proportion could be mustered of both.

F. Scott Fitzgerald, The Crack-Up 1936

Source: Edmund Wilson (ed), *The Crack-Up. F. Scott Fitzgerald* New York: New Directions Books, 1956, p. 69.

United Press International

351

For reflection

1. What was the most recent crisis you have experienced? Would you call it a normal life crisis?

2. What processes do you go through when you solve a crisis?

3. How did you learn to solve crises?

4. How does your father or mother resolve his or her crises?

5. What are the benefits of experiencing a crisis? What are the costs?

The process of adjustment involves growth that is caused by interaction with complex social environments, and growth that is caused by encounters with conflict and crisis. You will recall from Chapter 5 that we discussed coping as an important mechanism for adjustment. In crisis, coping skills are pushed to their limits. We see people using their own talents, their own concepts, and their own sense of self on painful or threatening life challenges.

The chapter focuses on normal life crises. These are the relatively predictable periods of conflict that happen when the person's skills are out of phase with cultural demands. The concept of normal crisis suggests that every person has moments of increased tension that tax personal resources. Anxiety, uncertainty, and conflict are part of every life history.

PSYCHOSOCIAL THEORY AND NORMAL LIFE CRISIS

Erik Erikson's psychosocial theory uses a stage approach to understanding the life span. Two assumptions about development dominate the theory. First, Erikson describes people at every life stage as having the ability to contribute to their own growth. People are not only governed by biological or environmental forces. They integrate, organize, and understand their own experiences so that they can protect themselves and so that they can grow. Second, one's social group actively contributes to the direction of personal growth. At every stage of life, cultural goals, expectations, and opportunities influence individual development. Societies encourage parenting, education, and attitudes toward sexuality, intimacy, and work that preserve and protect the culture.

The concept of psychosocial crisis was first introduced in Chapter 2. The concept of crisis refers to a normal set of stresses and strains rather than to an extraordinary set of events. The demands of each life crisis are growth-producing in that they encourage more effective use of new skills.

The crises of nine life stages

Table 5·2 lists the crisis of each of the stages of development, from infancy through later adulthood. The positive and negative ways of resolving each crisis are presented below:

Trust. A feeling of confidence that one's needs will be met and that one is valued by others.

Mistrust. Total doubt that needs will be met. An inability to experience physical and psychological comfort.

Autonomy. Pleasure and pride in doing things on one's own.

Shame and doubt. A sense that one's actions will result in the displeasure or disapproval of others. Constant anticipation of failure.

Initiative. Active inquiry, exploration, and experimentation within one's environment.

● *taboo*—a strong social norm prohibiting certain actions that are punishable by the group or community, by the supernatural, or by magical consequences.

Guilt. A self-imposed feeling that inhibits action and signals violation of a moral code or *taboo*.

Industry. An eagerness for building skills and for working.

Inferiority. Feelings of lack of worth, inadequacy, and incompetence.

Group identity. A sense of affiliation with a group which gives a comfortable fit between personal values and group values.

Alienation. Not belonging. A lack of commitment to any group and a sense that ways of becoming a member of a group are blocked.

Individual identity. An integration of past identifications, present competences and relationships, and future life goals which leads to a sense of oneself.

Role diffusion. Confusion and aimlessness. An inability to bring roles, skills, and goals into a coordinated sense of self.

Intimacy. Mutual understanding and regulation of needs in a close relationship.

Isolation. Inability to make a commitment to another person. Fears of personal dissolution prevent intense relations with others.

Generativity. A commitment to improving the quality of life for future generations.

● *self-aggrandizement*—making oneself appear greater or more powerful.

Stagnation. A lack of psychological growth characterized by preoccupation with *self-aggrandizement* and personal satisfaction.

Integrity. An ability to accept the facts of one's life and to accept death without great fear.

Despair. Feelings of regret, resentment, and depression.

The concept of normal life crises has three important implications for the study of adjustment. First, it tells us that growth is caused by psychological tension. The idea of normal crisis suggests that developmental anxiety (anxiety about one's ability to succeed at the tasks of development of each life stage) is always a part of life. This anxiety is a signal of the need for growth and change. It helps the person begin to focus on life experiences that are changing. We often think that anxiety is a negative sign, a sign of danger or threat. One implication of this notion of normal crisis is that anxiety can serve as a positive signal. It may even serve as a motivational force for growth.

A second implication of the notion of normal crisis is that the resolu-

John Penzari

At each life stage, new conflicts challenge the person's resources.

tion of each life crisis involves a balance between the possible positive and negative outcomes. Just like the moon, every person has a "dark" side. We all have many life experiences, feelings, and wishes that we think of as unacceptable. We all have a negative identity, a part of ourselves that we don't value. We may even deny that these represent anything important in our personality. The experiences of role diffusion, isolation, stagnation, and despair are strong influences in the psychology of adulthood. People who are doing well and who feel a great sense of personal fulfillment in their daily lives still have times of discouragement. They may see a difference between the intimacy they desire and the feeling of separateness they experience. They may sense frustration in trying to make contributions to their social group.

We must begin to understand the contribution of these experiences to personal growth. To what extent is the feeling of isolation an outcome of a well-defined personal identity? To what extent does stagnation represent a way of fending off the threat of dying? How might feelings of despair reflect a person's inability to accept the end of change and growth after a lifetime of seeking to grow? These thoughts suggest a need for greater understanding of the crises of adulthood. We must accept the fact that negative feelings occur for everyone and that they may help us to develop more fully.

A third point to be made about normal crises is that positive resolution of earlier crises may make later crises easier to resolve. We must also understand that this is not always true. At each stage, the challenges of development are great. The characteristics of one's spouse, the personalities of one's children, or the stresses and demands of the work setting may interfere with adult development. Adults may discover that they are unable to make a satisfying adjustment during middle adulthood even though they had made successful resolutions of earlier crises. In addition to everything else, it appears that the adult crises tend to pit the integrity of the individual's personal development against the social, economic, and political fluctuations of the historical period they live in.

FIGURE 12.1
The interplay of successive life stages

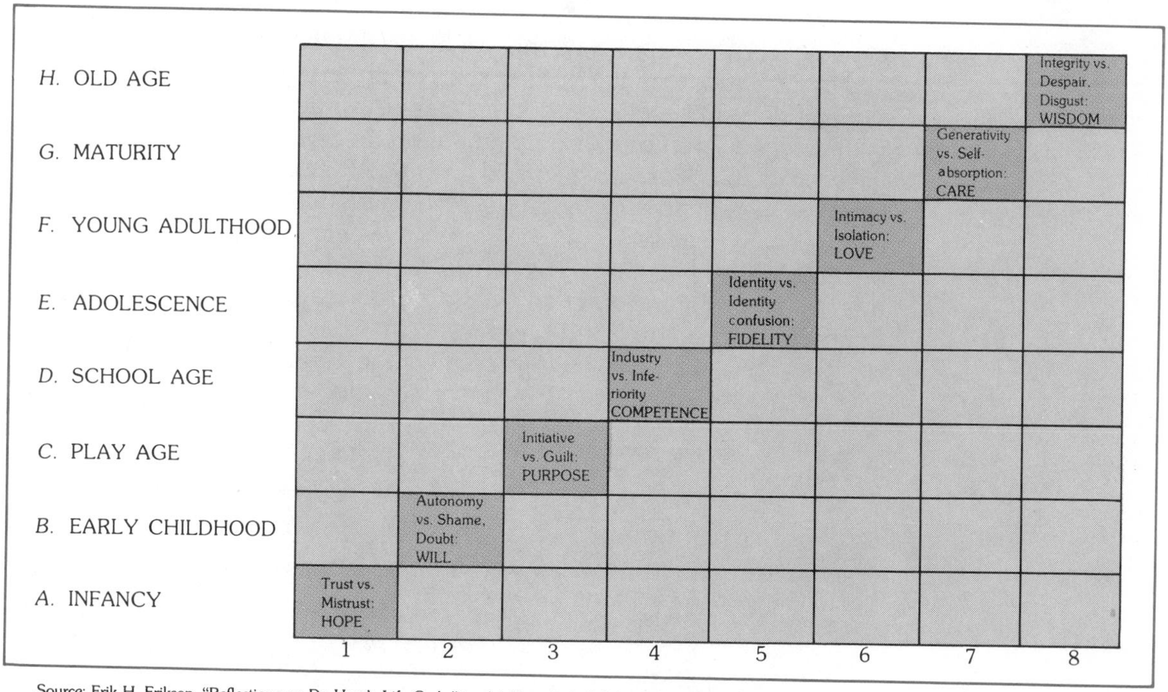

	1	2	3	4	5	6	7	8
H. OLD AGE								Integrity vs. Despair, Disgust: WISDOM
G. MATURITY							Generativity vs. Self-absorption: CARE	
F. YOUNG ADULTHOOD					Intimacy vs. Isolation: LOVE			
E. ADOLESCENCE				Identity vs. Identity confusion: FIDELITY				
D. SCHOOL AGE			Industry vs. Inferiority COMPETENCE					
C. PLAY AGE		Initiative vs. Guilt: PURPOSE						
B. EARLY CHILDHOOD	Autonomy vs. Shame, Doubt: WILL							
A. INFANCY	Trust vs. Mistrust: HOPE							

Source: Erik H. Erikson, "Reflections on Dr. Vorg's Life Cycle," in *Adulthood*, ed. Erik H. Erikson (New York: W. W. Norton & Co., Inc., 1978, 1976), p. 25. Reprinted with permission of W. W. Norton & Company, Inc. Copyright © 1978, 1976 by the American Academy of Arts and Sciences.

Adults who are trying to resolve the crises of intimacy, generativity, and integrity often need help with their historical perspective as well as with personal skills that will permit them to create a life pattern that is personally fulfilling.

Figure 12·1 illustrates the psychosocial view of personal growth. Erikson describes the positive outcome of a successful resolution of each psychosocial crisis. The achievement of a sense of trust produces hope about future interactions. The achievement of identity produces a capacity for fidelity or commitment. As the figure suggests, the achievements of earlier stages contribute to the possibility for later growth.

The central process for coping with crisis

Every psychosocial crisis reflects some gap between the developmental competences of the person at the beginning of the stage and the social pressures for more effective functioning. A central process for conflict resolution refers to the main context within which the conflict is resolved. At every life stage the relevant players and the relevant skills change. Certain kinds of psychological work and certain kinds of social interactions appear to be necessary in order for a person to continue to grow at each life stage.

● *mutuality*—ability of two people to meet each other's needs and share each other's concerns and feelings.

In infancy, for example, the central process is *mutuality* with the caregiver. In learning to count on the caregiver and in learning to control their own demands, infants learn to trust and to mistrust others. Eventually, they also learn to trust and mistrust themselves. During toddlerhood (two–four), we have identified imitation as the central mechanism for psychosocial growth. During this period of life, children have the opportunity to increase the range of their skills by imitating adults, siblings, television models, playmates, and even animals. Imitation provides toddlers with much satisfaction. Through imitation they can increase the similarity between themselves and admired members of their social group. They begin to experience the world as other people and animals experience it. They can exercise some control over events that may be frightening or confusing by imitating these events in their play. The movement toward a sense of autonomy is aided by the child's readiness to imitate and by the many models the child observes.

In Table 12·1 we have presented the central processes that lead to the acquisition of new psychosocial skills, to the resolution of the

TABLE 12·1
The central process for resolution of the psychosocial conflict

Life stage	Central process
Infancy (birth to 2 years)	Mutuality with the caregiver
Toddlerhood (2–4)	Imitation
Early school age (5–7)	Identification
Middle school age (8–12)	Education
Early adolescence (13–17)	Peer pressure
Later adolescence (18–22)	Role experimentation
Young adulthood (23–30)	Mutuality among peers
Middle adulthood (30–50)	Person-environment fit and creativity
Later adulthood (51–)	Introspection

psychosocial crisis, and to successful coping at each life stage. In the first three life stages, the central process involves interactions with parents or caregivers. In middle school age, the process widens. The educational process is influenced by a whole range of important people. Peer relations are central during early adolescence and young adulthood. In later adolescence and middle and later adulthood, the central process is a product of individual integration, analysis, and definition. During each of these stages, growth depends heavily on the person's own capacity to find meaning and value in their experience.

A family in conflict

The case of the Klaskins (see Case 12·1) shows the stress that can occur as each family member encounters psychosocial crisis.

Case 12·1

THE KLASKINS—A FAMILY IN CONFLICT

Family on the Move

A Manager's Transfers
Impose Heavy Burden
On His Wife, Children

*After 9 Moves, Mrs. Klaskin
Is Tired; Daughter Feels
She Doesn't Have a Home*

Husband: Is Job Worth It?

AUSTIN, Texas—Barbara Klaskin stares hard at her left tennis shoe and talks about her moves from Hyattsville, Md., to Beltsville, Md.; to Tujunga, Calif., to Wheaton, Md., to Randolph Township, N.J., to the Marshall Islands, to Potomac, Md., to here. She is 13 years old.

"I don't feel I have a home anywhere," she says, sitting stiffly on her living room sofa, "because I've grown up in so many different places, y'know? And I don't really want to go back anywhere because I don't think that would feel too great."

Her father, Roy Klaskin, 42, holds a middle-management job at International Business Machines Corp., which transferred him here last spring. He knows that the numerous transfers he

has made in his career have wounded his family. "There's a loss," he says. "I can't measure it."

Mr. Klaskin and his wife, Leona, were born and raised in Brooklyn. The move here was the seventh for Barbara, the eighth for her 16-year-old brother, Howard, and the ninth for Mr. and Mrs. Klaskin since their marriage 20 years ago. As has always been true, the Klaskin family is having difficulty adjusting to its latest move.

A slower life

The slower pace of life here bothers the Klaskins. "In the time the bag boy painstakingly loads the groceries," Mr. Klaskin says, "Leona could practically give birth." The atmosphere at school is different. "There's chewing tobacco everywhere," Howard says. The family misses items that are unavailable in this part of the country. "Sometimes I'd trade my arm," Mrs. Klaskin says, "for a Hebrew National salami." Overall, Barbara says, this was probably just one move too many.

Every year, companies transfer hundreds of thousands of employes. Many like Roy Klaskin, are relatively young men with school-age children. The Employee Relocation Council, a Washington consulting firm, says 96 percent of transferred employes are men; about half of them are in their 30s, and about one third have children aged 6 to 18. Almost 40 percent of the transferred employes have moved at least four times in their careers.

Generally, of course, a transfer benefits both the company and the employe. It usually means a promotion, resulting in increased status, more challenging work and a bigger paycheck. For companies, transfers are a way to season young executives by giving them varied management experience and familiarizing them with the company's operations in the field.

A heavy price

But the nomadic existence of America's managers sometimes exacts a heavy price, and most of it is paid by the wives and children of the men who are transferred.

Ronald Raymond, a Wilton, Conn. psychologist who specializes in helping such families, says a basic problem is the "loss of credentials" that wives and children undergo in moving. The husband enters the new community as a success, his status enhanced by his new job. Wives and children lack such symbols. "Suppose a teen-aged football player has rushed for 1,000 yards in a season," says Mr. Raymond. "How does he apply that credential in a new community without sounding like a braggart?"

For a close look at the stresses arising in a family because of a transfer, a reporter visited the Klaskins here and talked with each of them about the experience.

Barbara

After a painful adjustment in the fifth grade, Barbara seemed to blossom in the sixth and seventh grades. She had a lot of friends. Now she recalls fondly the times in Potomac when she always had someone to talk to, go to the movies with, or just "hack around" with at a nearby shopping mall, wandering among the shops and munching junk food.

For several months here in Austin, she didn't have any friends. She tells of boys taunting her at school,

ripping up her papers, knocking over her books. She became especially angry after school officials fumbled some paperwork from Maryland and thus forced her to repeat a three-hour standardized test. She turned sullen and withdrawn, and she dumped most of her anger on her father.

"It's all your fault," she would shout at him. When he tried to encourage her to form friendships in Austin, she shouted: "I have all the friends I'm ever going to get. There's no way I'm ever going to get any more. Leave me alone." Although she hadn't strongly opposed the move in the discussions back in Potomac, she now felt she had been "cornered" by other family members into acquiescing.

In those rough initial months here, her brother wasn't any help, she says. Howard, who also was tense and resentful, would "pick on me even more," she says. He called her names a lot and once threw her, fully clothed, into the swimming pool. Determined to get even, she sneaked into his bedroom and ransacked his drawers, scattering the contents on the floor. "I had a good time doing that," she says. "It made me feel so good."

Mrs. Klaskin says it took Barbara nearly six months to find a close friend. The two girls started going to movies together and Barbara seemed happier.

But Barbara still hasn't adjusted to the different atmosphere at the junior high school she attends here. In Potomac, girls her age dressed much like the boys, which suited her fine. She favors tennis shoes, blue jeans and rolled-up sleeves. In Austin, however, girls her age attend school in stockings, high heels, below-the-knee dresses and fake furs. They have elaborate "Farrah Fawcett" hairdos, and they're learning to use makeup, sometimes to excess.

"Sure," Barbara says, "girls back East sometimes got dressed up just for the heck of it. But they didn't go all out of their way, and wash their hair every morning, and get up an hour earlier before school just to put on their makeup." Barbara is doubly irritated about the sophisticated look—

which she so far refuses to adopt. Austin fashions, she contends, are "about four years behind" Washington-area fashions. "Skirts are starting to come back a little shorter," she says. "People down here don't know it yet."

Barbara has been bothered for months by a stomach problem. She believes it is probably "from living here." A doctor says she may be getting an ulcer, but her mother, although genuinely worried, doubts that diagnosis. On one point, however, Barbara's mother says she does agree with the doctor. "He said it's hard to be 13 anywhere, but it's particularly hard when you're where you don't want to be."

Howard

To hear Howard Klaskin tell it, a 16-year-old boy's life is pretty much the same wherever he lives. "There's nothing here that's really that much different from back East," he says. "The teen-age mind is programmed to do the same thing everywhere, I feel."

He acknowledges differences between the high school here and the one in Potomac. There, for example drugs were prevalent at school. "I could just walk into the hall and see kids giving each other money and drugs. It got so open I couldn't believe it. In every class there was somebody who was a drug freak. He wore the same clothes every day, and he stunk. The kid stunk like one big cigaret."

At L. C. Anderson High School here, Howard says there's hardly any drug use. But there is a lot of chewing tobacco. He says that either students have wads of it in their mouths or they have spit it in a variety of places: in water coolers, the corners of classrooms and garbage cans. "They even have announcements in class: 'Don't chew tobacco in class.'"

Howard gives the impression he is taking these changes and various others in stride. He doesn't want to talk much about the first few months here, but other family members say he found the move, about as troubling as the rest of them.

His parents recall that shortly after he arrived in Austin, he became depressed. Like the other family members, he had difficulty adjusting to Austin life and finding friends. It is his nature to clown and joke a lot, they say, but in those first months he was hostile and withdrawn.

After weeks of relative silence, says his mother, one night at the dinner table, Howard suddenly announced in a bitter tone—and using a graphic teen-age slang term—that he had decided he disliked Austin. Each night for a while, he repeated the basic conclusion, wording it a bit differently each time and enumerating fresh examples of what he found objectionable about Austin life.

A disconcerting result of the move for Howard is that, at 16, he needs only one more course to graduate. That means he is one or two years ahead of most of his peers. At his high school in Maryland, there were more class periods than here, and so he transferred a large number of credits. But he and his parents have agreed that he will stay at Anderson High School another year. They don't want him entering college with freshmen a year or two older than he.

Leona Klaskin

Mrs. Klaskin sips coffee at her kitchen table here and recalls that distant afternoon when she and her husband drove from Brooklyn to what now is Elmwood Park, N.J.—their first move. "It seemed like we were going to the other end of the world," she says; when she was a youngster, "to go to the Bronx was an adventure."

Nine moves later, she is tired of moving. She says the moves probably have worsened an ailment she has had since childhood. She grinds her teeth. "Other people get upset," Mrs. Klaskin says. "They throw things or they yell and scream. I have a fairly even temperament, and I just grind my teeth." It has taken a year of painful gum and root-canal work, as well as 13 caps, to restore her mouth. While she is sleeping or when she is working intently at something like painting a chair, she wears a retainer to preserve her teeth.

There have been other costs for her. "I've given up personal things," she says, "in the sense of a career, for example. You really can't do that when you move around." Her husband tends to blame himself for that. "In a way," he says, "I deliberately sacrificed her career." (She holds teacher certificates from two states and the Marshall Islands.) "Now it would be very hard for her to compete with the new teachers coming out of college," Mr. Klaskin says.

The stresses of setting up a new household fell most heavily on Mrs. Klaskin. In the move, lamps were shattered, sofas were ripped, dresser legs were broken, bikes were bent. Barbara's piano, a gift from Mrs. Klaskin's parents, arrived in pieces. Additionally, the movers lost the family's station wagon. When it was retrieved six weeks later, it was saturated with the putrid odor of 50 houseplants that had rotted while stored inside.

The Klaskin home here is an old house, in an established neighborhood, and those factors turned out to have a depressing effect on her. The house was so dirty that during the lengthy cleanup period, she tacked a beach towel to the wall behind her bed so her pillow wouldn't touch the dirt. She believes the neighborhood's established character contributed to her difficulty in finding friends.

"You have nothing in common with the people next door who have lived here for years," she explains. "They're really not interested in my problems. They know who to call when they need a plumber. Their kids are adjusted to school. They've lived here forever. So it's not the same."

She misses the Washington area's theaters, concerts and museums that she and her husband enjoyed together. And although the Texans she has met are friendly, she has found few couples who seem to "want to follow through on anything," such as an evening out together.

Mrs. Klaskin recognizes the importance of the moves to her husband, but she believes he would be more content if he accepted the viewpoint she expressed to him during those first weeks here.

"I told him that in his own way, he'd reached some sort of success," she says—"that he's never going to be president of the company and that he ought to accept that. If he could accept that, he could be happier."

As for future moves, Mrs. Klaskin says, "I would go anyplace with my husband, truthfully." But later, as they are joking together, she declares, "Roy's got one more move left, and that's it." Then she turns to her husband and playfully brandishes a fist.

Roy Klaskin

It began with job frustration. In late 1977, while living in Potomac, Mr. Klaskin started feeling that his work as an IBM senior programmer wasn't sufficiently interesting. Mrs. Klaskin says she noticed signs of boredom: He stopped working as late, and he rarely brought work home.

But when IBM mentioned the possibility of making him manager of the systems assurance department here, he was hesitant, despite the more challenging work at a higher salary. He thought immediately, he recalls, of the problems his family already had suffered because of what he calls his "restlessness."

Eventually, though, he decided he wanted the job, and he began discussing it with his family. None of the family members knew much about Austin, but each could think of reasons that the move was appealing. The Klaskins had never become attached to Potomac, the Washington suburb where they lived. Life there was hectic, and they disliked the showy affluence of the community. Several of their friends had moved away, further reducing the Klaskins' attachment to the area. With Howard acting as Austin's chief advocate in these family councils—a role he soon regretted—the Klaskins finally agreed to make the move.

A year later, Mr. Klaskin sits in his comfortable three-bedroom home here on a picturesque acre of land and reflects on the decision. "You wonder," he says, "whether the move you make is really good for your family. You wonder what the trade-offs are." He regrets that because of his frequent moves, his children never really got to know his father, who died recently. "To never know one's grandparents very well is a shame," he says.

And he is especially sensitive about his daughter's moodiness—her hair-trigger temper, crying spells and tendency to bolt into her bedroom when she is upset. He suspects that she plays on his sensitivity. "It's a little trick that little girls innately understand," he says.

The first few weeks after the move were especially hard for him because that's when his family seemed to have the roughest time. He became "quite lethargic," he recalls. "I would just sit on that beautiful porch there and watch that beautiful sunset. I felt that I'd really fouled up the family this time. The job wasn't worth it. What's the use of succeeding at work when I've screwed up my family?"

Source: A. Ramirez, "Family on the move," *The Wall Street Journal*, February 28, 1979, 59, pp. 1, 31. Reprinted by permission of *The Wall Street Journal*, © Dow Jones & Company, Inc. 1979. All Rights Reserved.

There are four members of the Klaskin family. Two are at the stage of middle adulthood, one is at the beginning of early adolescence, and one is at the end of early adolescence. The parents, Leona and Roy are involved in the crisis of generativity versus stagnation. They are doing some serious questioning about the purpose and meaning of their lives. Leona is becoming aware that she has given up certain opportunities for making important contributions beyond the family in order to achieve intimacy in early adulthood. Roy is asking himself about the values of his career moves. To what extent have they benefited anyone? Most important, he wonders, have they benefited or harmed his children? These are normal, if somewhat painful, questions that emerge from the crisis of generativity versus stagnation. They reflect these adult's appreciation of the "bigger picture" of life's purpose. The moves, especially the recent one, may have brought about the probing and questioning. However, psychosocial theory would suggest that a certain amount of this tension is predictable during middle adulthood. Adults experience stress as they strive to confront the society's expectation that they make a contribution to the quality of life for the next generation. The feelings of discouragement and frustration are part of the process through which the people evolve a philosophy of life within the framework of a spouse, and children. The pain that the Klaskins are experiencing can be viewed as normal developmental anxiety. It reflects their discovery that there is a need to clarify life goals and to reconsider what is important to them. Life does not go on forever. If choices that have been made in the past are not bringing fulfillment, there is a feeling of urgency about making sure that future life choices will.

Barbara Klaskin, at age 13, is just at the beginning of the crisis of group identity versus alienation. Her anger and her anxiety are linked to the uncertainties of peer group membership. The transfer was poorly timed for her. It disrupted her place in the informal social structure of her peer group. She had already established a set of preferences for dress and for activities that had tied her to a group of friends in Maryland. No comparable group exists in her new community. She had prepared

● **betrayal—being failed or deserted, especially in the time of need.**

herself for being with a peer group that is not available in her present situation. Her anger and her sense of *betrayal* stem from her frustration that she is not going to be able to be part of the group that would have included her if she remained in Maryland.

Howard Klaskin seems to have resolved the crisis of group identity versus alienation. He is aware of the underlying similarities in peer groups and the superficial nature of some of the peer group distinctions. Howard faces the challenge of individual identity. He responds to the move with

Living laboratory 12·1

PSYCHOSOCIAL THEORY AND NORMAL LIFE CRISIS

Purpose: To understand the psychosocial theory of the normal life crisis.

Method: Using Case 12·1 as an example, interview an individual who is in the life stage of middle adulthood and compile a case study of the person's life.

Results: Ask the following questions:

Are you questioning the purpose or meaning of your life? In what ways?

Have you made career changes (such as remaining at home to rear children, then joining the work force)? Why? When? How do you feel about the changes?

If you have not changed careers, why not? Do you ever think about such changes? What thoughts do you have?

How have these decisions, to change or not change careers, benefited or harmed other members of your family?

Have you felt a commitment to improve the quality of life for future generations? If so, how would you do it?

Have you felt a lack of psychological and/or personal growth? When? How frequently? Have you tried to overcome it? How?

What major decisions pertaining to your life have you made recently? Have you needed support from your family and friends in this decision-making process? Have you gotten it?

What aspects of your life do you feel really good about? What aspects would you like to change?

You may think of additional questions to ask the person in your case study.

Discussion: If the person in your case study is in a normative life crisis listed in Table 12·1, what are the implications for this person's process of adjustment? To what extent has the person resolved earlier crises? Why does resolution of earlier crises enhance the resolution of later crises?

Do you think it is important for people to be able to recognize the existence of crises? Why?

Could you recognize your own normative life crises? Do you have the skill and competences to resolve it?

depression. It is likely that the depression has more to do with his sense of the life choices ahead than about the move itself. Howard may also be identifying with his father, and showing his father's confusion and depression. In later adolescence, parents are important as models especially for sex role development and career commitment. If Mr. Klaskin is struggling with the wisdom of his decision, Howard may well be struggling with the challenge of evaluating his own father. He is trying to integrate earlier identifications which most likely idealized Roy with a new awareness of Roy's weaknesses.

A DIALECTIC VIEW OF CRISIS

The notion of a dialectic model of crisis refers to contradictory conditions that require new personal organization (Riegel, 1976). From a dialectic point of view, crisis is responsible for reorganization and growth. Underlying every major aspect of behavior there is a contradiction that gives the behavior meaning. For example, activity is meaningful in relation to passivity; stability is meaningful in relation to change. Growth results from continuous interaction between an active person and the active environment. Both the person and the environment change along many dimensions at once. At any time, the two can be in harmony, each responding appropriately and predictably to the needs of the other. Or, the two can be in discord, posing conflicts for one another.

Harmony and discord in life events

From a dialectic perspective, human adjustment involves changes in the following areas:

1. Inner-biological.
2. Individual-psychological.
3. Cultural-sociological.
4. Outer-physical.

Inner-biological changes refer to physical and sexual growth, development of motor skills, biological aging, and physical illness. Changes in the individual-psychological dimension would include cognitive growth, self-awareness, and the development of coping skills. Changes in the cultural-sociological dimension would include learning cultural roles and their accompanying norms of behavior, participation in cultural rites and rituals, or cultural change like changes in sex-role norms that have an impact on individuals. Changes in the outer-physical dimension would include epidemics, natural disasters, wars, or changes in climate.

From the dialectic view, personal development requires an interweaving of these four dimensions. That means it is impossible to understand the person without understanding the person's inner life, their immediate psychosocial environment, and the broader physical environment. Change can occur along any single dimension, but it is more likely that change occurs along more than one dimension at a time.

The dialectical theory looks at life crisis with respect to the harmony and discord in life events. Most people recall their past as a series of

"Every now and again I'm shocked at the things that don't shock me any more."

Reprinted by permission The Wall Street Journal

"structured sequences marked by 'disruptive' events." (Riegel, 1975). The disruptive events are the points of discord. Most crises are examples of discord between the individual-psychological dimension and the cultural-sociological dimension. Attempts by the culture to exploit, devalue, or ignore the person's worth can create crisis. Crisis may also occur if the person is unable or unwilling to change with changing cultural values or beliefs. Other crises can arise when either the inner-biological events or the outer-physical events are in discord with the individual-psychological dimension. Examples here would be illness or death, disaster, or war. Finally, several aspects of a single dimension may be in discord. Erikson's concept of role diffusion is a good example of discord at the individual level. The person experiences crisis because of an inability to bring together the many roles and commitments that contribute to their life.

Creative adaptations to life crises

Research on adjusting to stress over the life course illustrates the importance of a dialectic analysis of life crisis. Lowenthal and Chiriboga (1973) described the process of adjustment among people at four transitional periods of adult life:

1. High school seniors facing college, work, or marriage.
2. Newlyweds expecting their first child.
3. Middle-adult parents whose youngest child was about to leave home.
4. Pre-retirees.

Their findings support the dialectical perspective. First, those subjects who had a high level of life stress expressed more very positive and more very negative emotions than those with little stress. Second, middle adults who had experienced high levels of stress felt happier than those whose lives were less stressful. Third, people who had exposure to high stress but were not overwhelmed by it showed high morale. They felt happier than those who were quite preoccupied but had actually experienced little stress. Fourth, the balance of resources and deficiencies changed in its impact on happiness over the life course. The happiest adolescents had many resources and many deficiencies. The happiest among the pre-retirees had few resources and few deficiencies. With advancing years, the energy and resilience to combat deficiencies, especially physical symptoms or disorganization of cognitive or emotional functioning, decreases dramatically. At some point these deficits can be so severe that the available resources simply cannot compensate for the limits on activities and relationships.

Mary Howell— Imposing harmony on contradictions

Mary Howell is a pediatrician in Boston who has integrated life roles that some might view as quite incongruous (Albin, 1979). The discord between her career pattern as a physician and the cultural norms for the kinds of interests and services physicians are supposed to provide are striking.

The physician's role is usually viewed as expert. Both physician and patient tend to agree to view the physician as an expert. The physician is expected to provide the care and the patient is expected to get better. Few expect the physician to educate the patient or the patient to actively contribute to the cure. Mary Howell takes a different view of this role— a view that helps bring greater harmony to the roles she plays as professional, parent, spouse, and teacher.

The important part of Mary Howell's case is that she has succeeded in confronting these conflicts and imposing her own will on them (see Case 12·2). It is an example of adjustment in its best sense when individual insight and will dominate over cultural stereotypes.

Case 12·2

MARY HOWELL

After leaving Harvard in 1975, she opened a pediatric practice in York, Maine, set up to give child health care back to parents. Her third book, *Healing at Home,* is a memorial to the year she spent there.

At the Child Health Station, Howell ran her practice collectively with two nurses and an office manager. The team sent out a patient newsletter that informed parents of office policies, health problems, and treatment information. They created a parent's advisory group so that office staff could stay in touch with and respond to community needs.

Once in the office, kids listened to their own hearts and observed lab tests. Mothers whose children endured frequent ear infections learned to use an otoscope at home so that they could look into the ear. Staff wrote patient charts while mothers remained in the office so that they could take a copy home with them.

"Much of what doctors do in ordinary situations, you can learn to do at home," says Howell. "You can learn about your child's vulnerable body system—ear, eye or whatever—and can often treat it yourself. I don't tell parents not to call a doctor, but I tell them to ask themselves first, what they can do about the problem, and what help they want from professionals."

Socialization never took

Howell is not a conventional physician and she tries to explain the sources of that unconventionality. "It is easy for women to become socialized out of understanding how life is experienced by most other women. I began medical school after having life experiences very different from those of most medical students. I had been married and divorced, I had an infant son, I had become involved in the intellectual world of psychology. Whatever medical school is trying to teach us about professionalism is easy to teach young men cut off from all else. But I was not cut off and I confronted this socialization process with a backlog of some very basic life experiences. The medical socialization never took."

"Male professionals often work in isolation from mundane life," she continued. "Women, on the other hand, are more likely to remain so connected to other human beings that this connection infuses their work. Nobody an take an active role in managing a household and fail to learn how to be flexible. By the time you've figured out your child, the child has changed. Men have usually opted out of this experience, and don't acquire the readiness for contingencies that child rearing and life demand. My book chapter may take longer because I write as I have given this interview, amidst six children and their friends, and with bread rising and cookies in the oven. This is not a less efficient process but a very different one, with different results."

Source: R. Albin, "Snapshot: Mary Howell," APA Monitor, March 1979, p. 4.

NATURAL INTERVENTIONS: COPING WITH DISASTER

Other sources of life challenges are personal or community disasters. Natural catastrophies and community disasters are not predictable. Yet they occur with some degree of regularity. Not every person will experience a disaster, but some people may experience several. During wartime, civilians may encounter repeated disasters including destruction of their homes, separation of family members, epidemic disease, or famine. Certain dimensions of disasters make them especially painful:

1. They generally cannot be anticipated.
2. Their beginning or end cannot be controlled.

3. They often take away the victim's self-defining properties, either property, relationships, or both.

4. They may bring the threat of imminent death to oneself or a loved one.

5. They may involve either physical pain and fear, or both.

Those who survive a disaster are left with the fear that they might have to experience such an ordeal again. Images of what occurred, the sense of helplessness, guilt over how one acted are all psychological effects of disaster. These effects require continuous coping.

Case 12·3 illustrates the response of a mental health service to

---

Case 12·3

VICTIMS OF TERRORISM

The Takeover

"From March 9 to March 11, 1977, approximately 154 men and women were held hostage by members of the Hanafi Muslim sect at three locations in Washington, D.C. The largest group, consisting of more than 100 persons, was held in the B'Nai B'Rith National Headquarters Building. Eleven hostages were held at the Islamic Center, and the others were captive in the D.C. City Council Chambers. During the 39 hours of their captivity, the hostages were subjected to physical violence, threats, verbal abuse, sleeplessness, severe physical restraints, hunger, humiliation, and the continual threat of imminent death."

The response

The treatment format was short-term, crisis-oriented, broad-spectrum group behavior therapy. Treatment began within the week following the hostages' release, on the first day they were permitted to return to work. The sessions were held in the building that had served as both their work site and, most recently, their prison. Attendance was variable, fluctuating with work schedules and level of need. In all, approximately half of the B'Nai B'Rith hostages were seen in treatment. Group sessions were held twice weekly for four weeks. Following a three-month break after the initial series of group sessions, an additional group was run for six weeks for those still

requesting treatment. One additional session was conducted approximately one year after the takeover in an attempt to forestall any untoward anniversary reactions.

The range of symptoms experienced by the hostages extended through all *modalities,* including avoidance behavior, depression, fatigue and muscular cramps, horrifying images of concentration camps and mass slaughter, irrational thoughts of personal cowardice and humiliation, disrupted familial relations, and requests for minor tranquilizers and hypnotics. Not every victim experienced each symptom, but these were the most prevalent and directly related to the captivity.

The psychotherapy employed included specific treatments addressed to the particular symptoms presented. For example, *in vivo* and systematic *desensitization* were employed for avoidance behaviors; deep muscle relaxation was taught for sleep disturbances, anxiety attacks, multiple somatic complaints, and as a substitute for minor tranquilizers and hypnotic agents; assertion imagery and rational-emotive therapy were used for disturbing images and recurrent irrational thoughts; and assertiveness training and outside referrals were used for disrupted familial relations. Table 12·2 presents the symptoms and treatments in a multimodal format (Lazarus, 1976).

TABLE 12·2
Hostages' multimodal
profile

Modality	Problem	Treatment
Behavior	Avoidance (of stairwells, elevators, taxis, being alone, the work site).	In vivo and systematic desensitization.
	Crying, verbally snapping at others.	DMR, assertiveness.
	Fear of isolation.	Planned program of writing and sharing experience with others.
Affect	Muted affect.	Encouraged group sharing of experience or writing feelings.
	Mild depression.	Planning rewarding activities, reassurance.
	Anxiety attacks.	DMR, coping imagery, assertiveness training.
	Anger.	Assertiveness training.
Sensation	Sleep disturbance.	DMR, scheduling usual relaxing activities, exercise, coping imagery.
	Headaches.	DMR with concentration on muscles of the face, neck, and shoulders.
	Stomach and bowel disturbances, palpitations, muscle tightness, back pains.	DMR with concentration on trunk muscles.
	Fatigue.	Permission to sleep more and engage in less rigorous activity.
Imagery	Reliving of takeover and holocaust fantasies.	Substituting calming imagery, focus on release.
	Being vulnerable in all life situations.	Assertion imagery.
	Unable to testify in court.	Behavior rehearsal, organized review of events.
Cognitions	Obsessive rumination.	Thought stopping.
	"Awfulizing."	Encouraging feedback from group members on behavior during takeover.
	"This wouldn't have happened if only. . . ."	
	"I should have. . . ."	
	"You should have. . . ."	
	"I wasn't a hero and I should have been."	
	"Catastrophizing."	RET.
	"I'll never get over this."	
	"The Hanafis know my name and address and will come to kill me later."	
	"No place is safe anymore."	
	Isolation.	Group sharing, therapists providing limited information about the wide variety of human reactions to stress.
	"I'm the only one who had these reactions."	
Interpersonal	Increased dependency and desire for human contact.	Coping imagery, assertion training, permission to need the comfort of others.
	Suspicious of strangers.	Take more realistic precautions (lock car and home, etc.), in vivo desensitization.
	Marital and family conflict.	Assertion training, referral to family and conjoint therapists.
Drugs	Increased use of tranquilizers, sleeping medications, alcohol.	Substitution of DMR, exercise, RET, coping imagery, limited use of drugs when appropriate.
	Somatic disturbances.	Medical check after release and before rejoining families, medical follow-ups of new complaints or old ones exacerbated by stress.

Note: DMR—deep muscle relaxation; RET—rational-emotive therapy.
Source: L. I. Sank, Community Disasters: Primary Prevention and Treatment in a Health Maintenance Organization, *American Psychologist*, 1979, *34*(4), 335. Copyright 1979 by the American Psychological Association. Reprinted by permission.

victims of an act of terrorism. We learn some of the symptoms that develop during a crisis and some strategies for providing help. In Case 12·4, we discover that there is potential personal growth that could result from a crisis of this kind.

Case 12·4

SHIRLEY

Shirley is a 42-year-old white, married, Jewish female who was working as an administrative assistant for the B'Nai B'Rith on March 9, 1977. She was at her desk when several Hanafis burst into her work area. She was herded together with all her colleagues on the floor and was pushed into the stairwell to be marched up to the eighth-floor conference room that was to serve as her prison for 39 terror-filled hours. Shirley did not see the actual stabbing of another employee, but she did hear the screams and did see the bloodied machete of her Hanafi captor. She is not sure how she got past the bloody scene up to the eighth floor, feeling somewhat dazed by the preceding moments. The hours went by with events not clearly distinguished from one another. She remembers her body aching from the damp cold of the concrete floor and her head aching from repeated crying spells. She recalls vividly the men being separated from the women and being roughly bound. She also remembers the humiliation heaped on several of the men because one wept, another wet himself, and still another behaved too effeminately.

Shirley remembers many moments of overwhelming fear. The worst seemed to coincide with the appearances of Khaalis, the Hanafi leader, who would repeatedly threaten grisly death to specific individuals and then the entire group. Shirley recalls the images of bodies pressed against each other for comfort and protection and her annoyance at the petty grumbling about the sharing of food and floor space for sleeping. She also recalls the delirious first moments of freedom, the feelings of exhaustion mixed with exhilaration. There were the reunions with her husband and daughter, both of whom she had thought about continuously through the ordeal as she took stock of her life and her commitment to those she loved.

Shirley's ordeal was not over, however, once she was released by the Hanafis. For several months she experienced a number of symptoms related to the extreme stress she had undergone while held prisoner. Shirley had great difficulty returning to work; she found herself crying without explanation and intolerant of others. She felt considerable anxiety and a mild, persistent depression. She associated this emotional state with a sense of being exhausted much of the time, as if she "had mononucleosis again." Shirley slept poorly at first, reliving scenes of the building takeover, of bloodied faces and clothes. On a positive note, Shirley, like many of her fellow captives, came away from her imprisonment inspired "to do better" in her primary relationships with her husband and teen-age daughter. She recognized and spoke of positive feelings she had felt but not verbalized for years. Her release signaled an occasion for renewal. Apparently, both her husband and her daughter felt and acted similarly after their own ordeal of waiting."

Source: L. I. Sank, "Community Disasters: Primary Prevention and Treatment in a Health Maintenance Organization," *American Psychologist* (1979), *34*(4), 334–38. Copyright 1979 by the American Psychological Association. Reprinted by permission.

United Press International

Family and friends gather when Hanafi
Muslims release their hostages.

The events of this crisis had direct impact on the physical, emotional, and intellectual functioning of the victims. An important part of the intervention was that people did not hae to wait until severe symptoms developed before receiving help. The mental health services did not isolate the victims from one another. They did not remove the victims from the work context to which the disaster was linked. Sentiments of caring, concern, and help-giving toward the victims were expressed by co-workers, employers, and mental health professionals. One outcome of this disaster may, in fact, have been a new norm for responding to psychological needs within the organization. Just as Shirley's relationship with her loved ones was strengthened by the disaster, so as the organization's commitment to the lives of the employees.

Living laboratory 12·2

NORMAL LIFE CRISES

Purpose: To compare two views of life crises.

Method: Analyze the case study of the Klaskins from the perspective of Lewin's field theory and Erikson's psychosocial theory. You might organize the data as follows:

	Field theory	Psychosocial theory
Basic concepts/laws		
Stage versus nonstage		
Implications for adjustment		
Definition of crisis		
Circumstances responsible		
for the crisis		
Strategy for adjustment		

Results: Identify similarities and differences between the two viewpoints.

Discussion: Which model would you use to solve a personal crisis?

What are the strengths and weaknesses of each model?

How do people learn to resolve crises?

What would you do to help a friend solve a crisis?

Chapter summary

Crisis emphasizes that tension is an unavoidable part of life. Each view of crisis sees certain circumstances as primarily responsible for crisis. Each view also implies a unique strategy for adjustment. Taken as a whole these views confirm the growth potential of crisis. When limits are tested, crises promote new behaviors or new concepts. The person moves to a new level of harmony and control. At every life phase, the person's resilience is tested. At the heart of a response to any challenge is the need to protect the very core of self-continuity and self-esteem. Sometimes, the only way to protect the self also closes off channels for future growth. The consequences of these maladaptive responses will be considered further in Chapter 14.

Psychosocial theory emphasizes the normal life crises. They result when developmental competences are inadequate to meet social demands.

The dialectic view of crisis emphasizes the dynamic conflicts in all phases of life.

Disaster adds the totally unpredictable and uncontrollable to the picture. We do not teach people to anticipate the devastation of a flood, or plane crash, or an act of terrorism. People who spend a lot of thought anticipating these events are viewed as morbid, if not somewhat disturbed. When disasters occur, however, they strip us of resources. They leave us feeling painfully vulnerable to the random perversities of life. As such they teach a vital lesson about all aspects of adjustment. We discover that much of behavior is intended to preserve a sense of meaning, control and predictability in life.

SUGGESTED
READINGS

For further reading on coping with normal life challenges:

Datan, N., & Ginsburg, L. H.   *Life span developmental psychology: Normative life crises.* New York: Academic Press, 1975.

Dohrenwend, B. P., & Dohrenwend, B. S.   *Stressful life events: Their nature and effects.* New York: Wiley, 1974.

Goertzel, V., & Goertzel, M. G.   *Cradles of eminence.* Boston: Little Brown, 1962.

Several recent works have looked at personality development in response to normal life challenges in adulthood:

Gould, R. L.   *Transformations: Growth and change in adult life.* New York: Simon & Schuster, 1978.

Levinson, D. J.   *The seasons of a man's life.* New York: Knopf, 1978.

A popularized treatment of this same theme is:

Sheehy, G.   *Passages: Predictable crises of adult life.* New York: Dutton 1974, 1976.

Reading

A GLIMPSE OF SCIENTIFIC INVESTIGATION

A new point of view

As I repetitiously continued to go over my ill-fated experiments and their possible interpretation, it suddenly struck me that one could look at them from an entirely different angle. If there was such a thing as a single nonspecific reaction of the body to damage of any kind, this might be worth study for its own sake. Indeed, working out the mechanism of this kind of stereotyped "syndrome of response to injury as such" might be much more important to medicine than the discovery of yet another sex hormone.

As I repeated to myself, "a syndrome of response to injury as such," gradually, my early classroom impressions of the clinical "syndrome of just being sick" began to reappear dimly out of my subconscious, where they had been buried for over a decade. Could it be that this syndrome in man (the feeling of being ill, the diffuse pains in joints and muscles, the intestinal disturbances with loss of appetite, the loss of weight) were in some manner clinical equivalents of the experimental syndrome, the triad (adrenocortical stimulation, thymicolymphatic atrophy, intestinal ulcers) that I had produced with such a variety of toxic substances in the rat?

If this were so . . .

If this were so, the general medical implications of the syndrome would be enormous! Some degree of nonspecific damage is undoubtedly superimposed upon the specific characteristics of any disease, upon the specific effects of any drug.

If this were so, everything we had learned about the characteristic manifestations of disease, about the specific actions of drugs, would be in need of revision. All the actually observed biological effects of any agent must represent the sum of its specific actions and of this nonspecific response to damage that is superimposed upon it.

If this were so, it would mean that my first classroom impressions about the one-sidedness of medical thinking were quite justified and by no means sterile questions without practical answers. If the "damage syndrome" is superimposed upon the specific effects of all diseases and remedies, a systematic inquiry into the mechanism of this syndrome might well furnish us with a solid scientific basis for the treatment of damage as such.

If this were so, we had been examining medicine— disease and treatment—looking only for the specific, but through glasses tinted with the color of nonspecificity. Now that we had become aware of this misleading factor, we could remove the glasses and study the properties of disease and treatment apart from the color we saw through the glasses.

It had long been learned by sheer experience that certain curative measures were nonspecific, that is, useful to patients suffering from almost any disease. Indeed, such measures had been in use for centuries. One advises the patient to go to bed and take it easy; one tells him to eat only very digestible food and to protect himself against drafts or great variations in temperature and humidity.

Furthermore, there were all these nonspecific treatments that we had learned about in medical school, such as injection of substances foreign to the body, fever therapy, shock therapy, or bloodletting. They were unquestionably useful in certain cases. The trouble was that often they did not help, and sometimes they did much harm; since one knew nothing about the mechanism of their action, using them was like taking a shot in the dark.

If we could prove that the organism had a general nonspecific reaction-pattern with which it could meet damage caused by a variety of potential disease-producers, this defensive response would lend itself to a strictly objective, truly scientific analysis. By clearing up the mechanism of the response through which nature herself fights injuries of various kinds, we might learn how to improve upon this reaction whenever it is imperfect.

A change of mind

I was simply fascinated by these new possibilities and immediately decided to reverse my plans for the future. Instead of dropping the stress problem and returning to classical endocrinology, I was now prepared to spend the rest of my life studying it. I have never had any reason to regret this decision.

Discouragement

It may be worth mentioning that I often had to overcome considerable mental inhibitions in my efforts to carry on with this plan. Nowadays it is perhaps difficult to appreciate just how absurd this plan seemed to most people before I had more facts to show that it worked. For example, I remember one senior investigator whom I admired very much and whose opinion meant a great deal to me. I knew he was a real friend who seriously wanted to help me with my research efforts. One day, during these busy weeks, he asked me into his office for a good heart-to-heart talk. He reminded me that for months now he had attempted to convince me that I must abandon this futile line of research. He assured me that, in his opinion, I possessed all the essential qualifications of an investigator and that I could undoubtedly contribute something to the generally recognized and accepted fields of endocrinology, so why bother with this wild goose chase?

I met these remarks with my usual outbursts of uncontrolled youthful enthusiasm for the new point of view; I outlined again the immense possibilities inherent in a study of the nonspecific damage which must accompany all diseases and all but the mildest medications.

When he saw me thus launched on yet another enraptured description of what I had observed in animals treated with this or that impure, toxic material, he looked at me with desperately sad eyes and said in obvious despair, "But, Selye, try to realize what you are doing before it is too late! You have now decided to spend your entire life studying *the pharmacology of dirt!*"

Source: H. Selye, *The Stress of Life* (New York: McGraw-Hill Book Company, 1956). Reprinted with permission.

Chapter 13
Cultural Change

Throughout the past, as successive stages of social evolution unfolded, man's awareness followed rather than preceded the event. Because change was slow, he could adapt unconsciously, "organically." Today unconscious adaptation is no longer adequate. Faced with the power to alter the gene, to create new species, to populate the planets or depopulate the earth, man must now assume conscious control of evolution itself. Avoiding future shock as he rides the waves of change, he must master evolution, shaping tomorrow to human need. Instead of rising in revolt against it, he must, from this historic moment on, anticipate and design the future.

Alvin Toffler, *Future Shock*, 1970

The photography of H. Armstrong Roberts

For reflection

1. What special customs or events have been passed from one generation to the next in your family?

2. What aspects of your cultural heritage would you like to teach to your children or share with your friends?

3. Why does conflict exist between subcultural groups in our country?

4. Why do members of the Amish religious group reject automobiles and current dress styles?

In this chapter, crisis that is caused by cultural change is discussed. Cultural change involves all of the sources of conflict presented in the last chapter and more. It produces basic challenges to the assumptions we have about life and the process of living.

The concept of culture refers to the thoughts, speech, behaviors, and products of a social group. It includes beliefs and assumptions held by the group. It includes social behavior such as rituals, structures of family relationships, and norms for interaction. It includes the technology, art, music, science, and religion of the group. Culture is an abstraction. One can describe the components of culture rather objectively when discussing another culture. It is harder, however, to recognize culture-linked assumptions of our own cultural group in ourselves. Cultural characteristics are experienced as givens. They are like the air we breathe or the sunlight. We rarely think about the clothes we wear, the tools we use to eat, the labels we use to refer to one another (i.e., mother, father, uncle, cousin), or the morals which tell us what is right and what is wrong yet these would be noticeable and perhaps unacceptable in another culture.

The basic routines of life are different from culture to culture. Three kinds of cultural change are discussed in this chapter. First, culture change occurs when a person moves from one culture to another. Moving, going to college, changing jobs would all be examples. Second, a person might experience one subculture during childhood and a different subculture during adulthood. Differences in lifestyles between subcultures such as ethnic, religious, and socioeconomic groups would make adjustment an important task for one who changes. Third, adults experience the stress of culture change as a result of new norms and technology that have occurred between one period of their lives and another. Despite the widespread changes that may be involved, people and groups adjust to these kinds of culture changes. You have realized by this time that culture change does not only happen when one travels from one country to another. Traveling between cities, states, neighborhoods, and regions takes the American from culture to culture. Going from one job to another, to college or into the military also places us in new cultures. The United States is designed to allow many subcultures to live side by side. Many argue, in fact, that the subcultures provide our great diversity. The diversity of interests within the structure provided by the Constitution and the Bill of Rights provides energy for the development of the society.

MOVING FROM ONE CULTURE TO ANOTHER

In 1978, 25,000 refugees from Southeast Asia settled in the United States alone (Putman, 1979). Victims of religious persecution, political exile, or war seek safety in new countries all the time. For those who flee persecution or possible extermination, the desire for survival overcomes the fears that uncertainty about life in a new culture might involve. Millions of adolescents leave home and go to college each year. People like the Klaskins change their lives because of job changes in increasing numbers. The first thing that is noticed by many people in moving from one culture to another is culture shock.

Culture shock

Rainy day. An apartment in South Lincoln Park Housing Project. Four men sit watching the Indianapolis 500 race on television. The four— Ly Fu, Seng Lee, Ly Geu, Yang Chee—are Hmong tribesmen, lately of Laos. Ly Fu, 45, is a former major in the Royal Laotian Army.

The United States had no stauncher ally in the war in Southeast Asia than the Hmong, some three hundred and fifty thousand people dwelling in the mountains of northern Laos. The Pathet Lao, the Communists, had no stauncher enemy.

Then one day it ended: The Americans went home. When the Pathet Lao gained control of Laos, the Hmong began to flee. These men were lucky; they crossed into Thailand before crossings were restricted.

Hmong still manage to get out of Laos and into Thailand and onward. A couple had arrived in Denver only two weeks before. The city's Hmong colony now numbers 650. But countless others remain trapped in their homeland.

"We don't understand," said one of the men. "There is nothing in the newspapers here about Laos, about what is happening there. Why is there nothing?"

Outside, Ly Phoua, the major's 15-year-old daughter, stepped daintily around the mud puddles. She wore a traditional Hmong custome: black dress trimmed in blue, green, red; a tiara; a silver necklet; and a belt of coins—old French piasters—that rang like wind chimes.

The women brought older mementos: bamboo flutes, stamps, woven cloth. The major picked up one flute and began to play. It was a sweet melody: "You are your parents' daughter; you are beautiful." There was laughter and applause and the women began to talk with animation. The major kept playing, but seemed withdrawn. In his mind's eye, I was sure, he was seeing the green hills of northern Laos, green hills he was not likely to see again (Putman, 1979, pp. 396–400).

Culture shock is the term given to experiences that accompany rapid change from one culture to another. Even when the transition is temporary, as in a summer abroad or in an international assignment, people react to the cultural differences. Some reactions that are part of culture shock include:

1. Confusion and impaired decision making.
2. Feelings of isolation and loneliness.
3. Anxiety and feelings of vulnerability.
4. Grief for what has been left behind.

Culture shock can be a major barrier to adjustment. Immigrants come to a new country with hopes of improving life conditions or fleeing persecution. They may not anticipate the range of differences between their own culture and the culture of the new setting. College students often experience the same things. Feelings of alienation, anxiety, and confusion result from the move. They may make it difficult to explore the new setting or to reach out to new people. In fact, new people are likely to seek others from their homeland or home community. They settle in communities where they may know people from their culture. Most large cities in the United States have ethnic neighborhoods. In these communities, the shock of total emergence in a new culture is buffered by the support of others who share a common cultural heritage.

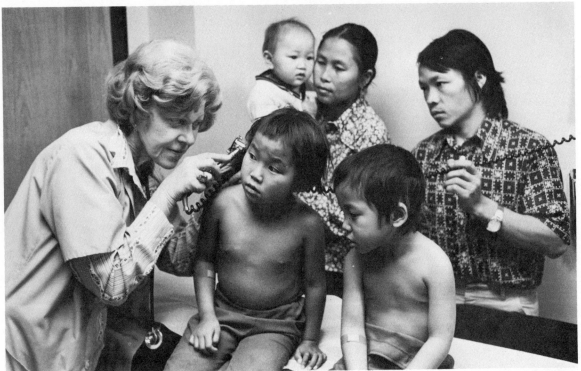

Donald Smetzer

A newly arrived Laotian family confronts American health care.

● *barrio*—a section or a neighborhood in a city or town occupied by Spanish-speaking people.

The *barrios* of Los Angeles, New York's Lower East Side, San Francisco's Chinatown are all examples of highly developed ethnic communities. The foods, the language, the holidays, and the family bonds of a distant country are transported to another culture. This strategy of adjustment reduces the demands for change. It permits a strong emotional and intellectual commitment to one's original culture. It allows people to take advantage of shared aspects of the mainstream culture. Finally, it creates barriers between the ethnic community and the mainstream culture. This strategy of adjustment is used by educational groups as well as ethnic groups. It is not uncommon in adult life to find "Harvard men" working and associating with each other. They gain support for culture acquired in college if not before.

Culture change does not always involve resistance to total involvement in the new culture. The Israelis have devised a plan for integrating immigrants from many cultures into Israeli life as rapidly as possible. The "Ulpan" is a system of orientation and integration through which all newcomers must pass. Orientation centers provide intense training in basic Hebrew, information about the history, politics, and economics of Israel. In order to aid adjustment, the centers provide assistance in finding housing, work, or retraining if necessary. Through the "Ulpan," newcomers to Israel have many opportunities to meet other newcomers, but they are not left to their own resources. Culture change is made easier by this planned, centrally organized effort to provide a welcome home to all new settlers. The Peace Corps has developed similar techniques for helping Americans reduce culture shock as they enter a variety of cultures.

Not all cultures are as committed to their newcomers as Israel, the Peace Corps, or the college discussed in Chapter 11 has been. For many, entry into a new culture brings humiliations and frustrations that cause intense stress. Newcomers are stripped of almost every significant social reference point. They do not know the language. They are often not able to make use of professional skills. They lose their community status. They may also lose a community to share the customs and the traditions of their past. In some cases, these losses are combined with an open resentment on the part of the residents toward the newcomers. New people are often ridiculed because of their language skills, their "ignorance" of customs, and their "peculiar ways." New people represent new competition for employment, social welfare resources, and rewards. In this country, we are learning that each new cultural group adds to the pool of talent that is important for our own culture to grow.

Acculturation

Few cultures are so totally isolated that they are unaware of the practices, beliefs, or things produced by other cultures. Just knowing about the ways of another culture is a form of acculturation. Knowledge of another way may change what we do or affect how we interpret our own culture. Technically, acculturation refers to observable ways that the blending of cultures leads to new, melded, cultural patterns. Acculturation takes place at the individual level as people take on the behaviors and beliefs of another culture as their own. This is an example of adjustment. When members of cultures borrow ways from each other and in the process create new ways that are better for all. This is a process of growth. The individual as well as the culture may benefit by the creation of new ways of doing things. Individuals may produce new ways of doing things which can help all members of the culture grow. In our times, the culture provides a great deal of input into each person's life. Few people give comparable input to the culture. Most people, therefore, spend much of their time throughout life adjusting to their culture.

One might think of acculturation as a gradual process whereby new ways are blended with old. Often, however, this process is neither smooth nor comfortable. Think of the problem of language. If adults move from a French- to an English-speaking culture, will they learn English or continue to speak French? If they choose to learn English, will they continue to speak French at home or with friends? If they have children, will

The decision to learn English is a major step in the acculturation of these Cambodian immigrants.

the children hear French or English spoken in the home? Will an adult totally abandon the language of their own childhood with all its poetry, stories, and mythology, never to share it with their own children? Giving up one's native language or refusing to teach that language to one's children can place a great barrier between the parent and the child. Acculturation is a process which produces a state of tension and crisis in the person and in the social groups. The tension is a source of stress which leads to very different outcomes for people and societies. Sometimes growth occurs, sometimes destruction is a product of the tension.

Sharp (1952) has described an example of acculturation in a group of Australian aboriginals called the Yir Yoront. The Yir Yoront lived at the level of a Stone Age technology. They were hunters and gatherers, with no farming. The dog was their only domestic animal. The stone ax was the main tool of the Yir Yoront culture, much like the automobile is important to our society. It served many functions at many levels of cultural organization.

Very briefly, the stone ax was linked to three main aspects of Yir Yoront culture:

> First, the stone axe was central for producing other aspects of the economy. It was used for cutting firewood, hunting, making other tools and weapons, and building shelters. This utility gave the axe concrete value. Only men were able to produce or own axes. Women and children could use them. Possession of a stone axe gave men special status.
>
> Second, the stone heads for the axes were taken from land 400 miles south of the Yir Yoront homeland. The stones were obtained through chains of trading partners. The trading pattern usually involved an exchange of spears for axe heads. These trading chains built lines of contact across regional groups. This also added status to the older men who had formed efficient trade relations.
>
> Third, the axe was a sacred *totem* of a certain Yir Yoront clan. This meant that the stone axe had mythical ties to the clan's origins. When sacred rituals were performed, only these clansmen could show a symbolic link between an ancient, ancestral period and the present (pp. 76–77).

● *totem*—an object serving as the emblem of a family or clan and often as a reminder of its ancestry.

Acculturation occurred when an Anglican mission was established in 1915 near the Yir Yoront territory. In order to raise the standard of life in this area, many artifacts were provided. Among them were steel axes. These axes were given as gifts, kept in stock for sale, and traded. They became desired objects. They were often used as an incentive for attending a mission meeting or doing chores for the missionaries. In Sharp's analysis, the steel-headed ax did not improve the economy of the Yir Yoront. Instead, it disturbed the basic structure of the culture. By giving so many axes indiscriminately, the dependence of women and children on men was disrupted. Trading relationships were disturbed. Older men lost status since they were no more likely to have steel axes than younger men. The special mythological link to the ancestral stonehead ax was dissolved. The steel-headed ax was not the only factor leading to the confusion that accompanied acculturation. It was a powerful factor that opened the way for change.

This is a situation that has occurred often over the past centuries. Cultures with more advanced technology have traveled to simpler cultures with less of a technological emphasis. The introduction of creations like the steel ax, the transistor radio, airplanes, and modern construction techniques produce great change in cultures. It is important to remember, however, that acculturation is a two-way process.

Preserving the best of one's culture

Not all outcomes of acculturation are negative. Among the Yir Yoront, the confusion and disruption were temporary periods leading to a freer life. Inkeles and Smith (1974) have demonstrated the link between economic development and personal development. In each of six developing countries including Argentina, Chile, India, Israel, Nigeria, and East Pakistan (Bangladesh) economic development was associated with positive psychosocial factors. These included more personal freedom, confidence, new skills, broadened perspectives on values, more information, higher personal aspirations, and frequent experiences of a sense of competence. The three elements of development that are most responsible for these changes are education, factory experience, and exposure to mass media.

Amidst the movement toward modernization, however, are those who try to preserve the integrity of a cultural heritage. This struggle is no simple effort. It requires continuous balancing of what is basic to the traditional way of life with what can be changed in the interest of modernization. In the United States, especially, the push toward assimilation is very great. Even though we recognize our diverse ancestry, most people strive to enter the "mainstream" of American culture.

Recently the sentiment for ethnic pride has become fashionable. Ethnic neighborhoods have existed in most communities for a long time. Now, these neighborhoods are openly celebrating their heritage. They resist giving up their language, their traditions, or their history. They are insistent on being accepted by the majority culture. Ethnic groups want to include more about their practices and history in their children's schools. Cultural groups are participating actively in the political leadership. They are fighting discrimination in housing, employment, and educational opportunities. The parish of Guadalupe in Denver, Colorado, is an example of this effort.

Guadalupe is the parish for 50,000 of those people. The church stands across the street from a sheet-metal company; Interstate 25 seals it off from downtown. Goats and sheep graze the side yard, pets for the children. There's a rich Mexican flavor in the tortillas prepared in the parish hall by the women, in the guitar and Mexcian dancing lessons, in the Mariachi

Mass at eleven each Sunday, when worshipers fill the aisles and flow down the steps.

It is a good place to follow the struggle of Denver's Mexican-Americans looking for a better chance.

Father Jose Lara, the rector, bearded, spectacled, slightly stooped, recalled his arrival in Denver in 1961. He and another young Spanish seminarian had been sent by their order to complete their studies in the United States.

"We had been two days on the train from New York, not knowing the language. Then at the railroad station here, we found a man who could speak Spanish, and with a special flavor. So we asked: 'Are you Mexcian?' Immediately there was a certain hesitancy. The priest who accompanied us took us aside, and in a gracious way said, 'You don't say that word here.'"

In time things began to change. Mexican-Americans, their numbers swelling, began to march, to demonstrate, to call on the mayor's office. They protested alleged police brutality, "liberated" the parks, picketed a newspaper that portrayed them in unflattering terms. They demanded jobs, a bilingual school program, Mexcian-American teachers, and an end to discrimination.

Father Lara marched with them. And when the Chicanos began to organize themselves politically, he was in the thick of it. A member of his congregation was the first Mexican-American to win a city-council seat. It was won in classic American style, after a hard-fought battle with an Italian-American incumbent.

So when I last visited Guadalupe—on Mother's Day, when the street by the church is closed off and there is music and beer and dancing and flowers for the mothers—Father Lara could introduce me not only to restaurant and hospital and construction workers, but also to the city councilman, a state senator, and a handful of rising young businessmen.

Many of Denver's Mexican-Americans have begun to enter the system. As they do so, other newcomers arrive (Putman, 1979, p. 396).

The stories of ethnic groups struggling to retain their identity and to take advantage of the things provided by the mainstream society go on all over America all the time. One of the primary theoretical breakthroughs for the preservation of ethnic identity came with the "black is beautiful" campaign. Developing a strong sense of ethnic pride and promoting yourself to the mainstream culture is a strategy that is working for many people in America today. It should also be noted that the thing that allows this to work in America is that the public settings are the property of everyone. Access is supposed to be equal. People with different ways of being, who feel good about themselves can compete for themselves with rights assured in the public settings and on their own property. The experiment of our society is based on this system working to promote the public welfare and to insure the common defense in an effective and efficient manner.

Living laboratory 13·1

PRESERVING THE BEST OF ONE'S CULTURE

Purpose: To increase awareness of one's ethnic heritage.

Method: Write down everything you can remember that reflects the special ancestry of your parents. This might include special expressions in another language, the celebration of special holidays, special stories that were told to you, clothing, artifacts (dishes, paintings, or antiques) that were a product of your ancestor's culture, certain meals or foods that have ethnic origins, or ethnic games, toys and songs.

Results: Try to assess how much of your own childhood was accented by the signs of ethnic identity. What feelings are attached to these memories? How well prepared are you to pass on this ethnicity to the next generation?

Discussion: Who is responsible for preserving the fragments of your family's ancestry?

Who teaches about your heritage?

What are the pressures to abandon ethnic identity? How well are those pressures resisted?

What are the advantages to you personally of giving up your ethnic identification? What are the costs?

CONFLICTS BETWEEN SUBCULTURES

The United States is not the only country to struggle with the problem of ethnic diversity. In Africa, not including the northern Mediterranean nations, there are an estimated 1,000 to 1,500 tribes. Each tribe claims tribal loyalties, uses a unique language or dialect, and controls specific territories. The terror of the Biafran War is a reminder of how strong these allegiances can be. During the three-year war, the Ibo (calling themselves the Republic of Biafra) seceded from the rest of Nigeria. Almost all the Ibo were eventually massacred. In recent days, the events in Iran have focused world attention on the various subcultures. These groups have been involved in actively changing Iran's society while blending into a new equilibrium.

Diversity of values across subcultures

In Kenya, the spirit of nationalism is struggling to blend the tribal bonds (Reader, 1979). In the schools, children learn about democracy, nationalism, government, and a national economy. But in private, the Kamba are not welcome in the homes of the Masai. The conflict between these tribes is, in part, the ecological conflict between farmers and herders. The conflict has been interwoven into tribal hostilities, vengencies, and ritual tests of manhood. When resources are plentiful, and when there is no drought, national interests can be tolerated. However, during drought or famine, economic survival of these two different cultures always places tribal bonds ahead of national commitment. The forces of cultural learning include a belief that one's own values, goals, and skills are the most important to preserve (Reader, 1979).

> The ability to keep cows alive and productive on marginal grasslands among lions and other predators produces a supreme self-assurance. The Masai believe there is no one better than themselves. Survival depends entirely upon the cow, so it is perhaps not surprising that the Masai believe every cow in the world belongs to them. This conveniently disposes of any moral problems involved with restocking. If drought, disease or predators should ravage the herd, you simply go and collect some from the folk settled on the hills—like the Kamba, for instance.
>
> Immediately following their circumcision during the years before World War II, Medoti and his age group took to the forests on the slopes of Kilimanjaro. They were men now, *moran,* warriors of the tribe. There were hundreds of them, says Medoti, camped out in groups of eight or ten, eating the bulls their fathers supplied, constantly testing their own strength and bravery; they killed buffalo and made shields from the hides; they killed lions and made headdresses from the manes. By the end of the year, says Medoti, they were all so highly strung and fierce that a questioning look was enough to start a fight. All this strength and tension was ultimately to be unleashed in a raid upon the Kamba farmers.
>
> It took place shortly after the long rains. Many Masai and Kamba were killed, he says, but altogether the raiders took several thousand head of cattle back to Masailand. Medoti's share of the spoils was 30 head (p. 44).

The clash between subcultures is one outcome of the diversity of values. We have seen this outcome often among ethnic groups in the United States. An intellectually advanced society recognizes that there are other ways for subcultures to behave toward each other. Ways are developed for groups with diverse values and interests to mix with each other. The methods are designed to channel the energy of conflict and use it to produce growth in the society.

Subcultural isolation

Subcultural isolation can occur by choice or because of barriers imposed by the mainstream culture. Isolation can be a firm effort by the subculture to ward off modernization of acculturation. On Mackinac Island in the upper peninsula of Michigan no automobiles are permitted. Once reaching the island by ferry, walking, bicycling, and horse-drawn carriage are the only means of transportation. The island struggles to maintain the pace and atmosphere that was typical of small communities at the late 19th century.

A more extreme form of cultural isolation is practiced by members of the Amish religious group. There are an estimated 22,000 baptized adult Amish plus adolescents and young children. The Amish are committed to continue the dress, the lifestyle, and the religious practices of their 17th-century ancestors. The Amish reject the use of telephones,

United Press International

*The Amish of Ohio gather for the funeral
of one of their church leaders.*

● *secular—**worldly.***

electric lights, automobiles, and modern forms of entertainment. They
wear a standard costume that makes them readily recognizable. Children
attend public elementary school, but they are not permitted to attend
high school. Amish traditionalism is a symbol of their devotion to religious
ideals. Their cultural isolation places enormous pressures on the young
children to resist forces toward acculturation. These forces are encountered daily during the elementary school years. However, the limit placed
on *secular* higher education allows the Amish to preserve their culture
from one generation to the next.

Enforced isolation occurs whenever the culture places barriers on
social interaction among subgroups. The Eastern European Shtetl or
ghetto was a carefully designated area where Jews were permitted to
live. Outside the shtetl, no Jew was allowed to own property. The Jewish
shtetl became a lively arena for Jewish study, music, art, and folklore.
However, opportunities for Jews and non-Jews to interact were minimized.

The Jews were always vulnerable to attack, plunder, or destruction. They
lived in terror of the ruler. At any time, soldiers might choose to raid
the shtetl and torment the inhabitants.

In our own country, racial segregation has created communities
similar to the shtetl. In black ghettos, residents are victims of economic

exploitation. They suffer from high unemployment, poor schools, over-crowded and run-down housing, and victimization by organized crime. Until recently black ghettos have been owned and managed by white entrepreneurs. Blacks in urban ghettos have begun to gather the resources to invest in their own businesses. They are claiming an active role in the managment of schools, and in political governance of their communities. Nevertheless, because of racial discrimination in educational opportunities, employment, and housing, many blacks continue to feel isolated. They despair of ever leaving the predictable poverty of the ghetto.

The frustration of educational, economic, and political isolation periodically leads to riot and revolution. In 1967, rioting in Detroit, Michigan, brought $250 million in property damage, 43 deaths, 4,000 arrests, and 5,000 homeless. Because of riots many middle-class residents left from the city, abandoning whole buildings. Crime rose as the population fled, adding to the isolation of those who remained. Despite community efforts to combat these destructive forces, unemployment remains a critical isolating factor. Without the hope of work, education is a hollow promise. Without education, the limit of employability is set even lower. One estimate projects that half of all black males growing up in Detroit will have no work experience by the time they are 25 years old.

Living laboratory 13·2

SUBCULTURAL ISOLATION

Purpose: To simulate the conditions of subcultural isolation. In this exercise, you will choose to isolate yourself from your peers by refusing to make use of a significant piece of modern technology.

Method: For one week, do not make or receive telephone calls. When asked, tell people that they can reach you by mail or in person but that the telephone is an intrusive force in your life. It interrupts concentration, it is out of your control, and it creates an impersonal mode of interaction.

Results: Keep a log of the number of interactions you have with others for two days before you begin. Then keep track of the number of interactions you have during the time when the telephone is not used. Try to record your feelings each day, especially feelings of loneliness, frustration, self-esteem, or personal freedom. Note how you feel about face-to-face interactions when the telephone has been excluded. Also note how others respond to your decision.

Discussion: What pressures are put to bear in order to get you to use the telephone?

How does the removal of this cultural tool influence your life?

What might be the long-term consequences of this form of isolation?

Does the data suggest that the number of interactions decreased by more than 20 percent?

Is the net effect really greater isolation or greater perceived isolation?

Whether it is imposed or elected, cultural isolation creates stress. In the former case there is the frustration of confronting social barriers to growth and personal improvement. Those who are isolated by choice are constantly bombarded with the fruits of modernization. They are plagued by doubts about whether their self-imposed isolation is meaningful.

GENERATIONAL CHANGE

No culture is totally static. Natural disasters, wars, specific chiefs or leaders, or the introduction of the new invention bring differences in the lives of each generation. In technological societies the rate of change is relatively rapid. Culture is the backdrop against which every person struggles to develop and preserve a value system and a set of life goals. Accelerating technical and social change is a source of anxiety for people in modern society (Toffler, 1970).

Only 30 years ago we were still enjoying the growth period of the 50s. There was no energy crisis, no concern about environmental protection, no electronic calculators, no microwave ovens, relatively few married women with children in the work force, no Concord jets, no man on the moon, no communication satellite, no court-ordered school desegregation, no discos, no skateboards, no color TV, no digital clocks, no women's liberation, and no Sesame Street.

What happens to people when they experience rapid changes in technology, leadership, norms about sexuality, sex roles, and the structure of their lifestyle? *Fortune Magazine* conducted interviews with 25-year-old business beginners in the 1950s and 1980. The author, Gwen Kinkead describes some of the similarities and differences between the two groups.

A quarter of a century ago, in the age of Ike, *Fortune* interviewed a large sampling of young men starting out in business and found them to be an optimistic, tractable, incurious lot, dedicated to family and community service. [See "The Confident Twenty-Five-Year-Olds," *Fortune,* February 1955.] This year, repeating the exercise, *Fortune* selected 82 25-year-olds from all over the United States and talked with them at length about their views of business and the world at large. Like the 1955 sample, the new one was chosen unscientifically, although we made an effort to find young people who had shown promise of becoming high-level managers and entrepreneurs. All the people interviewed—this time they included women—are or will be 25 some time this year. The results show that the adjective "confident" still applies; indeed, the confidence borders on brashness. These new heirs of the nation's product want a lot more of everything than the Eisenhower generation, and they plan to get what they want—both the tangibles and the intangibles—by driving hard and fast up the career path.

The going is apt to be arduous. Because they had the tough luck to be born in 1955, smack in the middle of the postwar baby boom, today's 25s face more competition for advancement in the corporate hierarchy than any generation in business history. Their progress will be impeded, if not blocked, by the many managers now in their mid-30s who were born at the beginning of the boom and, more indirectly, by older executives who are choosing to retire later. And behind the 25s bulks a horde of younger challengers born between 1956 and 1964, a span that included several peak years of the baby boom. The squeeze from fore and aft can only worsen when this class eventually vies for the few top positions at the apex of the hierarchy.

Yet, while the statistics portend a Hobbesian all-against-all future struggle, the realities are not nearly so grim. The prospective managers *Fortune* interviewed will progress more quickly into upper income brackets—which start at about $29,000 per household today—than most of their predecessors would have dreamed possible. Single 25-year-olds in the group are already earning a median of $20,000, well above the median U.S. family income, estimated at around $17,040. And those remarkable statistics pale beside another: the medican income of 20 married couples in the sample is $37,250. (Twenty-four of the 82 are married, but in four cases only one spouse works.) In other words, most of them are already well into the upper income bracket. As more of this group marry and achieve higher salaries, they will constitute a new "superclass." Whether all this conjugal earning power will compensate for what the demographics warn will be thwarted career ambitions remains to be seen.

All indicators suggest that it won't. Almost without exception these 25-year-olds are careerists, in the sense that they measure their self-worth according to the accomplishment of their professional goals. There is nothing new or unusual about this: some 25-year-olds have probably always viewed their lives this way. What is unusual is that it surfaces as the overriding characteristic of the entire group of promising young business people. They put their jobs ahead of most other diversions and commitments— including marriage, which many are in no hurry for, and children, which some claim they'll never want (*Fortune,* April 7, 1980, pp. 74, 75. Courtesy of *Fortune Magazine;* © 1980 Time Inc.).

A young executive illustrates one outcome of the questions of modern life:

> Dennis Eshleman, an associate product manager with General Goods, and his wife, Kathy, a paralegal, earn about $45,000. Eshleman calculates they would have to sell the two-bedroom house they just bought in Eastchester, New York, if she quit work now to raise children. "That would be a big adjustment," he says "I'm willing not to have a family if it disrupts my wife's career" (Kinkead, 1980).

One result of increased production of all kinds of things is that people want more things. To get more they are willing to work harder. The great variety of attractive things that we make stimulate people in ways that are pleasurable and produce feelings of competence. This stimulation leads us to want more things. Companies produce things with the idea of producing the most appealing product. Needs create products and products create needs. This is a motivational condition which may provide the motor mechanism for adjustment in modern society.

Try to think ahead just 20 years into the future. What will be the major social concerns in the year 2000? What will be the primary sources of personal or family conflict, the new technology, or the new opportunities? If you have trouble anticipating the future, then you along with most other people are facing the stress of rapid cultural change. How does one prepare for the future? What coping skills are most needed to deal effectively with the inability to predict? The basic coping competences needed to adjust in any situation are:

1. The capacity to acquire and analyze new information.
2. The capacity to maintain control over emotions at least long enough to evaluate the logic of a new direction (in other words to have some balance to nostalgia).
3. The capacity to maintain diverse interactions so that one gets many points of view.
4. The capacity to clarify one's own personal moral philosophy. This guiding philosophy serves as an antenna for picking out those directions that may dehumanize rather than enhance the quality of life.

Living laboratory 13·3

GENERATIONAL CHANGE

Purpose: To appreciate the pace of generational change and its impact on adjustment.

Method: Interview four people about the benefits and harms of television. Select people aged 10–12, 20–24, 45–50, and 65 or older. Find out about the person's own experiences watching television, including age at first viewing, number of hours of viewing, and present viewing pattern. Then ask about why television viewing might be good or harmful for children. Was television viewing good or harmful for them in any ways?

Results: Compare the early experiences with television across the four ages.

Consider age differences in attitudes toward the benefits and harms of television viewing.

Discussion: What are each generation's experiences with television?

What activities do you think were replaced by television?

What new attitudes about learning, about entertainment, or about national and international affairs might be a product of television viewing?

Is there anything special about American television that might help retain particularly American values or attitudes?

Chapter summary

Three kinds of cultural change are discussed. Each brings the stresses of discontinuity and uncertainty. Each tests the resources for coping and adjustment. Moving from one culture to another is perhaps most stressful in that it brings sudden and vast change. Culture shock which usually accompanies entry into a new culture includes physiological, emotional, and cognitive symptoms. Adjustment may take the form of seeking others who have a similar cultural background. Others adjust by trying eagerly to assimilate. The struggle to preserve what is meaningful of a past culture and to integrate aspects of the new culture is a difficult process. It often leads to value conflict, role confusion and some sense of alienation. In its most positive light, culture change can lead to an appreciation of those values and goals that go beyond culture. These values provide a sense of life's universal meaning.

Culture change is not always total or sudden. Acculturation is a more common form of cultural change. Although this gradual process is not usually perceived as stressful, it can disrupt a balanced cultural pattern. Disruption occurs when change brings new levels of uncertainty. When it includes new opportunities for education, employment, and diverse information acculturation generally brings new levels of personal freedom. It enhances one's world perspective. There is no doubt that these gains are made at the cost of increased uncertainty. Perhaps the point is that uncertainty and anxiety are unavoidable elements of psychosocial evolution.

Culture conflict offers another challenge to adjustment. In many societies rivalries exist between subcultures. The dominant culture may reject or devalue cultural subgroups. Prolonged periods of cultural conflict result in the establishment of complex adaptive mechanisms on the part of the rejected or isolated subgroup. These mechanisms serve to protect the rejected group and to maintain a core self.

SUGGESTED READINGS

For further reading in the area of culture change:

Toffler, A. *Future shock.* New York: Random House, 1970.

Mead, M. *Culture and commitment. The new relationships between the generations in the 1970s.* Garden City, N.Y.: Doubleday, 1978.

A text in cultural anthropology is:

Miller, E. S. *Introduction to cultural anthropology.* Englewood Cliffs, N.J.: Prentice-Hall, 1979.

Readings in anthropology can be found in:

Annual editions in anthropology. Guilford, Conn.: Dushkin, 1980–81. (These readings are revised yearly.)

Reading

CULTURAL DIVERSITY AND HUMAN SURVIVAL

There are far deeper problems than those that involve combating the immediate dangers of nuclear war, nuclear proliferation, permanent irreversible environmental damage, and deterioration of the quality of life. These hazards are very grave. The need to prevent the destruction of civilization, if not life itself, is urgent and overriding. Although survival is the absolute necessity for the further development of the human experience, too much concentration on survival, besides actively making that survival less likely, can in a subtle way blur our vision, because somehow we have demeaned ourselves in the process. To the statement, "Man does not live by bread alone," must be added, "Man does not live by life alone"—something the great religions have always preached, each in its limited, time-bound way.

There are new technological conditions within which a new initiative for the human race is possible. But it will not be found without a new vision. The historic figures of speech of "brotherhood" and "sisterhood," of loyalty to kin, which the great religions have used, are no longer enough. As my daughter Catherine Bateson has pointed out, the image of a group of brothers and sisters, although it has carried the great religions forward for several thousand years, is in fact too narrow and leaves out a group to which human beings have been equally bound throughout human evolution—those others whom they marry and brothers-in-law and sisters-in-law.

To the age-old vision of one's own home fires, one's own kin, one's own community, and one's own country, to be loved, defended, and sustained against all odds, we can now add a vision of a planetary community all living within one atmosphere, encircled by air currents that carry danger in one part of the world to another part, all of which must be protected if any are to be protected. And for the great religious vision which has been partially embodied in the idea of human brotherhood, we have now the vision of human community, male and female, kin and nonkin, who together make up the unity of the human race. Within such a vision, the contributions of each culture, of the search for spirituality and grace in some parts of the world and the search for good works and the earthly well-being of human beings in other parts of the world, can become complementary.

Such a vision and the search for music to hail it, figures of speech to interpret it, styles of life to embody it, should be enough to evoke the strongest commitment the world has ever seen. Our vision has enlarged as our political communities have enlarged; our capcity to call men "brothers" or "fellow citizens," no matter what their physique or whether we would recognize them if we met, has grown. Cultural evolution has been an enormous enlargement of the human spirit, an enlargement which has been intimately related to the number and diversity of those whom we could include within our expanding frontiers of shared dedication.

Chapter 14
Problems in adjusting to life

Following are excerpts from the hitherto secret private journal of Woody Allen, which will be published posthumously or after his death, which ever comes first.

Getting through the night is becoming harder and harder. Last evening, I had the uneasy feeling that some men were trying to break into my room to shampoo me. But why? I kept imagining I saw shadowy forms, and at 3 A.M. the underwear I had draped over a chair resembled the Kaiser on roller skates. When I finally did fall asleep, I had that same hideous nightmare in which a woodchuck is trying to claim my prize at a raffle. Despair.

Woody Allen, *Without Feathers*, 1976

Ken Firestone

For reflection

1. What happens to people who don't adjust successfully?

2. Why would you seek advice from a therapist, counselor, or psychiatrist rather than your mother, father, or best friend?

3. What personal characteristics should a counselor, therapist, or psychiatrist possess in order to provide effective therapy for a person needing help?

4. If you were the parent of a juvenile delinquent, what would you do?

Throughout this book we have focused on adjustment as an active, creative process. Adjustment results in feelings of effectiveness and personal satisfaction. The feelings produced by successful activity are pleasant. Every person encounters challenges and personal doubts that produce unpleasant feelings. So the well-adjusted person creates a well from which pleasant feelings will flow. The balance of pleasant and unpleasant feelings is likely to tip in favor of pleasant feelings for the well-adjusted person. The confidence, security, and relaxation produced by the pleasant feeling state helps the person to confront new situations successfully. There are many stumbling blocks in the path toward adjustment. For most people, these stumbling blocks provide the challenges and stimuli for continued growth. They are occasions for self-evaluation, for new concepts, and for creative action. Self-insight, flexibility in response to stress, and a more accurate reading of the social environment occur when coping is successful.

Some people do not make a positive adjustment to life's challenges. They are not able to retain flexibility in their responses to stress. Their responses become more and more rigid and off-target. Greater self-insight is not achieved. Rather, these people begin to distort their own personal qualities. They deny characteristics of the self or inaccurately estimate their talents. They do not seem to have an accurate assessment of the environment. They may be unable to predict the outcomes of their actions. They may be unable to have meaningful social interactions. They may see danger where it does not exist or fail to recognize changes in the environment when change has taken place.

Several words are used to describe the kinds of problems we consider here. Terms including *deviance, psychopathology, maladaptation,* or *mental illness,* are all used to refer to failure to make a successful adjustment to living. This failure can occur early in life in such conditions as autism, childhood schizophrenia, or childhood phobias. Failure can occur at any point in the life span, usually as a result of inadequate coping skills or unusual environmental stress. Failures in adjustment can be recognized by the pain they cause the person, or by the pain the person causes the community.

In this chapter three forms of unsuccessful adjustment or maladaptation are described: neurosis, psychosis, and behavior disorders. Not every form of maladaptation is considered. Enough patterns are described, however, to give a picture of the many ways that adaptation can fail to result in adjustment. Strategies for helping people to create more effective coping strategies are discussed at the end of the chapter. There are many techniques that have been developed to intervene in the lives of those who have reached the limits of their own resources.

NEUROSES

The psychoanalytic theory has contributed the most commonly used explanation for unsuccessful emotional adjustment. The term which is used for these kinds of disorders is neurosis. In the psychoanalytic view, neuroses emerge when the person develops restrictions against the expression of basic impulses. These two forces operating in opposing directions place the person in psychological conflict. The person must be able to express basic instincts like sex and aggression. At the same time, we learn to control or restrict expression of raw instinct. This conflict produces tension or anxiety in the person. In order to ward off these unpleasant feelings, some people begin to become maladaptive by developing temporary ways of gaining relief called symptoms. Symptoms may be effective in providing short-term relief of anxiety and tension. The person continues to need them because they do not really relieve the causes of the problem. These symptoms do not provide effective resolution for the person's conflicts about sex and aggression.

Repression, a defense mechanism that was first discussed in Chapter 5, is often used to shield the person from the unpleasant conflict. Repression blocks the impulses, the conflict, and the restrictions from the person's conscious awareness. The conflict continues to exist, however, and the impulses continue to seek expression, in the unconscious.

If repression was truly effective, the conflict would be retained totally in the unconscious. The fact that repression is not fully effective is what causes neurosis. This is a simple analysis. You would find more complex elements of the conflict become conscious or threaten to become conscious. This produces anxiety. Anxiety is experienced as unpleasant, and usually the person is driven to reduce it. Symptoms develop that provide temporary relief but do not resolve the conflict. Symptoms are thought to express the conflict at a very distorted level. The expression of impulses through symptomatic behavior is never enough to resolve the conflict because the symptoms only permit indirect and distorted expression.

Let's look at an example. Person X has strong sexul impulses and strong, internalized restrictions against the expression of sexuality. As X begins to experience sexual fantasies, strong guilt is also experienced. This combination upsets X. In order to protect itself, X's ego drives the sexual impulses and the restrictions on sexual expression out of consciousness. Now X begins to worry about cleanliness. Dirt and germs become preoccupations. In order to stay clean, X initiates hand washing. This gives X relief from the worry of contamination. The relief is short-lived, however. Thoughts of contamination occur again, and further hand washing is necessary. X washes three or four times an hour at first. After a while, 10–12 washings an hour are necessary. It becomes increasingly difficult for X to do much else.

After repression, X's thoughts of dirt and disease represent both the impulse and the restriction. Sexuality is "dirty." Thinking about dirt and contamination gives X an extremely distorted expression for unacceptable impulses. It is like thinking about sex. The thoughts of contamination also cast sexual impulses in a negative light. The preoccupation, or obsession with dirt, is one symptom. The anxiety becomes too strong for X and the behavior symptom develops. Hand washing provides X with both the pleasure of physical stroking and the restriction of physical pleasure by cleansing. The behavioral symptom represents the impulse, the restriction, and some resolution of the conflict.

Learning theorists take a different view of neuroses. They believe that neurotic behavior is learned over time through experiences of reinforcement. A person who experiences a stressful situation may become anxious in that situation. Fear persists even when the stressful stimuli are removed. The person is motivated to reduce the fear. Behaviors are developed to bring a reduction of fear. Over time these fear-reducing behaviors become firmly established as habits. When these behaviors are ineffective and peculiar, they are called neurotic.

There probably is validity to the psychoanalytic view that some neuroses are the result of ineffective attempts to deal with internal conflicts. There is also validity to the learning theorists' notion that neurotic behavior is a current behavior that emerged in response to a traumatic past event. In addition, neurotic behavior may be an attempt to reduce anxiety induced by environmental experiences that cannot be dealt with directly or effectively. An adolescent who cannot get along with an important teacher develops a strong fear of attending school. This fear leads to strain in the family and tension for the adolescent. Dealing with the teacher directly would be most appropriate. This strategy is not considered because of differences in status between the teacher and the student. The child and the parent may believe that it is legitimate for the teacher to be arbitrary or demeaning. They assume that such behavior is justified because of the teacher's status and expertise. Because of role discrepancies, they do not view direct confrontation an acceptable way of resolving the problem. The adolescent is fearful of confronting the teacher, but unable to escape the relationships. As the adolescent's fear and anxiety grow, school itself becomes a frightening experience.

We may, then, think of three kinds of neuroses: impulse neuroses, learned neuroses, and environmentally induced neuroses. Anxiety and the development of symptoms to reduce anxiety are common to all three forms. The origins of these neuroses are quite different. The first form is caused by difficulties in managing internal impulses. The second is caused by the development of ineffective and peculiar habits. The third is a result of difficulties in relating to the external environment. All three may result in similar behavioral symptoms. The inability to admit or to express sexual conflicts, a fearful past association to a setting, or a poor relationship with an important teacher may all lead to a strong fear of going to school—a school phobia. Although the causes may be very different, the outcomes in behaviors and thoughts may be very much the same.

Common experiences also provide some of the content for neurotic symptoms. Returning to the example of school phobia, this symptom is rarely seen in children from birth to the age of five or in adults beyond college age. People who attend school develop school phobias. Although some of these people may have problems that are caused by their school experience, not all of them do. The school is a setting in which all people of this age-group are involved. It serves as a target for phobias that may be caused by any of the three explanatory factors. In treating neuroses, the clinician must try to understand the cause of the problem as well as the symptoms. An analysis of the cause is necessary in order to guide the individual toward self-understanding, to dissolve the symptom patterns, and to establish new, more effective coping efforts.

Although neuroses may be extremely unpleasant and upsetting, they do not usually make a person unable to tell the difference between fantasy and reality. Neurotics may have some extremely unpleasant and upsetting fantasies. They may not be able to rid their minds of those fantasies. However, neurotics know that these mental experiences are fantasies. *Reality testing* is maintained. There are three exceptions. The first is anorexia nervosa, a condition that results in severe restrictions on food intake (Bruch, 1978). After prolonged starvation, a person may be unable to think logically. Too great a restriction of food intake for too long a time can result in death (Sours, 1969). The second condition is neurotic depression. Neurotic depression may involve thoughts of self-destruction. The anxiety, feelings of worthlessness, and the lack of prior experience with these feelings may lead people who suffer continual depression to conclude that they must try to take their own life (Yasin, 1973; Gallagher & Harris, 1976). We would argue that an attempt at suicide caused by thinking that is generated by depressive anxiety is a failure of the reality-testing mechanism. The third is dissociative reactions. Under some circumstances the person is not fully aware of major behavioral episodes. We would conclude, then, that although neurotics for the most part are able to test the difference between reality and fantasy, there may be occasional lapses of reality testing. In the remainder of this section, we will describe six of the common neuroses.

Anxiety reactions   Anxiety plays an important role in every neurosis. In anxiety reactions, emotional tension and high levels of anxiety are the main symptoms. The person feels apprehensive, but has no clear sense of what the threat

Richard Younker

The person who is neurotically anxious feels anxiety more often and more acutely than others.

is or where the anxiety comes from. The major symptoms are anxiety states. These states produce increased levels of anxiety and heightened activity in an already tension-filled person.

Most people experience emotional tension as part of life. The centrality of anxiety to adult experience was emphasized in Chapter 4, "Motives and Emotions," and again in the chapters on coping, normative life crises, and culture change. The person who is neurotically anxious simply feels more anxious more often. Such a person's capacities for relaxation and enjoyment are seriously diminished. Usually, anxious people accept their high levels of anxiety and adapt their lives to accommodate their tension (Cameron, 1963). This adaptation often exacts heavy costs.

Common symptoms of *chronic anxiety* include:

● **chronic anxiety—a painful or apprehensive uneasiness of mind over a long duration.**

1. A vigilant, unrelaxed attitude.
2. High levels of driven activity.

● *hypochondria—*
**preoccupation with
imagined illnesses.**

3. Aches, pains, and *hypochondria.*
4. Stomach or intestinal upset.
5. Shallow, irregular breathing.
6. Heart palpitation.
7. Sleep disturbances.
8. Depressed appetite, diarrhea, and constipation.
9. Sexual dysfunctions, including excessive masturbation, impotence, frigidity, and menstrual irregularities (Cameron, 1963; Gallagher & Harris, 1976; Coleman, 1976; Davison & Neale, 1978).

The neurotically anxious person constantly worries about danger (Beck, Lande, & Bohnert, 1974). Episodes of general, overwhelming tension sometimes occur. These are called anxiety attacks. An extremely severe anxiety attack is called a panic reaction. It is usually the end result of unbearable tension that has built up over a long period of time. Panic reactions may result in serious disorganization of the personality.

Phobias

Phobias are strong fears that are focused upon specific objects or situations. These objects and situations are then avoided as much as possible. Unlike people who have anxiety reactions, persons with phobias believe that they know what causes their strong, unpleasant anxiety attacks. They do not know why the object of their fear affects them as it does. Whereas people with anxiety reactions usually have many different symptoms, strong fear and avoidance of the feared are the main symptoms of phobias. Many phobics have only a single strong fear. Others have multiple phobias. A phobia usually plays an adaptive function for the phobic person. As long as the target of the phobia can be avoided, the phobic person can remain free from anxiety. Table 14·1 lists some of the common phobias. As you can see, there are numerous targets of fear.

Phobias are common at every stage of life. Cameron (1963) calls the phobia "the normal neurosis of childhood." Most of us can remember strong fears that we had as children. Darkness, monsters, certain animals, and school are some common targets of childhood phobias. We would extend Cameron's comment to call the phobia "the normal neurosis of life." Almost every person has one or two strong fears that are managed by avoiding the targets of the fear. If a person is made anxious, it is quite logical to try to identify the cause of the anxiety. A causative target is easy to select. Why the target causes the anxiety is less easily understood. If a person is experiencing conflict and anxiety because of unconscious impulses and restrictions, then the target of fear may be selected through the mechanisms of displacement and projection (Cameron, 1963). The target will have symbolic meaning. It will be something involved in the person's daily experience. For an early adolescent who is experiencing heightened sexual impulses and their corresponding restrictions, a strong fear of high places may develop. This target is selected because high

TABLE 14·1
Some common phobias

Accident phobia	Accidents, collisions, crashes, injury.
Acrophobia	High places—cliffs, roofs, high windows, airplanes, stairwells, ladders.
Agoraphobia	Open places—halls, wide streets, fields, parks, beaches (sometimes in recent years, a few of all places outside one's house).
Algophobia	Pain.
Anthropophobia	People.
Astraphobia	Natural dangers—storms, thunder, lightning.
Bacteriophobia	Bacteria.
Claustrophobia	Enclosed places—small rooms, closets, elevators, alleys, subways.
Cynophobia	Dogs.
Demonophobia	Demons, monsters.
Equinophobia	Horses.
Hematophobia	Blood.
Herpetophobia	Lizards or reptiles.
Mysophobia	Contaminants—dirt, germs, poisons, certain foods.
Monophobia	Being alone.
Nyctophobia	Darkness.
Ochlophobia	Public gatherings—crowds, meetings, lectures, theaters, stadiums, concerts, churches.
Ophidiophobia	Snakes.
Pathophobia	Disease.
Pyrophobia	Fire.
School phobia	School.
Strangophobia	Strangers, unfamiliar places, unidentified sounds and movements, the unknown.
Vehicle phobia	Cars, trains, planes, ships, buses, subways, escalators.
Weapons phobia	Guns, knives, scissors, bombs, clubs, axes.
Zoophobia	Animals.

places may have symbolic meaning for the adolescent. "Sexual activity in the dominant position is desired," or "high places generate a sensory experience that is similar to aspects of sexual activity." The fear represents punishment for unconscious impulses, and the avoidance of high places represents the appropriate restrictions on the impulses. The phobic symptom pattern is rather far removed from the actual topic of sexuality. However, it protects the person from having to deal with sexuality directly. The pattern also allows the person to avoid anxiety. If the sexual impulses become less intense or find mature expression, then the phobia will retreat. If the phobia remains the primary vehicle for dealing with sexual impulses and sexual impulses remain intense or increase, then the phobia will remain strong or will increase in intensity. The person might be unable to attend classes on upper floors of the school building or be unable to tolerate the upper floor of the home. If the phobic behavior interferes with the person's ability to function, then therapy may be necessary.

If, as a child, a person is on the upper floor of a building or the sight-seeing platform of a monument when a thunderclap, a sonic boom, or some other loud noise occurs, fear of high places may result. Over the years, the person may elaborate this fear as a simple kind of avoidance learning. The selection of a fear of high places is not symbolic. The learned habit of avoiding high places can be changed through a process of desensitization. In this process, the person is taught to remain relaxed while thinking of experiences in high places. Eventually the person will be able to relax and to overcome this early fear and the resulting habit pattern. For most people, early childhood fears never cause much restriction of behavior.

Neurotic depression

Neurotic depression is primarily a mood disturbance. It is a reaction to loss or threatened loss, to failure, discouragement, or disillusionment. The basic symptoms are self-evaluation of the dejection and appeals for reassurance. Neurotically depressed people lose interest in people, things, or activities. They give up their initiative. They repeatedly express feelings of inferiority, unworthiness, and hopelessness. However, the neurotically depressed do not totally relinquish relationships. They may find considerable reassurance from parents and friends who counter the claims of inferiority with arguments praising the person's worth. Judgment and reality testing may be somewhat distorted, but they are not seriously disturbed.

● **melancholia—** sadness or depression of mind or spirit.

In discussing depression, Freud (1957) stated: "The distinugishing mental features of *melancholia* are a profoundly painful dejection, cessation of interest in the outside world, loss of the capacity to love, inhibition of all activity, and a lowering of the self-regarding feelings to a degree that finds utterance in self-reproaches and self-revilings and culminates in a delusional expectation of punishment" (p. 244).

● **mood—**a feeling state.

Freud points out that there are many similarities between normal and neurotic depression. This should make the experience of the neurotic depression relatively easy for most people to understand because most of us have been depressed. Good days and bad days are common experiences that most people come to expect. As the song says, "Rainy days and Mondays always get me down." Normal, everyday *mood* disturbances may be caused by a bad grade; something someone says to you; the feeling that you didn't live up to personal expectations; the weather; or a girl friend/boyfriend, parent, or best friend taking a trip. Many daily experiences that involve some loss will cause depression. A major personal loss such as the death of a loved one will produce an intense depressive reaction in most people that may last for some time. Most people ultimately recover from the depression produced by such a loss. There is no doubt, however, that the death of a parent, a child, a spouse, or a grandparent will have a lifelong effect on the psychological development of the grieving person.

Self-depreciation evolves into a neurotic depressive reaction when persons are chronically preoccupied with their own worthlessness, failure, and hopelessness. Such people continue to feel dejected despite positive external experiences. They lose their personal initiative and their interest in activities and people. They often express feelings of despair and futility even when their personal situation does not warrant a lack of hope. Physical symptoms similar to those observed in anxiety reactions often occur (Cameron, 1963; Beck, 1967; Weiner, 1970; Coleman, 1976).

Hysterical reactions

Two main forms of hysterical neuroses have been identified: conversion reactions and dissociative reactions (American Psychiatric Association, 1980). Since the symptom patterns associated with these forms are quite different, we will discuss each form separately.

Conversion reactions. In a conversion reaction, unconscious conflict is transformed (converted) into a physical symptom. There is a physical reaction, but there is no physiological cause. The function of a part of the body is literally dedicated and sacrificed to the expression defense, denial, or punishment of a forbidden impulse. All of these meanings can be combined in a single symptom. Persons may develop a partial paralysis and then enjoy the care and support that the paralysis causes others to give. The symptom may persist because the person learns to use it for positive outcomes. A conversion reaction may develop as a way of avoiding some environmental situation that is too threatening to face. The reasons for a conversion reaction are not known to the person. The person is not pretending or practicing any form of conscious *deception.* In the conversion reaction, the person's anxiety is unconsciously transformed into physical disability. The meaning of the symptom is repressed. Often the person appears to be relatively anxiety free and unconflicted. The disability is the price that the person pays for relative freedom from anxiety (Sperling, 1973).

● *deception*—a falsehood.

There are many kinds of conversion reactions. We will list some in order to give you an idea of the variety of bodily symptoms that people use in order to resolve psychological conflict. Cameron (1963) presents an expanded discussion of each of these.

1. Loss of speech. As a conversion symptom, this may be quite complete and may last for several days. Stammering, stuttering, and the inability to speak above a whisper are less serious conversion reactions.
2. Muscular paralysis. As a conversion symptom, this will involve relatively serious and long-lasting loss of motor functions, including paralysis of the arms or legs.
3. Skin anesthesia. This is a relatively serious and long-lasting loss of feeling in some part or parts of the body, with no neurological impairment. Often, but not always, this accompanies conversion paralysis.
4. Visual disturbance. This is blindness, usually selective or in a single eye, which indicates that the person is blotting out the image of something threatening and anxiety provoking.

5. Deafness.   Sometimes it is complete, but usually partial. As with blindness, it is used to shut out threat.
6. Tremor.   It usually begins as a part of emotional excitement but persists because it symbolizes unconscious impulses. For example, trembling in the leg may keep an early adolescent from participating in sports where failure may be threatening.
7. Spasms or cramps.   These are sudden or painful muscle contractions that actively interfere with the performance of a skilled act. Writer's cramp may make it impossible for an adolescent to do homework.
8. Tics.   These are exaggerated gestures that recur intermittently.
9. Postural peculiarities.   They are unusual postures, such as a stoop, which, as a conversion reaction, are greatly exaggerated.

Dissociative reactions.   These are the kinds of hysterical reactions that most people are familiar with, because they have been popularized in literature and the mass media. Stevenson's *Dr. Jekyll and Mr. Hyde* is a fictional example, and the case of Eve, popularized as *The Three Faces of Eve,* is a rather dramatic real-life example (Lancaster & Poling, 1958; Thigpen & Cleckley, 1954, 1957). A recent case of multiple

Jean-Claude Lejeune

Emotional apathy is a form of dissociation.

personality describes the three faces of Evelyn both clinically and experimentally (Jeans, 1976; Osgood, Luria, & Smith, 1976). Dissociative reactions separate one or more components of the personality system from the rest (Cameron, 1963). They are ways of avoiding stress by escaping from conflicts, even though the separation that occurs may lead to unusual, dramatic, or peculiar outcomes. Abnormal dissociative reactions are rather rare, accounting for less than 2 percent of all neuroses (Abse, 1966; Coleman, 1976; Davison & Neale, 1978).

People often make use of dissociation in a normal way during extreme stress. When people learn of the death of a loved one or view a terrible accident, temporary distancing from emotion enables them to mobilize resources for more successful coping.

The various types of pathological dissociation include (Cameron, 1963):

1. Object estrangement.   There is an attempt to relieve anxiety by making the object world seem unfamiliar. Examples include an inability to listen to and understand what someone says and alterations in one's perception of objects.
2. Somatic estrangement.   The body, some part of the body, or the body image seems to be unfamiliar or unreal.
3. Depersonalization.   The person feels that some change in the self has occurred. The person feels that the self is unfamiliar, detached, or unreal. The early adolescent often experiences a sense of depersonalization because of actual bodily changes.
4. Sleepwalking.   This is relatively common in childhood and adolescence. Certain objects or experiences are sought without wakeful thought or inhibitions. This symptom can lead to dangerous situations, such as walking on a roof or a ledge.
5. Hysterical convulsions.   This is a nonphysiologically caused convulsive state in which the person becomes suddenly unaware of the surroundings while acting out some fantasy that has been repressed. The convulsive state allows anxiety to be obliterated while the person expresses the problem.
6. Trances.   People become immersed in regressive preoccupations which they cannot express in words. People are not easily aroused from trances.
7. Psychogenic stupor.   The person sits almost motionless and appears to be in a coma, but is preoccupied with internal, previously unconscious fantasies.
8. Massive amnesia without fugue.   The person wanders around near home but doesn't remember his or her identity or home environment.
9. Massive amnesia with fugue.   The person doesn't remember his or her identity or home environment and runs away from the home situation.
10. Dissociated personality.   This includes alternating personality, in

which two or more alternating personalities become almost completely dissociated from one another, double or multiple personality, in which one personality dominates while one or more other personalities occasionally take over in relatively childlike ways.

Dissociative reactions represent attempts to avoid experiencing anxiety by separating aspects of personality and experience (Briss, 1966). Although such reactions are relatively rare, they tend to be noticeable and dramatic.

Obsessive-compulsive reactions

● *sadism*—delight in cruelty.
● *masochism*—pleasure in being abused or dominated.

In obsessive-compulsive reactions, emotional tension and anxiety are expressed openly in what appear to be senseless repetitious thoughts, words, actions, rituals, ceremonies, doubts, or ruminations (Alchter et al., 1975). The major conflicts of obsessive-compulsive neurotics are love and hate, right and wrong, cleanliness and dirt, orderliness and disorder. *Sadism* and *masochism* are often expressed freely, and strong feelings of guilt are common. Magical thinking and superstitious behavior are often observed. Obsessive-compulsive individuals are usually aware that they are in conflict, although they usually don't understand what the conflict is about (Cameron, 1963).

The pattern of obsessive thoughts and compulsive behavior is illustrated in the following example: "A boy of twelve suffered from repetitious thoughts of calling his parents obscene names. He would control these impulses by saying 'Stop it! Stop it!' to himself out loud. Then he would repetitively swear at himself for having the obsessive thoughts" (Cameron, 1963, p. 373). In this example, the boy is obviously in conflict about love and hate feelings toward his parents. The boy's method for controlling anxiety and tension about this conflict involves the development of obsessive thoughts. The thoughts provide an expression of his forbidden impulses to aggress against his parents. The compulsive use of words to deny such expression also serves to punish him for having had the impulses in the first place. This pattern occurs over and over again. It becomes a predictable ritual that provides some relief from tension through a sequence of indulgence, restraint, and punishment.

Obsessive-compulsive behaviors are observable in normal people and in society as a whole. Freud (1955) believed that such ritualistic manners of behaving were very important in maintaining social order. Rules, orders, procedures, traditions, and customs characterize most well-run social organizations. Society places a high value on orderly, well-mannered people who obey rules and effectively organize their personal behavior. We are pleased when children and adolescents develop an interest in work and a corresponding interest in good work habits. This interest indicates a new level of social commitment and responsibility. Many people perform ritualistic behaviors before they undertake stressful work. Some students have certain rituals of behavior and dress that they use before taking exams. Some baseball pitchers perform repetitive ges-

United Press International

Mark Fidrych talks to the ball, telling it what to do and scolding it when it makes a mistake.

tures before each pitch. We carry good luck charms, feel nervous on Friday the 13th, and celebrate a holiday of superstition—Halloween.

Every culture makes use of ritual behaviors that resemble those of the obsessive-compulsive neurotic. The difference is that the neurotic is usually preoccupied with a specific conflict. This conflict produces symptoms that are highly related to the conflict and are usually great exaggerations of normal obsessions, compulsions, rituals, and doubts.

PSYCHOSES

Psychoses are more serious forms of psychopathology than neurotic reactions. These are the conditions that people usually refer to as mental

● **agitation—upset.**

illness or "craziness." Pronounced emotional disturbances ranging from extreme *agitation* to extreme emotional flatness may be observed. Uncontrolled, inappropriate fits of giddy laughter are common in some types of psychoses. Uncontrollable and inappropriate sadness may be seen in other types. Thought disorders are common in psychotic reactions. They include delusions, hallucinations, and psychotic logic. All of these disorders indicate the person's inability to differentiate between reality and fantasy.

Delusions are false cognitions. They continue to be believed even in the face of evidence that they are wrong. People who have delusions may truly believe that they are religious prophets, that they are from other planets, or that they are being watched by important government officials. Such people may act on the basis of their delusions, which often makes their behavior bizarre and unpredictable.

Hallucinations are visions, sounds, and feelings that are created by the person. People having hallucinations may hear voices or other sounds, feel things touching them, or see things that are not there. Hallucinations often persist over time. They are strong evidence of the failure of reality-testing mechanisms.

Psychotic logic involves profound violations of the rules of mature logical thought. A psychotic person may reason as follows: "A person is president of the United States. I am a person. Therefore I am president of the United States." The psychotic may respond to the sound of a word in a question rather than to the meaning of the question. "How are you feeling?" "Quite congealing." This is called a "clang" association. There are many other examples of flawed and distorted reasoning among psychotics.

Often, psychotic people experience problems in interpersonal relations. Some psychotics withdraw from others. Catatonics show extreme withdrawal. They may sit in a rigid physical position and not say a word to anyone for months or years. It is not usually the case that the psychotic can have good relations but simply does not want to. Rather, the psychotic's ability to make meaningful social responses is impaired.

Extreme disturbances of emotion, thought, and interpersonal relations produce a common quality of psychotic reactions—bizarre behavior. Other people easily note—and may be frightened by—a response of giddy laughter when a person is told that someone has died; the statement that a small rocket ship is hovering alongside one's head; or a rigid, withdrawn, noncommunicative posture. These kinds of symptoms are severe. They are signs of a serious inability to function in the world or to take care of oneself. Three psychoses are discussed below: schizophrenia; psychotic depression; and manic-depressive psychosis.

Schizophrenia

Schizophrenia is one of the most severe psychological disorders. The degree of disturbance of emotion, thought, interpersonal relations, and behavior is extensive. Sometimes a schizophrenic attack occurs very suddenly in someone who has never shown schizophrenic behavior before.

United Press International

There are many forms of schizophrenia.
Generally, thinking is disorganized, emo-
tions are distorted, and social relations are
erratic or nonexistent.

● *spontaneous*
remission—a cure that
takes place without
treatment.
● *chronic—lasting for a*
long time.

The episode may be highly disabling and filled with many symptoms. At other times, schizophrenic behavior may involve a pattern of personality disorganization that has developed slowly over the years. One of the main differences between these patterns of onset is with the outlook for recovery. When the onset of schizophrenic symptoms is sudden, there is a much better chance for recovery than when the condition has developed over a long period of time. Extreme and sudden schizophrenic reactions sometimes disappear after a relatively short period of time through *spontaneous remission*. In other cases, after intensive psychotherapy the individual makes a recovery and never experiences another episode. For some persons, however, the first episode is only the beginning of recurring episodes that lead to the development of *chronic* schizophrenia.

There are ten subtypes of schizophrenia. These are summarized in

Acute type	Characterized by a sudden onset of undifferentiated schizophrenic symptoms, often involving perplexity, confusion, emotional turmoil, delusions of reference, excitement, dream-like dissociation, depression, and fear. The individual seems to undergo a massive breakdown of filtering processes, with the result that experience becomes fragmented and disorganized, taking on the qualities of a nightmare.
Paranoid type	A symptom picture dominated by absurd, illogical, and changeable delusions, frequently accompanied by vivid hallucinations, with a resulting impairment of critical judgment and erratic, unpredictable, and occasionally dangerous behavior. In chronic cases, there is usually less disorganization of behavior than in other types of schizophrenia, and less extreme withdrawal from social interaction.
Catatonic type	Often characterized by alternating periods of extreme withdrawal and extreme excitement, although in some cases one or the other reaction predominates. In the withdrawal reaction there is a sudden loss of all animation and a tendency to remain motionless for hours or even days, in a stereotyped position. The clinical picture may undergo an abrupt change, with excitement coming on suddenly, wherein the individual may talk or shout incoherently, pace rapidly, and engage in uninhibited, impulsive, and frenzied behavior. In this state, the individual may be dangerous.
Hebephrenic type	Usually occurs at an earlier age than most other types of schizophrenia, and represents a more severe disintegration of the personality. Emotional distortion and blunting typically are manifested in inappropriate laughter and silliness, peculiar mannerisms, and bizarre, often obscene, behavior.
Simple type	An insidious depletion of thought, affect, and behavior, beginning early in life and gradually progressing until the individual impresses others as being curiously inaccessible, isolated, colorless, and uninteresting. Because psychological disorganization is typically less severe than in other types of schizophrenia and some superficial contact with reality is usually maintained, hospitalization is less frequent.
Schizo-affective type	Characterized by a mixture of general schizophrenic symptoms, in conjunction with more pronounced obvious depression or elation—not typical of the usual surface pattern of "flattened affect."
Latent type	Characterized by various symptoms of schizophrenia but lacking a history of a full-blown schizophrenic episode.
Chronic undifferentiated type	Although manifesting definite schizophrenic symptoms in thought, affect, and behavior, not readily classifiable under one of the other types.
Residual type	Mild indications of schizophrenia shown by individuals in remission following a schizophrenic episode.
Childhood type	Preoccupation with fantasy, and markedly atypical and withdrawn behavior prior to puberty.

Source: J. C. Coleman, *Abnormal Psychology and Modern Life*, 5th ed. (Glenview, Ill.: Scott, Foresman and Company, 1976), p. 308. © 1976 by Scott, Foresman and Company. Reprinted by permission.

TABLE 14·2
Summary of types
of schizophrenia

Table 14·2. Schizophrenia is characterized by disturbances of emotion, thought, interpersonal relations, and behavior. Table 14·3 compares schizophrenic adolescents with schizophrenic adults as to subtype. All subtypes appear in adolescence. There is a greater incidence of paranoid schizophrenia in adulthood. Acute, undifferentiated schizophrenia is more frequent in adolescence. One difficulty in diagnosing adolescent schizophrenia is that often the more serious condition is masked by what appears to be less serious symptoms. Eating disorders, delinquency, and school phobias may be hiding a much more serious schizophrenic distur-

TABLE 14·3
Subcategories of
schizophrenia in
adolescent and adult
patients terminated
from psychiatric clinics*

| | Adolescents† | | Adults‡ | |
Subcategory	Males	Females	Males	Females
Paranoid	18.6	14.5	39.2	34.4
Acute undifferentiated	11.6	16.4	5.3	6.7
Chronic undifferentiated	27.9	25.5	32.2	31.3
Childhood	20.9	12.7	§	§
Other	21.0	30.9	23.3	27.6

* Expressed as percentage of total.
† From B. M. Rosen et al., "Adolescent Patients Served in Psychiatric Clinics," *American Journal of Public Health*, Vol. 55 (1965), p. 1588, based on approximately 2,550 schizophrenic adolescents.
‡ From *Outpatient Psychiatric Clinics* (1963, pp. 150–51), based on approximately 17,000 schizophrenic adults.
§ Category not listed.
Source: L. B. Weiner, *Psychological Disturbances in Adolescence* (New York: Wiley-Interscience, 1970), p. 105. Reprinted by permission of John Wiley & Sons, Inc.

● *neurophysiological—*
functions of the nervous
system.

bance. Clinicians must be careful to distinguish between a less serious neurotic or behavior problem and a schizophrenic reaction.

Many questions are currently being studied in order to understand the causes of schizophrenic reactions. Is schizophrenia hereditary? Are there biochemical causes? Do schizophrenics have abnormal *neurophysiological* development? Is schizophrenia related to a particular form of family interaction or to socioeconomic status? Is schizophrenia caused by extreme stress or trauma? An abundant literature has developed around each of these questions. For the moment, it is safe to say that although we are concerned with the condition, we do not fully understand it. Hereditary, biological, psychological, and social factors may all interact with one another to produce schizophrenic reactions.

Currently, the outlook for the treatment of schizophrenics is not too good. There is no doubt about the extremely serious and disabling nature of a schizophrenic disturbance.

Psychotic depressive reactions

● *diagnostic*
interview—**an interview**
conducted to determine
the cause or nature of a
problem.

The picture of depression that was begun earlier in the chapter becomes intensified in psychotic reactions. The severity of depression is sometimes determined by *diagnostic interview* and sometimes by rating scales. Reports about degrees of sadness, self-dislike, and crying episodes, among other things, help to tell the neurotic and psychotic depressive reactions apart.

In psychotic depressive reactions dejection, guilt, and organized delusions of self-depreciation are overwhelming. Hallucinatory experiences are generally not part of the psychotic depressive reaction. The psychotic depressive shuts out others much more than the neurotic does. The neurotic depressive tries to manipulate others into support and praise in order to bolster low self-esteem. The psychotic depressive generally becomes preoccupied with delusions of unworthiness, inadequacy, and failure. These delusions are accompanied by strong feelings of guilt. The psychotic depressive exhibits less personality disorganization than the schizophrenic.

Psychotic depressives turn on themselves and shut out others in a savage manner. Their deep self-hate includes grandiose delusions concerning the extent of their wickedness. "I am the worst person in the world" and "I am the most sinful person in the world" are common statements. Along with the sense of guilt for this "wickedness" is a strong need for punishment. Plans for how to punish oneself and how to hurt oneself may be a major preoccupation for the psychotic depressive. Suicide (which will be discussed in detail later in this chapter) is a real risk. Parents, friends, relatives, children, and others who are close to the psychotically depressed person do not have any difficulty sensing the depth and seriousness of this type of depression. Extremely disturbed thoughts about one's worthlessness, self-injury, and repentance are so strong that they replace the person's ability to test reality or to make effective judgments.

Psychotically depressed people scorn others for trying to help them. They may wall themselves off from others. Thus, although they may not go unnoticed, they may go unhelped. This is a particularly serious problem because of the suicide risk. Psychotically depressed later adolescents are especially at risk. They are often outside the boundaries of former close support structures such as their families, but not yet engaged in their own intimate networks. As they become preoccupied with self-depreciation, guilt, and punishment, there may be no one to notice the loss of reality testing and judgment that is occurring. School or work failure, the death of a parent, or the loss of a lover may initiate a depression that goes unheeded. No one notices the clear development of increasingly serious symptoms. Roommates, co-workers, or new acquaintances may not feel like becoming involved in helping someone who shuns help at every turn. In fact, these people may not know how they can be of help. Who to go to? What to do? These questions are hard enough for parents, husbands, wives, and others who feel responsible for the safety and well-being of the psychotically depressed person. The questions may be too difficult, too time-consuming, and too unrewarding for a relatively uninvolved person to bother with. Psychotically depressed people may be left alone to fall deeper and deeper into the depths of the depression— to commit suicide or to isolate themselves from others.

Institutions such as colleges and many communities have developed crisis emergency services and telephone services. Isolated persons may obtain advice, brief therapy, plans for management, or appropriate referral through these services. These services often alert community services to serious psychotic disturbances as they are brewing. These services may help psychotic depressives who won't help themselves. In general, there is little adaptive value to psychotic depressive reactions. The condition induces a loss of effective functioning. It may drain the resources of the afflicted person's family, friends, and associates. As the condition deepens, it becomes increasingly serious and difficult to cure. Like the outlook for recovery from chronic schizophrenia, the chances for recovery from chronic psychotic depression is poor. Psychotic depressives often pose a real threat to themselves, and sometimes to others.

Manic-depressive psychotic reactions

● *mania*—extreme excitement.

● *euphoria*—a joyous feeling of well-being.

This category comprises two different symptom patterns. One of the patterns is characterized primarily by *mania*. In the other pattern, mania and depression alternate.

Manic reactions.   Cameron (1963) points out that although manic-depressive reactions have been described for centuries, manic reactions alone have been more prevalent in his clinical experience. Manic reactions are defined as mood disorders. Extreme *euphoria* is accompanied by self-assertion and delusions of self-importance. During manic reactions, people are often very talkative. It soon becomes apparent that their conversation is limited in scope, shallow, and rambling. A great deal of activity often accompanies manic reactions. A person who is having a manic attack may appear very happy and excited. After a while, it can be seen that like a little child, the person is having difficulty controlling excitement. Manic reactions often last for weeks or months (Cameron, 1963). People who are having a manic attack actually lose contact with reality. They become preoccupied with asserting internal states of self-importance and happiness. They may insist on planning self-aggrandizing activities that cannot possibly be carried out. The manic state is maintained in spite of pleas of friends and relatives for more rational behavior (Lichtenberg, 1959). Sometimes reality oriented comments from others evoke hostility or increased self-aggrandizement (Cohen et al., 1954).

The manic attack often masks or is used as a defense against a deep sense of depression (Cameron, 1963). Rather than become psychotically depressed, individuals deny the depressive aspects of their lives by self-assertion, self-aggrandizement, and euphoria. Although manic individuals experience very profound disturbances of reality testing and may represent a danger to themselves or others, they do serve an adaptive role in warding off deep depression.

Manic attacks may be mild or severe. They may occur only once or many times. Sometimes individuals will have a manic episode and then a depressive episode years later. At other times a manic attack is preceded by a mild initial depression (Cohen et al., 1954). The best chances for recovery are for people who have a single, mild manic attack. Mania usually indicates underlying difficulties with feelings of self-worth. Case 14•1 describes a manic attack of a college student.

Barry's case is a good example of the onset of a serious manic episode in a college student. This attack began after only a mild rejection by a girl whom he had been dating. The euphoria, high-activity level, and grandiosity of mania are well represented. Barry's attack lasted for several weeks. His judgment and reality testing were replaced by a strong belief in his delusional trip. Barry was finally hospitalized after his roommates called his parents to notify them about his condition.

Manic-depressive reactions.   It was once thought that the typical pattern of manic and depressive reactions involved alternations of mania and depression. More recently, it has been pointed out that either psychotic depression or mania are the more common cases (Cameron,

Case 14·1

THE MANIC ATTACK OF A COLLEGE STUDENT

Barry was a participant in a self-analytic group as part of a course in group dynamics at a large midwestern university. He was a moderate participant during the first several meetings. When he spoke, his contributions were appropriate to the discussion. When he talked about himself, he mentioned a lack of confidence in dating situations and a career interest in business administration. These disclosures are quite typical for someone his age.

Barry was absent for several sessions, which was clearly a violation of the group's norms. When he returned, other members wanted to know why he had been absent. Barry began to tell a story that lasted for the remainder of the two-hour session and from which he could not be distracted by the other group members.

He said that several weeks before, he had been awakened in the middle of the night by a phone call. The caller was a member of the Beatles, George Harrison. Harrison had told him to take the next available flight to London. He did this and was met upon arrival by the Beatles, who took him to their recording studio. They told

him that he was involved in a secret mission of international significance but that they could not disclose the reason to him until the mission had begun.

He said that he spent several days with the Beatles, and then one afternoon they told him that the mission was to get under way. They boarded a plane heading for the United States. It was a U.S. Air Force customized-jet. On board, along with several high-ranking Air Force officers and the Beatles, was Lyndon B. Johnson (then president of the United States). Barry was told that the mission was to "look for the hole in the ocean." Although he knew that this was a line from one of the Beatles songs, he said that he now believed that the Beatles were involved in some type of international intrigue. He realized that secrets were disclosed in their songs. At some point halfway across the Atlantic a huge chasm opened in the water. Everyone on board agreed that this was the hole in the ocean. The significance of the discovery was unclear to Barry. He was then flown to the university town and let off the plane. This had occurred several weeks before. He had been busy telling everyone he knew about his experience.

1963; J. C. Coleman, 1976). There are some instances, however, when a full-fledged manic attack leads directly into a full-fledged depression, or vice versa (Arieti, 1959). Some cases have even been reported in which there is a precise period for the two phases. Jenner et al. (1967) mention a manic-depressive reaction that had lasted for 11 years. A manic phase of exactly 24 hours was followed by a 24-hour depressive phase. Bunney et al. (1972) cite a case in which a woman alternated between manic and depressive periods every 48 hours for two years. Such precision is rare, however. In a more typical manic-depressive reaction, there is a period of one to ten days of relative normality between the end of the depressed period and the start of the manic period. The switch from mania to depression usually occurs more suddenly, with little warning.

Studies of manic-depressives find that such persons are achievement oriented, conventional in their beliefs and values, concerned about how

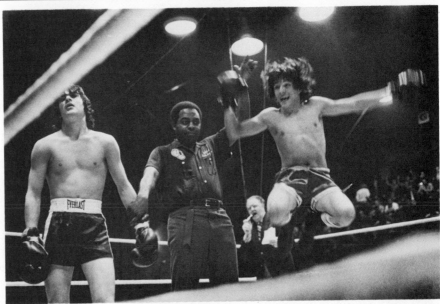

Richard Younker

*In manic depression, the extremes of elation
and despair shown on those two boys' faces
exist side by side in one person.*

others react to them, ambitious, sociable, and successful. They tend to have rather rigid consciences. They often find it difficult to express hostile feelings toward others. Self-depreciation and self-blame when things go wrong are often reported (Bagley, 1973; Schancke, 1974).

The personality pattern described above is not uncommon. Many people have such characteristics but do not become manic-depressives. The inability to express hostility and a family history of depression may begin to distinguish the manic-depressive from other sociable, achievement-oriented adults. It is obvious from the picture sketched above that there is a strong possibility of observing this type of reaction among college students. Extreme mood swings are not uncommon among students in high-pressure schools. For some, these mood swings are indicators of the first phases of manic-depressive disorders. Some clinicians argue that the major dynamic for the manic-depressive is a profound underlying depression (Cameron, 1963). Mania is seen as a defense against depression. When it does not work, the depression surfaces. When the person regains a defensive position, the mania is used to protect the person from depression.

**BEHAVIOR
DISORDERS**

Behavior disorders include a variety of problems in adjustment in which the person's behavior is in obvious conflict with cultural norms.

Behavior disorders do not include an inability to assess reality accurately or a distortion in self-perception. Frequently, the person who is described as having a behavior disorder knows full well that the behaviors run counter to social expectations. These behaviors are continued because they serve an important function for the person. Many behavior disorders, for example, alcoholism, sexual perversions, or extreme shyness and timidity are long-term patterns. They are totally embedded in the person's lifestyle. They are not easily changed, especially if they do not cause the person anxiety. Three examples of behavior disorders that are especially relevant during adolescence are discussed below: (1) juvenile delinquency, (2) adolescent suicide, and (3) substance abuse. This includes the use of alcohol and other drugs. In delinquency, the person directs hostile impulses outward to attack property or persons. In suicide, impulses are turned inward, hurting others by harming oneself. In substance abuse, impulses are altered so as to make them more bearable. Abuse becomes a way of harming the self.

Juvenile delinquency

The word *delinquency* is defined as "conduct that is out of accord with accepted behavior or the law" (Webster, 1977, p. 300). *Juvenile delinquency* is defined as "a status in a juvenile characterized by antisocial behavior that is beyond parental control and therefore subject to legal action" (Webster, 1977, p. 629). Delinquency can involve any of an array of actions that are unacceptable to society. Society takes this behavior as a sign that the person is out of parental control and must be controlled by society through its legal system. What is usually defined by the law as juvenile delinquency is behavior that would be criminal in an adult. The adult would be held fully responsible, but the child (usually under eight) is not considered intellectually mature enough to be responsible. The juvenile delinquent is thought to be *(a)* mature enough to be somewhat responsible for the deviant behavior; *(b)* out of parental control; and *(c)* in need of control, guidance, and rehabilitation from the society.

Many adolescents commit acts that would be considered delinquent. By and large these acts are not observed and those who commit them are not brought to the attention of juvenile authorities (Coleman, 1976; Sarason, 1976). The data from court records and similar sources underestimate the actual amount of delinquent behavior that exists during the early adolescent years. It is estimated that one out of every nine children will be brought to the attention of the juvenile authorities before their 18th birthday. J. C. Coleman (1976) and the Uniform Crime Reports (Federal Bureau of Investigation, 1975) provide estimates that 1 out of every 15 adolescents in the nation was arrested in 1974. The problem of juvenile delinquency is quite prevalent, but the problem of delinquent behavior among adolescents is even more widespread.

For most people who commit delinquent acts, the antisocial behavior is a brief, temporary experience. Among the reasons for episodes of delinquent behavior are:

1. The breakthrough of aggressive impulses.
2. Peer group coaxing.
3. Crowd behavior.
4. Rebellion.
5. A state of deprivation.
6. Thrill-seeking.
7. A reaction against depression.
8. Feelings of low self-esteem.

Many "one-timers" are not caught by the police. Often, however, the effect of such unobserved antisocial behavior is powerful. The behavior brings the issues of morality and problems in personal control to the adolescent's attention. Sometimes the delinquent behavior also comes to the attention of parents. The delinquent behavior itself and the fear of immorality are enough to bring an end to the behavior. Unobserved delinquent behavior warns the offender that there is a potential problem in behavioral control. The offender is able to use this information adaptively to prevent any new episodes.

The involvement of early adolescents in the total crime statistics in the United States is significant. In 1966, the FBI found that juveniles comprised 22.9 percent of all arrests in 1965 (Federal Bureau of Investigation, 1966). This figure has been rising faster than the rise in the proportion of adolescents in the population (Federal Bureau of Investigation, 1975). Between 1968 and 1975, arrests of persons under 18 years of age for serious crimes increased 100 percent. This was four times as fast as the rise in the size of the population of this age-group (Federal Bureau of Investigation, 1975; Coleman, 1976). In 1974, adolescents accounted for one out of three arrests for robbery, one out of five arrests for rape, and one out of ten arrests for murder (Federal Bureau of Investigation, 1975; Coleman, 1976).

More boys become delinquents than girls. An estimated 80 percent of delinquents are boys. The main crime areas for boys are theft, burglary, disorderly conduct, curfew violation, *vandalism,* auto theft, running away, and breaking liquor and drug laws. To a lesser degree, boys are also arrested for crimes against people. These include armed robbery and aggravated assault. The main crimes for girls are drug use, sexual offenses, running away from home, disorderly conduct, and theft (Lunden, 1964; Schimel, 1974; Coleman, 1976).

● *vandalism*—willful destruction of public or private property.

There is a developmental pattern to delinquent behavior. Delinquency is most frequently observed between the ages of 14 and 15. This is true for both boys and girls. The incidence of delinquent behavior at different ages may vary according to the kind of offense. At 14 the main kind of observed delinquent behavior is stealing. The ages of 16 and 17 are the peak years for malicious mischief, vandalism, auto theft, carrying an offensive weapon, and assaults (West, 1967). We find a pattern in which delinquency may be observed early (because of state laws, the age of 8 may be the earliest period of observation), increase to a peak at 15, and then decline. Less serious delinquent behavior is observed at earlier ages. More serious crime tends to be observed as children grow older. The evidence also suggests that those who commit delinquent acts at an early age are more likely to continue criminal behavior into adulthood (West, 1967; Sarason, 1976).

The patterns of delinquency suggest the following analysis. For the vast majority of adolescents who commit delinquent acts, the experience goes unobserved by agents of the society. The episode itself warns the youth to exert greater personal control over his or her behavior. The next largest number of adolescents who commit delinquent acts come to the attention of the police and the courts. This experience serves to warn such adolescents and their families to impose greater efforts for behavioral control. The smallest group begin to commit minor delinquent acts at an early age. They continue to perform delinquent acts of an increasingly serious nature. During the later adolescent years they develop into criminal personalities. Many more boys than girls are involved in this type of behavior problem, suggesting a greater ability by girls to impose behavioral control over aggressive and antisocial impulses.

Researchers and clinicians have described many types of delinquents (Weiner, 1970; Coleman, 1976; Sarason, 1976). We will describe five types in order to give you some idea of the complexity of delinquency. You will note that varied psychopathological problems find an outlet in antisocial behavior.

1. The psychopathic delinquent. This type of personality is characterized by impulsiveness, defiance, a lack of guilt, inability to learn from experience, and inability to maintain close social relationships. This kind of delinquent behavior is found in girls as well as boys. Many arrests and difficulties in changing personality structure are characteristic of this type.

2. The neurotic delinquent. This kind of delinquent behavior is thought to be a product of conflict and anxiety. Behavior results from: *(a)* needs that cannot be expressed otherwise, including needs for punishment, recognition, admiration, status, and help; *(b)* the effects of parental fostering of antisocial behavior; and *(c)* the effects of "scapegoating"— the selection of a child who receives the family's subtle encouragement to delinquency (Weiner, 1970).

3. The psychotic delinquent. Delinquent behavior of this type, often violent, is one sign of the person's inability to test reality, control personal impulses, or use good judgment (Weiner, 1970; Coleman, 1976).

4. The organic delinquent. The two main groups of organic delinquency are *(a)* mental retardation, in which low intelligence impedes judgment and makes the person a willing instrument for a brighter delinquent; and *(b)* brain damage, which interferes with behavioral control and may cause periodic displays of violence (Weiner, 1970; Coleman, 1976).

Richard Younker

Gang delinquency often involves protecting or claiming a territory.

5. The gang delinquent.   Once thought to be the typical delinquency pattern, current research finds gang delinquency to be less common than had been thought. Gang delinquency serves a social purpose. It involves the protection of territory and other resources. Just as social cliques like frats or preppies fill the social needs of their members for status, resources, and relationship, so juvenile gangs fill similar needs for their members.

There are many causes of delinquency. Some adolescents perform one or only a few delinquent acts. This behavior is often by the breakthrough of impulses. Most adolescents are able to heed this behavioral warning. They develop new coping skills as a result of it. For the organic delinquent, the causes are genetic and physical. For the neurotic and psychotic delinquent, the causes of delinquency are rooted in emotional turmoil and personality disorganization. The delinquent behavior is a symptom of these problems. The origins of the neuroses and psychoses of early adolescence have been discussed above.

The psychopathic delinquent is an integrated character structure that is the product of the following factors:

1. Rejection in childhood.
2. The experience and expectation of hostility and aggression from others as a part of this rejection.

3. Aggressive behavior as a reaction to rejection and to observing aggressive models.
4. Lack of support for social achievement in school.
5. Peer group rejection.

This combination of factors does not always lead to the development of a psychopathic personality. It is, however, commonly found in delinquents who have developed this type of personality structure.

The causes of gang delinquency seem to involve: (a) social rejection by high-status groups; (b) interaction with others who have also been rejected; (c) the formation of a socially meaningful group that provides a basis for group identity; and (d) the rejection by the group of common social means for attaining resources.

Adolescent suicide

Suicide is a most disturbing form of maladaptation during later adolescence. We are frustrated by the premature ending of life, by unrealized potential. We are agonized by our failure to prevent the act. We are haunted by the questioning and doubt that surround suicides. Suicides increase our own preoccupation with the meaning of life. They sensitize us to the amount of suffering or isolation that we are prepared to absorb into our own lives. The emotions of sadness, guilt, anger, and frustration that we feel in response to another's suicide are the same emotions that are associated with the suicide attempt itself.

Suicide is currently the second most common cause of death in the age-group 15–24 (Hendon, 1975). Among this age-group, about 4,000 deaths are attributed to suicide each year. Many more suicides are reported as accidents in order to protect the reputation of the adolescent or his or her family (Toolan, 1975; Miller, 1975). College students, black youth, and American Indians are more likely to commit suicide than others in their age-group. The rate of suicide for Indians is almost five times as high as the rate for other 15 to 24-year-olds (Frederick, 1973; Smith, 1976).

The pattern of suicide attempts is somewhat different from the pattern of suicides that actually result in death. Adolescents have a much higher attempted-to-completed suicide ratio than do older adults. Estimates of attempts to completions are as high as 120:1 in adolescent populations, whereas they are closer to 10:1 for older groups (Weiner, 1970; Rosenkrantz, 1978). This disproportion between attempted and completed suicides has been used as evidence that many adolescent suicides are cries for help. They are efforts to change the pattern of communication that exists between adolescents and significant others.

More females than males are likely to attempt suicide, but more males complete suicide. The most common way of accomplishing suicide among adolescents is firearms or explosives. The next most frequent methods are strangulation for males and poison for females. Among those who try but do not complete suicide, poison is by far the most common method (Weiner, 1970). Since the statistical distinction between attempted and completed suicides is based on the outcome, it does not take the intention into account. Some adolescents who plan a violent, immediate death are "saved." Some who do not think they have taken a lethal overdose of some drug actually die. There is clearly no truth to the myth that a person who attempts suicide and fails will not try again.

Coleman (1976) offers four stress factors that are associated with suicide:

1. Interpersonal crises including the loss of a loved one or the loss of an important person's love may lead to suicide.
2. Failure or shame may result in feelings of depression and self-blame that lead to suicide.
3. Inner conflict can lead to suicide if the person simply cannot accept some aspect of his or her own fate.
4. Loss of meaning or hope, especially in the case of a terminal illness or prolonged chronic pain, may lead to suicide.

The common theme of depression is found in all of these factors (Leonard, 1974; Weissman, Fox, & Klerman, 1973). The suicidal person is filled with feelings of hopelessness, a sense of isolation, or a lack of meaningful communication.

Some theorists have argued that adolescent suicide is an impulsive act. It occurs in reaction to a stress situation (Jacobinizer, 1960; Gould, 1965). In contrast, Weiner (1970) presents strong evidence for the view that adolescent suicide is a final response to a long series of problems. Usually the adolescent experiences feelings of alienation from family or feelings of failure and worthlessness. In many cases, other kinds of symptoms are observed before the suicide attempt. These include sleeplessness, psychosomatic illness, defiant acts, and declining school grades. However painful these symptoms may be, the majority of adolescents who commit suicide do not seek counseling. They do not have a history of diagnosed psychopathology (J. P. Miller, 1975; Temby, 1961). Their suicide attempt is a last response to a prolonged sequence of personal and interpersonal stress.

The most frequent theme associated with adolescent suicide is some disappointment or loss of intimacy and love. The following was written by a 19-year-old college student:

> Dear Jim:
> I've just emptied 40 capsules and put the powder in a glass of water. I'm about to take it. I'm scared and I want to talk to someone but I just don't have anybody to talk to. I feel like I'm completely alone and nobody cares. I know our breakup was my fault but it hurts so bad. Nothing I do seems to turn out right, but nothing. My whole life has fallen apart. Maybe if, but I know.
> I've thought about all of the trite phrases about how it will get brighter

tomorrow and how suicide is copping out and really isn't a solution and maybe it isn't but I hurt so bad. I just want it to stop. I feel like my back is up against the wall and there is no other way out.

It's getting harder to think and my life is about to end. Tears are rolling down my face and I feel so scared and alone. Oh Jim . . . if you could put your arms around me and hold me close . . . just one last time. . . . . . . J . . . . . m (Coleman, 1976, p. 607).

The end of a love relationship, the death of a parent, and the threat of parental abandonment are all kinds of interpersonal loss that can bring feelings of depression or worthlessness. If these events occur together with a history of prolonged stress and expressed plans of suicide or repeated fantasies of suicide, the risk of suicide becomes quite high (Griest et al., 1974).

Substance abuse   *Alcohol.* Except for a small number of complete abstainers, almost everyone has at least tried alcohol during later adolescence. There is

William S. Nawrocki

Alcohol is misused by young people in increasing numbers.

more variability about the legality of alcohol use in later adolescence than in early adolescence. In such states as New York, the legal drinking age is 18. In other states, such as Michigan, the legal drinking age is 21. Thus later adolescent drinking is legal in some places and illegal in other places. Whatever the legal status, the most widely used and abused drug in later adolescence is alcohol (Chafetz, 1974a; National Institute on Alcohol Abuse and Alcoholism, 1975). The National Institute on Alcohol Abuse and Alcoholism (Chafetz, 1974b) estimates that problem drinking is characteristic of 10 percent of the adult Americans who drink. Of the 18 to 20-year-olds who drink, 27 percent are problem drinkers. Of the 20 to 24-year-olds who drink, 18 percent are problem drinkers. Later adolescents who use alcohol are more likely to develop serious problems than are alcohol users of other ages. This situation becomes even more noteworthy when we realize that during the past 15 years there has been an ever-increasing use of alcohol among later adolescents. The use of marijuana and other hallucinogens increased until the late 60s, but since that time there has been a leveling off (and even some decline) in the use of these drugs. Alcohol use increased continuously throughout the first half of the 1970s (Kleinhesselink, St. Dennis, & Cross, 1976).

Alcohol is a central nervous system depressant. Although most people think that alcohol makes you "high," or intoxicated, at its highest level of concentration in the body it can cause death by depressing breathing. Even though this outcome is extremely rare, it is most often observed during late adolescence after "chugging" large amounts of alcohol. A recent report (*New York Times,* 1978) documents the death of a college student due to forced alcohol consumption during a fraternity initiation.

Death due to too great a concentration of alcohol in the blood is rare. There are two other extremely serious problems that involve alcohol and can lead to death. The first problem is the use of alcohol along with other drugs. Sometimes getting drunk is just a prelude to taking other drugs. Often alcohol is taken along with barbiturates or amphetamines in order to increase the effects of the drug experience. Impaired judgment due to drunkenness may lead to taking a fatal overdose of other drugs. The other problem is the use of alcohol while driving. It is a well-known and well-documented fact that alcohol use is involved in many automobile accidents. Approximately half of the 55,000 traffic deaths that occur each year are related to alcohol use. Nearly half of all pedestrians who are killed by automobiles have blood alcohol levels that lead them to be classified as intoxicated. The above examples demonstrate three ways in which the misuse and abuse of alcohol can end in death.

Sometimes the desire for new experiences, impaired judgment, thrill-seeking, peer taunting, or personality disorganization can have a fatal outcome. This danger is not necessarily confined to alcoholics. The warning is to be aware that: *(a)* if anyone's blood contains more than 0.55

percent alcohol, the outcome is lethal; *(b)* taking alcohol and other drugs can be dangerous because the interaction effects of the two substances may be more than the "sum of the two" and because impaired judgment may lead to taking an overdose of a dangerous drug; and *(c)* whether you drink a lot or only occasionally, you should not drive when you've been drinking and you should be careful where you are walking.

Most people who drink do so with moderation. Figure 14·1 presents the effects of various amounts of alcohol on most people. The majority of people who drink do it for the mild effects described in the figure, particularly the feelings of warmth and relaxation. This state may also ease social relations. One tends to be somewhat less shy and more talkative after having had a couple of drinks. Alcohol can be used in a responsible manner if it is used to improve social relationships and if it is not

FIGURE 14·1
Alcohol levels in the blood after drinks taken on an empty stomach by a 150-pound person

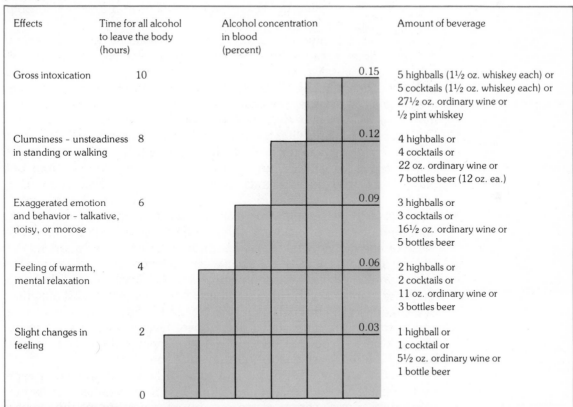

Effects	Time for all alcohol to leave the body (hours)	Alcohol concentration in blood (percent)	Amount of beverage
Gross intoxication	10	0.15	5 highballs (1½ oz. whiskey each) or 5 cocktails (1½ oz. whiskey each) or 27½ oz. ordinary wine or ½ pint whiskey
Clumsiness - unsteadiness in standing or walking	8	0.12	4 highballs or 4 cocktails or 22 oz. ordinary wine or 7 bottles beer (12 oz. ea.)
Exaggerated emotion and behavior - talkative, noisy, or morose	6	0.09	3 highballs or 3 cocktails or 16½ oz. ordinary wine or 5 bottles beer
Feeling of warmth, mental relaxation	4	0.06	2 highballs or 2 cocktails or 11 oz. ordinary wine or 3 bottles beer
Slight changes in feeling	2	0.03	1 highball or 1 cocktail or 5½ oz. ordinary wine or 1 bottle beer
	0		

Note: calories: 5½ ounces of wine—115, ounces of beer—170, 1½ ounces of whiskey—120.

Source: J. C. Coleman, *Abnormal Psychology and Modern Life*, 5th ed. (Glenview, Ill. Scott, Foresman and Company, 1978), p. 416. Copyright © 1976 by Scott, Foresman and Company. Reprinted by permission.

the primary activity. Moderate alcohol consumption may even be good for one's physical health. Later adolescents who are away at college, in military service, or in a new area of their hometown will probably engage in some social drinking to help themselves relax and to facilitate social participation.

Unfortunately, certain aspects of the college culture and of the later adolescent's self-concept are likely to encourage more than moderate alcohol consumption. Within the college community, many events are marked by celebrations that include the heavy use of alcohol. The "Thank God It's Friday" parties that celebrate the end of the week; football, basketball, or hockey victories (and sometimes defeats); the end of classes; the end of exams; graduation; and assorted college weekends (Winter Carnival, homecoming, Spring Fling) are all cultural occasions for "letting go." More than likely, part of letting go is getting drunk. What is more, the cultural approval of the use of alcohol for celebration seems to carry over the approval of alcohol to combat depression or frustration. In the same way that aspirin and lots of juices are seen as a cure-all for colds or the flu, a pitcher of beer or some bottles of wine are seen as a surefire way to handle a failing grade, a disappointment in a love relationship, or a rejection from graduate school.

The other component of this picture of potential alcohol abuse is the later adolescent's self-image. During later adolescence, young people tend to see themselves as vigorous, energetic, and somewhat impervious to harm. They perceive themselves as young and healthy. In fact, they are likely to be in better physical condition and less vulnerable to illness than they were during childhood or than they will be ten years later. This sense of personal vitality encourages later adolescents to scorn moderation. They will stay up late into the night and then engage in a full day of academic, athletic, and work activities. They will go from one party to the next on weekends, giving up sleep for celebration. They will take on responsibilities for a variety of committees, plan to drive a long trip without stopping for rest, or save two or three long papers until the last week of class and then do them all without sleeping. This sense of energy and vitality extends to the later adolescents' orientation toward alcohol. There is no special appreciation of moderation. The fun of drinking is the abandonment of limits. "Guzzling" or "chugalug-ging" are examples of the heroism attached to consuming great quantities of alcohol. Getting drunk is usually a part of the fun, a sign that caution and restraint were temporarily abandoned. Getting sick or passing out may not be as "cool" as being able to maintain a drunken ambience, but they are more acceptable than staying sober.

Other drugs. Drug use is a form of behavior in which people try to change their internal state for one reason or another. Drugs may be used for a wide variety of reasons, but in general terms the intent is always the same—to alter the physical or psychological state of the person. (We will not be at all concerned here with drugs that are used to combat infection and disease, such as antibiotics). Sometimes individuals will wish to become more aroused, and they will then use drugs that act as stimulants to the central nervous system. Such drugs are called "uppers." Sometimes they will wish to become more relaxed. In this case, they will elect drugs that act as depressants to the central nervous system. Sometimes people will wish to "expand their consciousness" or alter their perceptions. In these cases they will seek drugs that produce these effects on the central nervous system. Such drugs are called hallucinogens or psychodelics. Each of these types of drug effects can be induced in a mild, moderate, or severe form, depending upon the type of drug used and to some extent upon the dosage that is ingested.

State-altering drugs may be used in five different ways:

1. Proper use—when a drug is prescribed by a physician for a medical purpose.

2. Addictive use—when a person develops a physiological or psychological dependence upon the drug.

3. Misuse—when a drug is used by mistake, as when a child accidentally ingests medication or an adult takes a tranquilizer thinking that it is a Bufferin. This would also include the situation in which one unknowingly ingests a hallucinogen that someone has put in a drink.

4. Abuse—excessive use of a drug which a person is well aware is excessive, whether or not there is dependence. Excessive use often leads to dependence.

5. Illegal use—when it is against the law for (a) a person to use a drug, (b) a drug to be used, or (c) a particular behavior to be performed while the person is under the influence of the drug.

A drug may be used in more than one of these ways. Table 14·4 lists common drugs which are addictive and are abused, misused, or illegally used by adolescents. The table categorizes central nervous system depressants, stimulants, and hallucinogens of mild, moderate, and severe toxicity.

Early adolescents are involved in the use of every kind of drug. Since it is illegal for early adolescents to use all of these drugs, including alcohol, drug usage itself would have to be classified as a form of deviant behavior. Milman and Su (1973) substantiate this in a study of drug use in which they find that patterns of drug use are most pronounced in youth who deviate from "currently accepted norms of behavior and adjustment."

Why do young people get involved with drugs? As with the types of behavior problems discussed earlier, there seem to be a multitude of reasons. Often the reasons are directly related to the type of drug used and to the intensity of use.

Early adolescents are often introduced to drugs by friends who have already become involved in drug use (Johnson, 1973). Another reason for use has to do with the excitement of experimentation (Proskauer & Rolland, 1973). It is common knowledge that different drugs give different

TABLE 14·4
Common drugs of
abuse and addiction
(CNS intoxicants)
employed by adolescents

Usual toxic effects	Physical and psychological addiction: CNS depressants	Mainly psychological addiction	
		CNS stimulants	CNS hallucinogens*
Mild	1. Organic solvents (e.g., toluene, acetone, benzene, carbon tetrachloride, ether) 2. Alcohol (e.g., ethyl alcohol)	1. Xanthines (e.g., caffeine) 2. Sympathomimetics (e.g., ephedrine, isoprenaline)	1. Nutmeg (Myristica fragrans) 2. Morning glory seeds (Convolvulacea) 3. Cannabis (Cannabis sativa)
Moderate	Hypnotics-sedatives 1. Barbiturates (e.g., pentobarbitone [s-a], amylobarbitone [1-a], phenobarbitone [1-al]) 2. Miscellaneous (e.g., Mandrax = methaqualone and diphenhydramine; Doriden = glutethimide; Librium = chlordiazepoxide; Valium = diazepam; Equanil = meprobamate)	Anorectics 1. Amphetamines (e.g., Benzedrine = amphetamine; Dexedrine = dexamphetamine; Methedrine = methylamphetamine) 2. Miscellaneous (e.g., Preludin = phenmetrazine; Ritalin = methylphenidate; Tenuate = diethylpropion)	1. Mescaline (peyote) 2. Psilocybin (psylocybe) 3. DMT = dimethyltryptamine
Severe	Opiates 1. Natural or semisynthetic (e.g., opium (Papaver somniferum); morphine; heroin = diacetylmorphine) 2. Synthetic (e.g., methadone, pethidine)	Cocaine (Erythroxylum coca or truxillense)	1. LSD = Lysergic acid diethylamide (lysergide) 2. STP = 4-methyl-2,5-dimethoxy-alpha-methyl phenethylamine

* This word is chosen in preference to others, as it describes the most common manifestation. Other names given to these drugs include: psychotomimetics = producing psychotic manifestations, psychodysleptics = producing delusional manifestations, psychodelics = producing expansion and distortion of mental perceptions.

Source: P. R. Boyd, "Drug Abuse and Addiction in Adolescents," in J. G. Howells ed., *Modern Perspectives in Adolescent Psychiatry* (New York: Brunner/Mazel, Inc., 1971), p. 294. Reprinted by permission.

William S. Nawrocki

*These are some of the drugs and equipment
used by people who take drugs.*

kinds of "highs." The desire to experiment with new sensations leads
to exploring different drugs. An estimated 60 percent of seventh graders
and 71–93 percent of high school students are experimental users of
alcohol. Marijuana is another drug that a large number of early adolescents
experiment with. Estimates of the extent of marijuana use vary considerably. Most studies show a widespread use on an experimental (sometimes
only onetime) basis. In terms of use for experimentation, marijuana's
popularity increased considerably during the 60s and the early 70s and
the use of alcohol surged forward in the 70s.

Some early adolescents, depending on their degree of daring and
the preferences of their companions, will try other drug experiences for
experimentation and excitement. "Glue sniffing" and intoxication from
other organic solvents are most prevalent among 10 to 15-year-olds.
Organic solvents produce a quick, short state of intoxication along with
a wide variety of unpleasant side effects, including headache, nausea,
and vomiting. For this reason, most early adolescents abandon this habit
rather quickly. LSD, cocaine, or heroin are used experimentally for the
thrilling effects by some adolescents, but, we would argue, only by the
most daring under circumstances of availability and heavy peer pressure.

Amphetamines and barbiturates may also be used by thrill seekers when they are available. These drugs can become truly dangerous when used in conjunction with each other.

Using drugs for experimentation will be a single experience for most of the adolescents who try them. For the next largest group, moderate drug use will continue as a social experience in much the same way as it does for many adults. Drinking groups and marijuana smoking groups can be found in most high school cultures. The use of one drug or the other reflects availability, historic trends, and political orientations and attitudes. The next largest group of users would be the people who are seeking thrills, highs, and intoxication. They may be trying to escape from boredom, a stressful situation, or feelings of depression. Some early adolescents use drugs as a method for adapting to and expressing neurotic or psychotic conflicts and problems. Just as delinquent behavior or running away may be used as a behavioral expression of a neurotic or psychotic problem, so may taking drugs serve this purpose.

A final reason why some adolescents use drugs is because it is an aspect of the lifestyle of people like themselves. Jessor and Jessor and their co-workers (Jessor et al., 1968; Jessor et al., 1970; Jessor & Jessor; 1977) have described a group of psychosocial variables that are linked with adolescent drug use and other forms of deviant behavior. Psychologically the person feels helpless, hopeless, and socially isolated. This is called alienation. The person also feels that social norms and laws can be disregarded because there are no restrictions from parents or peers. This is called anomie. There must also be a tolerance for deviance and an access to opportunities to learn deviant behaviors. These factors combine to produce problem behavior as part of a deviant lifestyle. The so-called deviant behavior is really an integral part of the person's subcultural experiences. Coming from a lower-class home, having high exposure to opportunities for and models of deviant drug use, high personal dissatisfaction, and a sense that it is acceptable to engage in deviant drug use combine to account for drug use in a particular segment of the population. The absence of social controls seems to be the single best factor that predicts drug abuse. This lifestyle is related to delinquency and running away as well as to drug use. Where there is deprivation, alienation, anomie, tolerance for deviance, and lack of control, there is a strong likelihood of drug use and delinquency and running away from home.

There are many risks of drug use at every age and some particular risks for the early adolescent. Physiological or psychological dependence are serious consequences which often lead to heavy and continuous drug use. The need to support an illegal and often expensive habit sometimes leads to drug-related stealing. The heavy use of certain drugs may lead the person to neglect hygiene and nutrition, which can lead to a wide variety of health problems. The dangers of overdoses of many drugs, including alcohol, are particularly noticeable in early adolescents. Overdoses often lead to death, so that this risk is extremely serious. The impulsive use of drugs, including the combining of drugs to increase their potency, is common in early adolescents and can also be extremely dangerous, sometimes leading to death. The dangers of using solvents, including urinary tract infections, damage to the nasal and oral membranes, and brain damage, are almost exclusively dangers of the early adolescent period, as most other drug-using groups do not use solvents. Impulsive behaviors related to the drug experience, including reckless automobile driving and attempts to fly out of upper story windows are common. Such behaviors point to the risks of drug use for even very occasional users, who because of their unfamiliarity with a drug may make a decision that leads to death or serious injury.

Even though some general principles can be applied to all forms of substance abuse, each kind of drug seems to bring its own pattern of uses and hazards. Availability is probably the major determinant in beginning to use any particular drug. However, the pattern of use, the culture that surrounds drug use, and the hazards of drug use can differ depending on the substance involved. For that reason, we look in greater detail at three kinds of drugs and the ways they are used or abused by adolescents.

Marijuana use. Most evaluations have concluded that marijuana is a relatively harmless drug that has less negative or dangerous effects than alcohol (Brill, et al., 1973; Shafer, 1972). A presidential commission on marijuana recommended decriminalization of the private use of marijuana, but suggested a maintenance of laws prohibiting the manufacture or sale of the drug. The current status of marijuana in our society represents a dilemma of values that is bound to generate controversy. Thus, an understanding of the use of marijuana requires an appreciation of its status as an illegal drug as well as its intoxicating properties.

Marijuana is a widely used drug, especially among college students. There are an estimated 24 million marijuana smokers, of whom 1.5 million smoke marijuana daily (Rist, 1972). Estimates of college use range from 49 percent at a large midwestern university to 87 percent at a college in New England (Levy, 1973; Bonier & Hymowitz, 1972). In general, marijuana use among these later adolescents cannot really be considered deviant, even though it is formally illegal. Most college students who use marijuana believe it to be a harmless drug that provides a pleasant high, enjoyable sensory experiences, and feelings of relaxation. Heavy users (three or more times a week) also claim that marijuana increases self-awareness, changes their perceptions about time, and heightens sexual pleasure. Marijuana use is generally not associated with needs to escape reality or to avoid commitment. Studies of users and nonusers find no significant differences between the groups in personal adjustment, in the likelihood of dropping out of school, or in feelings of optimism and self-worth (Hochman, 1972; Knight Sheposh, & Bryson, 1974). Some studies have reported that the grade point averages of users are higher than those of nonusers. Marijuana use is most widespread among some of the more prestigious, competitive colleges. These findings clearly discourage any psychopathological interpretation of marijuana use.

On the other hand, there are some differences between marijuana smokers and nonsmokers that do suggest different patterns of adaptation. Marijuana smokers are usually introduced to the experience by friends who teach the novice how to smoke, what to look for as part of a "high," and how to enjoy the sensations of intoxication (Becker, 1953; Goode, 1970). The more one is involved in the use of marijuana, the more one is likely to associate with peers who also use it and who share the perceptual, political, and cognitive orientations that tend to be associated with heavy marijuana use. Chronic marijuana users are more likely than nonusers to have liberal or radical political views, to express pessimism about the future of the U.S. government, and to have experienced harassment, arrest, or questioning by the police (Levy, 1973). Because marijuana users are involved in illegal behavior, they are forced to confront the legal system more directly than are nonusers. They must deal with the reality of being suspected or even arrested for the sale or possession of marijuana. They must try to balance the illegality or marijuana use against the pleasure of the marijuana high. In this sense, chronic marijuana users are allied in their rejection of a part of the legal code. Being part of what may begin as inadvertent resistance, chronic users are likely to call into question other aspects of the political system, especially those involving areas of personal freedom and individual rights. Chronic users tend to be more rebellious, more antiauthoritarian, and more reckless or prone to other deviant behaviors than nonusers.

The area of marijuana use that has been least well evaluated is the effect of heavy, long-term use. This level of abuse would amount to being stoned all day long, every day. There is research which suggests that under this condition a variety of physical complications develop, including lung cancer, hormone deficiency, reduced immune responsiveness, and chromosomal damage. On the other hand, research comparing marijuana users and nonusers has not reported any specific health dangers that can be reliably associated with moderate marijuana use.

Halluncinogenic drugs.   The psychedelic or mind-expanding drugs provide vivid sense experiences, visual and occasionally auditory hallucinations, and a sense of self-detachment. The most commonly used and the most publicized of these drugs is LSD, or "acid" (lysergic acid diethylamide), which can be taken as a colorless liquid or powder. When doses of 100–55 micrograms are taken, the experience of an LSD high will last for as long as 10 to 12 hours. LSD has very powerful properties that are readily apparent on the first "trip." They do not have to be learned or socialized, as is the case with marijuana. There is, however, an important contextual component to the way the hallucinogens are used. Davis & Munoz (1968) distinguish between "freaks" and "heads" to clarify this aspect of hallucinogenic drug use. The freak uses the drug for kicks, or for satisfying excessive cravings or emotional needs. Freaks are likely to be highly anxious, aggressive, or paranoid. They are likely to use drugs to the exclusion of other activities or relationships. In contrast, the heads use hallucinogens to heighten their self-awareness or to gain insight into their genetic origins. They use LSD as a means of personal growth in conjunction with other self-expanding experiences. The heads may even give up hallucinogenic drugs in order to achieve this level of consciousness through meditation. One's orientation toward the use of LSD may depend on whether it is taken in the company of freaks or heads.

In general, the hallucinogens are not biologically addictive, although the freak user may become emotionally dependent on this kind of high. If the same dosage is taken several days in a row, the effects are dramatically reduced. Therefore, most users trip only periodically. The use of hallucinogens is very closely associated with the youth culture, especially the college-age population. Studies of college campuses have reported experimentation with these drugs by 2–18 percent of the students (Levy, 1973). In a study of marijuana use, it was found that only 1 percent of nonusers had tried LSD, whereas 29 percent of occasional users and 57 percent of chronic users had tried it (Hochman, 1972). Although the hallucinogens are not nearly as popular as marijuana or alcohol, many adolescents see them as an intriguing way of experimenting with the totality of conscious experience.

The negative consequences of LSD seem to fall into three categories. First, there is the unwanted trip. In this case, a person ingests LSD at a party or during an outdoor celebration without knowing that the drug was part of the "refreshments." The resulting hallucinations, sensory experiences, and sense of detachment are likely to set off an intense anxiety reaction and a fear of going crazy. Because the effects of the drug last so long and the source of the effects is unknown, the person may become convinced that he or she is psychotic. Even after the effects of the drug have worn off, the memory of the fear of madness and the power of some of the imagery may remain as a source of anxiety. Second, there are "bad trips" during which even experienced users become extremely anxious and paranoid. These trips may result in prolonged periods of psychotic thought, including hallucinations, frightening nightmares, and disorganization that can last for a few days or as long as a few months (Cohen, 1967). Third, there are adolescents who appear to experience prolonged or even permanent confusion or effectlessness after heavy use of hallucinogens (Kline, 1971). These changes have been attributed to potential brain damage or to the tendency of the hallucinogens to reduce the person's ability to defend against areas of existing pathology. The risks associated with LSD and other hallucinogens are disturbingly unpredictable. Heavy users can continue to trip periodically for several years with no observable negative consequences, and they can stop using the drug without any obvious withdrawal symptoms except for occasional "flashbacks" of vivid drug-related experience. On the other hand, a novice or an experienced user can encounter acute anxiety, paranoid delusions, terrifying hallucinations, or prolonged confusion as a result of just one dose. The promise that LSD holds of greater self-insight, which is so urgently important for adolescents who are at work on indentity, is tied to a threat of identity disruption or dissolution.

Addictive narcotics. This group of drugs, which includes heroin, cocaine, codeine, and opium, is considered addictive in the sense that abstinence creates physical discomfort and an intense preoccupation with trying to maintain access to a supply of the drug. "The opiate high provides relief from pain, including hunger, and a gratifying buzz, a feeling that has never been adequately described, of immediate pleasure and transient well-being" (Boyd, 1971, p. 304). The heroin high lasts for about two hours, and withdrawal symptoms begin after about four hours. These symptoms can include anxiety, irritability, sweating, nausea, cramps, vomiting, and diarrhea. A single dose of heroin does not lead to addiction. In fact, some people use heroin every once in a while without suffering unpleasant withdrawal symptoms. This may be because of the small amount of pure heroin that is contained in American heroin or because these drug users are also taking other drugs that mask the effects of heroin withdrawal.

Adolescent involvement with heroin and other addictive narcotics is relatively infrequent in comparison to their involvement with alcohol and marijuana. An estimated 1.3 percent of those 18 or over have tried heroin (National Commission on Marijuana and Drug Abuse, 1973). During the Vietnam War there was a significant increase in heroin use because the drug was readily available and inexpensive for American troops in Vietnam. In the United States, heroin is mixed with large quantities of other substances, including lactose. Because of the poor quality and high cost of the domestic supply, soldiers returning from Vietnam have been likely to give up their involvement in this form of drug use. Active methadone maintenance programs have been established to obtain the positive effects of the narcotic high with a clinic-administered substitute drug while providing skill training, recreational opportunities, and psychological counseling that will replace the heroin addict's emotional dependence on the narcotic high.

The controlled use of narcotics does not, in and of itself, create a maladaptive lifestyle. Rather, it is a convergence of the factors that surround the supply and application of narcotics that usually results in mental and physical distress. Generally, the narcotics purchased on the street are impure. Dirty syringes, unregulated dosages, and malnutrition all contribute to the physical complications associated with heroin use. These complications include tetanus, hepatitis, and local infections. Death may be a direct result of a heroin overdose or a complication of these other conditions. Because heroin use is illegal, the adolescent heroin user is thrown into contact with others who are involved in criminal activity and who perceive themselves as deviants. Often, in order to support the habit, heroin users become involved in illegal and violent activities. There are, however, no generally accepted differences in the personalities or degree of pathology present among users and nonusers. In fact, in one study of suburban, white, middle-class males, the 7 percent who used heroin were no different from nonusers in school grades, number of courses failed, frequency of cheating, or attitudes toward principals or teachers (Rathus, Siegel, & Rathus, 1976). The pathology of heroin addiction consists primarily in what the adolescent is willing to do to avoid withdrawal. There are no characteristics that predict who will become an addict, and there are no common psychological deficits among former addicts that link drug addiction to any of the commonly used categories of psychopathology.

THERAPIES: NEW RESOURCES FOR LIVING

In thinking about therapy, it is important to realize that the kinds of problems in adjustment and their causes are diverse. Should a person begin experiencing severe difficulties in adaptation or should a parent or friend observe these problems in a child or close friend, the first question that is usually raised is where to go for help. Most people who do not know about the mental health resources in a community will turn to a clergyman or a physician. These strategies may result in a referral to a clinic, a therapist, a social agency, a mental health center, or a self-help group.

At this point the most essential step in treatment is an accurate diagnosis. It is impossible to plan or to advise a course of therapy without an accurate assessment of the problem. Some disturbances that appear to be psychological in nature may have a specific physical cause. For example, a man who appears to be extremely suspicious, irritable, and has concerns that people are talking about him behind his back may be suffering from hearing loss, not paranoia. A whole variety of physical disturbances including hormone imbalance, tumors, sensory impairment, neurological damage, or bacterial or viral infections can all result in behavior or thought disturbances. In contrast, some seemingly physical conditions including ulcers, chronic pain, sensory impairment, nausea, or paralysis can have psychological causes.

In many communities, people resist the assistance of mental health professionals. They persist for a long time, trying to resolve the problem on their own. If a child has problems, parents may try to protect that child by increasing their vigilance, restricting the child's social encounters, or trying to provide additional support within the family. Without a diagnosis, however, there is no way of knowing whether these special efforts will improve the child's coping competences.

Once a diagnosis is made, the therapy or treatment depends on the assessment. In the case of the neuroses, treatment usually takes the form of some kind of *insight* therapy based around verbal interactions between the client and the therapist. Psychoanalytic therapy is probably the most well known and highly caricatured of the "talking" therapies.

● *insight*—a new idea or a new understanding.

In this model, the main technique is free association. Clients are encouraged to talk about whatever comes to mind, to keep nothing back even if it doesn't make sense. As part of the therapy, the therapist helps the client to bring to conscious thought wishes, fantasies, and fears from childhood. Relationships with parents, siblings, and significant others from childhood are especially central. The therapist uses the material from dreams, early memories, and free association to help build a picture of the unconscious wishes that might be expressed in the current neurotic symptoms.

Other insight therapies focus more on contemporary "here and now" causes of problems rather than childhood origins of conflict. Therapeutic techniques that stimulate insight include:

1. Reflection, in which the therapist echoes back or restates the client's feelings.
2. Role playing, in which the client is instructed to voice the thoughts and feelings of another person.
3. Conflict resolution, in which the client learns strategies for analyzing problems, planning solutions, and evaluating the consequences of solutions.
4. Assertiveness training, in which the client learns to express feelings directly, to identify and state personal preferences, and to overcome resistance or rejection by others.

Recently forms of "insight" therapy have been developed that make greater use of the person's own ability to make sense of his or her problems and to choose directions for change. Transactional analysis is an excellent example of a therapy that builds on the client's own resources. In that model, the assumption is made that every person carries voices of the child, the parent, and the adult roles. The child is demanding, unwilling to compromise, and in great need of comfort from others. The parent is critical, moralistic, and demands control and restraint. The adult is the voice of maturity. The adult can compromise and negotiate. The adult sees the points of view of others and strives to satisfy his or her own needs in ways that are not satisfying to others. Often, people participate in relationships where either the voice of the child or the voice of the adult are the only modes of interaction. The goal of transactional analysis is to identify the characteristic ways the client has of trapping himself or herself in either the parent or the child voices by analyzing the common qualities of his or her interactions. Then the goal is to replace these unflexible, unsatisfying roles with the role of the adult.

The other major therapeutic model for working with neurotic problems is behavior therapy. This model, built on principles of learning theory, emphasizes reinforcement of positive behaviors that are incompatible with negative behaviors. One of the major techniques includes desensitization. This method, which is especially useful in treating phobias and anxiety neurosis, helps clients to reduce their fears by training them to relax. Clients learn to retain calming images in the face of anxiety-provoking situations. In this technique, clients use relaxation and mental imagery to overcome anxiety.

Therapy for the psychoses is much less developed and more experimental. Many psychotics do not have an accurate assessment of reality, of themselves, or both. Therefore, the idea of insight therapy based on meaningful interactions between client and therapist is not very promising. For many psychotic clients, medication is the primary therapy. Other strategies include occupational therapy, *hydrotherapy,* and total residential inpatient treatment. Rosen et al. (1965) has developed a therapeutic technique called direct analysis for use with psychotic clients. In this method, fantasies and wishes are the content of the interactions. Rosen argues that psychotics have created an illusory world in which their fantasies are directly expressed instead of repressed or "hidden" from conscious thought. Rosen teaches his clients by feeding them with a bottle, rocking and cuddling them like an infant, or allowing the client to lash out at him in anger. After the first meaningful contacts are established at this primitive level, Rosen has a basis for developing more mature interactions.

Behavior disorders can be temporary problems in which case the act itself is enough to startle the person into a new behavior pattern. When the problem is chronic and the person does not have the resources to correct the problem, several therapeutic programs may be tried. Some delinquents experience insight therapy with a caseworker or therapist. Some are assigned to attend special classes or community activities. There are also special treatment centers for juvenile offenders. In extreme cases, detention centers function as prisons for young offenders.

For behavior disorders, one of the most successful forms of therapy has been the "self-help" group. Alcoholics Anonymous, Weight Watchers, and Synanon are some of the more well-known groups of this type. However, other groups including child abusers, ex-convicts, and families of runaways have joined together for mutual help. These groups usually are led by people who have experienced the particular problem themselves. They succeed by stating rather specific guidelines for behavior and by providing a social network that supports and encourages the person's efforts to change. Each participant must begin by owning or accepting their problem. Other group members may use confrontation, confession, condemnation, or comfort to build feelings of identification with the group and commitment to change. As the problem behavior comes under the person's control, he or she strengthens the new behavior by continuing to teach and support new members.

Suicide attempters may be treated with antidepressant drugs, insight therapy, or short-term hospitalization. They may be treated only for the physical harm they have inflicted and sent home. Crisis lines or walk-in clinics are designed to provide immediate help to those who are at the point of taking their own lives. Crisis-oriented resources are often successful. They influence people to seek help rather than to end their lives.

● *hydrotherapy*—the scientific use of water in the treatment of disease.

" "In the city this would be called a group therapy session and it would be costing us fifteen bucks apiece."

Reprinted by permission The Wall Street Journal

Most therapies, except for the extreme case of long-term hospitalization, are designed to bring the client to the point where the therapy is no longer needed. Most therapies try to build on existing strengths. They help the person learn new skills that can be used to address persistent life problems. At the heart of these therapies is a nonjudgmental professional. The therapist offers opportunities for meaningful, predictable, and accepting interactions. Once the client can function effectively within the therapeutic relationship, the next step is to bring those new strengths to other daily interactions. The therapy usually continues while the person is trying to cope with the daily life challenges that could not previously be surmounted. Adjustment after therapy is a continuous challenge. It requires the ability to apply new learning, and new behaviors to ongoing and new family, work, and community relationships.

Living laboratory 14·1

THERAPIES: NEW RESOURCES FOR LIVING

Purpose: To become acquainted with mental health professionals.

Method: Arrange an interview with a therapist, counselor, or psychiatrist. During the interview, gather the following information: educational background; the reasons for becoming a mental health professional; the best aspects of working with clients; the difficulties of working with clients; and the type of therapy they use.

Results: What educational experiences should a mental health professional obtain?

Why did this professional seek this career?

Did a special event or circumstance enhance interest in this field?

Why did the professional become a counselor rather than a therapist?

Why does the professional like working with clients?

What are the stresses or difficulties of this kind of work?

What type of therapy is used?

Discussion: What personal characteristics should a counselor, therapist, or psychiatrist possess in order to provide effective therapy?

Think of personal characteristics of clients and professionals. Would some clients work better with some mental health professionals than with others? Think about and describe "good matches" between clients and professionals.

Would some therapies be more appropriate for some problems, but not others?

Chapter summary

Problems in adjusting to life may stem from five major sources: (1) ineffective resources for coping with conflict; (2) inadequate developmental competences; (3) overwhelming environmental stress; (4) peer or parental models of maladaptation; and (5) organic disorders that disrupt effective functioning. At any point in the life span new problems in adjustment may pose challenges with which the person is unable to cope. In this sense, mental health resources are needed at every life stage from infancy through later adulthood.

Three forms of maladaptation were discussed: neuroses, psychoses, and behavior disorders. Each category is a very general term for an array of problems with their own unique symptom patterns. Five examples of neurosis were described: anxiety reaction, phobias, neurotic depression, hysterical reactions, and obsessive-compulsive neurosis. Chronic anxiety is a central component of most neuroses. It is this anxiety and the fear that one may be "losing one's mind" that usually motivate the person to seek help. Three examples of psychosis include schizophrenia, psychotic depression, and manic-depressive psychosis. Psychoses usually involve disruption of thinking, interpersonal relations, and behavior. Behavior disorders are well-developed behavior patterns that may interfere with daily functioning. They usually do not involve delusions, hallucinations, or chronic anxiety. Often, behavior disorders are more painful for others than they are for the person whose behavior is disrupted. The examples of juvenile delinquency, adolescent suicide, and substance abuse illustrate the peculiar and varied nature of behavior disorders. The behaviors obviously violate cultural norms. They may be a meaningful coping strategy from the person's point of view.

Strategies for helping people who are having problems in adjustment are as varied as the problems themselves. Help begins with an accurate diagnosis. Communities vary in the quality of mental health resources and their accessibility to all segments of the population. The therapy or treatment, whatever the mode, is closely tied to the diagnosis and the assumptions about the origin of the problem.

SUGGESTED READINGS

For some textbooks in abnormal psychology:

Coleman, J. *Abnormal psychology and modern life.* 5th ed. Glenview, Ill.: Scott, Foresman, 1976.

Davison, G. C., & Neale, J. M. *Abnormal psychology.* 2d ed. New York: Wiley, 1978.

Maser, J. D., & Seligman, M. E. P. *Psychopathology: Experimental models.* San Francisco: Freeman, 1977.

Readings in special areas include:

Becker, J. *Depression: Theory and research.* New York: Halstead, 1974.

Bruch, H. *The golden cage: The enigma of anorexia nervosa.* Cambridge, Mass.: Harvard University Press, 1978.

Swanson, D. W., Bohnert, P. J., & Smith, P. J. *The paranoid.* Boston: Little, Brown, 1970.

Shapiro, D. *Neurotic styles.* New York: Basic Books, 1965.

Reading

PERSONAL ADJUSTMENT IN A MENTAL HOSPITAL

Learning to live under conditions of imminent exposure and wide fluctuation in regard, with little control over the granting or withholding of this regard, is an important step in the socialization of the patient, a step that tells something important about what it is like to be an inmate in a mental hospital. Having one's past mistakes and present progress under constant moral review seems to make for a special adaptation consisting of a less than moral attitude to ego ideals. One's shortcomings and successes become too central and fluctuating an issue in life to allow the usual commitment of concern for other person's views of them. It is not very practicable to try to sustain solid claims about oneself. The inmate tends to learn that degradations and reconstructions of the self need not be given too much weight, at the same time learning that staff and inmates are ready to view an inflation or deflation of a self with some indifference. He learns that a defensible picture of self can be seen as something outside oneself that can be constructed, lost, and rebuilt, all with great speed and some equanimity. He learns about the viability of taking up a standpoint—and hence a self—that is outside the one which the hospital can give and take away from him.

The setting, then, seems to engender a kind of cosmopolitan sophistication, a kind of civic apathy. In this unserious yet oddly exaggerated moral context, building up a self or having it destroyed becomes something of a shameless game, and learning to view this process as a game seems to make for some demoralization, the game being such a fundamental one. In the hospital, then, the inmate can learn that the self is not a fortress, but rather a small open city; he can become weary of having to show pleasure when held by troops of his own, and weary of having to show displeasure when held by the enemy. Once he learns what it is like to be defined by society as not having a viable self, this threatening definition—the threat that helps attach people to the self society accords them—is weakened. The patient seems to gain a new plateau when he learns that he can survive while acting in a way that society sees as destructive of him.

A few illustrations of this moral loosening and moral fatigue might be given. In state mental hospitals currently a kind of "marriage moratorium" appears to be accepted by patients and more or less condoned by staff. Some informal peer-group pressure may be brought against a patient who "plays around" with more than one hospital partner at a time, but little negative sanction seems to be attached to taking up, in a temporarily steady way, with a member of the opposite sex, even though both partners are known to be married, to have children, and even to be regularly visited by these outsiders. In short, there is licence in mental hospitals to begin courting all

over again, with the understanding, however, that nothing very permanent or serious can come of this. Like shipboard or vacation romances, these entanglements attest to the way in which the hospital is cut off from the outside community, becoming a world of its own, operated for the benefit of its own citizens. And certainly this moratorium is an expression of the alienation and hostility that patients feel for those on the outside to whom they were closely related. But, in addition, one has evidence of the loosening effects of living in a world within a world, under conditions which make it difficult to give full seriousness to either of them.

The second illustration concerns the ward system. On the worst ward level, discreditings seem to occur the most frequently, in part because of lack of facilities, in part through the mockery and sarcasm that seem to be the occupational norm of social control for the attendants and nurses who administer these places. At the same time, the paucity of equipment and rights mean that not much self can be built up. The patient finds himself constantly toppled, therefore, but with very little distance to fall. A kind of jaunty gallows humor seems to develop in some of these wards, with considerable freedom to stand up to the staff and return insult for insult. While these patients can be punished, they cannot, for example, be easily slighted, for they are accorded as a matter of course few of the niceties that people must enjoy before they can suffer subtle abuse. Like prostitutes in connection with sex, inmates in these wards have very little reputation or rights to lose and can therefore take certain liberties. As the person moves up the ward system, he can manage more and more to avoid incidents which discredit his claim to be a human being, self-respect; yet when eventually he does get toppled—and he does— there is a much farther distance to fall. For instance, the privileged patient lives in a world wider than the ward, containing recreation workers who, on request, can dole out cake, cards, table-tennis balls, tickets to the movies, and writing materials. But in the absence of the social control of payment which is typically exerted by a recipient on the outside, the patient runs the risk that even a warmhearted functionary may, on occasion, tell him to wait until she has finished an informal chat, or teasingly ask why he wants what he has asked for, or respond with a dead pause and a cold look of appraisal.

References

Abse, D. W. *Hysteria and related mental disorders*. Baltimore: Williams & Wilkins, 1966.

Adams, B. N. Occupational position, mobility and the kin of orientation. *American Sociological Review,* 1967, *32*(3), 364–377.

Adams, B. N. *The family: A sociological interpretation*. New York: Rand, 1975.

Adams, R. L., & Philips, B. N. Motivational and achievement differences among children of various ordinal birth positions. *Child Development,* 1972, *43,* 155–164.

Adler, A. *Practice and theory of individual psychology*. New York: Harcourt, Brace & World, 1927.

Adler, A. The fundamental views of individual psychology. *International Journal of Individual Psychology,* 1935, *1,* 5–8.

Ainsworth, M. D. S. The development of infant-mother attachment. In B. Caldwell and H. Ricciuti (Eds.), *Review of child development research* (Vol. 3). Chicago: University of Chicago Press, 1973, 1–94.

Ainsworth, M. D. S., Bell, S. M. V., and Stayton, D. J. Individual differences in strange-situational behavior of one-year-olds. In H. A. Schaffer (Ed.), *The origins of human social relations.* London: Academic Press, 1971.

Albin, R. Snapshot: Mary Howell. *APA Monitor,* March 1979, p. 4.

Alchter, S., Wig, N. N., Varma, V. K., Pershad, D., & Varma, S. K. A phenomenological analysis of symptoms in obsessive-compulsive neurosis. *British Journal of Psychiatry,* 1975, *127,* 342–348.

Alexander, K. L., & Eckland, B. K. School experience and status attainment. In S. E. Dragastin & G. H. Elder, Jr. (Eds.), *Adolescence in the life cycle: Psychological change and social context.* New York: Wiley, 1975, 25–47.

Allport, G. W. *Becoming: Basic considerations for a psychology of personality*. New Haven, Conn.: Yale University Press, 1955.

Allport, G. W. *Pattern and growth in personality*. New York: Holt, 1961.

Allport, G. Personality: Contemporary viewpoints (I). In D. Sills (Ed.), *International encyclopedia of the social sciences.* New York: Macmillan, 1968.

American Psychiatric Association. *Diagnostic and statistical manual of mental disorders* (3d ed.). Washington, D.C.: American Psychiatric Association, 1980.

Appleyard, D., & Lintell, M. The environmental quality of city streets: The residents viewpoint. *Journal of American Institute of Planners,* 1972, *38,* 84–101.

Archibald, W., & Cohen, R. Self-presentation, embarrassment, and facework as a function of self-evaluation, conditions of self-presentation, and feedback from others. *Journal of Personality and Social Psychology,* 1971, *20,* p. 287–297.

Arieti, S. Manic-depressive psychosis. In S. Arieti (Ed.). *American handbook of psychiatry.* New York: Basic Books, 1959, 419–454.

Armstrong, C. M. Patterns of achievement in selected New York state schools. Albany, N.Y.: State Education Department, 1964.

Astin, A. W. *Preventing students from dropping out*. San Francisco: Jossey-Bass, 1975.

Astin, A. W. *Four critical years*. San Francisco: Jossey-Bass, 1977.

Atchley, R. C. The life course, age grading, and age-linked demands for decision making. In N. Datan & L. H. Ginsberg (Eds.), *Life-span developmental psychology: Normative life crises.* Washington, D.C.: Academic Press, 1975, 261–278.

Atchley, R. C. *The sociology of retirement*. New York: Wiley, 1976.

Athanasiou, R., Shaver, P., & Travris, C. Sex. *Psychology Today,* 1970, *4*(2), 39–52.

Atkinson, J. W., & Birch, D. *Introduction to motivation* (2d ed.). New York: Van Nostrand, 1978.

Atkinson, J. W., & Raynor, J. *Motivation and achievement*. Washington, D.C.: Winston, 1974.

Bach, G. R. Father-fantasies and father-typing in father-separated families. *Child Development,* 1946, *17,* 63–80.

Bachman, J. G., Green, S., & Wirtanen, I. D. *Youth intransition, Vol. III: Dropping out—Problem or Symptom.* Ann Arbor, Mich.: Institute for Social Research, 1971.

Back, K. W. Transition to aging and the self-image. *Aging and Human Development,* 1971, *2,* 296–304.

Bagley, C. Occupational class and symptoms of depression. *Social Science and Medicine,* 1973, *7,* 327–340.

Baird, L. L. Big school, small school: A critical examination of the hypothesis. *Journal of Educational Psychology,* 1969, *60,* 253–260.

Baird, L. L. The practical utility of measures of college environments. *The Review of Educational Research,* 1974, *44,* 307–330.

Baird, L. L. Entrance of women to graduate and professional education. Paper presented at the American Psychological Association meeting, Washington, D.C., 1976.

Baird, L. L. Men and women college seniors' images of five careers. Paper presented at the American Psychological Association meetings, San Francisco, Calif., 1977.

Baker, S. L., Fagan, S. A., Fischer, E. G., Janda, E. J., & Cove, L. A. Impact of father absence. III. Problems of family reintegration following prolonged father absence. Paper presented at American Orthopsychiatric Association meeting, Chicago, March 1968.

Baldwin, A. L. Changes in parent behavior during pregnancy. *Child Development,* 1947, *18,* 29–39.

Bandura, A. *Social learning theory.* Englewood Cliffs, N.J.: Prentice-Hall, 1977.

Bandura, A., Ross, D., & Ross, S. Imitation of film-mediated aggressive models. *Journal of Abnormal and Social Psychology,* 1963, *66,* 3–11.

Bandura, A., Ross, D., & Ross, S. A. Transmission of aggression through imitation of aggressive models. *Journal of Abnormal and Social Psychology,* 1961, *63,* 575–582.

Barker, R. G. *Habitats, environments and human behavior.* San Francisco: Jossey-Bass, 1978.

Barker, R. G. On the nature of the environment, *Journal of Social Issues,* 19, 1963, 17–38.

Barker, R. G., & Gump, P. V. Big school, small school. Stanford, Calif.: Stanford University Press, 1964.

Barker, R. G., & Wright, H. F. *Midwest and its children.* New York: Harper & Row, 1955. (Reprinted by Archon Books, Hamden, Conn., 1971.)

Barrett, T. C., & Tinsley, H. E. A. Vocational self-concept crystallization and vocational indecision. *Journal of Counseling Psychology,* 1977, *24,* 301–307.

Barry, W. A. Marriage research and conflict: An integrative review. *Psychological Bulletin,* 1970, *73*(1), 41–54.

Baumrind, D. Effects of authoritative parental control on child behavior. *Child Development,* 1966, *37,* 887–907.

Bayer, A. E. College impact on marriage. *Journal of Marriage and the Family,* 1972, *34*(4) 600–609.

Beck, A. T. *Depression: Clinical, experimental, and theoretical aspects.* Harper & Row, 1967.

Beck, A. T., Lande, R., & Bohnert, M. Ideational components of anxiety neurosis. *Archives of General Psychiatry,* 1974, *31,* 319–325.

Becker, H. S. Becoming a marijuana smoker. *American Journal of Sociology,* 1953, *59,* 235–243.

Becker, H. S., Geer, B., & Hughes, E. C. *Making the grade: The academic side of college life.* New York: Wiley, 1968.

Becker, W. C. Consequences of different kinds of parental discipline. In M. L. Hoffman & L. W. Hoffman (Eds.), *Review of child development research* (Vol. 1). New York: Russell Sage, 1964.

Bell, R. Q. Contributions of human infants to caregiving and social interaction. In M. Lewis & L. A. Rosenblum (Eds.), *The effect of the infant on its caregiver.* New York: Wiley, 1974, 1–20.

Bell, W. G. Community care for the elderly: An alternative to institutionalization. *The Gerontologist,* 1973 *13*(3, pt. I), 349–54.

Belmont, L., & Marolla, F. A. Birth order, family size, and intelligence. *Science,* 1973, *182*(4117), 1096–1101.

Bendo, A. A., & Feldman, H. A. Comparison of the self-concept of low-income women with and without husbands present. *Cornell Journal of Social Relations,* 1974, *9,* 53–85.

Bengtsson, A. *Environmental planning for children's play.* New York: Praeger, 1970.

Berg, D. H. Sexual subcultures and contemporary heterosexual interaction patterns among adolescent. *Adolescence,* 1975, *10*(40), 543–548.

Berkowitz, L. Control of aggression. In B. M. Caldwell & H. N. Ricciuti (Eds.), *Review of child development research* (Vol. 3). Chicago: University of Chicago Press, 1973, 95–140.

Bernard, J. The adjustment of married mates. In H. T. Christensen (Ed.), *The handbook of marriage and the family.* Chicago: Rand McNally, 1964.

Bernard, J. Marital stability and patterns of status variables. *Journal of Marriage and the Family,* 1966, *28,* 421–439.

Bernard, J. *The future of marriage.* New York: Crowell, 1971.

Bernard, J. *Women and the public interest.* Chicago: Aldine-Atherton, 1971.

Biblow, E. Imaginative play and the control of aggressive behavior. In J. L. Singer (Ed.), *The child's world of make-believe.* New York: Academic Press, 1973, 104–128.

Bikson, T. K., & Goodchilds, J. D. Old and alone. A paper for the Symposium Family Patterns: Social myth and social policy. Presented at the 86th annual meeting of the American Psychological Association, Toronto, Ontario, August 1978.

Biller, H. B. *Paternal deprivation,* Indianapolis, Ind.: Heath, 1974.

Biller, H., & Meredith, D. *Father power.* Garden City, N.Y.: Anchor/Doubleday, 1975.

Birch, D., Atkinson, J. W., & Bongort, K. Cognitive control of action. In B. Weiner (Ed.). *Cognitive views of human motivation.* New York: Academic Press, 1974.

Birnbaum, J. A. Life patterns and self-esteem in gifted family-oriented and career committed women. In M. T. S. Mednick, S. S. Tangri, & L. W. Hoffman (Eds.), *Women and achievement: Social and motivational analyses.* New York: Halsted, 1975.

Birns, B., Blank, M., & Bridges, W. H. The effectiveness of various soothing techniques on human neonates. *Psychosomatic Medicine,* 1966, *28,* 316–322.

Blaxall, M., & Reagan, B. *Women and the workplace.* Chicago: University of Chicago Press, 1976.

Blenkner, M. Social work and family relationships in later life with some thoughts on filial maturity. In E. Shanas & G. F. Streib, *Social structure and the family: Generational relations.* Englewood Cliffs, N.J.: Prentice-Hall, 1965, 46–59.

Blood, R. O. *The family,* New York: Free Press, 1972.

Blood, R. O., & Wolfe, D. M. *Husbands and wives.* New York: Free Press, 1960.

Bloom, B. L. *Community mental health.* Monterey, Calif.: Brooks/Cole, 1977.

Blos, P. *On adolescence: A psychoanalytic interpretation.* New York: Free Press, 1962.

Bonier, R. J., & Hymowitz, P. Marijuana and college students: Set, setting, and personality. Paper presented at American Psychological Association, Honolulu, September 1972.

Borke, H.   The development of empathy in Chinese and American children between three and six years of age: A cross-cultural study. *Developmental Psychology,* 1973, *9,* 102–108.

Borow, H.   Career development. In J. F. Adams (Ed.), *Understanding adolescence: Current developments in adolescent psychology* (3d ed.). Boston: Allyn and Bacon, 1976, 489–523.

Bowerman, C. E., & Bahr, S. J.   Conjugal power and adolescent identification with parents. *Sociometry,* 1973, *36,* 366–377.

Bowerman, C. E., & Dobash, R. M.   Structural variations in intersibling affect. *Journal of Marriage and the Family,* 1974, *36,* 48–54.

Bowlby, J.   The nature of the child's tie to his mother. *International Journal of Psychoanalysis,* 1958, *39,* 350–373.

Bowlby, J.   Separation anxiety. *International Journal of Psychoanalysis,* 1960, *41,* 69–113.

Boyd, P. R.   Drug abuse and addiction in adolescents. In J. G. Howells (Ed.), *Modern perspectives in adolescent psychiatry.* New York: Brunner/Mazel, 1971, 290–328.

Boyd, R. E.   Conformity reduction in adolescence. *Adolescence,* 1975, *10*(38), 297–300.

Brain, R.   Somebody else should be your own best friend. *Psychology Today,* 1977, *11,* 83–84.

Brazelton, T. B., Koslowski, B., & Main, M.   The origins of reciprocity: The early mother-infant interaction. In M. Lewis & L. A. Rosenblum (Eds.), *The effect of the infant on its caregiver.* New York: Wiley-Interscience, 1974, 49–76.

Bridgman, B.   Effects of test score feedback on immediately subsequent test performance. *Journal of Education Psychology,* 1974, *66,* 62–66.

Brill, H., Fioramonti, F., Fort, J., Goode, E., & Lang, I. L.   A panel discussion on marijuana. *Contemporary Drug Problems,* 1973, *2,* 267–302.

Brim, O.   Adult socialization. In J. Clausen (Ed.), *Socialization and society.* Boston: Little, Brown, 1968.

Brittain, C. V.   Adolescent choices and parent-peer cross pressures. *American Sociological Review,* 1963, *28,* 385–391.

Brittain, C. V.   An exploration of the bases of peer-compliance and parent-compliance in adolescence. *Adolescence,* 1967–68, *2,* 445–458.

Brittain, C. V.   A comparison of rural and urban adolescents with respect to peer versus parent compliance. *Adolescence,* 1969, *13,* 59–68.

Broman, S. H., Nichols, P. L., & Kennedy, W.   *Preschool I.Q.* Hillsdale, N.J.: Lawrence Erlbaum, 1975.

Bronfenbrenner, U.   Some familial antecedents of responsibility and leadership in adolescents. In L. Petrullo & B. M. Bass (Eds.), *Leadership and interpersonal behavior.* New York: Holt, 1961, 239–271.

Bronson, G. W.   Infants' reactions to an unfamiliar person. In L. J. Stone, H. T. Smith, & L. B. Murphy (Eds.), *The competent infant.* New York: Basic Books, 1973.

Broverman, I. K., Vogel, S. R., Broverman, D. M., Clarkson, F. E., & Rosencrantz, P. S.   Sex-role stereotypes: A current appraisal. *Journal of Social Issues,* 1972, *28*(2), 59–78.

Brown, B. F. (Ed.).   *The reform of secondary education: A report to the public and the profession.* The National Commission on the Reform of Secondary Education. New York: McGraw-Hill, 1973.

Brown, P., & Elliott, R.   Control of aggression in a nursery school class. *Journal of Experimental Child Psychology,* 1965, *2,* 103–107.

Brown, R.   *Social psychology.* New York: Free Press, 1965.

Bruch, H.   *The golden cage: The enigma of anorexia nervosa.* Cambridge, Mass.: Harvard University Press, 1978.

Brunner, J. S.   *Processes in cognitive growth: Infancy.* Worcester, Mass.: Clark University Press, 1968.

Bunney, W. E., Jr., Murphy, D. L., Goodwin, F. K., & Borge, G. F.   The "switch-process" in manic-depressive illness: A systematic study of sequential behavioral changes. *Archives of General Psychiatry,* 1972, *27,* 295–302.

Buss, A. & Plomin, R. A.   *A temperament theory of personality.* New York: Wiley, 1975.

Buss, A. R., & Poley, W.   *Individual differences: Traits and factors.* New York: Gardner Press, 1976.

Busse, E. W.   Psychoneurotic reactions and defense mechanisms in the aged. In Paul H. Hock and J. Zubin (Eds.), *Psychopathology of Aging.* New York: Grune & Stratton, 1961.

Calonico, J., & Calonico, B.   Classroom interaction: A sociological approach. *Journal of Educational Research,* 1972, *66*(4), 165–69.

Cameron, N.   *Personality development and psychopathology: A dynamic approach.* Boston: Houghton Mifflin, 1963.

Cameron, P., & Biber, H.   Sexual thought throughout the life span. *The Gerontologist,* 1973, *13,* 144–147.

Campbell, A.   The American way of mating: Marriage si, children only maybe. *Psychology Today,* May 1975, *8,* 37–40.

Campbell, A., Converse, P. E., & Rogers, W. L.   *The quality of American life.* New York: Russell Sage, 1976.

Campbell, A.   Subjective measures of well-being. *American Psychologist,* 1976, *31*(2), 117–125.

Canter, D., & Canter, S.   Close together in Tokyo. *Design and Environment,* 1971, *2*(2), 60–63.

Caplan, G.   *Principles of preventive psychiatry.* New York: Basic Books, 1964.

Caplan, G.   *The theory and practice of mental health consultation.* New York: Basic Books, 1970.

Carns, D. E.   Talking about sex: Notes on first coitus and the double sexual standard. *Journal of Marriage and the Family,* 1973, *35,* 677–688.

Cartwright, L. K.   Continuity and noncontinuity in the careers of a sample of young women physicians. *Journal of the American Medical Womens Association,* 1977, *32,* 316–321.

Cavior, N., & Dokecki, P. R.   Physical attractiveness, perceived attitude similarity, and academic achievement as contributors to interpersonal attraction among adolescents. *Developmental Psychology,* 1973, *9,* 44–54.

Centra, J., & Rock, D.   College environments and student academic achievement. *American Educational Research Journal,* 1971, *8,* 623–634.

Chabaud, J. *The education and advancement of women.* Paris: UNESCO, 1970.

Chafetz, M. Alcoholism: Drug dependency problem number one. *Journal of Drug Issues,* Winter 1974, 64–68. (a)

Chafetz, M. *Alcohol and health: New knowledge.* Second special report to the U.S. Congress from the secretary of health, education, and welfare. Reprint edition. Washington, D.C.: U.S. Government Printing Office, 1974. (b)

Children's Defense Fund. *Children out of school in America.* Cambridge, Mass.: Children's Defense Fund of the Washington Research Project, Inc., 1974.

Chombart de Lauwe, Y. M. J. Le group familial et l'enfant. In *Psychopathologie sociale de l'enfant inadapte.* Paris: Centre National de la Recherche Scientific, 1959, 175–210.

Circirelli, V. G. Effects of mother and older sibling on the problem-solving behavior of the younger child. *Developmental Psychology,* 1975, *11,* 749–756.

Clanton, G. The contemporary experience of adultery: Bob and Carol and Updike and Rimmer. In R. W. Libby & R. N. Whitehurst (Eds.), *Marriage and alternatives: Exploring intimate relationship.* Glenview, Ill.: Scott, Foresman, 1977, 112–130.

Clark, R. A., Nye, F. I., & Gecas, V. Husbands' work involvement and marital role performance. *Journal of Marriage and the Family,* 1978, *40,* 9–21.

Clausen, J. A. Research note on family size, sib order, and socialization influences. Unpublished paper, 1965.

Clausen, J. A. Family structure, socialization, and personality. In L. W. Hoffman & M. L. Hoffman (Eds.), *Review of child development research* (Vol. 2). New York: Russell Sage, 1966.

Clayton, R. R., & Voss, H. L. Shacking up: Cohabitation in the 1970s. *Journal of Marriage and the Family,* 1977, *39*(2), 273–283.

Clifford, E. Body satisfaction in adolescence. *Perceptual and Motor Skills,* 1971, 33, 119–125.

Cohen, M., et al. An intensive study of twelve cases of manic-depressive psychosis. *Psychiatry,* 1954, *17,* 103–137.

Cohen, S. Psychomimetic agents: *Annual Review of Pharmacology,* 1967, *7,* 301.

Cohen, S., Glass, D. C., & Singer, J. E. Apartment noise, auditory discrimination, and reading ability in children. *Journal of Experimental Social Psychology,* 1973, *9,* 407–422.

Coleman, J. C. *Abnormal psychology and modern life* (5th ed.). Glenview, Ill.: Scott, Foresman, 1976.

Coleman, J. L. *The adolescent society.* New York: Free Press, 1961.

Coleman, J. S. How do the young become adults? *Review of Educational Research,* 1972, *42,* 431–439.

Coles, R. Like it is in the alley. *Daedalus,* Fall 1968, *97,* 1315–1330.

Conger, J. J. Sexual attitudes and behavior of contemporary adolescents. In J. J. Conger (Ed.), *Contemporary issues in adolescent development.* New York: Harper & Row, 1975, 221–230.

Costanzo, P. R., & Shaw, M. E. Conformity as a function of age. *Child Development,* 1966, *37,* 967–975.

Cottle, T. J. *College: Reward and betrayal.* Chicago: University of Chicago Press, 1977.

Coward, R. T., & Kerckhoff, R. K. *The rural elderly: Program planning guide.* Ames, Iowa: North Central Regional Center for Rural Development, 1978.

Cozby, P. C. Self-disclosure: A literature review. *Psychological Bulletin,* 1973, *79,* 73–91.

Crandall, V. C. Reinforcement effects of adults reactions and nonreactions on children's achievement expectations. *Child Development,* 1963, *34,* 335–354.

Cuber, J. F. Adultery: Reality versus stereotype. In G. Neubeck (Ed.), *Extramarital Relations.* Englewood Cliffs, N.J.: Prentice-Hall, 1969.

Curtis, R. L. Adolescent orientations toward parents and peers: Variations by sex, age, and socioeconomic status. *Adolescence,* 1975, *10,* 483–494.

Cutright, P. Income and family events: marital stability. *Journal of Marriage and the Family,* 1971, *33,* 291–306.

Dale, P. S. *Language development: Structure and function.* (2d ed.) New York: Holt, 1976.

Damon, W. The development of peer group interaction in children from four to ten. Paper presented at the American Psychological Association meetings in Washington, D.C., 1976.

Daniel, P., & Lachman, M. The prime of life. In F. Rebelsky (Ed.), *Life: The continuous process.* New York: Knopf, 1975, 52–60.

Darwin, C. On the origin of species by means of natural selection, or the preservation of favored races in the struggle for life. London: J. Murray, 1859.

Darwin, C. The descent of man and selection in relation to sex, (2 vol.). London: J. Murray, 1871.

Davis, F., Munoz, L. Heads and freaks: Patterns and meanings of drug use among hippies. *Journal of Health and Social Behavior,* 1968, *9,* 156–164.

Davison, G. C., & Neale, J. M. *Abnormal psychology: An experimental clinical approach* (2d ed.). New York: Wiley, 1978.

Deal, T. E., & Roper, D. A. Dilemma of diversity: The American high school. In J. G. Kelly (Ed.), *Adolescent boys in high school: A psychological study of coping and adaptation.* Hillsdale, N.J.: Lawrence Erlbaum, 1979, 15–34.

deBeer, G. R. Evolution. Macropaedia (Vol. 7). *The New Encyclopaedia Britannica.* Chicago: Encyclopaedia Britannica, Inc., 1974, 7–23.

Dennis, W. Creative productivity between the ages of twenty and eighty years. *Journal of Gerontology,* 1966, *21,* 1–8.

Derlega, V. J., & Chaikey, A. L. Privacy and self-disclosure in social relationships. A paper presented at the meetings of the American Psychological Association, San Francisco, 1977.

Deveck, C. S., & Bush, E. S. Sex differences in learned helplessness: I. Differential debilitation with peer and adult evaluators. *Developmental Psychology,* 1976, *12,* 147–156.

Dinklage, L. B. *Student decision-making studies, studies of adolescents in the secondary schools. Report No. 6.* Cambridge, Mass.: Harvard Graduate School of Education, 1969.

Dollard, J., & Miller, N. E. *Personality and psychotherapy: An analysis in terms of learning, thinking and culture.* New York: McGraw-Hill, 1950.

Douglas, J. W. B. *The home and the school: A study of ability and attainment in the primary school.* London: MacGibbon and Kee, 1964.

Douglas, J. W. B., & Bloomfield, J. M. *Children under five.* London: Allen and Unwin, 1958.

Douvan, E., & Adelson, J. *The adolescent experience.* New York: Wiley, 1966.

Doyle, W., Hancock, G., & Kifer, E. Teachers' perceptions: Do they make a difference? Paper presented at the annual meeting of the American Educational Research Association, 1971.

Drabman, R. S., & Thomas, M. H. Does media violence increase children's toleration of real-life aggression? *Developmental Psychology,* 1974, *10,* 418–421.

Dunphy, D. C. The social structure of urban adolescent peer groups. *Sociometry,* 1963, *26,* 230–246.

Dweck, C. S. The role of expectations and attribution in the alleviation of learned helplessness. *Journal of Personality and Social Psychology,* 1975, *31,* 674–685.

Dweck, C. S., & Bush, E. S. Sex differences in learned helplessness: I. Differential debilitation with peer and adult evaluators. *Developmental Psychology,* 1976, *12,* 147–156.

Dweck, C. S., & Gilhard, D. Expectancy statements as determinants of reactions to failure: Sex differences in persistence and expectancy change. *Journal of Personality and Social Psychology,* 1975, *32,* 1077–1088.

Dworkin, R. H., Burke, B. W., Maher, B. A., & Gottesman, I. I. A longitudinal study of the genetics of personality. *Journal of Personality and Social Psychology,* 1976, *34*(3), 510–518.

Dwyer, J., & Mayer, J. Psychological effects of variations in physical appearance during adolescence. *Adolescence,* 1968–69, *3,* 353–368.

Edwards, D. W., & Kelly, J. G. A longitudinal field test of the person-environment transaction model: Coping and adaptation. Unpublished manuscript, 1977.

Edwards, T. J. Looking back on growing up black. In R. W. Pugh (Ed.), *Psychology and the black experience.* Monterey, Calif.: Brooks/Cole, 1972.

Egbert, L., Battit, C., Welch, C., & Bartlett, M. Reduction of postoperative pain by encouragement and instruction of patients. *New England Journal of Medicine,* 1964, 270, 825–27.

Ekman, P. Universal and cultural differences in facial expressions of emotions. In J. K. Cole (Ed.), *Nebraska Symposium on Motivation* (Vol. 19), Lincoln: University of Nebraska Press, 1972.

Elder, G. H., Jr. Family structure: The effects of size of family, sex composition and ordinal position on academic motivation and achievement. *In adolescent achievement and mobility aspirations.* Chapel Hill, N.C.: Institute for Research in Social Science, 1962, 59–72.

Elder, G. H., Jr. Parental power legitimization and its effect on the adolescent. *Sociometry,* 1963, *26,* 50–65.

Elder, G. H., Jr., Age differentiation and the life course. *Annual Review of Sociology,* 1975, *1,* 165–190.

Elder, G. H., Jr., & Bowerman, C. E. Family structure and child-rearing patterns: The effect of family size and sex composition. *American Sociological Review,* 1963, *30,* 81–96.

El-Khawas, E., & Bisconti, A. *Five and ten years after college entry.* Washington, D.C.: American Council on Education, 1974.

Elliott, D. S., Voss, H. L., & Wendling, A. Capable dropouts and the social milieu of the high school. *Journal of Educational Research,* 1966, *60,* 180–186.

Ellis, A. C., & Hall, G. S. A study of dolls. *Pedagogical Seminary,* 1896, *4,* 129–175.

Ellis, M. J. Play: Theory and research. In W. J. Mitchell (Ed.), *Environmental design: Research and practice.* Proceedings of Environmental Design Research Association 3/AR8 Conference. Los Angeles: University of California Press, 1972.

Epstein, S. The self-concept revisited: Or a theory of a theory. *American Psychologist,* 1973, *28,* 404–416.

Erikson, E. H. *Childhood and Society.* New York: Norton, 1950.

Erikson, E. H. The problem of ego identity. *Psychological Issues,* 1959, *1*(1), 101–164.

Erikson, E. H. *Dimensions of a new identity.* New York: Norton, 1974.

Erikson, E. H. Reflections on Dr. Borg's life cycle. In E. H. Erikson (Ed.), *Adulthood.* New York: Norton, 1978, 1976.

Erlick, A. C., & Starry, A. R. *Vocational plans and preferences of adolescents, Poll 94.* West Lafayette, Ind.: Purdue University, 1972.

Escalona, S. K., & Leitch, M. and others. *Early phases of personality development: A nonnormative study of infant behavior,* Monograph, Society for Research in Child Development, 17, No. 1, serial No. 54, 1952.

Estep, R. E., Burt, M. R., & Milligan, H. J. The socialization of sexual identity. *Journal of Marriage and the Family,* 1977, *39*(1), 99–112.

Faust, V., Weidman, M., & Welmer, W. The influence of meterological factors on children and youths: A 10% random selection of 16,000 pupils and apprentices of Basle City, Switzerland. *Acta Paedopsychiatrica,* 1974, 40, 150–156.

Federal Bureau of Investigation, U.S. Department of Justice. *Uniform crime reports for the United States.* Washington, D.C.: U.S. Government Printing Office, 1966.

Federal Bureau of Investigation, U.S. Department of Justice. *Uniform crime reports.* Washington, D.C.: U.S. Government Printing Office, 1975.

Feldman, H., & Feldman, M. Natural intervention: An alternative method for the social sciences. Adapted from a paper presented at the American Psychological Association Meetings. New Orleans, 1974.

Feldman, H., and Feldman, M. The family life cycle: Some suggestions for recycling. *Journal of Marriage and the Family,* 1975, *37,* 277–284.

Feldman, H., & Feldman, M. Personal communication, 1977.

Feldman, K. A., & Newcomb, T. M. *The impact of college on students.* Vol. 1: *An analysis of four decades of research.* San Francisco: Jossey-Bass, 1969.

Ferrell, M. Z., Tolone, W. L., & Walsh, R. H. Maturational and societal changes in the sexual double-standard: A panel analysis (1967–1971; 1970–1974). *Journal of Marriage and the Family,* 1977, *39*(2), 255–271.

Feshbach, S. The catharsis hypothesis and some consequences of interaction with aggressive and neutral play objects. *Journal of Personality,* 1956, *24,* 449–462.

Finger, J. A., Jr., & Silverman, M. Changes in academic performance in the junior high school. *Personnel and Guidance Journal,* 1966, *45,* 157–164.

Fitzsimmons, S. J., Cheever, J., Leonard, E., & Macunovich, D. School failures: Now and tomorrow. *Developmental Psychology,* 1969, I, 134–146.

Flanagan, J. C. A research approach to improving our quality of life. *American Psychologist,* 1978, *33,* 138–147.

Flanders, N. A. *Analyzing teacher behavior.* Reading, Mass.: Addison-Wesley, 1970.

Flerx, V. C., Fidler, D. S., & Rogers, R. W. Sex-role stereotypes: Developmental aspects and early intervention. *Child Development,* 1976, *47*(4), 998–1008.

Ford, E. B. *Ecological genetics* (4th ed.). New York: Halsted, 1975.

Frederick, C. J. *Suicide, homocide, and alcoholism among American Indians.* U.S. Department of Health, Education, and Welfare Publication no. ADM 74-42. Washington, D.C.: U.S. Government Printing Office, 1973.

Freedman, D. G., & Freedman, N. C. Behavioral differences between Chinese-American and European-American newborns. *Nature,* 1969, 224, 1227.

Freedman, J. L. *Crowding and behavior.* San Francisco: W. H. Freeman, 1975.

Freud, A. *The ego and mechanisms of defense.* New York: International Universities Press, 1936.

Freud, A. *Normality and pathology in childhood.* New York: International Universities Press, 1965.

Freud, A., & Dann, S. An experiment in group upbringing. In R. Eissler, A. Freud, H. Hartmann, & E. Kris (Eds.), *The psychoanalytic study of the child* (Vol. 6). New York: International Universities Press, 1951.

Freud, S. Three essays on the theory of sexuality. In J. Strachey (Ed.), *The standard edition of the complete psychological works of Sigmund Freud* (Vol. 7). London: Hogarth Press, 1953. (1st ed., 1905.)

Freud, S. Notes upon a case of obsessional neurosis. In J. Strachey (ed.), *The standard edition of the complete psychological works of Sigmund Freud* (Vol. 10). London: Hogarth Press, 1955. (Originally published in German in 1909). (b)

Freud, S. Mourning and melancholia. In J. Strachey (Ed.), *The standard edition of the complete psychological works of Sigmund Freud* (Vol. 14). London: Hogarth Press, 1957. (Originally published in 1917.) 243–258.

Freud, S. Formulations on the two principles of mental functioning. In J. Strachey (Ed.), *The standard of the complete psychological works of Sigmund Freud* (Vol. 12). London: Hogarth Press, 1958. (Originally published in 1911.)

Freud, S. The sexual enlightenment of children. In J. Strachey (Ed.), *The standard edition of the complete psychological works of Sigmund Freud* (Vol. 9). London: Hogarth Press, 1959. (Originally published in German in 1907.) (a)

Freud, S. On the sexual theories of children. In J. Strachey (Ed.), *The standard edition of the complete psychological works of Sigmund Freud* (Vol. 9). London: Hogarth Press, 1959. (Originally published in German in 1908.) (b)

Freud, S. The dissolution of the Oedipus-complex. In J. Strachey (Ed.), *The standard edition of the complete psychological works of Sigmund Freud* (Vol. 19). London: Hogarth Press, 1961. (Originally published in 1924.)

Freud, S. Introductory lectures on psycho-analysis. In J. Strachey (Ed.), *The standard edition of the complete psychological works of Sigmund Freud* (Vols. 15 and 16). London: Hogarth Press, 1963. (Originally published in German in 1917.)

Freud, S. New introductory lectures on psychoanalysis. In J. Strachey (Ed.), *The standard edition of the complete psychological works of Sigmund Freud* (Vol. 22). London: Hogarth Press, 1964. (Originally published in German in 1933.)

Gagnon, J. H., & Greenblat, C. S. *Life designs: Individuals, marriages, and families.* Glenview, Ill.: Scott, Foresman, 1978.

Gallagher, J. R., & Harris, H. J. *Emotional problems of adolescents.* (3d ed.). New York: Oxford University Press, 1976.

Gallese, L. R. Women managers say job transfers present a growing dilemma. *The Wall Street Journal,* May 4, 1978.

Gardell, B. Psychosocial aspects of the working environment. *Working Life in Sweden,* 1977, *1.*

Gecas, V. The socialization and child care roles, in F. I. Nye (Ed.), *Role structure and analysis of the family.* Beverly Hills, Calif.: Sage, 1976, 33–60.

George, V., & Wilding, P. *Motherless families.* London: Routledge and Kegan Paul, 1972.

Gillis, J. R. *Youth and history.* New York: Academic Press, 1974.

Ginzberg, E. Toward a theory of occupational choice: A restatement. *Vocational Guidance Quarterly,* 1972, 20, 169–176.

Ginzberg, E. et al. *Occupational Choice.* New York: Columbia University Press, 1951.

Glass, D. C., & Singer, J. E. *Urban stress.* New York: Academic Press, 1972.

Glick, P. C. Some recent changes in American families. U.S. Bureau of the Census, Current Population Reports, Series P-23, No. 52, Washington, D.C.: U.S. Government Printing Office, 1976.

Glick, P. C. Updating the life cycle of the family. *Journal of Marriage and the Family,* 1977, *39*(1), 5–114.

Glick, P. C., & Norton, A. J. Marrying, divorcing, and living together in the United States today. *Population Bulletin,* 1977, 32(5), 3–39.

Glueck, S., & Glueck, E. *Family environment and delinquency.* Boston: Houghton Mifflin, 1962.

Goertzel, V., & Goertzel, M. G. *Cradles of eminence.* Boston: Little, Brown, 1962.

Goethals, G. W., & Klos, D. S. *Experiencing youth: First person accounts* (2d ed.). Boston: Little, Brown, 1976.

Gold, S. Nonuse of neighborhood parks. *Journal of American Institute of Planners,* 1972, 38, 369–378.

Goldberg, G., & Mayerberg, C. K. Effects of three types of affective teacher behavior on student performance. *Child Study Journal,* 1975, 5, 99–105.

Goldberg, R., Kaye, G., Groszko, M., Hichenberg, A., & Kelly, J. G. A comparative analysis of the social characteristics of the four schools selected. Appendix F: Adaptive behavior in varied high schools environments. Research proposal (ROI-MH-15606-04) submitted as a privileged communication to the National Institute of Mental Health, 1967.

Goode, E. *The marijuana smokers.* New York: Basic, 1970.

Goodman, N., & Feldman, K. A. Expectations, ideals, and reality: Youth enters college. In S. E. Dragastin and G. H. Elder, Jr. (Eds.), *Adolescence in the life cycle: Psychological change and social context.* Washington, D.C.: Hemisphere Publishing Company, 1975, 147–169.

Gordon, I. J. *Children's views of themselves.* Washington, D.C.: Association for Childhood Education International, 1972.

Gordon, J. E., & Cohen, F. The effects of affiliation drive arousal on aggression in doll interviews. *Journal of Abnormal and Social Psychology,* 1963, 66, 301–307.

Gornick, V. Consciousness. *New York Times Magazine,* January 10, 1971.

Gottlieb, B. H. The contribution of natural support systems to primary prevention among four social subgroups of adolescent males. *Adolescence,* 1975, 10, 207–220.

Gould, R. E. Suicide problems in children and adolescents. *American Journal of Psychotherapy,* 1965, 19, 228–246.

Gould, R. L. The phases of adult life: A study in developmental psychology. *American Journal of Psychiatry,* 1972, 129, 521–531.

Gould, R. L. Adult life stages: Growth toward self-tolerance. *Psychology Today,* February 1975.

Grant, W. V., & Lind, C. G. *Digest of education statistics.* Washington, D.C.: U.S. Government Printing Office, 1976.

Gregg, C., Clifton, R. K., & Haith, M. M. A possible explanation for the frequent failure to find cardiac orienting in the newborn infant. *Developmental Psychology,* 1976, 12(1), 75–76.

Griest, J. H., Gustafson, D. H., Strauss, F. F., Rowse, G. L., Loughren, T. P., & Chiles, J. A. Suicide risk prediction: A new approach. *Life-Threatening Behavior,* 1974, 4(4), 212–223.

Gump, P. The behavior setting. A promising unit for environmental designs. *Landscape Architecture,* 1971, 61, 130–134.

Gump, P. Ecological psychology and children. In E. M. Hetherington (Ed.), *Review of child development research* (Vol. 5). Chicago: University of Chicago Press, 1975, 75–126.

Gurin, G., Veroff, J., & Feld, S. *Americans view their mental health: A nationwide interview survey.* New York: Basic Books, 1960.

Haith, M. M. Visual scanning in infants. Paper presented at the Society for Research in Child Development, Clark University, March 1968.

Hall, G. S. *Adolescence: Its psychology and its relations to phys-iology, anthropology, sociology, sex, crime, religion and education* (Vols. 1 and 2). New York: Appleton, 1904.

Hamlin, R. M. Restrictions on the competent aged. Paper presented at the 85th annual meetings of the American Psychological Association, San Francisco, August 26–30, 1977.

Hansen, C. F. *The four track curriculum.* Englewood Cliffs, N.J.: Prentice-Hall, 1964.

Hansen, S. L. Dating choices of high school students. *The Family Coordinator,* 1977, 26, 133–138.

Hare, A. P. *Handbook of small group research.* New York: Free Press, 1962.

Harmon, L. W. The childhood and adolescent career plans of college women. *Journal of Vocational Behavior,* 1971, 1, 45–56.

Harren, V. A. An overview of Tiedeman's theory of career decision making and summary of related research. Unpublished manuscript, Southern Illinois University—Carbondale, 1976.

Harren, V. A., & Kass, R. A. The measurement and correlates of career decision making. Paper presented at the American Psychological Association meeting, San Francisco, 1977.

Hartmann, H. *Essays on ego psychology: Selected problems in psychoanalytic theory.* New York: International Universities Press, 1964.

Hauser, R. M., & Featherman, D. L. Socioeconomic achievements of U.S. men, 1962 to 1972. *Science,* 1974, 185, 4148, 325–331.

Havens, E. M. Women, work and wedlock: A note on female marital patterns in the United States. *American Journal of Sociology,* 1973, 78, 975–981.

Havighust, R. Human development and education. New York: Longmans, 1953.

Havighurst, R. J. Youth in exploration and man emergent. In H. Borow (Ed.), *Man in a world at work.* Boston: Houghton Mifflin, 1964.

Havighurst, R. J. Unrealized potentials of adolescents. National Association of Secondary School Principals Bulletin, 1966, 50, 75–96.

Havighurst, R. J. Youth in social institutions. In R. J. Havighurst and P. H. Dreyer (Eds.), *Youth,* the 74th yearbook of the National Society for the Study of Education. Chicago: University of Chicago Press, 1975, 115–144.

Havighurst, R. J., & Dreyer, P. H. (Eds.). *Youth,* the seventy-fourth yearbook of the National Society for the Study of Education. Chicago: University of Chicago Press, 1975.

Hawkes, G. R., Burchinal, L., & Gardner, B. Size of family and adjustment of children. *Marriage and Family Living,* 1958, 20, 65–68.

Hawkins, J. L., Weisberg, C., & Ray, D. L. Marital communication style and social class. *Journal of Marriage and the Family,* 1977, 39(3), 479–490.

Heckman, N. A., Bryson, R., & Bryson, J. B. Problems of professional couples: A content analysis. *Journal of Marriage and the Family,* 1977, 39(2), 323–330.

Hendon, H. Student suicide: Death as a life-style. *Journal of Nervous and Mental Disorders,* 1975, 160, 204–219.

Hendricks, J., & Hendricks, C. D. *Aging in mass society: Myths and realities.* Cambridge, Mass.: Winthrop, 1977.

Hess, R. D. High school antecedents of young adult achievement. In R. E. Grinder (Ed.), *Studies in adolescence*. New York: Macmillan, 1963, 401–416.

Hetherington, E. M. Effects of paternal absence on sex-typed behaviors in Negro and white preadolescent males. *Journal of Personality and Social Psychology,* 1966, *4,* 87–91.

Hicks, J. M., Edwards, K. T., & Sgan, A. D. Attitudes toward school as related to nongrading and intelligence. *Psychological Reports,* 1973, *33,* 739–742.

Hill, K. T., & Sarason, S. B. The relation of test anxiety and defensiveness to test and school performance over the elementary school years: A further longitudinal study. *Monographs of the Society for Research in Child Development,* 1966, *31,* 2, 1–76.

Hiller, D. V., & Philliber, W. W. The derivation of status benefits from occupational attainments of working wives. *Journal of Marriage and the Family,* 1978, *40*(1), 63–68.

Hjelle, L. A., & Ziegler, D. J. *Personality.* New York: McGraw-Hill, 1976, 256.

Hobson v. Hansen, 269 F. Supp. 401 (1967). Washington, D.C.: U.S. Government Printing Office.

Hochman, J. S. *Marijuana and social evolution.* Englewood Cliffs, N.J.: Prentice-Hall, 1972.

Hoffman, L. W. Effects of maternal employment on the child. In L. W. Hoffman and F. I. Nye (Eds.), *Working mothers.* San Francisco: Jossey-Bass, 1974, 126–166.

Hoffman, L. W., & Nye, F. I. (Eds.). *Working mothers.* San Francisco: Jossey-Boss, 1974.

Hoffman, M. L. Developmental synthesis of affect and cognition and its implications for altruistic motivation. *Developmental Psychology,* 1975, *11,* 607–622.

Hotchner, A. E. *Papa Hemingway.* New York: Random House, 1966.

Hughes, D. C. An experimental investigation of the effects of pupil responding and teacher reacting on pupil achievement. *American Educational Research Journal,* 1973, *10,* 21–37.

Hull, C. L. *Principles of behavior.* New York: Appleton-Century-Crofts, 1943.

Hunt, M. *Sexual behavior in the seventies.* Chicago: Playboy Press, 1974.

Huxley, J. *The uniqueness of man.* London: Chatto and Windus, 1941.

Huxley, J. *Evolution: The magic synthesis.* New York: Harper Bros., 1942.

Hyman, H. H., Wright, C. R., & Reed, J. S. *The enduring effects of education.* Chicago: University of Chicago Press, 1975.

Iacovetta, R. G. Adolescent-adult interaction and peer-group involvement. *Adolescence,* 1975, *10*(39), 327–336.

Ihinger, M. The referee role and norms of equity: A contribution toward a theory of sibling conflict. *Journal of Marriage and the Family,* 1975, *37,* 515–525.

Inkeles, A. *What is sociology?* Englewood Cliffs, N.J.: Prentice-Hall, 1964.

Inkeles, A., & Smith, D. H. *Individual change in six developing countries.* Cambridge, Mass.: Harvard University Press, 1974.

Ittelson, W. H., Proshansky, H. M., Rivlin, L. G., & Winkel, G. H. *An introduction to environmental psychology.* New York: Holt, 1974.

Jackson, D. W. The meaning of dating from the role perspective of non-dating preadolescents. *Adolescence,* 1975, *10*(37), 123–126.

Jacobinizer, H. Attempted suicides in children. *Journal of Pediatrics,* 1960, *56,* 519–525.

Jacobs, J. *Death and life of great American cities.* New York: Vintage, 1961.

Jacobson, E. *The self and the object world.* New York: International Universities Press, 1964.

Jahoda, G. A note on Aslianti names and their relation to personality. *British Journal of Psychology,* 1954, *45,* 192–195.

Jamison, D., Suppes, P., & Wells, S. The effectiveness of alternative instructional media: A survey. *Review of Educational Research,* 1974, *44,* 1–67.

Janis, I. Psychological effects of warnings. In G. W. Baker & D. W. Chapman (Eds.), *Man and society in disaster.* New York: Basic Books, 1962.

Janis, I. Vigilance and decision making in personal crises. In G. V. Coelho, D. A. Hamburg, & John E. Adams (Eds.), *Coping and adaptation.* New York: Basic Books, 1974, 139–175.

Janis, I. L., & Feshbach, S. Effects of fear-arousing communication. *Journal of Abnormal and Social Psychology,* (1953) *48,* 78–92.

Janis, I. L., & Mann, L. Coping with decisional conflict. *American Scientist 64*(6), 1976, 657–667.

Janis, I. L., Mohl, G. F., Kagan, J., & Holt, R. R. *Personality: Dynamics, development, and assessment.* New York: Harcourt, Brace & World, 1969.

Jeans, R. F. An independently validated case of multiple personality. *Journal of Abnormal Psychology,* 1976, *85,* 249–255.

Jenner, F. A., Gjessing, L. R., Cos, J. R., Davies-Jones, A., & Hullen, R. P. A manic-depressive psychotic with a 48 hour cycle. *British Journal of Psychiatry,* 1967, *113,* 859–910.

Jessor, R., Graves, T. D., Hanson, R. C., & Jessor, S. *Society, personality, and deviant behavior.* New York: Holt, 1968.

Jessor, R., & Jessor, S. L. *Problem behavior and psychosocial development.* New York: Academic Press, 1977.

Jessor, R., Jessor, S. L., & Finney, J. A social psychology of marijuana use: Logitudinal studies of high school and college youth. *Journal of Personality and Social Psychology,* 1973, *26,* 1–15.

Jessor, R., Young, H. B., Young, E., & Tesi, G. Perceived opportunity, alienation, and drinking behavior among Italian and American youth. *Journal of Personality and Social Psychology,* 1970, *15,* 215–222.

Johnson, B. D. *Marijuana users and drug subcultures.* New York: Wiley-Interscience, 1973.

Jones, M. C. A study of socialization patterns at the high school level. *Journal of Genetic Psychology,* 1958, *93,* 87–111.

Jones, N. B. *Ethological studies of child behavior.* London: Cambridge University Press, 1972.

Jones, S. High school social status as a historical process. *Adolescence,* 1976, *11*(43), 327–333.

Jourard, S. M., & Secord, P. F. Body-cathexis and the ideal female figure. *Journal of Abnormal and Social Psychology,* 1955, 50, 243–246.

Jyrkila, F. Society and adjustment to old age. In *Transactions of the Westmarck Society,* Vol. 5. Turlsu: Maksgaard, 1960.

Kagan, J. The concept of identification. *Psychological Review,* 1958, *65*(5), 296–305.

Kagan, J. Emergent themes in human development. *American Scientist,* 1976, *64,* 186–196.

Kamens, D. H. The college "charter" and college size: Effects on occupational choice and college attrition. *Sociology of Education,* 1971, *44,* 270–296.

Kandel, D. B. Similarity in real-life adolescent friendship pairs. *Journal of Personality and Social Psychology,* 1978, *36,* 306–312.

Kandel, D. B., & Lesser, G. S. *Youth in two worlds.* San Francisco: Jossey-Bass, 1972.

Kasl, S. V., & Harburg, E. Perceptions of the neighborhood and the desire to move out. *Journal of the American Institute of Planners,* 1972, *38,* 318–324.

Keller, A. B. Psychological determinants of family size in a Mexican village. *Merrill-Palmer Quarterly,* 1973, *19,* 289–299.

Kelly, J. G. (Ed.). *Adolescent boys in high school: A psychological study of coping and adaptation.* Hillsdale, N.J.: Lawrence Erlbaum, 1979.

Kelly, J. G. Ecological constraints on mental health services. *American Psychologist,* 1966, *21,* 535–539.

Kelly, J. G. Naturalistic observations in contrasting social environments. In E. P. Williams & H. L. Raush (Eds.), *Naturalistic viewpoints in psychological research.* New York: Holt, 1969, 183–199.

Kelly, J. G. Towards an ecological conception of preventive interventions. In J. W. Carter, Jr. (Ed.), *Research contributions from psychology to community mental health.* New York: Behavioral Publications, 1968, 75–99.

Kelly, J. G., in collaboration with Edwards, D. W., Fatke, R., Gordon, T. A., McClintock, McGlee, D. P., Newman, B. M., Rice, R. R., Roistacher, R., & Todd, D. M. The coping process in varied high school environments. In M. J. Feldman (Ed.), *Theory and research in community mental health.* (Studies in Psychotherapy and Behavioral Change, no. 2). Buffalo: State University of New York at Buffalo, 1971.

Kifer, E. The impact of schooling on perceptions of self. Paper presented at the self-concept symposium. Boston, September 1978.

Kimmel, D.C. *Adulthood and aging.* New York: Wiley, 1974.

King, K., Balswick, J. O., & Robinson, I. E. The continuing premarital sexual revolution among college females. *Journal of Marriage and the Family,* 1977, *39,* 455–459.

Kinkead, G. On a fast track to the good life. *Fortune,* April 7, 1980, 74–75.

Kinsey, A. C., Pomeroy, W. B., & Martin, C. E. *Sexual behavior in the human male.* Philadelphia: Saunders, 1948.

Kinsey, A. C., Pomeroy, W. B., Martin, C. E., & Gebhard, P. H. *Sexual behavior in the human female.* Philadelphia: Saunders, 1953.

Kleinhesselink, R. R., St. Dennis, R., & Cross, H. Contemporary drug issues involving youth. In J. F. Adams (Ed.), *Understanding adolescence: Current developments in adolescent psychology* (3d ed.). Boston: Allyn and Bacon, 1976. Pp. 369–411.

Kline, N. S. The future of drugs and drugs of the future. *Journal of Social Issues,* 1971, *27*(3), 73–87.

Knight, R. C., Sheposh, J. P., & Bryson, J. B. College student marijuana use and societal alienation. *Journal of Health and Social Behavior,* 1974, *15*(1), 28–35.

Koch, H. L. Sibling influence on children's speech. *Journal of Speech Disorder,* 1956, *21,* 322–328.

Koch, H. L. The relation of certain formal attributes of siblings to attitudes held toward each other and toward their parents. *Monographs* of the Society for Research in Child Development, 1960, *25,* 4.

Kohlberg, L. Development of moral character and moral ideology. In M. L. Hoffman & L. W. Hoffman (Eds.), *Review of child development research* (Vol. 1). New York: Russell Sage, 1964.

Komarovsky, M. Cultural contradictions and sex role: The masculine case. *American Journal of Sociology,* 1973, *78*(4), 873–884.

Kon, I. S., & Losenkov, V. A. Friendship in adolescence: Values and behavior. *Journal of Marriage and the Family.* 1978, *40*(1), 143–156.

Konopka, G. *Young girls: A portrait of adolescence.* Englewood Cliffs, N.J.: Prentice-Hall, 1976.

Koriat, A., Melkman, R., Averill, J. R., & Lazarus, R. S. The self-control of emotional reactions to a stressful film. *Journal of Personality,* 1972, *40*(60), 1–19.

Korner, A., & Grobstein, R. Visual alertness as related to soothing in neonates: Implications for maternal stimulation and early deprivation. *Child Development,* 1966, *37,* 867–876.

Kroeber, A. L. *Race, language, culture, psychology, prehistory* (rev. ed.). New York: Harcourt, Brace & World, 1948.

Kuhn, D. Relation of two Piagetian stage transitions to I.Q. *Developmental Psychology,* 1976, *12,* 157–161.

Kurlesky, W. P., Thomas, K. A. Social ambitions of Negro boys and girls from a metropolitan ghetto. *Journal of Vocational Behavior,* 1971, *1,* 177–187.

Lamb, M. E. Twelve-month-olds and their parents interaction in a laboratory playroom. *Developmental Psychology,* 1976, *12*(3), 237–245.

Lancaster, E., & Poling, J. *The final face of Eve.* New York: McGraw-Hill, 1958.

Larson, D. L., Spreitzer, E. A., & Snyder, E. E. Social factors in the frequency of romantic involvement among adolescents. *Adolescence,* 1976, *11,* 7–12.

Larson, L. E. The influence of parents and peers during adolescence: The situation hypothesis revisited. *Journal of Marriage and the Family,* 1972, *34,* 67–74. (a)

Larson, L. E. The relative influence of parent-adolescent affect in predicting the salience hierarchy among youth. *Pacific Sociological Review,* 1972, *15,* 83–102. (b)

Lazarus, A. A. *Multimodal behavior therapy.* New York: Springer, 1976.

Lazarus, R. S. Cognitive and coping processes in emotion. In B. Weiner (Ed.), *Cognitive views of human motivation.* New York: Academic Press, 1974.

L'Ecuyer, R. The development of the self-concept through the life-span. Paper presented at the Self-Concept Symposium, Northeastern University, Boston, Mass., September 28–October 1, 1978.

Lee, L. C. Toward a cognitive theory of interpersonal development: Importance of peers. In M. Lewis & L. A. Rosenblum (Eds.), *Friendship and peer relations.* New York: Wiley, 1975, 204–222.

Lehman, I. J. Conformity in critical thinking, attitudes and values from freshman to senior years. *Journal of Educational Psychology,* 1963, *54,* 305–315.

Leonard, C. V. Depression and suicidality. *Journal of Consulting and Clinical Psychology,* 1974, *42,* 98–104.

Lerner, R. M., & Weinstock, A. Note on the generation gap. *Psychological Reports,* 1972, *31,* 457–458.

Lesser, G. S., & Kandel, D. Parent-adolescent relationships and adolescent independence in the United States and Denmark. *Journal of Marriage and the Family,* 1969, *31,* 348–358.

Levinger, A. A social psychological perspective on marital dissolution. *Journal of Social Issues,* 1976, *32,* 21–47.

Levinson, D. The mid-life: A period of adult psychosocial development. *Psychiatry,* 1977.

Levinson, D. J., in collaboration with C. M. Darrow, E. B. Klein, M. H. Levinson, & B. McKee. *The seasons of a man's life,* New York: Knopf, 1978.

Levy, L. Drug use on campus: Prevalence and social characteristics of collegiate drug users on campuses of the University of Illinois. *Drug Forum,* 1973, *2*(2), 141–171.

Lewin, K. *A dynamic theory of personality.* New York: McGraw-Hill, 1935.

Lewin, K. *Principles of topological psychology.* New York: McGraw-Hill, 1936.

Lewin, K. Behavior and development as a function of the total situation. In L. Carmichael (Ed.), *Manual of child psychology,* New York: Wiley, 1946, 791–844.

Lewin, K. *Field theory in social science: Selected theoretical pages.* (D. Cartwright, ed.). New York: Harper & Row, 1951.

Lewin, K., Lippit, R., & White, R. Patterns of aggressive behavior in experimentally created "social climates." *Journal of Social Psychology,* 1939, *10,* 271–299.

Lewis, M., Young, G., Brooks, J., & Michalson, L. The beginning of friendship. In M. Lewis & L. A. Rosenblum (Eds.), *Friendship and peer relations.* New York: Wiley, 1975, 27–66.

Libby, R. W. Creative singlehood as a sexual life-style: Beyond marriage as a rite of passage. In R. W. Libby & R. N. Whitehurst (Eds.), *Marriage and alternatives: Exploring intimate relationships.* Glenview, Ill.: Scott, Foresman, 1977, 37–61.

Lichtenberg, J. D. Theoretical and practical considerations of the management of the manic phase of the manic-depressive psychosis. *Journal of Nervous and Mental Disorders,* 1959, *129,* 243–281.

Lieberman, G. L. Children of the elderly as natural helpers: Some demographic differences. *American Journal of Community Psychology.* 1978, *6*(5), 489–498.

Liebow, E. *Tally's corner.* Boston: Little, Brown, 1967.

Lippitt, R., & Gold, M. Classroom social structure as a mental health problem. *Journal of Social Issues,* 1959, *15,* 40–58.

Littlewood, J., & Sale, R. *Children at play: A look at where they play and what they do on housing estates.* London: Department of Environment, 1972.

Long, B. H., Henderson, E. H., & Ziller, R. C. Developmental changes in the self-concept during middle childhood. *Merrill Palmer Quarterly,* 1967, *13,* 201–215.

Lopata, H. Z. *Widowhood in an American city.* Cambridge, Mass.: Schenkman, 1973.

Lopata, H. Z. Widowhood: Social norms and social integration. In H. Z. Lopata (Ed.). *Family factbook.* Chicago, Ill.: Marquis Academic Media, 1978, 217–226.

Lovaas, O. I. Effects of exposure to symbolic aggression on aggressive behavior. *Child Development,* 1961, *32,* 37–44.

Lowenthal, M. R., & Chiriboga, D. Social stress and adaptation: Toward a life-course perspective. In C. Eisdorfer & M. P. Lawton (Eds.), *The psychology of adult development and aging.* Washington, D.C.: American Psychological Association, 1973, 281–310.

Lowenthal, M. J., & Haven, C. Interaction and adaptation: Intimacy as a ritual variable. *American Sociological Review,* 1968, *33*(1), 20–30.

Lunden, W. A. Statistics on delinquents and delinquency. Springfield, Ill.: Charles C. Thomas, 1964.

Lunneborg, P. W. Sex and career decision-making styles. Paper presented at the American Psychological Association meetings, San Francisco, 1977.

Lynn, D. B. The process of learning parental and sex-role identification. *Journal of Marriage and the Family,* 1966, *28,* 466–470.

Maccoby, E. E., & Jacklin, C. N. *The psychology of sex differences.* Stanford, Calif.: Stanford University Press, 1974.

Mächtlinger, V. Psychoanalytic theory: Preoedipal and oedipal phases with special reference to the father. In M. E. Lamb (Ed.), *The role of the father in child development.* New York: Wiley, 1976, 277–306.

Macklin, E. D. Cohabitation in college: Going very steady. *Psychology Today,* November 1974, *8,* 53–59.

Maddi, S. R. *Personality theories: A comparative analysis.* Homewood, Ill.: Dorsey, 1976.

Maehr, M. C., & Stallings, W. M. Freedom from external evaluation. *Child Development,* 1972, *43,* 177–185.

Mair, L. P. Native marriage in Buganda, the International Institute of African Languages and cultures, *Memorandum 19,* 1940.

Mann, R. D., Arnold, S. M., Binder, J., Cytrynbaum, S., Newman, B. M., Ringwald, B., Ringwald, J., & Rosenwein, R. *The college classroom: Conflict, change, and learning* New York: Wiley, 1970

Marcia, J. E. Development and validation of ego identity status. *Journal of Personality and Social Psychology,* 1966, *3,* 551–558.

Market Opinion Research. *American women today and tomorrow.* National Commission on the Observance of the International Women's Year. Washington, D.C. U.S. Government Printing Office, 1977.

Martell, G. Class bias in Toronto schools. The Park School Community Council brief. *This Magazine Is about Schools,* 1971, *5*(4), 7–35.

Martin, B. Parent-child relations in F. D. Horowitz (Ed.). *Review of child development research* (Vol. 4). Chicago: University of Chicago Press, 1975, 463–540.

Maslow, A. H. *Motivation and personality.* New York: Harper & Row, 1954.

Maslow, A. H. Toward a humanistic biology. *American Psychologist,* 1969, *24,* 724–735.

Maslow, A. H. *Toward a psychology of being.* New York: Van Nostrand, 1962.

Masters, J. C., & Wilkinson, A. Consensual and discriminative stereotyping of sex-type judgements by parents and children. *Child Development,* 1976, *47*(1), 208–218.

McCall, R. B., Appelbaum, M. I., & Hogarty, P. S. Developmental changes in mental performance. *Monographs of the Society for Research in Child Development.* Serial No. 150, 1973, *38*(3).

McCandless, B. R., Roberts, A., & Starnes, T. Teachers' marks, achievement test scores, and aptitude relations with respect to social class, race and sex. *Journal of Educational Psychology,* 1972, *63,* 153–159.

McCary, J. L. *Human sexuality* (3d ed.). New York: Van Nostrand, 1978.

McCleam, G. E. Genetic influences on behavior and development. In P. H. Mussen (Ed.), *Carmichael's manual of child psychology* (Vol. 1). New York: Wiley, 1970, 39–76.

McClelland, C. D. The achieving society. Princeton, N. J.: Van Nostrand, 1961.

McCormick, N. B. Power strategies in sexual encounters. Paper presented at American Psychological Association meetings, San Francisco, 1977.

McKeachie, W. J., Doyle, C. L., & Moffett, M. M. *Psychology.* Reading, Mass.: Addison-Wesley, 1976.

Mead, M. On grandparents as educators. In H. J. Leichter (Ed.), *The family as educator.* New York: Teachers College Press, 1975.

Mead, M., & Newton, N. Cultural patterning of perinatal behavior. In S. A. Richardson & A. F. Guttmacher (Eds.), *Childbearing—Its social and psychological aspects.* Baltimore: Williams and Wilkin, 1967, 142–244.

Mebrabian, A. The development and validation of measures of affiliative tendency and sensitivity to rejection. *Educational and Psychological Measurement,* 1970, *30,* 417–428.

Messinger, L. Remarriage between divorced people with children from previous marriages: A proposal for preparation for remarriage. *Journal of Marriage and Family Counseling,* 1976, *2*(2), 193–200.

Michigan Alumnus, *What are you getting out of college?* February 1978, 5–8.

Milburn, T. W., Bell, N., & Koeshe, G. F. Effect of censure or praise and evaluative dependence on performance in a free-learning task, *Journal of Personality and Social Psychology,* 1970, *15,* 43–47.

Miller, A. L., and Tiedeman, D. V. Decision making for the 70's: The cubing of the Tiedeman paradigm and its application in career education. *Focus on Guidance,* 1972, *5*(1).

Miller, D. *Adolescence: Psychology, psychopathology, and psychotherapy.* New York: Jay Aronson, 1974.

Miller, J. G. Sensory overloading. In B. E. Flaherty (Ed.), *Psychophysiological aspects of space flight.* New York: Columbia University Press, 1961.

Miller, J. P. Suicide and adolescence. *Adolescence,* 1975, *10,* 11–24.

Millham, J., & Jacobson, L. I. The need for approval. In H. Londan and J. E. Exmer, Jr. (Eds), *Dimensions of personality.* New York: Wiley, 1978. 365–390.

Milman, D. H., & Su, W. Patterns of illicit drug and alcohol use among secondary-school students. *Journal of Pediatrics.* 1973, 314–320.

Moll, R. W. The college admissions game. *Harper's,* March 1978, 24–30.

Montague, E. K. The role of anxiety in serial role learning. *Journal of Experimental Psychology,* 1953, *45,* 91–96.

Montemayor, R., & Eisen, M. The development of self-conceptions from childhood to adolescence. *Developmental Psychology,* 1977, *13*(4), 314–319.

Moore, P. What we expect and what it's like. *Psychology Today,* August 1975, 29–30.

Moos, R. H. The human context: Environmental determinants of behavior. New York: Wiley, 1976.

Moreland, J. R. Career decision making within life-span human development. Paper presented at the American Psychological Association meetings, San Francisco, 1977.

Moriarty, A. E., & Toussieng, P. W. *Adolescent coping.* New York: Grune and Stratton, 1976.

Morris, R. The development of parallel services for the elderly and disabled. *The Gerontologist,* 1974, *14*(1), 14–19.

Mueller, C. W., & Campbell, B. G. Female occupational achievement and marital status: A research note. *Journal of Marriage and the Family,* 1977, *39*(3), 587–593.

Murdock, G. P. *Our primitive contemporaries.* New York: Macmillan, 1934.

Murdock, G. P. World ethnographic sample, *American Anthropologist,* 1957, *59.*

Murphy, L. B. *The widening world of childhood.* New York Basic Books, 1962.

Murphy, L. B. Coping, vulnerability and resilience in childhood. In G. V. Coelho, D. A. Hamburg, & J. E. Adams (Eds.), *Coping and adaptation.* New York: Basic Books, 1974, 69–100.

Murphy, L. B., & Moriarty, A. E. *Vulnerability, coping and growth.* New Haven, Conn.: Yale University Press, 1976.

Murray, H. A. (and collaborators). *Explorations in personality.* New York: Oxford, 1938.

Murray, W. The sound of the future. *The New Yorker,* September 16, 1972, 85–93.

Mussen, P. H., Conger, J., & Kagan, J. *Child development and personality.* New York: Harper & Row, 1979.

National Commission on Marijuana and Drug Abuse. *Drug use in America: Problem in perspective.* Washington, D.C.: U.S. Government Printing Office, 1973.

National Institute on Alcohol Abuse and Alcoholism. *A national study of adolescent drinking behavior, attitudes, and correlates.* Final report prepared by Research Triangle Institute, Research Triangle Park, North Carolina, 1975.

Neimark, E. D. Longitudinal development of formal operations thought. *Genetic Psychology Monographs,* 1975, *91,* 171–225.

New York Times. L.I. youth dead, 2 others hospitalized after party for fraternity's pledges. February 26, 1978, section 1, p. 27.

Newcomb, T. M. Student peer group influence. In N. Sanford (Ed.), *The American College.* New York: Wiley, 1962, 469–488.

Newman, B. M. Characteristics of interpersonal behavior among adolescent boys. *Journal of Youth and Adolescence,* 1975, *4*(2), 145–153.

Newman, B. M., & Newman, P. R. *Infancy and childhood: Development and its contexts.* New York: Wiley, 1978.

Newman, B. M., & Newman, P. R. *Development through life: A psychosocial approach* (2d ed.). Homewood, Ill.: Dorsey, 1979. (a)

Newman, B. M., & Newman, P. R. *An introduction to the psychology of adolescence.* Homewood, Ill.: Dorsey, 1979. (b)

Newman, G., & Nichols, C. R. Sexual activities and attitudes in older persons. *Journal of the American Medical Association,* 1960, *173,* 33–35.

Newman, O. *Defensible space.* New York: Macmillan, 1972.

Newman, P. R. The effects of varied high school environments on student socialization. Appendix K: Adaptive behavior in varied high school environments. Research proposal (ROI-MH-15606-04) submitted to the National Institute of Mental Health, 1970.

Newman, P. R. Persons and settings: A comparative analysis of the quality and range of social interaction in two suburban high schools. Unpublished doctoral dissertation, University of Michigan, 1971.

Newman, P. R. Persons and settings: A comparative analysis of the quality and range of social interaction in two suburban high schools. In Kelly, J. G. (Ed.), *Adolescent boys in high school: A psychological study of coping and adaptations;* Hillsdale, N.J.: Lawrence Erlbaum, 1979.

Nichols, W. C., Jr. The marriage relationship. *Family Coordinator,* 1978, *27*(2), 185–191.

Nicol, T. L., & Bryson, J. B. Intersex and intrasex stereotyping on the Bem Sex Role Inventory. Paper presented at the meeting of the American Psychological Association, San Francisco, 1977.

Norton, A. J., & Glick, P. C. Changes in American family life. *Children Today,* 1976, *5*(3), 2–4. (a)

Norton, A. J. & Glick, P. C. Marital instability: Past, present, and future. *The Journal of Social Issues,* 1976, *32,* 5–20. (b)

Nye, I. *Role structure and analysis of the family.* Beverly Hills, Calif.: Sage Publications, 1976.

O'Connor, M. The nursery environment. *Developmental Psychology,* 1975, *11*(5), 556–562.

O'Leary, V. E. The widow as female household head. Paper presented at the 85th annual meeting of the American Psychological Association, San Francisco, August 26–30, 1977.

Oppenheimer, V. K. The sex-labeling of jobs. *Industrial Relations,* 1968, *7,* 187–248.

Osgood, C. E., Luria, Z., & Smith, S. W. A blind analysis of another case of multiple personality using the semantic personality technique. *Journal of Abnormal Psychology,* 1976, *85,* 256–270.

Papanek, H. Men, women and work: Reflections on the two-person career. *American Journal of Sociology,* 1973.

Papousek, H., & Papousek, M. Mirror image and self-recognition in young human infants, 1. A new method of experimental analysis. *Developmental Psychobiology,* 1974, *7,* 149–157.

Parsons, J. E. Attributional factors mediating female underachievement and low career aspirations. Paper presented at the American Psychological Association Meetings, San Francisco, 1977.

Parsons, J. E., Frieze, I. H., & Ruble, D. N. Intrapsychic factors influencing career aspirations in college women. Mimeo, 1975.

Parsons, J. E., Ruble, D. N., Hodges, K. L., & Small, A. W. Cognitive-developmental factors in emerging sex differences in achievement-related expectancies. *The Journal of Social Issues,* 1976, *32,* 47–61.

Parsons, T. The kinship system of the contemporary United States. *American Anthropologist,* 1943, *45,* 22–38.

Parsons, T. Family structure and the socialization of the child. In T. Parsons & R. F. Bales (Eds.), Family, socialization and interaction process. Glencoe, Ill.: Free Press, 1955.

Pepitone, E. A., Loeb, H. W., & Murdock, E. M. *Social comparison and similarity of children's performance in competitive situations.* Paper presented at the 85th annual meeting of the American Psychological Association. San Francisco, August 26–30, 1977.

Peplau, L. A., & Perlman, D. Blueprint for a social psychological theory of loneliness. In M. Cook & G. Wilson (Eds), *Love and attraction: An international conference.* Oxford: Pergeman, in press.

Peplau, L. A., Russell, D., & Helm, M. An attributional analysis of loneliness. In I. Frieze, D. Bar-Tol & J. Carroll (Eds.), *New approaches to social problems.* San Francisco: Jossey-Bass, 1979.

Peretti, P. O. Closest friendships of black college students: Social intimacy. *Adolescence,* 1976, *11*(43), 395–403.

Perrella, V. C. Employment of recent college graduates. *Monthly Labor Review,* February 1973, 41–50.

Petroni, F. A. Teenage interracial dating. *Trans-action,* September 1971.

Phillips, L. *Human adaptation and its failures.* New York: Academic Press, 1968.

Piaget, J. *The moral judgment of the child.* Glencoe, Ill.: Free Press, 1948. (Originally published, 1932.)

Piaget, J. *Play, dreams, and imitation in childhood.* New York: Norton, 1951. (Originally published in French in 1945.)

Piaget, J. *The child's conception of physical causality.* Paterson, N.J.: Littlefield, Adams, 1960. (Originally published in French in 1927.)

Piaget, J. *The moral judgment of the child.* New York: Free Press, 1965.

Piaget, J. Piaget's theory, in P. H. Mussen (Ed.), *Carmichael's manual of child psychology* (Vol. 1). New York: Wiley, 1970, 703–732.

Pines, A., & Kafry, D. Burn out and life tedium in three generations of professional women. Paper presented at the 85th Annual Convention of the American Psychological Association, San Francisco, August 26–30, 1977.

Pierson, E. C., & D'Antonio, W. V *Female and male: Dimensions of human sexuality.* Philadelphia: Lippincott, 1974.

Pitcher, E. G., & Prelinger, E. *Children tell their stories.* New York: International Universities Press, 1963.

Place, D. M. The dating experience for adolescent girls. *Adolescence,* 1975, *10*(38), 157–174.

Plomin, R. A. *A temperament theory of personality development: Parent-child interactions.* Unpublished doctoral dissertation, University of Texas, 1974.

Plumb, J. H. The great change in children. *Horizon,* Winter 1971, 153–166.

Pope, B. Socioeconomic contrasts in children's peer culture prestige values. *Genetic Psychology Monograph,* 1953, *48,* 157–220.

Poppei, J. *Toddlers' use of peer imitation for problem solving.* Unpublished doctoral dissertation, University of Chicago, 1976.

Porter, J. W. *The adolescent, other citizens, and their high schools: A report to the public and the profession.* Task Force 1974, A National Task Force for High School Reform. New York: McGraw-Hill, 1975.

Poveda, T. G. Reputation and the adolescent girl: An analysis. *Adolescence,* 1975, *10,* 127–136.

Powers, E. A., & Goudy, W. J. Examination of the meaning of work to older workers. *International Journal of Aging and Human Development,* 1971, *2,* 38–45.

Proshansky, H. M., Ittelson, W. H., & Rivlin, L. G. *Environmental psychology: People and their physical settings* (2d ed.). New York: Holt, 1976.

Proskauer, S., & Rolland, R. S. Youth who use drugs. *Journal of the American Academy of Child Psychiatry,* 1973, *12,* 32–47.

Pugh, R. W. *Psychology and the black experience.* Monterey, Calif.: Brooks/Cole, 1972.

Putman, J. J. Denver, Colorado's Rocky Mountain High. *National Geographic.* March 1979, *155,* 396–397, 400.

Quinn, R. P., & Staines, G. L. *The 1977 quality of employment survey.* Ann Arbor, Mich.: Institute for Social Research, 1979.

Ragan, P. K., & Dowd, J. J. The emerging political consciousness of the aged: A generational interpretation. *Journal of Social Issues,* 1974, *30,* 137–158.

Rainwater, L. *Behind ghetto walls: Black families in a federal slum.* Chicago: Aldine, 1970.

Ramirez, A. Family on the move. *The Wall Street Journal,* February 28, 1979, *59*(94), 1 & 31.

Rathus, S. A., Siegel, L. J., & Rathus, L. A. Attitudes of middle-class heroin abusers toward representatives of the educational system. *Adolescence,* 1976, *11,* 1–6.

Raush, H. L., Barry, W. A., Hertel, R. K., & Swain, M. A. *Communication, conflict, and marriage.* San Francisco: Jossey-Bass, 1974.

Reader, J. Microcosm of a continental force: Tribalism in Kenya. *Smithsonian,* 1979, *10,* 44.

Redbook Magazine. Mail Questionnaire Study. October 1975.

Reed, E. Genetic anomalies in development. In F. D. Horowitz (Ed.), *Review of child development research* (Vol. 4). Chicago: University of Chicago Press, 1975, 59–100.

Renne, K. S. Correlates of dissatisfaction in marriage, *Journal of Marriage and the Family,* 1970, *32,* 54–67.

Renshaw, J. R. An exploration of the dynamics of the overlapping worlds of work and family. *Family Process,* March 1976.

Rice, R. R., & Marsh, M. The social environments of the two high schools: Background data. In J. G. Kelly (Ed.), *Adolescent boys in high school: A psychological study of coping and adaptation.* Hillsdale, N.J.: Lawrence Erlbaum, 1979.

Rich, H. E. The liberalizing influence of college: Some new evidence. *Adolescence,* 1977, *12,* 200–211.

Riegel, K. F. Adult life crises: A dialectic interpretation of development. In N. Datan & Leon H. Ginsberg (Eds.), *Life-span developmental psychology: Normative life crises.* New York: Academic Press, 1975.

Riegel, K. F. The dialectics of human development. *American Psychologist,* 1976, *31*(10), 689–700.

Riley, M. W., & Foner, A. *Aging and society, I: An inventory of research findings.* New York: Russell Sage, 1968.

Rist, R. C. Marijuana and the young: Problem or protest? *Intellect Magazine,* 1972, *101,* 154–156.

Roebuck, J., & Spray, S. The cocktail lounge: A study of heterosexual relations in a public organization. *American Journal of Sociology,* 1967, *72,* 388–395.

Rogers, C. *On becoming a person: A therapist's view of psychotherapy.* Boston: Houghton Mifflin, 1961.

Rogers, C. A. A theory of therapy, personality, and interpersonal relationships, as developed in the client-centered framework. In S. Koch (Ed.), *Psychology: A study of a science* (Vol. 3). New York: McGraw-Hill, 1959, 184–256.

Rollins, B. C., & Fledman, H. Marital satisfaction over the family life cycle. *Journal of Marriage and the Family,* 1970, *32,* 20–27.

Roper, B. S., & Labeff, E.   Sex roles and feminism revisited: An intergenerational attitude comparison. *Journal of Marriage and the Family,* 1977, *39*(1), 113–119.

Roos, P. D.   Jurisdiction: An ecological concept. *Human Relations,* 1968, *21,* 75–84.

Rosen, B. C.   Family structure and achievement motivation. *American Sociological Review,* 1961, *26,* 574–585.

Rosen, B. C., D'Andrade, R. G.   The psychological origin of achievement motivation. *Sociometry,* 1959, *22,* 185–218.

Rosen, B. M., Bahn, A. K., Shellow, R., & Bower, E. M.   Adolescent patients served in outpatient psychiatric clinics. *American Journal of Public Health,* 1965, *55,* 1563–1577.

Rosen, C. E.   The effects of socio-dramatic play on problem-solving behavior among culturally disadvantaged preschool children. *Child Development,* 1974, *45,* 920–927.

Rosenfeld, G. W.   Changing self-esteem by including selective attention to successes and failures. Paper presented at the American Psychological Association meeting in Toronto, Canada, August 28, 1978.

Rosenkrantz, A. L.   A note on adolescent suicide: Incidence, dynamics, and some suggestions for treatment. *Adolescence,* 1978, *13,* 211–214.

Rossi, A. S.   Transition to parenthood. *Journal of Marriage and the Family.* 1968, *30,* 26–39.

Rovee, C. K., & Rovee, D. T.   Conjugate reinforcement of infant exploratory behavior. *Journal of experimental child psychology,* 1969, *8,* 33–39.

Rubin, K., & Maioni, T.   Play preference and its relationship to egocentrism, popularity and classification skills in preschoolers. *Merrill-Palmer Quarterly,* 1975, *21,* 171–180.

Rubin, Z.   *Liking and loving: An invitation to social psychology.* New York: Holt, 1973.

Rule, B. G., Rule D., and Rehill, D.   Direction and self-esteem effects on attitude change. *Journal of Personality and Social Psychology,* 1970, *15,* 359–365.

Sagi, A., & Hoffman, M. G.   Empathic distress in the newborn. *Developmental Psychology,* 1976, *12*(2), 175–176.

Salamon, S.   Family bounds and friendship bonds: Japan and West Germany. Journal of Marriage and the Family. 1977, *39*(4), 807–820.

Sank, L. I.   Community distasters: Primary prevention and treatment in a Health Maintenance Organization, *American Psychologist,* 1979, *34*(4), 334–338.

Sarason, J. G.   *Abnormal psychology: The problem of maladaptive behavior* (2d ed.). Englewood Cliffs, N. J.: Prentice-Hall, 1976.

Sarason, S. B.   *The psychological sense of community.* San Francisco: Jossey-Bass, 1974.

Scanzoni, J. H.   *Opportunity and the family.* New York: Free Press, 1970.

Schaefer, E. S.   A circumplex model for maternal behavior. *Journal of Abnormal and Social Psychology,* 1959, *59,* 226–335.

Schafer, W. E., and Olexa, C.   *Tracking and opportunity: The locking-out process and beyond.* Scranton, Pa.: Chandler, 1971.

Schaffer, H. R., & Emerson, P. E.   The development of social attachments in infancy. *Monographs of the Society for Research in Child Development,* 1964, *29*(3) (Serial No. 94).

Schancke, D. A.   If you're way, way down—or up too high. *Today's Health,* 1974, *52*(5), 39–41, 65–67.

Schapera, I.   *The Khorsan peoples of South Africa.* London: Routledge and Kegan Paul, 1930.

Schimel, J. L.   Problems of delinquency and their treatment. In G. Caplan (Ed.), *American handbook of psychiatry* (2d ed.), Vol. 2: *Child and adolescent psychiatry, socio-cultural and community psychiatry.* New York: Basic Books, 1974, 264–274.

Schmitt, R. C.   Implications of density in Hong Kong. *Journal of the American Institute of Planners,* 1963, *24,* 210–217.

Schmuck, R. A., & Schmuck, P. A.   *Group processes in the classroom* (2d ed.). Dubuque, Iowa: Wm. C. Brown, 1975.

Scott, R., & Seifert, K.   Family size and learning readiness profiles of socioeconomically disadvantaged preschool whites. *Journal of Psychology,* 1975, *89,* 3–7.

Seashore, S.   *Group cohesiveness in the industrial work group.* Ann Arbor, Mich.: Institute for Social Research, 1954.

Severance, L. J., & Gottsegen, A. J.   Modeling influences on the achievement of college men and women. Paper presented at the American Psychological Association meetings, San Francisco, 1977.

Shafer, R.   *Marijuana: A signal of misunderstanding.* National Commission on Marijuana and Drug Abuse. New York: New American Library, 1972.

Shafer, S. M.   Adolescent girls and future career mobility. In R. E. Grinder (Ed.), *Studies in adolescence* (3d ed.). New York: Macmillan, 1975, 114–125.

Shantz, C. U.   The development of social cognition. In E. M. Hetherington (Ed.), *Review of child development research* (Vol. 5). Chicago: University of Chicago Press, 1975, 257–324.

Shapiro, H. D.   Do not go gently. *New York Times Magazine,* February 6, 1977, 36–54.

Sharp, L.   Steel axes for Stone Age Australians. In E. H. Spicer (Ed.), *Human problems in technological change: A casebook.* New York: Russell Sage, 1952.

Sheehy, G.   *Passages: Predictable crises of adult life.* New York: Dutton, 1974, 76.

Sidel, R.   *Women and child care in China.* New York: Farrar, Straus, and Giroux, 1972.

Silber, E., Hamburg, D., Coelho, G., Murphy, E., Rosenberg, M., & Pearlin, L.   Adaptive behavior in competent adolescents: Coping with the anticipation of college. *Archives of General Psychiatry,* 1961, *5,* 354–365.

Simmer, M. L.   Newborns response to the cry of another infant. *Developmental Psychology,* 1971, *5,* 136–150.

Simmons, R. G.; Blyth, D., & Bush, D.   The impact of junior high school and puberty upon self-esteem. Paper presented in a symposium entitled sociocultural aspects of puberty, Chariman, Jeanne Brooks. At the biennial meeting of the

Society for Research in Child Development, New Orleans, March 17–20, 1977.

Simmons, R. G., Rosenberg, F., & Rosenberg, M. Disturbance in the self-image at adolescence. *American Sociological Review,* 1973, *38,* 553–568.

Simon, K. A., & Frankel, M. M. *Projections of education statistics to 1984–85.* Washington, D.C.: U.S. Government Printing Office, 1976.

Simon, W., Berger, A. S., & Gagnon, J. H. Beyond anxiety and fantasy: The coital experiences of college youth. *Journal of Youth and Adolescence,* 1972, *1*(3), 203–221.

Simonton, D. K. Creative productivity, age, and stress: A biographical time-series analysis of 10 classical composers. *Journal of Personality and Social Psychology,* 1977, *35,* 791–804.

Simos, B. G. Adult children and their aging parents. *Social Work,* 1973, *18,* 78–85.

Singer, J. L. *Daydreaming: An introduction to the experimental study of inner experience.* New York: Random House, 1966.

Singer, J. L. *The child's world of make-believe: Experimental studies of imaginative play.* New York: Academic Press, 1973.

Siqueland, E. R., & DeLucia, C. A. Visual reinforcement of non-nutritive sucking in human infants. *Sciences,* 1969, *165,* 1144–1146.

Smith, C. P. The origin and expression of achievement-related motives in children: In C. P. Smith (Ed.), *Achievement-related motives in children.* New York: Russell Sage, 1969.

Smith, D. F. Adolescent suicide: A problem for teachers? *Phi Delta Kappa,* April 1976, 195–198.

Smith, M. B. Competence and socialization. In John A. Clausen (Ed.), *Socialization and society.* Boston: Little, Brown, 1968, 270–320.

Sorenson, R. C. *Adolescent sexuality in contemporary America: Personal values and sexual behavior, ages 13–19.* New York: World, 1973.

Sours, J. A. Anorexia nervosa: Nosology, diagnosis, developmental patterns, and power control dynamics. In G. Caplan and S. Lebovici (Eds.), *Adolescence: Psychosocial perspectives.* New York: Basic Books, 1969, 185–212.

Southworth, M. The sonic environment of cities. *Environment and Behavior,* 1969, *1,* 49–70.

Speegle, J. College catalogs: An investigation of the congruence of catalog descriptions of college environments with student perceptions of the same environments as revealed by the College Characteristics Index. Unpublished doctoral dissertation, Syracuse University, 1969.

Sperling, M. Conversion hysteria and conversion symptoms: A revision of classification and concepts. *Journal of the American Psychoanalytic Association,* 1973, *21,* 745–771.

Spitz, R. A. Hospitalism: An inquiry into the genesis of psychiatric conditions in early childhood in R. S. Eissler et al. (Eds), *The psychoanalytic study of the child* (Vol. 1), New York: International Universities Press, 1945, 53–74.

Spitz, R. A. Hospitalism: A follow-up report. In R. S. Eissler et al. (Eds.) *The psychoanalytic study of the child* (Vol. 2), New York: International Universities Press, 1946, 113–117.

Spock, B. *Baby and child care.* (Rev. Ed.). New York: Hawthorne, 1976.

Stafford, R., Backman, E., & Dibona, P. The division of labor among cohabiting and married couples. *Journal of Marriage and the Family,* 1977, *39*(1), 40–47.

Stainback, W. C., & Stainback, S. B. A close look at the variety of reinforcers. *Training School Bulletin,* 1972, *69,* 131–135.

Starr, J. R., & Carns, D. E. Singles in the city. *Society,* 1972, *9,* 43–48.

Stein, A. H., & Bailey, M. The socialization of achievement orientation in females. *Psychological Bulletin,* 1973, *80,* 346–366.

Stein, M. *Lovers, friends, slaves.* New York: Berkeley Publishing, 1974.

Stephens, W. N. *The family in cross-cultural perspective.* New York: Holt, 1963.

Stetar, J. M. Community colleges and the educational needs of older adults. *Education Digest,* April 1975.

Stodgill, R. Group productivity, drive and cohesiveness, *Organizational behavior and human performance,* 1972, *8*(1), 26–43.

Stolz, L. M. *Father relations of war-born children.* Stanford, Calif.: Stanford University Press, 1954.

Stone, L. J., & Church, J. *Childhood and adolescence.* New York: Random House, 1979.

Stone, W. F. Patterns of conformity in couples varying in intimacy. *Journal of Personality and Social Psychology,* 1973, *27*(3), 413–419.

Streib, G. Are the aged a minority group? In B. Neugarten (Ed.), *Middle age and aging.* Chicago: University of Chicago Press, 1968.

Strong/Campbell Interest Inventory, SC II, Newark, N.J.: Roche Psychometric Service, 1974.

Sullivan, H. S. *The collected works of Harry Stack Sullivan* (Vols. 1 and 2). New York: Norton, 1949.

Sussman, M. B. Relationships of adult children with their parents in the United States. In E. Shanas & G. F. Streib (Eds.), *Social structure and the family.* New York: Prentice-Hall, 1965.

Suttles, G. *The social order of the slum: Ethnicity and territory in the inner city.* Chicago: University of Chicago Press, 1968.

Sutton-Smith, B. A syntax for play and games. In R. E. Herron and B. Sutton-Smith (Eds.), *Child's play.* New York: Wiley, 1971, 298–310.

Sutton-Smith, B., & Rosenberg, B. G. Sixty years of historical change in the games of American children. *Journal of American Folklore,* 1961, *74,* 17–46.

Sutton-Smith, B., & Rosenberg, B. G. *The sibling.* New York: Holt, Rinehart & Winston, 1970.

Swain, M. *Husband-wife patterns of interaction at three stages of marriage.* (Doctorial dissertation, University of Michigan, 1969, University Microfilms).

Tangri, S. S. Determinants of occupational role innovation among college women. *Journal of Social Issues,* 1972, *28*(2), 177–199.

Tanner, D. *Schools for youth: Change and challenge in secondary education.* New York: Macmillan, 1965.

Temby, W. D. Suicide. In G. R. Blaine and C. C. McArthur (Eds.), *Emotional problems of the student.* New York: Appleton-Century-Crofts, 1961, 133–152.

Terkel, S. *Working: People talk about what they do all day and how they feel about what they do.* New York: Random House, 1972, 74.

Thaw, J., & Efran, J. S. The relationship of need for approval to defensiveness and goal setting behavior: A partial replication. *Journal of Psychology,* 1967, *65,* 41.

Thigpen, C. H., & Cleckley, H. M. A case of multiple personality. *Journal of Abnormal and Social Psychology,* 1954, *49,* 135–151.

Thigpen, C. H., & Cleckley, H. M. *The three faces of Eve.* New York: McGraw-Hill, 1957.

Thistlethwaite, D. L. College press and student achievement. *Journal of Educational Psychology,* 1959, *50,* 183–191.

Thistlethwaite, D. L. *College press and changes in study plans of talented students. Journal of Educational Psychology,* 1960, *51,* 222–239.

Thomas, P. *Down these mean streets.* New York: Knopf, 1967.

Thomas, R. M., & Thomas, S. M. *Individual differences in the classroom.* New York: David McKay, 1965.

Thompson, J. D., & Goldin, G. *The hospital: A social and architectural history.* New Haven, Conn.: Yale University Press, 1975.

Thompson, S. K. Gender labels and early sex role development. *Child Development,* 1975, *46,* 339–347.

Tidball, M. F. Perspective on academic women and affirmative action. *Educational Record,* 1973, *54,* 130–135.

Tiedeman, D. V. Decision and vocational development: A paradigm and its implications. *Personnel and Guidance Journal,* 1961, *40,* 15–21.

Tiedeman, D. V., & Miller-Tiedeman, A. Choice and decision processes and careers. Paper presented at the Conference on Career Decision Making, American Institute of Research, March 1975.

Tiedeman, D. V., & O'Hara, R. P. *Career development: Choice and adjustment.* New York: College Entrance Examination Board, 1963.

Toffler, A. *Future shock.* New York: Random House, 1970.

Toolan, J. M. Suicide in children and adolescents. *American Journal of Psychotherapy,* 1975, *29,* 339–344.

Trall, L. E. The family of later life: A decade review. *Journal of Marriage and the Family,* 1971, *33,* 263–290.

Turner, B. F. The self-concepts of older women. A paper presented at the 85th annual meeting of the American Psychological Association, San Francisco, August 26–30, 1977.

U.S. Bureau of Labor Statistics. "Employment of School Age Youth," 1966, 1970, Special Labor Force Report, No. 87, 1967; Special Labor Force Report, No. 135, 1971.

U.S. Bureau of Labor Statistics, *Monthly Labor Review, 102,* 10, "Working Mothers in the 1970s: A look at the statistics." Washington, D.C.: U.S. Government Printing Office, 1979, 39–49.

U.S. Department of Commerce, Bureau of the Census. *Current population reports.* Series P-20, No. 285, Mobility of the Population of the United States: March 1970 to March 1975. Washington, D.C.: U.S. Government Printing Office, 1975b.

U.S. Department of Commerce, Bureau of the Census. *Current population reports,* Series P-20, no. 306. Washington, D.C.: U.S. Government Printing Office, 1977.

U.S. Department of Commerce, Bureau of the Census. *Current population reports.* Series P-20, No. 307, Population Profile of the United States: 1976. Washington, D.C.: U.S. Government Printing Office, 1977, 12.

U.S. Department of Commerce, Bureau of the Census. Census of Population: *Detailed characteristics,* Final Report PC (1)—D Series. Washington, D.C.: U.S. Government Printing Office, 1970.

U.S. Department of Commerce, Bureau of the Census. Households and families by type: March, 1976, *Current population reports,* Series P-20, No. 296. Washington, D.C.: U.S. Government Printing Office, 1976. (a)

U.S. Department of Commerce, Bureau of the Census. Marital status and living arrangements: March 1975. *Current population reports,* Series P-20, No. 287. Washington, D.C.: U.S. Government Printing Office, 1975.

U.S. Department of Commerce, Bureau of the Census. Number, timing, and duration of marriages and divorces in the United States, June 1975. *Current population reports.* Series P-20, No. 297. Washington, D.C.: U.S. Government Printing Office, 1976. (b)

U.S. Department of Commerce, Bureau of the Census. Prospects for American Fertility, *Current population reports,* Series P-20, No. 300. Washington, D.C.: U.S. Government Printing Office, 1976. (c)

U.S. Department of Commerce, Bureau of the Census. *Statistical Abstract of the United States 1978,* (99th edition). Washington, D.C.: U.S. Government Printing Office, 1978, Table 259.

Vaillant, G. E. *Adaptation to life.* Boston: Little, Brown, 1977.

Veroff, J., Melnick, H., & Kulka, R. Personal, situational and interpersonal attributions of causes or critical life problems. Paper presented at the American Psychological Association Meetings, San Francisco, 1977.

Waber, D. P. Sex differences in cognition: A function of maturation rate? *Science,* 1976, *192*(4239), 572–573.

Wade, G. R. A study of free-play patterns of elementary school-age children in playground equipment areas. Unpublished master's thesis, Pennsylvania State University, 1968.

Waller, W. The rating and dating complex. *American Sociological Review,* 1937, *2,* 727–734.

Walters, R. H. Parke, R. D., & Cane, V. A. Timing of punishment and the observation of consequences to others as determinants of response inhibition. *Journal of Experimental Child Psychology,* 1965, *2,* 10–30.

Ward, R. A. The impact of subjective age and stigma on older persons. *Journal of Gerontology,* 1977, *32,* 227–232.

Warren, R., & Warren, D. *The neighborhood organizer's handbook.* Notre Dame, Ind.: University of Notre Dame Press, 1976.

Webster's New Collegiate Dictionary. Springfield, Mass.: G. and C. Merriam, 1977.

Weiner, B.   *Cognitive views of human motivation.* New York: Academic Press, 1974.

Weiner, I. B.   *Psychological disturbances in adolescence.* New York: Wiley-Interscience, 1970.

Weinstock, A., & Lerner, R. M.   Attitudes of late adolescents and their parents toward contemporary issues. *Psychological Reports,* 1972, *30,* 239–244.

Weiss, R. S.   *Loneliness: The experience of emotional and social isolation.* Cambridge, Mass.: MIT Press, 1973.

Weissman, M. M., Fox, K., & Klerman, G. L.   Hostility and depression associated with suicide attempts. *American Journal of Psychiatry,* 1973, *130,* 450–455.

Wellemeyer, M.   Reassessment time for the Forty-Niners, *Fortune,* May 21, 1979, 118–122.

Wells, L. E., & Marwell, G.   *Self-esteem: Its concepualization and measurement.* Beverly Hills, Calif.: Sage Publications, 1976.

West, D. J.   *The young offender.* New York: International Universities Press, 1967.

White, B. C., & Watts, J. C.   *Experience and environment* (Vol. 1). Englewood Cliffs, N.J.: Prentice-Hall, 1973.

White, R. W.   Competence and the pscychosexual stages of development. In M. R. Jones (Ed.), *Nebraska Symposium on Motivation.* Lincoln: University of Nebraska Press, 1960, 97–141.

White, R. W.   Strategies of adaptation: An attempt at systematic description. In G. V. Coelho, D. A. Hamburg, & J. E. Adams (Eds.), *Coping and adaptation.* New York: Basic Books, 1974.

Whiting, B. B., & Whiting, J. W. M.   *Children of six cultures: A psychocultural analysis.* Cambridge, Mass.: Harvard University Press, 1975.

Willerman, L.   Activity level and hyperactivity in twins. *Child Development,* 1973, *44,* 288–293.

Williams, C. D.   The elimination of tantrum behavior by extinction procedures. *Journal of Abnormal and Social Psychology,* 1959, *59,* 269.

Willis, S., & Brophy, J.   Origins of teachers' attitudes toward young children. *Journal of Educational Psychology,* 1974, *66,* 520–529.

Wilson, R. S.   Twins: Mental development in the preschool years. *Developmental Psychology,* 1974, *10,* 580–588.

Wilson, R. S.   Twins: Patterns of cognitive development as measured on the Wechsler preschool and primary scale of intelligence. *Developmental Psychology,* 1975, *11,* 126–134.

Winch, R. F.   The functions of dating. From R. F. Winch, *The Modern Family* (Rev. Ed.), New York: Holt, 1971.

Winch, R. F.   *The modern family* (3d ed.). New York: Holt, 1971.

Winch, R. F.   Some observations on extended familism in the United States. In R. F. Winch, & G. B. Spanier (Eds.), *Selected Studies in Marriage and the Family* (4th ed.). New York: Holt, 1974, 147–160.

Winsborough, H. H.   The social consequences of high population density. *Law and Contemporary Problems,* 1965, *30,* 120–126.

Winterbottom, M. R.   The relation of need for achievement to learning experiences in independence and mastery. In J. W. Atkinson (Ed.), *Motives in fantasy, action and society.* Princeton, N.J.: Van Nostrand, 1958.

Wolff, C. T., Friedman, S. B., Hofer, M. A., & Mason, J. W.   Relationship between psychological defenses and mean urinary 17-hydroxycorticosteroid excretion rates: I. A predictive study of parents of fatally ill children. *Psychosomatic Medicine,* 1964, *26,* 576–591.

Wolman, B. B.   *Victims of success: Emotional problems of executives.* New York: Quadrangle/The New York Times Book Co., 1973, 7.

Wylie, R.   *The self-concept.* Lincoln, Neb.: University of Nebraska Press, 1961.

Wylie, R. C.   *The self-concept.* (Rev. ed.) (Vol. 1). Lincoln: University of Nebraska Press, 1974.

Yamamoto, Kaaru (Ed.).   *The child and his image: Self-concept in the early years.* Boston: Houghton Mifflin, 1972.

Yang, R. K., Federman, E. J., & Douthitt, T. C.   The characterization of neonatal behavior: A dimensional analysis. *Developmental Psychology,* 1976, *12*(3), 204–210.

Yarrow, L. J.   The development of focused relationships during infancy. In J. Hellmuth (Ed.), *Exceptional infant* (Vol. 1). (Special Child Publications), New York: Bruner/Mazel, 1967, 428–442.

Yarrow, L. J.   Research in dimensions of early maternal care. *Merrill-Palmer Quarterly,* 1963, *9,* 101–114.

Yarrow, L. J.   Separation from parents during early childhood. In M. L. Hoffman & L. W. Hoffman (Eds.)   *Review of child development research* (Vol. 1). New York: Russell Sage, 1964, 89–136.

Yasin, A. S.   Attempted suicide in an adolescent—The resolution of an anxiety state. *Adolescence,* 1973, *8,* 17–28.

Yearbook of Higher Education, 1979–80 (11th edition). Chicago: Marquis—Who's Who, 1979, 605.

Young, A. M.   The high school class of 1972: More at work, fewer in college. *Monthly Labor Review,* 1973, *96,* 26–32.

Zellner, M.   Self-esteem, reception, and influencability. *Journal of Personality and Social Psychology,* 1970, *15,* 87–93.

Zey-Ferrell, M., Tolone, W. L., & Walsh, R. H.   The intergenerational socialization of sex-role attitudes: A gender or generation gap? *Adolescence,* 1978, *13*(49), 95–108.

Glossary-index

Index

This book has been set VideoComp, in 11 and 10 point Souvenir Light, leaded 1 point. Part numbers and titles and chapter numbers and titles are 24 point Souvenir Demi-Bold. The size of the type page is 37 by 48 picas.